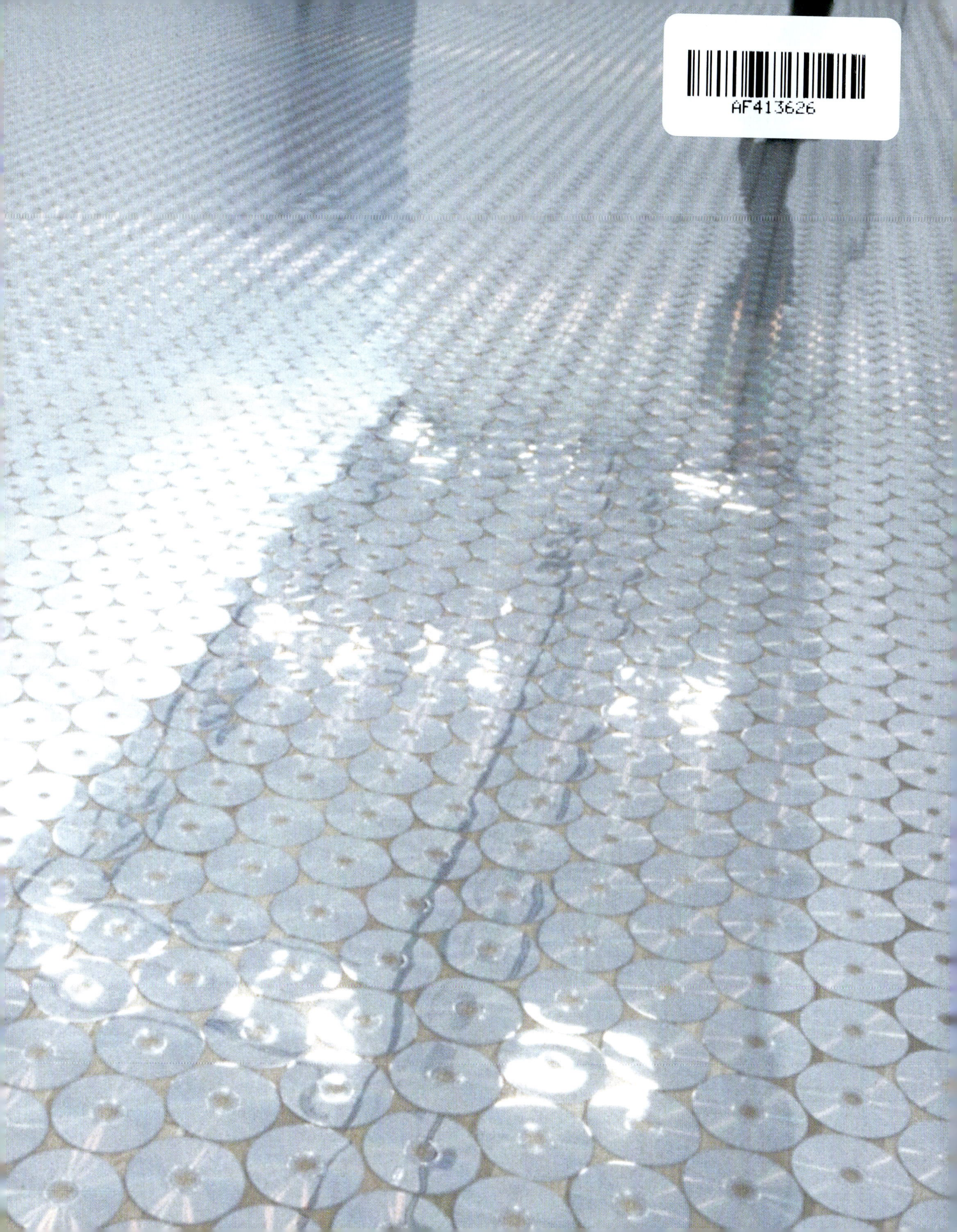
AF413626

20 YEARS OF PARKETT: 32 Extraseiten/Special Pages:
Essay von/by Johanna Burton; Interview mit/with Franz West; Artists' Pages
ANNIVERSARY EDITION FOR PARKETT: FRANZ WEST

DIE PARKETT-REIHE MIT GEGENWARTSKÜNSTLERN / THE PARKETT SERIES WITH CONTEMPORARY ARTISTS

Book Series with contemporary artists in English and German, published three times a year. Each volume is created in collaboration with artists, who contribute an original work specially made for the readers of Parkett. The works are reproduced in the regular edition and available in a limited and signed Special Edition.

Buchreihe mit Gegenwartskünstlern in deutscher und englischer Sprache, erscheint dreimal im Jahr. Jeder Band entsteht mit Künstlern oder Künstlerinnen, die eigens für die Leser von Parkett einen Originalbeitrag gestalten. Diese Werke sind in der gesamten Auflage abgebildet und zusätzlich in einer limitierten und signierten Vorzugsausgabe erhältlich.

PARKETT NR. 71 ENTSTEHT IN COLLABORATION MIT • OLAF BREUNING, RICHARD PHILLIPS, KEITH TYSON • WILL BE COLLABORATING ON PARKETT NO. 71

JAHRESABONNEMENT (DREI NUMMERN) / ANNUAL SUBSCRIPTION (THREE ISSUES) SFR. 116.– (SCHWEIZ), € 78 (BRD), € 82 (ÜBRIGES EUROPA), US$ 80 (USA AND CANADA ONLY)

ZWEI- UND DREIJAHRESABONNEMENTPREISE SIEHE GELBE BESTELLKARTE IM HEFT / FOR TWO & THREE YEAR RATES, PLEASE CONSULT YELLOW ORDER FORM.

Zürichsee Druckereien AG (Stäfa)   Satz, Litho, Druck/Copy, Printing, Color Separations

PARKETT-VERLAG AG   ZÜRICH   MAI 2004   PRINTED IN SWITZERLAND   ISBN 3-907582-20-9   ISSN 0256-0917

Cover / Umschlag: WILHELM SASNAL, UNTITLED, 2004, ink on paper / Tusche auf Papier.
Cover flap & page 1 / Umschlagklappe & Seite 1: CHRISTIAN MARCLAY, ECHO AND NARCISSUS, 1992–1999, Tokyo Opera City, 1999.
Inner cover flap: WILHELM SASNAL, UNTITLED, 2003, oil on canvas / Öl auf Leinwand.
Back cover / Rückseite: GILLIAN WEARING, TRAUMA, 2000, production still. (MAUREEN PALEY ART INTERIM, LONDON)
All images slightly cropped / Alle Bilder leicht beschnitten.

PARKETT   Zürich   New York

Bice Curiger Chefredaktorin/Editor-in-Chief; **Jacqueline Burckhardt** Redaktorin/Senior Editor; **Cay Sophie Rabinowitz** Redaktorin USA / Senior Editor US; **Suzanne Schmidt** Textredaktion und Produktion /Editing and Production; **Hanna Koller · Simone Eggstein** Graphik/Design, **Trix Wetter** Graphisches Konzept/Founding Designer (–2001); **Catherine Schelbert** Englisches Lektorat/ Editorial Assistant for English; **Claudia Meneghini Nevzadi** Korrektorat/Proof Reading

Beatrice Fässler Vorzugsausgaben, Inserate/ Special Editions, Advertising; **Nicole Stotzer** Buchvertrieb, Administration / Distribution, Administration; **Mathias Arnold** Abonnemente /Subscriptions; **Priya Bhatnagar** Redaktionsassistenz USA / Assistant Editor US; **Monika Condrea** Vorzugsausgaben, Inserate und Abonnemente USA / Special Editions, Advertising, and Subscriptions US; **Zoe Jackson** Praktikantin USA/Intern US; **Adrian Koerfer** Deutsche Verlagsvertretung/German Representative

Jacqueline Burckhardt – Bice Curiger – Dieter von Graffenried Herausgeber/Parkett Board;
Jacqueline Burckhardt – Bice Curiger – Dieter von Graffenried – Walter Keller – Peter Blum Gründer/Founders

Dieter von Graffenried Verleger/Publisher

www.parkettart.com

PARKETT-VERLAG AG, QUELLENSTRASSE 27, CH-8031 ZÜRICH, TEL. 41-1-271 81 40, FAX 41-1-272 43 01
PARKETT, NEW YORK, 155 AV. OF THE AMERICAS, N.Y. 10013, PHONE (212) 673-2660, FAX (212) 271-0704

Im Zentrum unseres Projektes steht seit dem Beginn vor zwanzig Jahren die Nähe zu den Künstlerinnen und Künstlern, als deren Partner wir uns verstehen. Deren Engagement wiederum manifestiert sich in den Collaborations, die wesentlich zum Renommee von Parkett beigetragen haben. In zwanzig Jahren sind so siebzig Bände mit Künstlerbeiträgen in Form von 150 Editionen und 62 Inserts entstanden. Ebenso massgeblich ist Parkett durch seine ausgewählte, internationale Autorenrunde geprägt. Die bis heute über tausend Essays, die jeweils aus verschiedenen Sprachen ins Deutsche und Englische übersetzt wurden, zeugen auch von einem lebendigen transkontinentalen Austausch.

Was ist heute anders als vor 20 Jahren? Natürlich haben Fax und E-Mail den Redaktionsalltag gründlich verändert, aber in der Kunst? Zum Geburtstag wollen wir die Leser – und auch ein bisschen uns selber – dreimal hintereinander (in jeder Ausgabe des Jubiläumsjahrgangs) mit einem kleinen «Heft im Heft» beschenken: Unter dem Titel *(IM)MATERIAL?* soll der aktuelle Materialbegriff in der Kunst beleuchtet werden. Den Anfang macht Johanna Burton mit ihrem Essay «Der urmaterielle Drang».

Wenn Franz West danach in einem (per E-Mail geführten) Gespräch sein archaisches Verhältnis zu Materialien betont, aber auch, wie Sprachliches und Psychologisches darin aufgeht oder mitbestimmend ist, so verweist er bewusst auf einen erweiterten Materialbegriff, der nicht nur die Materie zum Anfassen meint. Ganz angemessen also, dass Franz West zum Jubiläum als Special Edition ein Büchergestell für die Parkettbände der vergangenen u n d kommenden 20 Jahre schuf.

Ehemalige Collaboration-Künstlerinnen und -Künstler griffen auf unsere Anfrage hin «Parkett» als assoziatives Spielmaterial auf, um spezielle Künstlerseiten zu gestalten, ein Projekt, das ebenfalls in den nächsten beiden Ausgaben fortgesetzt wird.

Gerne imaginiert man sich mit solcherart geschultem Metablick ein musikalisches Geburtstagsständchen von Christian Marclay beim Betrachten der Collaboration-Beiträge im vorliegenden Band. Musik in ihrer Abwesenheit, aber auch in ihrer Potenzialität ist ein grosses Thema in Marclays Arbeit. Die Existenz ganz konkret in ihren vielfältigen Masken und Kleidern, die ihre Gefährdung auch kaschieren, ist in Gillian Wearings Werken überall präsent. In Furcht erregender Weise sind auch Wearings Masken Instrumente, die mit existenzieller Note vom schrillen Missklang der Identitäten künden. Und wenn Gordon Burns zu Wearing schreibt, «Wir alle sind Geschöpfe der elektronischen Vorhölle» (S.122), so trifft dies auch für Wilhelm Sasnal zu: In seiner Malerei herrscht ein derart gesteigerter freier Austausch von Bildern, Medien, Stilen, dass die Quellenlage in dumpfe Ferne rückt. Deshalb ist es obsolet, seine Motive oder Anlehnungen an Darstellungsweisen auf einen soliden Ursprung zurückführen zu wollen. Alles ist in Fluss geraten und mündet in grosser Ruhe in die düster schöne Präsenz der Malerei.

Our core objective, since we first started 20 years ago, has been to work closely with contemporary artists, for we consider them partners in a joint venture. They, in turn, have consistently demonstrated their commitment in collaborations that contribute substantially to the renown of Parkett. For the 70 volumes published over the past 20 years, our artists have designed and created 150 editions and 62 inserts. An international roster of eminent writers has played an equally substantial role in defining the character of Parkett. Well over 1000 essays, translated from a variety of languages into German and English, testify to a sustained and dynamic transcontinental exchange.

What is different now than it was two decades ago? E-mail and the electronic highway have, of course, profoundly changed day-to-day production, but what about art? To celebrate our birthday, we have decided to give our readers—and ourselves—a booklet within a book, which will be bound into each of our anniversary issues. Entitled *(IM)MATERIAL?*, it will debate the current concept of material in art, beginning with Johanna Burton's discerning essay on "The 'Urmaterial' Urge."

Franz West follows suit (in a conversation conducted by e-mail), discussing not only his archaic relationship to materials but also their ability to embody or even define linguistic and psychological content. He deliberately stretches the concept of material to include not only matter that can be touched. What could be more appropriate, then, but Franz West's Special Edition for our anniversary: a bookcase with room for 20 years of Parkett, past a n d future.

In response to our invitation, many former collaboration artists have explored "Parkett" as a sourcebook of associations in order to design a page for our anniversary feature— a project to be continued in the next two issues as well.

We take pleasure in imagining what it would be like to listen, with a similar, well-trained meta-view, to a birthday serenade by Christian Marclay while studying the contributions to this volume of Parkett. Music as absence, but also as potential, is a salient aspect of Marclay's work. Physical existence, along with all the masks and clothing that disguise its vulnerability, is the stuff of Gillian Wearing's oeuvre. Her masks are indeed frightening instruments whose existential tones bear witness to the shrill dissonance of identities. As Gordon Burns puts it, "We are all creatures of the electronic limbo" (p. 114), a comment that might also be applied to Wilhelm Sasnal. Sasnal's painting shows such an intense and uninhibited commerce between imagery, media and styles that the question of origin fades into distant obscurity. Wanting to trace his motifs or modes of representation to specific sources is, therefore, an antiquated enterprise. Nothing is fixed; everything flows into the darkly forbidding beauty of painting which is a law unto its own.

BICE CURIGER

Rebecca Warren:
SHE

EVERY ASPECT OF BITCH MAGIC (1996) was one of Rebecca Warren's earliest artworks to come to wide public attention and it remains a touchstone for what has followed. I observed her install the piece in an exhibition, "Material Culture," which I co-curated with Michael Archer at the Hayward Gallery in London in 1997. The show considered different approaches to the object in British art of the past two decades. Even among such a deliberately heterodox assortment, Warren's approach commanded special notice. She had created the work in her bedroom over a period of three months. This biographical information is relevant since the work's contents and meanings are intimate and compacted. She started with a white plinth onto which she placed and replaced a selection of objects that were variously to hand. These included a jar containing a dead bee that a friend had brought to her. A scrunchie (an elastic band used to hold back hair) was stretched over the jar for safekeeping. Other items that came to rest on the plinth's surface included a shell, a shard of green glass, a pair of underpants, and a safety pin. Warren constructed a wooden frame as a sketch for a Perspex cover. She never made the cover but kept the indicative frame. On it rested a large white envelope over which she had stretched another pair of

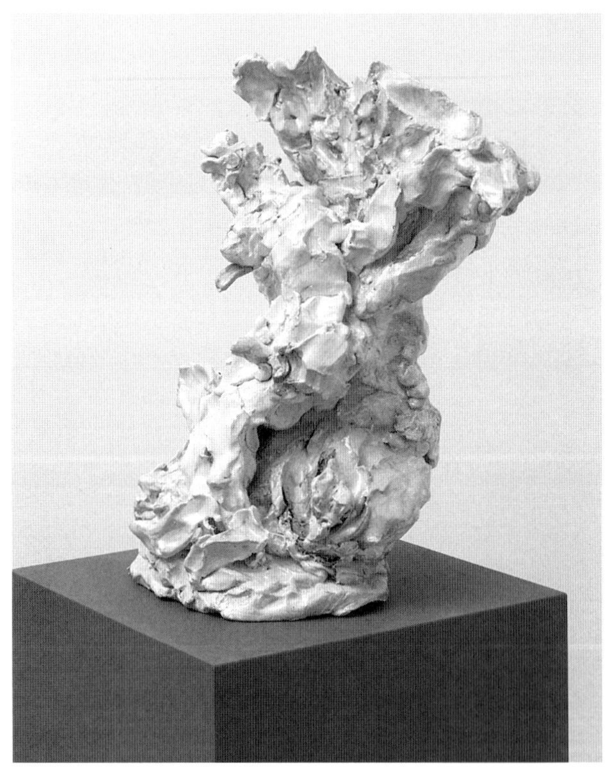

REBECCA WARREN, 10–4, 2000,
unfired painted clay and plinth, $7^{1}/_{8}$ x $7^{1}/_{8}$ x $11^{7}/_{8}$" /
ungebrannter bemalter Ton mit Sockel, 18 x 18 x 30 cm.
(PHOTOS: MAUREEN PALEY INTERIM ART, LONDON)

GREG HILTY is a curator and writer and currently Director of Visual Arts & Literature at Arts Council England in London.

underpants, its crotch gently padded with fluff from a washing machine. The envelope itself was also padded out with slides of the artist's work.

Description is not criticism and accumulation is in itself not art. Warren's accretion of apparently incidental elements, just described, nevertheless conjured up both the completeness and the "bitch magic" of her title. The work betrays an urge to art that predates that of mimesis or symbolism: the impulse to endow raw matter with spirit or meaning and so to transform it. Such a process, which might as well be called "magic," depends as much on the nature of the transformative act as on its objects. Warren took pains to make her collection as simple as she could while avoiding the simply mundane. Her efforts were repeated in the exhibition installation, which took about a week. Warren clocked in daily at the gallery to spend hours tweaking the relative position of her sculptural ingredients. One sensed strongly that she was searching not for any formal or conceptual resolution to the piece but rather a conclusion of the opportunity available to work on it. This is not a trivial motive. It was clear that she took her role as a creative maker seriously and that the work would not be finished until the role was over, rather than the other way around.

Last summer, Warren unveiled her latest work in her second gallery show at Maureen Paley Interim Art in London. The show was intriguingly titled "SHE" and was introduced with two overt references. First, the 1887 novel of the same name by Rider Haggard and the Hammer Studios film based on it, starring Ursula Andress as the eponymous embodiment of female power and beauty. Second, a black and white photograph reproduced on the exhibition's invitation, showing Sigmund Freud among a gathering of besuited and bespectacled professional colleagues. Neither reference explains the works shown but both act as allusive counterpoints. The show comprised six large sculptures in unfired clay. These sculptures are approximately life-sized and female but wildly free in their anatomical exaggeration, abbreviation, and expressiveness. Breasts, buttocks, and hands appear as prominent focal points. Heads seem to have fallen victim to evolutionary redundancy. In spite of or because of their deformities the figures possess an uncanny psycho-physiological rectitude and a purposeful energy. Their surfaces are rough and at times seem barely modeled from the raw blocks of clay out of which they emerge. "SHE" unashamedly evokes and engages with a powerful history of expressive figurative sculpture stretching from Degas and Rodin through Boccioni to Fontana, taking in Picasso and the German expressionists for good measure. Warren seems to want to grapple with this lineage of male masters on their own terms, rather than women sculptors of the female form such as Elizabeth Frink. Warren's references to popular culture and to psychology show that she is culturally conscious, but neither irony nor critique is a significant motive behind these works. They can be elucidated by comparisons but they cannot be read as essays. They are not hewn from lard or chocolate nor will they disintegrate through sustained exposure to the climate of East London. Their most up-to-date feature is their placement on studio trolleys. This gives the sculptures an added measure of dynamism (they could scoot off anywhere) and informality (they are not rooted) but was initially a practical step on the part of the artist (they cannot otherwise be moved).

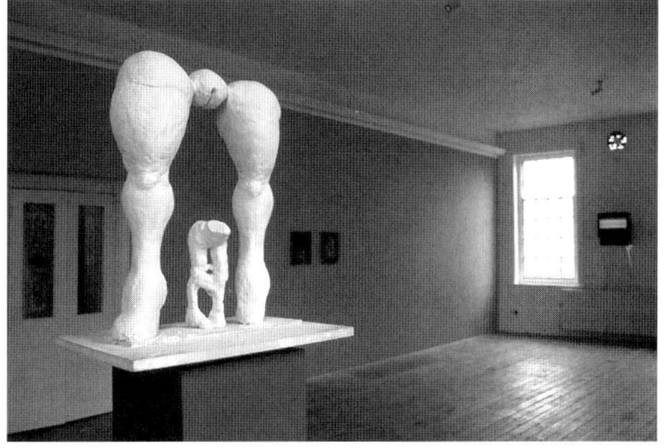

REBECCA WARREN, HELMUT CRUMB, 1998, installation view, "It's a Curse, It's a Burden" at The Approach, London, 1999.

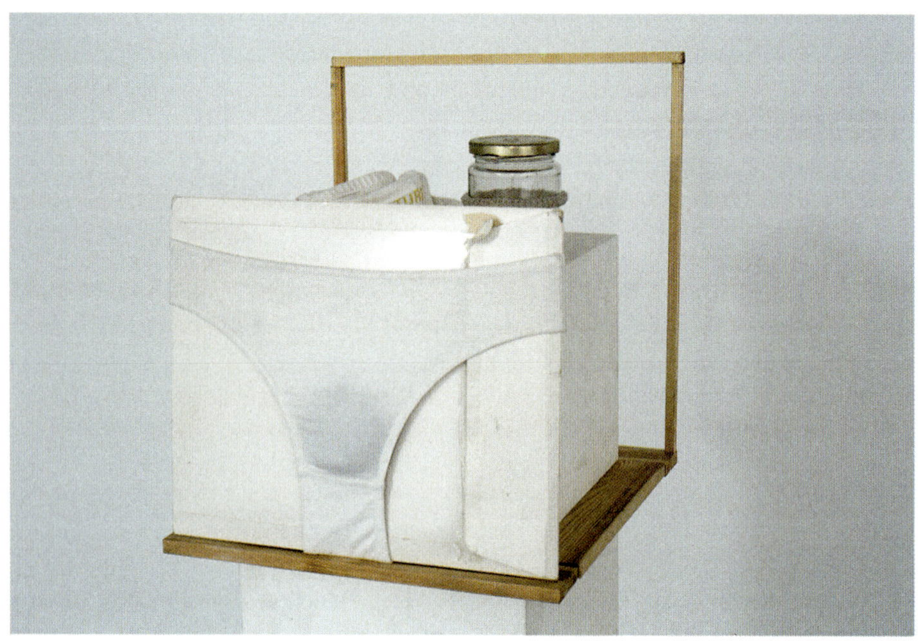

Immediately engaging and persuasive as they are, these sculptures challenge us to place them in a contemporary context and to connect with the signs sent out from EVERY ASPECT OF BITCH MAGIC seven years earlier.

Clues are provided by two groups of works that relate closely to that work and to *SHE* respectively while also possessing their own integrity. Examples of each were displayed together, for the first time, in Warren's exhibition last autumn at the Donald Young Gallery in Chicago. The first is a series of collages, approached like the surface of the BITCH MAGIC plinth turned vertically and hung on the wall. Their contents are perhaps more abstract and even more allusive than those of the earlier work: pieces of wood, wire, pompoms. They evoke however the same mental landscape of everyday arcana, the resonance of abstracted conversations where much is revealed by talking about small subjects close to hand. The

emotional range of these works is extended in wall assemblages like FRAUENSCHADE or F.S.1 (both 2003) that introduce a more sculptural third dimension along with features including small neon lights. The piece that connects them all is BITCH MAGIC: THE MUSICAL (2001–2003), a delightful reprise of the early work but this time with the absurd sumptuousness of a full-length Perspex sheath and sharp injections of color: the electric red of a neon tube and a pompom, a gold-painted plaster off-cast that lies like a molten ingot on top of the Perspex cover. With more than a hint of wry self-awareness Warren the bedroom magician parades her skills as a gallery virtuoso.

The second relevant group consists of a series of unfired clay figurines, collectively titled TOTEMS (2002). They resemble the *SHE* series in their material and free modeling but are smaller, designed for display on plinths and decorated with painted glazes. Rather than single figures they suggest pairs or groups, though engaged in such close erotic coupling that they more often appear unitary clumps of merged matter. Color is used in a manner privileged to porcelain as erogenous indicator, more spice than sustenance. Warren has continued making work in this vein since her surprising 1998 presentation of the piece HELMUT CRUMB, an appropriately obscene hybrid inspired by Helmut Newton and Robert Crumb. The genre was further developed in "The Agony and the Ecstasy," her wide-ranging playful first show at Maureen Paley Interim Art in 2000. The somewhat larger single figures DEUTSCHE BANK (2002–2003) and BUNNY (2003) later paved the way for the *SHE* series and for the similar group of three works, TEACHER (M.B.), TEACHER (R.), and TEACHER (W.), all 2003, included in her Chicago show.

Warren maintains an odd but revealing fiction about these figure works. She would like us to imagine them as having been made by a mildly perverted teacher at a regional English art college. This image conveys (rightly or wrongly) the impression of both artistic and sexual frustration. Repression and liberation characterize and justify most erotic art, both good and bad. Somewhere in between are the films of Russ Meyer, particularly his *Supervixens* series in which spectacularly over-endowed women maintain a droning narrative of withheld desire while periodically bursting out across the screen and each other. The particular relevance to Warren's work is that they do so against a background of blasted desert landscapes strewn with run-down shacks and jeeps and populated with feckless men who talk big but deliver little. While by no means the same as Warren's world, Meyer's mundane mythologizing helps illustrate the profound layers of desire and restraint that run through her work.

Warren's alter ego is a curiously powerful and positive proxy for a young woman artist working today to invoke. It carries certain resonances of Salvador Dalí's obsession with "putrefaction" in the mid-twenties; Warren's posture, like Dalí's, consciously mingles disdain and admiration for her artistic antecedents. This in turn leads to sophisticated, if apparently aberrant, strategies for producing new work faced with all that have come before. Dalí wrote, in terms that seem directly relevant to Warren's artistic proj-

ect, "Form is always the product of an inquisitorial process of matter—the specific reaction of matter when subjected to the terrible coercion of space choking it on all sides, pressing and squeezing it out, producing the swellings that burst from its life to the exact limits of the rigorous contours of its own originality of reaction."[1] However Warren defines the physical and historical contours of her originality, her impetus to exceed those limits remains consistently compelling.

1) Salvador Dalí, *The Secret Life of Salvador Dalí*, trans. Haakon M. Chevalier (1942), (London: Vision Press, 1968), p. 3.

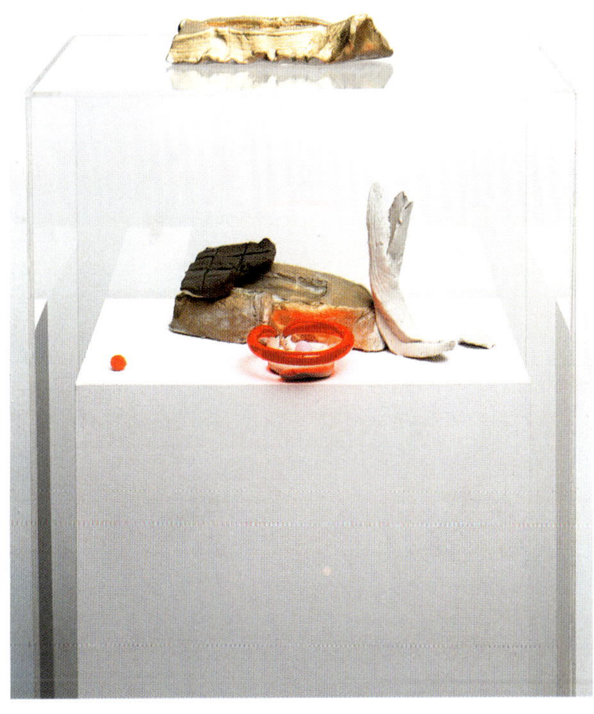

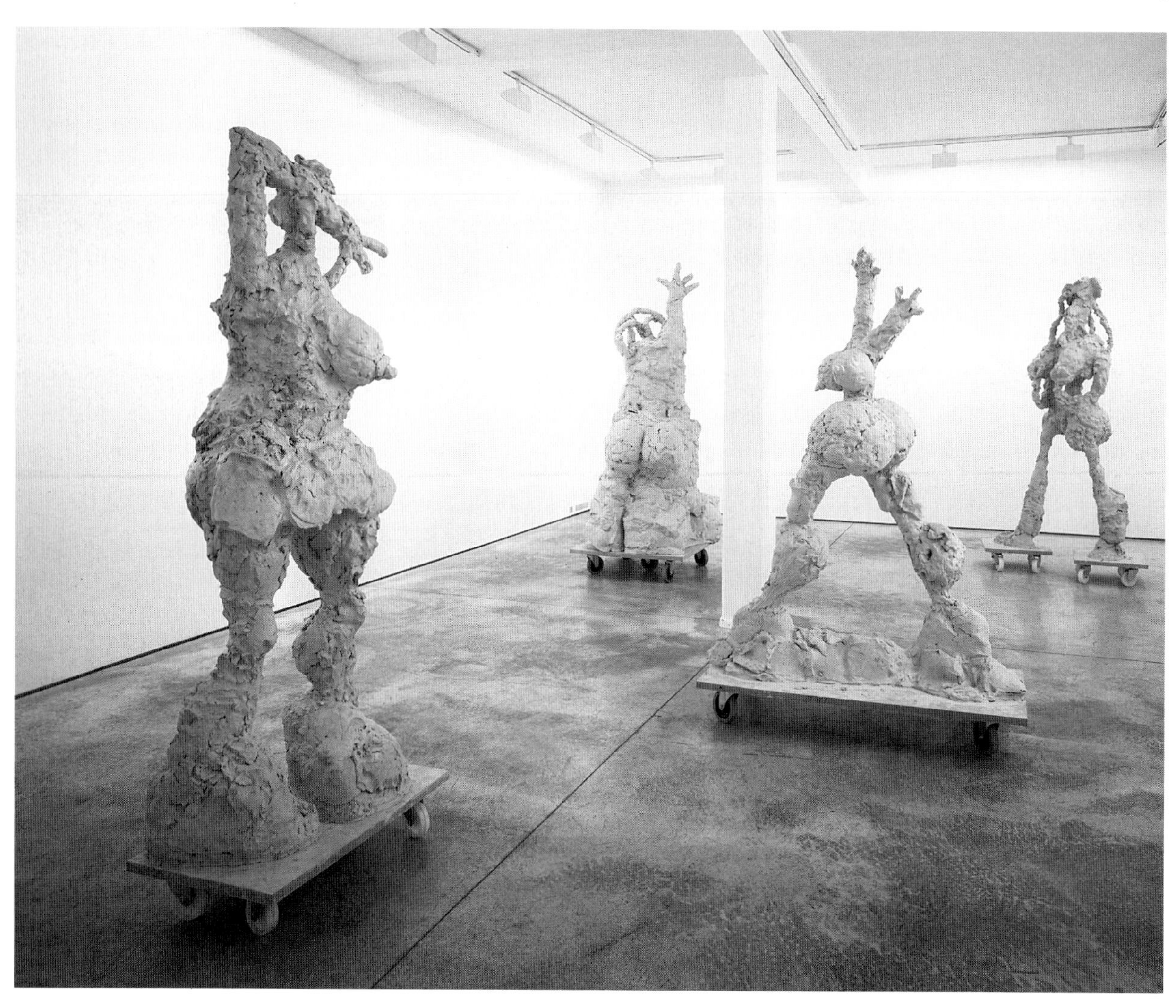

REBECCA WARREN, "SHE," 2003, installation view at Maureen Paley Interim Art, London; clockwise from left: HOMAGE TO R. CRUMB; MY FATHER; SOUTH KENT; NO. 6 / im Uhrzeigersinn von links: HOMMAGE AN R. CRUMB; MEIN VATER; SOUTH KENT; NR. 6.

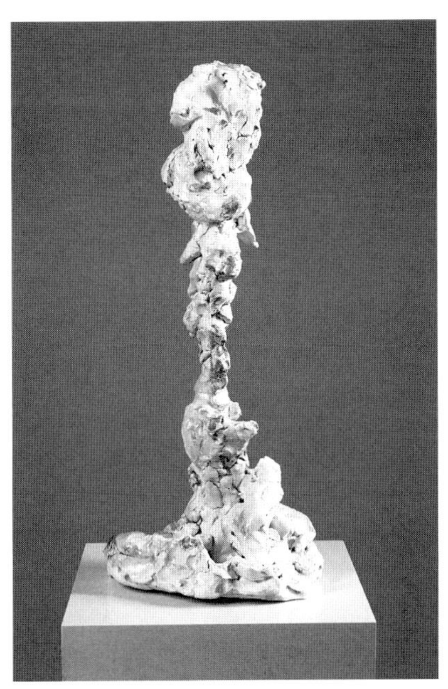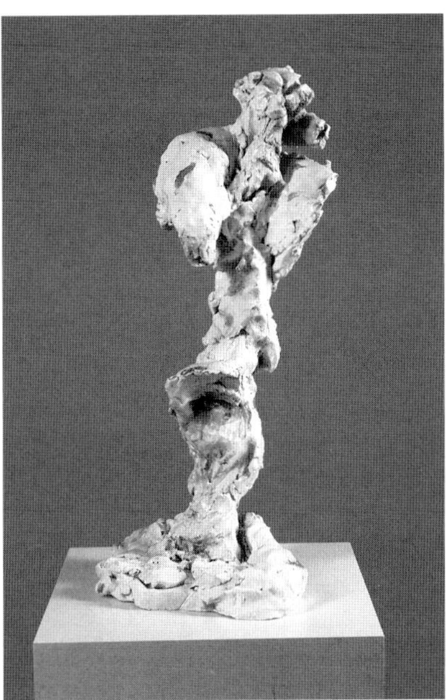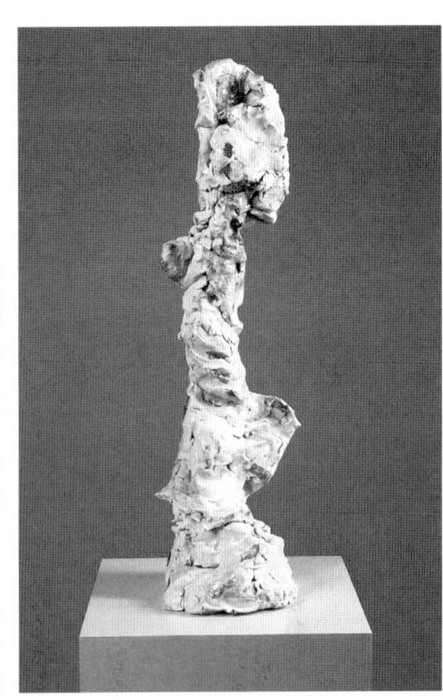

REBECCA WARREN, TOTEMS, 2003, self-hardening clay; height: a) 23$^1/_2$”, b) 22”, c) 25$^1/_2$” /

selbsthärtender Ton; Höhe: a) 60 cm, b) 56 cm, c) 64,8 cm.

11

GREG HILTY

Rebecca Warren: SHE

EVERY ASPECT OF BITCH MAGIC (Ludermagie in all ihren Aspekten, 1996) war eines der ersten Werke von Rebecca Warren, das bei einem breiteren Publikum Beachtung fand, es bleibt ein Markstein für alles, was danach kam. Ich sah zu, wie sie die Arbeit installierte, und zwar im Rahmen der Ausstellung «Material Culture» in der Hayward Gallery in London 1997, die ich gemeinsam mit Michael Archer als Kurator betreute. Die Ausstellung untersuchte verschiedene Arten des Umgangs mit Objekten in der britischen Kunst der letzten zwei Jahrzehnte. Aber selbst in einem so betont heterogenen Umfeld blieb Warrens Vorgehen auffällig. Sie hatte die Arbeit im Lauf von drei Monaten in ihrem Schlafzimmer geschaffen. Dieser biographische Hintergrund ist wichtig, weil Inhalt und Bedeutung des Werks sehr persönlich und kompakt sind. Sie begann mit einem weissen Sockel, auf den sie allerlei Objekte, die gerade verfügbar waren, stellte und wieder auswechselte. Darunter war auch ein Marmeladeglas mit einer toten Biene drin, das Geschenk einer Freundin. Zur Sicherheit war ein elastisches Haarband darüber gespannt. Andere Gegenstände, die ihren Platz auf dem Sockel fanden, waren eine Muschel, eine grüne Glasscherbe, ein Paar Unterhosen und eine Sicherheitsnadel. Als Entwurf für eine Plexiglashaube

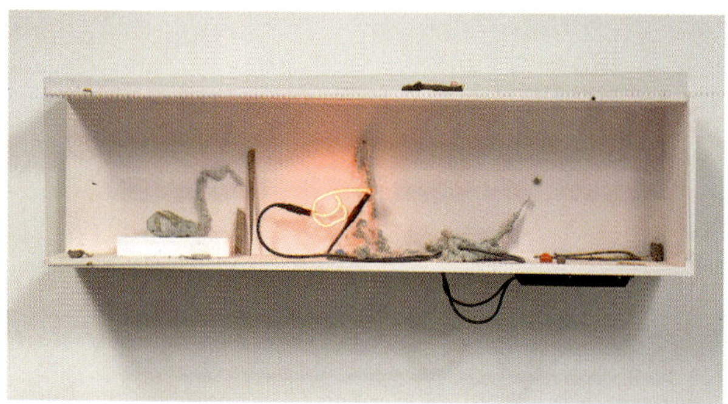

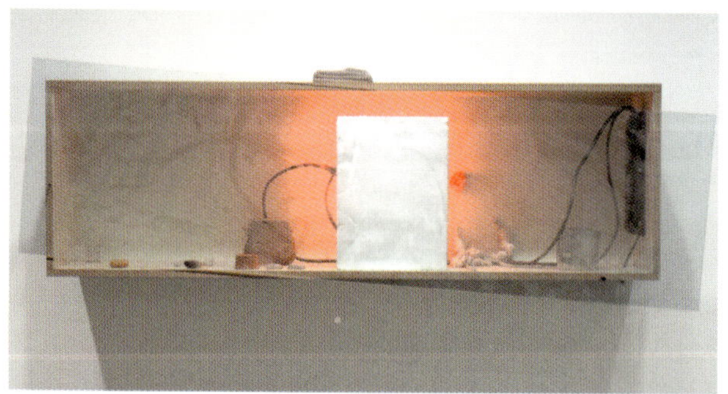

Top / Oben: REBECCA WARREN, FRAUENSCHADE, 2003, mixed media, 16 ³/₄ x 54 ⁵/₁₆ x 11 ¹/₄" / 42,5 x 138 x 28,5 cm. Bottom / Unten: F.S.1, 2003, mixed media, 17 ¹/₄ x 53 ¹/₂ x 11 ¹/₄" / 43,8 x 135,9 x 28,5 cm.

(PHOTOS: MAUREEN PALEY INTERIM ART, LONDON)

GREG HILTY ist Publizist und Kurator sowie Director of Visual Arts and Literature des Arts Council England in London.

baute Warren einen Holzrahmen dazu. Diese Haube stellte sie dann nie her, aber den stellvertretenden Rahmen behielt sie bei. Auf dem Rahmen lag ein grosser weisser Briefumschlag, über den sie wiederum ein Paar Unterhosen gespannt hatte, deren Schritt sorgfältig mit Flusen aus einem Wäschetrockner ausgepolstert war. Der Briefumschlag selbst war ebenfalls ausgestopft, und zwar mit Dias vom Werk der Künstlerin.

Eine Beschreibung ist noch keine Kritik und eine Ansammlung von Dingen an sich noch keine Kunst. Dennoch beschwor Warrens Anhäufung scheinbar zufälliger Elemente allein schon durch ihre Beschreibung die im Titel angesprochene Vollständigkeit und Magie herauf. Die Arbeit verrät einen Drang zur Kunst, der älter ist als jede Mimesis und jeder Symbolismus: nämlich den Impuls, der rohen Materie Geist einzuhauchen oder Bedeutung zu verleihen und sie dadurch zu verwandeln. Ein solcher Prozess, den man auch «magisch» nennen kann, ist ebenso von der Art des Verwandlungsaktes abhängig wie von den zu verwandelnden Objekten. Warren setzte alles daran, ihre Sammlung so einfach wie möglich zu halten und gleichzeitig das allzu Profane zu vermeiden. Diese Anstrengung wiederholte sich beim Einrichten der Ausstellung, das etwa eine Woche in Anspruch nahm. Warren tauchte jeden Tag in den Ausstellungsräumen auf und verbrachte Stunden damit, die skulpturalen Elemente ihrer Arbeit im richtigen Verhältnis zueinander zu platzieren. Es war deutlich zu spüren, dass sie nicht nach einer formalen oder konzeptuellen Lösung suchte, sondern nach einem Abschluss der Möglichkeit daran zu arbeiten. Das ist kein trivialer Beweggrund. Es war klar, dass sie ihre kreative Rolle ernst nahm und dass das Werk nicht vollendet sein würde, bis sie diese Rolle erfüllt hätte, und nicht etwa umgekehrt.

Letzten Sommer enthüllte Warren ihr jüngstes Werk in ihrer zweiten Galerieausstellung bei Maureen Paley Interim Art in London. Die Ausstellung trug den verführerischen Titel «SHE» (Sie) und stand unter dem Zeichen zweier offensichtlicher Referenzen: erstens, des gleichnamigen Romans von Rider Haggard und seiner Verfilmung durch die Hammer Studios, mit Ursula Andress als Verkörperung weiblicher Macht und Schönheit in der Hauptrolle; zwei-

tens, einer Schwarzweissphotographie, die auf der Einladungskarte abgebildet war und Sigmund Freud in einer Versammlung Brillen tragender Professorenkollegen in schwarzen Anzügen zeigte. Keine dieser Referenzen erklärt die ausgestellten Werke, aber beide fungieren als kontrapunktische Anspielungen. Die Ausstellung umfasste sechs grosse Skulpturen in ungebranntem Ton. Diese Skulpturen sind ungefähr lebensgross, weiblich, aber völlig frei, ja wild in ihren anatomischen Übertreibungen, Vereinfachungen und ihrer Expressivität. Vor allem die Brüste, Hinterteile und Hände ziehen die Blicke auf sich. Die Köpfe scheinen einer evolutionären Redundanz zum Opfer gefallen zu sein. Trotz oder gerade wegen ihrer Deformierungen besitzen die Figuren eine unheimliche psycho-physiologische Richtigkeit und eine zielgerichtete Energie. Ihre Oberflächen sind rau und scheinen manchmal kaum modelliert, das heisst, sie unterscheiden sich kaum von den rohen Tonklötzen, aus denen sie entstanden sind. Unerschrocken verweist «SHE» auf die grosse Tradition der expressiven figurativen Bildhauerei von Degas und Rodin bis hin zu Boccioni und Fontana und schliesst auch gleich noch Picasso samt den deutschen Expressionisten mit ein. Warren scheint lieber mit dieser Ahnenreihe männlicher Meister zu deren Bedingungen fertig werden zu wollen, als sich auf weibliche Bildhauerinnen wie etwa Elizabeth Frink zu beziehen. Warrens Verweise auf die Populärkultur und Psychologie zeigen, dass sie kulturell bewandert ist, aber weder Ironie noch Kulturkritik bilden ein wesentliches Motiv ihrer Arbeiten. Sie lassen sich durch Vergleiche erhellen, können aber nicht als Essays verstanden werden. Sie sind weder aus Speck oder Schokolade gehauen, noch werden sie sich auflösen, wenn man sie über längere Zeit dem Klima East Londons aussetzt. Das einzig offensichtlich Zeitgenössische an ihnen ist ihre Platzierung auf Rollsockeln. Dies verleiht den Skulpturen eine zusätzliche Dynamik (sie könnten irgendwohin wegflitzen) und Zwanglosigkeit (sie sind nicht verwurzelt), war ursprünglich jedoch eine rein praktische Massnahme der Künstlerin (weil sich die Figuren nur so bewegen lassen).

So unmittelbar einnehmend und überzeugend diese Skulpturen sind, wir sind aufgefordert, sie in einen zeitgenössischen Kontext einzuordnen und

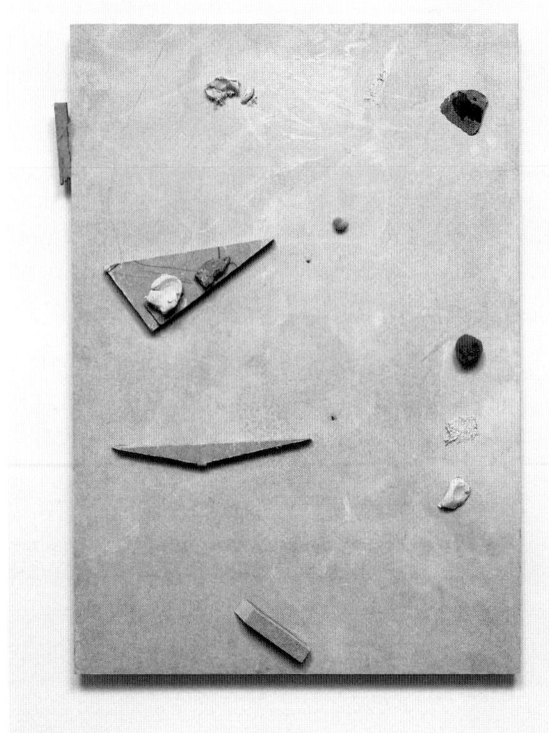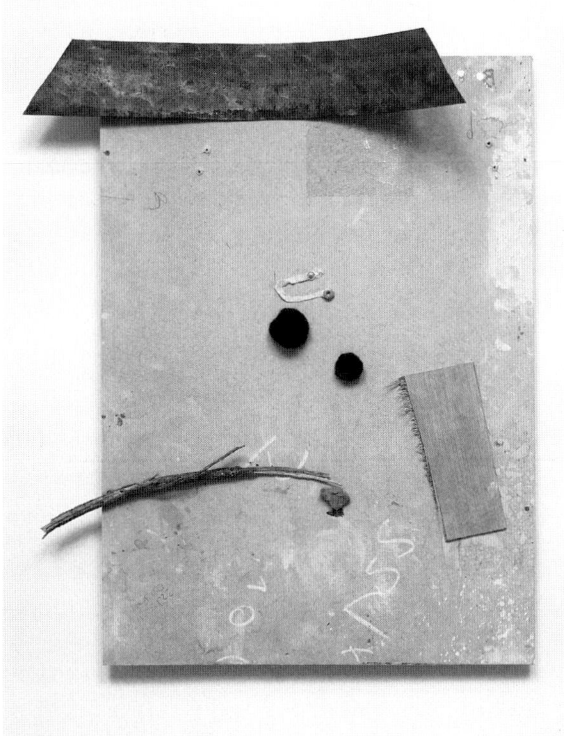

Left / Links: REBECCA WARREN, COLLAGE, 2003, mixed media on MDF, 24 x 20 x 5" / diverse Materialien auf MDF, 61 x 51 x 12,7 cm.
Right / Rechts: COLLAGE, 2003, 24 $^1/_2$ x 16 x 1 $^3/_4$" / 62,2 x 40,7 x 4,5 cm.

eine Verbindung zu jenen Zeichen herzustellen, welche die sieben Jahre früher entstandene Arbeit EVERY ASPECT OF BITCH MAGIC gesetzt hat.

Hinweise dazu liefern zwei Gruppen von Werken, die eine gleichermassen enge Beziehung zu jener Arbeit und zu «SHE» aufweisen und dabei gleichzeitig über eine eigene Integrität verfügen. Beispiele beider Gruppen waren erstmals im letzten Herbst zusammen ausgestellt, und zwar im Rahmen von Warrens Ausstellung bei Donald Young in Chicago. Die erste ist eine Serie von Collagen, die gleichsam die in die Vertikale gekippte und an die Wand gehängte Oberfläche des BITCH-MAGIC-Sockels zeigen. Ihr Inhalt ist vielleicht abstrakter und sogar noch anspielungsreicher als jener des älteren Werks: Holzstücke, Draht, Pompons. Beide beschwören jedoch dieselbe geistige Landschaft aus Alltagsmysterien, ein Nachhallen zerstreuter Unterhaltungen, in denen vieles

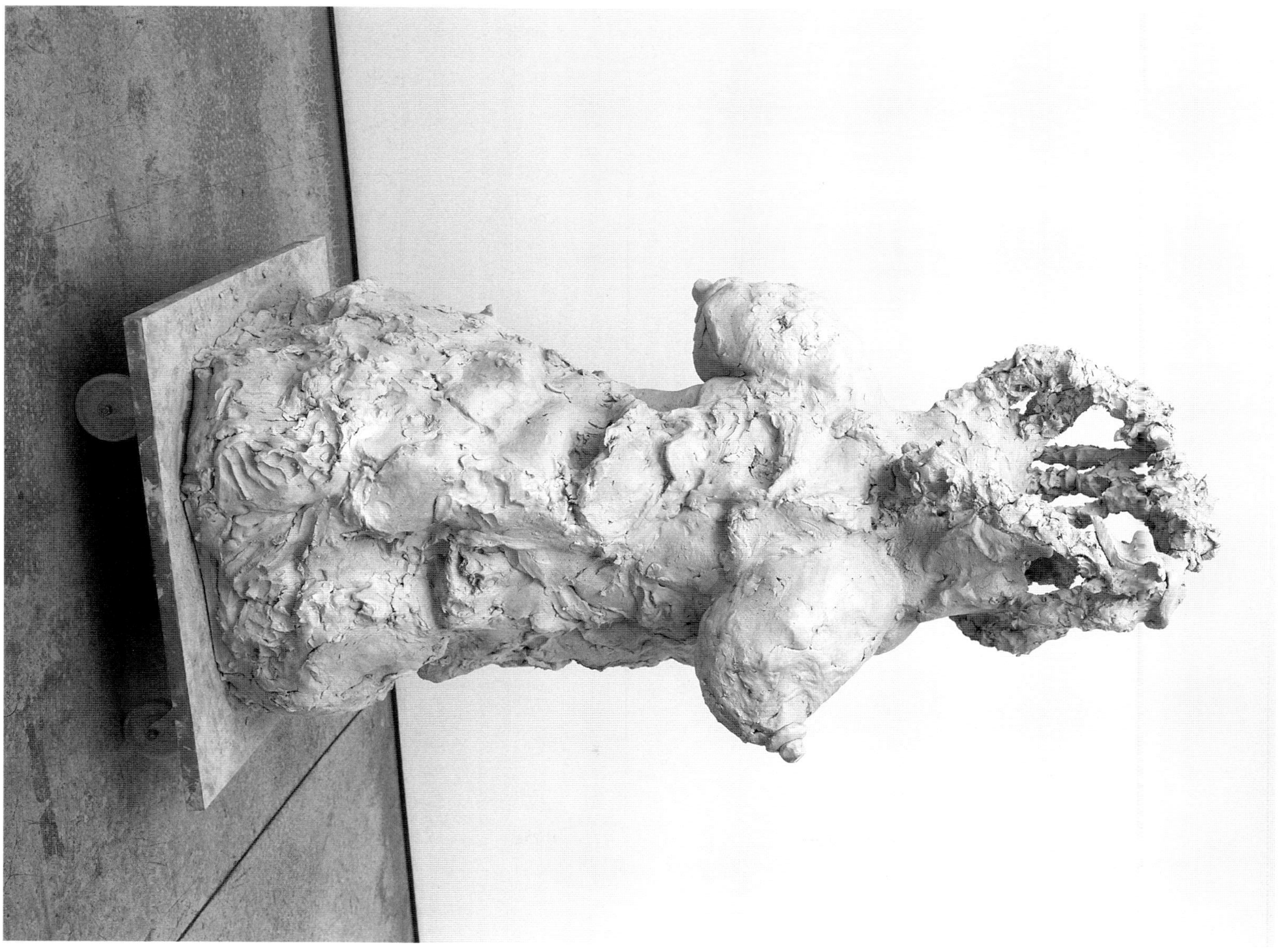

REBECCA WARREN: DEUTSCHE BANK, 2002, unfired clay, MDF and wheels, 26 x 29⅛ x 29⅛" / ungebrannter Ton, MDF und Räder, 66 x 74 x 74 cm.

beim Sprechen über kleine und nahe liegende Dinge offenbar wird. Die emotionale Bandbreite dieser Arbeiten wird noch erweitert in Wandassemblagen wie FRAUENSCHADE oder F.S.1 (beide 2003), die noch deutlicher eine plastische dritte Dimension einführen und Dinge wie kleine Neonlampen. Das Werk, das alles miteinander verbindet, ist BITCH MAGIC: THE MUSICAL (2001–2003), eine vergnügliche Wiederaufnahme der früheren Arbeit, aber diesmal mit der absurden Luxuriosität einer umfassenden Plexiglasverkleidung und knalligen Farbtupfern: dem elektrisierenden Rot einer Neonröhre und eines Pompons; einem golden bemalten Gipsabguss, der wie ein echter Goldbarren auf der Plexiglashaube liegt. Mit mehr als nur einem Hauch Selbstironie demonstriert Warren, die Magierin des Schlafzimmers, ihre Virtuosität beim Bespielen der Galerie.

Die zweite wichtige Werkgruppe besteht in einer Serie ungebrannter Tonfiguren mit dem gemeinsamen Titel TOTEMS (2002). Sie ähneln den Figuren der *SHE*-Serie, was Material und Freiheit des Modellierens angeht, aber sie sind kleiner, für das Ausstellen auf Sockeln gedacht, obwohl sie oft in so enger erotischer Umarmung begriffen sind, dass sie meist eher wie ein einziger Klumpen verschmolzener Materie wirken. Farbe wird auf eine Weise eingesetzt, die sonst dem Porzellan vorbehalten ist, als erogenes Signal, mehr würzige Zutat denn wesentlicher Bestandteil. Warren pflegt diese Werklinie seit ihrer überraschenden Präsentation von HELMUT CRUMB (1998), einer angemessen obszönen Kreuzung von Helmut Newton und Robert Crumb. Dasselbe Genre entwickelte sie weiter in «The Agony and the Ecstasy», ihrer vielseitig verspielten ersten Ausstellung bei Maureen Paley Interim Art im Jahr 2000. Die etwas grösseren Einzelfiguren DEUTSCHE BANK (2002–2003) und BUNNY (2003) bereiteten den Weg für die Serie *SHE* sowie eine ähnliche Dreiergruppe – TEACHER (M.B.), TEACHER (B.) und TEACHER (W.), alle 2003 –, die ebenfalls in Chicago zu sehen war.

Warren hat eine seltsame, aber aufschlussreiche Phantasie zu diesen figurativen Werken. Sie möchte, dass wir uns vorstellen, sie stammten von einem leicht perversen Lehrer an einer englischen Kunstschule in der Provinz. Dieses Bild erweckt (ob zu Recht oder zu Unrecht) den Eindruck künstlerischer

und sexueller Frustration. Unterdrückung und Befreiung kennzeichnen und rechtfertigen fast jede erotische Kunst, egal ob sie gut oder schlecht ist. Irgendwo dazwischen sind die Filme von Russ Meyer, insbesondere seine *Supervixens*-Serie, in der spektakulär üppig ausgestattete Frauen eine eintönige Handlung unterdrückten Begehrens in Gang halten, das immer wieder ausbricht, indem sie die Leinwand zu sprengen drohen und übereinander herfallen. Der Bezug zu Warrens Arbeit liegt darin, dass dies vor verbrannten Wüstenlandschaften stattfindet, die mit baufälligen Schuppen und Jeeps übersät sind und bevölkert von kraftlosen Männern, die zwar das Maul aufreissen, aber sonst nicht viel taugen. Und obwohl ihre Welten ganz und gar nicht dieselben sind, liefert Meyers profane Mythologie eine hilfreiche Illustration der tieferen Schichten von Begehren und Unterdrückung, denen wir in Warrens Werk begegnen.

Warrens Alter Ego ist ein seltsam kraftvoller und konkreter Stellvertreter für eine junge Künstlerin unserer Tage. Es erinnert ein bisschen an Salvador Dalís «Fäulnis»-Fimmel Mitte der 20er Jahre; wie Dalí vereint Warren Verachtung und Bewunderung für ihre künstlerischen Vorläufer ganz bewusst. Das führt zu raffinierten, wenn auch scheinbar ausgefallenen Strategien der Produktion neuer Werke angesichts all jener, die vorangegangen sind. Dalí schrieb, in Worten, die einen direkten Bezug zu Warrens künstlerischer Tätigkeit zu haben scheinen, «Form ist immer das Produkt eines inquisitorischen Prozesses der Materie – die spezifische Reaktion von Materie, die dem schrecklichen Zwang des Raumes unterworfen wird, der sie von allen Seiten würgt, presst und ausquetscht und die Beulen hervortreibt, die sich aus ihrem Leben bis exakt zu den Grenzen der strengen Konturen ihrer Reaktionseigenart entladen.»[1] Warren definiert jedoch die physischen und historischen Konturen ihrer eigenen Ursprünglichkeit, und ihr Impuls diese Grenzen zu überschreiten ist und bleibt überzeugend.

(Übersetzung: Wilma Parker)

1) Salvador Dalí, *Das geheime Leben des Salvador Dalí*, Übers. Ralf Schiebler, Schirmer/Mosel, München 1990, S. 12–14.

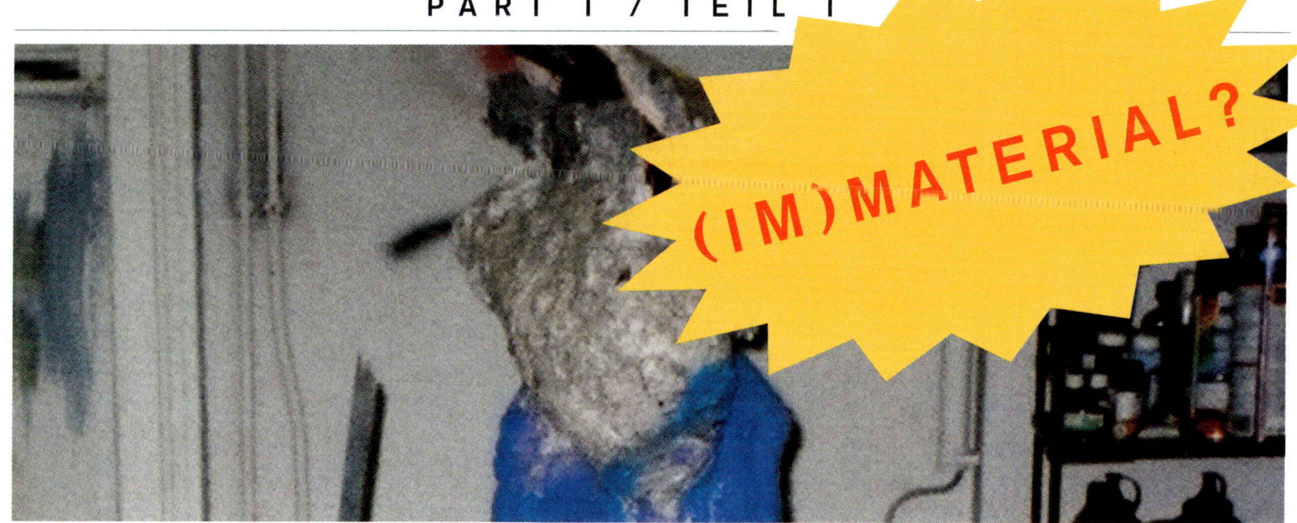

THE FIRST OF THREE ESSAYS ON THE WHYS AND WHEREFORES OF MATERIALS IN CONTEMPORARY ART, IN CELEBRATION OF PARKETT'S 20TH ANNIVERSARY / DER ERSTE VON DREI ESSAYS ZUM MATERIALBEGRIFF IN DER GEGENWARTSKUNST ANLÄSSLICH DES 20-JÄHRIGEN JUBILÄUMS VON PARKETT

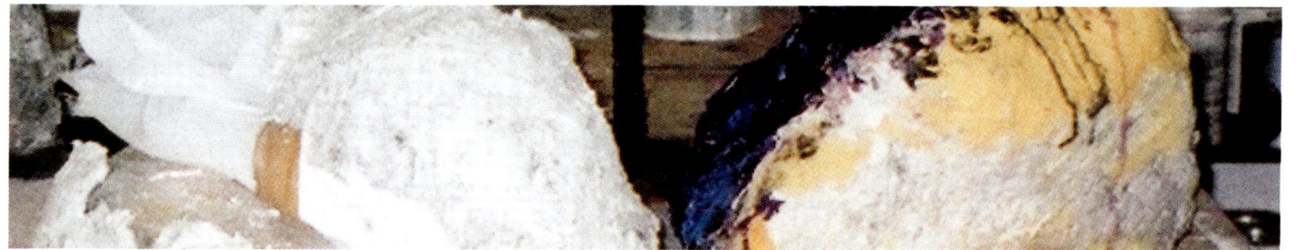

WITH A SPECIAL COLLABORATION BY / MIT EINER EXTRA-COLLABORATION VON

FRANZ WEST

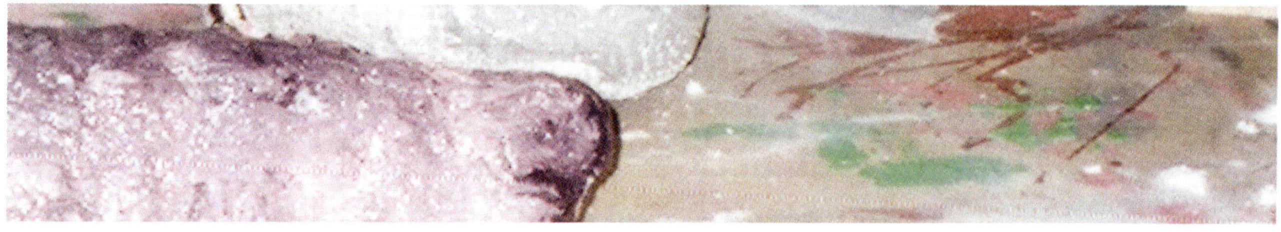

AND ARTISTS' PAGES / UND KÜNSTLERBEITRÄGEN

INHALT

THE "URMATERIAL" URGE

JOHANNA BURTON

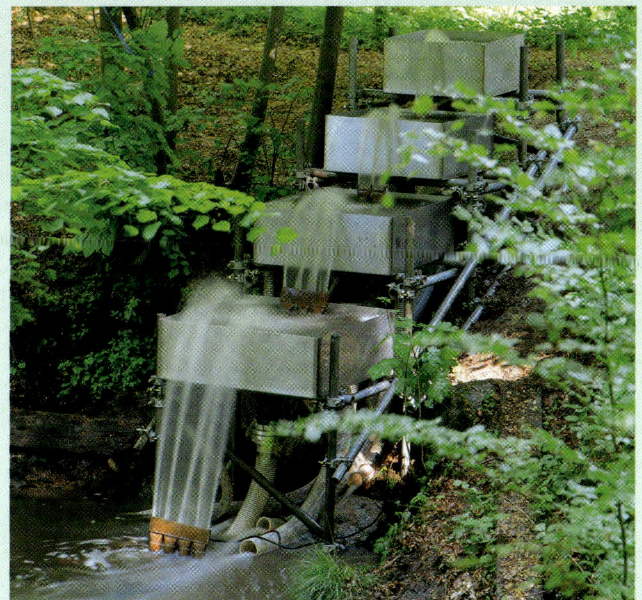

OLAFUR ELIASSON, YET UNTITLED,
1998/2000, reversed waterfall,
installation at the Wanas Foundation,
Knislinge, Sweden / NOCH OHNE TITEL,
umgekehrter Wasserfall.

"We still do not know how much less 'nothing' can be. Has an ultimate zero point been arrived at with black paintings, white paintings, light beams, transparent film, silent concerts, invisible sculpture…? It hardly seems likely."[1] These are the closing lines from Lucy Lippard's famous 1968 rumination on "The Dematerialization of Art," and they pose a kind of modern-day Zeno's paradox. It seemed that if the very definition of early postmodern art was increasingly linked to a gradual dissolution of the object and a visible distancing of idea from material, it would logically follow that soon the most advanced contemporary works might no longer be recognized as art at all—at least not according to any of its previous conceptions. At the same time, conceptual or performance-based practices (those two strains of postmodern art that Lippard saw as contributing to the dematerialization, and thus potential obsolescence, of the object) simultaneously stood as totems of art's future. That is, while exceeding, even counteracting, the formerly established terms of art, these new modes offered the possibility that art itself remain vital and viable, pleasurable and critical, relevant in the face of an ever-more voracious spectacle culture. But, however you read the equation: as the end of art or as its rebirth by way of burgeoning postmodern condition, Lippard's essay concluded with her productive pontification on the limits of the zero point, which I'll simply rephrase as: Just how low can you go?

One answer (and this was: lower, much lower) was given by way of a rotated axis, as Jean-François Lyotard shifted from the vertical measure of dematerialization to the horizontal spread of the "immaterial." In his mammoth 1985 exhibition at the Centre Georges Pompidou, titled "Les Immatériaux," Lyotard presented a notion of immateriality that took on the micro-features inherent to viral sprawl. Indeed, "immateriality," as such, didn't announce the disappearance of the object altogether—it rather posed questions about the radically new relationship between object and maker, in part by suggesting that there were "materials" that already shimmered in and out of comprehension as such. "Immaterial" materials were associated specifically with the technological revolution—prosthetic skin is one handy example—and neatly illustrated what Lyotard saw as an increasingly wide cleft altering what had been, since the Enlightenment, a straightforward relationship of man's mastery over objects. Lyotard argued that the terms of creation were, in both theological and artistic terms, in the process of being radically retooled; the reassuring Hegelian notion that objects of art could be understood as providing mirror reflections of human subjects could simply no longer be ascribed to. In fact, having lost control of the creative process, man had relinquished mastery and become just one more element in a sea of immateriality, no longer central but rather one more interchangeable cog.

Perhaps most importantly, Lyotard offered yet another model of materiality on the move—one not, as with Lippard's, gradually emptying itself of symbolic freight, but instead rather violently exploding, bursting, effectively atomizing itself into particles. Where dematerialization was, to an extent, a kind of experiment in seeing how long a body could live after its head had been chopped off—think of Kosuth's paintings of dictionary definitions—immaterialization proposed something else. There was, it seemed, a counterintuitive anti-entropy at work, in which material broke down into smaller and smaller components in order to keep circulating (rather than winding down)—and these microscopic parts, operating by way of constant displacement, could no longer, even clumsily, be sutured together (even as, paradoxically, the boundaries between them dizzyingly blurred). No wonder, then, that Lyotard filled the galleries of the Pompidou with anything he felt might embody immaterial materials, these all equally part of an "immanent and, as it were, 'flat' network of areas of in-

quiry"[2]: from artworks to architectural plans; from computer programs to scientific trials; from conceptual experiments to theoretical data. Here, any remaining notion of "material" manifested itself as a knife's edge—paradoxically reducing everything to immaterial indistinguishability and yet spontaneously producing unexpected relationships and patterns within its chaotic nebula. For Lyotard, then, if there was a way to productively rethink aesthetics, it was by unmooring the visible from representation (or meaning), to introduce a kind of hiccup between the two, and to thus allow for the possibility of the "presentation of the unpresentable."[3] (It is not inconsequential that Duchamp was one of Lyotard's favorite artists.) Lyotard's earlier *Postmodern Condition* notion of "incommensurability" (which provided an opportunity to discombobulate the act of seeing, as it were, to abruptly release objects and words from pre-assigned meanings and to render both momentarily—if not perpetually—strange) looked to have evolved into a radical "imcommensurability," in which notions of measure and proportion necessarily undid themselves altogether.[4]

Briefly mapping this trajectory makes one thing clear. No less in 1985 than in 1968 and whether joined by an anxious "de-" or an ambiguous "im-" ("immaterials" can, after all, be equally read as not-materials or knot-materials), materiality itself was very much the shakily privileged term, as terms in states of useful crisis often seem to be. And this is no less the case today—the prefix that would, however, best describe the relationship of artistic practice to material product (or byproduct) might be the German "ur," making ours perhaps the moment of "urmateriality." Indeed, considering many recent engagements with, and extensions of, materiality, as such, it's tempting to rethink materiality in the new millennium as a kind of psychic construction rather than any palpable substance, no matter how malleable or divested of meaning. The prefix "ur"—with its connotations of original, primitive, ancient, or archetypal—offers a way of thinking materiality as phantasmatic space, or to be more precise, phantasmatic nonspace. Take two recent projects done in the Tate Modern's cavernous Turbine Hall in just the last two years. (Indeed, the hall's existence itself is conducive to a rethinking of materiality—liminal, cave-like, and striving for sublimity, the space exerts an unspoken "urmaterial" imperative on any artwork taking up residence there.)

In October 2002, Anish Kapoor unveiled MARSYAS, an installation work that nearly filled the hall's 550-foot long, 75-foot wide, 115-foot high expanse. In keeping with Kapoor's oeuvre, however, the work managed to utilize materials in such a way that, while undeniably taking up space, it

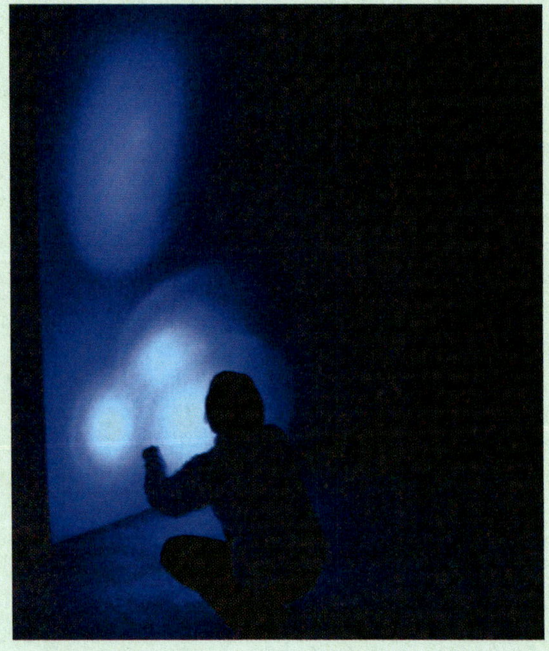

DAVID HAMMONS, CONCERTO
IN BLACK AND BLUE, 2002,
installation view, Ace Gallery, New York /
KONZERT IN SCHWARZ UND BLAU.
(PHOTO: ACE GALLERY, NEW YORK)

simultaneously created an alternate space—this one extending both literally and figuratively to suggest a kind of shared skin between artwork and viewer. MARSYAS (the title of which refers to the satyr flayed alive by Apollo) was a monumental membrane, a kind of corporeal möbius that disallowed rational binaries, such as inside and outside, horizontal and vertical, here and there. This tautly pulled deep-red epidermis was folded into an undulating shape not unlike a monumental eardrum, with each end twisting into a conch-like spiral and offering virtual access to those canals within. The work could hardly be called a sculpture in any traditional sense, though it did use materials in order to sculpt the viewer's experience of space, as did minimalist works of the sixties. Yet, here that sculpted space rendered the body experiencing it into a synaesthetic membrane itself, as the gargantuan corpus transmitted sensory data to any body in its proximity. Indeed, here sight became invariably mixed up with sounds produced from the hollows and planes of the membrane, just as color called up taste and smell. Kapoor's stake in what I'm calling "urmateriality" has almost nothing to do with the nuts and bolts of its fantastic edifice—constructed using one immense sheet of PVC membrane. Rather, such "urmateriality" exists in the kind of archetypal synaesthetic space in which bodies were self-reflexively unmoored from language and had to give into a kind of inverted monumentality. There is hardly an image that the piece calls to mind more than the womb—that first space of "materiality" that is indubitably linked to "maternity." Here, "urmateriality" might be seen as a conduit for the experiential—ungrounding the viewer through the most deeply familiar, yet deeply unnamable, space.

Olafur Eliasson's work for the Turbine Hall, which opened there in October 2003, operates in a slightly different "urmaterial" mode. The Nordic artist has been celebrated for his ability to conjure the sublime through banal mechanical means, and he often lays bare the mechanisms of clichés of the "natural" by multiplying their Romantic (and thus artificial) effects—perhaps at once a critique and a celebration of such long-standing pleasures. Indeed, such works as a waterfall that runs uphill and strobe-lit artificial rain call attention not only to conventionally represented nature but, perhaps more importantly, to habituated patterns of seeing. In THE WEATHER PROJECT, Eliasson goes so far as to render such subtle retoolings as a kind of immersive mirage. Here, the hall is occupied by no recognizable "materials" but is instead emptied of its architectural status and recoded as an outdoor—or perhaps otherworldly—environment. A huge "sun" is constructed as thousands of mono-frequency lights form a half-arc that is completed by its twin reflection in the mirrored ceiling. A fine mist is emitted, and it gathers and dissipates, approximating the behavior of clouds. Viewers congregate in the space, lolling on the cement ground beneath them as though it were a grassy hill, formally invited by the artist to contemplate contemplation itself. If the intellectual and mnemonic aims of the project aren't readily clear, given its components, the Tate's website makes them explicit, inviting audience members to contribute their own weather stories, these presumably recalled and illuminated by Eliasson's atmospheric doppelganger. If "urmateriality" is a means for Kapoor to access a literally originary space (pre-language, where bodies are not yet distinguishable from one another— a kind of primordial prehistory), for Eliasson it works to establish a hallucinatory collective memory. Indeed, there is no one for whom an evocation of a misty day—sun bursting through— will not call up myriad memories, longings, and fantasies, many of them imposed by the media or other shared texts. "Urmateriality" works to call attention to the everyday events (here, the weather) that, activated, reveal themselves as communally binding.

In 1915, Freud coined the term "Urphantasien" (primal phantasies), in part to explain how certain psychic realities are not necessarily in line with physical ones.[5] For Freud, it was possible that primal phantasies—scenes of sexual intercourse between parents, seduction, and castration, among them—could be explained phylogenetically. He argued that such phantasies had, in fact, been acted out in the larger archaic history of humanity (entering into a kind of collective memory) and thus, even when not experienced by an individual directly, could find themselves incorporated into an individual's psychic history. While I hardly want to argue that works by, say, Eliasson and Kapoor are attempts to tap into such a dubious collective pool, as Freud suggests, I do think that the term affords a number of ways of thinking about the current stakes of materiality in art-making. So many artists are turning toward a communal pool of information, experience, or history as the primary "materials" for their practices that one might fruitfully ask just how such projects—these relying on a common human denominator, whether physical or cultural—must necessarily proceed by way of the "urmaterial." This needn't mean returning to a primordial soup, or even to the womb, but more widely to a notion of shared—if not always firsthand—experience. The word "immersive" is used again and again to describe installations like those above, and this language only affirms the way "urmaterials" work, suggesting, as they do, that one's bodily and psychic responses are not merely reactions to the work but are, in fact, the work itself.

Such tendencies can be seen in David Hammons's 2003 CONCERTO IN BLACK AND BLUE, a work that literally didn't exist without its audience, which was asked to circumnavigate a 20,000-square-foot space guided only by tiny LED flashlights that emitted pinpoints of blue light. The piece, then, was the eventual interaction of tiny beams—yours within a ready-made community of other participants—and the realization that the only object to be seen was your own mostly blinded journey as it intersected with others. On the opposite aesthetic pole, "urmateriality" might be said to operate in Thomas Hirschhorn's lovingly constructed, abundantly cluttered altars and kiosks—these pedagogical weigh-stations designed to house temporary communities of readers who share philosophical and cultural history, if seemingly little else. Here, as with works by, say, Philippe Parreno, Pierre Huyghe, Rirkrit Tiravanija, and others "urmateriality" works not so much through the material substance engaged within the space of any one work—whether redeployed Japanese anime character, xeroxed Marxist text, or steaming pot of Thai noodles—but rather by way of the strata of another phantasmatically constructed communal history.

This needn't manifest itself as utopic, critical, or even socially prescriptive though some artists—Hirschhorn, for example—do utilize such "urmaterial" manifestations to address the current political climate, just as others use that mode to levy cultural analysis. (Hammons, for example, has addressed racist capitalism head on by way of the "urmaterial.") Rachel Harrison, not clearly condemning or celebrating, deploys the "urmaterial" by calling upon commonly held cultural and social signifiers (photos of Liz Taylor, cans of olives, middle America home furnishings) and then severing the link between a construction of primal phantasy around those objects and their contemporary relevance. Pairing minimalist sculpture gone *informe* with generally lowbrow commodity items, Harrison's "urmateriality" stalls its viewers in the umbilical space between temporalities, forcing them to contemplate contemplation, as does Eliasson, but to intentionally frustrated (rather than elated) ends.

This sort of ambivalent urge appears in work by a number of artists who take their materials from art and cultural history in order to simultaneously call them forth (and thus keep them present, in circulation, and relevant) and cancel them out (negating them and thus denying them a sanctimonious history). Wade Guyton, an artist who works "across" mediums, performs such literal "double-crossings," simultaneously marking appropriated imagery as significant and negligible. In his series of *Printer Drawings*, for instance, he rips pages from (usually decades old) art and architecture books, then runs them through his printer, palimpsesting iconic geometric shapes, such as Xs and Us, onto their surfaces. Such historical collapsing is also present in work by Kelley Walker who, like Guyton, avoids authorial mark and, rather, takes up older cultural history only to coolly mark it as existing in the now. Walker's images exist primarily as digital imagery, and while they were plucked from a kind of continuously evolving "urmaterial" archive to begin with, they are immediately put back into circulation there. Having altered an image of, say, Warhol's already-appropriated RED RACE RIOT (1963) by pairing it with ectoplasmic whorls produced by spreading toothpaste and mouthwash on his scanner, Walker might sell digital editions of the image with the explicit directive that its buyers continue to tweak the image as they like. In such cases, the literal manifestation of "urmateriality" implies a kind of ongoing morphing process that, nonetheless, acutely acknowledges—and even exposes—the primal phantasies into which it taps.

A rather unexposed element of this "urmaterial" moment, however, appears to manifest itself in the connective tissue evident—if generally repressed—between the "material" and the "maternal" to which I alluded briefly at the beginning of this essay. "Immersive urmateriality," a brand of contemporary installation that constructs an alternate embodied space for its viewer (à la Eliasson, for instance) usurps a maternal model only to deploy its effects using an equally appropriated, culturally valorized, vocabulary of the sublime. In effect, then, such "immersive" sites provide a (however temporary) "place" for their viewers. In her famous 1984 *Ethique de la différence sexuelle* (An Ethics of Sexual Difference), Luce Irigaray argues persuasively that women have historically occupied a paradoxical position: The "maternal feminine"—in Irigaray's terminology—has provided a place for man (both literally and figuratively "enveloping" him) while simultaneously allowing for no place of her own.[6] A bodily metaphor of spatiality, then, appears to be easily usurped by male artists, as is evidenced by the monumental space-providing or space-producing works discussed here. An alternate, and often more internally complicated, approach to "urmateriality" might be seen in works by artists such as Angela Bulloch and Isa Genzken, who display an inherently uneasy relationship to space. Genzken literally turns commonly held perceptions of space inside-out, allowing disoccupation. In a work such as OHR (2002), in which Genzken set a large-scale print of a female ear into the exterior panels of a building, the bodily debt inherent in architecture was made overt—if obstinately unavailable for occupation. Genzken's forays into the "urmaterial" operate at an intentional remove, disallowing immer-

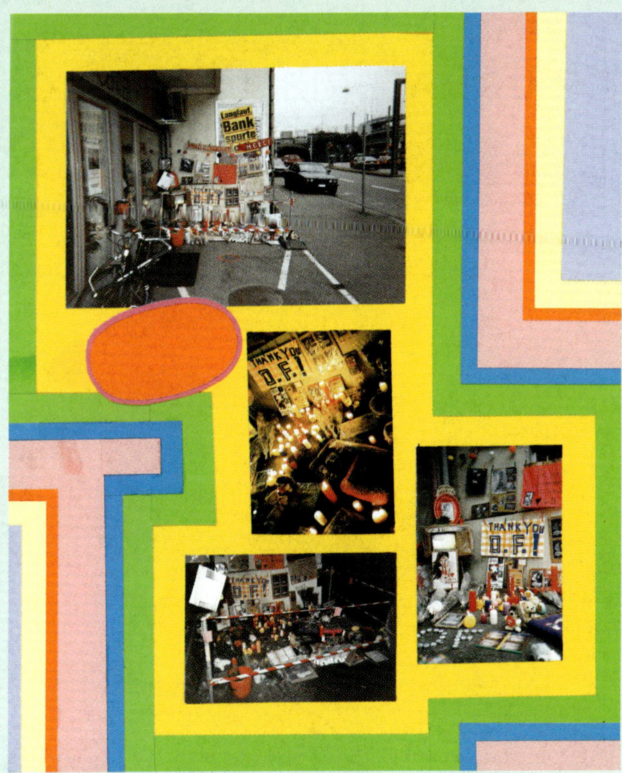

THOMAS HIRSCHHORN, OTTO FREUNDLICH ALTAR, 1998,
group exhibition «Non lieux», Kaskadenkondensator,
Basel (Wiedergabe einer vom Künstler
gestalteten Seite in Parkett 57 / reproduction
of a page in Parkett 57 designed by the artist).

sion and aggressively upending the gendered mechanics of spatial constructions—artistic and otherwise.

To necessarily conclude, then, if we are indeed living in an "urmaterial" era, it's safe to say that "materials" exist both everywhere and nowhere at once—artists establish the subjects of their work as existing not only between a kind of necessarily fictional rendition of the past (whether cultural, psychical, or physical) and present but also between audience and artwork. Indeed, if there is a uniquely positive potential inherent to such an extended description of materiality, it is the hope that such abundance will yield contemplative practices that remain self-reflexive (if not always critical) of their own (material and social) conditions. The very real danger of such an "urmaterial urge," however, is that immersive urmateriality will—as a natural extension of Lippard's "zero point" and Lyotard's "immanent and, as it were, 'flat' network of areas of inquiry"—simply suck everything, hook, line, and sinker, right back to from whence it came.

JOHANNA BURTON
is an art historian and critic living in New York City.

1) Lucy Lippard and John Chandler, "The Dematerialization of Art," *Art International* (February 1968, vol. XII, No. 2). Reprinted in Lippard, *Changing; essays in art criticism* (New York: Dutton, 1971), pp. 255–276.
2) Jean-François Lyotard, *The Postmodern Condition*, trans. Geoff Bennington and Brian Massumi (Minnesota: University of Minnesota Press, 1984), p. 39.
3) Ibid., pp. 80–81 (Appendix).
4) See the double volume catalogue accompanying "Les Immatériaux," published on the occasion of the exhibition: *Les Immatériaux: album et inventaire* and *Les Immatériaux: épreuves d'écriture* (Paris: Centre Georges Pompidou, 1985). Also see Jean-François Lyotard, op. cit. (note 2).
5) See Sigmund Freud, "A Case of Paranoia Running Counter to the Psycho-Analytic Theory of the Disease," (1915), Standard Edition, vol. XIV, p. 269. and *Introductory Lectures on Psycho-Analysis* (1916–17), Standard Edition, vol. XVI, p. 371.
6) See Luce Irigaray, *Ethique de la différence sexuelle* (Paris: Les Editions de Minuit, 1984) translated from the French by Carolyn Burke and Gillian C. Gill as *An Ethics of Sexual Difference* (Cornell: Cornell University Press, 1993).

DER URMATERIELLE DRANG

JOHANNA BURTON

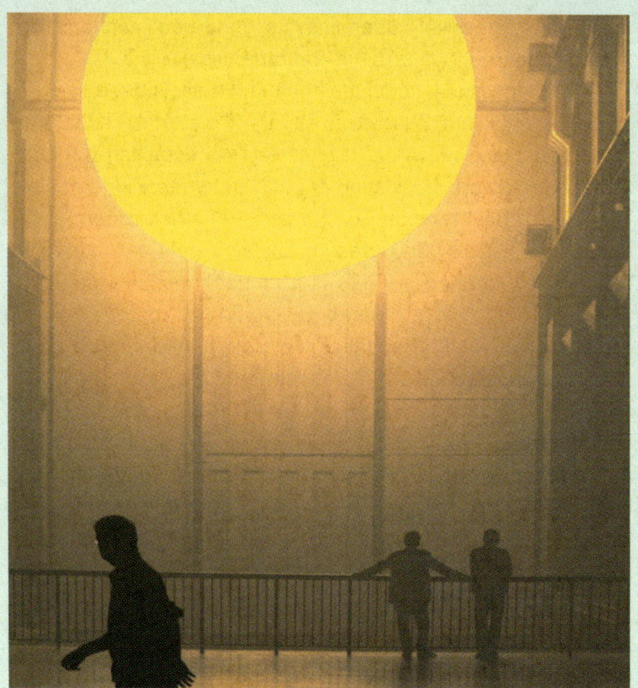

OLAFUR ELIASSON, THE WEATHER
PROJECT, 2003, Tate Modern Turbine Hall,
London, 16 October 2003–21 March 2004.
(PHOTO: TATE MODERN, LONDON)

«Noch immer wissen wir nicht, wie viel weniger nichts sein kann. Ist der definitive Nullpunkt erreicht mit schwarzen Bildern, weissen Bildern, Lichtstrahlen, transparenter Folie, stillen Konzerten, unsichtbaren Skulpturen…? Es erscheint wenig wahrscheinlich».[1] So lauten die Schlusszeilen von Lucy Lippards berühmten Reflexionen über «Die Entmaterialisierung der Kunst» und sie laufen auf eine Art modernes Pendant zu Zenons Paradoxien hinaus. Da die frühe postmoderne Kunst *per definitionem* mit einer schrittweisen Auflösung des Objekts und einem sichtbaren Auseinanderdriften von Idee und Material einherging, erschien es nur logisch, dass früher oder später die konsequentesten zeitgenössischen Werke gar nicht mehr als Kunst erkennbar sein würden – zumindest nicht im Sinn irgendeiner bis dahin gültigen Vorstellung von Kunst. Gleichzeitig galten die konzeptuellen oder auf der Performance aufbauenden Kunstformen (jene beiden Zweige der postmodernen Kunst, die Lippard als für die zunehmende Entmaterialisierung – und folglich das potenzielle obsolet Werden – des Objekts mitverantwortlich betrachtete) quasi als Totems, welche das Fortbestehen der Kunst sichern würden. Das heisst, diese neuen Kunstformen erlaubten, obwohl sie bestehende Kunstbegriffe sprengten oder ihnen sogar zuwiderliefen, dass die Kunst selbst lebendig, lebensfähig, attraktiv, kritisch und, angesichts einer immer reisserischeren Spektakelkultur, von Be-

deutung bleiben konnte. Aber egal, wie man die Gleichung versteht, als Ende der Kunst oder als ihre Wiedergeburt im Aufblühen der Postmoderne, Lippards Essay schliesst mit einer produktiven Abhandlung über die Grenzen des Nullpunkts, die ich wie folgt zusammenfassen möchte: «Wie tief hinunter kann man überhaupt gehen?»

Eine Antwort (die lautete: «tiefer, viel tiefer») erfolgte durch eine Achsendrehung, als Jean-François Lyotard von der vertikalen Messung der Entmaterialisierung zur horizontalen Ausdehnung des «Immateriellen» überging. In seiner Mammutausstellung «Les Immatériaux» im Centre Georges Pompidou, 1985, führte Lyotard einen Begriff von Immaterialität ein, der die Mikro-Eigenschaften der viralen Verbreitung angenommen hatte. Tatsächlich führte die «Immaterialität» als solche noch nicht zum völligen Verschwinden des Objekts – sie warf eher Fragen auf über das radikal neue Verhältnis zwischen dem Objekt und seinem Schöpfer, teilweise durch die Andeutung, dass es «Materialien» gebe, die an sich schon an oder jenseits der Grenze unseres Begriffshorizonts flimmerten. «Immaterielle» Stoffe wurden insbesondere mit dem technologischen Fortschritt in Verbindung gebracht – im Labor gezüchtete Haut ist ein gutes Beispiel dafür – und sie veranschaulichten deutlich, was Lyotard meint, wenn er von einer sich immer weiter öffnenden Kluft spricht, welche die seit der Aufklärung angenommene klare Herrschaft des

Menschen über die Dinge verändern werde. Lyotard argumentiert, dass der Schöpfungsbegriff sowohl in theologischer wie künstlerischer Hinsicht gerade einen radikalen Wandel durchmache; es sei schlicht unmöglich geworden, sich auf die beruhigende Hegelsche Vorstellung zu berufen, dass Kunstwerke als Spiegel des menschlichen Subjekts fungierten. Tatsächlich habe der Mensch längst die Kontrolle über den Schaffensprozess verloren, habe die Herrschaft abgetreten und sei einfach zu einem weiteren Element im Meer des Immateriellen geworden, er stehe nicht mehr im Zentrum der Dinge, sondern sei lediglich ein auswechselbares Rädchen im Getriebe.

Aber das Wichtigste ist vielleicht, dass Lyotard noch ein anderes Modell des sich verändernden Wesens der Materie anbot, ein Modell, demzufolge sich die Materie nicht wie bei Lippard allmählich ihrer symbolischen Überfrachtungen entledigt, sondern selbst gewaltsam explodiert, birst und sich tatsächlich in ihre kleinsten Partikel auflöst. Während die Entmaterialisierung in gewissem Mass ein Experiment war, um zu sehen, wie lange ein Körper weiter lebte, nachdem man ihm den Kopf abgeschlagen hatte – man denke etwa an Kosuths Bilder lexikalischer Definitionen –, bedeutet die Immaterialisierung etwas anderes. Da war, wie es schien, eine kontraintuitive Anti-Entropie am Werk, in welcher das Stoffliche in immer kleinere Komponenten zerfiel, und zwar eher um die Zirkulation aufrechtzuerhalten als um sie herunterzuschrauben. Und diese mikroskopisch kleinen Bestandteile, die ihre Funktion durch fortwährendes In-Bewegung-Sein erfüllten, liessen sich nicht mehr, auch nur annähernd zusammenfügen (dies, obwohl die Grenzen zwischen ihnen paradoxerweise verwirrend unscharf geworden waren). Wen wundert es also, dass Lyotard die Ausstellungsräume des Centre Pompidou mit Dingen füllte, von denen er dachte, sie könnten immaterielle Materialien verkörpern, die alle gleichermassen zu einem «immanenten, sozusagen 'flachen' Netz von Forschungen»[2] gehörten: Kunstwerke und Baupläne; Computerprogramme und wissenschaftliche Versuche; konzeptuelle Experimente und theoretische Daten. Hier wurde jede noch haltbare Materialvorstellung zur messerscharfen Schneide, die paradoxerweise alles bis zur immateriellen Ununterscheidbarkeit reduzierte und dennoch spontan unerwartete Bezüge und Regelmässigkeiten innerhalb des chaotischen Nebels aufzeigte. Sollte es überhaupt eine Möglichkeit geben, die Ästhetik neu zu denken, so, laut Lyotard, nur indem man das Sichtbare aus seiner Verbindung mit der Repräsentation (oder Bedeutung) löst, um eine Art Schluckauf zwischen beiden herbeizuführen und damit die «Darstellung des nicht Darstellbaren»[3] zu ermöglichen. (Es ist kein Zufall,

dass Duchamp einer von Lyotards Lieblingskünstlern war.) Lyotards früherer, in *Das postmoderne Wissen* eingeführte Begriff der «Inkommensurabilität» (der erlaubte, den Akt des Sehens aufzusprengen, um Objekte und Worte abrupt von ihren vorgegebenen Bedeutungen zu befreien und beides – wenn auch nicht dauerhaft, so doch einen Moment lang – fremd erscheinen zu lassen) schien sich zu einer radikaleren «Imkommensurabilität» entwickelt zu haben, in welcher sich alle Mass- oder Proportionsvorstellungen vollständig auflösten.[4]

Fasst man diesen Wandlungsprozess kurz zusammen, wird eines klar. Wie 1968 war der Begriff des Materiellen auch 1985, ganz gleich ob ihm ein besorgtes «de-» oder ein zweideutiges «im-» vorangestellt wurde («immateriell» kann schliesslich sowohl Nicht-Materielles wie Innermaterielles bezeichnen), bereits ein etwas wackeliger, aber beliebter Begriff, wie das bei Begriffen, die sich in einer produktiven Krise befinden, oft der Fall ist. Und genauso ist es auch heute, auch wenn das Präfix, das die Beziehung zwischen künstlerischer Praxis und materiellem Produkt (oder Nebenprodukt) am besten trifft, heute eher das deutsche «ur» sein dürfte, was unsere Zeit vielleicht zu einer der «Urmaterialität» macht. Tatsächlich ist es angesichts der jüngsten Behandlungsweisen und Erweiterungsversuche des Materialbegriffs verlockend, materielle Beschaffenheit im neuen Jahrtausend eher als psychische Konstruktion denn als – egal wie geschmeidige und jeder Bedeutung entledigte – greifbare Substanz zu verstehen. Die Vorsilbe «ur» mit ihren Konnotationen «original», «ursprünglich», «alt» oder «archetypisch» eröffnet zudem die Möglichkeit das Wesen des Materiellen als phantastischen Raum zu begreifen, oder genauer: als phantastischen Nicht-Raum. Betrachten wir zwei neuere Projekte, die im Lauf der letzten zwei Jahre in der geräumigen Höhlung der Turbinenhalle in der Tate Modern realisiert wurden. (Tatsächlich zeugt die Existenz dieser Halle an sich schon von einem neuen Begriff von Materialität: Als eine Art Höhle oder Passage mit einem deutlichen Hang zum Erhabenen stellt sie für jedes Kunstwerk, das dort ausgestellt werden soll, eine unausgesprochene «urmaterielle» Herausforderung dar.)

Im Oktober 2002 enthüllte Anish Kapoor seinen MARSYAS, eine Installation, die den rund 170 Meter langen, 23 Meter breiten und 35 Meter hohen Raum fast vollständig ausfüllte. Im Einklang mit seinem übrigen Werk gelang es Kapoor, sein Material so einzusetzen, dass es, obwohl es sehr viel Raum einnahm, zugleich einen neuen Raum entstehen liess – einen, der sich buchstäblich und metaphorisch zwischen Werk und Betrachter aufspannte wie eine beiden gemeinsame Haut. MARSYAS (der Titel nimmt Bezug auf die

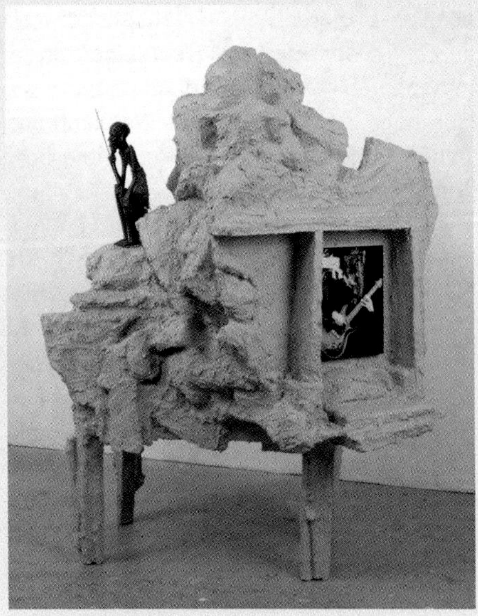

RACHEL HARRISON, UNTITLED, 2002,
mixed media, 54 x 21 1/2 x 36" / OHNE TITEL,
diverse Materialien, 137,2 x 54,6 x 91,5 cm.
(PHOTO: GREENE NAFTALI GALLERY, NEW YORK)

antike Sage des von Apollo bei lebendigem Leibe gehäuteten, gleichnamigen Satyrs) war eine monumentale Membran, eine Art Möbiusschleife, die keine rationalen Dualitäten wie innen und aussen, horizontal und vertikal, hier und dort zuliess. Die straff gespannte, tief rote Epidermis bildete eine, einem monumentalen Ohr nicht unähnliche, wellenförmige Gestalt, deren Enden sich zu einer muschelartigen Spirale drehten und einen virtuellen Zugang zu den inneren Gängen boten. Man kann dieses Werk kaum mehr als Skulptur im herkömmlichen Sinn bezeichnen, obwohl darin – wie schon in der Minimal Art der 60er Jahre – Materialien verwendet werden, um die Raumerfahrung des Betrachters zu formen. Hier verwandelte der geformte Raum jedoch den ihn erfahrenden Körper selbst in eine synästhetische Membran, indem der gigantische Korpus jedem Körper in seiner Nähe sensorische Daten übermittelte. Tatsächlich vermischte sich der visuelle Eindruck unweigerlich mit den durch die Höhlungen und Flächen der Membran hervorgerufenen Tönen, genauso, wie auch die Farbe den Geschmacks- und Geruchssinn auf den Plan rief. Kapoors Interesse für das, was ich «Urmaterialität» nenne, hat fast nichts zu tun mit den konkreten Materialien seiner phantastischen Konstruktion (aus einer einzigen riesigen PVC-Plane). Diese «Urmaterialität» besteht vielmehr in dem gewissermassen archetypischen, synästhetischen

Raum, in dem die menschlichen Körper von der Sprache losgelöst auf sich selbst zurückgeworfen wurden und sich einer Art invertierter Monumentalität überlassen mussten. In ihrer Form erinnert die Arbeit stark an die der menschlichen Gebärmutter – jenen ersten Raum der «Materialität», der zweifellos mit Mutterschaft (Maternität) zu tun hat. Hier liesse sich die «Urmaterialität» als Kanal für das mit der eigenen Erfahrung Verbundene verstehen: Dem Betrachter wird der Boden unter den Füssen entzogen mittels jenes Raumes, der ihm der ursprünglich vertrauteste und unaussprechlichste zugleich ist.

Etwas anders ist die «urmaterielle» Wirkung von Olafur Eliassons Arbeit für die Turbinenhalle (THE WEATHER PROJECT, Eröffnung im Oktober 2003). Der nordeuropäische Künstler ist berühmt für seine Fähigkeit Sublimes mit banalen mechanischen Mitteln heraufzubeschwören. Oft enthüllt er die Mechanismen von Natürlichkeitsklischees, indem er ihre romantischen (ergo künstlichen) Wirkungen überhöht – vielleicht zugleich als Kritik und Würdigung dieser langlebigen Freuden. Tatsächlich lenken Werke wie ein aufwärts stürzender Wasserfall oder ein künstlicher Regen im Lichtgewitter die Aufmerksamkeit nicht nur auf das konventionelle Bild der Natur, sondern auch, und das ist vielleicht wichtiger, auf festgefahrene Wahrnehmungsmuster. In seinem WEATHER PROJECT geht Eliasson so weit, dass er die subtile technische Inszenierung zu einer Illusion werden lässt, in die man eintauchen kann. Diesmal ist die Halle nicht mit erkennbaren «Materialien» ausgestattet, sondern wird stattdessen ihres architektonischen Status enthoben und neu als Aussenraum definiert – vielleicht sogar als ausserweltlicher Raum. Eine gigantische Sonne bestehend aus Tausenden von Monofrequenzlampen, die, in einem vertikalen Halbkreis angeordnet, durch die Reflexion in der verspiegelten Decke zu einem ganzen Kreis werden. Ein feiner Nebel wird erzeugt, der sich beinah wolkenhaft verdichtet und wieder auflöst. Die Besucher versammeln sich im Raum, lümmeln auf dem Betonboden unter der Sonne herum, als wäre es ein grüner Hügel; der Künstler fordert quasi dazu auf, über das Wesen der Kontemplation selbst nachzudenken. Und wenn die intellektuellen und mnemotechnischen Ziele des Projekts angesichts seiner Komponenten auch nicht gleich auf der Hand liegen, die Website der Tate Gallery legt sie offen, indem sie das Publikum auffordert, seine eigenen Wettergeschichten zu erzählen, welche wohl Eliassons atmosphärischer Doppelgänger ins Gedächtnis rufen und illustrieren soll. Während die «Urmaterialität» bei Kapoor dazu dient, den Zugang zu einem buchstäblich ursprünglichen Raum zu eröffnen (ein vorsprachlicher Raum, in dem sich Körper noch nicht vonei-

WADE GUYTON, UNTITLED PRINTER DRAWING (SOMAINI, P. 78), 2003, inkjet on bookpage, 11 x 9" / DRUCKERZEICHNUNG OHNE TITEL (SOMAINI, S. 78), Inkjet auf Buchseite.

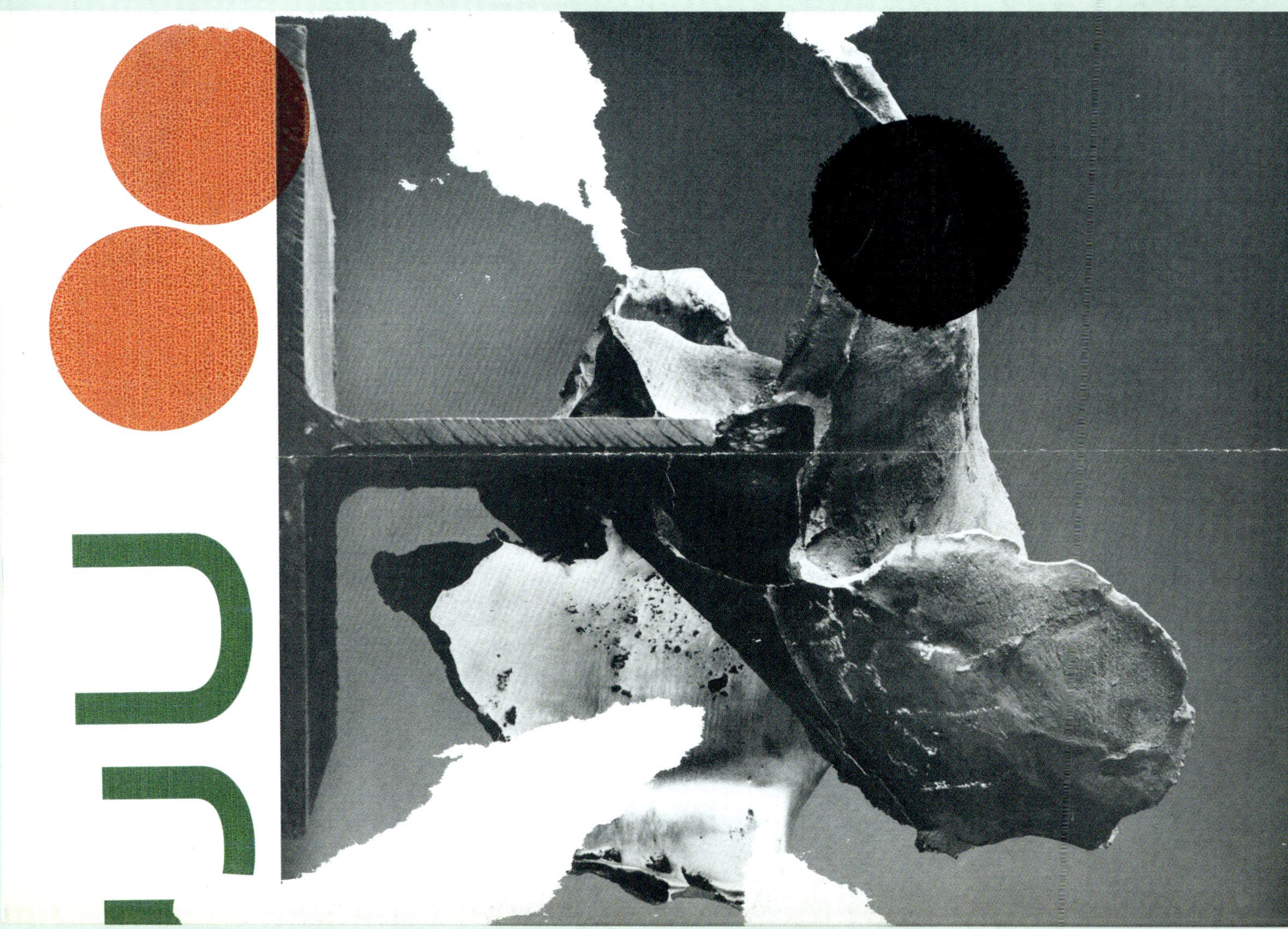

nander unterscheiden – eine Art ursprüngliche Vorgeschichte), dient sie Eliasson dazu, ein halluzinatorisches kollektives Gedächtnis heraufzubeschwören. Tatsächlich gibt es niemanden, bei dem das Bild eines nebligen Tages mit durchbrechenden Sonnenstrahlen nicht unzählige Erinnerungen, Sehnsüchte und Phantasien wachriefe, wobei viele davon den Medien oder anderen gemeinsamen Kontexten entstammen dürften. Der «Urmaterialität» gelingt es, die Aufmerksamkeit auf Alltägliches (hier das Wetter) zu lenken, das sich, einmal aktiviert, als gemeinschaftsbildend erweist.

1915 prägte Freud den Begriff «Urphantasien», teilweise um zu erklären, warum gewisse psychische Realitäten nicht unbedingt mit den physischen übereinstimmen.[5] Für Freud waren Urphantasien, etwa jene des elterlichen Liebesaktes, der Verführung oder der Kastration phylogenetisch erklärbar. Er vertrat die These, dass solche Phantasien in der menschlichen Urgeschichte tatsächlich ausagiert worden seien (und damit Eingang ins kollektive Unbewusste gefunden hätten); deshalb war es möglich, dass sie eine Rolle in der Entwicklung der individuellen Psyche spielen konnten, obwohl das Individuum selbst sie nie erlebt hatte. Nun will ich nicht behaupten, dass Arbeiten wie die von Eliasson oder Kapoor aus einem solch dubiosen kollektiven Tümpel, wie Freud ihn annimmt, zu schöpfen versuchen, aber ich glaube, dass dieser Begriff uns helfen kann darüber nachzudenken, welche Rolle Material und Materialität in der heutigen Kunst spielen. So viele Künstlerinnen und Künstler greifen für das Ausgangsmaterial ihrer Arbeit auf einen allgemeinen Pool der Informationen, Erfahrungen oder Geschichte zurück, dass es fruchtbar sein mag, zu fragen, wie es kommt, dass diese Projekte, die einen gemeinsamen menschlichen, physischen oder kulturellen Nenner haben, unbedingt auf das «Urmaterielle» angewiesen sind. Das muss nicht heissen, dass man zur Ursuppe zurückkehrt, oder gar zum weiblichen Schoss, sondern eher weiter gefasst: zur Vorstellung einer gemeinsamen Erfahrung, die nicht immer aus erster Hand sein muss. Der Ausdruck «eintauchen» oder «Immersion» wird immer wieder verwendet im Zusammenhang mit Installationen wie den oben geschilderten. Und diese Sprache bestätigt lediglich die Art, wie «Urmaterialien» wirken, indem sie uns nämlich vermitteln, dass unsere körperlichen und seelischen Reaktionen nicht nur durch das Werk ausgelöst wurden, sondern das Werk selbst sind.

Diese Tendenz sieht man etwa in David Hammons' CONCERTO IN BLACK AND BLUE (Konzert in Schwarz und Blau, 2003), einer Arbeit, die buchstäblich nicht existiert ohne das Publikum, welches aufgefordert wurde, einen knapp 2000 Quadratmeter grossen Raum zu umgehen, wobei ledig-

lich winzige blaue LED-Blitzlichter als Orientierungshilfe dienten. Das Werk bestand also aus der gelegentlichen Interaktion winziger Lichtstrahlen – jedes einzelnen Teilnehmers innerhalb der sich gerade ergebenden (Readymade-)Besuchergemeinschaft – und seine Realisierung darin, dass das einzig Sichtbare der jeweils eigene vorwiegend blind zurückgelegte Weg war, der sich mit anderen kreuzte. Am entgegengesetzten ästhetischen Pol finden wir die «Urmaterialität» von Thomas Hirschhorns liebevoll aufgebauten, üppig bestückten Altären und Kiosks, diese pädagogischen Wiegestationen, die dazu bestimmt sind, temporäre Lesergemeinschaften mit gemeinsamem philosophischem oder kulturellem Hintergrund zu beherbergen, auch wenn sie sonst wenig gemein haben. In diesem Fall, wie auch bei einem Philippe Parreno, Pierre Huyghe oder Rirkrit Tiravanija, wird die «Urmaterialität» nicht so sehr durch das im einzelnen Werk verwendete Material wirksam – sei dies eine weiterentwickelte *Anime*-Figur, ein photokopierter marxistischer Text oder ein dampfender Topf Thai-Nudeln –, sondern durch das Einweben von Schichten einer anderen, mit phantastischen Mitteln konstruierten, gemeinsamen Geschichte.

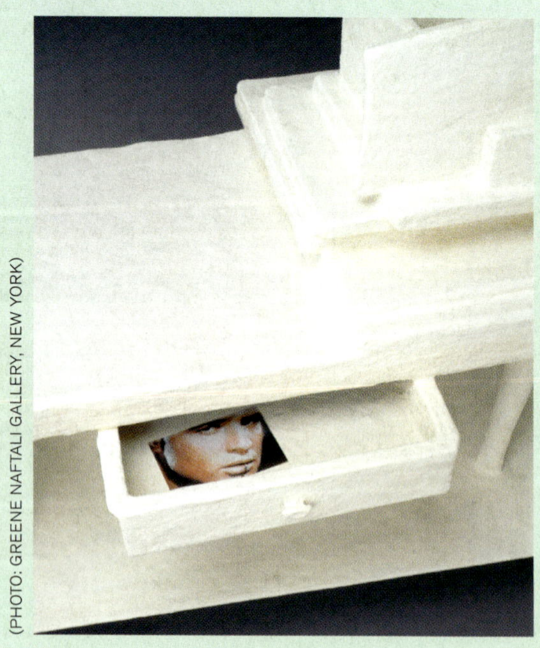

RACHEL HARRISON, MARLON AND INDIAN, 2002, mixed media and c-print, 47 1/2 x 51 1/2 x 32 1/2" / MARLON UND INDIANER, diverse Materialien und C-Print, 120,7 x 130,8 x 82,6 cm.

(PHOTO: GREENE NAFTALI GALLERY, NEW YORK)

Das muss nicht utopisch, kritisch, oder gar als soziale Vorschrift in Erscheinung treten, obwohl einige Künstler – Hirschhorn, zum Beispiel – mit solch «urmateriellen» Gesten auch das aktuelle politische Klima ansprechen, während andere es eher als mögliches Mittel der Kulturkritik sehen. (Hammons hat mit dem «Urmateriellen» gearbeitet, um den rassistischen Kapitalismus zu entlarven.) Rachel Harrison verwendet das «Urmaterielle» ohne damit eine Bewertung vorzunehmen, um allgemein verbreitete kulturelle und soziale Sinnbilder zu beschwören (Photos von Liz Taylor, Olivendosen, mittelamerikanische Inneneinrichtungselemente) und dann die Verbindung zu kappen zwischen der Urphantasie, die diese Objekte umgibt, und deren Bedeutung im tatsächlichen Leben. Indem sie unförmig gewordene Minimal-Skulpturen mit gewöhnlichen billigen Konsumgütern kombiniert, drängt Harrison das Publikum mit ihrer «Urmaterialität» in einen nabelschnurartigen Raum zwischen den Zeiten und zwingt es ebenfalls über Kontemplation nachzudenken, aber im Gegensatz zu Eliasson mit eher frustrierender als berauschender Wirkung.

Dieser ambivalente Drang taucht in den Arbeiten zahlreicher Künstler auf, die ihren Stoff in der Kunst- oder Kulturgeschichte finden, um dieselbe gleichzeitig anzurufen (und damit gegenwärtig, lebendig und bedeutungsvoll zu erhalten) und auszulöschen (indem sie sie negieren und ihr die historischen Weihen verweigern). Wade Guyton ein Künstler, der intermedial arbeitet, nimmt solche buchstäblichen Doppelkreuzungen vor, indem er bestehende Bildsprachen übernimmt und sie als bedeutungsvoll und unbedeutend zugleich brandmarkt. In seiner Reihe *Printer Drawings* (Druckerzeichnungen) reisst er zum Beispiel Seiten aus (meist jahrzehntealten) Kunst- und Architekturbüchern und bedruckt sie auf seinem Drucker mit geometrischen Zeichen, etwa X- oder U-Formen. Ein ähnlicher geschichtlicher Kollaps findet auch im Werk von Kelley Walker statt, der wie Guyton jede auktoriale Handschrift vermeidet und stattdessen lieber die ältere Kulturgeschichte aufnimmt, um sie lediglich lässig als im aktuellen Moment existierende zu kennzeichnen. Walkers Bilder existieren in erster Linie als digitale Bilderwelt, und obwohl sie anfangs aus einer Art fortwährend sich entwickelndem Archiv des «Urmaterials» gepflückt wurden, werden sie sofort wieder dorthin zurückversetzt und erneut in Umlauf gebracht. Hat er beispielsweise ein Bild von Warhols bereits appropriiertem RED RACE RIOT (Rote Rassenunruhen, 1963) verändert, indem er es mit Ektoplasma-Spiralen kombiniert hat, die durch das Auftragen von Zahnpasta und Mundwasser auf seinem Scanner entstanden sind, verkauft Walker womöglich eine digitale Edition dieses Bildes mit der direkten Aufforde-

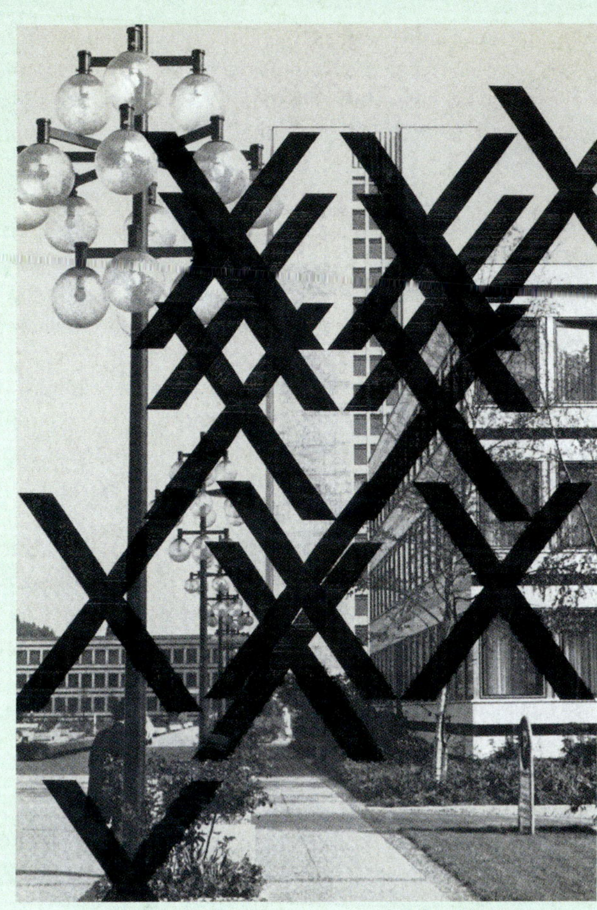

WADE GUYTON, UNTITLED PRINTER DRAWING, 2003, inkjet on book page, 10 x 7" / DRUCKERZEICHNUNG OHNE TITEL, Inkjet auf Buchseite, 25,4 x 17,8 cm.

rung an die Käufer, das Bild weiter nach Belieben zu verzerren. In diesen Fällen impliziert die buchstäbliche «urmaterielle» Qualität einen fortwährenden Wandlungsprozess, der jedoch die Urphantasien, von denen er lebt, eingesteht oder sogar vorführt.

Ein eher verborgeneres Element dieses «urmateriellen» Moments scheint allerdings in der offensichtlichen – wenn auch gern verdrängten – Verflechtung zwischen dem «Materiellen» und dem «Maternellen» wirksam zu sein. Ich habe zu Beginn dieses Essays kurz darauf angespielt. «Immersive Urmaterialität» ist das Markenzeichen einer zeitgenössischen Installationskunst, die für ihre Betrachter einen alternativen körperhaften Raum schafft (wie Eliasson) und dabei ein Modell des Mütterlichen in Anspruch nimmt, um ihre Wirkungen mittels eines ebenfalls übernommenen, kulturell abgestützten Vokabulars des Erhabenen zu entfalten. Tatsächlich geben solche Stätten zum «Eintauchen» ihren Betrachtern (wenn auch nur temporär) Raum. In ihrer berühmten *Ethik der sexuellen Differenz* (1984) argumentiert Luce Irigaray sehr überzeugend, dass die Frauen in der Geschichte eine paradoxe Stellung innehätten: Laut Irigaray gibt das Mütterlich-Weibliche dem Mann einen Ort (umschliesst ihn buchstäblich und metaphorisch), während es selbst keinen Ort hat.[6] Eine körperliche Raummetapher wird von männlichen Künstlern daher offenbar leichter in Anspruch genommen, was die monumentalen Raum greifenden und Raum schaffenden Werke, von denen hier die Rede ist, zu bestätigen scheinen. Einen anderen, oft innerlichen und komplizierteren Umgang mit «Urmaterialität» findet man in den Arbeiten von Künstlerinnen wie Angela Bulloch und Isa Genzken, die beide ein gebrocheneres Verhältnis zum Raum erkennen lassen. Genzken verkehrt gängige Raumauffassungen, indem sie das Innere nach aussen stülpt und auch das Unbewohnte zulässt. In einer Arbeit wie OHR (2002), bei der Genzken einen übergrossen Farbdruck eines weiblichen Ohrs auf der Aussenfassade eines Gebäudes anbrachte, wird offenkundig, was die Architektur dem Körper verdankt, auch wenn sie es letztlich nicht besetzen und einlösen kann. Genzkens Streifzüge ins «Urmaterielle» arbeiten mit einem bewussten Abstand, sie verweigern das Eintauchen in aggressiver Verkehrung der geschlechtsspezifischen Techniken räumlicher Konstruktion, egal ob im künstlerischen oder einem anderen Kontext.

Wenn wir tatsächlich in einer Ära des «Urmateriellen» leben, so lässt sich mit Sicherheit sagen, dass «Materialien» überall und nirgends zugleich existieren. – Künstler setzen den Gegenstand ihrer Arbeit als einen, der nicht nur zwischen einer notwendig fiktionalen Wiedergabe der (kulturellen, psychischen oder physischen) Vergangenheit und der Gegenwart existiert, sondern auch zwischen dem Publikum und dem Kunstwerk. Sollte in einem derart erweiterten Materialbegriff wirklich ein einmaliges positives Potenzial schlummern, so ist es die Hoffnung, dass diese Fülle eine kontemplative Praxis begünstigen wird, die sich selbst (wenn auch nicht immer kritisch) und ihre eigenen Bedingungen (materieller und sozialer Art) reflektiert. Die sehr reale Gefahr eines solchen «urmateriellen» Drangs ist jedoch, dass die zum Eintauchen einladende Urmaterialität – wie eine natürliche Erweiterung von Lippards Nullpunkt oder Lyotards immanentem, flachem Netz der Forschungsrichtungen – einfach alles mit Haut und Haar verschlingt und dorthin zurücksaugt, woher es einst kam.

Übersetzung: Suzanne Schmidt

JOHANNA BURTON
ist Kunsthistorikerin und -kritikerin. Sie lebt in New York City.

1) Lucy Lippard, John Chandler, «The Dematerialization of Art», *Art International*, Vol. XII, Nr. 2, Februar 1968. Reprint in Lippard, *Changing; Essays in Art Criticism*, Dutton, New York 1971, S. 255–276.

2) Jean-François Lyotard, *Das postmoderne Wissen*, hrsg. v. Peter Engelmann, Edition Passagen, Wien, S. 116.

3) Engl.: «presenting the unpresentable»: vgl. Jean-François Lyotard, *The Postmodern Condition*, University of Minnesota Press, Minnesota 1984, S. 80–81. (Die englische Ausgabe enthält im Anhang eine Übersetzung von Lyotards Aufsatz «Réponse à la question: qu'est-ce que le postmoderne?», der ursprünglich in der französischen Zeitschrift *Critique*, Nr. 419, April 1982, erschien und in der deutschen Ausgabe von *Das postmoderne Wissen* nicht enthalten ist.)

4) Vgl. den zweibändigen Katalog zur Ausstellung: *Les Immatériaux: album et inventaire; Les Immatériaux: épreuves d'écriture*, Centre Georges Pompidou, Paris 1985; sowie Jean-François Lyotard, op. cit.

5) Sigmund Freud, «Mitteilung eines der Psychoanalytischen Theorie widersprechenden Falles von Paranoia», in *Gesammelte Werke*, Bd. X, S. Fischer Verlag, Frankfurt 1999, S. 242, und *Vorlesungen zur Einführung in die Psychoanalyse, Gesammelte Werke*, Bd. XI, S. 386.

6) Luce Irigaray, *Ethik der sexuellen Differenz*, übers. v. Xenia Rajewsky, Edition Suhrkamp, Frankfurt am Main 1991.

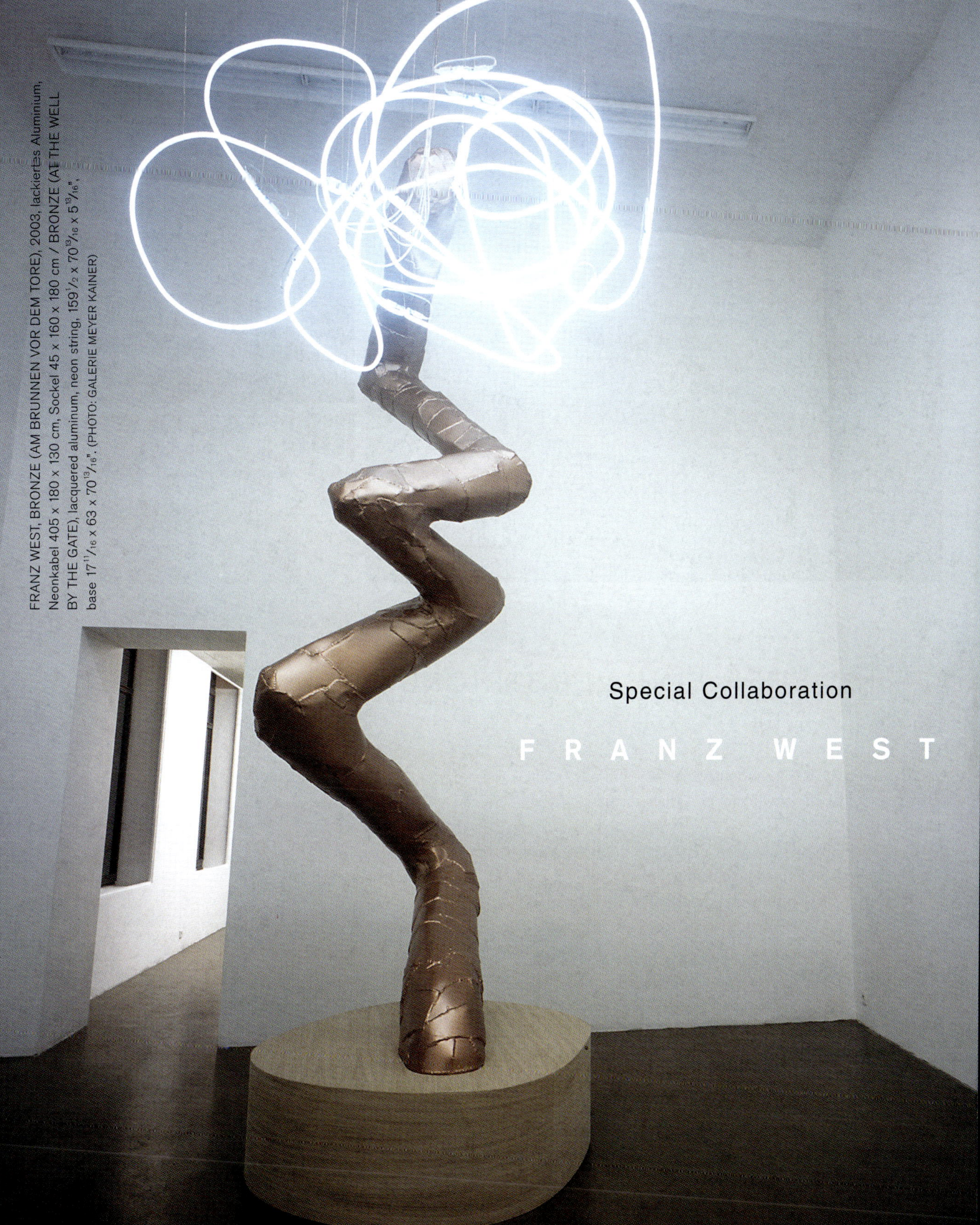

FRANZ WEST, BRONZE (AM BRUNNEN VOR DEM TORE), 2003, lackiertes Aluminium, Neonkabel 405 x 180 x 130 cm, Sockel 45 x 160 x 180 cm / BRONZE (AT THE WELL BY THE GATE), lacquered aluminum, neon string, 159 1/2 x 70 13/16 x 5 13/16", base 17 11/16 x 63 x 70 13/16". (PHOTO: GALERIE MEYER KAINER)
Special Collaboration
F R A N Z   W E S T

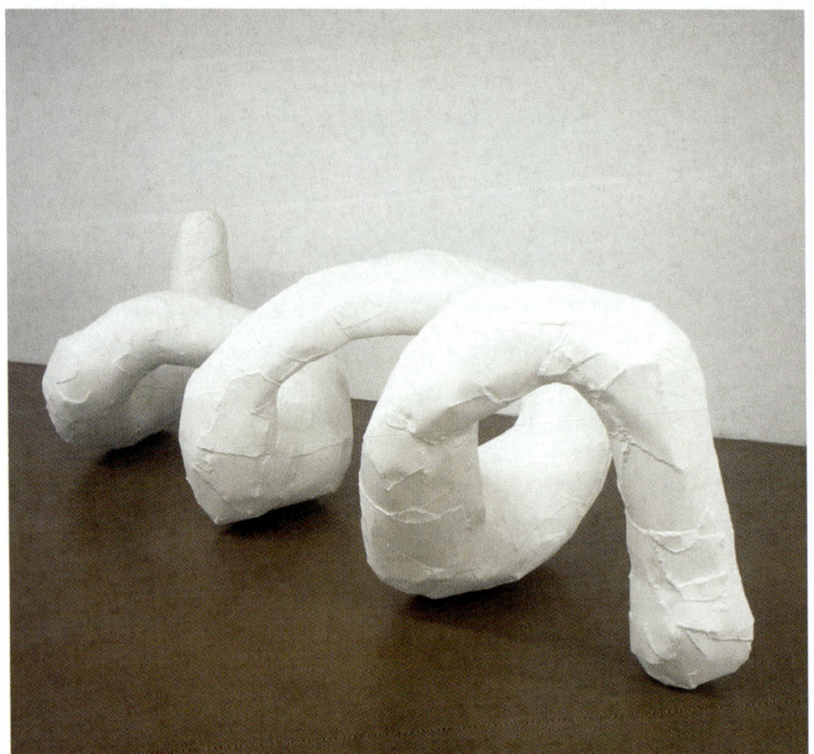

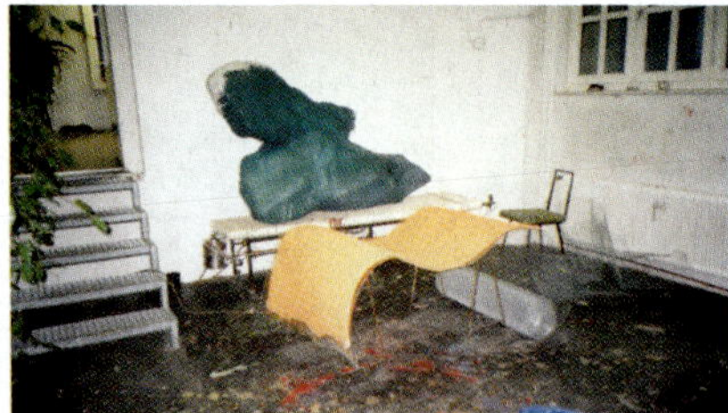

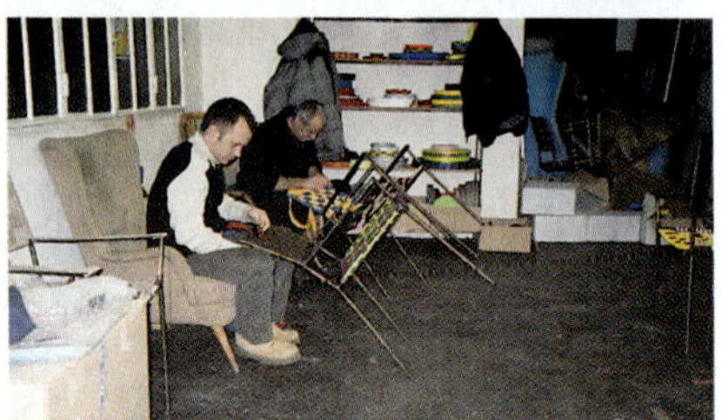

FRANZ WEST, GARTENMÖBEL, 2003,
lackierte Aluminiumskulptur, 65 x 435 x 315 cm /
GARDEN FURNITURE, lacquered
aluminum sculpture, 25 5/8 x 17 15/16 x 124".
(PHOTO: GALERIE MEYER KAINER, WIEN)

Im Atelier von Franz West /
Views of Franz West's studio.

«ES IST EHER EINE VERSTRICKUNG…»

EIN GESPRÄCH MIT FRANZ WEST

BICE CURIGER: Du arbeitest mit einer relativ reichen Palette von Materialien. Könntest du ewas aus deiner ganz alltäglichen Praxis erzählen. Wie beeinflussen Materialien deine Entscheidungen?

FRANZ WEST: Im Gegensatz zu einer anfänglichen Skepsis und zynischen Verachtung jeglicher Form von «Materialfetischismus» erfuhr ich im Lauf der Jahrzehnte, dass den jeweiligen Eigenschaften des Materials nachzugehen das Meinige ist.

BC: Nehmen wir also Papiermaché und Gips versus Metall, oder bedruckte Stoffe und Teppiche versus Spiegel, dann ergibt sich zunächst ein Gegensatz zwischen weich und hart. Aber natürlich ist auch der Arbeitsprozess mit angesprochen. Wie folgst du den jeweiligen Eigenschaften des Materials?

FW: Unbestimmt! Weder Negation noch Affirmation verweist auf das, was immer schon vorausgeht. Wer fügt sich denn schon einer Logik?

BC: Ist der marxistische Gegensatz Materialismus versus Idealismus noch brauchbar? Hat er für dich je eine Bedeutung gehabt?

FW: Nein, ich kenne mich noch nicht so gut aus.

BC: Du hast mal deine Enttäuschung über Duchamps FLASCHENTROCKNER (1914) geäussert, er sei ein schlecht ausgeführtes Objekt, mit zu vielen hässlichen Schrauben versehen.

FW: Halten wir zumindest vorläufig fest: Kunst ist wesentlich die Kenntnis des Nicht-Bekannten, Nicht-Seienden oder allgemeiner: die Beziehung zum Unbekannten, Entzogenen!

BC: Welche seriell fabrizierten Alltagsgegenstände faszinieren dich besonders?

FW: Einmachgläser.

BC: Man könnte auch Lücken, Löcher, Zwischenräume als Material bezeichnen.

FW: Ich begehre das, was der, der begehrt, nicht braucht, was ihm nicht fehlt, was er nicht zu besitzen wünscht. Es ist das Begehren nach dem, was unzugänglich und fremd bleibt. Das Begehren nach Anderem als Anderes, ganz nüchtern. Schau, beispielsweise baue ich mit Heimo Zobernig ein BATEAU IMAGINAIRE, ein von Heimo erarbeiteter Kubus, auf dem vier oder fünf Stühle von mir stehen. Er ist im circa drei Meter tiefen Wasser verankert und wird anlässlich einer «Biennale» einige Kilometer von Paris entfernt in einem See schwimmen. Der Kubus wird so hoch sein, dass es für eine schwimmende Person nicht möglich ist, zur Oberfläche, auf der die Stühle stehen, emporzuklimmen, und es gibt weder eine Leiter noch Stufen, Griffe etcetera. Die Wasserqualität lässt den Impuls, dort ein Bad zu nehmen, gar nicht erst aufkommen.

BC: Aus welchem Material soll der Kubus sein?

FW: Möglich wäre Kunststoff, Holz oder Metall – Heimo will scharfe Kanten, daher Metall. Also ich komme nicht vom Material, sondern vom Stück her und nehme dann das, was mir oder jemand Beteiligtem am geeignetsten erscheint.

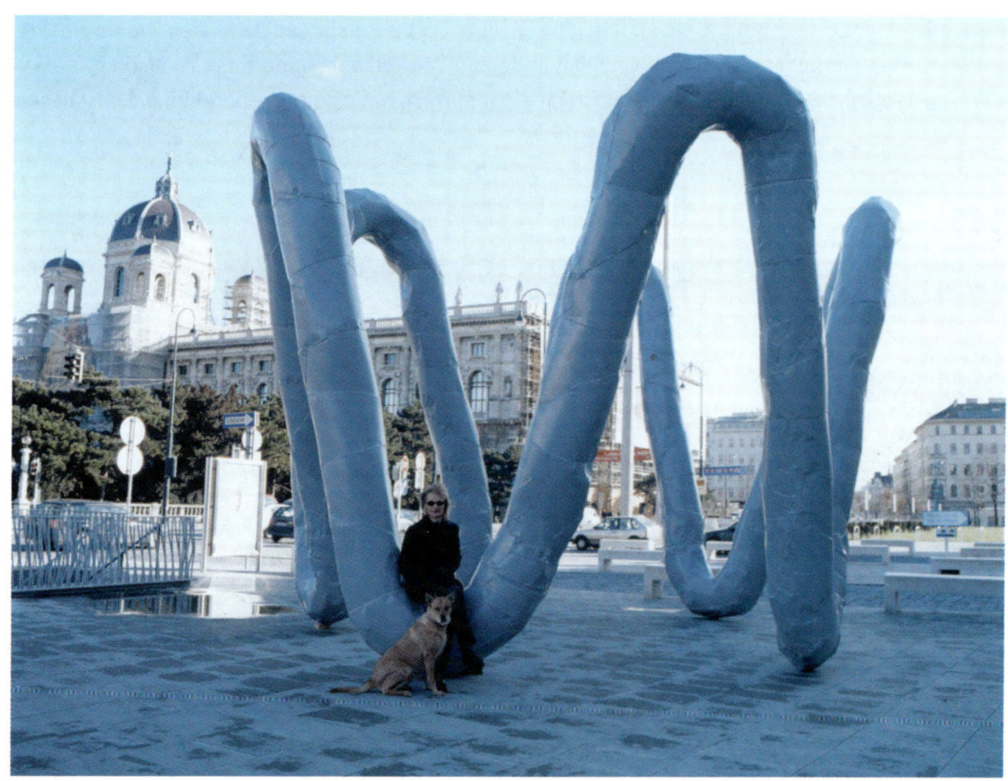

FRANZ WEST, CORONA, 2002, lackiertes Aluminium, 500 x 700 x 700 cm, Museumsquartier Wien, 2003 / lacquered aluminum, 196 $^7/_8$ x 275 $^5/_8$".
(PHOTO: ROBERT RUBAK)

BC: Reden wir von deinen Möbeln. Sie sehen prekär aus, erfüllen aber alle funktionalen Ansprüche.

FW: Sie sind ungewöhnlich dünn, das macht es aus. Die Tektonik ist unsichtbar. Es hält eigentlich nur dadurch, dass es verschweisst ist. Der klassische Stuhl ist dicker. Die Stühle sind unerwartet hoch, nicht dem Zeitgeist entsprechend.

BC: Inwiefern spielt bei dir die Vorstellung der «Beseelung» des Materials eine Rolle? Oder umgekehrt gefragt: Gibt es die Materialisierung von Vorstellungen?

FW: Wie gesagt, früher hielt ich Material für unbeseelt. Jedoch LSD-Erfahrung und Wittgenstein-Lektüre belehrten mich, dass alles lebt.

BC: Die Menschen, die mit und in deinen Skulpturen erscheinen, gehören als weitere «Seelen» ganz natürlich dazu. Sie sind dominant in deinen Papiercollagen. Fühlt man sich da wie ein göttlicher Zauberer, der über die Geschicke des irdischen Personals schalten und walten kann?

FW: Distanz erst eröffnet die Möglichkeit menschlicher Erkenntnis und Selbsterkenntnis. Wir sind, was wir noch nicht sind. Das Unbestimmte ist das Noch-nicht-Bestimmte, aber keineswegs das Unbestimmbare.

BC: Es geht also um ein Herantasten als Arbeitsmotto. Hat dein Tun etwas Befreiendes für dich?

FW: Es ist eher eine Verstrickung als eine Befreiung.

BC: In der Kunst der 70er Jahre spielte eine gewisse Archaik im Einsatz des Materials eine Rolle. Man denke an Richard Serra, die Arte Povera oder Joseph Beuys. Selbst in der betonten Faktizität der Minimal Art kommt dies zum Tragen. Heute scheint man sich davon sehr weit entfernt zu haben. Wie siehst du das?

FW: Trotz aller revidierten Skepsis bin ich nach wie vor einer von diesen Fernen.

BC: Wirklich? Ist es nicht so, dass du zwar das archaische Potenzial im Material anerkennst, jedoch aus einer Distanz heraus schaffst? Gebiert diese Distanz noch anderes? Das Karnevaleske, die Maskerade im Sinne von Bachtin scheint in deinen Werken auch eine Rolle zu spielen.

FW: Der Wertzerfall, von dem Hermann Broch einst sprach, hat sich nun endgültig erfüllt. Dieser

Im Atelier von Franz West / Views of Franz West's studio. (PHOTOS: BICE CURIGER)

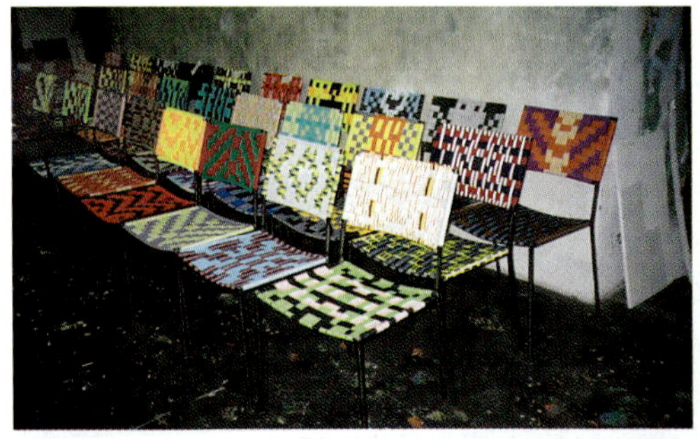
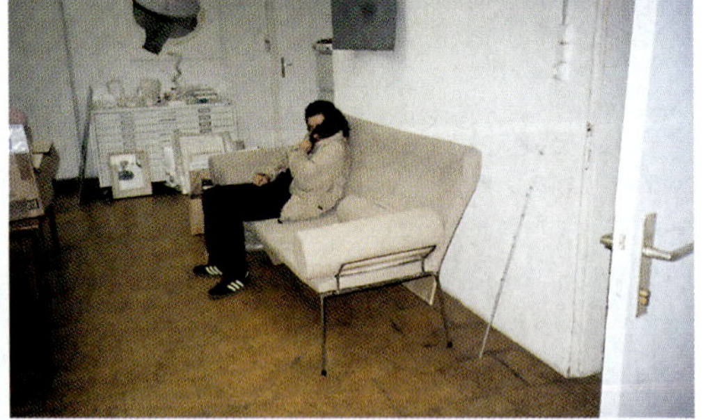
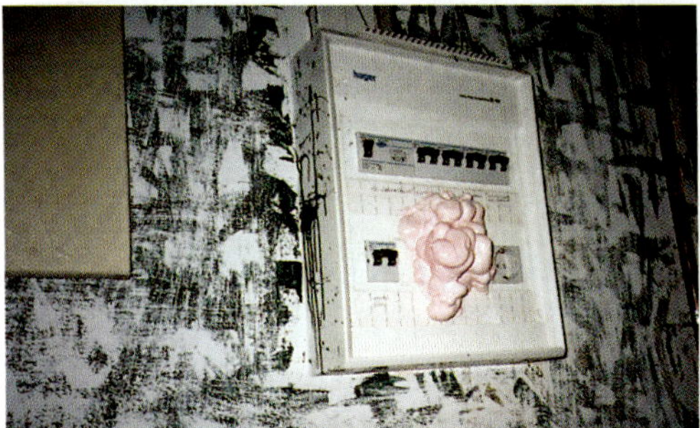
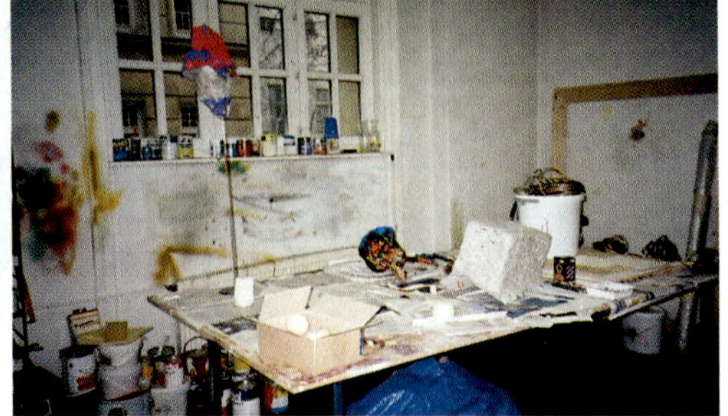

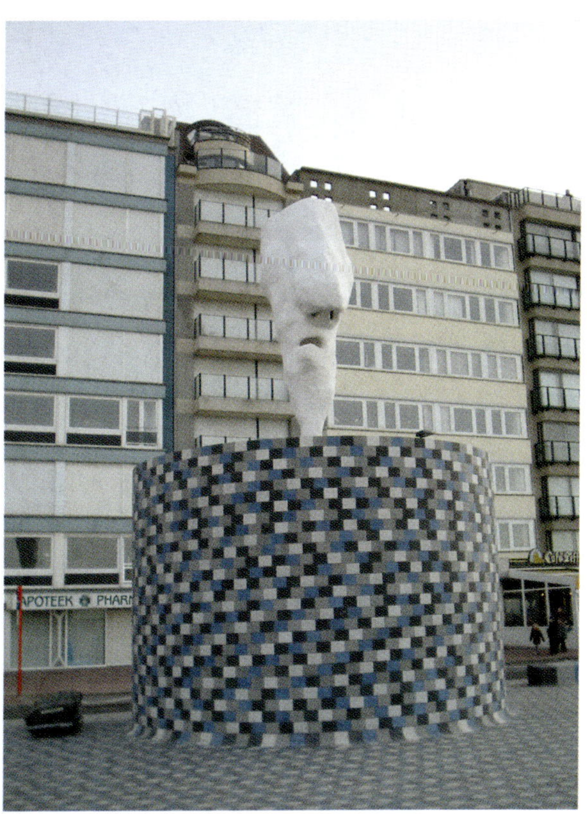

FRANZ WEST, 2 LEMUREN, 2003,
Rubens Plein, Knokke / 2 LEMURES
(PHOTO: TIM VAN LAERE, ANTWERPEN)

tote Punkt ist aber kein Grund zur Resignation, sondern Anlass, wieder erfinderisch zu werden.

BC: Magst du Meteoriten?

FW: Nur in lauen Sommernächten am Traunsee.

BC: Auch durch Farbgebung lässt sich eine gewisse Distanz, zumindest ein Vertuschen der darunter liegenden Materialität erzielen. Du hast mal die Farbe Rosa mit der Neurose in Verbindung gebracht, auch mit dem Zahnfleisch. Ist Rosa deine meist verwendete Farbe?

FW: Wir leben in einer echt dürftigen Zeit. Die Politik hat versagt und versagt täglich aufs Neue. Die Fundamentalismen sind doch nichts anderes als kompensative Verzweiflungsideologien. Die Wissenschaft – ganz und gar unfröhlich – hat sich von ihren Ursprüngen verabschiedet, um damit dem zynischsten aller Spiele zu entkommen. Das Rosa ist also ein fremdes Gewand, ein mehr und mehr dahintautologisierender, rein farbphysiologischer Diskurs, eine schlecht oder echt dynastische Disziplin, die sich mit dem Leistungsprinzip liiert hat. Alles Sonstige gibt auch kaum Grund zu dieser Farbe.

BC: Wucherungen, die «Abart», der Wildwuchs ergeben rein phänomenologisch ein Bild von Individualität – interessiert dich dieser Zusammenhang?

FW: Selbstverständlich.

BC: Deine ins Spiel gebrachten Materialien sind ja auch «immateriell», wenn ich an die Sprache, die Lektüreverweise, die Gedanken und Zitate denke, die in deinen Werken ebenso viel Raum wie das «Handfeste» einnehmen.

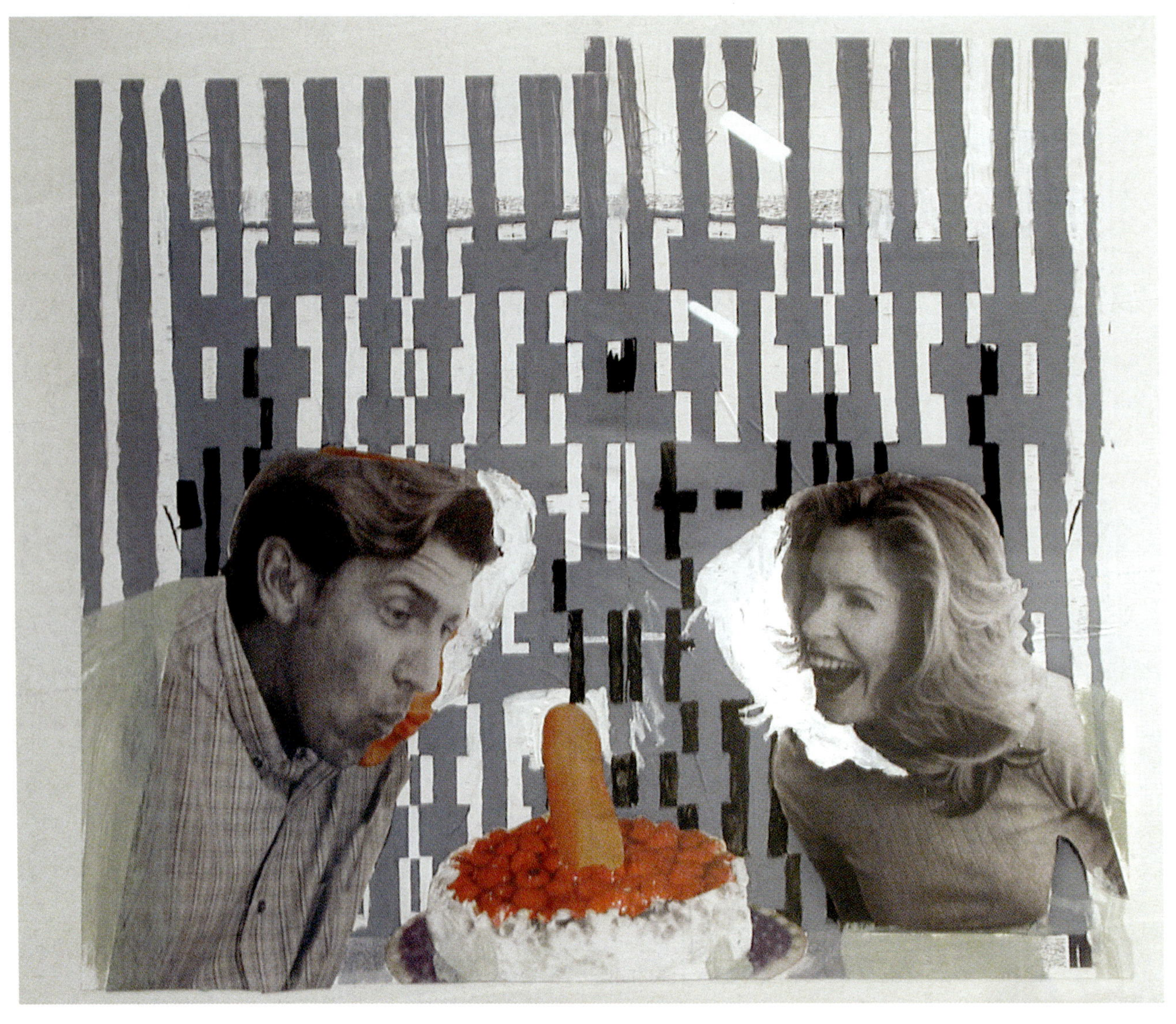

FRANZ WEST, OHNE TITEL (TORTE/EINLADUNGSPLAKAT), 2003, 44 x 49 cm / UNTITLED (FANCY CAKE/INVITATION POSTER), $17^{5}/_{16}$ x $19^{3}/_{8}$".
(PHOTO: GALERIE MEYER KAINER, WIEN)

FW: Künstler und Museen müssen ihre gesellschaftliche Funktion, ihre historisch gewachsene Rolle radikal überdenken und dürfen dabei das Experimentelle, Expeditive, den Hasardismus nicht scheuen, um ihre eingebüsste Glaubwürdigkeit wiederzuerlangen.

BC: Es gibt eine Wärme in all deinen Arbeiten. Für *Parkett* hast du 1993 ein «Tascherl» gemacht, eine Schutzhülle für das Buch. Kommt dieser Eindruck von Wärme von der Tatsache, dass der Aspekt des Handwerklichen oder Handgemachten im Vordergrund steht?

FW: Nein, sicher nicht, es ist ja kein Handschuh, sondern eine Ballspende.

BC: Anlässlich deiner Ausstellung im Portikus in Frankfurt 1988 hast du vom Moment des Umstülpens als Eintritt der «vierten Dimension» gesprochen, und zwar beobachtet beim Ausziehen des Handschuhs, den du für die Herstellung der Papiermaché-Objekte verwendet hast. Es gibt die Friktionen zwischen Körper und Körper (Objekten und Menschen), zwischen Haut und Haut (auch Netzhaut), zwischen kalt und warm. Inwiefern wird schon im Machen nicht bloss die Betrachtung, sondern auch der «Umgang» mit deinen Werken mitgedacht?

FW: Das Evidente – das Schöne, das Richtige, das Stimmige (als seine bestimmenden Gegensätze) sind uneinholbar. Es ist dem Voraus-Sein, dem Kalkül, dem Entwurf, der Bestimmung um genau das voraus, was deren Nützlichkeit begründet. Es ist museal: wertlos, weil nicht reproduzierbar gewordene Realität. Unsere Zeit braucht neue Mythologien der Immanenz, eine Kultur der Heiterkeit, andere Feiertage!, Freuden, Vermählung von Ethik und Phantasie, ein Fest des Lebens in den Schulen, unseren pädagogischen Institutionen und höheren Bildungsanstalten, denen wir unsere Kinder anvertrauen: neben Mathematik und Grammatik einen neuen Eros, der das Private und Öffentliche vereinigt, sich aus den unvereinbaren Gegensätzen speist.

BC: Sind Formen, die unzähmbar erscheinen, die grösseren, gefährlicheren, schöneren Energien im Raum?

FW: Unzähmbar ist das Züngeln einer Flamme.

BC: Goethe schrieb seinen *Westöstlichen Diwan* als Vermittler fremder Kultur. Du hast Perserteppiche und afrikanische Stoffe verwendet. Ist das dein westöstlicher oder nordsüdlicher Diwan?

FW: Ich versuche mich an den *Westöstlichen Diwan* zu erinnern… Ich würde meine Skulpturen lieber unter materialistischen Gesichtspunkten sehen. Mir ist diese Interpretation grundsätzlich zu poetisch. Es ist wie ein Transfer, aber nicht unbedingt wie ein poetischer Transfer.

BC: Deine Werke scheinen wie aus einer Metamaterie gemacht – platzieren sich wie prononcierte Kunstkörper zwischen die lebendigen und die fabrizierten Alltagskörper. Wie siehst du das?

FW: Das tut mir leid, so erschien's mir auch schon manchmal, aber dafür kann ich nichts.

Im Atelier von Franz West / Views of Franz West's studio.

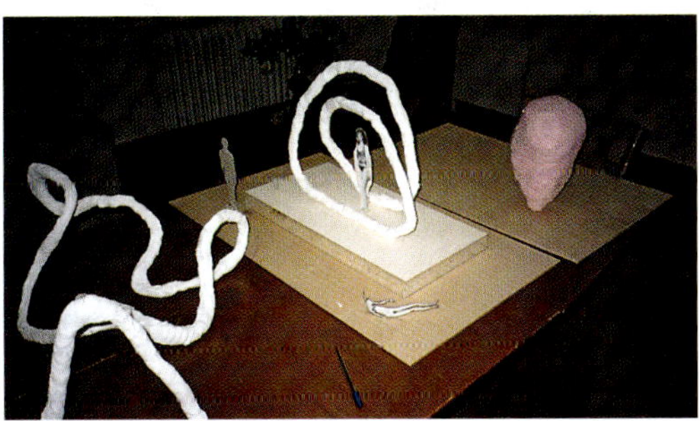
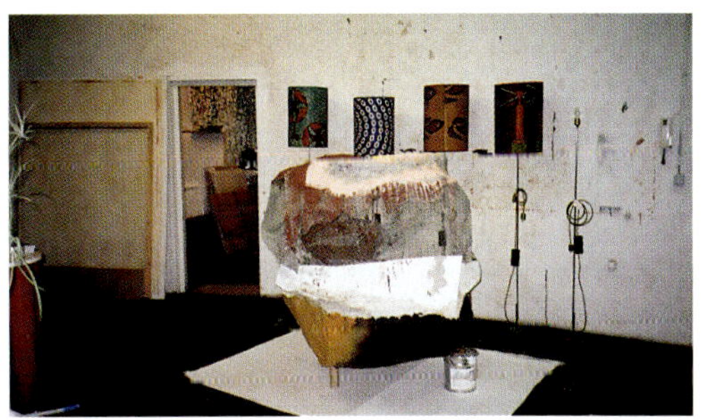

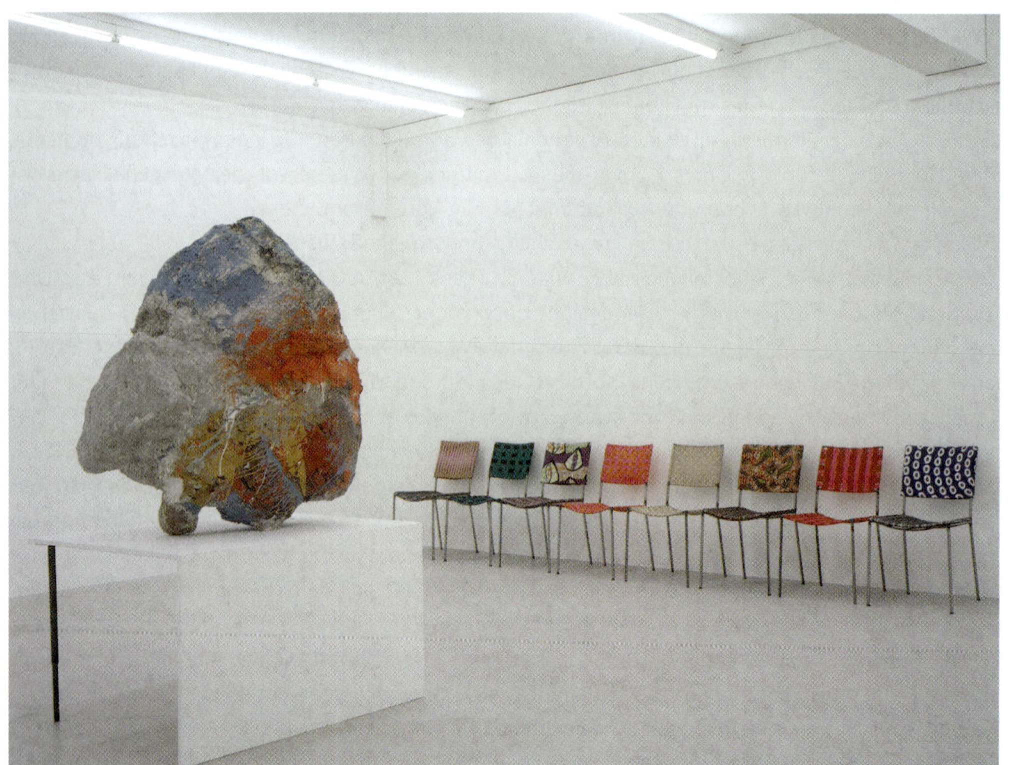

"IT'S MORE LIKE BEING ENTANGLED..."

A CONVERSATION WITH FRANZ WEST

BICE CURIGER: You work with a relatively broad range of materials. Can you say something about how you go about your everyday work? How do materials influence your decisions?

FRANZ WEST: In contrast to an initial skepticism and cynical contempt of any kind of "material fetishism," I have come to realize, over the years, that exploring the respective qualities of a material is, in fact, precisely what I want.

BC: Let's take papier-mâché and plaster versus metal, or printed fabrics and carpets versus a mirror: the first thing that comes to mind is the contrast between soft and hard. But then there is also the difference in working with such materials. How do your materials affect your work?

FW: Undefined! Neither negation nor affirmation refers to what happens beforehand anyway. And in any case, who would bow to logic?

BC: Does the Marxist opposition between materialism and idealism still work? Or did it ever mean anything to you?

FW: No, I'm not that well informed yet.

BC: You once expressed disappointment in Duchamp's BOTTLE RACK (1914); it was a poorly made object with too many ugly screws.

FW: Let's say for the moment that art is essentially the knowledge of the non-known, of non-

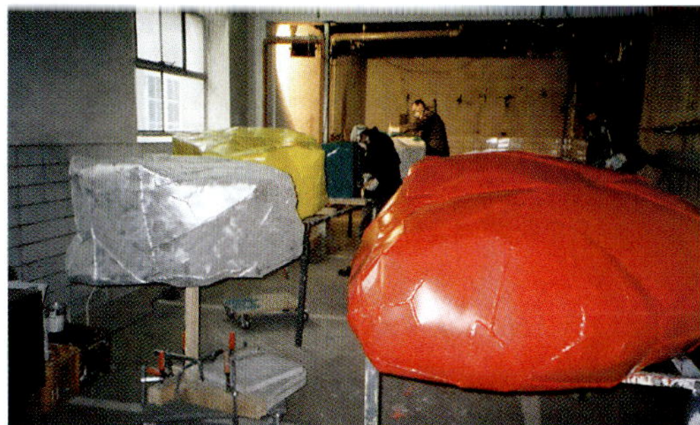

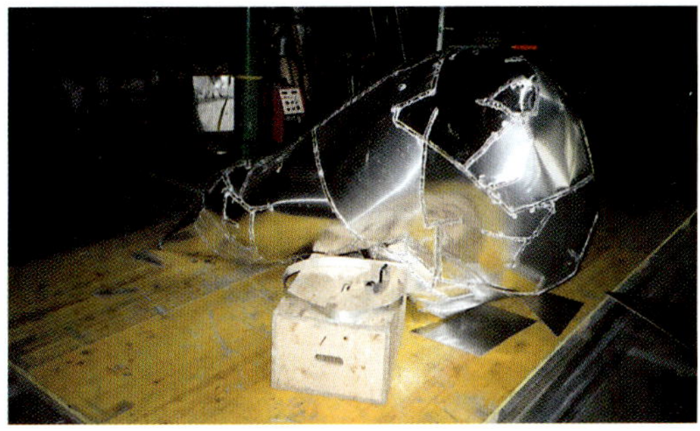

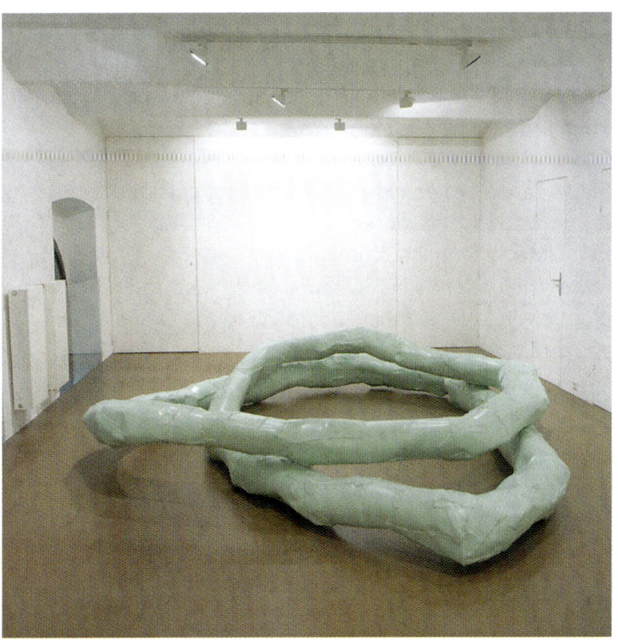

FRANZ WEST, GARTENMÖBEL, 2003, lackierte Aluminiumskulptur, 130 x 410 x 130 cm / GARDEN FURNITURE, lacquered aluminum sculpture, 51 $^{3}/_{16}$ x 161 $^{7}/_{16}$ x 51 $^{3}/_{16}$". (PHOTO: GALERIE MEYER KAINER)

being, or more generally: the relationship to the unknown, the inaccessible!

BC: Which serially manufactured everyday objects do you find especially fascinating?

FW: Pickling jars.

BC: Gaps, holes, interstices could also be called material.

FW: I desire the things that one who desires doesn't need, doesn't lack, and doesn't wish to possess. It is a desire for that which remains unapproachable and alien. A desire for otherness as difference, plain and simple. Look, I build a "bateau imaginaire" with Heimo Zobernig, for example, a cube that Heimo has created with four or five chairs of mine on top of it. It's anchored in water about 10 feet deep and it will float on a lake a few miles outside of Paris on the occasion of a "biennial." The cube will be so high that it will be impossible for a swimmer to climb up on top where the chairs are placed and there will be no ladder or steps or handles, etc. The quality of the water is such that no one will have the impulse to go swimming there anyway.

BC: What will the cube be made of?

FW: Possibilities include plastic, wood, or metal—Heimo wants sharp edges, therefore metal. I'm not approaching it in terms of material, of the metal, but rather in terms of the piece, and then taking what seems most appropriate to me or to anyone involved.

BC: Let's talk about your furniture. It looks precarious but it satisfies all the requirements of function.

FW: It's unusually thin; that's the important point. The engineering is invisible. It works only because it's welded. A regular chair is thicker. The chairs are unexpectedly tall, not in the spirit of the times.

BC: To what extent does the idea of investing material with life play a role for you? Or, conversely: do you materialize ideas?

FW: As said, I used to think material is lifeless. But experience with LSD and reading Wittgenstein taught me that everything lives.

BC: The people who appear with and in your sculptures are naturally part of them as additional "souls." They are dominant in your paper collages. Does that make one feel like a divine magician toying with the fate of his personnel?

FW: Detachment is a prerequisite of insight into others and into oneself. We are what we are yet to be. The undefined is the non-yet-defined, but certainly not the undefinable.

BC: So you take a probing approach to your work. Is there something liberating for you about what you do?

FW: It's more like being entangled than liberated.

BC: In the art of the seventies, there was something archaic about the use of materials as in the work of, say, Richard Serra, Arte Povera artists, or Joseph Beuys. You can even observe it in the deliberate facticity of Minimal Art. Today art seems to have moved a long way away from that approach. What do you think?

FW: Despite the revised skepticism, I am still one of those who have moved a long way away.

BC: Really? Wouldn't you say that you recognize the archaic potential of materials, but approach it with detachment? Does that detachment generate other things? Carnival, masquerading in the sense of Bakhtin also seems to play a role in your works.

FW: The disintegration of values that Hermann Broch once talked about has finally come true. But that's no reason to resign; it should actually encourage a renaissance of inventiveness.

BC: Do you like meteorites?

FW: Only on balmy summer nights at Traunsee Lake.

BC: Coloring can also produce a certain detachment or at least a concealment of the material underneath. You once associated pink with neurosis, and with gums. Is pink the color you use most?

FW: We live in pretty wretched times. Politics fail and keep failing, day after day. Fundamentalist movements are nothing but acts of desperation, compensatory ideologies. Sciences—deadly earnest—ignore their origins in order to escape the most cynical of all games. Pink is therefore an alien guise, an increasingly tautologically aligned discourse on color physiology, a poor or pure dynastic discipline affiliated with the performance principle. There's nothing else that's likely to justify that color.

BC: Rampant growth, "deviance," proliferation yield a purely phenomenological picture of individuality—are you interested in this association?

FW: Obviously.

BC: You also bring "immaterial" materials into play like language, literary references, thoughts, and quotations that take up just as much room in your works as the "solid" things do.

FW: Artists and museums have to radically re-evaluate their social function and the role they play, which has evolved historically, but without shunning experimental, expeditious, or speculative ventures in order to recover the credibility they've lost.

BC: All of your works convey warmth. In 1993 you created a tote bag for Parkett, a protective pouch for the book. Is this impression of warmth generated by the emphasis on handicraft or making things by hand?

FW: No, certainly not, it's not a glove but rather a donation for a charity ball.

BC: At your 1988 exhibition at Portikus in Frankfurt, you described turning things inside out as entering the "fourth dimension," an observation based on pulling off the glove that you had used to make your papier-mâché objects. There is friction between body and body (object and person), between skin and skin (the retina as well), and between cold and warm. To what extent is not just

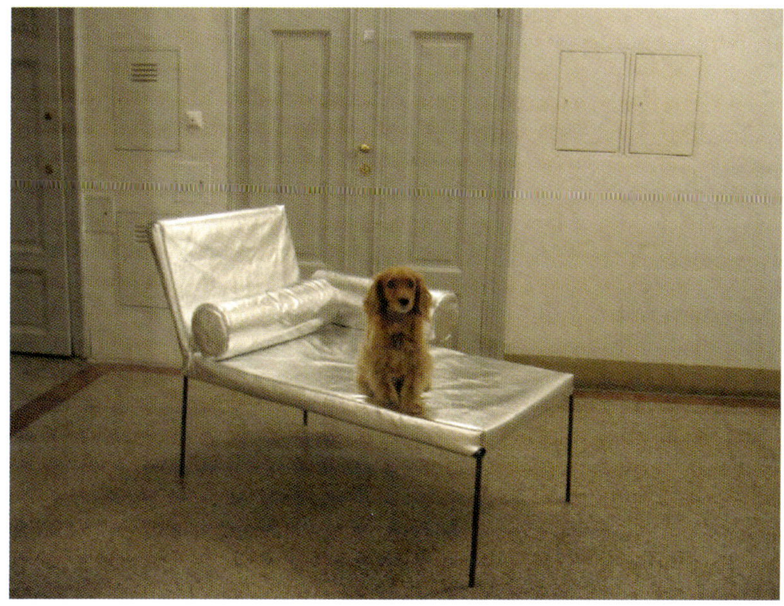

FRANZ WEST, CHAISELONGUE, 2003, Metall, Schaumstoff, Leinen, Carbon Kevlar,
ca. 153 x 95 x 90 cm / metal, rubber foam, canvas, Carbon Kevlar, ca. 60$^{1}/_{4}$ x 37$^{3}/_{8}$ x 35$^{7}/_{16}$".

the viewing but also the "handling" of your works involved in the process of making them?
FW: You can't catch up with things that are evident—beautiful, right, definitely compelling (as their defining opposites). It's a matter of being ahead of calculation or design or definition by exactly that distance that establishes their usefulness. It's museological: worthless because it's become a nonreproducible reality. Today we need new mythologies of immanence, a culture of serenity, different holidays!, joys, the wedding of ethics and fantasy, a celebration of life in schools, in the educational institutions and universities to which we entrust our children: a new Eros in addition to mathematics and grammar that unites the private and public and is nurtured by irreconcilable opposites.
BC: Forms that seem to be untamable—are they the larger, more dangerous, more beautiful energies in space?
FW: The flickering of a flame is untamable.

BC: Goethe wrote his *Westöstlicher Diwan* as a link with foreign cultures. You've used Persian carpets and African fabrics. Is that your west-east or north-south divan?
FW: I'm trying to remember the *Westöstlicher Diwan*… I would rather see my sculptures in material terms. The other interpretation is essentially too poetic for me. — It's like a transfer, but not necessarily a poetic transfer.
BC: Your works seem to be made out of meta-matter, they settle down like pointedly artificial bodies among the living and manufactured bodies of everyday life. How do you see that?
FW: My apologies, they look like that to me sometimes, too, but I can't do anything about it.

Translation: Catherine Schelbert

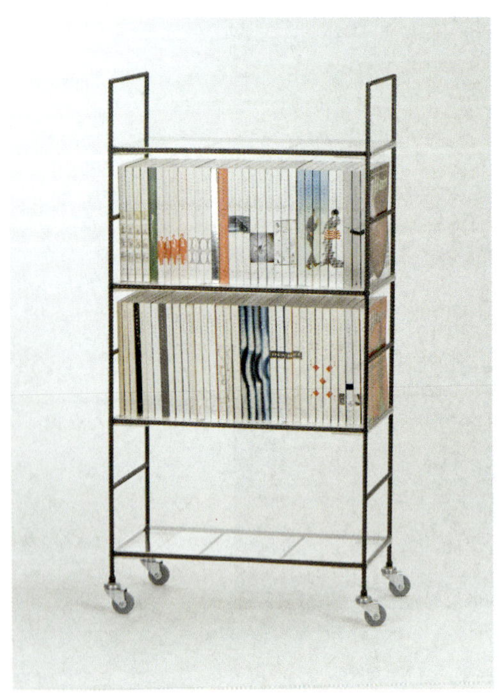

ANNIVERSARY EDITION FOR PARKETT

FRANZ WEST

2 x 20 JAHRE PARKETT, 2004
Büchergestell. Armierungsstahl, Plexiglas, vier Räder,
120 x 60 x 30 cm.
Auflage: 99, signiertes und nummeriertes Zertifikat.

2 x 20 YEARS OF PARKETT, 2004
Bookshelf. Reinforcing steel, Plexiglas, four wheels,
$47^{1}/_{4}$ x $23^{5}/_{8}$ x $11^{13}/_{16}$".
Edition of 99, signed and numbered certificate.

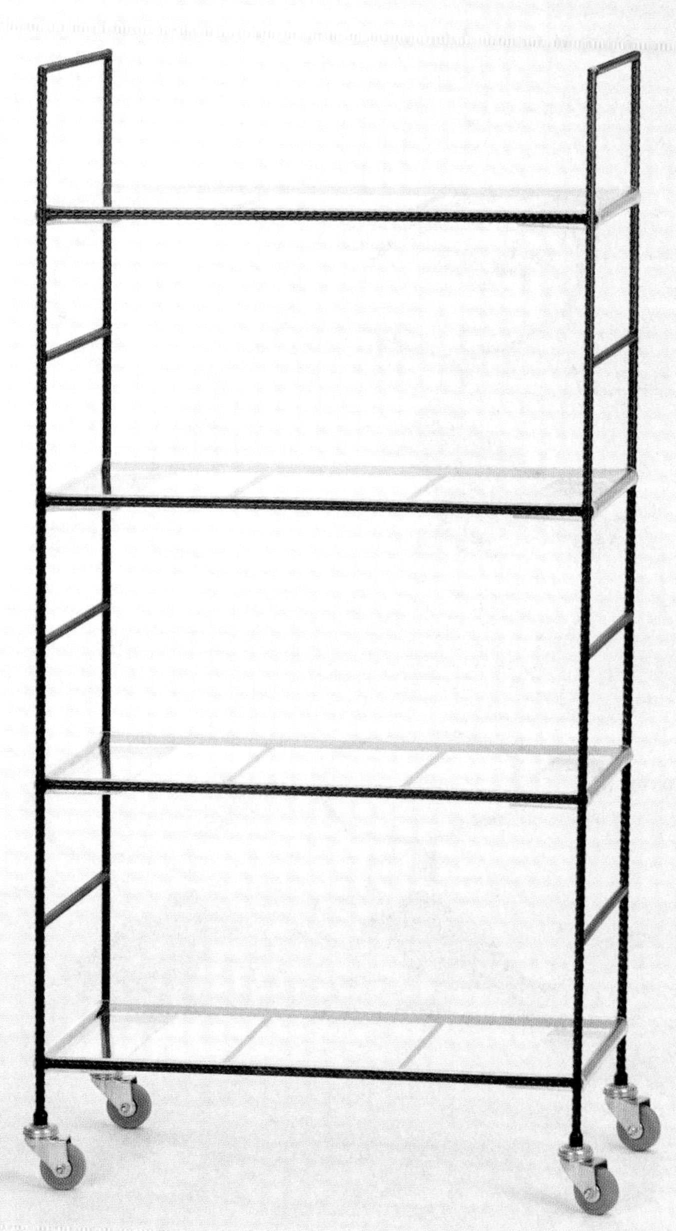

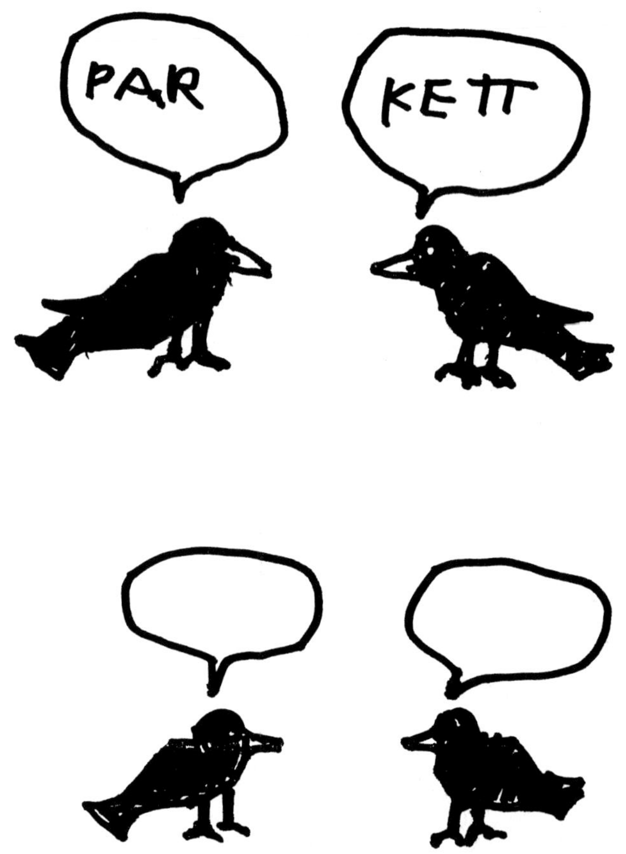

ALEX KATZ, 2004

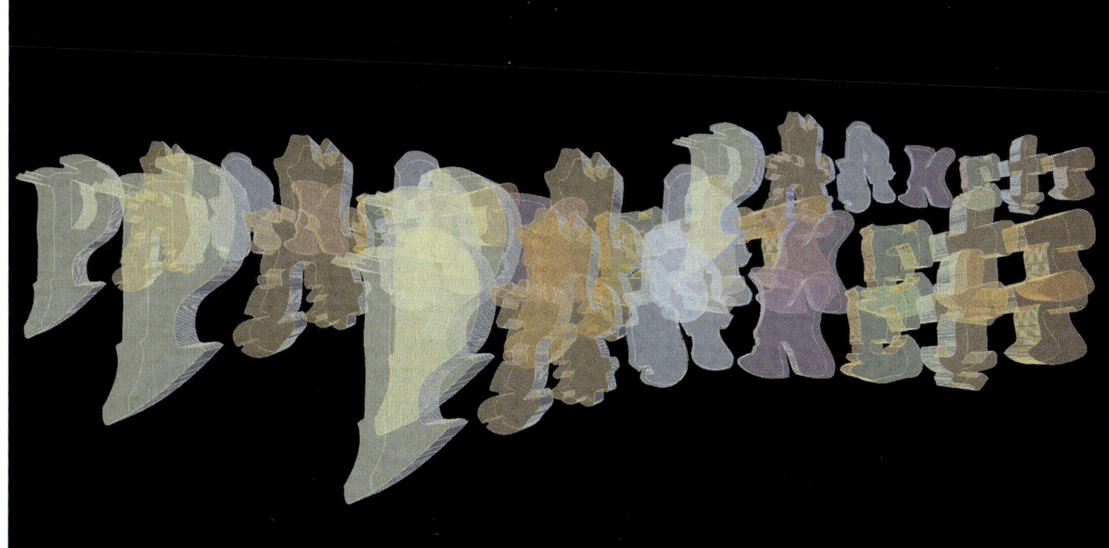

Parkett
1/sfr12/dm34/us$56

Patrick Frey/Gilbert & George
Oskar Bätschmann/Hans Belting
Dieter Meier/Christian Dior
Jacqueline Burckhardt/Dana Reitz
Jean-Christophe Ammann/Enzo Cucchi
Bice Curiger/Marja Bloem/Enzo Cucchi
Theodora Vischer/Vivian Suter
Johannes Gachnang/Meret Oppenheim
Les Infos du Paradis
Barbara Kruger/Roger Spottiswood
Gianfranco Verna/Cumulus
Peter Suter/Theo Modespacher
Balkon

collaboration/Enzo Cucchi

FROM THE ORCHESTRA FLOOR
(PARKETT)
MOST THINGS SEEM POSSIBLE

LAWRENCE WEINER   2004

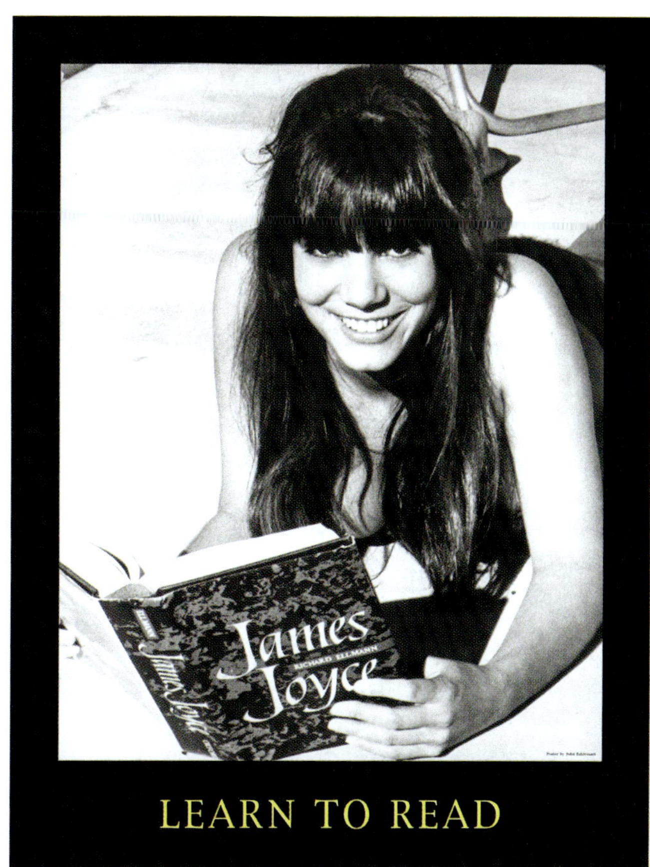

JOHN BALDESSARI, 2004

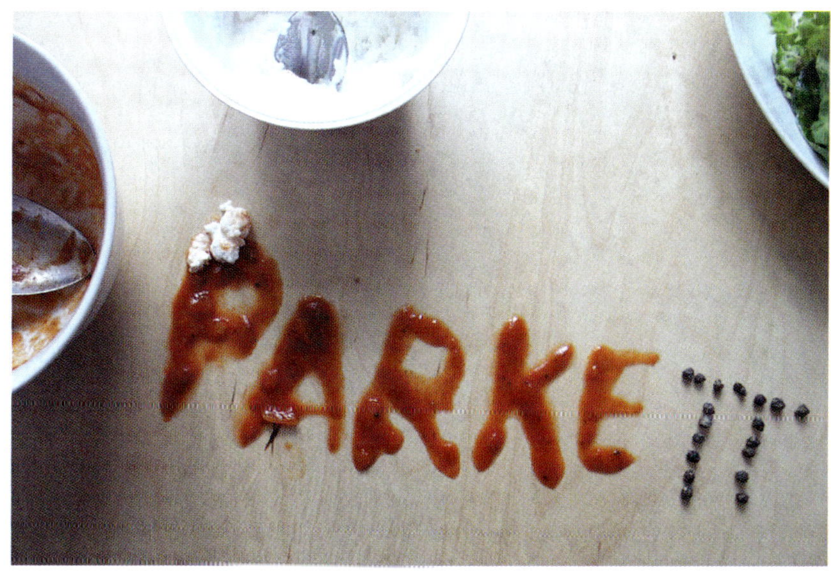

JOHN BOCK, 2004

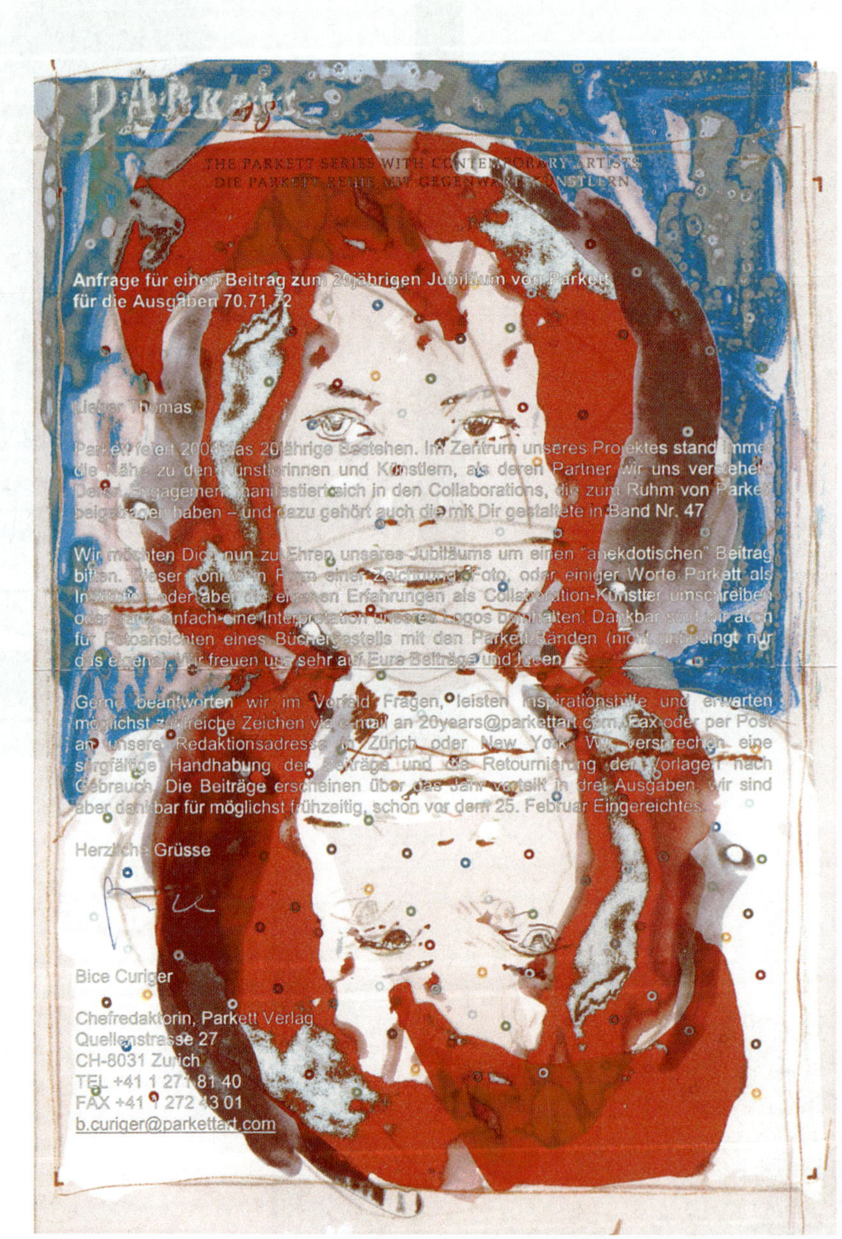

THOMAS SCHÜTTE, 2004

Christian Marclay

born 1955 in San Rafael, California, lives and works in New York / geboren 1955 in San Rafael, Kalifornien, lebt und arbeitet in New York.

Wilhelm Sasnal

born 1972 in Tarnów, Poland, lives and works in Tarnów / geboren 1972 in Tarnów, Polen, lebt und arbeitet in Tarnów.

Gillian Wearing

born 1963 in Birmingham, England, lives and works in London / geboren 1963 in Birmingham, England, lebt und arbeitet in London.

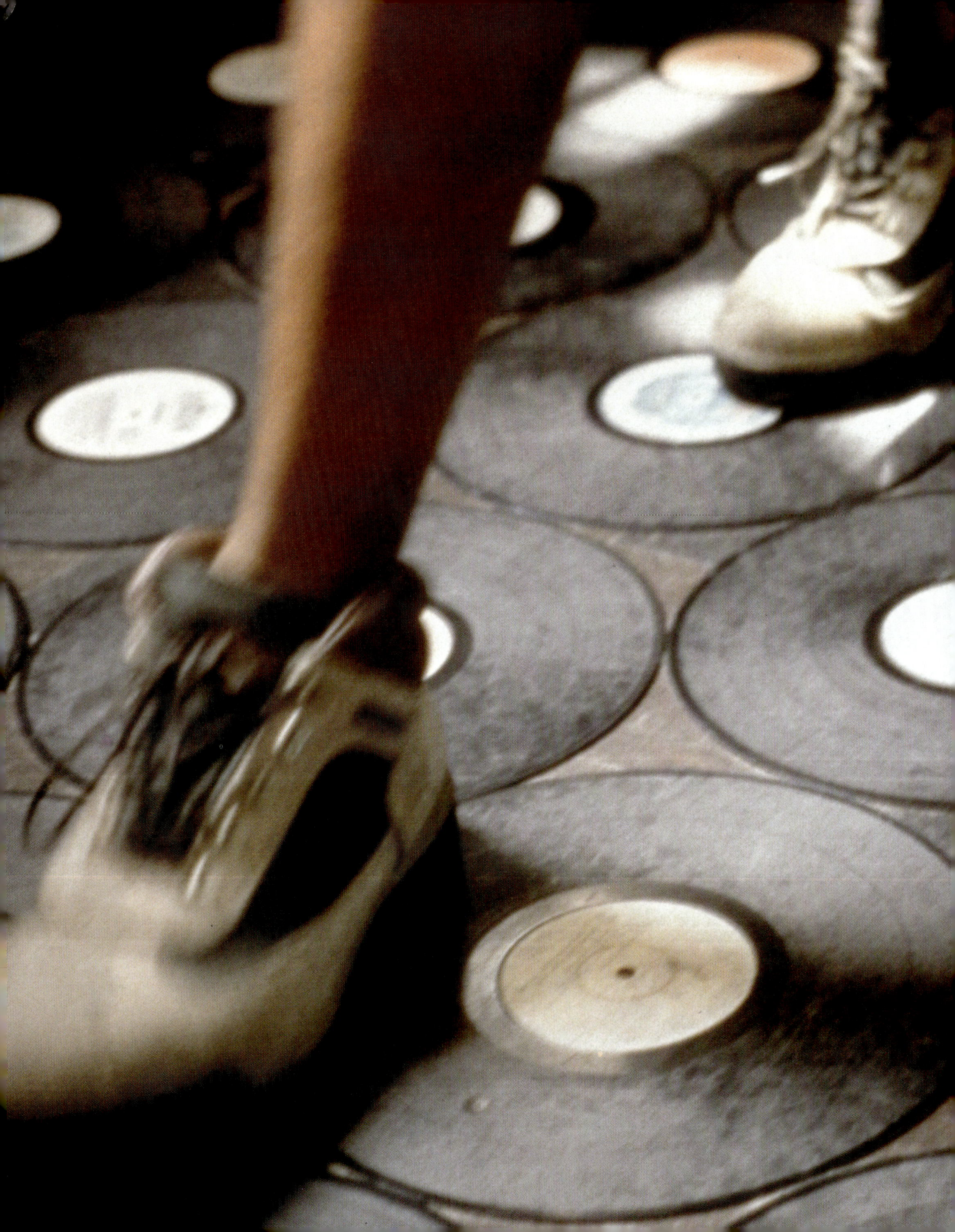

CHRISTIAN MARCLAY

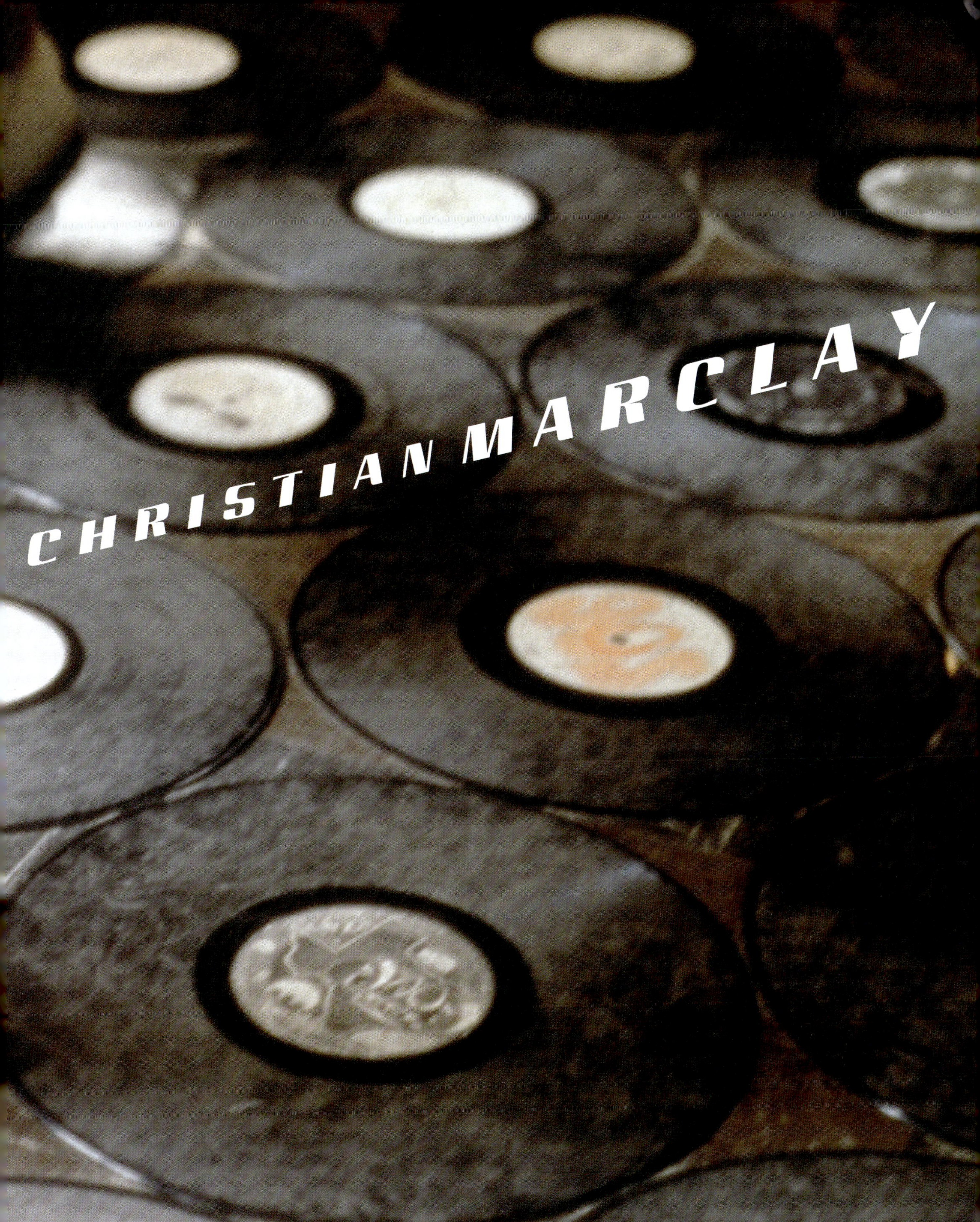

CHRISTIAN MARCLAY, MEMORY LANE, 2000, vinyl records, installation, P.S.1 Contemporary Arts Center, New York / GEDENKWEG, Schallplatten.

CHRISTIAN MARCLAY'S

PHILIP SHERBURNE

Taking the musical world as his primary material, Christian Marclay fuses the documentary with the imaginary, merging the public and private worlds of listening. Many sound artists have traversed the limits of silence—beyond John Cage, of course, see Francisco López, or Reynols, or Richard Chartier—but Marclay's work is different. It either emits sound or it does not. His inaudible works may be said, metaphorically, to hum with cultural resonances, but this is ultimately only a metaphor. A great deal of Marclay's output, possibly the majority of it, is visual or plastic in nature. And yet even this is as much about sound—about the c u l - t u r a l universe of sound—as any recording; perhaps more so, because it concerns the ubiquity of sound in culture. Marclay's work is about the socially inscribed "flip side" of sound; it is about the very fact that I could use the phrase "flip side" as unthinkingly as I just did, realizing only as I typed it that the term derives from records, and is thus infinitely apropos for use here.

Before we consider Christian Marclay in more detail, two recent incidents serve as coincidental introductions to his work. Widely reported in the North American media, they hone in on Marclay's practice as surely as the turntable stylus winds concentrically toward the center of the disc.

Several weeks ago, I received an email—a forward of a forward of a forward, in the curiously passive manner of Internet activism—alerting me that unscrupulous businessmen were planning an act of wanton destruction, and enlisting my assistance in opposing them. A company called Master Tape Collection had come into possession of the original studio master of Elvis Presley's "That's All Right," recorded during the 1954/55 Sun Sessions, and was planning to cut the tape into two-inch segments, mount the strips on commemorative plaques, and sell them to collectors for $ 495 a pop.

The uproar, reported the following week in *The New York Times,* was not surprising, and the *Times* article quoted both horrified archivists and defensive Master Tape representatives, who alleged that the tape's deterioration had rendered it unplayable.[1] (The archivists, though,

---

PHILIP SHERBURNE is a San Francisco-based critic, photographer, and DJ.

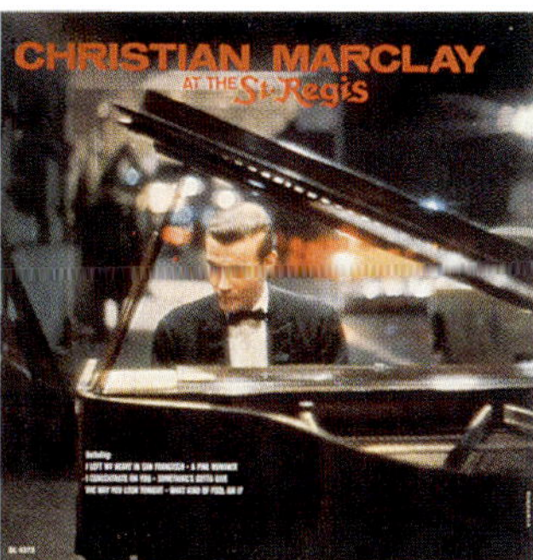

CHRISTIAN MARCLAY, CHRISTIAN MARCLAY AT THE ST. REGIS
(IMAGINARY RECORDS), 1981, paint,
Letraset on record cover / Farbe und Letraset auf Plattenhülle.

COCHLEAR IMPLANTS

seemed to have the stronger argument: as fragile as the tape might be, that was no excuse for shredding and selling it, denying future attempts at preservation or reconstruction.)

Less than a week later, an unrelated story in *The New York Times* reported another curious incident in the annals of sound recording. Digging for rare funk LPs in a thrift store, two record collectors had stumbled upon a trove of handmade records credited to an unknown artist named Mingering Mike. The sleeves were painstakingly faked, complete with hand-lettered liner notes, spine titles, nonexistent catalogue numbers, and occasionally even shrink wrap and price stickers; the records themselves were but cardboard discs with hand-drawn grooves and labels. Mingering Mike, it turned out, was a real person, if not the accomplished recording artist his imaginary records made him out to be; a dreamer with fantasies of fame, he had produced his archive of covers, he said, so that "if it all came together one day, I'd be ready."[2]

Anyone familiar with Marclay's work will immediately be reminded of certain examples from his "Imaginary Records" series as well as the poster project FALSE ADVERTISING (1994). In "Imaginary Records" like CHRISTIAN MARCLAY AT THE ST. REGIS (1981), the artist doctored mass-produced record sleeves by blotting out the performers' names with his own; for FALSE ADVERTISING, he designed fake concert posters billing himself in any number of contexts—jazz saxophonist, heavy metal guitarist—and wheat-pasted the handbills all over town. Both projects offered a pastiche of the graphic styles associated with various musical genres, and perhaps played with common teenage dreams of fame. (As an adolescent, I fashioned intricate logos for many an imaginary band that I was sure would one day propel me into the spotlight.) Mingering Mike had taken the Art Brut approach to the same idea, using his creations to insert himself in the pop-culture spectrum—even if his only audience, until two crate-diggers came along, was in his own imagination.

The Elvis incident, while hardly such a feel-good tale, resonates just as surely with Marclay's approach to the recorded object. The story struck me for the way it highlighted a number of issues—the fragility of the recorded object, the status of the original within a system of mechanical reproduction, the desire to o w n the aura by means of a relic—which have remained unresolved since Walter Benjamin articulated them in his critical touchstone, *The Work of Art in the Age of Mechanical Reproduction*. For the duration of his career, Marclay has worked deep within this nexus of issues, exploring the space where music, mechanical reproduction, popular culture, commodified desire, and the imaginary collide.

Marclay's projects may never have aroused quite the anxiety that the Master Tape incident did—quite to his credit, I might add—but he has often alluded to this kind of object-oriented anxiety in his work. FOOTSTEPS (1989), for example, covered a gallery floor with 3,500 records, requiring museumgoers to walk upon them. For anyone who came of age in a pre-digital era, such an action is tantamount to asking a patriot to tread upon the flag. RECORD WITHOUT A COVER (1985) was simply a vinyl record containing one of Marclay's recordings, distributed and sold as indicated. Designed to be damaged in its commercial journey from the pressing plant to the consumer's home, it thumbed its nose at the fetishization of the vinyl object even as it reveled in its very material being, soaking up traces of its experience on the market in the form of scuffs and clicks, and becoming perhaps the most literal example of "pop music" ever. Perhaps even more pertinent to the Master Tape incident is Marclay's SECRET (1988)—an update of Duchamp's A BRUIT SECRET (With Hidden Noise, 1916)—, a 7-inch metal master disc with an affixed padlock, short-circuiting the system of mechanical reproduction and forever sealing the sounds within, which nonetheless remain tantalizingly visible in the grooves on the record.

While both "real life" stories' correspondence to certain of Marclay's works may be accidental, the way they harmonize with his practice underscores an important point. Marclay, who has often referenced Duchamp, is frequently noted for his sculptural use of readymade objects, from collaged record covers to cut and glued vinyl discs to actual musical instruments like the conjoined tuba and pocket trumpet in LIP LOCK (2000). But reading outward from his work to Mingering Mike and then to the Master Tape Collection—or perhaps it would be better to say, cross-cutting between the three—it becomes apparent that Marclay's entire career consists of readymade i n t e r v e n t i o n s that put the subtlest spin on everyday activities. By framing them, putting them on a pedestal, as it were, Marclay highlights our own participation in a never-ending system of cultural circulation. This is profoundly fitting, of course, for an artist tutored as much in the DIY trenches of late seventies punk rock as in the traditions of Duchamp and Fluxus. Despite the theoretical complexity and art historical allusions of much of Marclay's work—even his first band, The Bachelors, Even, was named after a Duchamp sculpture—it resonates as powerfully as it does because it retraces the aesthetic choices and emotional investments of its audience.

Marclay is routinely described as a "sound artist." This is due in part to the fact that his work, which spans sculpture, DJing, performance, painting, installation, video, and more, takes as its primary subject matter the world of recorded music and its accompanying imagery—even though he often works silently, through allusion alone. Marclay's reputation as a sound artist is also no doubt due to the fact that sound art is enjoying unprecedented institutional acceptance. But Marclay is not a traditional sound artist. Instead of constructing sonic installations or recording CDs of abstract tone investigations, he typically divides his

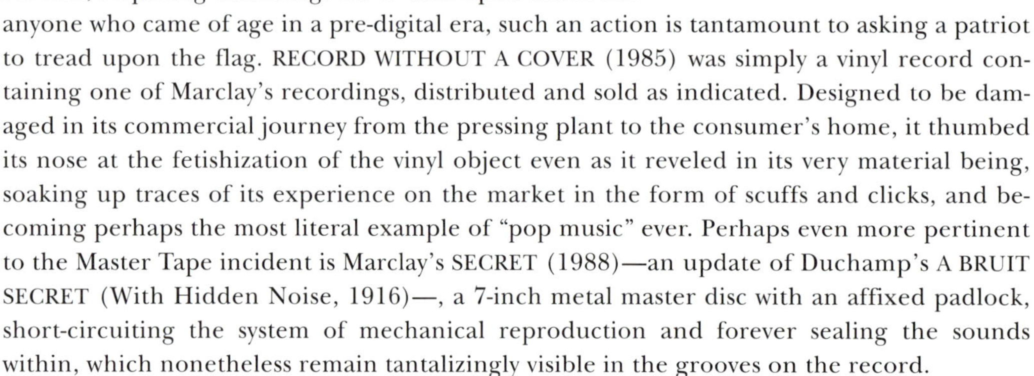

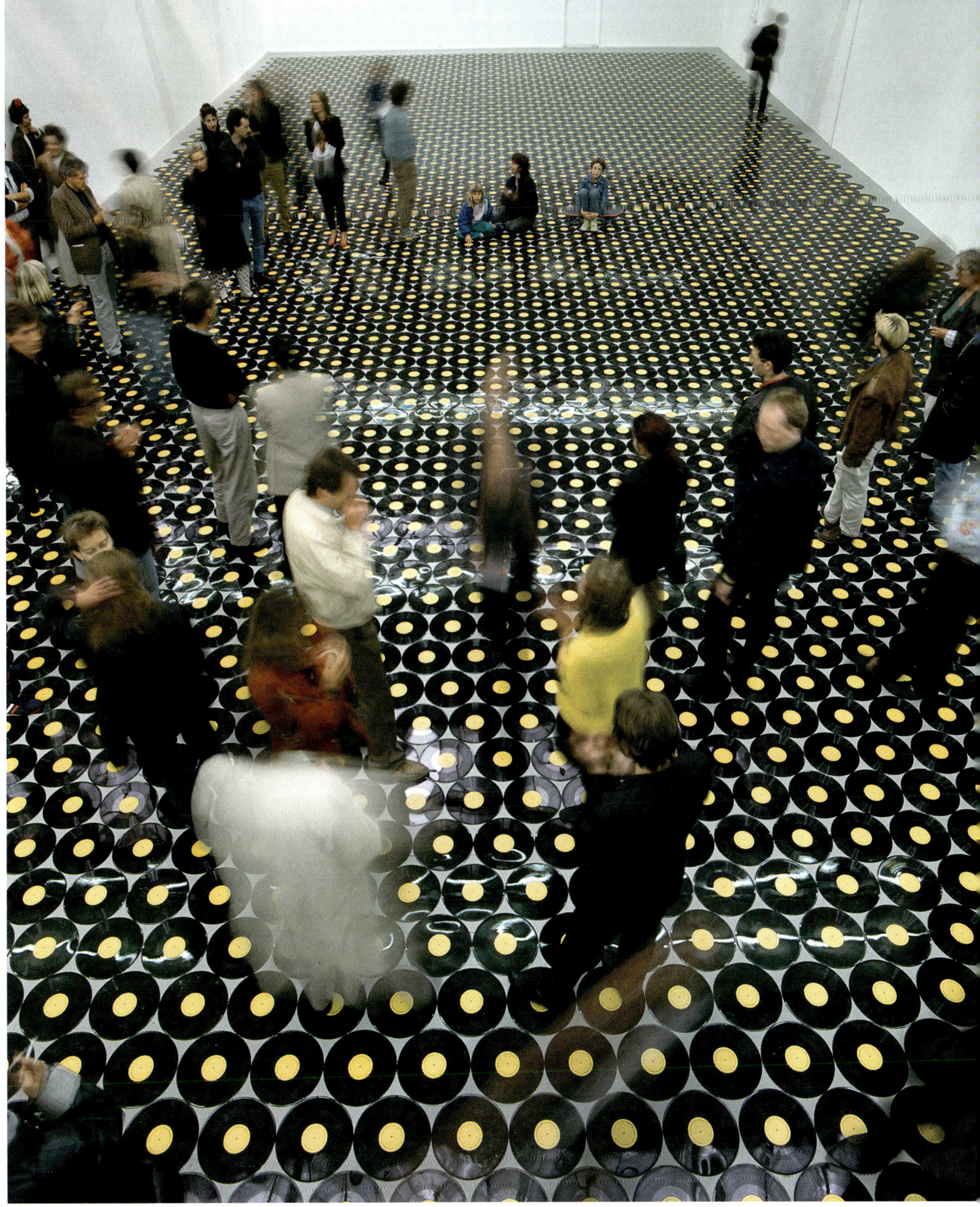

CHRISTIAN MARCLAY, FOOTSTEPS, 1989, 3500 vinyl records, installation, Shedhalle Zürich / FUSSSTAPFEN, 3500 Schallplatten. (PHOTO: WERNER GRAF)

23

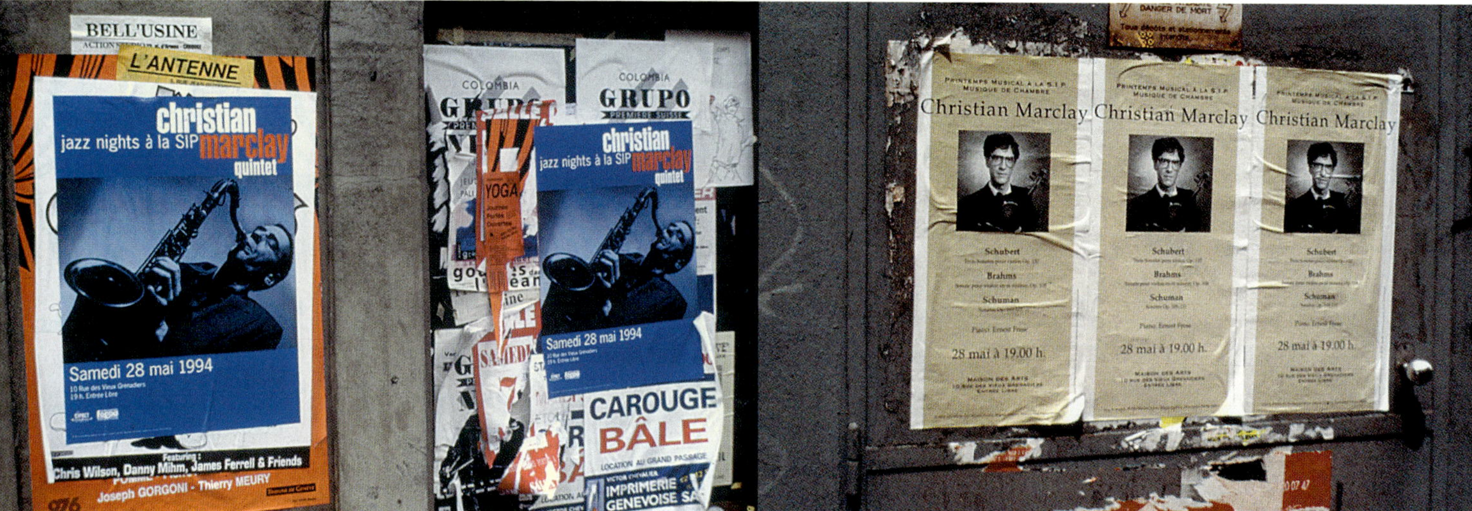

CHRISTIAN MARCLAY, FALSE ADVERTISING, 1994, *poster series /*
FALSCHE WERBUNG, Plakatserie.

work between live DJ performances and visual and plastic artworks with no audible content at all. There are exceptions: among his video and installation pieces, VIDEO QUARTET (2002), UP AND OUT (1998), TAPE FALL (1989), and GUITAR DRAG (2002) all contain audio elements. But, crucially, even his sound-inclusive works are not about sound per se. If most "sound art" is about sound's relationship to space, Marclay's work is always about music as a locus of mediated information, cultural capital, and overdetermined signs.

Seldom—almost never—does Marclay work with sound that does not signify musically. The only piece that comes to mind is TAPE FALL, in which a reel-to-reel recorder perched on a ladder and missing its take-up reel slowly spills its tape in a growing pile below; as it runs, it plays back the sound of running water, an unusually mimetic sound within Marclay's oeuvre. But even here, this naïve soundtrack is overdetermined, and what flows is not a flow (*pace*, Gertrude Stein) but rather a pool of allusions intermingling references to the water music of Cage, Satie, Takemitsu, and others.

There is a substrain within Marclay's work that concerns itself with telephones—either in sculptural configurations like BONEYARD (1990) or in video work like TELEPHONES (1995), in which Marclay has spliced together numerous cinematic fragments of people speaking on telephones. Even here, though, sound fills a communicative (or miscommunicative) role. Likewise, UP AND OUT, which marries the soundtrack from Brian De Palma's *Blow Out* (1981) to the visuals of Michelangelo Antonioni's *Blow-Up* (1966), plays out like a triple detective flick in which the audience's role is to fill in the gaps between sound and vision.

Even when considering Marclay as a DJ—and Marclay, a formidable performer, is the godfather of an entire movement of experimental turntablists working today—few commentators actually discuss the s o u n d of his work, preferring to concentrate on his technique (multiple turntables, frenetic jump-cuts) and material (such as the thousands of Christmas records utilized since 1999 in his ongoing performance project THE SOUNDS OF CHRIST-MAS). In part this is because Marclay's recordings, by intention, are incomplete—their real-

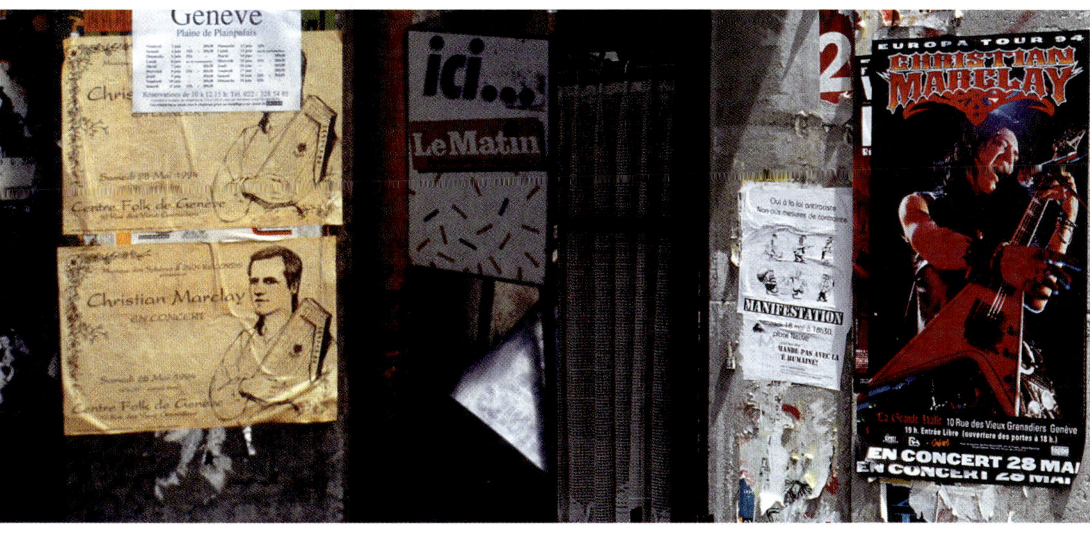
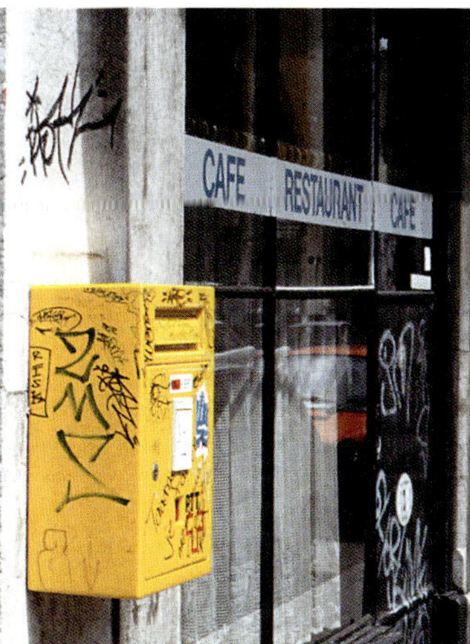

CHRISTIAN MARCLAY, THE SOUNDS OF CHRISTMAS (1999–),
ongoing performance project / WEIHNACHTSKLÄNGE, andauerndes Performanceprojekt.

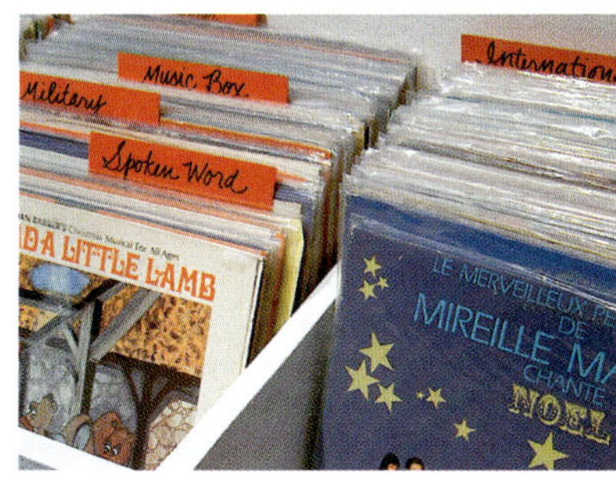
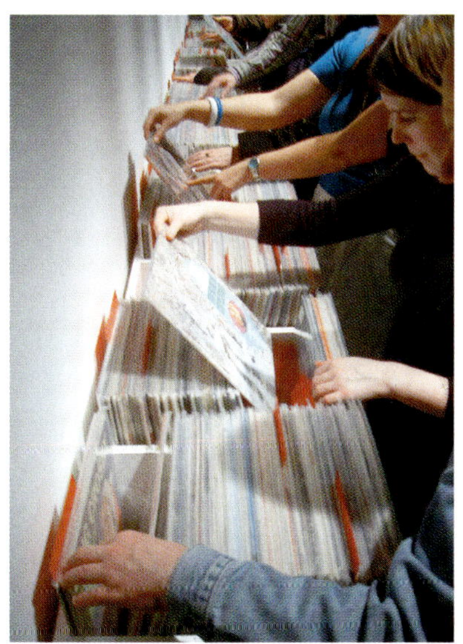

ization happens only in a live context. While he rehearses certain transitions and prepares his records by affixing tape and stickers to create anticipated loops, most of his performance is unplanned. Notably, his discography features few studio recordings; most of his recorded output is in the form of collaborative improvisations with other instrumentalists.

While sound artists like Stephen Vitiello, Richard Chartier, or Francisco López concentrate on sound's spatial, textural, and immersive properties, Marclay's work as a DJ has tended to be primarily allusive in nature, whether remixing artists from Jimi Hendrix to Louis Armstrong on his *More Encores* (1988) record or zigzagging from genre to genre within the ensembles like John Zorn's. Marclay's allusive effects outstrip even his intentions. As he once explained to me, discussing his performances, "People recognize things that I'd never played. Because they were expecting recognition, I would create this dense mix and they would recognize a recording, and they would come up after the gig and say, 'Oh, you played this…' Well, no."[3] Even the ghosts in Marclay's music come singing of the known world. In his silences resonate the strains of a version of an Elvis song nevermore to be reproduced; in his dizzying collisions of familiar songs, even Mingering Mike might hear his own voice rumbling deep in the mix.

1) Robin Pogrebin, "All Shook Up Over Cutting and Selling of Elvis Tape," *The New York Times,* January 28, 2004.
2) Neil Strauss, "A Well-Imagined Star," *The New York Times,* February 2, 2004.
3) Conversation with the author, November 5, 2003.

CHRISTIAN MARCLAYS

PHILIP SHERBURNE

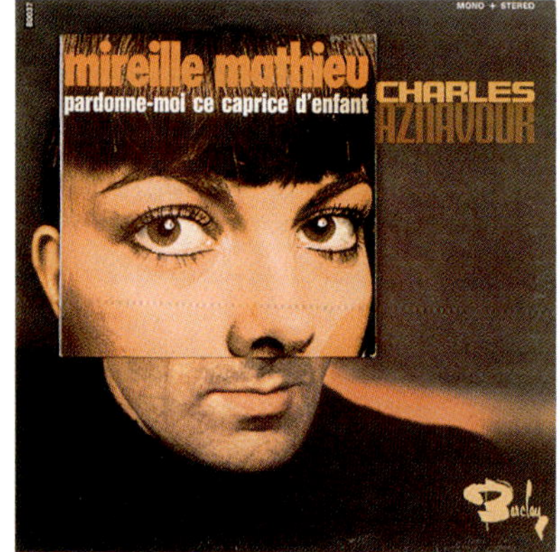

Christian Marclay, dessen grundlegendes Arbeitsmaterial aus der Welt der Musik stammt, verbindet das Dokumentarische mit dem Fiktiven und verschmilzt die öffentliche mit der privaten Welt des Hörens. Zahlreiche Klangkünstler haben die Grenzen der Stille überschritten – John Cage natürlich, aber auch Leute wie Francisco López, die argentinische Band Reynols oder Richard Chartier –, Marclays Werk aber ist anders. Es kann Geräusche aussenden oder auch nicht. Im übertragenen Sinn könnte man sagen, dass seine nicht hörbaren Arbeiten von kulturellen Resonanzen widerklingen, doch ist dies letztlich eben nur eine Metapher. Ein grosser, vielleicht sogar der überwiegende Teil von Marclays Werk ist dem Wesen nach visuell oder plastisch. Dennoch geht es auch in diesen Arbeiten ebenso sehr um Klänge – um das k u l t u r e l l e Universum der Klänge – wie bei jeder Plattenaufnahme, ja vielleicht sogar noch stärker, weil sie die kulturelle Allgegenwart von Klängen ansprechen. Marclays Werk handelt von der gesellschaftlich geprägten «Kehrseite» der Klangwelt – in passender Anspielung auf die Schallplatte könnte man auch sagen: von der «B-Seite».

Bevor wir näher auf Christian Marclay eingehen, sollen uns zwei Begebenheiten aus jüngster Zeit als uns vom Zufall bescherte Einführung in sein Werk dienen. Sie wurden von der nordamerikanischen Presse weitherum zur Kenntnis genommen und kreisen Marclays künstlerische Praxis genauso zielsicher ein, wie die Nadel am Tonarm in konzentrischer Bewegung aufs Zentrum der Scheibe zugleitet.

Vor mehreren Wochen erhielt ich eine E-Mail – eine, in der seltsam passiven Art der Internet-Aktivität x-fach weitergeleitete Nachricht –, die mich darauf aufmerksam machte, dass skrupellose Geschäftsleute einen Akt mutwilliger Zerstörung planten, und um meine Mithilfe bei der Vereitelung dieses Vorhabens bat. Eine Firma namens Master Tape Collection war in den Besitz der Originalstudioaufnahme von Elvis Presleys «That's All Right» gelangt, einer Aufnahme aus der Zeit der Sun Sessions 1954–55, und plante, das Tonband in

---

PHILIP SHERBURNE ist Kritiker, Photograph und DJ und lebt in San Francisco.

INNENOHR-IMPLANTATE

fünf Zentimeter lange Schnipsel zu zerschneiden, diese dann auf Erinnerungsplaketten zu kleben und für 495 Dollar das Stück an Sammler zu verkaufen.

Der Aufschrei der Empörung, über den in der Woche darauf die *New York Times* berichtete, war nicht verwunderlich; der Artikel zitierte sowohl entsetzte Archivare als auch apologetische Vertreter der Firma Master Tape Collection, wobei Letztere behaupteten, das Band sei auf Grund seines schlechten Zustandes ohnehin nicht mehr abspielbar.[1] (Das Argument der Archivare wirkte jedoch stichhaltiger: Auch wenn das Tonband in noch so miserablem Zustand sei, sei dies kein Grund, es zu zerschnippeln und zu verkaufen, denn dies vereitle definitiv jede allenfalls später mögliche Konservierung oder Rekonstruktion.)

Eine knappe Woche später erschien in der *New York Times* ein anderer Artikel, der über eine weitere kuriose Begebenheit in den Annalen der Tonaufzeichnung berichtete, die mit der ersten weiter nichts zu tun hatte. Zwei Plattensammler waren beim Durchstöbern eines Secondhandladens nach alten Funk-LPs mit Sammlerwert auf eine echte Rarität gestossen: eine Reihe handgefertigter Schallplatten mit Aufnahmen eines unbekannten Musikers namens Mingering Mike. Die Plattenhüllen waren minutiös nachgebildet, bis hin zu handgeschriebenen Erläuterungstexten, Rückenbeschriftung, nicht existierenden Katalognummern und in einigen Fällen sogar Plastikfolie und Preisaufklebern. Die Schallplatten selbst waren blosse Pappscheiben mit von Hand aufgemalten Rillen und Labels. Mingering Mike war, wie sich herausstellte, eine real existierende Person, wenn auch nicht der begnadete Musiker, als den seine fiktiven Platten ihn darstellten, sondern ein Phantast, der vom Ruhm träumte und seine eigene Plattenserie geschaffen hatte, um, wie er sagte, «bereit zu sein für den Fall, dass eines Tages alles zusammenpasst».[2]

Wer Marclays Werk kennt, wird sich sogleich an bestimmte Beispiele aus der Serie *Imaginary Records* (Fiktive Schallplatten) sowie an sein Plakatprojekt FALSE ADVERTISING (Falsche Werbung, 1994) erinnert fühlen. Bei den *Imaginary Records,* etwa CHRISTIAN MARCLAY AT THE ST. REGIS (1981), verfremdete er kommerziell hergestellte Plattenhüllen, indem er die Namen der Musiker durch seinen eigenen Namen ersetzte. Für FALSE ADVERTISING entwarf er fiktive Konzertplakate, auf denen er seinen eigenen Auftritt in völlig verschiedenen

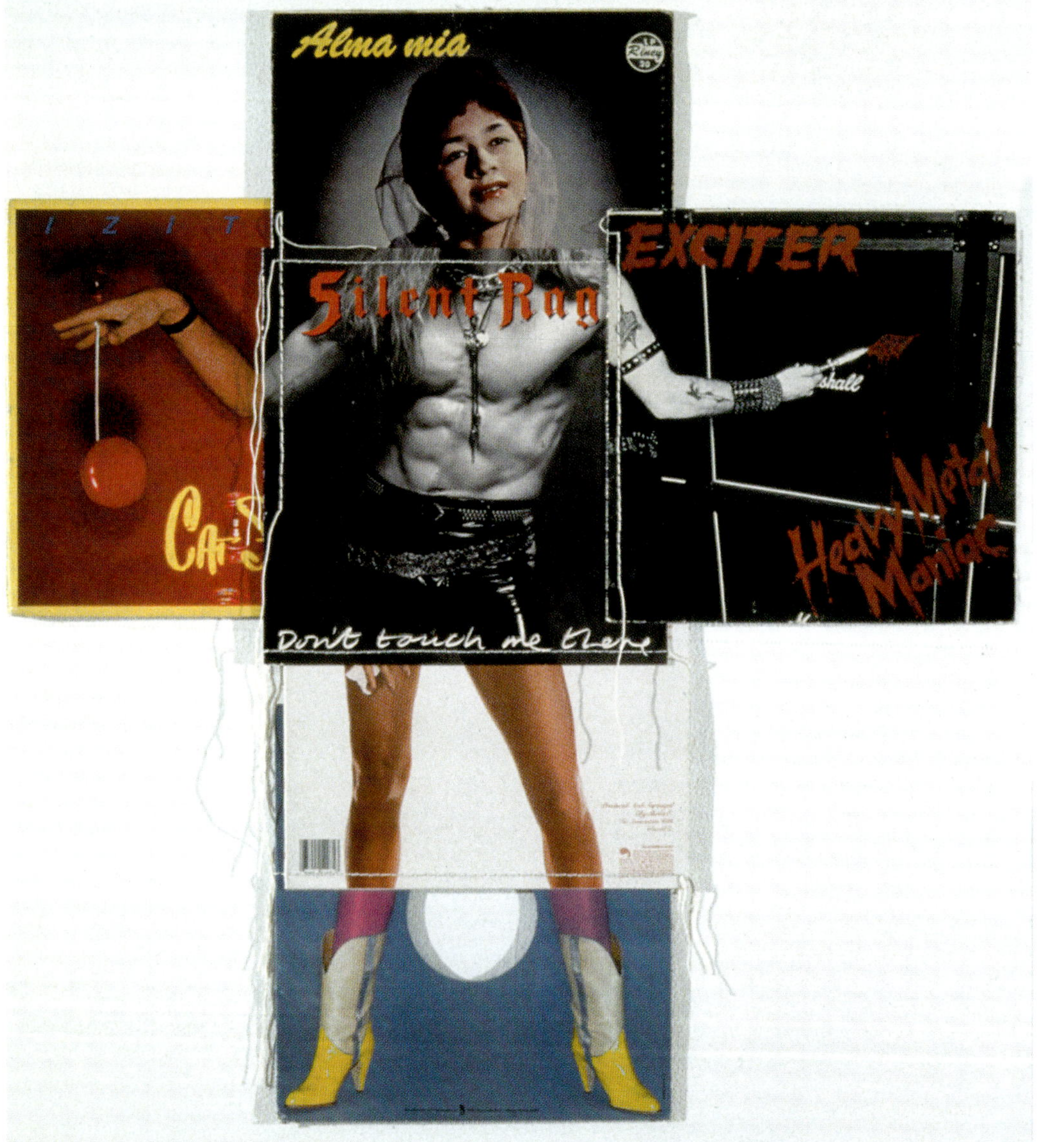

CHRISTIAN MARCLAY, ALMA MIA, 1991, record covers and thread, 33 x 31" / Plattenhüllen und Bindfaden, 83,8 x 78,8 cm.

Kontexten ankündigte – als Jazzsaxophonist ebenso wie als Heavymetal-Gitarrist –, und verteilte diese in der ganzen Stadt. Beide Projekte imitierten die graphischen Gestaltungsstile, die man mit den verschiedenen Musikrichtungen in Verbindung bringt, und spielten vielleicht auch mit den üblichen Starphantasien von Teenagern. (Als Heranwachsender entwarf ich aufwendige Logos für manch eine fiktive Band, die mich eines Tages, da war ich mir sicher, ins Scheinwerferlicht des Ruhms katapultieren würde.) Mingering Mike hatte mit den Mitteln der Art Brut dieselbe Idee verfolgt und sich mit Hilfe seiner Kreationen unter die Popstars eingereiht, auch wenn sein Publikum lediglich in seiner eigenen Phantasie existierte, zumindest bevor die beiden Spürnasen auf den Plan traten.

Die etwas weniger heitere Geschichte mit den Elvis-Bändern erinnert nicht minder unverkennbar an Marclays Umgang mit Tonaufzeichnungen. Was mich an dieser Geschichte

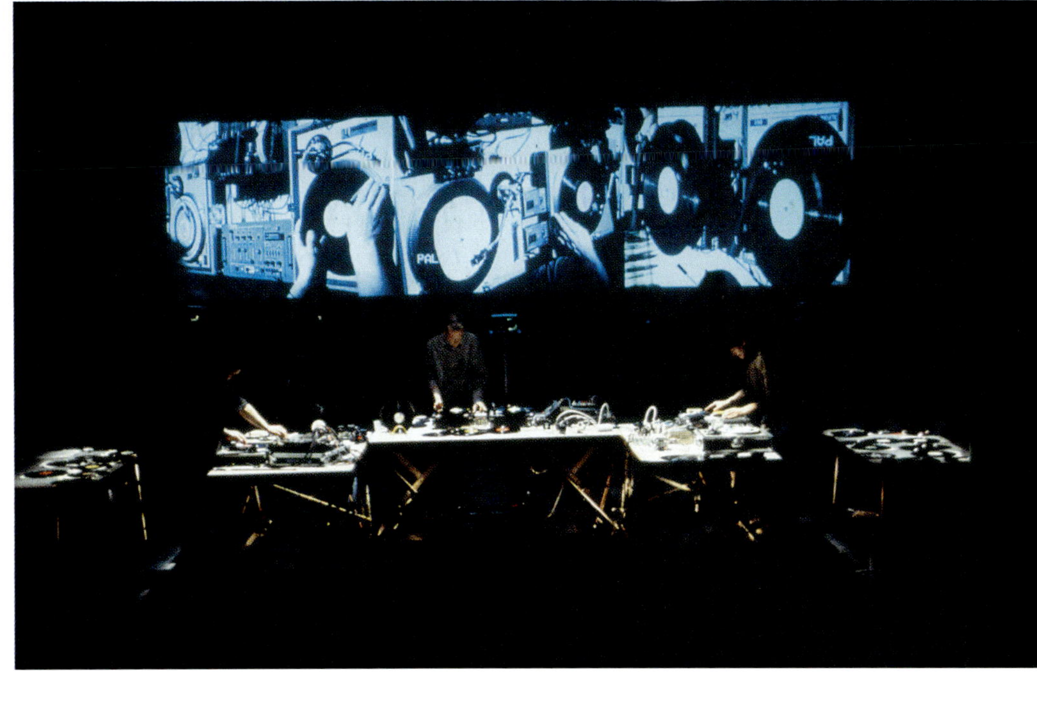

djTRIO, Christian Marclay, DJ Olive, Erik M., February 2000, Centre Georges Pompidou, Paris.
(PHOTO: B. PREVOST)

beeindruckte, war, dass sie eine Reihe von Problemen ins Blickfeld rückte – die Zerbrechlichkeit des Aufgezeichneten; den Stellenwert des Originals innerhalb eines Systems mechanischer Reproduktion; das Bedürfnis, über ein Relikt (eine Reliquie) in den Besitz der damit verbundenen Aura zu gelangen –, welche, seit Walter Benjamin sie in seinem Essay *Das Kunstwerk im Zeitalter seiner technischen Reproduzierbarkeit* erstmals auf den Punkt brachte, ungelöst geblieben sind. Marclay hat sich im Lauf seiner künstlerischen Laufbahn eingehend mit diesem Themenkomplex auseinander gesetzt und den Bereich untersucht, wo Musik, mechanische Reproduktion, Massenkultur, verdinglichtes Begehren und das Imaginäre aufeinander prallen.

Marclays Projekte mögen nie so viel Aufregung ausgelöst haben wie der Vorfall um das Originalband von Elvis – und das spricht wohlgemerkt durchaus für ihn –, er hat in seiner

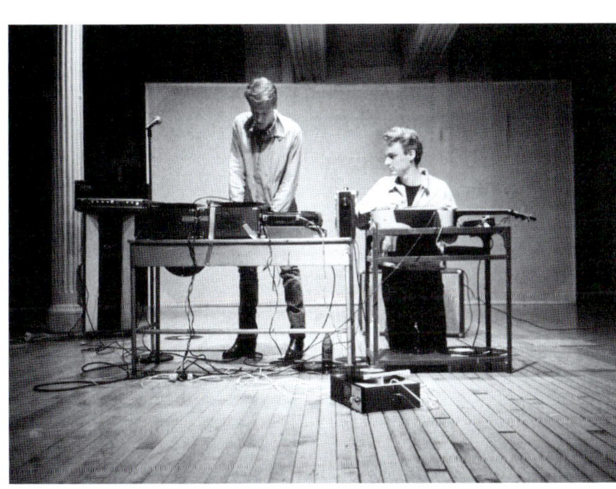

THE BACHELORS, EVEN, performance at / Auftritt im P.S. 122, New York, 1980.
(PHOTO: PAULA COURT)

Arbeit jedoch oft auf solche objektbezogenen Ängste Bezug genommen. So bedeckte er etwa für die Arbeit FOOTSTEPS (Fussstapfen, 1989) den Fussboden eines Ausstellungsraums mit 3500 Schallplatten, so dass die Museumsbesucher auf die Platten treten m u s s t e n. Jedem, der in vordigitaler Zeit aufgewachsen ist, muss solch ein Akt genauso ungeheuerlich erscheinen wie einem Patrioten die Aufforderung, die Nationalfahne mit Fussen zu treten. RECORD WITHOUT A COVER (1985) war einfach eine Vinylplatte mit einer Aufnahme von Marclay, die wie der Titel sagt, ohne Hülle vertrieben und verkauft wurde. Die Platte, deren Beschädigung auf dem Handelsweg von der Plattenpresse zum Plattenspieler des Konsumenten vorprogrammiert war, mokierte sich über die Fetischisierung des Vinylobjektes, obwohl sie gleichzeitig ihre eigene Materialität zelebrierte, indem sie die Spuren dessen, was ihr im Handel widerfuhr, in Form von Kratzern und Klickgeräuschen in sich aufnahm und so vielleicht zum besten Beispiel von «Popmusik» im wahrsten Sinn des Wortes wurde. Eine Arbeit, die einen vielleicht noch deutlicheren Bezug zur Affäre um das Elvis-Tape aufweist, ist SECRET (Geheimnis, 1988) – Marclay nahm damit Duchamps A BRUIT SECRET (Mit verborgenem Geräusch) aus dem Jahr 1916 auf und übertrug es in seine zeitgemässe Form: die metallene Originalpressung einer Singleplatte, an der ein Vorhängeschloss angebracht war, so dass das System der mechanischen Reproduktion kurzgeschlossen wurde und die Klänge, die als Plattenrillen nach wie vor sichtbar lockten, für alle Zeiten unerreichbar eingeschlossen waren.

Die Analogie dieser beiden «wahren» Geschichten zu einzelnen Arbeiten Marclays mag zufällig sein, aber dass sie so gut zu seiner künstlerischen Praxis passen, macht etwas Wichtiges deutlich. Marclay, der oft Duchamp zitiert, ist bekannt für seine Skulpturen aus Readymade-Objekten, von seinen Collagen aus Plattenhüllen oder zerschnittenen und zusammengeleimten Vinylplatten, bis hin zu eigentlichen Musikinstrumenten wie in LIP LOCK (2000), einer mit einer Taschentrompete verschweissten Tuba. Wenn wir aber von Marclays Werk ausgehend auf Mingering Mike und die Master Tape Collection schauen – oder vielleicht treffender ausgedrückt: alle drei miteinander kurzschliessen –, so wird klar, dass Marclays gesamte Künstlerlaufbahn aus solchen Readymade-Interventionen besteht, die alltägliche Aktivitäten mit einem subtilen Dreh «verfremden». Indem er ihnen einen neuen Rahmen gibt, sie gleichsam auf einen Sockel hebt, rückt Marclay unsere eigene Beteiligung am unendlichen System des kulturellen Kreislaufs ins Blickfeld. Das passt natürlich ausgezeichnet zu einem Künstler, der seine Sporen auf dem *Do-it-yourself*-Schlachtfeld des Punkrock der 70er Jahre abverdient hat, aber auch mit Duchamp und Fluxus grossgeworden ist. Und obwohl theoretische Komplexität und kunsthistorische Anspielungen für weite Teile von Marclays Werk kennzeichnend sind – selbst seine erste Band (*The Bachelors, even*) ist nach einer Skulptur Duchamps benannt –, verdankt es seine starke Ausstrahlung der Tatsache, dass es den ästhetischen Vorlieben und dem emotionalen Engagement seines Publikums nachspürt.

Marclay wird gewöhnlich als «Klangkünstler» bezeichnet. Das ist zum Teil darauf zurückzuführen, dass das zentrale Thema seines Werkes, welches plastische Arbeiten, DJ-Auftritte, Performance, Malerei, Installationen und Video umfasst, die Welt der aufgezeichneten Musik und der damit verbundenen Bildsprache ist – auch wenn er oft ganz auf den Ton verzichtet und nur mit Hilfe von Anspielungen arbeitet. Sein Ruf als Klangkünstler ist zweifellos auch darauf zurückzuführen, dass diese Sparte sich gegenwärtig einer nie dagewesenen institutionellen Anerkennung erfreut. Marclay ist jedoch kein Klangkünstler im herkömmlichen Sinn. Statt Klanginstallationen aufzubauen oder abstrakte Klangexperimente auf CD aufzunehmen, wechselt er in seiner Arbeit hin und her zwischen Liveauftritten als DJ und Bildern oder plastischen Arbeiten, welche keine hörbaren

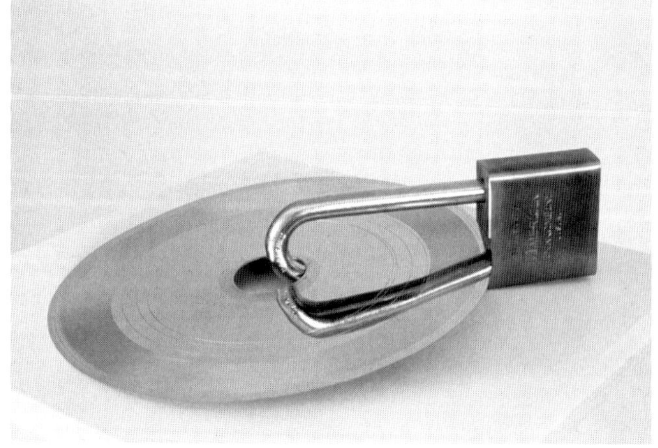

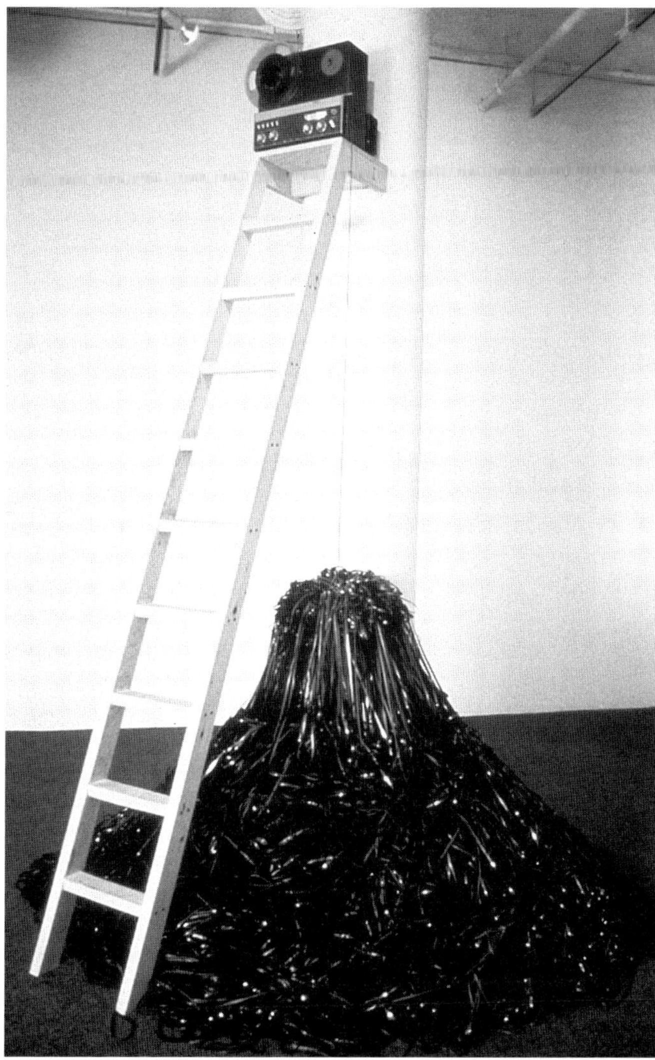

CHRISTIAN MARCLAY, TAPE FALL, 1989,
Revox player, audio tape, ladder / TONBANDFALL,
Revox-Tonbandgerät, Tonband, Leiter.

Elemente enthalten. Es gibt Ausnahmen: Videoarbeiten und Installationen wie VIDEO QUARTET (Videoquartett, 2002), UP AND OUT (Auf und aus, 1998), TAPE FALL (Tonbandfall, 1989) und GUITAR DRAG (Gitarrentravestie, 2002) weisen alle Audioelemente auf. Entscheidend ist aber, dass es selbst bei den Arbeiten mit Ton nicht unbedingt um den Ton als solchen geht. Während «Klangkunst» meist das Verhältnis von Klang und Raum thematisiert, dreht sich Marclays Werk immer um die Musik als Ort der vermittelten Information, des kulturellen Kapitals und der überdeterminierten Zeichen.

Marclay arbeitet selten oder nie mit Klängen aus dem nicht-musikalischen Bereich. Die einzige Arbeit, die mir dazu einfällt, ist TAPE FALL, bei der ein Tonbandgerät mit Ab- aber ohne Aufwickelspule am oberen Ende einer Leiter angebracht ist. Das Tonband läuft, gleitet zu Boden und türmt sich allmählich zu einem Haufen. Dabei gibt es das Geräusch fliessenden Wassers wieder, ein für Marclays Werk ungewöhnliches, mimetisches Geräusch. Doch selbst hier ist die naive Tonaufzeichnung überdeterminiert, und was fliesst, ist hier – Gertrude Stein zum Trotz – kein Fluss, sondern vielmehr ein Wust von Zitaten und Anspielungen auf die Wassermusik von Cage, Satie, Takemitsu and anderen.

Es gibt eine Seitenlinie in Marclays Werk, die sich mit dem Telefon befasst, sei es in skulpturalen Arrangements wie BONEYARD (Friedhof, 1990) oder einer Videoarbeit wie TELEPHONES (1995), in welcher der Künstler Szenen aus bekannten Filmen zusammenmontiert hat, die klingelnde Telefonapparate und Menschen beim Telefonieren zeigen. Doch selbst da spielt der Ton vor allem eine kommunikative (oder die Kommunikation störende) Rolle. Und auch die Arbeit UP AND OUT, die den Soundtrack von Brian De Palmas *Blow Out* (1981) mit den Bildern aus Michelangelo Antonionis *Blow-Up* (1966) verknüpft, funktioniert wie ein Krimi mit drei Ebenen, wobei das Publikum aufgefordert ist, die Kluft zwischen Ton und Bild zu schliessen.

Selbst unter den Kritikern, die sich mit Marclay als DJ befassen – und Marclay ist dank seinen beeindruckenden Auftritten der geistige Vater einer ganzen Bewegung heute aktiver experimenteller DJ-Virtuosen –, gehen nur wenige wirklich auf die Klangkomponente seines Werks ein, meist steht stattdessen sein technisches Vorgehen (mehrere Plattenspieler und jähe *jump-cuts*) im Mittelpunkt, oder aber sein Material (etwa die Tausenden von Weihnachtsplatten, die seit 1999 in seinem laufenden Performanceprojekt THE SOUNDS OF CHRISTMAS Verwendung fanden). Das hängt auch damit zusammen, dass Marclays Tonaufnahmen be-

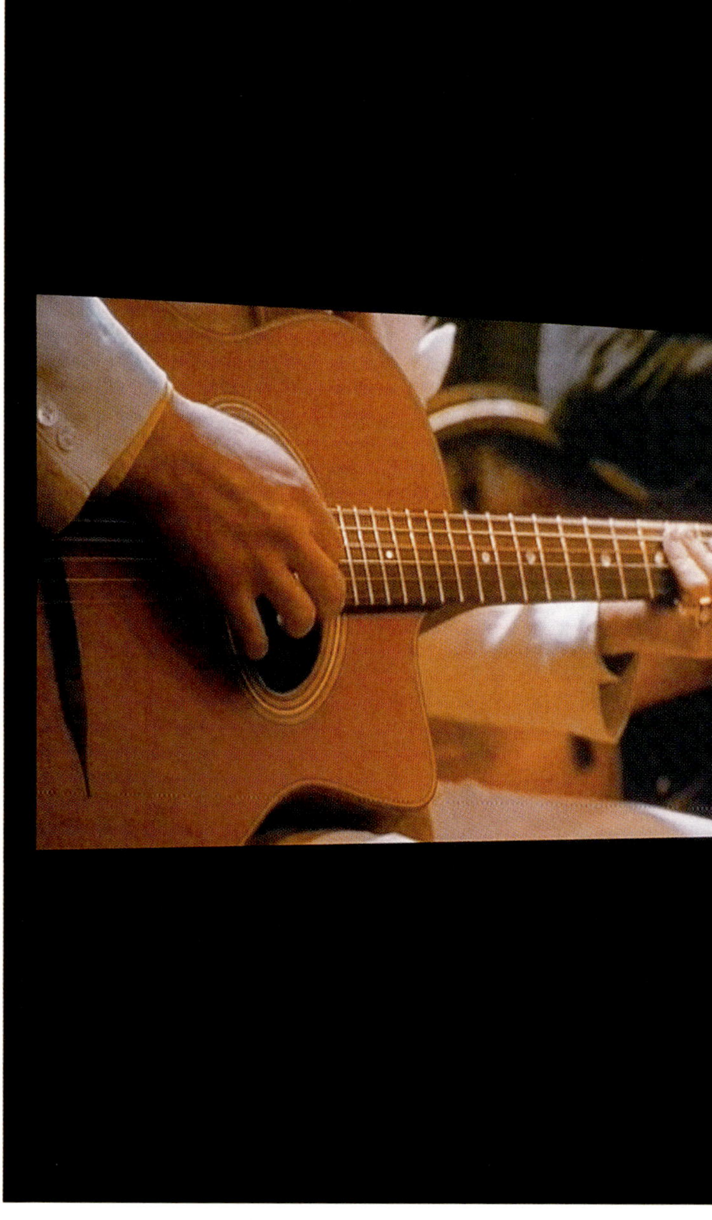

CHRISTIAN MARCLAY, VIDEO QUARTET, 2002,
4-channel DVD projection with sound, 96 x 480" /
VIDEOQUARTETT, 4-Kanal-DVD-Projektion mit Ton,
243,8 x 1219,2 cm. (PHOTO: STEPHEN WHITE)

wusst unvollständig sind: Erst im Kontext des Live-Auftritts gelangen sie zur vollen Realisation. Marclay probt zwar bestimmte Übergänge und bereitet seine Platten vor, indem er sie mit Klebstreifen und Auf-klebern versieht, um bestimmte Loops herbeizuführen, der grösste Teil seiner Darbietung ist jedoch nicht geplant. In seiner Diskographie finden sich denn auch nur wenige Studioaufzeichnungen; die meisten seiner Aufnahmen, sind gemeinsame Improvisationen mit anderen Instrumentalisten.

Während Klangkünstler wie Stephen Vitiello, Richard Chartier oder Francisco López sich auf die räumlichen Eigenschaften, die Strukturen und die Tiefendimension von Klängen konzentrieren, arbeitet Marclay als DJ vor allem mit Zitaten, etwa beim Remix verschiedener Musiker von Jimi Hendrix bis Louis Armstrong auf seiner Platte *More Encores* (1988) oder beim Wechsel zwischen den Musikrichtungen mit Ensembles wie dem von John Zorn. Dabei entstehen zum Teil unwillkürliche Bezüge, die so gar nicht beabsichtigt waren. «Die Leute erkennen Sachen wieder, die ich nie gespielt habe», erklärte er mir gegenüber einmal, als wir über seine Auftritte sprachen. «Weil sie damit rechneten, etwas wiederzu-

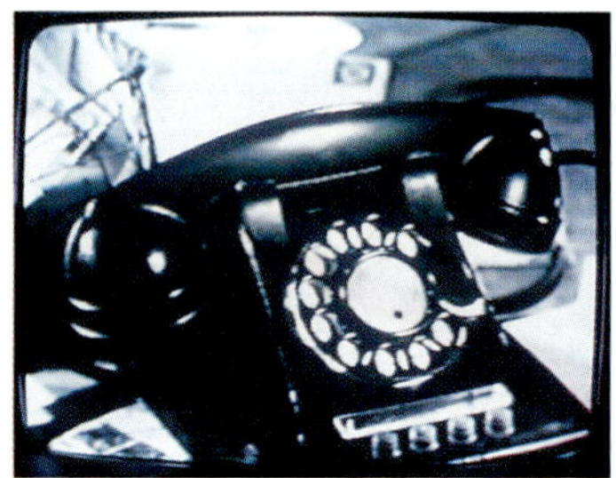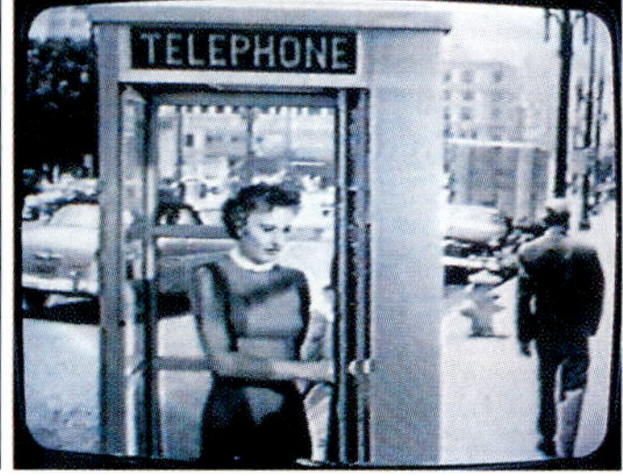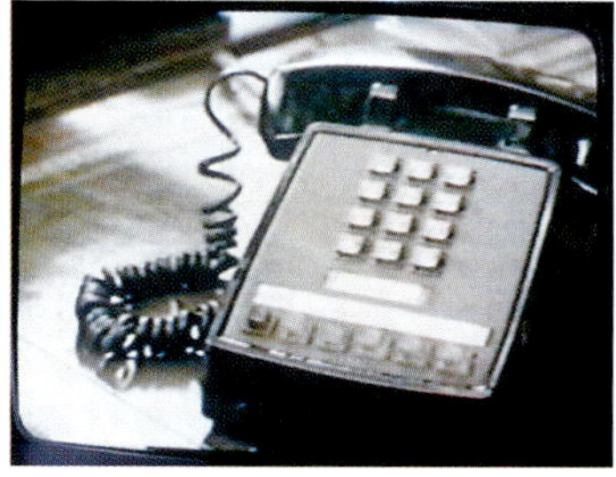

CHRISTIAN MARCLAY, TELEPHONES,
1995, stills from the 7 1/2-min. video /
Bilder aus dem 7 1/2-minütigen Video.

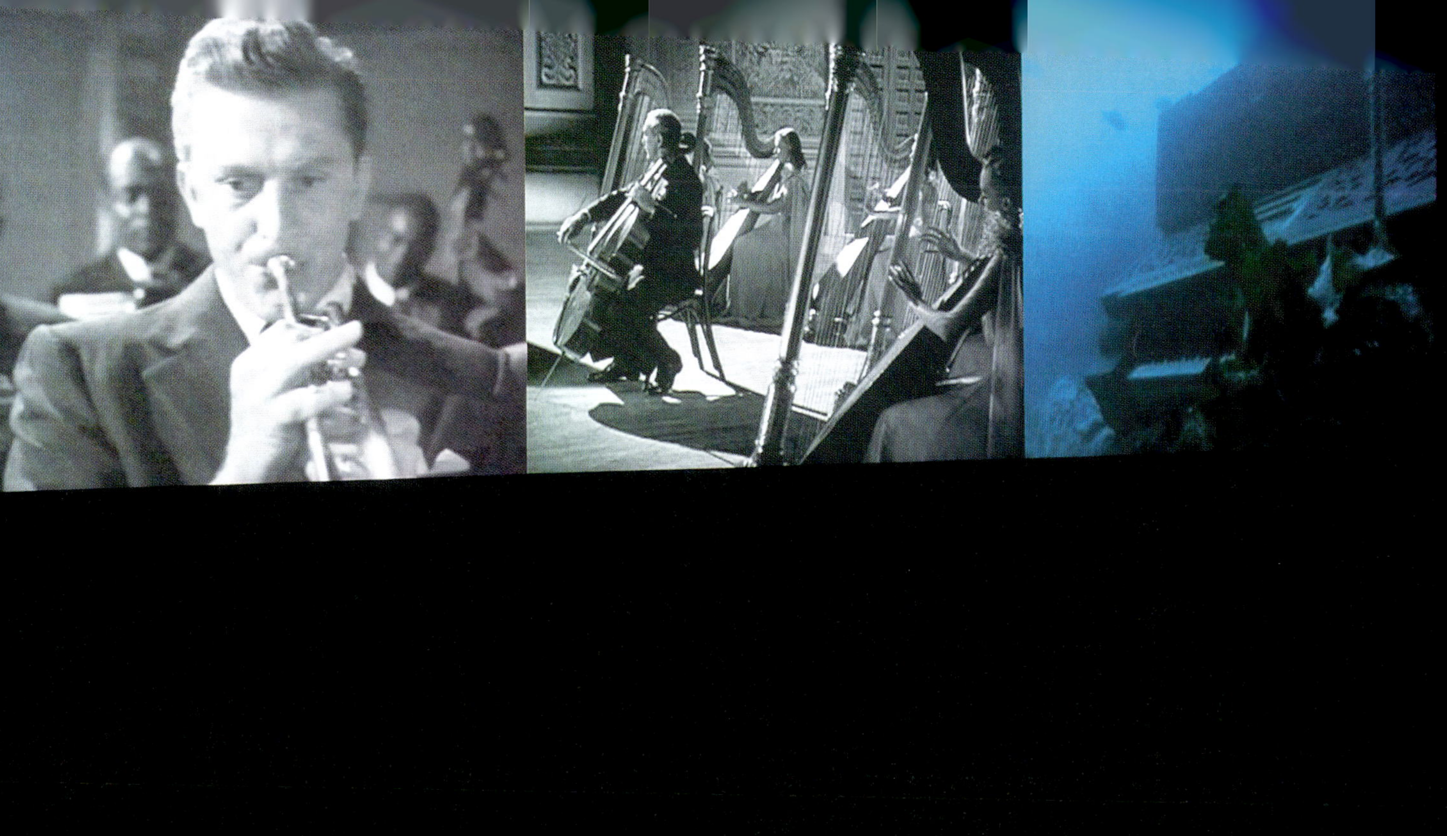

erkennen, machte ich einen besonders komplexen Mix, und sie glaubten prompt, eine bestimmte Aufnahme wiederzuerkennen, kamen nach dem Gig zu mir und sagten: ‹Ah, du hast das und das gespielt.› – Tut mir Leid, nein.»[3] Selbst die Geister in Marclays Musik singen von der Welt, wie wir sie kennen. In seinen stillen Momenten hallen die Klänge eines Elvis-Songs nach, der sich nie mehr reproduzieren lässt, und im Schwindel erregenden Aufeinanderprallen vertrauter Songs hört vielleicht sogar Mingering Mike seine eigene Stimme im Dickicht des Mixes rauschen.

(Übersetzung: Bram Opstelten)

1) Robin Pogrebin, «All Shook Up Over Cutting and Selling of Elvis Tape», *The New York Times,* 28. Januar 2004.
2) Neil Strauss, «A Well-Imagined Star», *The New York Times*, 2. Februar 2004.
3) Christian Marclay im Gespräch mit dem Autor, 5. November 2003.

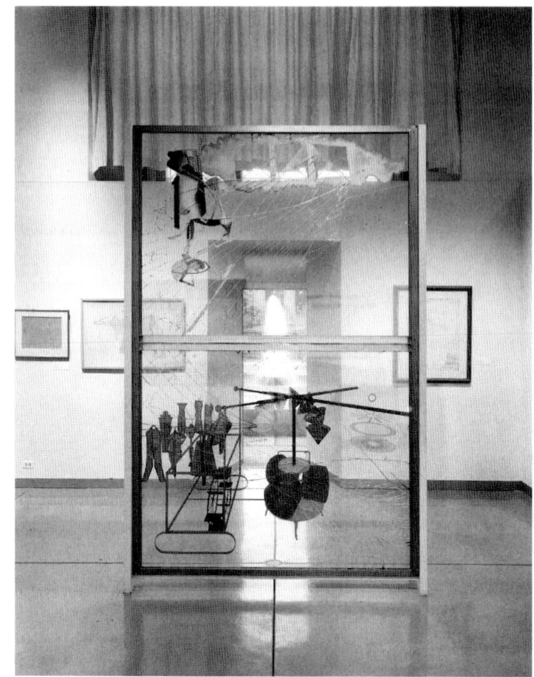

INGRID SCHAFFNER

Wise Cracks

Christian Marclay's project THE BELL AND THE GLASS (2003) is composed of coincidences and correspondences that build to an exquisite state of tension between two Philadelphia monuments, both cracked. At one point in the installation's two-screen video projection, we watch Marcel Duchamp tell an interviewer how THE LARGE GLASS (1915–23) came to be shattered—"do you remember how it happened in 1926?"—juxtaposed with an image of light streaming through the magnificent fissure in the Liberty Bell. The relationship quickly gets erotic. The silhouette of the bell appears as a pendulous pair of buttocks, or a vagina—complete with clitoris, given the little round plug in the crack near the lip. The two projections are stacked vertically on top of one another, like the panes of Duchamp's famous work, the full title of which is THE BRIDE STRIPPED BARE BY HER BACHELORS, EVEN (THE LARGE GLASS). The curvaceous bell (or *belle*) appears on the top screen, which corresponds to "The Bride's Domain," according to the work's complex iconography. On the bottom screen, in the lower portion relegated to those pathetic little gizmos, "The Bachelor Apparatus," is Duchamp. Looking admiringly up at his work, he muses, "The more I look at it, the more I like it. I like the breaks the way they come, the cracks."

INGRID SCHAFFNER is Senior Curator at the Institute of Contemporary Art, University of Pennsylvania, Philadelphia, where she is currently working on an exhibition about "nothing."

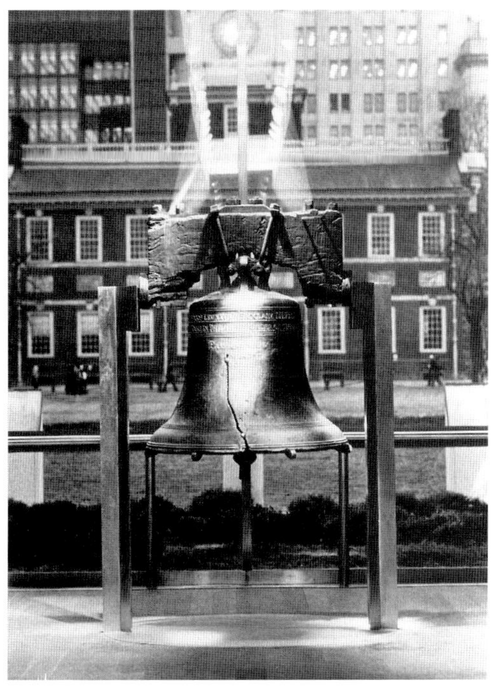

Liberty Bell in Liberty Bell Pavilion in front
of Independence Hall, Philadelphia, 1976 /
Die amerikanische Freiheitsglocke in ihrem Pavillon
vor der Independence Hall.
(PHOTO: INDEPENDENCE HALL, PHILADELPHIA)

The bell cracked shortly after it arrived in Philadelphia from England, but was recast in 1753. Never a pretty-sounding thing, it tolled frequently to summon colonists, who were complaining about the awful noise as early as 1772. On July 8, 1776, the bell rang to summon citizens to the first public reading of the Declaration of Independence. Only then did the common bell begin its apotheosis into a national symbol—though not exclusively of liberty. (The abolitionist, women's suffrage, and civil rights movements all adopted the bell as a sign of equality denied.) By 1835, it was considered too fragile to strike regularly, though the exact circumstances of the bell's second cracking are not precisely known. Until 2001, when someone struck it with a sledgehammer,

the bell could be touched, or even kissed—something which its skirt shape and democratic meaning seemed to call out for visitors to do. Today it stands out of reach, mute, and on display at the Liberty Bell Center (since 1976) like an object in a museum.

By the time Marcel Duchamp's LARGE GLASS arrived at the Philadelphia Museum of Art (PMA) in 1954, its cracks were legend. The damage was discovered in 1931, five years after the work was returned from an exhibition. The collector Katherine Dreier was devastated: this was Duchamp's masterpiece, an exquisite and coarse summation of the erotics, strategies, mechanics, and play of the creative act, which had taken him six years to make. The artist accepted the event with alacrity. After all, he had declared the piece had reached a "definitive stage of incompletion" in 1921, but not that it was done. He was thus at liberty to continue a process that could now incorporate the work's destruction into its formal and conceptual context. In 1936 he spent three months tenderly ministering to the fractured work of art, sandwiching it between two sheets of heavy glass. Since the two panes of glass had been traveling and bouncing on top of one another, the cracks mirrored each other in such a way that Duchamp observed a "curious intention that I'm not responsible for, readymade intention, in other words, that I respect and love." Today THE LARGE GLASS stands in front of a window, as part of a permanent installation of works by Duchamp that constitutes one of Modernism's pilgrimage destinations.

Christian Marclay had made the reverential journey from New York many times, prior to a coincidental pair of invitations. The first came in 2001 from Relâche, Philadelphia's new music ensemble under the artistic direction of Thaddeus A. Squire, who approached Marclay about their "Future Sounds" series of new work. A conceptual artist with a Duchampian turn of mind, Marclay has always been as involved with making sounds as objects. When he came to New York in 1977 to study art, he hooked into the punk and downtown club scene. (During the eighties he even played in a band called The Bachelors, even.) The second came from the PMA, where curator Ann Temkin asked him to participate in their Museum Studies series of artist's projects based on the

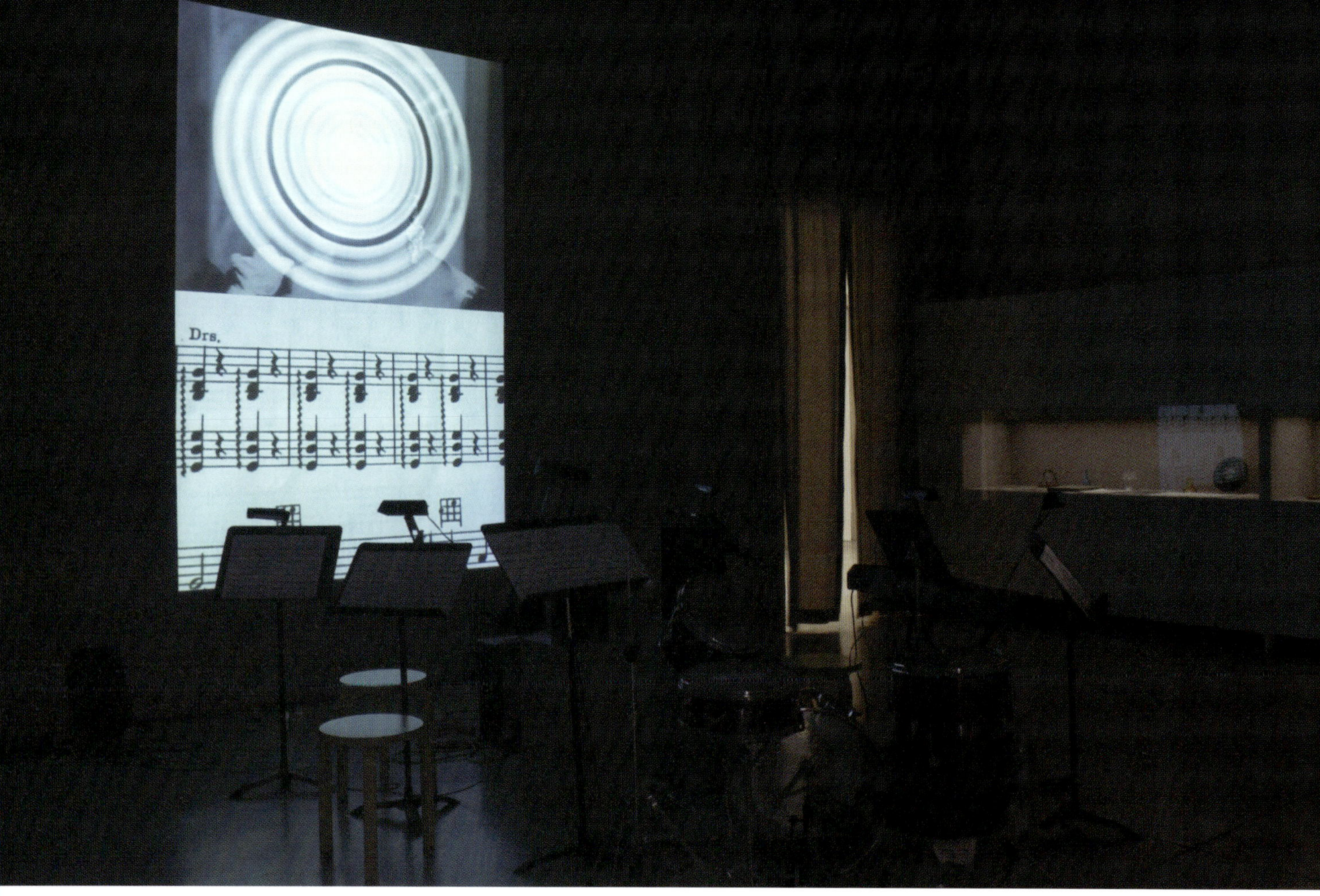

CHRISTIAN MARCLAY, THE BELL AND THE GLASS, 2003, video score installation / DIE GLOCKE UND DAS GLAS, Videoinstallation.
(PHOTO: PHILADELPHIA MUSEUM OF ART)

permanent collection. As synthesized by Marclay into one project, THE BELL AND THE GLASS has four constituent parts. Besides the video projections, there are display cases filled with objects compiled by the artist of Duchamp material (from the museum) and souvenir glass Liberty Bells (from historic collections and e-bay), and an artist book (edited by PMA curator Susan Rosenberg). This book and the video became a musical score based on the pitch of Duchamp's voice transcribed into musical notes and played by members of Relâche, who also improvised by taking cues from the video. Altogether, these parts produced a constellation of collaborations and associations—visual and acoustic, silly and profound, found and forged—too dynamic to be contained by any single form or, for that matter, description.

Take just a quick flip through the artist book. In Marclay's picture essay, you'll find scores for old time ditties, like "You're A Grand Old Bell," and musical compositions by Marclay based on Duchamp's statements about the GLASS. A 1969 press photo of two lovely patriots ceremoniously cleaning the bell after it served as the backdrop for an anti-Vietnam War protest appears next to Man Ray's 1920 photograph of THE LARGE GLASS, titled DUST BREEDING. The photograph was taken of the surface of the glass after it sat around in Duchamp's studio for five years. A shower-curtain version of THE LARGE GLASS (by artists Victor Bouillon and Susan Emerling) stands page-to-page with a showerhead in the form of the Liberty Bell (from Ronald Reagan's bathroom). Turn to the essay, a transcription of a conversation between Marclay, Squire, Temkin, and Thomas Y. Levin, a professor of Germanic languages, to overhear an erudite repartee that links the glass to the bell by way of the toilet that Duchamp, who considered plumbing and bridges America's great contribution to culture, dubbed a FOUNTAIN (1917). They touch on war (bells and cannons were manufactured by the same foundries), religion (cracks are like wounds, to be revered), and individual freedom (Duchamp and the bell both speak of it). Meanwhile, the entire transcript is peppered with many annotations, a textual trellis of side-notes and subsequent footnotes by the participants that adds further twists (the theorist Paul Virilio, who observed that every technology contains its own accident, originally trained as a stained-glass artist).

Packed with information, apropos and elliptical, the book is to THE BELL AND THE GLASS as THE GREEN BOX (1934) is to THE LARGE GLASS. Duchamp intended his box of facsimile notes to function as a guide, sparking the conceptual links which he considered the essential experience of the work, and distracting the viewer from the painting's "retinal aspect that I don't like." THE GREEN BOX is the better known of two companion pieces, the second being IN THE INFINITIVE (THE WHITE BOX). Issued as an edition in 1967, it's no coincidence that THE WHITE BOX came out two years before The Beatles' *White Album.* The album's famously monochrome cover was actually a conceptual work of art by Richard Hamilton, the translator of Duchamp's 1934 box of notes into English. Nor is it by chance that Marclay, who once crocheted and stuffed a pillow with The Beatles' complete taped works, made his own "White Album." In 1990, he had time-battered Hamilton jackets blind embossed with lyrics to create his *White Album* series. But now we're drifting… always a hazard when one starts following the riffs in Marclay's art.

To return to THE BELL AND THE GLASS, the printed patter of the catalogue is nothing compared to the video, which spins at a light pace over the two screens that merge and separate into a seamless, looping whole. There are clips from all kinds of films: silent (a lady robot, a mechanical bride, from *Metropolis*), Hollywood (Tarzan dropping from a vine, which of course reads in this context like a crack). There is documentary footage of Duchamp ("I didn't care," he twinkles) as well as Marclay's own tape (hands piecing together Liberty Bell and LARGE GLASS jigsaw puzzles—the latter Marclay had to make for the purpose). There is an overall pulse (the throb of a Rotorelief, the spin of a roulette wheel), orchestrated to a spare symphony of sounds (a pneumatic hiss, the scratch of a glazier's wheel) with a leitmotif of water (as transparent as glass). There is a sexual narrative (imperious "brides" teasing pathetic "bachelors") that escalates (lots of running up and down staircases—though not by any nudes), churns (Duchamp's CHOCOLATE GRINDER, 1914), climaxes (real chocolate squirting into vibrating Liberty Bell molds), then concludes in scenes of kissing couples collapsing into union. You can almost hear the bells peal. That is, if your head hasn't exploded.

With every element of THE BELL AND THE GLASS, Marclay creates so much syntactical energy, it's almost a relief to turn away. I knew it was time to switch off the flywheel when I found myself trying to make something more of the coincidence that just moments before encountering it in Marclay's work, I had just been listening to a recording of Marcel Duchamp's music, which I discovered at the bottom of a box of forgotten CDs. Yet again, this is the work's great success. The pressure Marclay produces by connecting two things that ultimately have nothing to do with one another, is enough to create exactly that thing which has been seen to unite them. The more the Liberty Bell and THE LARGE GLASS come together, the closer one's conceptual capacity to keep them either together or apart comes to cracking.

For the collage artist Joseph Cornell, the notion of "correspondences" was the glue that held his art together—even when there was no adhesive involved. His DUCHAMP DOSSIER (1942–53) is a portrait based on many kinds of evocative ephemera—a dry-cleaning tag that Cornell probably snatched out of Duchamp's trash, various images of the Mona Lisa—all held loosely in a battered cardboard box. (In 1999, the DOSSIER was displayed as the centerpiece of a fantastic exhibition held at the PMA that explored an ongoing dialogue between the two artists' work.) It was also part of a unique and small body of work within Cornell's oeuvre, one that posed a question, a question which also comes up with THE BELL AND THE GLASS: how do you not make collage? How do you make art that contains all the vast correspondences one detects and collects from across modern and contemporary culture—like Marclay, Cornell was as avid for book, music, film, popular, entertainment culture of all kinds, as he was for art—without gluing things down? According to the DOSSIER, which has more in common with the art historian Aby Warburg's open-ended picture atlas than with the rest of Cornell's collage, the answer is archiving. Archiving is also the essential impulse behind THE BELL AND THE GLASS. But Marclay's new work takes this approach to making art in the age of mechanical reproduction and pitches it into a digital practice.

As visually complex as it appears, the video component of THE BELL AND THE GLASS was made on a home computer and edited using Final Cut Pro. You might say it was stitched together, thereby calling to mind Marclay's sewn record jackets of the early nineties. These put together the famous (male) faces of music with nameless (female) bodies that sell music, to create a truly exquisite corpus of work. Stitching is also the way to make a sampler, a practical example of needlework that gives a homey, feminine origin for the hip-hop, homeboy technique of mak-

ing music by mixing it, scratching it, off records. And as hip-hop exploded into mainstream culture, so does sampling become the predominant construct of our day. It's part of the syntax of everyday life: scanning, streaming, scrolling. And while collage is an aesthetic of fragments and ruptured meaning, sampling is about the potential for making sense from correspondences, however discordant or coincidental. Performing as a DJ and as a musician who plays turntables, Marclay has been sampling for years: a recorded piece from the eighties, DUST BREEDING (1982), used four turntables to make a sampler-style chamber piece. But this is just a minor note compared to his most recent VIDEO QUARTET (2002) where he has orchestrated both the sounds and the images from hundreds of Hollywood films into a seamless four-screen panoramic projection. At the end of this fourteen-minute epic, people clapped. In its way, THE BELL AND THE GLASS is also a remarkably accessible and entertaining work of art. Sampled off the Liberty Bell and THE LARGE GLASS, it is an extremely site-specific work. It's hard to imagine it being as scintillating an experience viewed outside of Philadelphia, where the presence of the objects themselves is part of the resonance of the piece. And here seems to be an opportunity to applaud the artist, who, in being invited to make a fresh work, created a new monument for a city that loves its breaks.

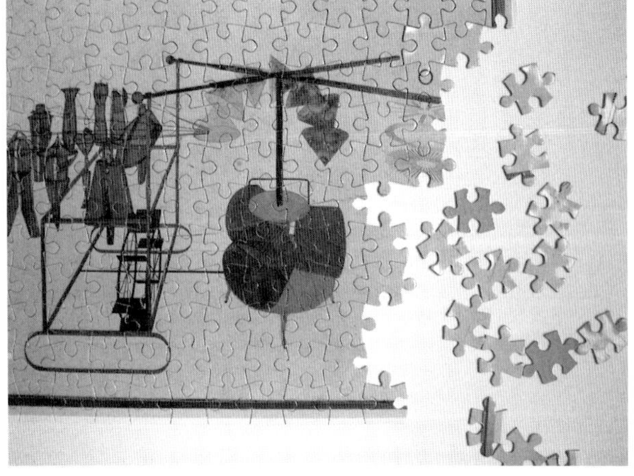

CHRISTIAN MARCLAY, jigsaw puzzle prototype of
THE LARGE GLASS, 2003/ DAS GROSSE GLAS-Puzzle, Prototyp.
(PHOTO: PHILADELPHIA MUSEUM OF ART)

THE SYMMETRY

Marcel Duchamp interviewed by James Johnson Sweeney, Philadelphia, 1955.

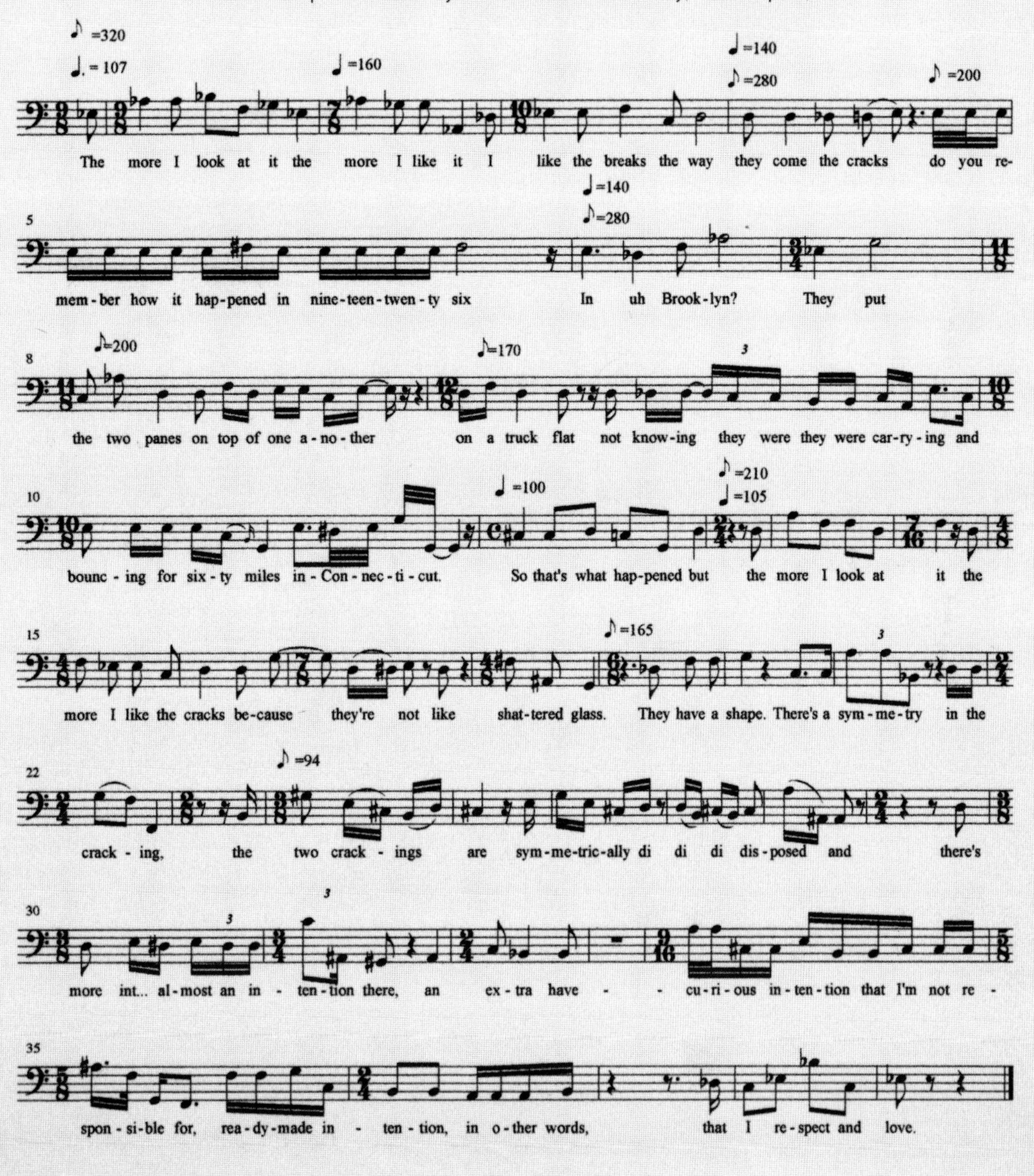

Christian Marclay

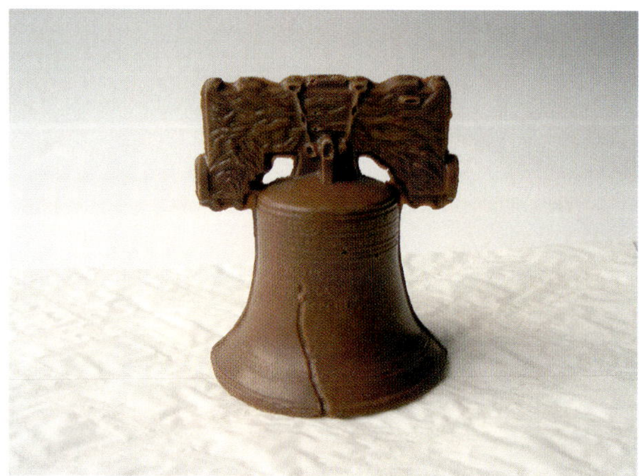

INGRID SCHAFFNER

Bruchstellen und Gedanken- sprünge

Christian Marclays Projekt THE BELL AND THE GLASS (Die Glocke und das Glas, 2003) besteht aus Zufällen und Entsprechungen, welche eine feine Spannung zwischen zwei Kunst-Ikonen Philadelphias erzeugen, die beide geborsten sind beziehungsweise Sprünge aufweisen. In der Videoprojektion auf zwei Leinwänden, die Teil dieser Installation ist, taucht in einer Szene Marcel Duchamp auf und erklärt einem Interviewer, wie LE GRAND VERRE (Das grosse Glas,

1915–23) zu seinen Sprüngen kam: «Erinnern Sie sich noch, wie das 1926 passiert ist?» Gegenüber sieht man ein Bild, auf dem das Licht durch den wunderbaren Sprung in der Freiheitsglocke strömt. Bald entwickelt sich daraus eine erotische Beziehung. Der Umriss der Glocke gleicht einem Paar birnenförmiger Pobacken oder einer Vagina samt Klitoris, denn im Spalt neben der Lippe befindet sich ein kleiner runder Pflock. Wie die Glasplatten in Duchamps berühmtem Werk – mit dem vollständigen Titel LA MARIÉE MISE À NU PAR SES CÉLIBATAIRES, MÊME (LE GRAND VERRE) / Die Neuvermählte, selbst von ihren Junggesellen entkleidet

INGRID SCHAFFNER ist Senior Curator am Institute for Contemporary Art der University of Pennsylvania, wo sie eine Ausstellung über «nichts» vorbereitet.

(Das grosse Glas) – sind auch die projizierten Bilder vertikal aufeinander gestapelt. Die Schöne (Glocke) mit ihren Kurven (vgl. das Wortspiel *bell / belle*) erscheint auf der oberen Leinwand, welche in der komplexen Bildsprache dieser Arbeit der «Domäne der Braut» entspricht. Duchamp ist auf die untere Leinwand verbannt, die den erbärmlichen kleinen Dingern zugeordnet ist, die die «Junggesellenmaschine» ausmachen. Er blickt bewundernd zu seinem Werk hoch und sinniert: «Je länger ich es betrachte, desto besser gefällt es mir. Mir gefällt, wie die Bruchstellen verlaufen, diese Risse.»

Die Glocke war in Philadelphia kurz nach ihrer Ankunft aus England zersprungen, wurde aber 1753 wieder neu gegossen. Sie hatte nie einen schönen Klang, wurde jedoch häufig geläutet, um die Kolonisten zusammenzurufen, die sich bereits 1772 über den schrecklichen Lärm beklagten. Am 8. Juli 1776 rief sie dann die Bürger zur ersten öffentlichen Verlesung der Unabhängigkeitserklärung. Erst zu diesem Zeitpunkt begann der Aufstieg der ganz gewöhnlichen Glocke zum nationalen Symbol – das durchaus nicht nur die Freiheit verkörperte. (Gegner der Sklaverei, Frauenrechtlerinnen und AnhängerInnen der Bürgerrechtsbewegung betrachteten die Glocke eher als Symbol einer vorenthaltenen Gleichheit.) 1835 hielt man es bereits für zu riskant, sie regelmässig zu läuten, aber es ist nicht bekannt, wann und warum die Glocke zum zweiten Mal gesprungen ist. Bevor sie 2001 mit einem Vorschlag-

CHRISTIAN MARCLAY, THE BELL AND THE GLASS, 2003: GLASS OBJECTS, installation view /
GLASOBJEKTE. (PHOTO: PHILADELPHIA MUSEUM OF ART)

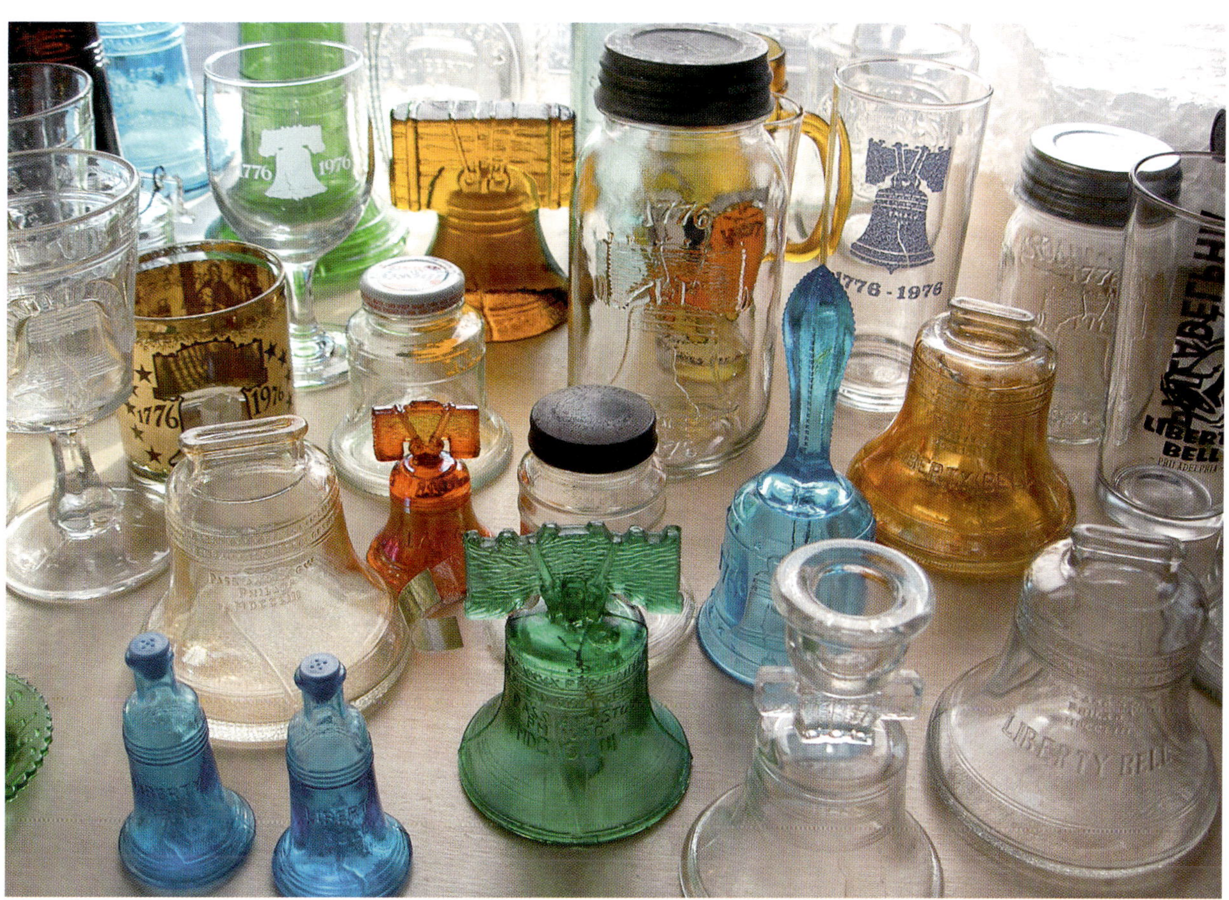

hammer attackiert wurde, durfte man sie auch berühren, ja sogar küssen – wozu ihre Rockform und demokratische Aura ja auch buchstäblich einluden. Seit 1976 steht sie als Museumsstück stumm und unberührbar im Liberty Bell Center in Philadelphia.

Als Duchamps LE GRAND VERRE im Jahr 1954 im Philadelphia Museum of Art (PMA) eintraf, waren seine Risse bereits legendär. Entdeckt hatte man den Schaden 1931, fünf Jahre nachdem die Arbeit von einer Ausstellung zurückgekommen war. Die Sammlerin Katherine Dreier war untröstlich: Schliesslich handelte es sich um Duchamps Hauptwerk, eine einzigartige, krude Summe aller erotischen Momente, Strategien, Mechanismen und Möglichkeiten des kreativen Aktes, an dem er sechs Jahre lang gearbei-

tet hatte. Der Künstler selbst nahm es eher erheitert zur Kenntnis. Schliesslich hatte er 1921 erklärt, die Arbeit habe ein «endgültiges Stadium der Unfertigkeit» erreicht, nicht aber, dass sie vollendet sei. Es stand ihm also frei, einen Prozess fortzusetzen, der die Zerstörung des Werkes in dessen formale und abstrakte Konzeption integrierte. 1936 widmete er sich drei Monate lang liebevoll dem beschädigten Kunstwerk und legte es zwischen zwei schwere Glasscheiben. Da die beiden Glasplatten beim Transport aufeinander gelegen und gegeneinander gestossen waren, standen ihre Bruchstellen in einem spiegelbildlichen Verhältnis zueinander, und Duchamp sah darin eine seltsame Intention, für die er nichts könne, quasi eine Readymade-Intention, die er respek-

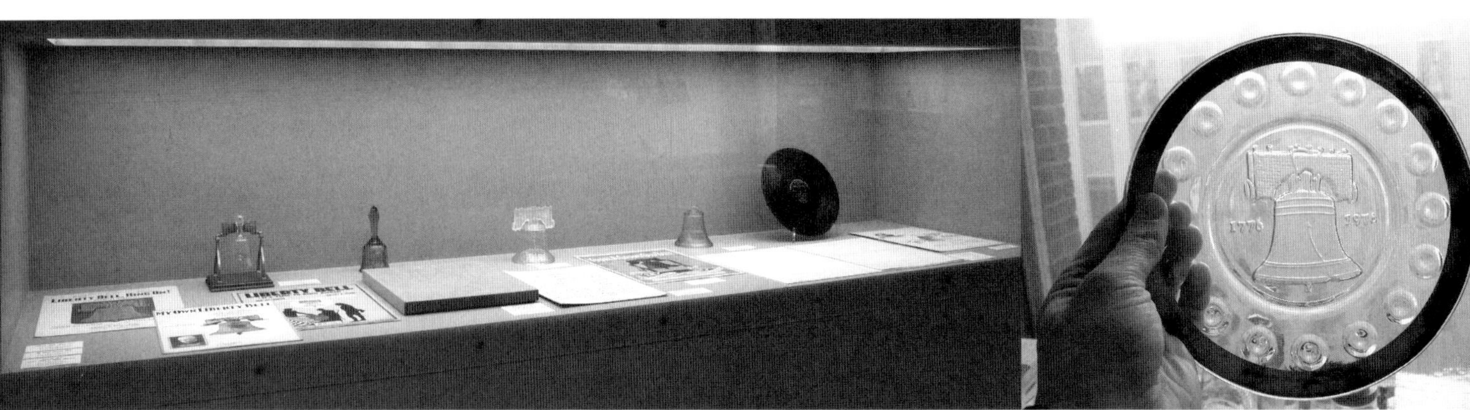

CHRISTIAN MARCLAY, THE BELL AND THE GLASS, 2003, installation view, Philadelphia Museum of Art /
DIE GLOCKE UND DAS GLAS. (PHOTO: PHILADELPHIA MUSEUM OF ART)

tiere und die ihm gefalle. Heute steht LE GRAND VERRE vor einem Fenster des Museums, und zwar im Rahmen einer permanenten Ausstellung der Werke Duchamps, welche mittlerweile zu einer Pilgerstätte der Klassischen Moderne geworden ist.

Auch Christian Marclay war mehrmals dorthin gepilgert, bevor er zufällig gleich zwei Einladungen nach Philadelphia erhielt. Die erste kam 2001 von Relâche, Philadelphias neuem Musikensemble unter der künstlerischen Leitung von Thaddeus A. Squire, der im Zusammenhang mit seiner neuen Reihe *Future Sounds* (Zukunftsklänge) mit Marclay Verbindung aufnehmen wollte. Als Konzeptkünstler im

Sinne Duchamps, hatte Marclay sich schon immer gleichermassen mit Sound und mit Objekten beschäftigt. Als er 1977 zum Kunststudium in New York eintraf, tauchte er tief in die Punk- und Downtown-Club-Szene ein. (In den 80er Jahren spielte er sogar in einer Band namens *The Bachelors, even*.) Die zweite Einladung kam von der Kuratorin des Philadelphia Museum of Art, Ann Temkin: Sie bat ihn, bei einem Museumsstudienprojekt mitzumachen, einer Projektreihe, in deren Rahmen sich Künstler mit der ständigen Sammlung des Museums auseinander setzen. Die aus diesem Anlass von Marclay zu einer einzigen Arbeit kondensierte Installation THE

BELL AND THE GLASS besteht aus vier Grund-elementen. Neben den Videoprojektionen gibt es Vitrinen, die der Künstler mit Duchamp-Material (aus den Beständen des Museums) und gläsernen *Souvenir Liberty Bells* (aus historischen Sammlungen und E-bay-Angeboten) gefüllt hat, sowie ein (von PMA-Kuratorin Susan Rosenberg herausgegebenes) Künstlerbuch. Aus Buch und Video wiederum entstand ein Musikstück, dem die in Notenschrift transkribierte Tonaufnahme von Duchamps Stimme zugrunde liegt; einige Musiker von Relâche spielten das Stück und liessen sich vom Video zu Improvisationen anregen. Insgesamt ergeben diese Elemente (die visuell und akustisch, albern und tiefschürfend, zufällig und manchmal auch an den Haaren herbeigezogen sind) ein komplexes Gebilde von Kollaborationen und Assoziationen, das von einer solchen Dynamik ist, dass es unmöglich in einer einzigen Form (geschweige denn Beschreibung) erfasst werden könnte.

Beim Blick in das Künstlerbuch findet man in Marclays Bildessay Notationen alter Lieder, etwa von «You're A Grand Old Bell», und musikalische Kompositionen des Künstlers, denen Duchamps Äusserungen zu LE GRAND VERRE zugrunde liegen. Neben einem Photo mit dem Titel DUST BREEDING (Staubvermehrung), das Man Ray 1929 von LE GRAND VERRE gemacht hatte, ist ein Pressephoto von 1969 abgebildet, auf dem zwei liebenswerte Patrioten feierlich die Freiheitsglocke reinigen, nachdem sie als Hintergrund für eine Demonstration gegen den Vietnamkrieg hat herhalten müssen. Rays Bild zeigt den Zustand der Glasplatte, nachdem das Werk fünf Jahre in Duchamps Atelier herumgestanden hatte. Eine Duschvorhangversion von LE GRAND VERRE (von Victor Bouillon und Susan Emerling) erscheint Seite an Seite mit einem Duschkopf in Form der Freiheitsglocke (aus Ronald Reagans Badezimmer). Aber wenden wir uns dem Text zu – einer transkribierten Unterhaltung zwischen Marclay, Squire, Temkin und Thomas Y. Levin, einem Germanistikprofessor – um in den Genuss eines intelligenten Schlagabtausches zu kommen, in welchem das Pissbecken (LA FONTAINE, 1917) von Duchamp, für den sanitäre Anlagen und Brücken die grösste zivilisatorische Leistung Amerikas dar-

stellten, als Verbindungselement zwischen Glas und Glocke bezeichnet wird. Der Krieg kommt zur Sprache (Glocken und Kanonen wurden in denselben Giessereien hergestellt), aber auch die Religion (Sprünge sind wie Wundmale mit Ehrfurcht zu behandeln) und die Freiheit des Individuums (sowohl bei Duchamp wie bei der Glocke geht es um diese). Die gesamte Transkription ist mit Anmerkungen übersät, die ein textuelles Gitterwerk aus Randbemerkungen und Fussnoten aller Beteiligten bilden, das wiederum ganz neue Aspekte eröffnet (so war beispielsweise der Philosoph Paul Virilio, der bemerkte, dass jede Technologie ihre eigenen Unfälle in sich berge, ursprünglich Glaskünstler).

Das mit relevanten und kryptischen Informationen gespickte Buch ist für THE BELL AND THE GLASS, was LA BOÎTE VERTE (Die grüne Schachtel, 1934) für LE GRAND VERRE. Duchamps Schachtel mit den Faksimiles handschriftlicher Notizen sollte eine Art Anleitung sein zum Wachkitzeln der gedanklichen Zusammenhänge, die für ihn das Wesentliche des Werks darstellten; sie sollte den Betrachter vom rein optischen Eindruck, der ihm nicht gefiel, wegführen. LA BOÎTE VERTE ist das bekanntere von zwei Begleitwerken; der Titel des zweiten lautet À L'INFINITIF (LA BOÎTE BLANCHE) – Im Infinitiv (Die weisse Schachtel). Es kam 1967 als Edition heraus, und es ist kein Zufall, dass LA BOÎTE BLANCHE zwei Jahre vor dem *Weissen Album* der Beatles erschien: Das berühmte monochrome Albumcover wurde nämlich vom Konzeptkünstler Richard Hamilton gestaltet, der Duchamps Zettelkasten von 1934 ins Englische übersetzt hatte. Genauso wenig ist es ein Zufall, dass Marclay, von dem auch ein gehäkeltes und mit Tonbändern sämtlicher Beatles-Songs gefülltes Kissen stammt, sein eigenes «Weisses Album» machte. 1990 hatte er für seine *White Album*-Serie mehrere, im Lauf der Zeit ziemlich abgegriffene Plattenhüllen von Hamilton in farblosem Prägedruck mit lyrischen Texten versehen. Doch wir schweifen ab… diese Gefahr besteht immer, wenn man den verschlungenen Motiven in Marclays Kunst nachspürt.

Aber kommen wir auf THE BELL AND THE GLASS zurück: Die gedruckte Version des Katalogs lässt sich natürlich überhaupt nicht mit dem Video vergleichen, das leichthin über die beiden Leinwände flimmert, die sich zu einem nahtlosen, eine Schleife bildenden Ganzen vereinen und alsbald wieder trennen. Es kommen Ausschnitte aus allen möglichen Filmen vor: aus Stummfilmen (ein weiblicher Roboter und eine mechanische Braut aus *Metropolis*), Hollywoodfilmen (Tarzan, der sich an einer Liane heruntergleiten lässt, die in diesem Kontext wie ein Sprung im Bild wirkt). Hinzu kommt dokumentarisches Filmmaterial von Duchamp («Mir war das egal», sagt er augenzwinkernd), aber auch Marclays eigene Aufnahme (Hände, die Puzzles von der Freiheitsglocke und LE GRAND VERRE zusammensetzen – Letzteres musste Marclay erst selbst anfertigen). Man hört ein ständiges Pulsieren (das Pochen eines Rotoreliefs, das Surren eines Roulette-Rads), das zu einer kargen Klangsymphonie (ein pneumatisches Zischen, das Kratzgeräusch eines Glasschneiders) mit dem Leitmotiv Wasser (transparent wie Glas) komponiert ist. Es gibt auch eine sexuelle Thematik (gebieterische «Neuvermählte», die ziemlich klägliche «Junggesellen» aufzureizen suchen); diese gewinnt an Momentum (hektisches Auf und Ab in Treppenhäusern – aber keine nackten Menschen), kocht hoch (Duchamps BROYEUSE DE CHOCOLAT / Schokoladenmühle, 1914), kommt zum Orgasmus (echte Schokolade spritzt in die vibrierenden Gussformen der Freiheitsglocke) und endet mit Szenen sich küssender und vereint zu Boden sinkender Paare. Man kann beinah die Glocken läuten hören, vorausgesetzt, der Kopf ist einem nicht geplatzt.

Mit jedem Element von THE BELL AND THE GLASS setzt Marclay so viel syntaktische Energie frei, dass man sich fast erleichtert abwendet. Mir wurde bewusst, dass ich das Rad anhalten musste, als ich es nicht länger als Zufall ansehen wollte, dass ich mir, kurz bevor ich Marclays Videoprojektion sah, eine Aufnahme von Marcel Duchamps Musik angehört hatte, auf welche ich in einer Schachtel mit vergessenen CDs gestossen war. Aber genau dies macht den Erfolg des Werkes aus. Der Druck, den Marclay erzeugt, indem er zwei Dinge miteinander verbindet, die eigentlich nichts miteinander zu tun haben, genügt, um genau das entstehen zu lassen, was sie offensichtlich einmal verbunden hat. Je mehr sich Freiheitsglocke und LE GRAND VERRE annähern,

desto mehr sprengt es unser Begriffsvermögen, sie entweder zusammenzubringen oder aber auseinander zu halten.

Für den Collagekünstler Joseph Cornell waren «Korrespondenzen» das Bindemittel, das seine Kunst zusammenhielt – auch wenn keinerlei Kleber im Spiel war. Sein DUCHAMP DOSSIER (1942–53) ist ein Porträt aus vielen aufschlussreichen, Alltagsgegenständen – etwa dem Etikett einer chemischen Reinigung, das Cornell wahrscheinlich aus Duchamps Abfall gefischt hatte, oder diversen Mona-Lisa-Bildern –, die lose in einem alten Karton aufbewahrt wurden. 1999 bildete das DOSSIER den Mittelpunkt einer grossartigen Ausstellung im Philadelphia Museum of Art, die den ständigen Dialog im Werk dieser beiden Künstler zum Gegenstand hatte. Und es bildet auch eine einzigartige kleine Einheit innerhalb von Cornells Œuvre, welche eine Frage aufwirft, die sich auch im Zusammenhang mit Marclays THE BELL AND THE GLASS stellt: Wie lässt sich eine Collage vermeiden? Wie kann man Kunst machen, die all die weit reichenden Korrespondenzen erfasst, die sich in der modernen und zeitgenössischen Kultur finden – wie Marclay begeisterte sich auch Cornell nicht nur für bildende Kunst, sondern auch für Bücher, Musik, Film, Populärkultur und jede Art von Unterhaltung –, ohne die Dinge festzunageln? Cornells DOSSIER zufolge, das mehr mit dem offenen Bildatlas des Kunsthistorikers Aby Warburg gemeinsam hat als mit seinen übrigen Collagen, lautet die Antwort: durch Archivieren. Das Archivieren ist auch die treibende Kraft hinter THE BELL AND THE GLASS. Aber Marclays neue Arbeit übernimmt diese Methode künstlerischer Gestaltung im Zeitalter der technischen Reproduzierbarkeit und erweitert sie zu einem digitalen Verfahren.

Trotz seiner visuellen Komplexität entstand der Videoteil von THE BELL AND THE GLASS auf einem einfachen Personalcomputer und für den Schnitt wurde das Programm Final Cut Pro verwendet. Man könnte meinen, der Film sei zusammengeheftet, was wiederum an Marclays zusammengenähte Plattenhüllen aus den frühen 90er Jahren erinnert. Jene kombinierten die Gesichter berühmter (männlicher) Musikstars mit namenlosen verkaufsfördernden (weiblichen) Körpern und liessen so etwas wirklich

Aussergewöhnliches entstehen. Zusammengestückelt wird auch beim Musiksampling, ein anschauliches Beispiel von Handarbeit, das auf den weiblichen, hausgemachten Ursprung des Hip-Hop verweist, bei dem Musik gemacht wird, indem man sie mixt und buchstäblich von den Platten kratzt. Und wie der Hip-Hop in der Massenkultur aufging, setzt sich auch Sampling allgemein als beherrschendes Verfahren unserer Zeit durch. Es ist längst Teil unseres Alltags: Wir scannen, streamen und scrollen. Und während die Collage eine Ästhetik der Fragmente und der aufgesplitterten Bedeutung ist, geht es beim Sampling um die Möglichkeit, aus Korrespondenzen einen Sinn herauszufiltern, sei er noch so widersprüchlich und zufällig. Marclay, der als DJ und Musiker am Plattenteller stand, hat Jahre lang gesampelt: In einer Aufnahme aus den 80er Jahren, DUST BREEDING (1982), setzte er vier Plattenspieler ein, um eine Art Kammermusik im Sampler-Stil zu erzeu-

gen. Dies war jedoch nur ein bescheidenes Beispiel im Vergleich zu seinem jüngst entstandenen VIDEO QUARTET (Videoquartett, 2002), in welchem er aus den Klängen und Bildern von Hunderten von Hollywoodfilmen eine nahtlose Panoramaprojektion auf vier Leinwänden komponierte. Am Ende dieses vierzehnminütigen Epos klatschte das Publikum. Aber auch THE BELL AND THE GLASS ist ein bemerkenswert leicht zugängliches und unterhaltsames Kunstwerk. Mit seiner Kombination von Freiheitsglocke und LE GRAND VERRE ist es gleichzeitig extrem ortsspezifisch. Es würde wohl ausserhalb von Philadelphia, wo die Präsenz der Originalobjekte einen grossen Teil seiner Wirkung ausmacht, kaum dieselbe Faszination ausüben. Auch dafür gilt es, dem Künstler Beifall zu zollen: Er hat mit seinem kreativen Beitrag eine weitere Ikone für eine Stadt geschaffen, die ihre eigenen Brüche liebt.

(Übersetzung: Uta Goridis)

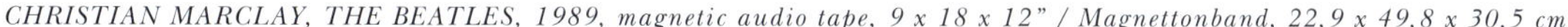

CHRISTIAN MARCLAY, THE BEATLES, 1989, magnetic audio tape, 9 x 18 x 12" / Magnettonband, 22,9 x 49,8 x 30,5 cm.

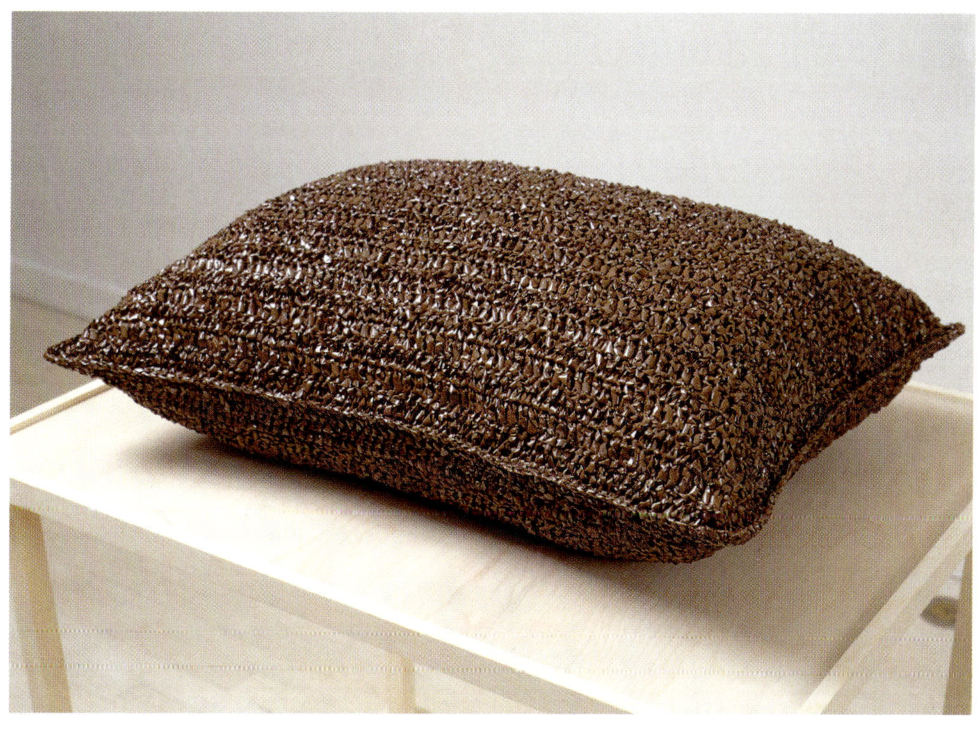

The Bride, Revived by Her Bachelors, on a Dissecting Table, between a Sewing Machine and an Umbrella

PHILIPPE VERGNE

Leave it up to chance… By a fortuitous turn of events in the form of an assisted readymade, Christian Marclay has just completed a project that wasn't really one, and that originated (unbeknownst to him) on the shores of the Mediterranean, from which the European avant-gardes sailed to the United States during the Second World War.

In 1995, Christian Marclay and the musician Otomo Yoshihide gave a concert—a duel of turntables—at the Musée d'Art Contemporain de Marseille. Moved by a cross-disciplinary impulse that has been at the core of Marclay's work since its very first developments, the performance was organized in the museum galleries, where crates containing the works from "In the Spirit of Fluxus" (an exhibition conceived and organized by the Walker Art Center) were packed for shipping. The two artists had installed their turntables on top of an improvised assemblage of these crates containing the works, the history, the testimonies, and the relics of the Fluxus movement—whose utopian ambition it was to make life more interesting than art, by reconciling the spectacle, the stage, and the performing arts with the visual arts.

Insofar as Marclay emerged after (and perhaps out of) the Fluxus movement, there could not have been a better "stage" for him than this locked-up history. Crated and kept under climate control by the museum committed to preserving its treasures, this may seem an absurd collection of works to conserve. Fluxus paradoxically intended to consume itself until its own extinction, as well as that of the institution that today protects and ensures its permanence. Quite innocently, what this DJ performance displayed "with hidden noise" (to paraphrase Marcel Duchamp), was a critical, bemused, and quietly subversive look at the fetishism attached to the "relics" that constitute the stuff of art history, Fluxus or otherwise.

This year, Christian Marclay is invited by the Walker Art Center in Minneapolis to realize a series of concerts and artworks to be both seen and heard, while the Walker itself is shut down, boxed up for a building expansion. It thus becomes, for this institution whose mission is to be cross-disciplinary, a question of conceiving the presentation of an artist's work in new spatial and temporal terms; or, to be precise, of conceiving the experience of a work freed from the constraints attached to the idea of an exhibition. Incidentally, the Walker has the privilege to count among its collections an important number of Fluxus objects, both multiples and unique pieces. Marclay turned this Fluxus collection into the subject, the object, and the matrix of a sound installation of video actions overlapping and playing simul-

PHILIPPE VERGNE is Senior Curator, Visual Arts, at the Walker Art Center in Minneapolis, Minnesota.

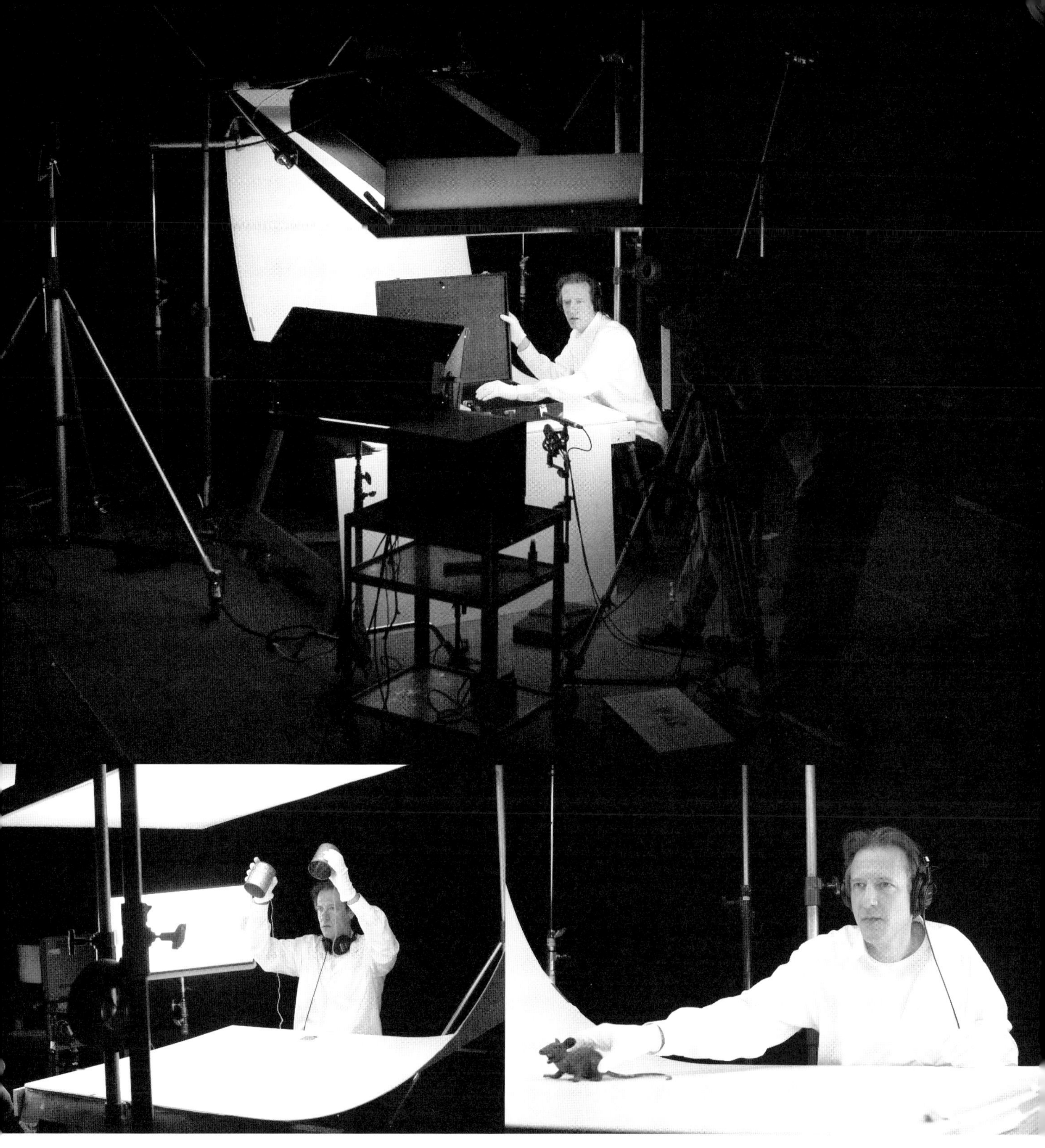

CHRISTIAN MARCLAY, SHAKE RATTLE & ROLL (FLUXMIX), 2004, Walker Art Center, Minneapolis, production stills.
(PHOTOS: CAMERON WITTIG)

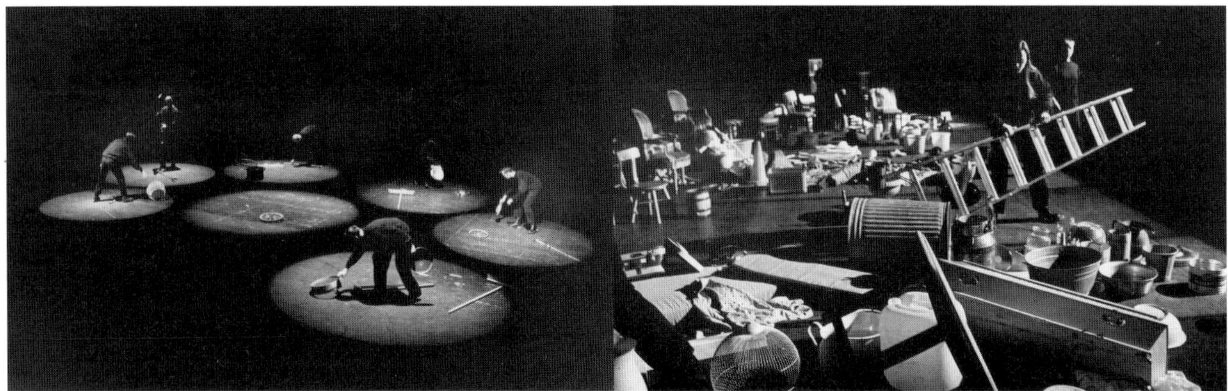

CHRISTIAN MARCLAY, LES SORTILÈGES:IM BANN DES ZAUBERS, 1996, performance at Marstall Theater, Munich /
Performance im Marstall-Theater, München. (PHOTO: LINDELL THORSEN)

taneously. We shall attempt to analyze the nature and content of this project from the angle of Marclay's working process.

Similar to ARRANGED AND CONDUCTED (1997) at Kunsthaus Zürich and LES SORTILÈGES (1996) at the Munich Marstall Theater, Marclay's project has its origin in a variant of the notion of "site-specificity" by engaging a public collection. It also reveals a critical and aesthetic practice that, beyond its original "micro-context," is absolutely coherent with the program, and the syntax, that Marclay has developed in the last twenty years, from the days of his band, The Bachelors, even, to his most recent works, in particular VIDEO QUARTET (2003). First, Marclay identified hundreds of objects made by the Fluxus group: Georges Brecht boxes, absurd card decks, prepared musical instruments, a violin destroyed by Nam June Paik, a green violin by Joseph Beuys, Ben Vautier's chamber pot, Philip Corner music scores, object poems by Yoko Ono, an anthology by Jackson McLow, etc., in other words, a collection of mass-produced objects available for a ridiculously low price at the time, and whose purpose was to invade and humorously subvert a somewhat stilted daily reality.

The paradox of these objects, like that of the introduction of Fluxus in the museum, lies in the fact that their very purpose is negated by the anaesthetic protocol of the vitrine, the "Do Not Touch" dictatorship and the hypochondriac neurosis of the registrar's white gloves. Marclay counters this paradox by

opening the crates on top of which he had performed a few years earlier and by questioning, with both sarcasm and subtlety, the validity of this kind of museological embalming. To this end, Marclay decided to make music with the Fluxus works and to film himself handling each object and revealing its potential for sound. A process is put in place by which the artist, wearing the reglementary white gloves, "stages" a manipulation of the collection. Placed in an environment that evokes, in my opinion, the obverse of the scenery of Marcel Duchamp's ÉTANT DONNÉS (1946–66) at the Philadelphia Museum of Art, he caresses, shakes, lets fall, or almost erotically strokes one by one each of the little relics of a bygone utopia, making them produce a sound that goes against their function. As a musician, he "interprets" these objects, systematically producing an unexpected sound, a countersound. The result is an absurd symphony, absurd because it is absolutely literal, where what you see is what you hear, or what you hear is really what you see. The real seems to have lost its double, its representation. Marclay has staged a principle of absolute tautology, which, in a culture dominated by image-making, makes us stumble on the real, for it is too shallow and too profuse at the same time.

If anything is staged in this work, it is a double process: both a desacralizing and a reviving. A desacralizing, insofar as Marclay attacks not only the museum as institution, but also the physical integrity of the objects in question. He violates them, like an artist who would open a can of shit by Piero Manzoni in order to know the reality of its contents; or like an artist who would attempt to unravel the ball of twine of Marcel Duchamp's WITH HIDDEN NOISE (1916) in order to finally identify the object at its center. But entwined with this desacralizing process is a reviving or reactivating process, as evidenced by the quasi-clinical aesthetic of the work (white background, white gloves, white shirt), and the quasi-medical care with which the artist manipulates these deaf and silent objects. It is a little bit as though Marclay were passing behind the scenery of Duchamp's ÉTANT DONNÉS in order to revive the motionless corpse lying at the center of the sculpture; a little bit as though (to remain with Duchamp) the Bride were revived by her bachelors, even.

All of this, of course, makes no sense, and so much the better. In a certain way, what Marclay is attempting to revive is a disruptive capacity to no longer make sense, an urgent call to 'stop making sense' reminiscent of the historical avant-gardes, the same who sailed from Marseilles to New York. By opening its doors to it, the museum turned Fluxus into the fossilized icon of a bygone freedom of spirit, in spite of the fact that this movement seems always to have preferred liberation (a process, a dynamic state of alert) to liberty (an ideal). In the end, when Christian Marclay extracts a plaintive sound from Vautier's chamber pot, he may be inviting us, through an absurd detour, to stay alert.

After carefully considering his recent retrospective exhibition organized by the UCLA Hammer Museum and carefully listening to his discography, the entire language and syntax that Marclay develops, in a space where our aesthetic categories (of the visible and the audible, of the original and the appropriated or interpreted copy) come to naught, tends likewise to erode our certainties, to revive our attention to the codes of representation and their validity. His appropriations and distortions of Fluxus objects, his samplings of sounds and readymade images, his command of production and distribution formats (soundtrack, film, sculpture, installation, photography, publications), far from satisfying themselves with an aesthetically pleasing and seductive use of

the available visual and aural cultural material, are critical tools, sowing the seeds of doubt within the status quo. Thus, when he elaborates the movie of a soundtrack, as opposed to the soundtrack of a movie, when he invents a sound image to respond to a moving or a fixed image, when he sculpts sound and invites us to listen to a sculpture, he is literally and metaphorically shattering the symphonic, orchestrated linearity of the discourses that constitute us. When he has Mallarmé's "A Throw of the Dice" sung,[1] Christian Marclay serenely suggests that images, discourses, exhibitions, and information lie, that the world isn't the complex sum of completed things, but a score of layered and constantly mutating representations and processes that defies the universality of logical concepts, but that can be as beautiful and as liberating as "the chance meeting on a dissecting table of a sewing machine and an umbrella."[2]

(Translation from the French by Anthony Allen)

The installation resulting from Christian Marclay's residency at the Walker will be exhibited from June 26 to August 14, 2004 at Franklin Art Works in Minneapolis.

1) This refers to the poem "Un coup de dés jamais n'abolira le hasard" (1897) by Stéphane Mallarmé.
2) "Beau comme la rencontre fortuite sur une table d'opération d'une machine à coudre et d'un parapluie": in connection with Surrealism's often-quoted phrase from third verse of Le Comte de Lautréamont's *Les Chants de Maldoror* (Paris, 1869).

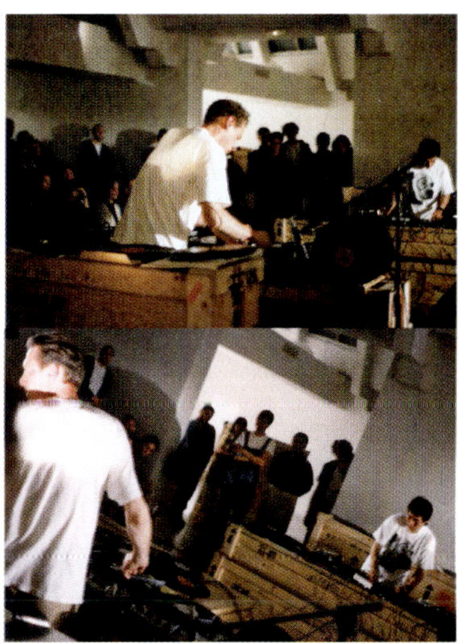

Christian Marclay and Otomo Yoshihide at the / im Musée d'Art Contemporain, Marseille, 1995.

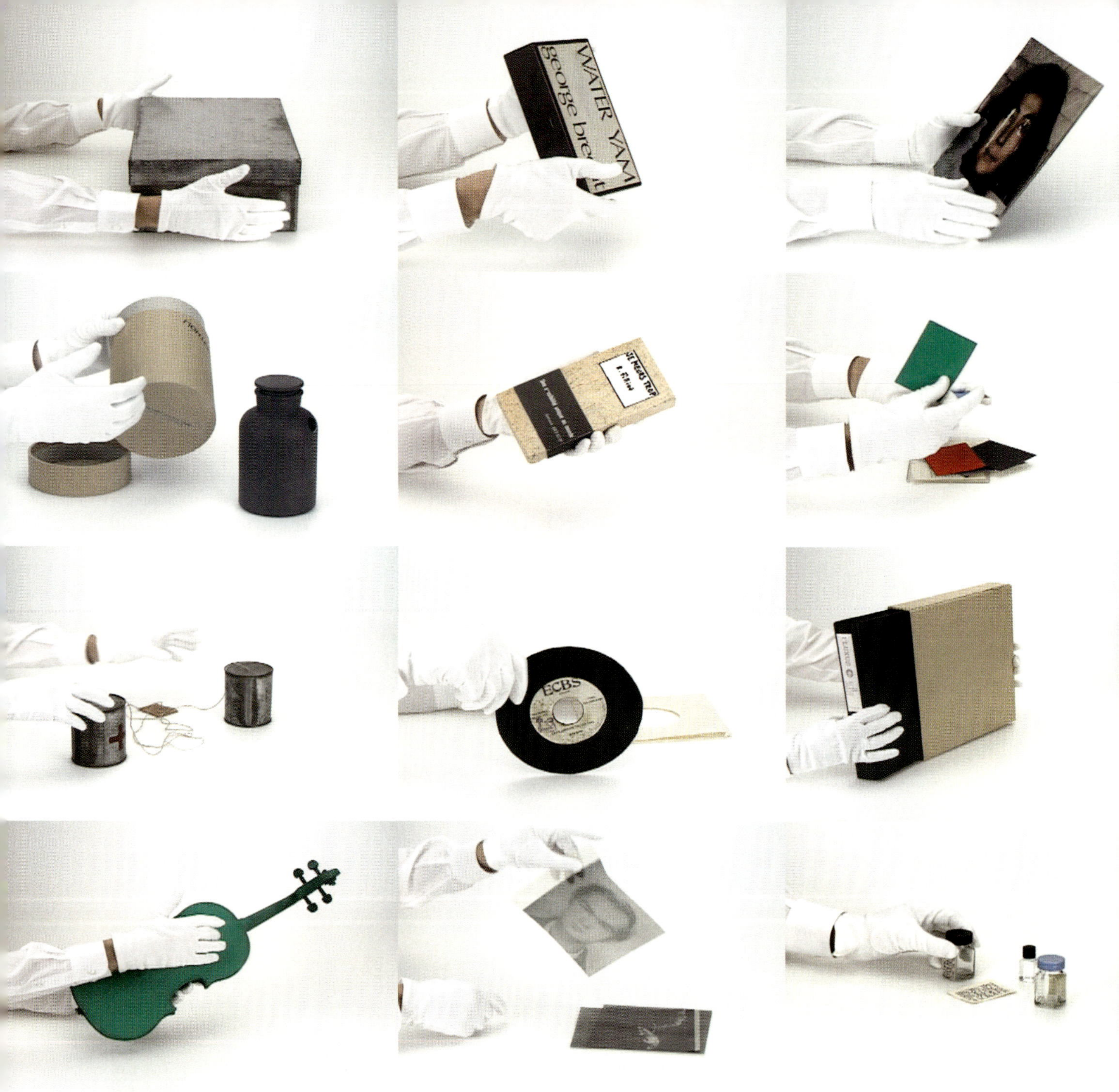

CHRISTIAN MARCLAY, SHAKE RATTLE & ROLL (FLUXMIX), 2004, Walker Art Center, Minneapolis, video stills.

Die von ihren Junggesellen wieder zum Leben erweckte Neuvermählte auf einem Seziertisch zwischen Näh- maschine und Regenschirm

PHILIPPE VERGNE

Der Zufall macht seine Sache gut. Dank eines glücklichen Zusammentreffens in Form eines *ready-made assisté* ist Christian Marclay ein Projekt zugefallen, das so nicht geplant gewesen war und seinen unfreiwilligen Anfang an der Küste des Mittelmeers nahm, dort, wo die europäische Avantgarde im Zweiten Weltkrieg an Bord ging, um in die Vereinigten Staaten zu emigrieren.

1995 gab Christian Marclay zusammen mit dem Musiker Otomo Yoshihide ein Konzert im Musée d'Art Contemporain de Marseille; sie lieferten sich quasi ein Duell am Plattenteller. Im Interesse der Interdisziplinarität, die in Marclays Arbeit schon immer eine zentrale Rolle spielte, fand die Performance in den Sälen des Museums statt, in denen die versandfertigen Kisten mit den Werken der vom Walker Art Center konzipierten und organisierten Ausstellung «In the Spirit of Fluxus» herumstanden. Die beiden Künstler hatten ihre Platten und Plattenspieler auf dieser improvisierten Kistenlandschaft installiert, welche Werke, Geschichte, Zeugnisse und

Reliquien der Fluxusbewegung in sich barg, deren Ziel und Utopie es einst gewesen war, durch die Versöhnung der bildenden Kunst mit dem Spektakel, der Bühne und der Performancekunst das Leben interessanter erscheinen zu lassen als die Kunst.

Insofern als er ein Nachgeborener (vielleicht auch ein später Nachfolger) der Fluxusbewegung ist, hätte es für Marclay keine geeignetere Bühne geben können als dieses Stück in Kisten verpackte Geschichte, die hier klimatisch kontrolliert gelagert wurde. Im Fall dieser Bewegung wirkt die Anstrengung des Museums, deren Philosophie und Ästhetik vollständig zu konservieren, besonders absurd, weil sie sich doch gerade ausleben und erschöpfen wollte bis zur Auslöschung ihrer selbst, aber auch jener Institution, die sie heute schützt, pflegt und ihr Fortbestehen sichert. Ganz unschuldig inszenierte diese Performance, dieses Duell am Plattenteller, *à bruit secret*, mit verborgenem Lärm – um mit Duchamps Worten zu reden –, einen kritischen, amüsierten und leise subversiven Blick auf den Fetischismus, der mit den «Reliquien» getrieben wird, die im Grunde die Kunstgeschichte ausmachen, egal ob es sich um Fluxus handelt oder etwas anderes.

PHILIPPE VERGNE ist Kurator des Walker Art Center in Minneapolis.

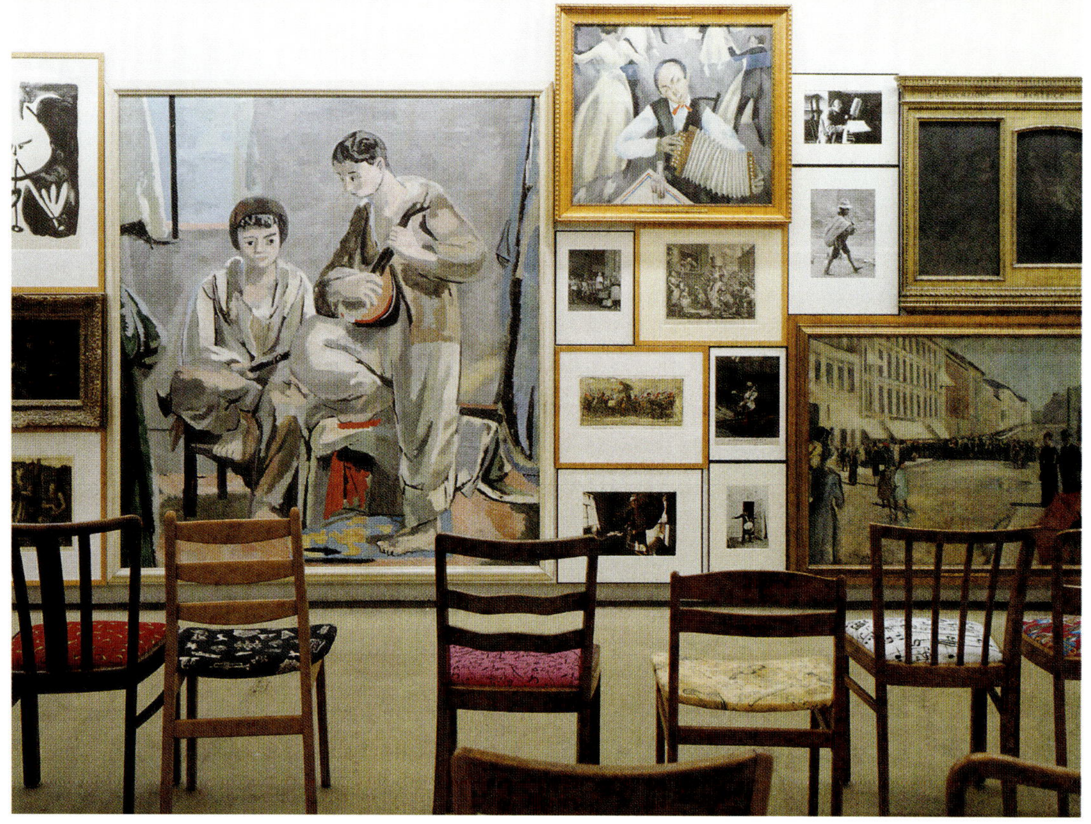

Dieses Jahr wurde Christian Marclay vom Walker Art Center in Minneapolis zur Realisierung einer Reihe von Projekten eingeladen, darunter Konzerte, aber auch andere Werke, die geeignet wären, ausgestellt, gezeigt und gehört zu werden, während das Walker Art Center selbst wegen Erweiterungsbauarbeiten geschlossen und in Kisten verpackt sein würde. Dieser Institution, die sich zum Ziel gesetzt hat interdisziplinär zu sein, geht es darum, in anderen als nur räumlichen und zeitlichen Begriffen zu denken, und darum, w i e man die Arbeit eines Künstlers zeigt; genauer noch, sich die Begegnung mit einem Werk frei von jenen Zwängen vorzustellen, die mit der Idee einer Ausstellung verbunden sind. Im Übrigen hat das Walker Art Center das Privileg, eine Sammlung etlicher wichtiger Objekte des Fluxus zu besitzen, sowohl Multiples als auch Originalwerke. Diese Sammlung hat Christian Marclay zum Thema, Gegenstand und Ausgangspunkt einer Soundinstallation gleichzeitig laufender und sich überlappender Videoaktionen gewählt. Ich will versuchen Art und Inhalt dieses Projektes an-

hand von Marclays Vorgehen bei dessen Realisierung zu analysieren.

Ähnlich wie im Fall von ARRANGED AND CONDUCTED (Arrangiert und dirigiert, 1997) im Kunsthaus Zürich oder LES SORTILÈGES: IM BANN DES ZAUBERS (1996) im Münchner Marstall-Theater bringt Marclay in diesem Projekt eine Variante des Begriffs der *site specificity* ins Spiel, indem er eine öffentliche Sammlung mit einbezieht. Es zeugt jedoch auch von einer kritischen und ästhetischen Praxis, die sich über diesen Mikrokontext der Herkunft hinaus absolut bruchlos ins Programm und die Syntax einfügt, die Christian Marclay seit rund zwanzig Jahren pflegt, von seiner Band *The Bachelors, even*, bis hin zu einem seiner jüngsten Werke, VIDEO QUARTET (Videoquartett, 2003). Zunächst einmal hat Christian Marclay Hunderte von Fluxus-Objekten identifiziert: Kisten von Georges Brecht, absurde Kartenspiele, speziell präparierte Musikinstrumente, eine von Nam June Paik zerstörte Geige, eine grüne Geige von Joseph Beuys, den Nachttopf von Ben Vautier, Partituren von Philip Corner, Objektgedichte von Yoko Ono, eine Anthologie von Jackson McLow und so weiter, kurz: eine Sammlung von Gegenständen jener Zeit, Massenprodukte, die damals zu einem geradezu lächerlichen Preis zu haben waren und den etwas tristen Alltag erobern und humoristisch unterwandern sollten.

Genau wie im Fall des Einzugs von Fluxus ins Museum besteht das Paradoxe dieser Objekte darin, dass ihre Brisanz entschärft wird durch die narkotisierende Wirkung der Vitrine, die Diktatur des «Nicht berühren!» und die hypochondrische Neurose des Archivars, alles nur mit weissen Handschuhen anzufassen. Marclay begegnet diesem Paradox, indem er die Kisten öffnet, auf denen er einige Jahre zuvor in Marseille aufgetreten ist, und den Sinn der musealen Aufbahrung ebenso subtil wie sarkastisch hinterfragt. Zu diesem Zweck beschliesst er mit den Fluxusobjekten Musik zu machen und sich dabei filmen zu lassen, wie er das Klangpotenzial eines jeden dieser Objekte vorführt. Darauf folgt ein Prozess, in dessen Verlauf der Künstler ordnungsgemäss weisse Handschuhe tragend die Manipulation dieser Sammlung «inszeniert». Inmitten einer Szenerie, die, wie mir scheint, geradewegs an die Rückseite des Dekors von Marcel Duchamps ÉTANT DONNÉS (1946–66) im Philadelphia Museum of Art erinnert, steht Marclay und streichelt und schüttelt die kleinen Überbleibsel einer längst entschwundenen Utopie, ja er liebkost sie auf beinah erotische Art und Weise und entlockt ihnen Töne, die nichts mit ihrer Funktion zu tun haben. Als Musiker «interpretiert» er die Objekte und ruft systematisch einen unerwarteten Ton, quasi einen Gegenton hervor. Dabei entsteht eine absurde Symphonie, absurd, weil sie absolut nüchtern ist, weil man sieht, was man hört, oder hört, was man sieht. Der Wirklichkeit scheint ihr Double, die Repräsentation, abhanden gekommen zu sein. Marclay hat ein Prinzip der absoluten Tautologie eingeführt, das uns in unserer bildlastigen Kultur über die Realität stolpern lässt, weil sie gleichzeitig zu schal und zu üppig ist.

Wenn diese Arbeit etwas demonstriert, so ist es der doppelte Prozess einer gleichzeitigen Entweihung und Reanimation: Eine Entweihung findet insofern statt, als Marclay sich nicht nur gegen die Institution des Museums wendet, sondern auch gegen die Integrität der Objekte als solche. Er tut ihnen Gewalt an, genau wie ein Künstler, der eine Büchse von Piero Manzonis MERDA D'ARTISTA (1961) öffnen würde, um ihren Inhalt zu überprüfen, oder einer, der versuchte, das Fadenknäuel von Duchamps A BRUIT SECRET (1916) aufzurollen, um endlich herauszufinden, was in seinem Inneren als Spule dient. Aber gleichzeitig mit dieser Entweihung und dank dieser quasi klinischen Ästhetik, die Marclay inszeniert (weisser Hintergrund, weisse Handschuhe, weisses Hemd), und der fast medizinischen Sorgfalt, die er den «taubstummen» Objekten angedeihen lässt, findet eine Wiederbelebung, eine Reaktivierung statt. Es ist ein wenig, als ob er hinter die Kulissen von Duchamps ÉTANT DONNÉS (1966) schlüpfte, um den leblosen Körper, der im Zentrum jenes skulpturalen Arrangements ruht, wieder zu beleben; ein wenig, um bei Duchamp zu bleiben, als ob «la Mariée était réanimée par ses célibataires, même…» (als ob die Neuvermählte von ihren Junggesellen selbst wieder zum Leben erweckt würde).

All das hat, wohlverstanden und zum Glück, überhaupt keinen Sinn. Christian Marclays Arbeit ist gewissermassen ein Versuch zur Wiederbelebung jener Fähigkeit des Abbrechens, des keinen Sinn mehr Habens, und jenes Drangs mit dem Sinn aufzuräumen, die für die historische Avantgarde typisch war, für jene Künstler also, die in Marseille das Schiff nach New York bestiegen. Als das Museum dem Fluxus seine Tore öffnete, liess es ihn zur Ikone einer geistigen Freiheit erstarren, die nicht mehr existiert, obwohl doch diese Bewegung gerade das Prozesshafte, das Dynamische, die wache Aufmerksamkeit, das Phänomen der «Befreiung» über das starre Ideal der «Freiheit» als Zustand gestellt hatte. Kurz, wenn Christian Marclay dem Nachttopf von Ben Vautier einen schrillen Ton entlockt, so bringt er uns vielleicht dank der Absurdität dieses Tuns dazu, wach zu bleiben.

Beim sorgfältigen Studium seiner jüngsten Retrospektive im Armand Hammer Museum, Los Angeles, und beim wiederholten Anhören seiner Platten kommt man zum selben Schluss: Marclays ganze Sprache, die Syntax, die er in einem Raum entwickelt, in welchem sich unsere ästhetischen Kategorien gegenseitig aufheben – das Sichtbare und das Hörbare, das Original und die Kopie als Appropriation oder Interpretation –, alles ist darauf ausgerichtet, unsere Sicherheiten zu durchkreuzen und unsere Aufmerksamkeit wieder auf die Codes der Repräsentation und deren Stellenwert zu lenken. Seine Appropriation und Distorsion von Fluxus-Objekten, sein Sampling von Klängen und Readymade-Bildern, sein Beherrschen der unterschiedlichsten Produktions- und Vermittlungsformen (Tonband, Film, Skulptur, Installation, Photographie, gedruckte Publikationen), all das ist weit davon entfernt, sich lediglich in der ästhetischen und verführerischen Anwendung der visuellen und audiovisuellen Mittel zu erschöpfen, sondern dient ihm als kritisches Werkzeug, das den Status quo in Frage stellt. Zum Beispiel, wenn er den Film zu einem Tonband erarbeitet, und nicht etwa den Ton zu einem Film; wenn er als Antwort auf ein bewegtes oder unbewegtes Bild ein Tonbild erfindet; wenn er den Ton modelliert und uns dazu anregt, eine Skulptur anzuhören: So zerschlägt er buchstäblich und auch im übertragenen Sinn die symphonische, orchestrierte Linearität der Diskurse, durch die wir uns definieren. Wenn er «Un coup de dés»[1] unbedingt singen lassen will, deutet Christian Marclay auf heitere Weise an, dass Bilder, Gespräche, Ausstellungen und Informationen lügen und dass die Welt nicht die komplexe Summe aller vollendeten Dinge ist, sondern eine Partitur vielschichtiger und ständig wechselnder Repräsentationen und Prozesse, die den Universalitätsanspruch des logischen Denkens Lügen straft, jedoch so schön und befreiend sein kann wie «die zufällige Begegnung einer Nähmaschine und eines Regenschirms auf einem Seziertisch.»[2]

(Übersetzung aus dem Französischen: Suzanne Schmidt)

Die in Zusammenarbeit mit dem Walker Art Center entstandene Installation wird vom 26. Juni bis 14. August 2004 bei Franklin Art Works in Minneapolis ausgestellt sein.

1) Gemeint ist das Gedicht «Un coup de dés jamais n'abolira le hasard» (1897) von Stéphane Mallarmé.
2) «Beau comme la rencontre fortuite sur une table d'opération d'une machine à coudre et d'un parapluie»: im Zusammenhang mit dem Surrealismus gern zitierte Zeile aus der 3. Strophe von Lautréamonts *Les Chants de Maldoror* (Paris, 1869).

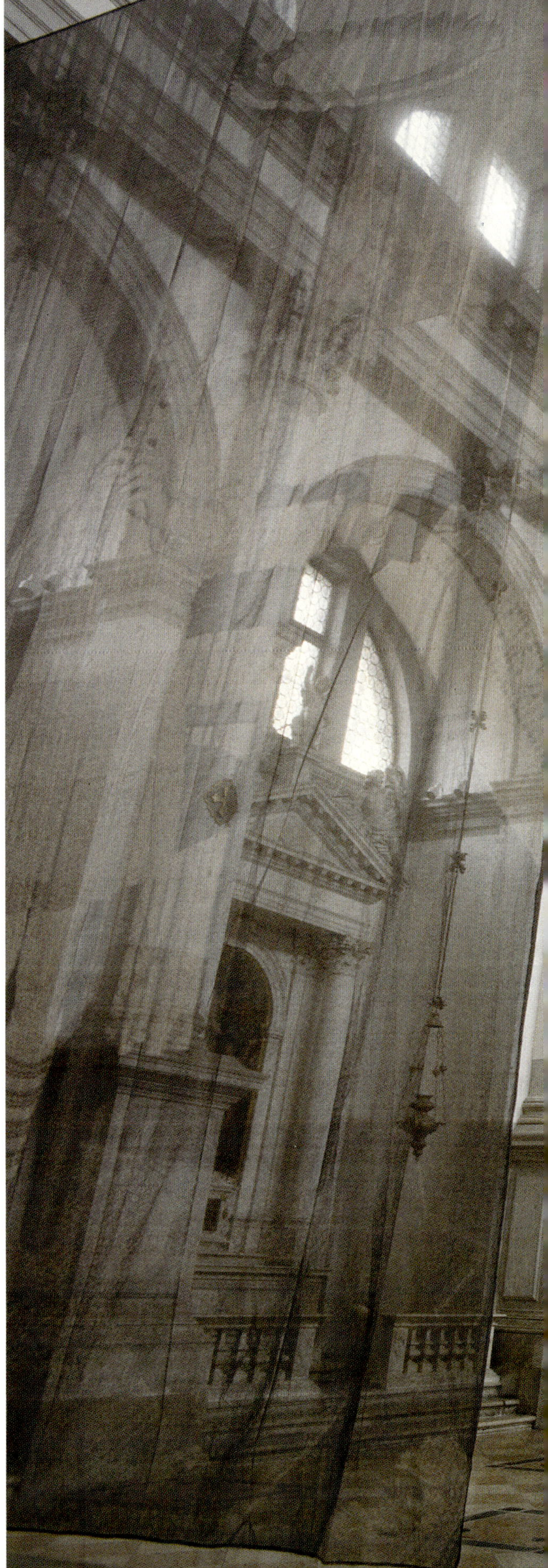

CHRISTIAN MARCLAY, AMPLIFICATION, 1995, *Chiesa di San Staë, Venice Biennale / VERSTÄRKUNG, Biennale Venedig*. (PHOTO: PIERRE-ANTOINE GRISONI)

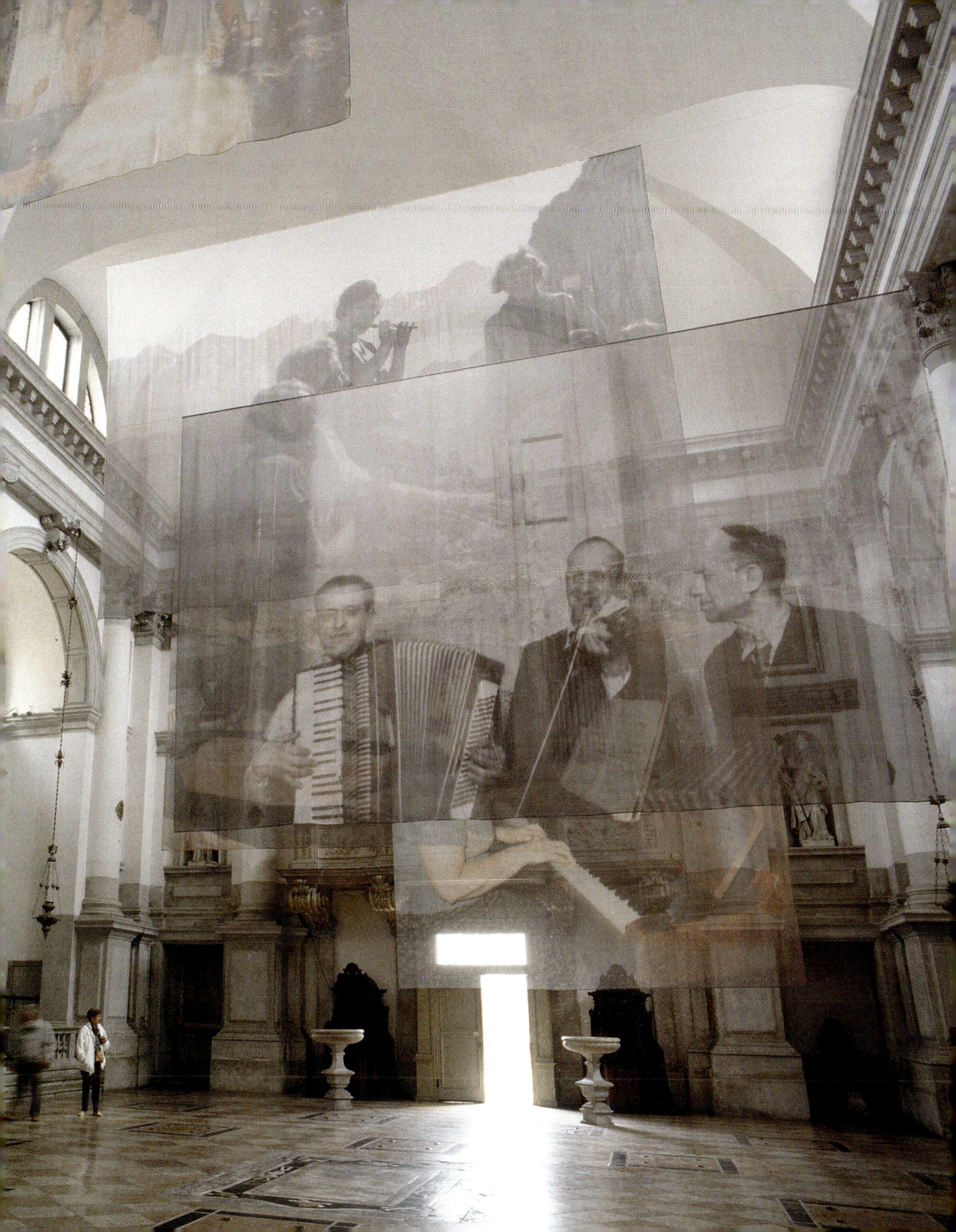

Edition for Parkett CHRISTIAN MARCLAY

My Bad Ear, 2004

Life-size bronze cast

by Modern Art Foundry, Astoria, NY.

Edition of 60, signed and numbered.

Mein schlechtes Ohr, 2004

Bronzeabguss im Massstab 1:1.

Guss: Modern Art Foundry, Astoria, NY.

Auflage: 60, signiert und nummeriert.

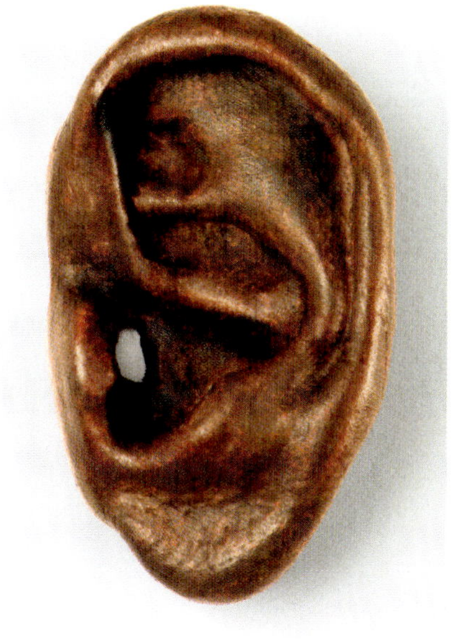

(PHOTO: MANCIA/BODMER, FBM STUDIO, ZÜRICH)

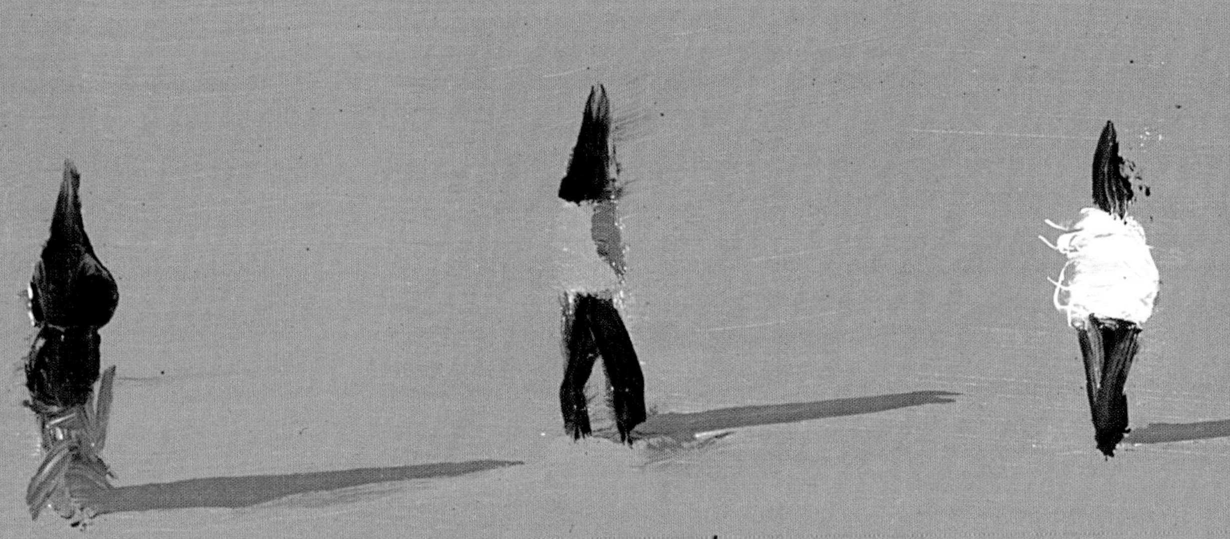

WILHELM SASNAL, UNTITLED, 2004, oil on canvas, 9½ x 11⅞" / OHNE TITEL, 2004, Öl auf Leinwand, 24 x 30

W i l h e l m

Sasnal

PAINTING RECORDING

MEGHAN DAILEY

"I feel unusually susceptible to pictures," Wilhem Sasnal confessed in a recent interview.[1] This is not a surprising admission for an artist with such an acute awareness of so many different images and visual forms. Sasnal's work utilizes news photographs, snapshots, films or animation, graphic motifs, comic books, his own drawings, and the work of other artists as points of origin. From these diverse sources, his works may further draw upon art historical styles ranging from Pop to geometric abstraction, and encompass (and sometimes subvert) genres of portraiture and landscape. Or his paintings and drawings might not refer to any preexisting image, but are derived instead from the artist's own imagination or an episodic personal memory. Sasnal has an uncanny ability to adopt any style he chooses and the heterogeneity of his output almost demands that works be viewed en masse, in order to absorb the full range, as well as the meaning, of that diversity. It is not merely to promote difference for its own sake that Sasnal will juxtapose, in a single gallery show, milky gray-and-white toned photographically derived paintings with boldly colored design-driven compositions and portraits. For all the vast number of images in the world, there are as many ways of seeing and apprehending them, and at least as many ways to paint them. This "everystyle" has become Sasnal's own style, a marker of his burgeoning identity as an artist.

And so while his remarking on his susceptibility toward pictures was not surprising, it has stuck with me. With that comment Sasnal was, I think, referring not only to the eagerness with which he responds to the readily available crop of images around him but also to the act of making pictures. He has completed hundreds and hundreds of paintings large and small in the past four or five years. While he makes numerous drawings (and some of his paintings do look deliberately drawn rather than painted), and has completed a few Super-8 films, Sasnal concentrates his efforts for the most part on painting with oil on canvas. As a student in Krakow, he painted everything in his immediate surroundings: Stereolab and Sonic Youth album covers; domestic objects, such as appliances or a kitchen chair; portraits of his girlfriend; and a rendering of the small dormitory room they shared. At that time, Sasnal was part of the Ladnie group, a loose collective of artists in Krakow who painted similarly ordinary subjects from everyday life. *Ladnie* is Polish for "pretty" but the gentle irony of the works exhibited under the label is that they were not always so pretty (the exteriors of dull apartment blocks and the mundane contents of their interiors). Sasnal's work also utilized motifs from advertising and popular culture, like a kind of neo-Pop without any of Pop's shiny exuberance. In 2001, Sasnal completed *Everyday Life in Poland Between 1999 and 2001,* an account

---

MEGHAN DAILEY is a writer and editor living in Brooklyn.

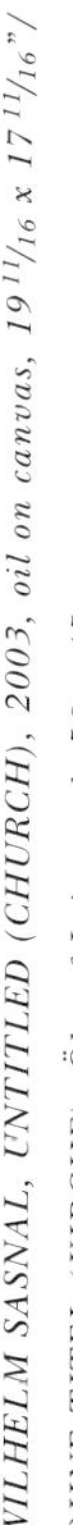

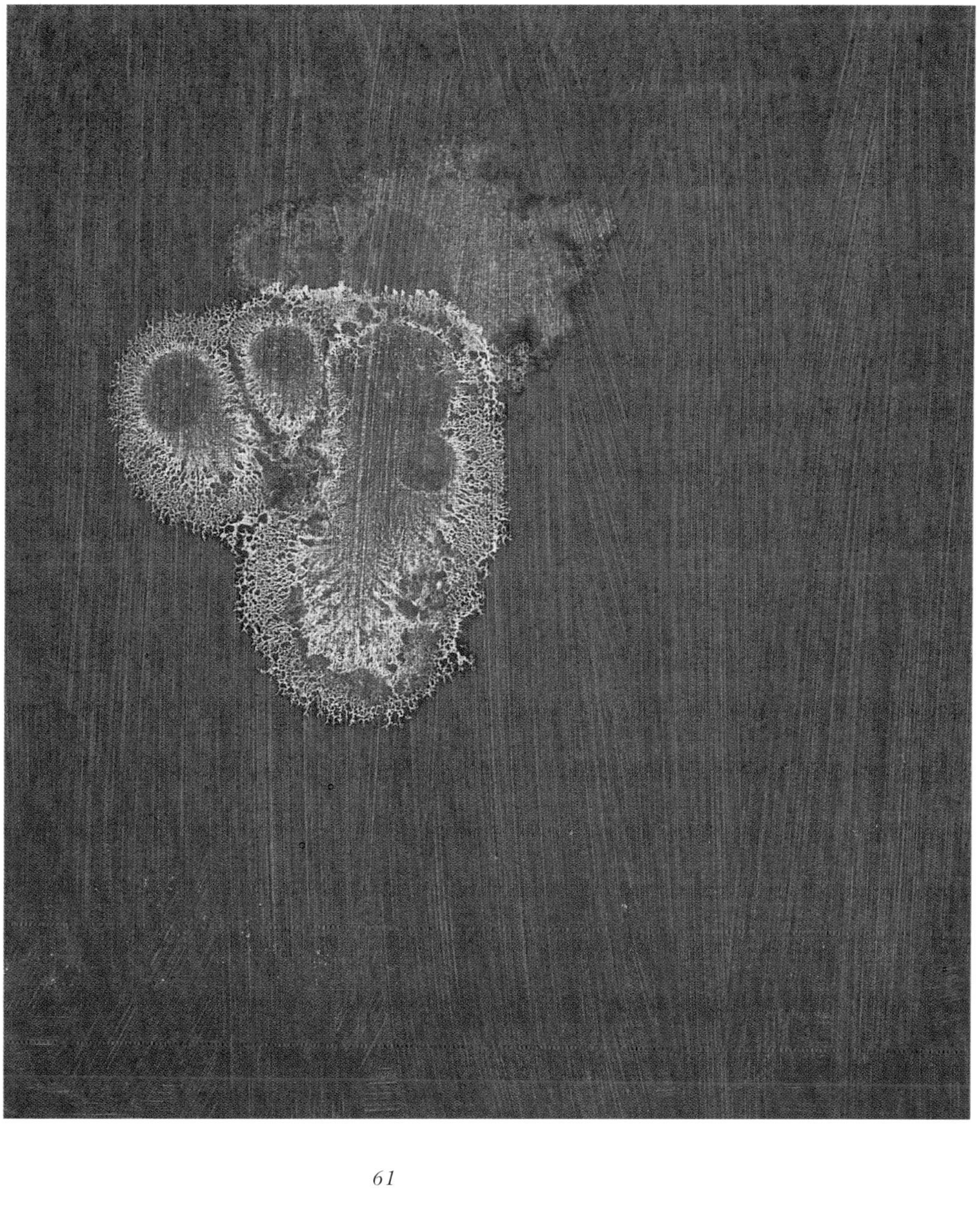

WILHELM SASNAL, UNTITLED (CHURCH), 2003, oil on canvas, 19 ¹¹/₁₆ x 17 ¹¹/₁₆" / OHNE TITEL (KIRCHE), Öl auf Leinwand, 50 x 45 cm.

WILHELM SASNAL, BECK, 2002, oil on canvas, 13 x 10 $^5/_8$" / Öl auf Leinwand, 33 x 27 cm.

in words and pictures of a year in the artist's life that also very much reflected the conditions of his generation, as if Henri Lefebvre had written his *Critique of Everyday Life* in graphic novel form.

The hermetic, personal side of Sasnal's practice reveals him as an artist who will capitulate to every impulse he feels to paint something, as if he simply has to. It is not the romantic idea of an artist driven to make art by some unseen force, but a more practical need, his contribution, his work. In its suggestion of a daily labor, Sasnal's practice is reminiscent of another Polish artist, Roman Opalka. Since 1965, Opalka has devoted himself to recording every number from one to infinity in endless rows in paint on canvas, each one the same size, each surface completely covered. Initiated during the Cold War, Opalka's lifelong existential project can be interpreted as a metaphor for the artist/individual working in isolation behind the Iron Curtain. More generally, the endeavor could be read as a way of imparting a fixed identity for Poland itself, which has been described as drifting in a nebulous "gray zone" in Europe (the artist's palette is also restricted to gray, white, and black), its sensibility and geography incompletely defined as somewhere between East and West. But ultimately Opalka's project transcends such associations; it is about life, both living and dying, and it's a way of recording the self, be it through numbers or album covers or the passing of shadows on the grass.

The artist to which Sasnal is most frequently compared is Gerhard Richter, mostly based upon a shared stylistic heterogeneity and use of photography. One might also see similarities in their respective backgrounds. Sasnal grew up in communist Poland in the seventies. Richter came of age under one dictatorship, fled a second as an adult, and developed a profound skepticism toward any kind of ideology, be it political or artistic; painting delivers no truths, it can only fulfill desires, one desire being the impulse to paint. The interrogation of the authenticity of images is the thread that connects Sasnal to Richter, and indeed that line of inquiry is one that many painters have followed since. Although it would be of little use to categorize their similarities or to suggest that Sasnal is somehow following in Richter's footsteps, it seems worth noting that while separated by nationality and a generation, their approaches to history reveal a similar means, and both artists simultaneously question the nature of memory, representation, and painting. Richter has wrestled with Germany's fascist past and postwar identity, particularly the collective inability to address that recent past directly, as in UNCLE RUDI (1965), based on a snapshot of Richter's uncle as an SS man. The inarticulable magnitude of the Holocaust made it impossible to represent it in an unmediated form. Nearly forty years after Richter's earliest works, it is still impossible; in Poland, questions of complicity, victimhood, guilt, and blame remain unanswered. A feeling of uncertainty prevails as to whether too much time has passed or not enough: "I constantly get the feeling that we are not living in the post-1989 generation, but the post-1945 period," Sasnal has said.[2)]

To address the Polish position during the German occupation, Sasnal turned to Art Spiegelman's reinterpretation of the Holocaust, *Maus* (begun in 1986). Instead of "copying" Spiegelman's characterizations (Jews as mice, Nazis as cats, Poles as pigs), Sasnal depicted only the background of settings within a concentration camp, such as a barracks interior, in stark black and white rendered in the stylized mode of a comic book. At an even further remove from its source is a group of three works entitled FOREST. In FOREST (2002), nature is rendered as an undefined, gestural mass of green strokes. Humankind is depicted as tiny in its midst. Another FOREST (2003) depicts a woman wearing a lilac colored garment with a mass of ebony hair, her facial features all but obscured by an almost opaque shadow of paint.

A third FOREST (2003) resembles a gray-on-gray Rorschach test that is probably a painting of the shadow cast by a tree. Connected only by title, these works are all based on scenes from Claude Lanzmann's epic documentary *Shoah* (1985). Sasnal's "forest of signs" amounts to his interpretation of the filmmaker's impressions of the recollections of others.

Sasnal's work itself can have a filmic quality, but it shows least in those works that make a direct cinematic reference, such as the three FOREST paintings. It is a quality that reveals itself in the way he uses light and shadow, the quality of interruption that some works have, or in his portraits, which are like characters captured in a moment of narrative uncertainty. The sensibility is somewhat akin to the German artist Eberhard Havekost, whose work alludes self-consciously to cinematic camera techniques by staging tricky points of view usually seen on screen: angles, cropping, close-ups, and so on. Both Sasnal's and Havekost's work are in dialogue with film and photography and the ways in which those mediums have affected not only the practice of painting, but also of looking. The film-still quality in Havekost's work would be from an action movie and in Sasnal's like something out of Bergman.

WILHELM SASNAL, A-BOMB, 2003,
oil on canvas, 33 ½ x 39 ⅜" / ATOMBOMBE,
Öl auf Leinwand, 85 x 100 cm.

Looking at Sasnal's paintings, we often get a bit of formal or symbolic shorthand and intuitively fill in the blanks with what remains, as with Robert Mangold's incomplete geometric forms. In one untitled picture of an airplane about to land, there are only disembodied wheels; the body of the plane exists intellectually, but not pictorially. Pictures fluctuate between abstraction and representation, though what is shown is often more symbolic than literal. In one, an expanse of white paint nearly fogs over the entire surface of the composition, leaving only snatches of more textured, sandy colored paint visible at the borders. This painterly mediation acquires new meaning when its title, A-BOMB (2002), is attached to it—suddenly the white is a toxic, obliterating cloud. The white expanse of paint used to conceal something beneath it is used elsewhere to different effect. In BECK and BEASTIE BOYS (both 2002), the performers are completely obscured by a rectangle smack in the middle of the frame.

Overriding everything, ultimately, is Sasnal's interrogation of painting's limits and capabilities. In his hands, the medium is a potent means of exploring how and what the eye sees. Many works primarily objectify the painting process through changes in density and application, such as when he uses a rag or his hands to apply pigment. However much the object or subject of the painting disappears or is rendered unfixed, painting itself is always the constant, the thing that one always sees. Even when he has derived a composition from another medium, Sasnal's paintings amount to approximations of the images to which they refer, very often taking narrative or representation to the realm of ideation.

1) Wilhelm Sasnal in conversation with Andrzej Przywara, in *Night Day Night*, exh. cat., Kunsthalle Zürich/Westfälischer Kunstverein Münster (Ostfildern-Ruit: Hatje Cantz, 2003), p. 38.
2) Ibid, p. 39.

MALEREI ALS AUFZEICHNUNG

MEGHAN DAILEY

«Ich bin aussergewöhnlich empfänglich für Bilder», gestand Wilhelm Sasnal kürzlich in einem Interview.[1] Dieses Eingeständnis ist nicht überraschend für einen Künstler, der so viele unterschiedliche Bilder und andere visuelle Erscheinungsformen so präzise wahrnimmt. Sasnal geht in seinen Arbeiten von Nachrichten, Photographien, Schnappschüssen, Filmen oder Trickfilmen, graphischen Motiven und Comic-Büchern aus, aber auch von eigenen Zeichnungen oder Werken anderer Künstler. Zusätzlich zur Benützung diverser Quellen machen seine Arbeiten mitunter auch Anleihen bei verschiedenen kunsthistorischen Stilen, von der Pop-Art bis zur Geometrischen Abstraktion, und wenden sich (manchmal durchaus subversiv) auch Gattungen wie der Porträt- oder Landschaftsmalerei zu. Seine Bilder und Zeichnungen nehmen dabei nicht unbedingt Bezug auf ein bereits existierendes Bild, sie können auch der Phantasie des Künstlers oder einem persönlichen Erinnerungsmoment entsprungen sein. Sasnal hat eine unheimliche Fähigkeit sich jeden beliebigen Stil anzueignen, und die Heterogenität seiner Produktion erfordert fast schon, dass man seine Arbeiten *en masse* betrachten kann, um ihre ganze Bandbreite und den Sinn ihrer Verschiedenheit zu erfassen. Wenn Sasnal in ein und derselben Ausstellung milchig wirkende, von der Photographie abgeleitete Bilder in grauweissen Tönen knallbunten Kompositionen und Porträts gegenüberstellt, die von der Grafik her kommen, so geht es ihm nicht um diese Differenz als solche. Der ungeheuren Zahl von Bildern auf der Welt entsprechen genauso viele Betrachtungs- und Wahrnehmungsmöglichkeiten und mindestens ebenso viele Weisen sie zu malen. Diese «Stilvielfalt» ist zu Sasnals eigenem Stil geworden, zum Markenzeichen seiner quicklebendigen Künstleridentität.

Deshalb ist mir Sasnals Bemerkung über seine hohe Empfänglichkeit für Bilder, auch wenn sie nicht überraschen mag, im Gedächtnis haften geblieben. Ich glaube, dass er damit nicht nur seine grosse Reaktionsbereitschaft auf die abrufbare Bilderfülle um sich herum gemeint hat, sondern auch den Akt des Bilder Machens selbst. In den letzten vier oder fünf Jahren hat er Hunderte und Aberhunderte von grossen und kleinen Bildern geschaffen. Obwohl er viele Zeichnungen macht (und manche seiner Bilder sehen auch so aus, als seien sie bewusst mehr gezeichnet als gemalt) und auch einige Super-8-Filme gedreht hat, konzentriert sich Sasnal hauptsächlich auf die Malerei mit Öl auf Leinwand. Als Student in Krakau

MEGHAN DAILEY ist Publizistin und Redaktorin, sie lebt in Brooklyn, New York.

PARKETT 70 2004

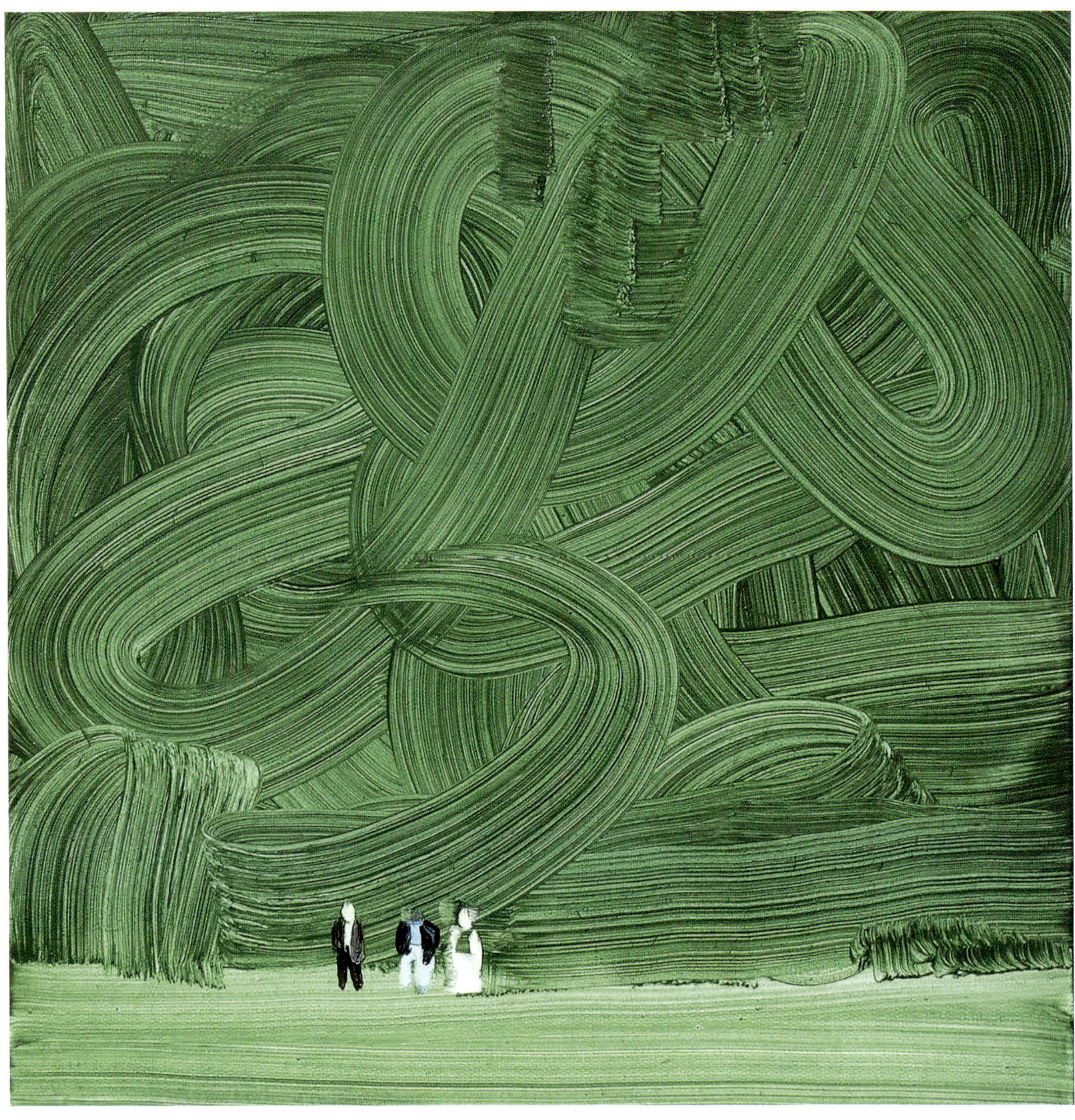

WILHELM SASNAL, UNTITLED (FOREST), 2003, oil on canvas, 17 $^{11}/_{16}$ x 17 $^{11}/_{16}$" / OHNE TITEL (WALD), Öl auf Leinwand, 45 x 45 cm.

malte er alles in seiner unmittelbaren Umgebung: Stereolab- und Sonic Youth-Plattencovers; Gegenstände im Haushalt wie Küchengeräte oder einen Küchenstuhl; Porträts seiner Freundin und ein Bild ihres gemeinsamen kleinen Schlafzimmers. Damals war Sasnal Mitglied der Ladnie Gruppe, einer losen Vereinigung von Krakauer Künstlern, die ebenfalls unspektakuläre Sujets aus dem Alltag malten. *Ladnie* ist das polnische Wort für «hübsch»; die sanfte Ironie der Arbeiten, die unter diesem Label ausgestellt wurden, war jedoch, dass sie durchaus nicht immer so hübsch waren (etwa die Aussenansichten öder Wohnblöcke und deren banale Innenausstattung). Sasnal verwendete auch Motive aus Werbung und Populärkultur, eine Art Neo-Pop, aber ohne die glitzernde Fülle der Popkultur. 2001 vollendete Sasnal *Everyday Life in Poland Between 1999 and 2001* (Alltagsleben in Polen zwischen 1999 und 2001), einen Bericht in Worten und Bildern über einen Zeitraum im Leben des Künstlers, der auch die Lebensbedingungen seiner Generation widerspiegelte, als ob Henri Lefebvre seine *Kritik des Alltagslebens* in der Form eines graphischen Romans geschrieben hätte.

Die hermetische, persönliche Seite von Sasnals Kunst zeigt ihn als Künstler, der jedem Impuls etwas zu malen nachgibt, als könne er gar nicht anders. Das ist nicht die romantische Idee des Künstlers, der von einer unsichtbaren Macht zur Kunst angetrieben wird, sondern das viel praktischere Bedürfnis, seinen Beitrag, seine Arbeit zu leisten. In ihrer Verwandtschaft mit der täglichen Arbeit erinnert Sasnals Kunst an einen anderen polnischen Künstler, Roman Opalka. Seit 1965 widmet sich Opalka der Aufgabe, jede Zahl von Eins bis Unendlich in endlosen Reihen mit Farbe auf Leinwand festzuhalten, wobei jede Leinwand gleich gross und vollständig mit Zahlen bedeckt ist. Begonnen während des Kalten Kriegs kann Opalkas lebenslängliches Projekt als Metapher für die individuelle isolierte Arbeit des Künstlers hinter dem Eisernen Vorhang verstanden werden. Allgemeiner betrachtet könnte man das Projekt als Versuch verstehen, Polen selbst eine feste Identität zu verleihen, einem Land, das als nebulös fliessende «Grauzone» innerhalb Europas beschrieben wurde (auch die Farbpalette des Künstlers ist auf Grau, Weiss und Schwarz beschränkt) und dessen kultureller und geographischer Ort, irgendwo zwischen Ost und West, unscharf definiert ist. Letztlich übersteigt jedoch Opalkas Projekt all diese Assoziationen; es handelt vom Leben, vom lebendigen wie vom sterbenden, und es ist eine Art Aufzeichnung des Selbst, sei es durch Zahlen, Plattencovers oder durch das Vorbeihuschen von Schatten im Gras.

Sasnal wird oft mit Gerhard Richter verglichen, meist aufgrund der ihnen gemeinsamen stilistischen Heterogenität und ihrer Verwendung der Photographie. Man könnte auch auf Ähnlichkeiten des jeweiligen Backgrounds verweisen. Sasnal wuchs in den 70er Jahren im kommunistischen Polen auf. Richter wurde in einer Diktatur volljährig, entfloh als Erwachsener einer weiteren Diktatur und entwickelte eine tiefe Skepsis gegenüber jeglicher Ideologie, egal ob politischer oder künstlerischer Art; die Malerei enthüllt keine Wahrheiten, sie kann nur Begierden stillen, und eine davon ist der Impuls zu malen. Die Hinterfragung der Authentizität von Bildern ist das Band, das Sasnal mit Richter verbindet; dies ist eine Stossrichtung, die seither von vielen Malern verfolgt wurde. Auch wenn es wenig Sinn macht, ihre Gemeinsamkeiten aufzulisten, oder aufzuzeigen, dass Sasnal irgendwie in Richters Fussstapfen tritt, so erscheint es doch bemerkenswert, dass sie die Geschichte – obwohl sie aus verschiedenen Ländern und Generationen stammen – mit ähnlichen Mitteln angehen und dass beide das Wesen der Erinnerung, der Darstellung und der Malerei zugleich befragen. Richter rang mit der faschistischen Vergangenheit Deutschlands in und nach dem Krieg, insbesondere mit der kollektiven Unfähigkeit diese jüngste Vergangenheit direkt anzusprechen, mittels versteckter Bezugnahmen, etwa in ONKEL RUDI (1965), das aufgrund eines Schnapp-schusses seines Onkels als SS-Mann entstand. Die unaussprechliche Tragweite des Holocaust machte jede unvermittelte Darstellung unmöglich. Und beinah vierzig Jahre nach Richters ersten Bildern ist dies noch immer so; auch in Polen blieben Fragen um Komplizenschaft und Opferrolle, um Schuldgefühle und Schuldzuweisungen unbeantwortet. Man weiss nicht recht, ob seither schon z u v i e l Zeit vergangen ist oder n o c h n i c h t g e n u g : «Ich habe laufend das Gefühl, dass wir nicht in der Generation nach 1989 leben, sondern in der nach 1945», meint Sasnal.[2]

Um die Stellung Polens während der deutschen Besetzung anzusprechen, wandte sich Sasnal Art Spiegelmans Reinterpretation des Holocaust zu, dem 1986 begonnenen Comic *Maus.* Aber statt Spiegelmans charakteristische Rollenverteilung (Juden als Mäuse, Nazis als Katzen, Polen als Schweine) zu übernehmen, bildete er nur den szenischen Hintergrund im Konzentrationslager ab, etwa das Innere einer Baracke, in groben Zügen und schwarzweiss wie in einem Comic. Noch grösser ist die Distanz zur ursprünglichen Vorlage in einer Grup-pe von drei Werken mit dem Titel FOREST (Wald): In FOREST (2002) ist die Natur als undefi-nierte, gestische Masse aus grünen Strichen wiedergegeben. Die Menschen sind lediglich et-was Winziges mittendrin. Ein anderes, FOREST (2003) zeigt eine Frau in einem lilafarbenen Kleid mit einer Masse schwarzen Haares, die Gesichtszüge sind beinah vollständig verdeckt durch einen fast opaken Farbschatten. Das dritte Bild (ebenfalls 2003) gleicht einem Grau-in-Grau-Rorschachtest, vielleicht das Bild eines Baums und seines Schattens. Scheinbar nur durch den Titel verbunden beruhen diese Arbeiten alle auf Szenen aus Claude Lanzmanns Dokumentarfilmepos *Shoah* (1985). Sasnals *forêt de symboles* (Baudelaire) besteht also aus In-terpretationen der in diesem Film vermittelten Impressionen der Erinnerungen anderer.

Sasnals Arbeit selbst hat oft filmische Qualität, aber diese zeigt sich am wenigsten dort, wo er direkt auf den Film Bezug nimmt wie in den drei FOREST-Bildern. Sie zeigt sich eher da-rin, wie er Licht und Schatten verwendet, oder im Anschein von etwas Unterbrochenem, den manche Bilder vermitteln, oder aber in seinen Porträts, die wirken wie in einem Moment narrativer Ungewissheit eingefangene Figuren. Diese Art von Sensibilität erinnert ein biss-chen an den deutschen Künstler Eberhard Havekost, dessen Werk bewusst Kameratechniken des Kinos aufnimmt, indem es ausgefallene Ansichten inszeniert, die man sonst nur im Film sieht: besondere Blickwinkel, Bildbeschneidungen, extreme Nahaufnahmen und so weiter. Sasnals wie Havekosts Werk steht im Dialog mit Film und Photographie sowie mit der Art und Weise, wie diese Medien nicht nur die Malerei, sondern auch unser Sehen beeinflusst haben. Das Filmische in Havekosts Werk scheint jedoch dem Actionfilm entnommen, während Sas-nals Gemälde eher an Bergman erinnern.

Beim Betrachten von Sasnals Bildern erhalten wir oft einen stenographischen, formalen oder symbolischen Hinweis und füllen die Lücken intuitiv mit dem Fehlenden aus wie bei Robert Mangolds unvollständigen geometrischen Figuren: So sind in einem Bild ohne Titel, das ein im Landen begriffenes Flugzeug zeigt (UNTITLED, 2002), nur lose Räder zu sehen; der Flugzeugkörper existiert nur in der Vorstellung, nicht auf dem Bild. Sasnals Bilder bewe-gen sich fliessend zwischen Abstraktion und Repräsentation, obwohl das Gezeigte meist eher symbolisch denn konkret ist. In einem der Bilder vernebelt eine weisse Farbfläche fast die ge-samte Bildkomposition und lässt nur wenige stärker strukturierte, sandfarbene Stellen an den Rändern erkennen. Dieser malerische Effekt erhält eine neue Bedeutung, sobald man den Titel, A-BOMB (Atombombe, 2002), damit in Verbindung bringt: Plötzlich wird das Weis-se zur giftigen, alles verschlingenden Wolke. An anderer Stelle wird die weisse Fläche, die etwas versteckt, mit anderer Wirkung eingesetzt: In BECK und BEASTIE BOYS (beide 2002) verschwinden die Protagonisten völlig hinter einem Rechteck inmitten der Bildfläche.

Wichtiger als alles andere ist aber letztlich Sasnals Auslotung der Grenzen und Möglichkeiten der Malerei. In seinen Händen wird das Medium zu einem effektiven Werkzeug, mit dem er untersucht, wie und was das Auge sieht. Viele Arbeiten objektivieren in erster Linie den Malprozess selbst mittels Veränderungen der Dichte und des Auftrags, wenn etwa das Pigment mit einem Lappen oder den Händen aufgetragen wird. Aber egal in welchem Mass das Bild als Objekt oder das Sujet des Bildes entschwindet und aufgelöst wird, die Konstante ist die Malerei selbst; sie ist es, die immer im Blick bleibt. Sogar wenn Sasnal eine Komposition aus einem anderen Medium entlehnt, sind seine Bilder stets Annäherungen an jene Bilder, auf die sie Bezug nehmen, wobei sie oft das Narrative oder Repräsentative ins Ideelle verlagern.

(Übersetzung: Suzanne Schmidt)

1) Wilhelm Sasnal im Gespräch mit Andrzej Przywara (poln./engl.), in *Night Day Night*, Ausstellungskatalog, Kunsthalle Zürich/Westfälischer Kunstverein, Münster (Ostfildern-Ruit: Hatje-Cantz, 2003), S. 38.
2) Ebenda, S. 39.

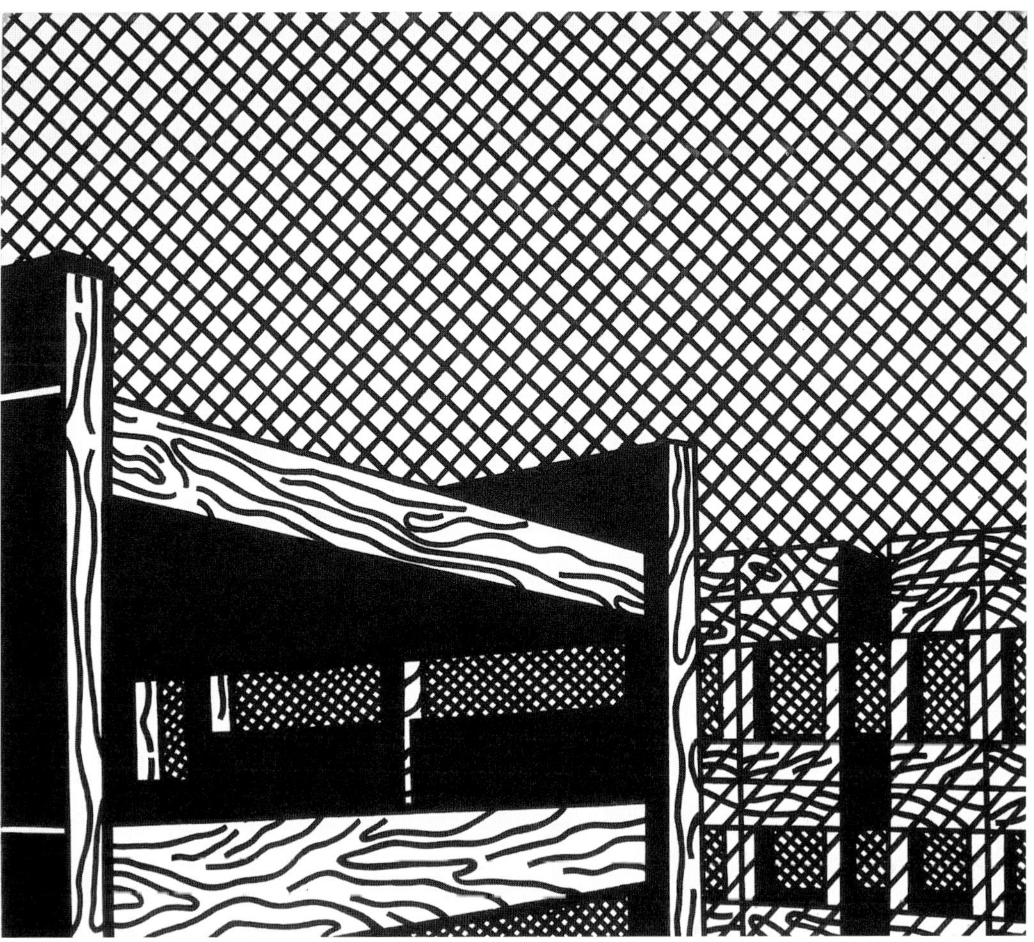

WILHELM SASNAL, UNTITLED (MAUS), 2001, oil on canvas, 45 ⁵/₁₆ x 5 ¹³/₁₆" / OHNE TITEL (MAUS), Öl auf Leinwand, 115 x 130 cm.

WILHELM SASNAL, E.B., 2003, oil on canvas, 21^5/$_8$ x 21^5/$_8$" / Öl auf Leinwand, 55 x 55 cm.

ADAM SZYMCZYK

S C H L A M M

Die frühen, vor 2000 entstandenen Bilder von Wilhelm Sasnal stellen oft einzelne Objekte dar: irgendein Lebensmittel, ein Werkzeug, ein Schallplattencover. Das Inventar der abgebildeten Sujets stammt aus der unmittelbaren Umgebung; manchmal haben diese Dinge einen Preis, dann gleichen die Bilder Werbeplakaten von Supermärkten. Aber auch Ereignisse sind solch vorgegebene Daten: die Katastrophe eines russischen Unterseeboots, ein Gipfeltreffen, die zufällige Begegnung mit einem Freund auf der Strasse. Die Aufzählung stellt eine gewisse Ordnung in der Welt her, bringt sie aber gleichzeitig auch durcheinander. Die Welt in diesen Bildern ist die eines zugleich aufmerksamen und zerstreuten Beobachters der sinnlich wahrnehmbaren Wirklichkeit, ist jedoch manchmal von Ironie, Untertreibungen, Lügen und Irrsinn durchzogen. Es ist eine flüchtig katalogisierte und in synthetischen Formen festgehaltene Welt, in Umrissen nachgezeichnet und benannt – sehr persönlich und eigenwillig, aber doch unter Verwendung eines allgemein verständlichen Vokabulars aus Medienzitaten, Songtexten und realen Elementen.

Die neueren Bilder sehen etwas anders aus. Anstelle der gegenständlichen Ansichten mit ihrer plakativen Kraft zeigen sie rätselhafte dicke Farbspritzer oder die Sicht verdeckende Wischer, undeutliche Stellen und weiss gehöhte Flächen. Das Konkrete hat an Bedeutung verloren, die Farben sind dunkler geworden, ehemals unverblümt raue Flächen haben nun einen fettigen Glanz und der Farbauftrag lässt Spuren breiter Pinsel oder eines Stofflappens erkennen. Diese Bilder wirken in ihrer ganzen Lebendigkeit und narzisstischen Selbstgenügsamkeit wesentlich weniger zurückhaltend, dennoch scheint dieser befreite malerische Gestus auf die schiere Diskreditierung jeglicher Form malerischen Ausdrucks ab-

zuzielen. Manche Bilder zeigen etwa eine «durchhängende, Falten werfende Leinwand» oder eine schlaffe, schlecht aufgespannte Leinwand; andere sind mit dramatischen Rissen übersät; wieder andere sind im Prinzip monochrome Bilder oder vielmehr ziemlich schlecht gemalte Kopien monochromer Leinwände in Schwarz oder Grau. Dabei wird ein ganzes Repertoire an Mitteln aufgeboten, um die ursprünglich wohl «ziemlich guten» Bilder zu «zerstören»: Porträts, bei denen die Gesichter ausgelöscht und durch «ausgeschnittene» weisse Rechtecke ersetzt sind; monochrome Bilder mit Fingerabdrücken darauf, wie wenn sich ein Blinder an ihnen entlang-

---

ADAM SZYMCZYK ist Leiter der Kunsthalle Basel und lebt in Basel.

getastet hätte; Leinwände, die aufgeschlitzt, durchgerieben, löchrig oder sonstwie beschädigt sind; Bilder, die Verfaulendes, Verschüttetes zeigen, organische Säfte, die versickern, oder aber das pockennarbige Antlitz Martin Luthers. Eine Seuche ist ausgebrochen und frisst die gemalte Welt von innen auf. In den drei Jahren, seit sie einem internationalen Publikum bekannt sind, haben Sasnals Bilder eine heftige Metamorphose durchgemacht, eine Art kontrollierte Schwindsucht. Die neueren Bilder sind insofern barocker als ihre Vorgänger, als sie von Würmern zerfressen und dem Verfall preisgegeben sind. Häufig stossen wir darin auf primitivere Lebensformen wie Pilze, Schimmelpilze, Algen. Das Parasitäre ist das Leitprinzip dieser Malerei, die sich am liebsten dort einnistet, wo das Leben einst üppig gedieh und voller Bedeutung war, heute jedoch abhanden gekommen, erstorben und erstarrt ist.

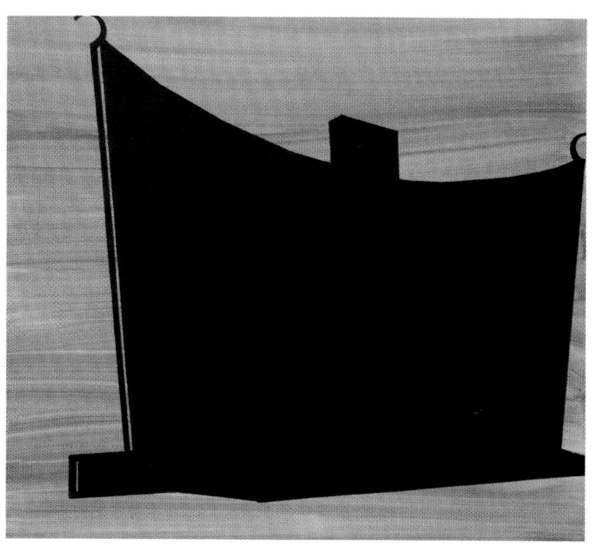

WILHELM SASNAL, UNTITLED, 2004, oil on canvas, 43 ⁵/₁₆ x 51 ³/₁₆" / OHNE TITEL, Öl auf Leinwand, 110 x 130 cm.

So ein Ort ist zum Beispiel die Kirche, und zwar aus vielerlei Gründen. Die auf den Kopf gestellten bläulichen Kuben polnischer modernistischer Kirchen, von denen die Farbe herunterläuft (etwa UNTITLED, 2001), wirken – wie die Darstellungen toter Tiere in anderen Bildern – blasphemisch, ja beinah elegisch. Auf einem drei Jahre später entstandenen Bild, UNTITLED (2004), erinnert die schwarze Fassade einer Kirche an den ausgebreiteten Mantel von Batman mit dunkelblauem Himmel im Hintergrund und fledermausartigen Krallen, die an den Ecken des gotischen Gebäudes vorspringen. Innen und aussen sind die Kirchen entvölkert, dafür voller Details von persönlicher Bedeutung: ein banales Bodengitter im Kirchenschiff, «in welches der Priester einst eine Hostie fallen liess»; ein düsterer, an eine mittelalterliche Festung erinnernder Beichtstuhl; eine schwarze Fensterrosette, die wie ein Visier oder Suchradar Gottes aussieht; Lampen in der Sakristei, die zu Insektenköpfen schrumpfen; ein krummer Blitzableiter, der über einer Landschaft mit sich dahinschlängelndem Fluss aufragt; ein Seiteneingang in der grauen Mauer wie die Schiessscharte eines verlassenen Bunkers. Die Kirche ist eine menschenleere Maschine, die militärisch wirkt und Entfremdung produziert. Zur Serie der Bilder mit Kirchendetails gehört auch das Porträt eines weissen Ziegenbocks vor einem grünen Hintergrund aus breiten Pinselstrichen. Das Teufelswesen ruht gelassen und würdig wie ein Lamm.

Zur Landkarte dieser Malerei gehören aber auch noch andere Orte: Museen und ihre Exponate, etwa die Seeminen und Maschinengewehre der Gedenkstätte auf der Westerplatte in Danzig, wo der Zweite Weltkrieg begann; Zoos, die mit ihrer künstlichen Felsenarchitektur dem Betrachter die überspannte Vision einer dem Menschen völlig untergeordneten Natur präsentieren; ausgestopfte Tiere, die als naturhistorische Ausstellungsstücke vergangenes Leben simulieren. Aber auch Schauplätze von Naturkatastrophen oder Kriegen, Ölpfützen, Lachen aus diversen sich vermischenden Flüssigkeiten: Rohöl aus einem Tanker, Flugbenzin, Salzwasser aus dem Toten Meer, Schweiss aus dem durchgeschwitzten T-Shirt nach einem Rockkonzert. Nahaufnahmen von menschlichen Haaren, menschlicher Haut und bild-

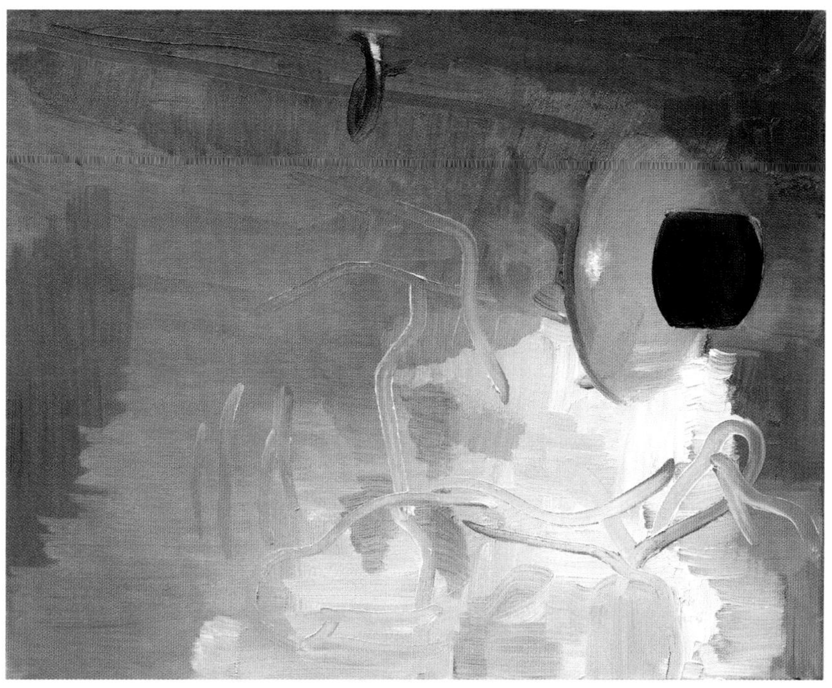

WILHELM SASNAL, SADDAM'S BASEMENT, MY BASEMENT, 2003, oil on canvas, 15 ³/₄ x 19 ¹¹/₁₆" / SADDAMS KELLER, MEIN KELLER, Öl auf Leinwand, 40 x 50 cm.

füllenden organischen Oberflächen, die völlig unlesbar und unpersönlich werden. Körper werden ebenso zu Handlungsschauplätzen, wie geographische Orte, Landschaften oder Gebäude. Gewöhnlich nimmt der Körper so viel Raum ein, dass er sich jeder Beschreibung entzieht: Die Person füllt das Bild aus, etwa in E. B. (2003) – die Sängerin Erykah Badu –, wo man nur eine riesige schwarze Wolke und daneben etwas Helleres sieht, vielleicht eine Afromähne und ein Hals. Zweifel stellen sich ein bezüglich der Überprüfbarkeit der Angaben, die ein Medienereignis ausmachen und schliesslich eine «historische Tatsache» schaffen, die uns gewöhnlich in Form einer Photographie, Fernsehaufzeichnung oder eines Diagramms erreicht. SADDAM'S BASEMENT, MY BASEMENT (2003) ist ein dunkles Loch, in dem man etwas erkennen kann, was die militärische Presseverlautbarung als Ventilator bezeichnet; das Bild zeigt aber eigentlich nur ein paar graue Flecken und einige verschmierte Linien. Gegenüber der Präzision des Titels wirkt die mangelhafte Genauigkeit und Glaubwürdigkeit des Bildes selbst schon fast komisch. Die

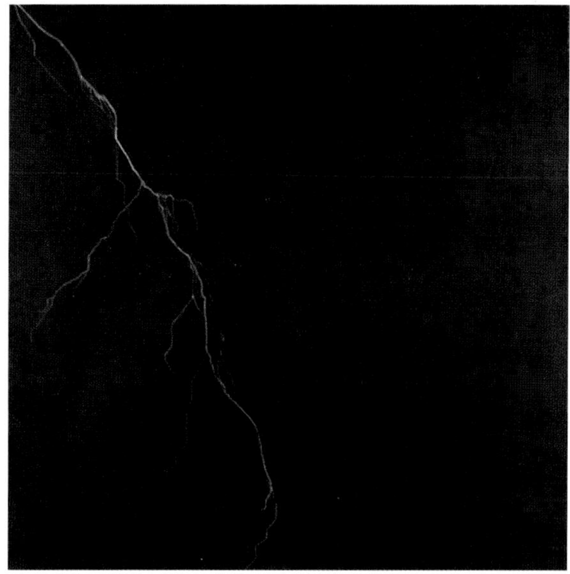

WILHELM SASNAL, UNTITLED, 2004, oil on canvas, 59 x 59" / OHNE TITEL, Öl auf Leinwand, 150 x 150 cm.

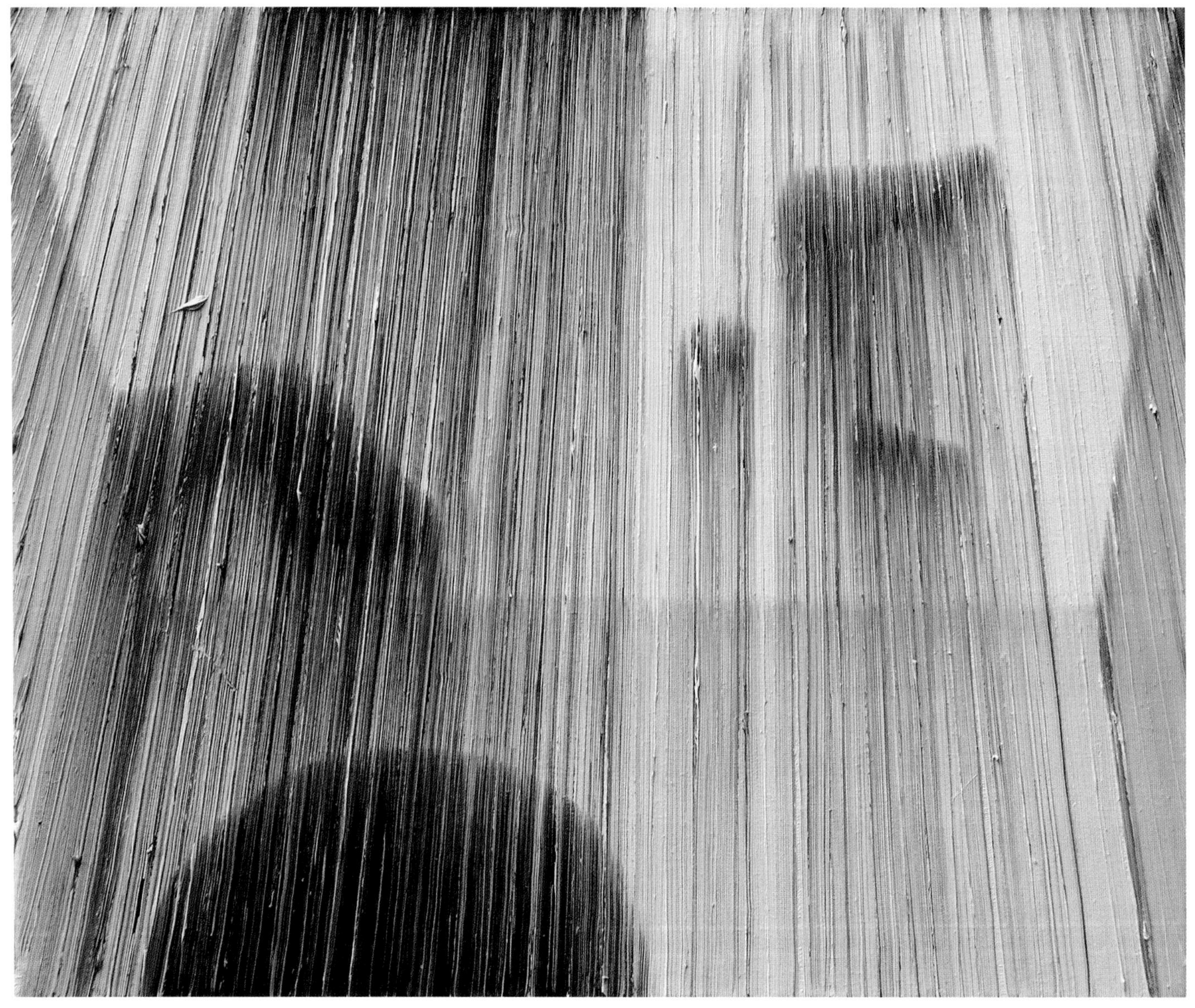

Repräsentation kommt ins Schlingern, entwischt und bleibt in der Farbe stecken.

Auch wenn die jüngsten Bilder stärker verschlüsselt und schwerer zu entziffern sind, haben sie vieles mit den früheren gemein. Nach wie vor ist da die Zuneigung zum isolierten Motiv: ein Gesicht, eine Gestalt, das Detail eines Raumes, ein Tier. Viele Bilder sind von der Photographie beeinflusst. Der Vordergrund ist über- oder unterbelichtet. Manchmal ist es, als wäre «zu wenig Licht» vorhanden, ein Vorwand für komplizierte Texturen, die nun zu einer Art Ersatzthema werden, nachdem das eigentliche Thema im Dunklen verschwunden ist. Es ist das Standardrepertoire der modernen Malerei – Motive von

Archivphotos, von Bildern aus dem Internet, Film-szenen. Das Archiv ist nicht nach irgendwelchen allgemeinen Regeln organisiert, es umfasst einfach Dinge, die dem Künstler aufgefallen sind. Manchmal hilft die Kenntnis der Quelle etwas zu verstehen, verhindert aber gleichzeitig jede andere Lesart: Liegt diesem Bild ein Schwarzweissphoto von Robert Smithson mit einem Bein über der Sessellehne zugrunde? Oder doch das Bild von Robert Downey Jr. in derselben Pose auf dem Titelblatt einer Zeitschrift aus dem letzten Jahr?

Neuere Bilder zeigen Gestalten, die sich mühsam vom Boden zu erheben versuchen, die auf allen Vieren kriechen, die zusammenbrechen oder ausruhen. Diese nicht sonderlich erfolgreichen Übungen entsprechen irgendwie dem Herumwühlen in der Farbe. Die Erde ist schlamm- oder staubbedeckt und die Farbschlieren, die Umriss und Körper einer Figur markieren, verschmelzen mit dem Hintergrund, den Schatten.

Ganz gleich, welches Motiv sie haben – Porträt, Landschaft, Innenansicht, Werkzeug oder abstrakte Darstellung –, die Bilder sind mit egozentrischer Intensität gemalt, von ganz nah und wie um zu zeigen, dass man bei aller technischen Fertigkeit etwas letztlich nie genau und wirklichkeitsgetreu erzählen kann. Wassertropfen am Badewannenrand und ein Donaustaudamm verdienen gleichermassen unsere Aufmerksamkeit. Das Porträt eines Freundes- oder Liebespaares (A. & E., 2004) verbirgt mehr, als es zeigt: Die Profile überlagern sich und die Münder sind verwischt. Ein Bild, dessen Titel aus Vor- und Nachnamen des Autors besteht, zeigt den schwarzen Umriss eines Kopfes vor dem Hintergrund eines Zimmers oder Gebäudes. Diese Malerei liefert nur wenig Information, obwohl sie im Grunde figurativ ist. Und in jüngster Zeit wird sie zunehmend apophatisch: Sie verbirgt ihre Obsessionen in Figuren der Abwesenheit, der Distanz, des Mangels und der Leere. Früher war sie transparent, zeigte profane Dinge, Konsum- und Kulturgüter, Personen des öffentlichen Lebens, Dinge, die allen vertraut waren. Nach und nach rückten diese vertrauten Dinge immer näher oder wichen zurück und gerieten aus dem Blickfeld, oder aber sie blockierten es völlig. Es ist kein Zufall, dass wir in den Bildern häufig Anspie-

lungen auf die Blindheit finden, etwa im Umriss eines Kopfes ohne Gesicht, bei dem anstelle des Auges das Fragment eines anderen, kleineren Gesichtes mit zwei Augen zu erkennen ist. Und es ist auch kein Zufall, dass die meisten neueren Bilder oft mit den Fingern vollendet wurden, als ob der Tastsinn das Sehen abgelöst hätte. Auf einem der Collage-Bilder aus der Serie *Polska* (Polnische Serie), die Photos aus einer Werbebroschüre und malerische Interventionen verbindet, ist das Gesicht eines Wissenschaftlers, der ein Präparat zur Untersuchung unter dem Mikroskop vorbereitet, schwarz übermalt: Es ist wie ein Hinweis darauf, dass derjenige, der die Dinge genau sehen will, einen Preis dafür bezahlen muss.

NARUTOWICZ (2003) ist vielleicht das komplexeste Beispiel aus der Serie *Spät beweinte Persönlichkeiten*. Gabriel Narutowicz, der erste Präsident der Republik Polen, war dank den Stimmen der Linken und verschiedener Minderheitsgruppen gewählt worden. Er war kaum eine Woche im Amt, als er am 16. Dezember 1922 bei einer Vernissage in der Warschauer Nationalgalerie Zach'ta von einem fanatischen Anhänger der Rechten (Volksnationale Union), dem Maler Eligiusz Niewiadomski, erschossen wurde. Der Saal, in dem der Präsident starb, wurde später nach ihm benannt. Der Maler wurde zum Tode verurteilt. Ein Porträt Narutowiczs achtzig Jahre später ist eine Geste und der Versuch, eine alte Rechnung zu begleichen, ein symbolisches Akzeptieren eines Teils der Schuld.

Es gibt aber auch Bezüge zu zeitlich näheren Begebenheiten, zum Beispiel in dem Bild, das die riesigen schwarzen Umrisse einer Skisprungschanze zeigt, die sich drohend über der grauen Landschaft von Kielce erhebt, ein indirekter Hinweis auf Adam Malysz – den polnischen Sporthelden der letzten Jahre. Das Nebeneinander dieser beiden Porträts, des politischen Mordopfers einerseits und des Sportidols andrerseits, könnte unangemessen erscheinen. Aber diese Malerei schert sich nicht um politische Korrektheit: Sie lebt von den Bildern, die diese Zeit und dieser Ort hervorbringen, und verändert sie nach ihren eigenen verworrenen und unbeständigen Regeln.

(Übersetzung aus dem Polnischen: Martin Zastrozny)

ADAM SZYMCZYK

S L U D G E

Wilhelm Sasnal's earlier paintings (done before 2000) often depict individual objects: an item of food, a tool, an album cover. The outside world provides material for an inventory of images; sometimes things have a price and the paintings resemble flyers announcing supermarket sales. Likewise, events are given dates: a Russian submarine disaster, a summit conference, a chance encounter with a friend. Enumeration introduces a degree of order into the world while disorganizing it at the same time. The world in these paintings is that of an attentive and absent-minded observer of sensory reality, with occasional strands of irony, understatement, falsehood, and

madness running through it. It is a world cursorily catalogued and recorded in synthetic forms, outlined and named—idiosyncratically yet with the use of commonplace vocabulary, quotes from the media, song lyrics, outtakes of reality.

Recent paintings are a little different. Obvious representations, poster-like in their forcefulness, have been replaced by enigmatic splashes of thick paint or view-obscuring smudges, blurs, and whitewash. The specific now matters less, colors have darkened, once rough and unambiguous surfaces have assumed a greasy sheen, traces of thick brushes or cloth are evident in the layers of paint. These paintings, with their vibrancy and narcissistic self-containment, seem much less restrained, and yet the goal of this liberation of painterly gesture appears to be the utter discreditation of the forms expression takes in painting. Some paintings depict "drooping, crumpled canvas," or sagging canvas nailed sloppily onto the stretcher; others are covered with theatrical cracks; others still are essentially monochromes, or rather imperfectly painted copies of monochrome canvases in black or gray. This end is achieved through a whole range of devices "spoiling" what were probably "perfectly good" paintings: portraits where the faces have been erased and replaced with "cutout" white rectangles; monochrome paintings with fingermarks on the canvas as if a blind person had been groping and feeling his way along a wall; paintings that have been slashed, worn through, pierced, or otherwise damaged; paintings showing things rotting, liquid spilling, organic substances oozing, or the pockmarked face of Martin Luther. Disease has broken out and is gnawing away at the painted world.

In the three years since they became known by the international public, Sasnal's paintings have undergone a convulsive metamorphosis, a controlled waning of sorts. Recent paintings are more Baroque than their predecessors in that they have become infested

---

ADAM SZYMCZYK is the director of the Kunsthalle Basel and lives in Basel, Switzerland.

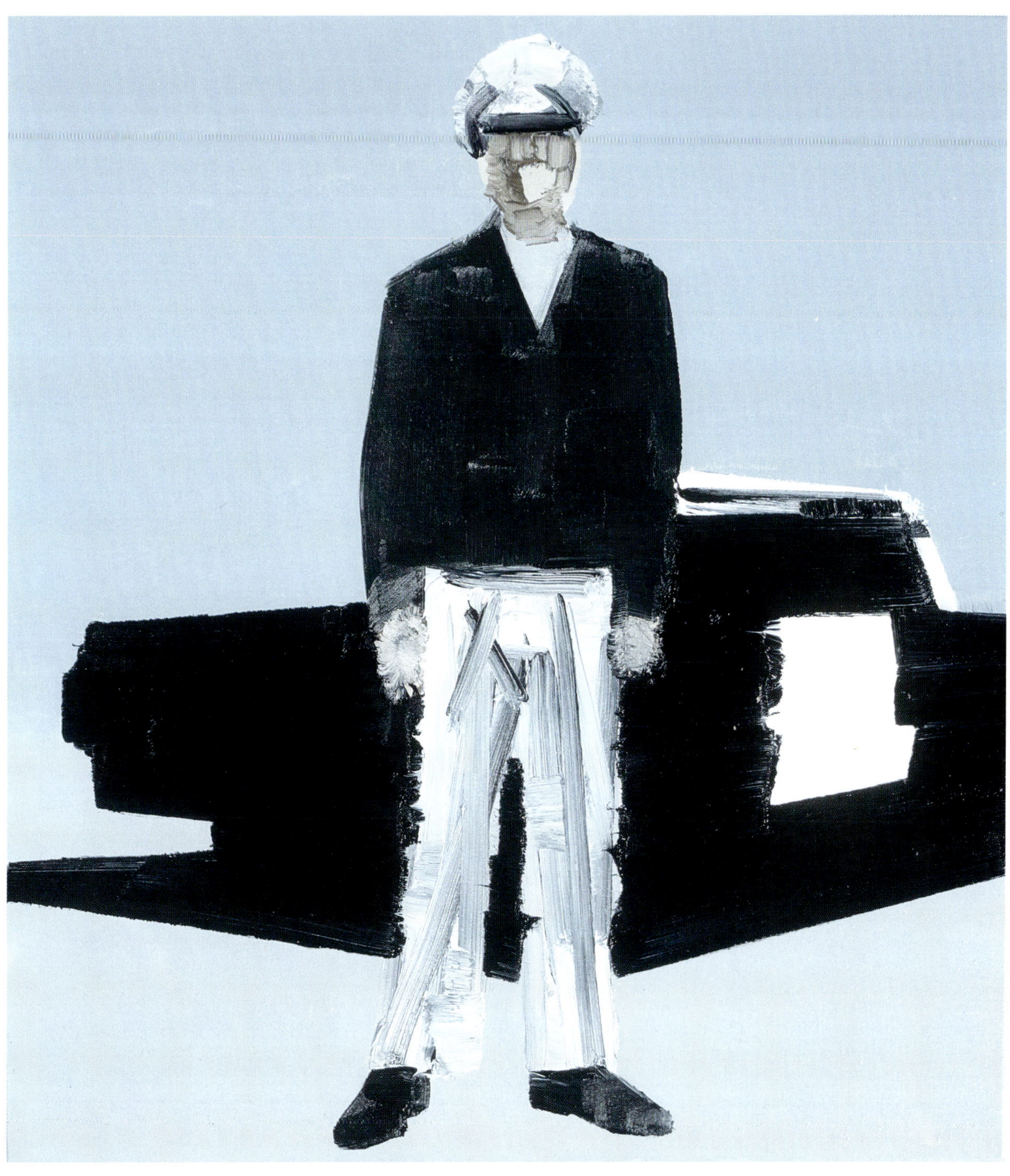

WILHELM SASNAL, UNTITLED, 2004, oil on canvas, 21 5/8 x 17 11/16" / OHNE TITEL, Öl auf Leinwand, 55 x 45 cm.

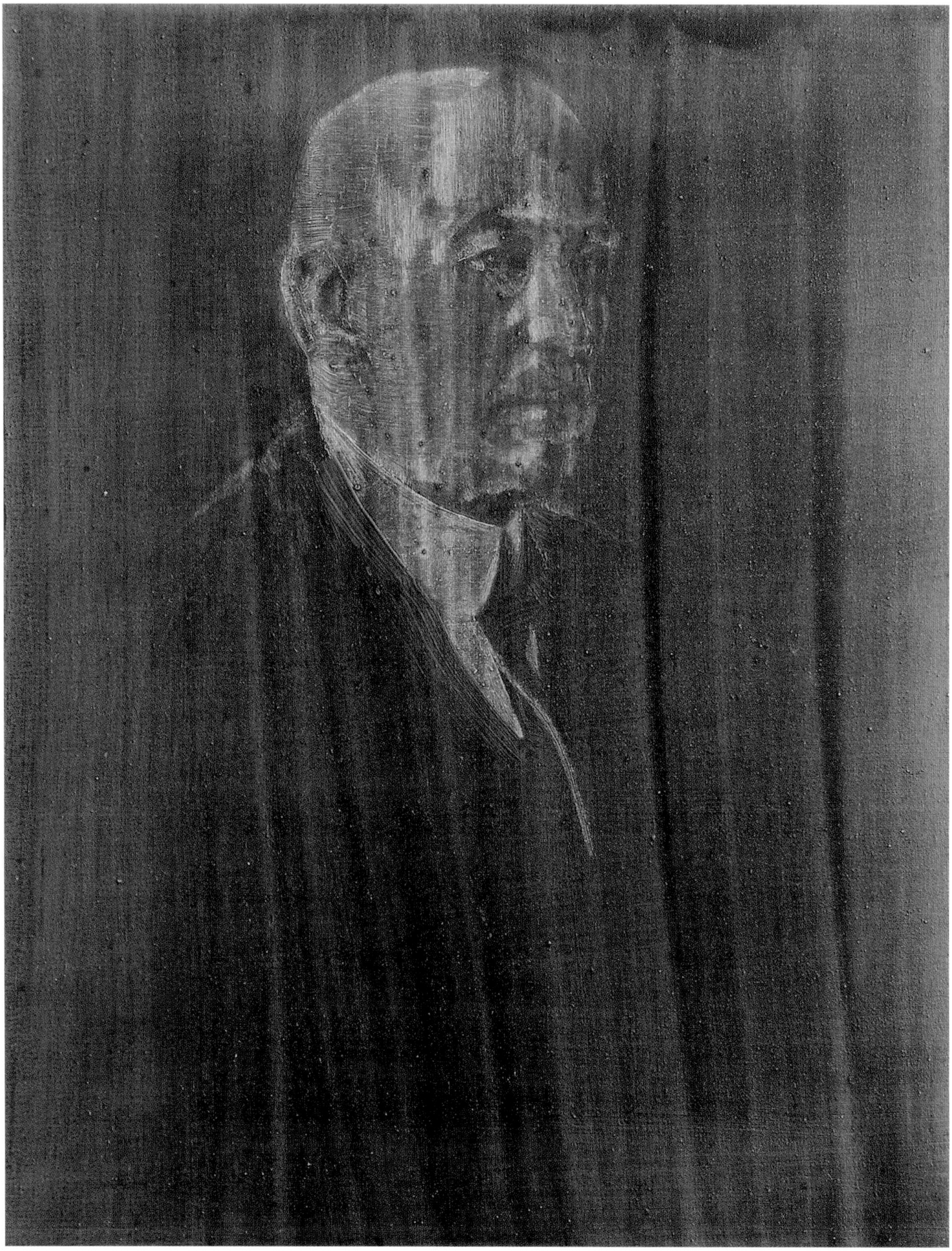

WILHELM SASNAL, NARUTOWICZ, 2003, oil on canvas, 19 $^{11}/_{16}$ x 15 $^{3}/_{4}$" / Öl auf Leinwand, 50 x 40 cm.

with worms, riddled with decay. Lower forms of life: fungi, mold, and algae appear surprisingly often here. A parasitic modus operandi is the guiding principle of this painting, which dwells on areas where life—once real, abundant, and full of meaning—has withdrawn, paused, come to a standstill.

Churches are one such place, and for many reasons. The upside-down bluish blocks of modernist Polish churches with paint running down their sides are, like the images of dead animals in other paintings, both blasphemous and nearly elegiac. In a painting done three years later the black facade of a church resembles a batcape spread out against the dark blue sky with bat-like claws protruding from the corners of the Gothic edifice. Church interiors and exteriors are barren, rife with details of a personal significance such as a banal grate in the floor of the aisle "into which the priest once dropped the Host," a dark confessional resembling a medieval fortress, a black rose-window looking like the sight of God's rifle or a radar screen, lamps in the sacristy morphing into insect heads, a twisted black lightning rod looming above a landscape with a meandering river, or the side entrance in a gray wall like the gunner's slit of an abandoned bunker. The church is a desolate machine of military aspect producing alienation. Another painting belonging to the series of church details is the portrait of a white billy goat on a background of broad green brushstrokes. The diabolical animal reclines with the poise and dignity of a lamb.

There are other places on the map of Sasnal's paintings: museums with exhibits such as the sea mines and machine guns at the Hall of Memory in Westerplatte where the first shots of World War II were fired, zoos with their make-believe stone architecture offering an exalted vision of Nature totally subject to Mankind, or stuffed animals at natural history exhibitions simulating bygone existence. Sites of natural disaster or war, oil slicks, puddles of spilt liquids flow into one another: it could be crude oil from a tanker, jet fuel, the salt water of the Dead Sea, or sweat drenching a mosher's T-shirt. Close-ups of human hair and skin, of organic surfaces, fill the canvas until it becomes illegible and impersonal. Bodies are the scene of the action to the same extent as geographical locations, landscapes, and architecture.

Usually the body takes up so much space that it defies description; the person fills the canvas entirely, as in E.B. (2003)—Erykah Badu—where all that is seen is an enormous black cloud with something lighter off to one side: an Afro and a nape? Doubts arise as to the verifiability of data which comprise a media event and ultimately create a "historical fact" which we usually absorb in the form of a photograph, a diagram, or television footage. SADDAM'S BASEMENT, MY BASEMENT (2003) is a dark pit in which we can identify what the military press release referred to as a ventilator, but the picture primarily depicts a patchwork of gray blots with a handful of smeared lines. Contrasted with its title, the image's lack of precision and credibility produces an almost comical effect. The representation slips, slides, and gets stuck in the paint.

Though more deeply coded and harder to decipher, the latest paintings have much in common with earlier ones. An affinity for the discrete motif: a face, a figure, a detail of an interior, an animal. Many paintings were inspired by photography: the foreground is over- or underexposed: it is often as if the painting "lacked light," and this provides an excuse to complicate the texture which acts as something of a surrogate subject now that the proper one has been obscured. This is the standard repertoire of contemporary painting—motifs taken from archival photographs, images found on the Internet, film stills. The archive is not organized according to any general principles; it contains various items that have caught the eye. Sometimes familiarity with the source aids in understanding while precluding other readings: was this image taken from a black-and-white photograph of Robert Smithson seated in a chair with his leg hanging over the armrest or from the cover of last year's magazine showing Robert Downey, Jr. in the same pose?

Recent paintings depict figures struggling to get to their feet, crawling around on all fours, collapsing, or resting. These not entirely successful exercises correspond in some way to sloshing around in paint. The ground is covered in mud or in dust, smears of paint delineating the outline and body of a figure blend in with the background and the shadows.

Whatever their subject—a portrait, a landscape, an interior, a device, or an abstraction—the works are all painted with an egoistic intensity, up close, showing that, technical prowess notwithstanding, little can be done to render something exactly and faithfully. Drops of water flowing down the edge of a tub and the river Danube are equally worthy of attention. A portrait of two friends or lovers (A.&E., 2004) conceals more than it exposes: the profiles overlap and the mouths are smudged. One painting, the title of which is the painter's name and surname, depicts a black outline against the background of what is either a room or a building. Precious little information can be gleaned from painting despite its essentially figurative nature. Recently its idiom has grown apophatic: concealing its obsessions in figures of absence, remoteness, deficit, and emptiness. Earlier it had been transparent, depicting mundane objects, consumer goods, the products of culture, public figures, things known to all. Gradually these familiar things came closer or receded, going beyond the field of vision or blocking it entirely. It is no coincidence that the paintings contain numerous references to blindness, as in the outline of a faceless head that has part of a smaller face with two eyes placed where its eye should be. Nor is it a coincidence that the finishing touches on the most recent paintings have been done with the fingers, as if touching had replaced looking. One of the collage paintings in the *Poland* series of painted over photographs from a promotional album is the face of a scientist preparing a specimen for viewing under a microscope, which has been painted black as if to indicate that there is a price to be paid in exchange for seeing things clearly.

NARUTOWICZ (2003) is perhaps the most complex image in the "late lamented figures" series. Gabriel Narutowicz was the first president of the Republic of Poland, and owed his election to left-wing and minority voters. His term in office lasted barely a week. On December 16, 1922, Narutowicz was shot dead at an opening in Zach'ta, Warsaw's national art gallery, by a right-wing fanatic, the painter Eligiusz Niewiadomski. The room in which the President was killed now bears his name. The painter was sentenced to death. A portrait of Narutowicz eighty

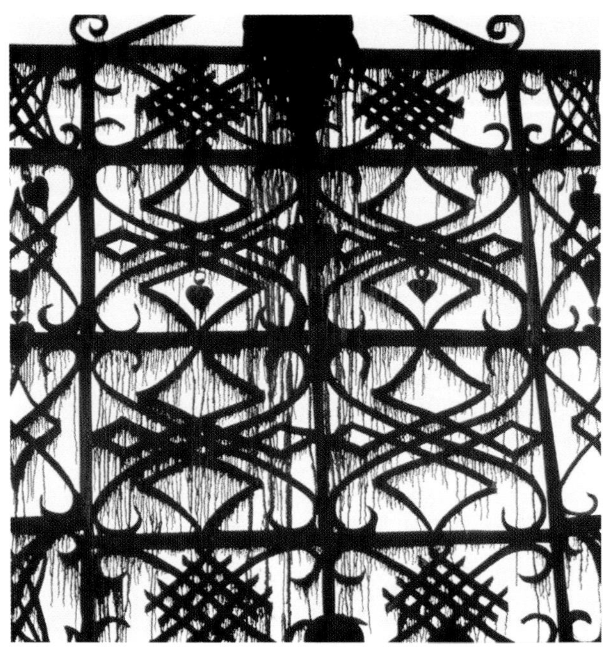

WILHELM SASNAL, UNTITLED (CHURCH), 2003,
oil on canvas, 59 x 59" /
OHNE TITEL (KIRCHE), Öl auf Leinwand, 150 x 150 cm.

years later is an attempt at settling the score, a symbolic acceptance of one's share of the blame.

There are also references to more contemporary events, as in the painting with the huge black bulk of the old ski jumping tower looming over the gray landscape of Kielce, which indirectly alludes to Adam Malysz—the Polish sports hero of the last few seasons. However inappropriate juxtaposing portraits of a victim of political assassination and a sports idol might seem, this painting cares little for political correctness. It feeds on images produced by this time and place, and modifies them according to its own baffling, ever-changing rules.

(Translation from the Polish: Artur Zapalowski)

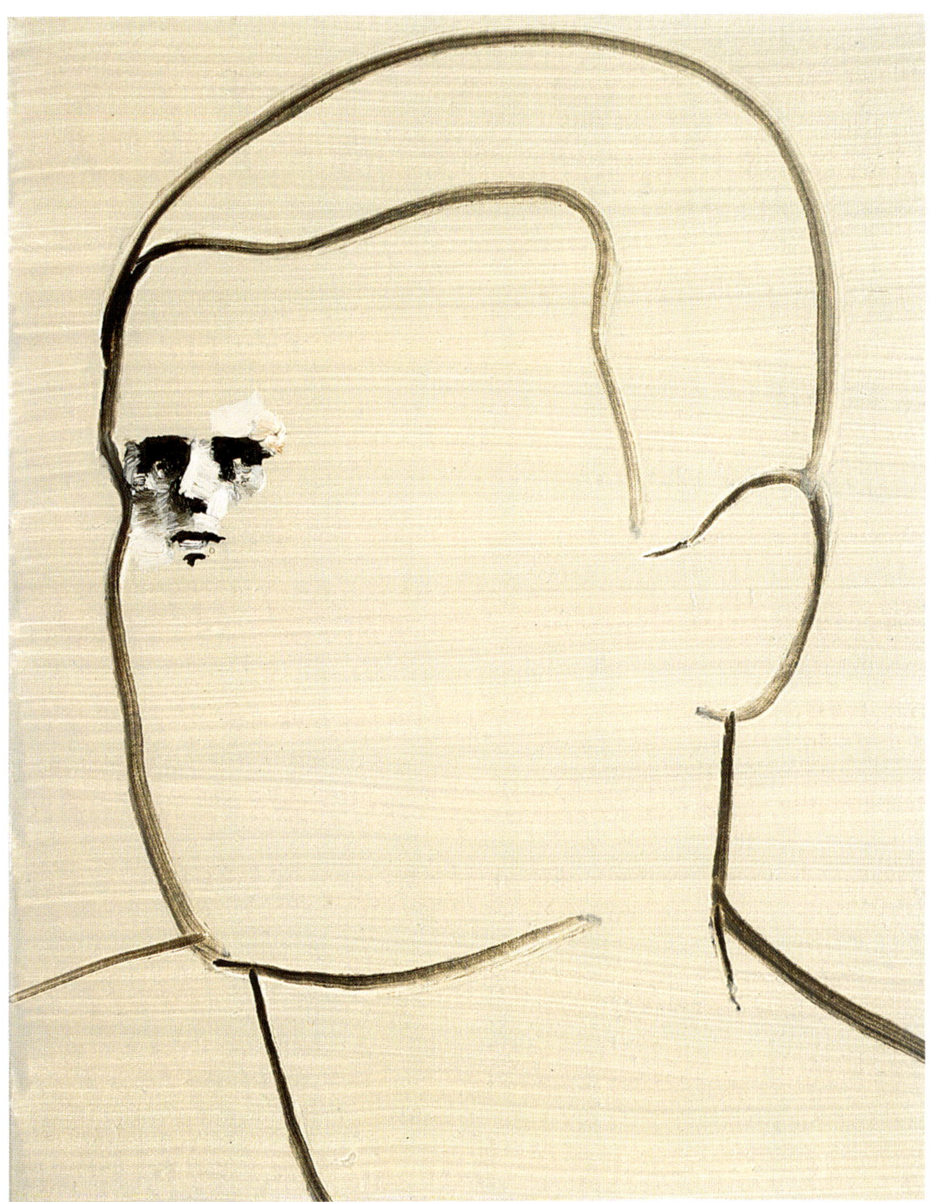

WILHELM SASNAL, UNTITLED, 2004, oil on canvas, 11 ¹³/₁₆ x 9 ⁷/₁₆" / OHNE TITEL, Öl auf Leinwand, 30 x 24 cm.

PETITE
SENSATION

GREGOR JANSEN

Der Tag, an dem die Farbe verblasste. Die Welt in klaren Kontrasten, gereinigt vom Schleier der künstlichen Konstruktion farblicher Reflexionsmuster, ein pures Wahr-Nehmen. Eine Gnade des Sehens oder eher ein Defekt, Achromatopsie, Farbenblindheit genannt, eine bestimmte Gehirnregion, den untersten Teil des Hinterhauptlappens betreffend? Eine Assoziation jedenfalls, die mir bei den Bildern Wilhelm Sasnals immer als erstes ins Bewusstsein kam – neben einer Neubetrachtung der Pop-Art. Hieran wurde mir bewusst, wie kurzfristig die Vorstellung wirkt, beziehen wir doch deduktiv immer den Umraum und Erinnerungen mit ein. Die Sinneseindrücke aus der visuellen Welt sind Andeutungen für unser Bewusstsein, wodurch wir auch eine verblassende Welt eine Zeit lang mit der erlernten Farberfahrung ergänzen.

Ein Flugzeug landet, doch wir sehen nur die Räder (UNTITLED, 2002), da ist der Rücksitz eines Autos (BACK SEAT, 2002), dann ein alter Silberpfeil (1939, 2002) oder ist es Batmans Batmobil aus der Vogelperspektive? Ein paar geometrische Formen und grüne Schlieren und wir entziffern eine Hängebrücke, ein grosser schwarzer Tuschefleck unter ein paar Strichen wird zum LKW und einer Landbegrenzung gegenüber dem Himmel, und wir erkennen Robert Smithsons ASPHALT RUNDOWN von 1969.

GREGOR JANSEN ist Dozent und Kunstwissenschaftler. Er lebt in Aachen.

Häuser, Autos, Jäger, Porträts; das Spiel liesse sich lange fortspinnen und auch die Erzählungen zu den zeichenhaft verkürzten Informationsrudimenten sind erstaunlich ausdehnbar. Woher stammt unser erkennendes Sehen als wieder erinnertes Wissen, woher die Bilder in unserem Kopf und wo werden diese gespeichert? Wie entsteht so etwas wie visuelle Kultur oder gar visuelle Intelligenz? Ist Kultur immer auch eine Frage der richtigen Bilder, ihrer Funktion und Identität? In den Gemälden von Wilhelm Sasnal eröffnet sich schlagartig und unvermittelt das Unverständnis der visuellen Kultur gegenüber einer Bilderhoheit, wie sie in geradezu aufdringlicher Partikularität und Popularität von den Massenmedien besetzt wird.

Sasnal arbeitet in einer einfachen, klar reduzierten und direkten Farben- und Formensprache.[1] In seinen Bildern ist beinahe alles gelöscht, was die unnatürliche Qualität einer «verblassenden Betrachtung» trüben könnte. Allein die wesentlichen Elemente wie Licht und Schatten, Konturen oder schematische Formen sind sichtbar, bestimmt durch wenige, einheitliche Farben, herausgelöste oder herangezoomte Details, letztlich mitunter ergänzt durch gestisch-expressive Schlieren, Kreisel, Tupfer, Craquelés, Farbläufe. «What you see is what it is!» Und das Etikett Neuer Realismus gegenüber diesem Reduktionismus ist beredt genug, um leichtfüssig von einer Faszination und Kritik an medialer Bild-

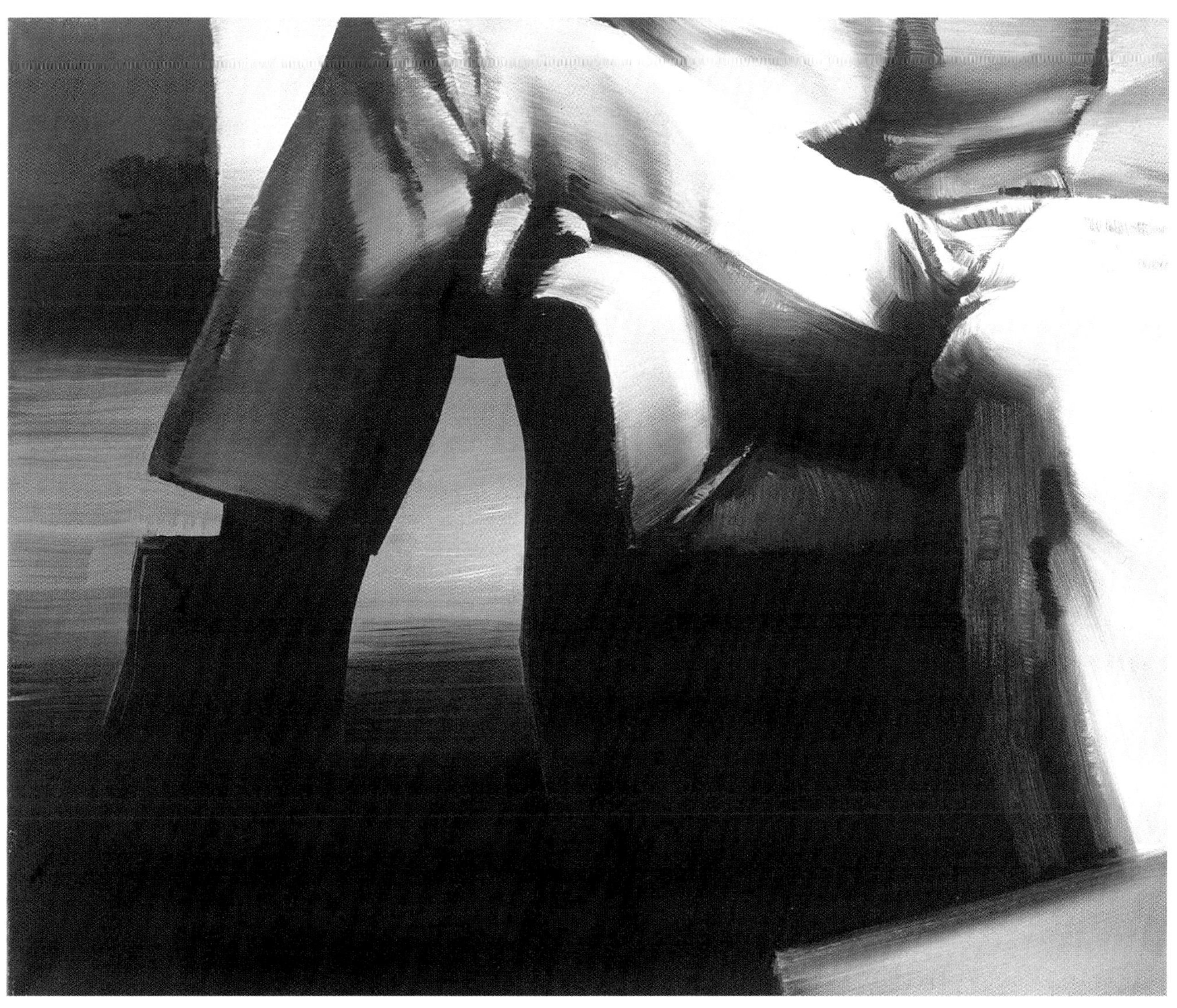

WILHELM SASNAL, R. SMITHSON, 2002, *oil on canvas, 21 $^5/_8$ x 25 $^5/_8$"/ Öl auf Leinwand, 55 x 65 cm.*
(PHOTO: C.&H. BASTIAN, BERLIN)

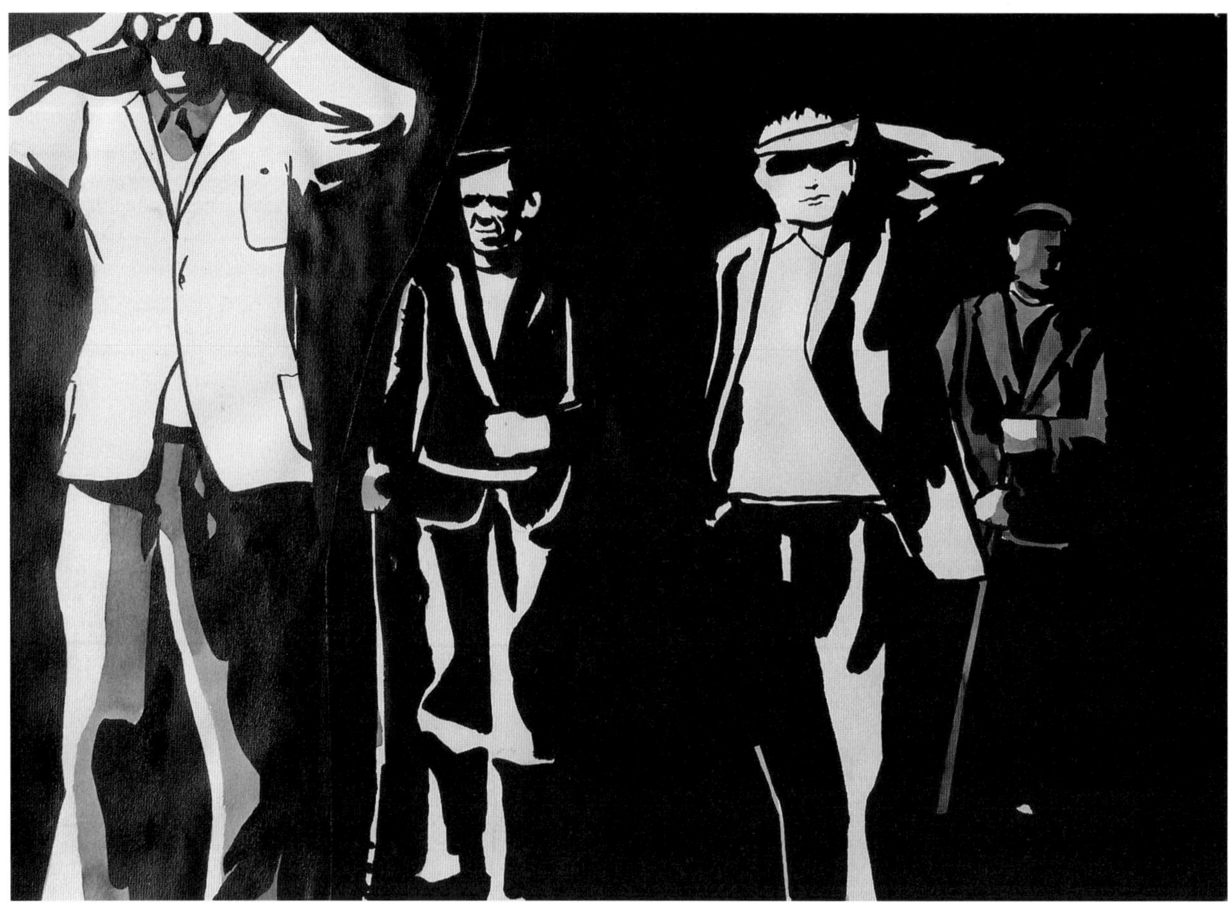

WILHELM SASNAL, 1939, 2003, ink on paper, 11 ^{11}/$_{16}$ x 16 ^{1}/$_{2}$" / Tusche auf Papier, 29,7 x 42 cm.

kultur auf die Begriffe Einbildungskraft und Ge-
meinschaftssinn zu kommen. Die bis auf wenige Ausnahmen zumeist kleinen, damit handlich und privat
wirkenden Gemälde und Zeichnungen Sasnals sind
von einer offensichtlichen, paradoxen Weltzuge-
wandtheit, in der bereits existierende Bilder einer
Neubetrachtung, Aneignung, Überprüfung und er-
neuten Egalisierung unterworfen werden. Die aus
Zeitungen, dem Fernsehen, Kino oder Plakaten, privaten Kontexten oder aus der Kunstgeschichte, Com-
puterspielen, Comics, Büchern stammenden Motive
sind alle gleichwertig, gleich interessant, aussagekräftig, bedeutungsvoll und relevant. Sasnal überführt sie ohne zu werten in ein Wechselverhältnis,
zeigt sie zugleich als banal, flüchtig, trivial, ober-

flächlich oder ordinär. Die unendliche, bunte Welt
der Bilder. Hierin zeigt sich die Ambiguität als welt-
umspannende *Lingua franca,* die uns zu stillen, stau-
nenden und abergläubischen Kulturteilhabern, aber
gleichzeitig auch zu sprachlosen und universalen,
nämlich identitätslosen Kulturbanausen macht.

Gleichwohl steht Sasnal in der Tradition des
Mediums Tafelbild, die er über den Verlust eines Re-
ferenzrahmens im Bild selber umgeht, was beinahe
der kubistischen Forderung Jacques Rivières zur
Abschaffung und Ersetzung von Beleuchtung und
Perspektive gleichkommt.[2] Zum anderen stellt sich
die vermutlich sogar hieraus resultierende Präsen-
tationsfrage, da bei Hängung vieler Bilder eine negative Überlagerung des Nicht-Referenziellen zum

Verlust der *petite sensation,* des kleinen Gefühls, führt. Andererseits wäre ein einziges Bild ebenso wenig aussagekräftig, fast verloren. Das eklektizistische Verfahren steht in einem positiven Verhältnis zur profanen Weltsicht eines jeden, weil der Maler die Dinge extrahiert, interpoliert und transformiert. Er überführt sie in ihr fragwürdiges Wesen als Entität. Dies ist so lange tragbar, wie etwas als erkennbares Motiv genug relativ konkreten Stoff oder Stofflichkeit bereithält, um auf die abstrakten Bilder anzuspielen.[3] Eine distanzierte Nahsicht im Sinn von Edward Hopper, eine kühle Sachlichkeit als eine *conditio humana,* die einen Rahmen als Träger, als Identität benötigt, den Sasnal sehr bewusst ignoriert. Denn hier ist Gemeinschaft und Einbildungskraft plötzlich Melancholie, Einsamkeit und Perspektivlosigkeit gewichen. Was den zweiten Kritikpunkt streift: die Verdrängung des Mehrwertes durch das Mehr an Bildern. Das Phänomen entsteht, wenn zu viele Gemälde nebeneinander hängen, und führt zum Verlust einer auratischen Identität, weil heute über die Einbildungskraft das Wissen um alle Identitäten die eigentliche Identität ersetzt hat.

«Was wir über unsere Gesellschaft, ja über die Welt, in der wir leben, wissen, wissen wir durch die Massenmedien.»[4] Der Glaube an sie ist unerschütterlich, obwohl wir auch wissen, «dass wir diesen Quellen nicht trauen können», betont Niklas Luhmann, was jedoch letztlich keine Rolle spielt, «da das den Massenmedien entnommene Wissen sich wie von selbst zu einem selbstverstärkenden Gefüge zusammenschliesst».[5] Beim Schock und der Katastrophe sind es zumeist schon die Ortsnamen, die metonymisch das Geschehen als Bild darstellen. Durch die Bilderflut von vermeintlich authentischen Abbildungen entsteht unbemerkt eine zweite Realität, die medial vermittelte Wirklichkeit als sich selbst verstärkendes Gefüge. Dieser Effekt ist irritierend, denn es geht nicht um ein sich auflösendes Geheimnis, wenn nur lange genug analysiert würde, sondern es handelt sich hierbei um die Eigenart von Medien *per se.* Die Magie der Dinge und ihrer von Apparaten oder von Hand gemachten Abbildungen, ihrer Darstellung als Repräsentation bildet sich also erst durch den Kosmos dieser technologischen oder individuellen Bildkultur entsprechend aus.

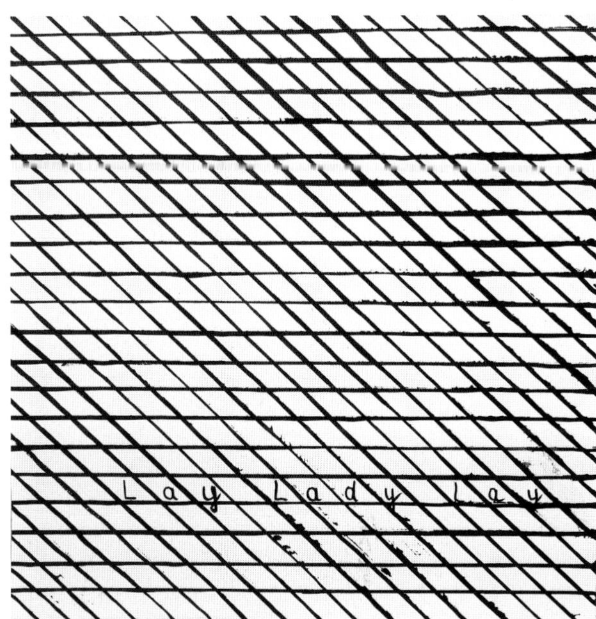

WILHELM SASNAL, UNTITLED, 2004, ink on paper, 11 ⁷/₁₆ x 11 ⁷/₁₆" / OHNE TITEL, Tusche auf Papier, 29 x 29 cm.

Unter Einbezug des rezeptionsästhetischen Kalküls einer mediatisierten Bildkultur zwischen ferner Katastrophe und naher Alltagsstimmung entflieht Wilhelm Sasnal auch der Langeweile.[6] Er beschreibt sein singuläres Problem, was letztlich auf ein allgemeines Phänomen verweist. Im Reflex einer medialen Kultur der Massen geht es ihm weniger um das zurückliegende Etwas, welches seinen Widerschein in der Realität des Bildes erfährt, sondern um die in der Ästhetik des Medialen fixierte Anwesenheit von Privatem, Banalem und Sensationellem als feste Grösse in einem individuellen und kollektiven Bildergedächtnis. Dieses wird nur ein wenig anders gelagert und somit neu verankert. Die Motive sind diesen Umstand reflektierende banale, skizzenartige, fast schematisierte und abstrahierte Umcodierer des «selbstverstärkenden Gefüges» populärer Kultur. Sie werden mit der Malerei anders sehenswürdig, ob-

Wilhelm Sasnal

WILHELM SASNAL, UNTITLED, 2003, oil on canvas, 51 ³/₁₆ x 59" / OHNE TITEL, Öl auf Leinwand, 130 x 150 cm.

wohl es eigentlich wenig Sehenswertes gibt. Unsichtbar neben den «ausgenüchterten Motiven» bildnerischer Handarbeit erwacht unsere Einbildungskraft. In einem auf Gerhard Richter rekurrierenden kritischen Kapitalistischen Realismus mit heterogenen Wirklichkeiten[7] – bei dem die Farben ebenfalls stark verblassten – entwirft auch Wilhelm Sasnal «einen Zugang zur Wirklichkeit, einen Realismus, der sich zugleich engagiert und kapituliert. [...Sein] Gesamtwerk entwirft eine ästhetische Parallelwelt, die sich in dem Widerspruch zwischen Verweis und Autonomie gegenüber der Alltagswirklichkeit ansiedelt.»[8] Es steht damit in einem «(von Sasnal aber nicht als Wahrheit formulierten) konstruktiven Konflikt mit einem Vollzug an Wirklichkeit in der Produktion von Bildern als kritische Praxis des Subjekts».[9] In der visuellen Entität erleben wir eine freie Eigengesetzlichkeit der Malerei. Wir erfahren in der seriellen Beweisführung aber auch etwas über die Umstände von Entitätsbildung und Realitätserfassung, obwohl doch eigentlich das technische Medium Photographie diese Funktion gesellschaftlicher Repräsentation von Wirklichkeit in der Malerei ausgelöscht hatte.

Die Ökonomie von Wilhelm Sasnal besteht darin, dass er den Betrachter an dieser ungelösten Ambivalenz und tragischen Sehnsucht nach naiver Erfassung des Unfassbaren permanent teilhaben lässt.[10] Eine Ambivalenz, die man wohl als die Basis von Sasnals Darstellung eines visuellen Befindens von Identität, oder eben als eine Art Defekt des Wahrnehmungsapparates bezeichnen kann. Seine Bilder sträuben sich trotz schneller «Lesbarkeit» gegen eine Deutung und sind dennoch geradezu von mentalitätsgeschichtlicher, subkultureller und oppositioneller Tragweite. Nicht nur wenn es um seine nationale Identität, Musikideologie oder um den Holocaust geht. Gerade in der Auseinandersetzung mit der Rolle Polens im Holocaust wirken die brutalen Symbolbezüge, in pop-ästhetische Abstraktionen überführt, dem Vorwurf der Unangemessenheit des Mediums Comic und der leichtfertig-naiven Brechungen von Art Spiegelman entgegen.[11] Mithilfe der Malerei eignet sich Sasnal visuelle Kultur an und holt sie damit aus dem mediatisierten Weltverständnis. Wir sehen die erfasste Teiltotalität einer nur noch scheinmenhaft erkennbaren, zersplitterten Netzhaut-Wirklichkeit. Die auf Cézanne zurückgehende *petite sensation* erfährt bei Wilhelm Sasnal durch die rahmenlose, gelöste Referenz einen Identitätsverlust, der für unsere Gesellschaft konstitutiv ist. Wir können die gemalten Motive nur über die mediale Reproduktion eines In- und Von-dieser-Welt-Seins sehen, wahrnehmen und verstehen. Die kleine Sensation, die sanfte Stimmung ist wie so vieles im Zusammenspiel von Kunst und Leben letztlich eine Frage der Dosierung.

1) Ein Nominalismus, dem ich wieder das Pikturale als Konzept vorstellen würde. Vgl. Thierry de Duve, *Pikturaler Nominalismus. Marcel Duchamp. Die Malerei und die Moderne*, Schreiber, München 1987, und: Ulrich Loock, «Sasnals Nominalismus» (dt. u. engl.), in *Wilhelm Sasnal. Night Day Night*, Ausstellungskatalog, Kunsthalle Zürich/Westfälischer Kunstverein Münster, Hatje-Cantz, Ostfildern-Ruit 2003, S. 97–108.

2) Jacques Rivière, «Gegenwärtige Strömungen in der Malerei» (1912), in: Edward Fry, *Der Kubismus,* DuMont, Köln 1966, S.82–87. Aber auch Gerhard Richter ist zu nennen (vgl. Anm. 7).

3) Oder den realen Stoff, bei dem Sasnal die Schweissränder seines T-Shirts nach einem Rockkonzert malte (aber auch das Shirt wurde auf Keilrahmen aufgezogen). Letztlich sehen wir dann in (bei)den (kristallinen) Weisshöhungen des Schweisses nur noch diese Geschichte – mithin eigene Erinnerungen an verklärte Momente ikonenhafter Musikverehrung, obwohl die Farben – synonym für Erinnerungen – verblassen.

4) Dieser Satz leitet die lesenswerte Studie *Die Realität der Massenmedien* von Niklas Luhmann ein. (Westdt. Verlag, Opladen 1996, S. 9.)

5) Ebenda.

6) Vgl. das Interview mit dem Künstler von Andrzej Przywara, in *Wilhelm Sasnal. Night Day Night,* op. cit. (Anm. 1), S. 33–40 (poln. u. engl.). Wilhelm Sasnal: «[...] I am scared of repeating myself, of defining. Whenever I go anywhere, I always try to return by another route. It's fear of boredom.» AP: «And is life in Tarnow boring?» WS: «Not if you're painting.»

7) Sehr erhellend sind die Notizen (und Bilder) von Gerhard Richter von 1964–1965, in: ders., *Text: Schriften und Interviews,* Insel-Verlag, Frankfurt am Main 1994, S. 25–33.

8) Carina Plath, «Moscice», in *Wilhelm Sasnal. Night Day Night,* op. cit. (Anm. 1), S. 9–16, hier: 16.

9) Beatrix Ruf, «Dokumente der Beunruhigung», in *Wilhelm Sasnal. Night Day Night,* op. cit. (Anm. 1), S. 17–23, hier: 18.

10) Vgl. Svetlana Alpers, «Interpretation ohne Darstellung – oder: Das Sehen von Las Meniñas, in: Wolfgang Kemp (Hrsg.), *Der Betrachter ist im Bild. Kunstwissenschaft und Rezeptionsästhetik,* DuMont, Köln 1985, S. 91–109, besonders: 103.

11) Völlig anders als z. B. bei Luc Tuymans, der das gemalte Bild auratisch erhöht. Vgl. auch Sasnals Interesse an der polnischen Kultur, insbesondere am Film der 60er Jahre. Ebenda, S. 20–23.

PETITE
SENSATION

GREGOR JANSEN

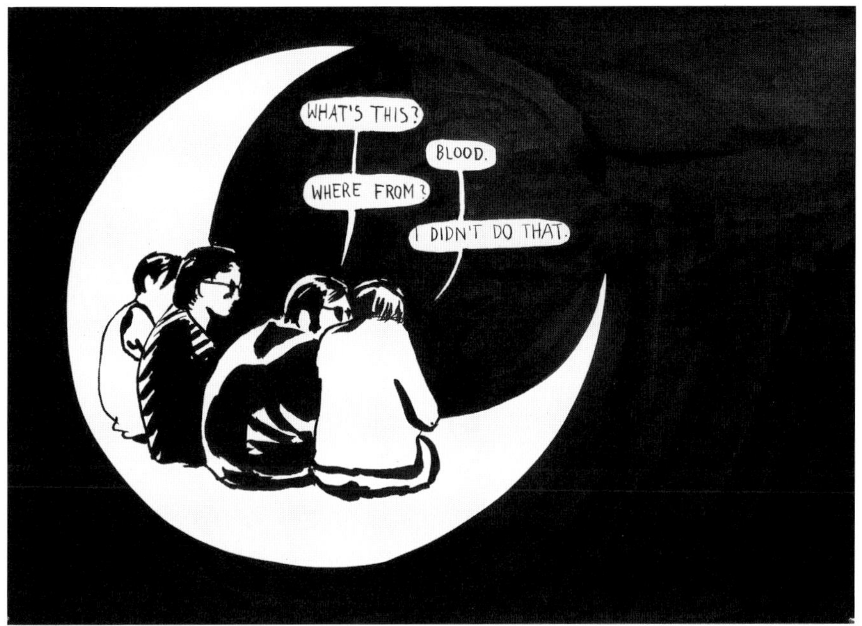

WILHELM SASNAL, UNTITLED, 2004, ink on paper, 8¹/₄ x 11 ¹¹/₁₆" / OHNE TITEL, Tusche auf Papier, 21 x 29,7 cm.

The day that color faded. A world clearly contrasted; the artificial construction of colored patterns of reflection, a haze that has been cleared away; seeing through pure per-ception. Is it the grace of seeing or rather a defect, achromatopsia, as color blindness is called, concerning a specific region of the brain, the dominant inferior occipital lobe? In any case, it's the first association that always occurs to me when I look at Wilhelm Sasnal's paintings—in addition to a visual renegotiation of Pop Art. It made me realize how short-term is the effect of the imagination, for we always deductively incorporate context and memories. Sensual impressions from the visual world are intimations for our consciousness, through which we also complement a fading world, for a while, with learned color experience.

An airplane lands, but we only see the wheels (UN-TITLED, 2002), there's the back seat of a car (BACK SEAT, 2002), then an old Silver Arrow (1939, 2002)—

GREGOR JANSEN is a lecturer and art historian, based in Aachen.

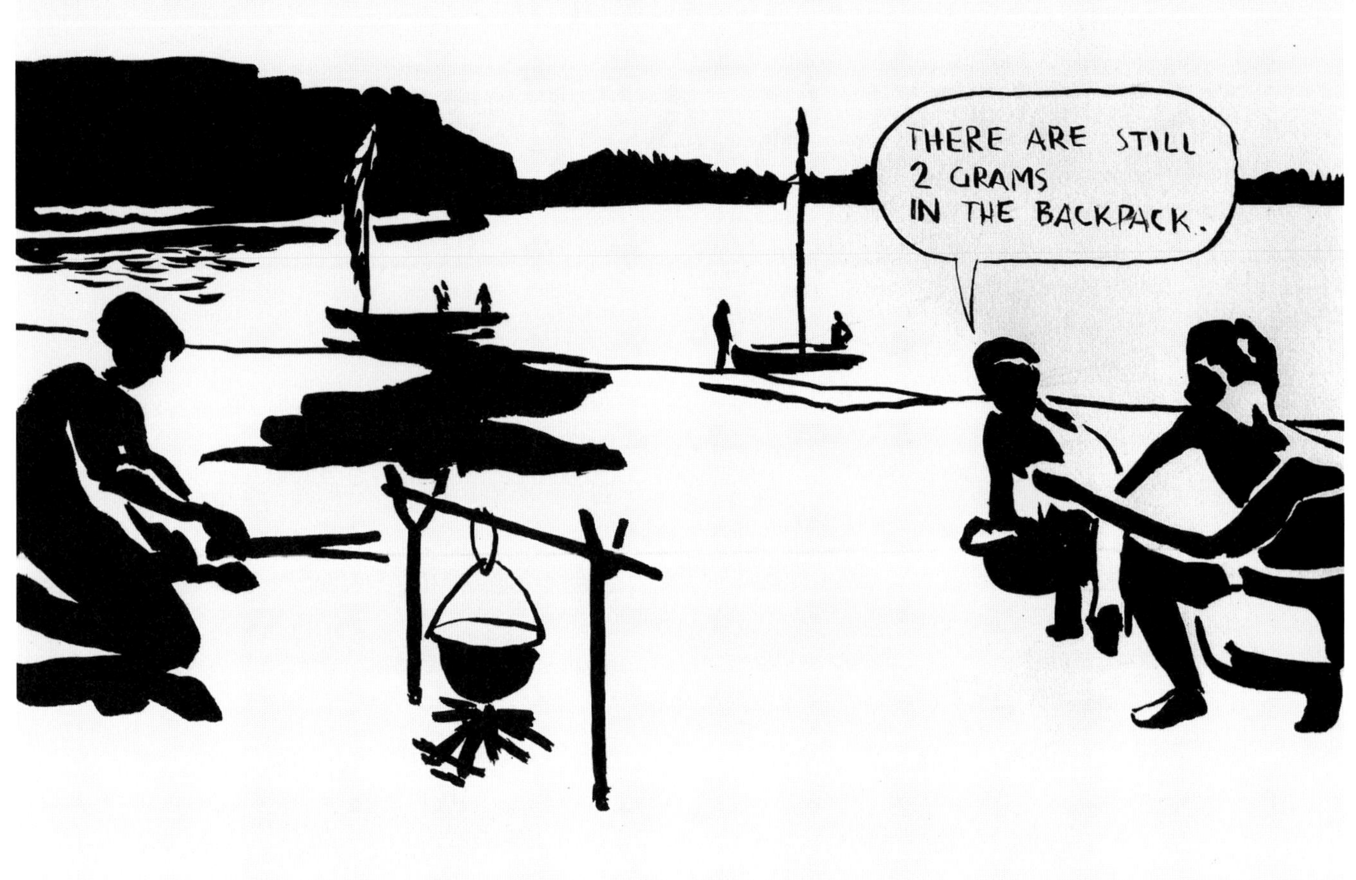

WILHELM SASNAL, UNTITLED, 2004, ink on paper, 8 ¹/₄ x 11 ¹¹/₁₆" / OHNE TITEL, Tusche auf Papier, 21 x 29,7 cm.

or is it a bird's-eye view of Batman's Batmobile? A few geometric shapes and green streaks and we decipher a suspension bridge, a big black splotch of ink under a few lines that make a truck on land delimited against the sky and we recognize Robert Smithson's ASPHALT RUNDOWN of 1969, buildings, cars, hunters, portraits; we can spin out the game endlessly, where narratives for the emblematically abbreviated rudiments of information lend themselves to astonishing elaboration. Where does it come from, the re-remembered knowledge of our cognitive vision, where do the pictures in our heads come from and where are they stored? How does something like a visual culture or even visual intelligence evolve? Is culture also a question of the right pictures, an inquiry into their function and identity? In Wilhelm Sasnal's paintings, we are instantly confronted head-on with visual culture's inability to understand the supremacy of pictures, as appropriated with positively intrusive particularity and popularity by the mass media.

Sasnal works with a simple, clearly reduced, and direct language of colors and shapes.[1] He eliminates just about everything in his pictures that might trouble the unnatural quality of "fading observation." Only essential elements like light and shadow, contours or stylized shapes are visible, defined by a few uniform colors, isolated or zoomed-in details, and complemented only with gesturally expressive streaks, circles, dots, craquelé, or dripping paint. "What you see is what it is!" And the label of New Realism in view of this reductionism is sufficiently eloquent to facilitate the light-footed transition from a fascination with and critique of medial visual culture to the concepts of imagination and social consciousness. Sasnal's paintings and drawings are, with few exceptions, small, handy, and seemingly intimate, yet characterized by an obvious, paradoxical worldliness, in which existing images are subjected to renegotiation, appropriation, examination and renewed leveling. Motifs taken from newspapers, television, movies, posters, and personal contexts, from art history, computer games, comics, and books are all equivalent, all equally interesting, expressive, significant, and relevant. Consistently nonjudgmental, Sasnal subjects them to changing situations, shows

them as being simultaneously banal, ephemeral, trivial, superficial, or vulgar. The infinitely colorful world of pictures. The works demonstrate the ambiguity of a global lingua franca that reduces us to mute, awed, superstitious participants in culture as well as speechless and universal cultural philistines, who therefore have no identity.

Even so, Sasnal works within the medium of the traditional painting, but circumvents it by eliminating the referential framework in the pictures themselves. This, in turn, is essentially tantamount to Jacques Rivière's Cubist call to repeal and replace lighting and perspective.[2] On the other hand, and presumably as a direct consequence of that elimination, the works raise the question of presentation, since a negative layer of nonreferentiality is superimposed on many of the pictures when they are hung, which leads to the loss of the *petite sensation*. But one picture in isolation would probably say just as little and would be almost lost. The eclectic procedure relates positively to a commonly held profane worldview be-

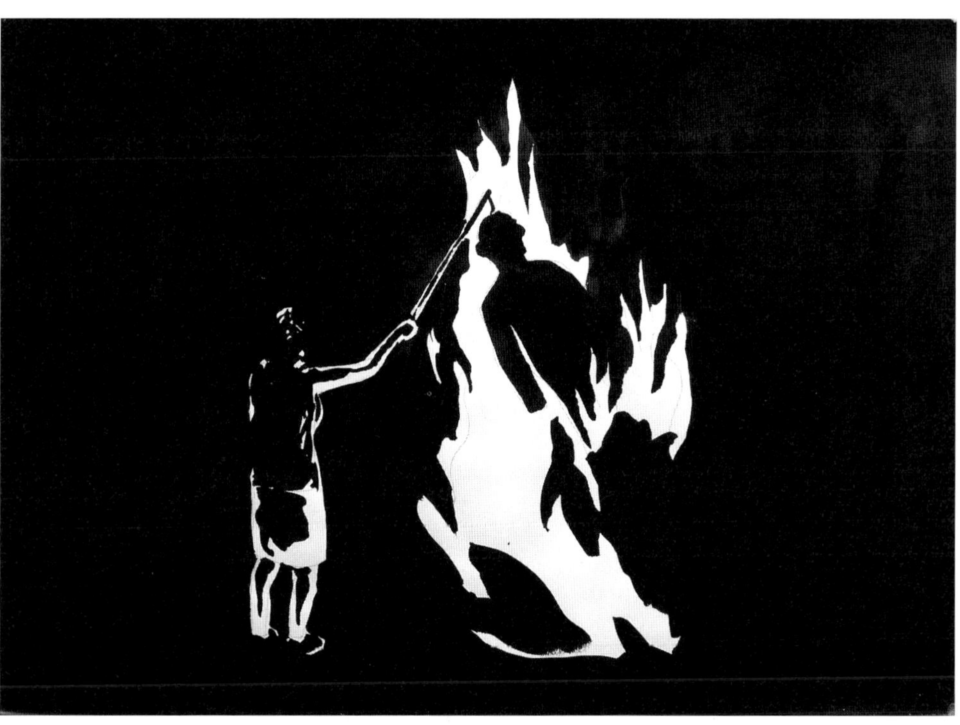

WILHELM SASNAL, UNTITLED, 2004, ink on paper, 11 ¹¹/₁₆ x 16 ¹/₂″ / OHNE TITEL, Tusche auf Papier, 29,7 x 42 cm.

cause the painter extracts, interpolates, and transforms his subject matter. He processes the debatable essence of his works as entities. This is viable as long as a recognizable motif offers enough relatively concrete material or materiality to allude to the abstract pictures:[3] a detached close-up, reminiscent of the moods conveyed by Edward Hopper, cool and matter-of-fact, a reflection on the human condition that requires a framework as a vehicle, an identity quite consciously ignored by Sasnal. For, in his case, the sense of community and the power of the imagination suddenly give way to melancholy, loneliness, and a lack of perspective. Which touches on the second critical point: the displacement of added value through the additive accumulation of pictures, a phenomenon that arises when too many paintings are hung next to each other. The result is the loss of an auratic identity because today, through the power of the imagination, a knowledge of all identities has replaced identity itself.

"Whatever we know about our society, or indeed about the world in which we live, we know through the mass media."[4] Our belief in them is unshakable although we are aware, as Niklas Luhmann emphasizes, "that we are not able to trust these sources. ... yet no consequences of any import ensue because knowledge acquired from the mass media merges together as if of its own accord into a self-reinforcing structure."[5] After the shock of a catastrophe, place names alone usually suffice to picture the event in metonymical representation. The flood of supposedly authentic images produces a second, unnoticed reality, a medially transmitted reality as a self-reinforcing structure. This effect is disturbing because the mystery—being intrinsic to the medium itself—cannot be resolved no matter how long we analyze it. The magic of things and their mechanical or manual reproduction, their representation, take suitable shape only through the cosmos of this technological or individual visual culture.

By deliberately incorporating the received aesthetics of a mediatized visual culture between distant catastrophe and the close-up of quotidian moods, Wilhelm Sasnal also escapes boredom.[6] He describes a singular problem that embraces a universal phenomenon. His study of a media culture of the masses does not focus on something left behind that comes to life again in the reality of the picture but rather on the presence of things personal, banal, and sensational, anchored in an aesthetics of the media as a given entity of individual and collective pictorial memory. Sasnal simply lifts the anchor, shifts it slightly, and drops it again. The motifs contemplate these concerns as banal, sketchy, and almost diagrammatically abstract recodifications of the "self-reinforcing structure" (Luhmann) of popular culture. The paintings make them worth seeing even though there's not actually very much that is worthy of being seen. Our imagination awakes imperceptibly next to the "sobered-up motifs" of artistic manual labor. Within the framework of a critical Capitalist Realism with heterogeneous realities that recurs to Gerhard Richter[7] (whose colors, incidentally, also faded substantially), Wilhelm Sasnal also "delineates an approach to reality, a realism, which at once engages and capitulates. ... [His] oeuvre delineates an aesthetic parallel universe, which situates itself in the contradiction between reference and autonomy vis-à-vis the reality of everyday life."[8] It is thus "placed in a conflict that is perhaps constructive (though Sasnal does not formulate it as a truth) with an implementation of reality in the production of images as a critical practice of the subject."[9] The visual entity gives us the experience of free, autonomous painting. But the serial evidence also tells us something about the circumstances that lead to the formation of entities and the grasp of reality, despite the fact that the technical medium of photography has essentially undercut painting's function of representing social reality.

Wilhelm Sasnal's economy lies in the fact that he consistently allows his viewers to share in this unresolved ambivalence and the tragic, naive longing to grasp the ungraspable.[10] An ambivalence that might be described as the basis of Sasnal's visual stock-taking of identity or, to repeat, as a kind of defect of the faculty of perception. Despite their easy "legibility," his pictures resist interpretation while still being of great significance in terms of historical mentality, subculture and opposition—and not only when his national identity, music ideology, or the Holocaust are involved. In fact, specifically in addressing the role of Poland in the Holocaust, the artist's brutal

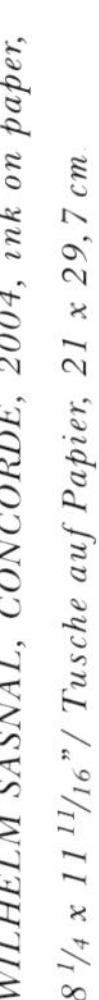

WILHELM SASNAL, CONCORDE, 2004, ink on paper, 8 1/4 x 11 11/16" / Tusche auf Papier, 21 x 29,7 cm

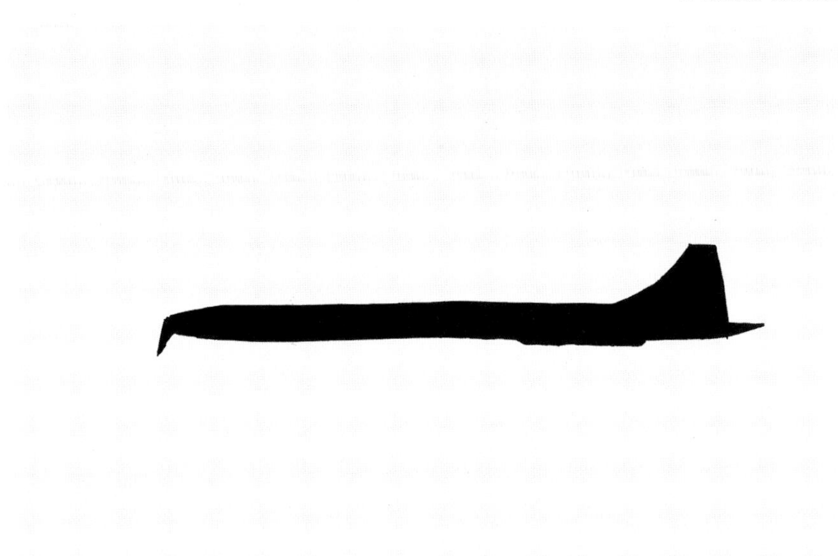

symbolic references, couched in the aesthetics of Pop Art abstraction, effectively parry the critique that comics and the thoughtlessly naive refractions of Art Spiegelman are not appropriate.[11] Abetted by painting, Sasnal assimilates visual culture and removes it from the confines of mediatized understanding. We see the partial totality of a hazy, barely distinguishable, splintered retinal reality. Wilhelm Sasnal's frame-less, detached referentiality subjects Cézanne's *petite sensation* to a loss of identity that is constitutive of our society. We can see, perceive, and understand the painted motifs only via the medial reproduction of being-in and of-this-world. Like so many other things in the interplay of art and life, the little sensation, the gentle mood, is ultimately a question of dosage.

(Translation: Catherine Schelbert)

1) A nominalism that I would have precede the pictorial again. Cf. Thierry de Duve, *Pictorial Nominalism: On Marcel Duchamp's Passage from Painting to the Readymade*, transl. Dana Polan (University of Minnesota press, 1991); and Ulrich Loock, "Sasnal's Nominalism," in *Wilhelm Sasnal. Night Day Night*, exh. cat., Kunsthalle Zürich/Westfälischer Kunstverein Münster (Ostfildern-Ruit: Hatje-Cantz, 2003), pp. 97–108 (German & English).
2) Jacques Rivière, "Present Tendencies in Painting" (1912), transl. Jonathan Griffin, in Edward Fry, ed., *Cubism* (London: Thames & Hudson, 1966). But Gerhard Richter is relevant in this respect as well, see note 7.
3) Or the real material that Sasnal painted, namely the perspiration outlined on his T-shirt after a rock concert (as well as mounting the shirt itself on a stretcher). In the (crystalline) white highlights of the sweat, we ultimately see only the story and, along with it, our own memories of rapturous moments of iconic musical adoration, although the colors—synonymous with memory—fade.
4) This sentence introduces Niklas Luhmann's commendable study on *The Reality of the Mass Media,* transl. Kathleen Cross (California: Stanford University Press, 2000), p. 1.
5) Ibid.
6) Cf. Andrzej Przywara's interview with the artist in *Wilhelm Sasnal. Night Day Night*, op. cit., pp. 33–40 (Polish & English). WS: "[…] I am scared of repeating myself, of defining. Whenever I go anywhere, I always try to return by another route. It's fear of boredom." AP: "And is life in Tarnow boring?" WS: "Not if you're painting."
7) Gerhard Richter's notes (and pictures) of 1964–65 are very illuminating. See idem., *Text: Schriften und Interviews* (Frankfurt am Main: Insel-Verlag, 1994), pp. 25–33.
8) Carina Plath, "Moscice," in *Wilhelm Sasnal. Night Day Night,* op. cit., p. 16.
9) Beatrix Ruf, "Documents of Concern," ibid., pp. 17–18.
10) Cf. Svetlana Alpers, "Interpretation ohne Darstellung – oder: Das Sehen von Las Meninas," in Wolfgang Kemp, ed., *Der Betrachter ist im Bild. Kunstwissenschaft und Rezeptionsästhetik* (Cologne: DuMont, 1985), pp. 91–109, esp. p. 103.
11) In great contrast to, say, Luc Tuymans, who auratically enhances the painted picture. Cf. Sasnal's interest in Polish culture, esp. films of the sixties. Ibid., pp. 20–23.

Edition for Parkett   W I L H E L M   S A S N A L

Concorde Is Dead, 2004
Color contact print from engraved negative
on Kodak paper, 12 ⅝ x 18 ⅞".
Edition of 60, signed and numbered.

Farbphotographie mit (auf dem Negativ) eingravierter Schrift,
Kontaktabzug auf Kodakpapier, 32 x 48 cm.
Auflage: 60, signiert und nummeriert.

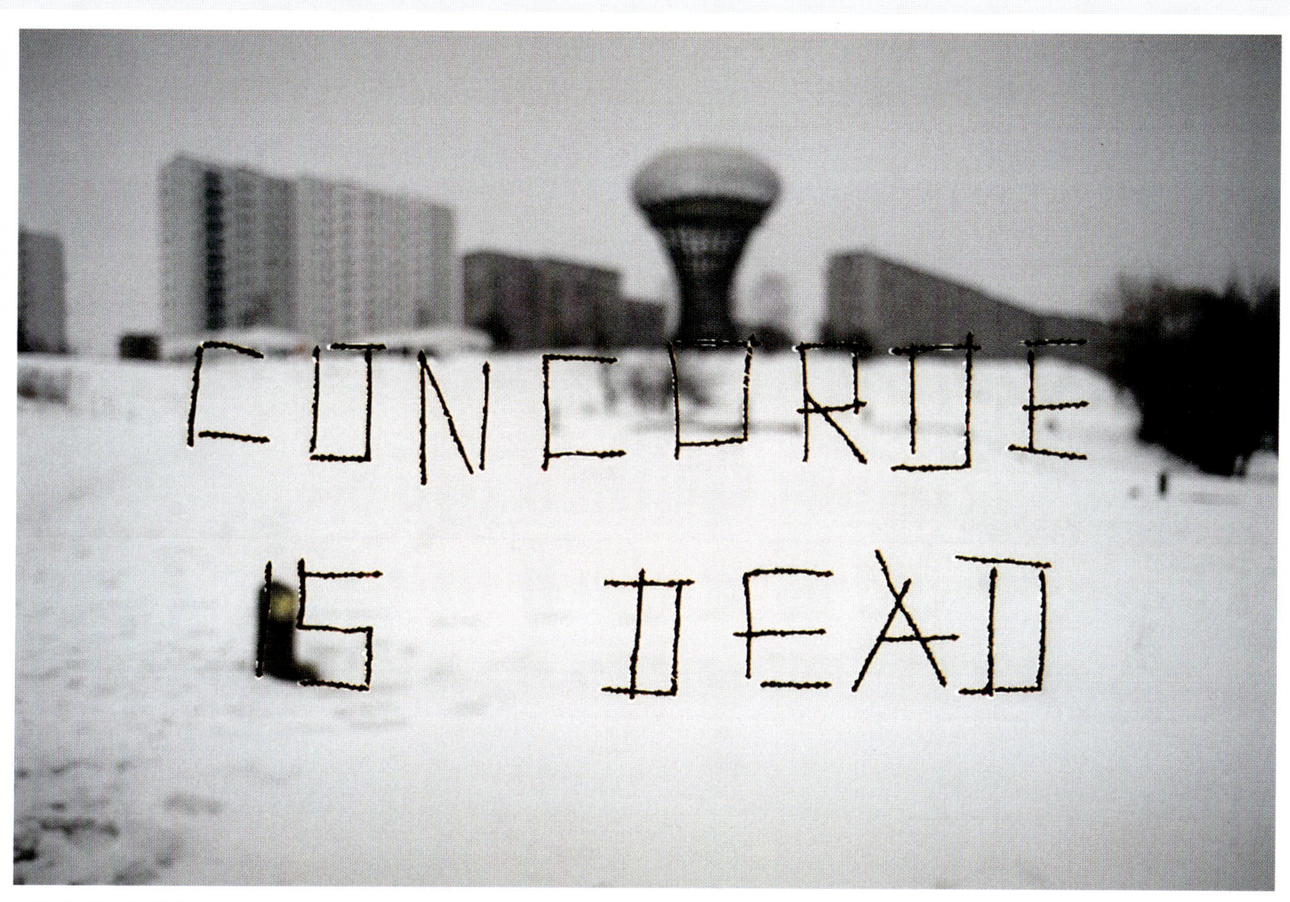
CONCORDE
IS DEAD

Gillian Wearing

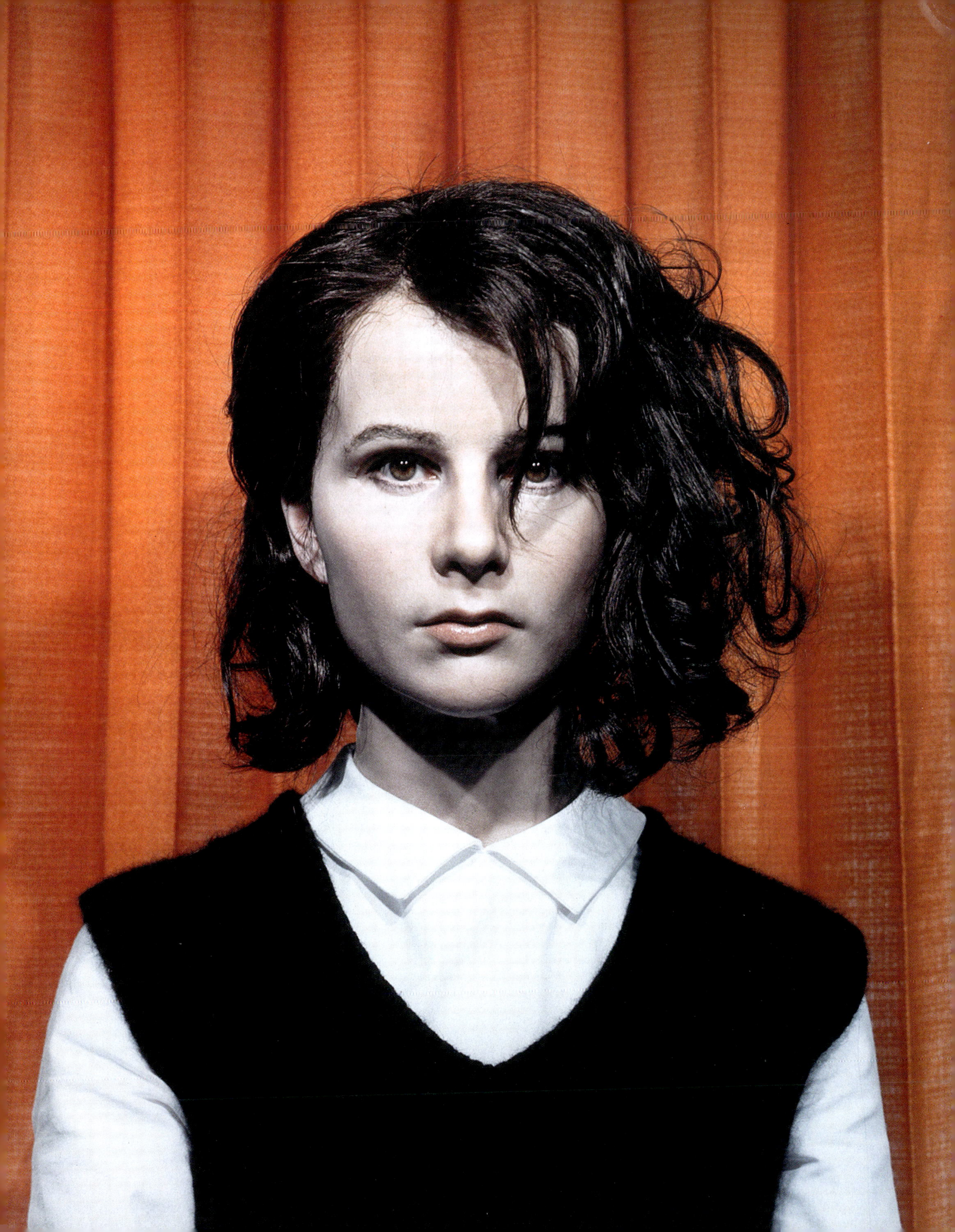

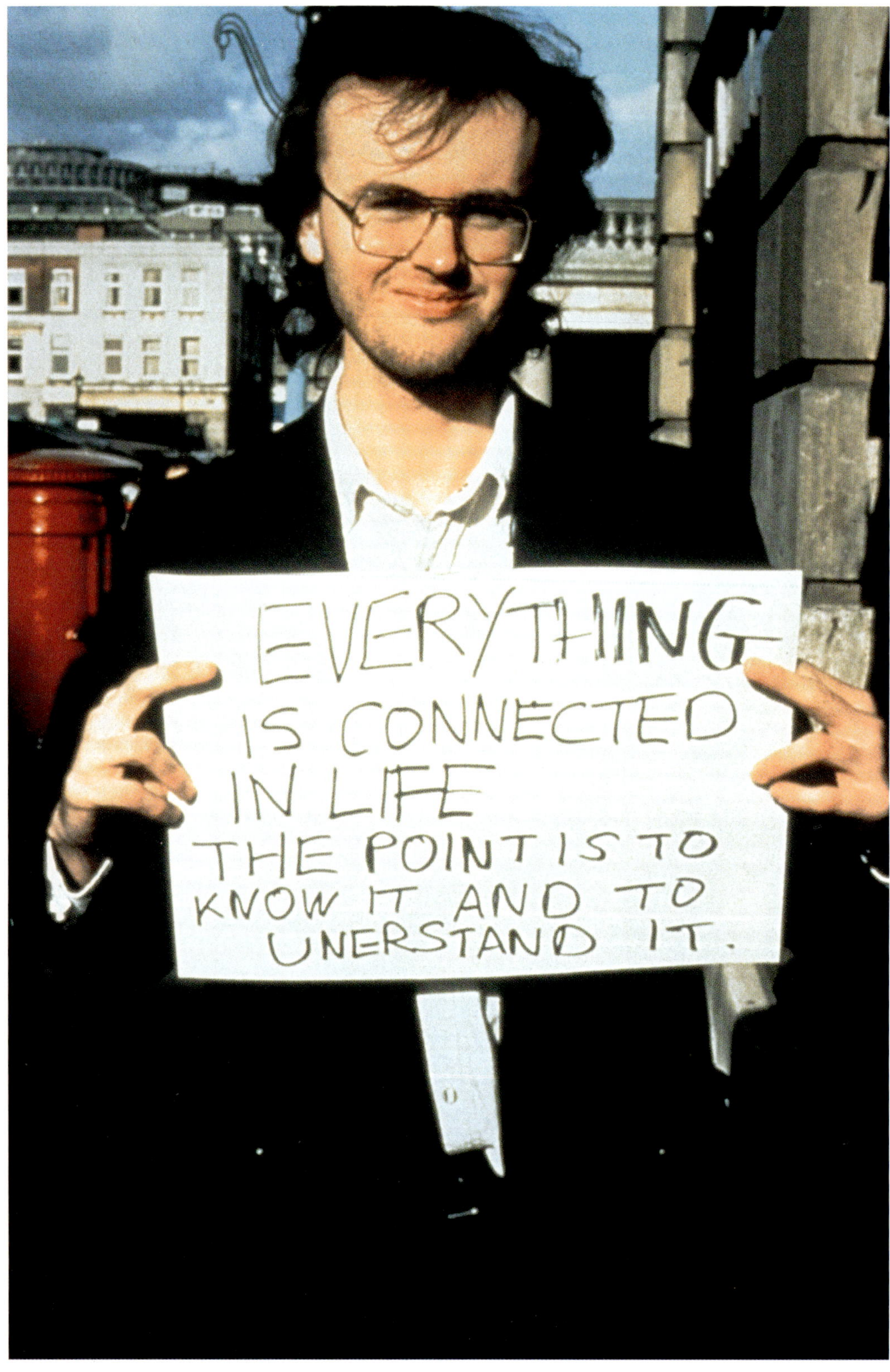

GILLIAN WEARING, SIGNS THAT SAY WHAT YOU WANT THEM TO SAY AND NOT SIGNS THAT SAY WHAT SOMEONE ELSE WANTS YOU TO SAY, 1992–1993, c-type prints, 15 ³/₄ x 11 ¹³/₁₆" / SCHILDER, DIE DAS SAGEN, WAS MAN WILL, UND NICHT SCHILDER, DIE SAGEN, WAS JEMAND ANDERER WILL, DASS SIE SAGEN, C-Prints, 40 x 30 cm.

I'm Desperate

GILLIAN WEARING'S ART OF TRANSPOSED IDENTITIES

DAN CAMERON

Each of us, at one point in time or another, has felt the compelling urge to become another person. But whether or not we hope to be someone in particular, or merely somebody other than ourselves, or whether we envision this change for an evening or a lifetime, the impulse to negate our own reality in favor of another's is not, in fact, a terribly alluring proposition. Considering how immensely difficult it is for many of us to establish a deep empathy for another person's point of view, it would seem to be exponentially more difficult to actually inhabit their skin. To truly feel someone else's emotions and sensations in place of our own, to open one's mouth to speak and have another's voice emerge, would involve such a profound displacement of one's sense of self that afterwards it might be impossible to fully regain per-

spective as a unified self. Worse still, we might never again be satisfied with staying within the confines of our individual shells.

Despite its versatility and resourcefulness, Gillian Wearing's art seems to be dedicated to the sole proposition that the possibility of entering into another person's reality can be both instructive and deeply disturbing. Using multiple perspectives and techniques, Wearing continuously revisits the same set of issues, probing the delicate border zone where her individuality ends and another's begins. Beginning with the work that first established her as an artist of consequence, SIGNS THAT SAY WHAT YOU WANT THEM TO SAY AND NOT SIGNS THAT SAY WHAT SOMEONE ELSE WANTS YOU TO SAY (1992–93), Wearing set out to undermine the hidden dynamics of the documentary, in which the purported objectivity of the form is in fact a subtle means of manipulating the subject while the author remains safely off-camera. Inviting passersby to create their own text, which she

DAN CAMERON has been Senior Curator at the New Museum of Contemporary Art since 1995, and most recently served as the curator for the 2003 Istanbul Biennial.

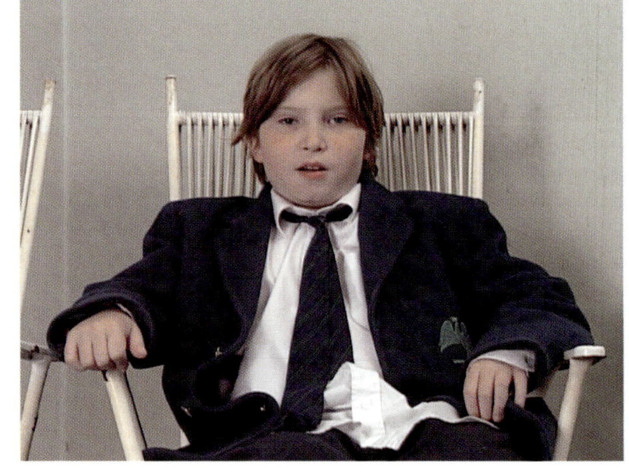

GILLIAN WEARING, 2 INTO 1, 1997, 4 min. 30 sec. video with sound; video still of Lawrence speaking with Hilary's voice / 2 IN 1, 4¹/₂-Minuten-Video mit Ton; Videostill von Lawrence, der mit Hilary's Stimme spricht.

then recorded with her camera, Wearing ensures that the eventual viewer of the piece becomes implicitly aware of the negotiations that took place behind the scenes. Wearing is not showing us what she found in the world and asking us to accept it as an objective fact; rather, she has enlisted others in the completion of a task, while making it clear that she is fully complicit in the outcome. If the results surprise us by revealing much more than one expects to see from photographs of strangers in a neutral setting, this is largely due to the degree to which the conventions of the photographic document have become so deeply rooted in our cultural experience. At first we think we are seeing something that falls safely within those conventions, only to discover that the rules have been emphatically turned upside down.

Many of Wearing's works provoke a marked degree of discomfort in the viewer, by creating perspectives that produce in us a feeling of unexpected intimacy with her subjects. Rather than deflecting or shielding that intimacy, however, the slippage of identity that is central to Wearing's project reminds us that we don't need to know who someone is to feel that we've trespassed on their most intimate thoughts and feelings. In one of her more harrowing videos, 2 INTO 1 (1997), she delves into the emotional conflicts between a mother and her two sons by inviting both sides to discuss their situation frankly and openly, then switching their roles, so that the mother

appears to speak in the sons' voices and vice versa. Because each side ends up representing the other's point of view, the dilemma becomes at once more upsetting and more vulnerable. We find ourselves embracing the illusion that the ability to speak in another's voice gives us the power to internalize their feelings, even when the fairly straightforward device Wearing uses conspires to make the divide more dramatic.

At a certain level, Wearing's work appears to question just how fixed our grasp on our respective identities really is. Through such devices of exchanged identities and masks, she enables us to literally experience two people at once, with the subsequent ambiguity between speaker and subject serving as a charged reminder of just how unsettlingly fluid the exchange can be. 10–16 (1997), one of her most celebrated videos, began life with a series of tape-recorded interviews with children from the ages of ten to sixteen, exploring the problems of growing up and trying to adjust to the shifting demands of family, friends, and school. After editing the audio portion of the work, Wearing then contracted adult actors to lip-synch to the children's voices on video, giving the distinct impression that the former have grown up to become the individuals whose faces we see. In this way, "the child is father to the man," one of psychoanalysis' central precepts, is taken as a point of departure for an elaborate fiction that nonetheless conveys a poignant fable of childhood's fears

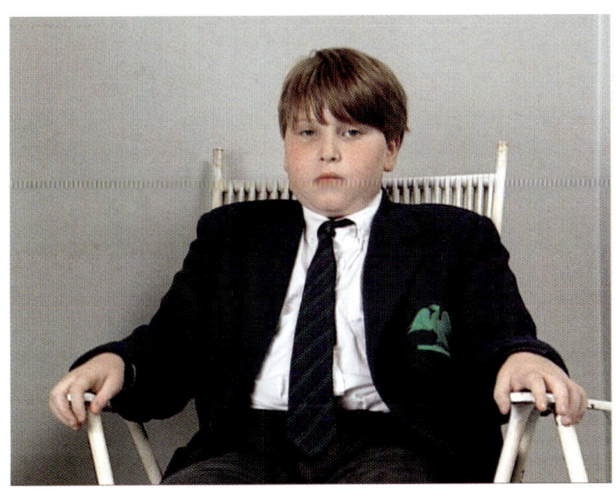

GILLIAN WEARING, 2 INTO 1, 1997, 4 min. 30 sec. video with sound; video still of Alex speaking with Hilary's voice / 2 IN 1, 4¹/₂-Minuten-Video mit Ton; Videostill von Alex, der mit Hilary's Stimme spricht.

and anxieties simmering below the surface of adulthood's travails. Similarly, in CONFESS ALL ON VIDEO. DON'T WORRY, YOU WILL BE IN DISGUISE. INTRIGUED? CALL GILLIAN (1994), Wearing uses anonymity as a tool to entice people to reveal their darkest secrets. Rather than showing them as identity-less, however, Wearing leaves the choice of mask to the confessor, thereby setting up a two-tiered reality in which the story and the disguise intersect in unexpected and jarring ways.

Following her success using the lives of other people, it was probably inevitable that Wearing would eventually turn her powers of examination to the subject of her own identity. With her most recent series of photographs, ALBUM (2003), Wearing engages in her most elaborate masquerade to date, in which an array of prosthetic masks, makeup props and scenography are used to transform herself into each member of her family. The challenge here was not merely to represent her parents, siblings, and other close relations, but to duplicate their likenesses as they appear in specific family photographs. Thus, it is not enough that Wearing becomes her father's double—she must become him as he is seen in a particular photograph, one that he has accepted as a token of his likeness at a particular moment in time. In the final version of the work, with all six photographs together, one can appreciate that each of the sitters is in fact the artist, but only by looking closely into her eyes. Certainly,

Wearing also wants us to be aware that within a family, the separation between self and others is a more subtle distinction, since in purely genetic terms we are the result of the mixing of our two parents. Yet, rather than serve as a release from the tension of ALBUM, the similarities between Wearing and her kin make the impersonation more disturbing, as if she was, at some level, creating a simulation of herself from the components of her actual self.

As Wearing's art has evolved, its deeper messages have emerged with more clarity, subjecting the constant scrutiny of self within society to an open-ended campaign of skepticism and doubt. One of the most astute artists focusing today on the contours and borderlines of identity, Wearing's importance is tied directly to the fact that she approaches her investigations in an unwavering spirit of experimentation. She makes art not to reinforce already held convictions, but to investigate the extent to which even the most firmly rooted belief systems are tied into a core of identity that can be shattered through trauma or dissolved by crisis. As part of an information-driven society wherein the protocols of status are determined by the unshakeable knowledge that one is who one claims to be, Wearing's art opens up the possibility of greater benefits (but also heightened uncertainty) to be derived from the possibility that one is a composite of many people at once, including the anonymous stranger in the street.

GILLIAN WEARING, SIGNS THAT SAY WHAT YOU WANT THEM TO SAY AND NOT SIGNS THAT SAY WHAT SOMEONE ELSE WANTS YOU TO SAY, 1992–1993, c-type prints mounted on aluminum, 15 ³/₄ x 11 ¹³/₁₆" / SCHILDER, DIE DAS SAGEN, WAS MAN SAGEN WILL, UND NICHT SCHILDER, DIE SAGEN, WAS JEMAND ANDERER WILL, DASS MAN SAGT, C-Prints auf Aluminium aufgezogen, 40 x 30 cm.

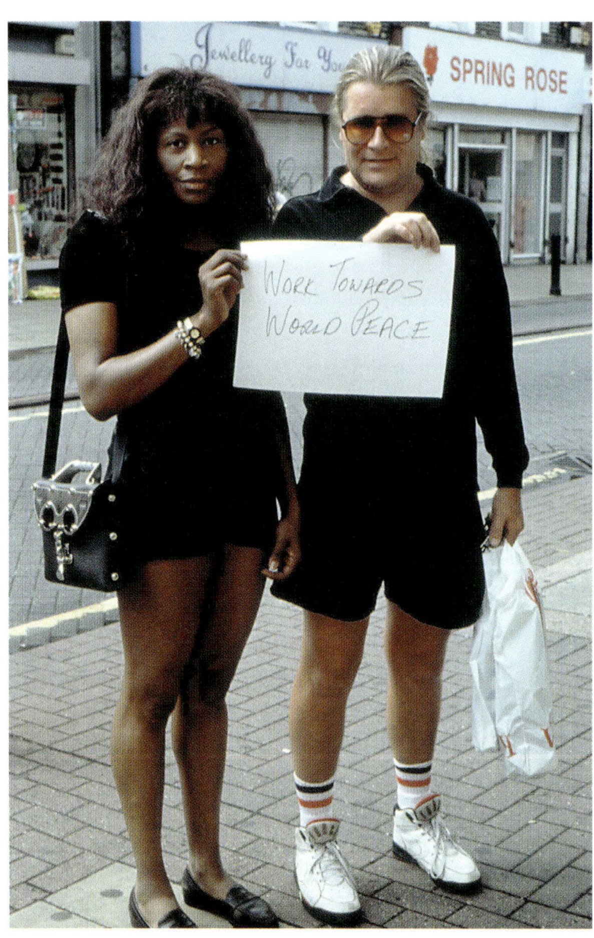

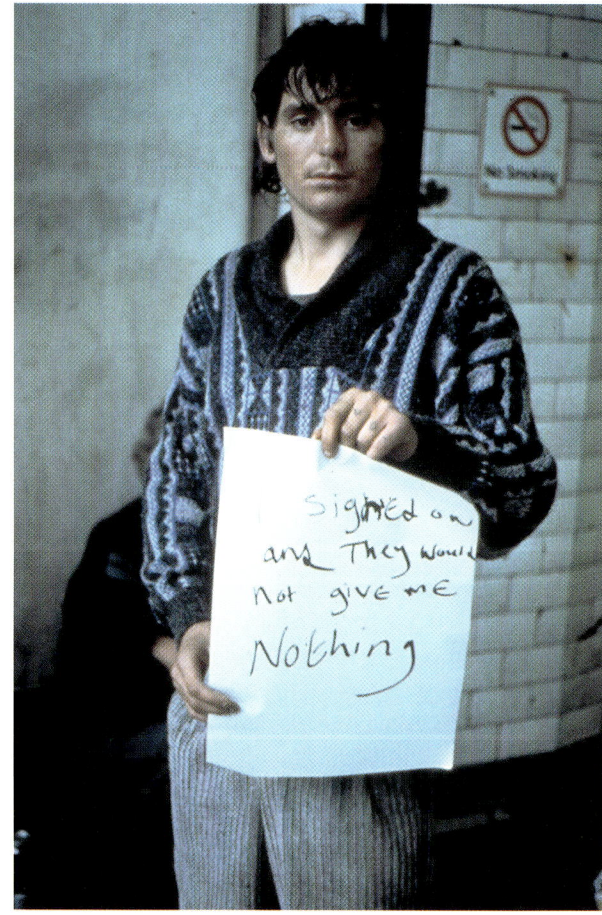

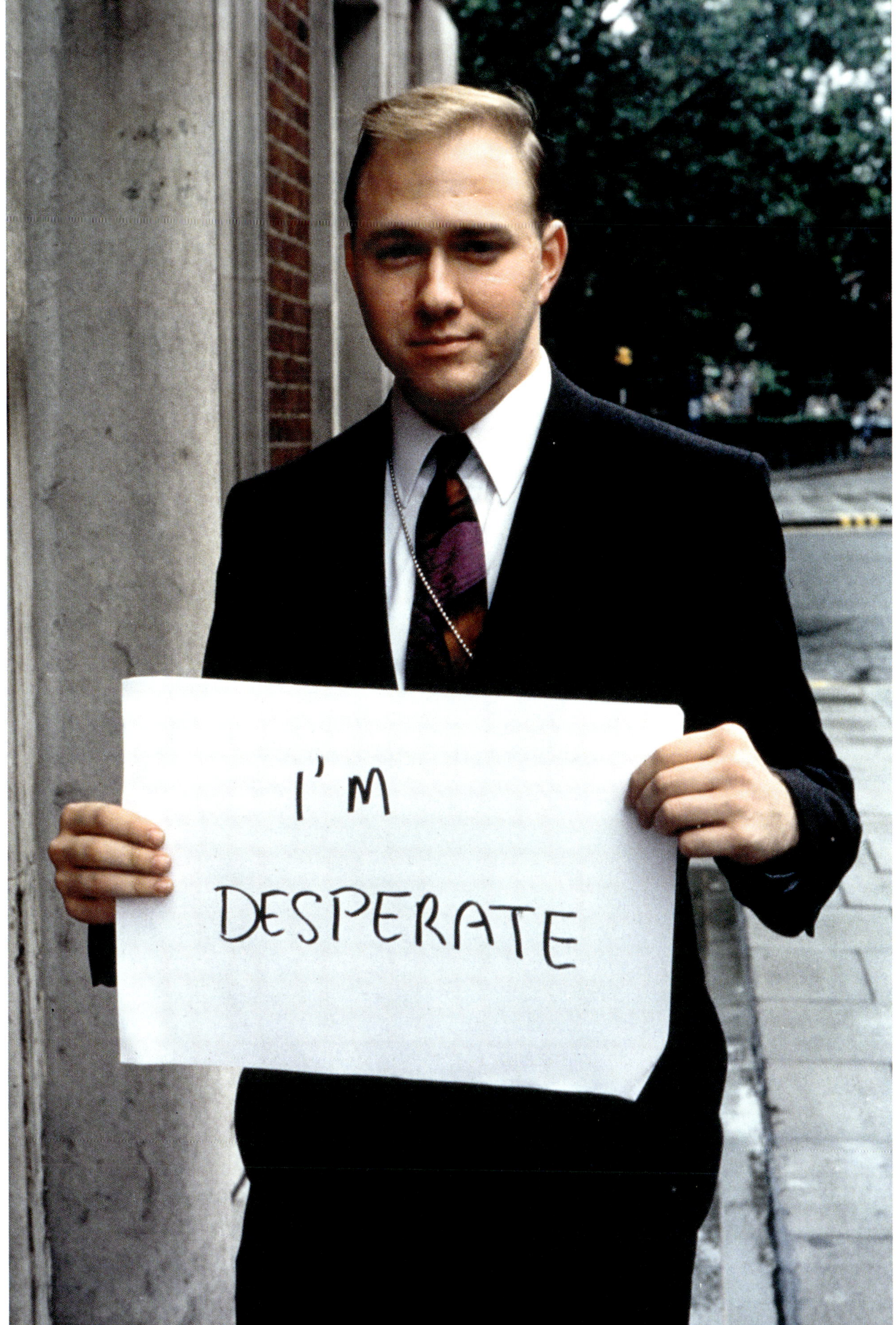
I'M
DESPERATE

Ich bin verzweifelt

GILLIAN WEARINGS SPIEL MIT WECHSELNDEN IDENTITÄTEN

DAN CAMERON

Jeder und jede von uns hat irgendwann einmal das Bedürfnis verspürt, unbedingt jemand anderer sein zu wollen. Aber, egal, ob wir uns wünschen eine bestimmte Person zu sein oder nur jemand anderer als wir selbst, und egal, ob wir diesen Wechsel nur für einen Abend ins Auge fassen oder für das ganze Leben, der Einfall, unsere eigene Realität zugunsten jener eines anderen Menschen zu verleugnen, ist eigentlich gar kein so unwiderstehliches Angebot. Bedenkt man, wie extrem schwer es vielen von uns fällt, den Standpunkt eines anderen Menschen wirklich nachzuempfinden, um wie viel schwieriger dürfte es erst sein, tatsächlich in seine Haut zu schlüpfen? Würde man wirklich anstelle der eigenen Gefühle und Empfindungen jene eines anderen erleben, also auch den Mund aufmachen und beim Sprechen die Stimme des anderen hören, so bedeutete dies eine so starke Erschütterung unseres Selbsterlebens, dass wir uns danach vielleicht nie wieder als einheitliches Ich würden fühlen können. Oder noch schlimmer, wir würden uns vielleicht nie wieder damit zufrieden geben können, innerhalb der Grenzen unserer individuellen Körperhülle bleiben zu müssen.

DAN CAMERON ist seit 1995 Senior Curator des New Museum of Contemporary Art in New York und war Kurator der Biennale Istanbul 2003.

Obwohl Gillian Wearings Kunst überaus vielseitig und einfallsreich ist, scheint es in ihren Arbeiten immer um diesen einen Gedanken zu gehen, dass es ebenso lehrreich wie zutiefst verstörend sein kann, in die Realität einer anderen Person zu schlüpfen. Unter vielerlei Gesichtspunkten und unter Einsatz verschiedenster Techniken wendet sich Wearing immer wieder demselben Themenkomplex zu und untersucht den fragilen Grenzbereich, wo die eigene Persönlichkeit endet und jene eines anderen beginnt. Seit SIGNS THAT SAY WHAT YOU WANT THEM TO SAY AND NOT SIGNS THAT SAY WHAT SOMEONE ELSE WANTS YOU TO SAY (Schilder, die das sagen, was man sagen will, und nicht Schilder, die sagen, was jemand anderer will, dass man sagt, 1992–93)– also jener Arbeit, mit der sie definitiv den Durchbruch schaffte – hat Wearing versucht, die verborgene Dynamik des Dokumentarischen zu unterlaufen: nämlich, dass die angebliche Objektivität der Form in Wirklichkeit dazu dient, das Thema subtil zu manipulieren, während der Autor sich fein säuberlich aus dem Bild heraus hält. Indem Wearing Passanten bittet ihren eigenen Text aufzuschreiben und diesen dann mit der Kamera aufzeichnet, stellt sie sicher, dass einem allfälligen Betrachter der Arbeit die hinter den Kulissen getroffenen Vereinbarungen implizit bewusst werden. Wearing führt uns nicht vor,

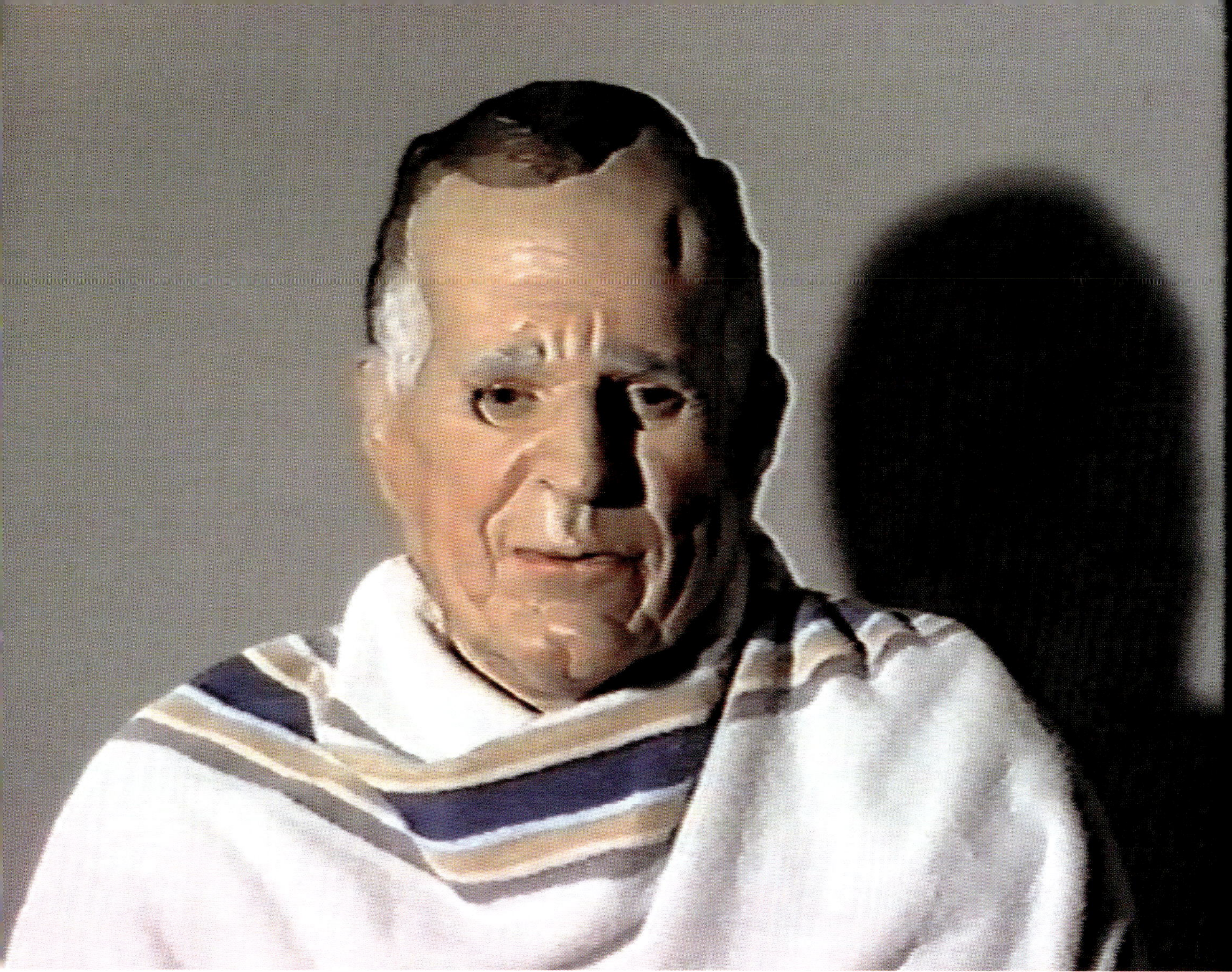

worauf sie in der Welt gestossen ist, und verlangt, dass wir dies als objektive Tatsache annehmen; vielmehr hat sie anderen eine Aufgabe gestellt und legt dabei völlig offen, dass sie am Endresultat kräftig mitmischt. Wenn die dabei entstehenden Bilder uns überraschen und viel mehr verraten, als man von Photographien fremder Leute vor neutralem Hintergrund erwarten würde, so rührt dies vor allem daher, dass die Konventionen des Photodokuments inzwischen so tief in unserer kulturellen Erfahrung verwurzelt sind: Zunächst meinen wir etwas zu sehen, was diesen Konventionen absolut entspricht, müssen jedoch alsbald feststellen, dass sämtliche Regeln rigoros über den Haufen geworfen worden sind.

Viele Werke Wearings rufen beim Betrachter tiefes Unbehagen hervor, weil sie Blickwinkel wählt, die uns in eine unerwartet intime Nähe zu ihren Sujets rücken. Statt diese Intimität zu umgehen oder zu schützen erinnert uns der für Wearings Arbeit so zentrale Wechsel der Identität daran, dass wir nicht wirklich wissen müssen, wer jemand ist, um das Gefühl zu haben, wir seien zu Unrecht in seine oder

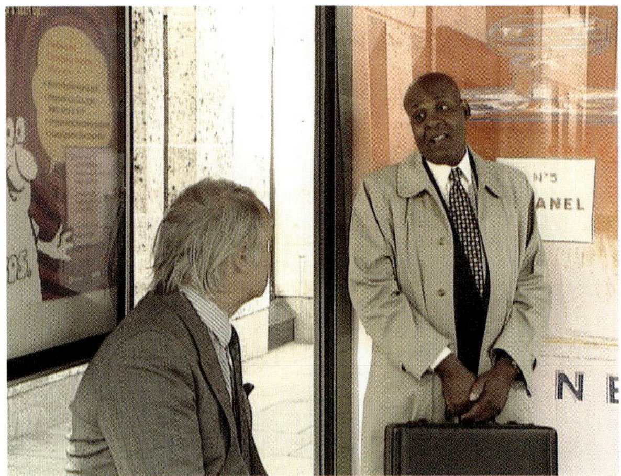

GILLIAN WEARING, 10–16, 2001, stills from 24-min.
DVD for back projection. Scene at busstop (top),
Tony (bottom), Richard looking at camera (top right),
eating women (bottom right).

ihre geheimsten Gedanken und Empfindungen ein-
gedrungen. In einem ihrer quälenderen Videos,
2 INTO 1 (2 in 1, 1997), taucht sie in die emotionalen Konflikte zwischen einer Mutter und ihren beiden Söhnen ein, indem sie beide Seiten einlädt, ihre
Situation offen und ehrlich zu besprechen und
danach die Rollen zu tauschen, so dass die Mutter
mit der Stimme ihrer Söhne zu sprechen scheint und
umgekehrt. Gerade weil jede Partei am Ende den
Standpunkt der anderen darstellt, erscheint das Dilemma plötzlich noch beunruhigender und die Ver-
letzlichkeit noch grösser. Wir verfallen der Illusion,
dass die Fähigkeit mit der Stimme eines anderen zu
sprechen uns auch die Macht verleiht seine Gefühle
zu verinnerlichen, obwohl doch das recht offene Vorgehen, das Wearing wählt, eher dazu geeignet scheint,
das Trennende besonders drastisch hervorzuheben.

Auf einer bestimmten Ebene scheinen Wearings
Arbeiten danach zu fragen, wie stark wir eigentlich
auf unsere jeweilige Identität fixiert sind. Mittels solcher Wechsel von Masken und Identitäten erlaubt sie
uns, buchstäblich zu erleben, wie es ist, zwei Personen zugleich zu sein, wobei uns die damit verbundene Spaltung von Sprecher und Subjekt nachhaltig
daran erinnert, wie beängstigend fliessend dieser
Übergang sein kann. 10–16 (1997), eines ihrer meist-
gefeierten Videos, begann zunächst mit einer Reihe

auf Band aufgenommener Interviews mit Kindern
im Alter zwischen zehn und sechzehn; es ging um die
Probleme des Erwachsenwerdens und darum, den
wechselnden Erwartungen von Familie, Freunden
und Schule gerecht zu werden. Nachdem sie die
Tonaufnahme fertig bearbeitet hatte, zog Wearing
erwachsene Schauspieler bei, um die Kinderstim-
men auf Video im Playback nachzusprechen, was den
Eindruck erweckte, die Kinder seien mittlerweile zu
eben den Individuen herangewachsen, deren Gesichter wir sprechen sehen. So wird das Kind zum Vater des Mannes, womit einer der zentralen Sätze der
Psychoanalyse als Ausgangspunkt einer komplizierten
Fiktion dient, die letztlich dennoch nichts anderes
ist als ein bedrückendes Gleichnis von den Ängsten
und Schrecken der Kindheit, die unter der Oberfläche des mühevollen Erwachsenendaseins lauern. Auf
ähnliche Art verwendet Wearing in CONFESS ALL ON
VIDEO, DON'T WORRY, YOU WILL BE IN DISGUISE.
INTRIGUED? CALL GILLIAN (Beichten Sie alles auf
Video, keine Angst, Sie werden maskiert sein. Interessiert? Rufen Sie Gillian an, 1994) die Anonymität
als Köder, um Leute dazu zu verleiten, ihre dunkels-
ten Geheimnisse zu verraten. Statt sie jedoch identi-
tätslos zu präsentieren, überlässt Wearing die Wahl
der Maske der jeweils beichtenden Person, womit sie
eine zwiespältige Realität erzeugt, in der Geschichte
und Maske unerwartet und widersprüchlich zusam-
menspielen.

Nach der erfolgreichen Anwendung auf das Leben anderer Leute war es wohl unausweichlich, dass

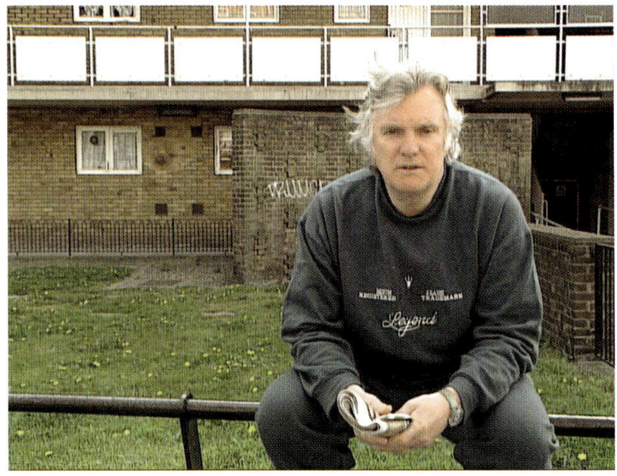

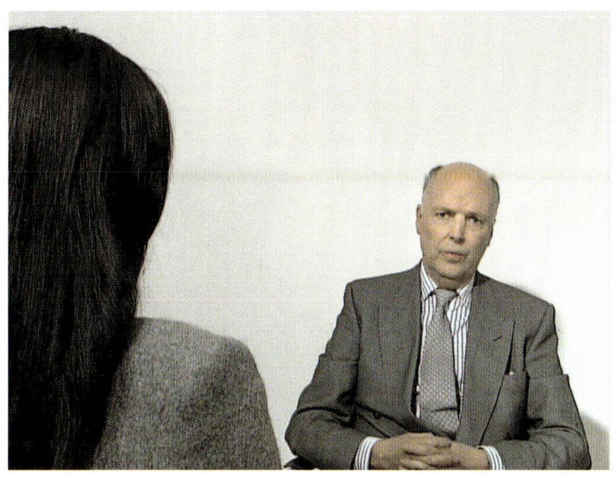

GILLIAN WEARING, 10–16, 2001, Szenen aus der 24-minütigen
DVD für Rückprojektion. An der Bushaltestelle (oben links),
Tony (unten links), Richard schaut zur Kamera (oben),
essende Frauen (unten).

Wearing früher oder später auch das Thema ihrer eigenen Identität unter die scharfe Lupe ihrer Beobachtungsgabe nehmen würde. Mit ihrer jüngsten Photoserie, ALBUM (2003), hat Wearing ihre bisher raffinierteste Maskerade in Angriff genommen; dabei verwendet sie eine Reihe von Prothesen, Masken, Make-up-Kniffs und Theaterrequisiten, um sich in jedes Mitglied ihrer Familie zu verwandeln. Die Herausforderung bestand nicht nur darin, ihre Eltern, Geschwister und andere nahe Verwandte darzustellen, sondern deren Erscheinungsbild, so wie sie auf bestimmten Familienphotos aussehen, präzis wiederzugeben. So genügt es Wearing nicht, dass sie zum Double ihres Vaters wird, nein, sie muss er selbst werden, wie er auf einem bestimmten Photo aussieht, und zwar auf einem, das er selbst als Beispiel dafür akzeptiert, wie er zu einem bestimmten Zeitpunkt ausgesehen hat. In der letzten Version der Arbeit, in der alle sechs Photos zusammen zu sehen sind, kann man sich vergewissern, dass jedes der photographierten Modelle die Künstlerin ist, aber nur, wenn man ihr genau in die Augen schaut. Natürlich will Wearing uns auch vermitteln, dass die Unterscheidung zwischen dem Ich und den anderen innerhalb der Familie noch feiner ist, weil wir ja schon rein genetisch eine Mischung unserer Eltern sind. Statt jedoch zur Auflösung der Spannung in ALBUM

beizutragen, lässt die Ähnlichkeit zwischen Wearing und ihren Verwandten das Rollenspiel noch beunruhigender erscheinen, als ob sie mit Elementen ihres tatsächlichen Ichs quasi eine Simulation ihrer selbst erschaffen würde.

Im Laufe ihrer Entwicklung traten die tieferen Botschaften in Wearings Kunst immer deutlicher zutage. Sie hat die unablässige Beobachtung des Ichs in der Gesellschaft einer endlosen skeptischen Befragung unterzogen. Wearing ist eine der raffiniertesten unter jenen Kunstschaffenden, die sich heute mit den Umrissen und Grenzen der persönlichen Identität befassen, und ihre Bedeutung hängt direkt damit zusammen, dass sie ihre Untersuchungen unerschrocken als Experimente angeht und versteht. Sie macht nicht Kunst um vorgefasste Überzeugungen zu bestätigen, sondern will untersuchen, wie weit selbst tief verwurzelte Glaubenssysteme an einen Identitätskern gebunden sind, der durch Traumata oder Krisen erschüttert und aufgelöst werden kann. In einer informationsbesessenen Gesellschaft, in der die protokollarischen Zuständigkeiten durch das unerschütterliche Wissen darum bestimmt sind, dass man ist, wer man zu sein behauptet, eröffnet Wearings Kunst die Chance zu grösserem Lustgewinn (aber auch grösserer Ungewissheit), der sich aus der Möglichkeit ergibt, dass man ein Konglomerat verschiedener Leute zugleich sein kann, einschliesslich des anonymen Mannes auf der Strasse.

(Übersetzung: Suzanne Schmidt)

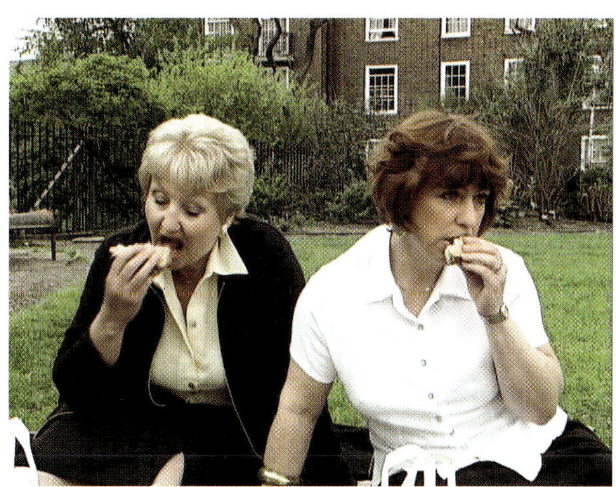

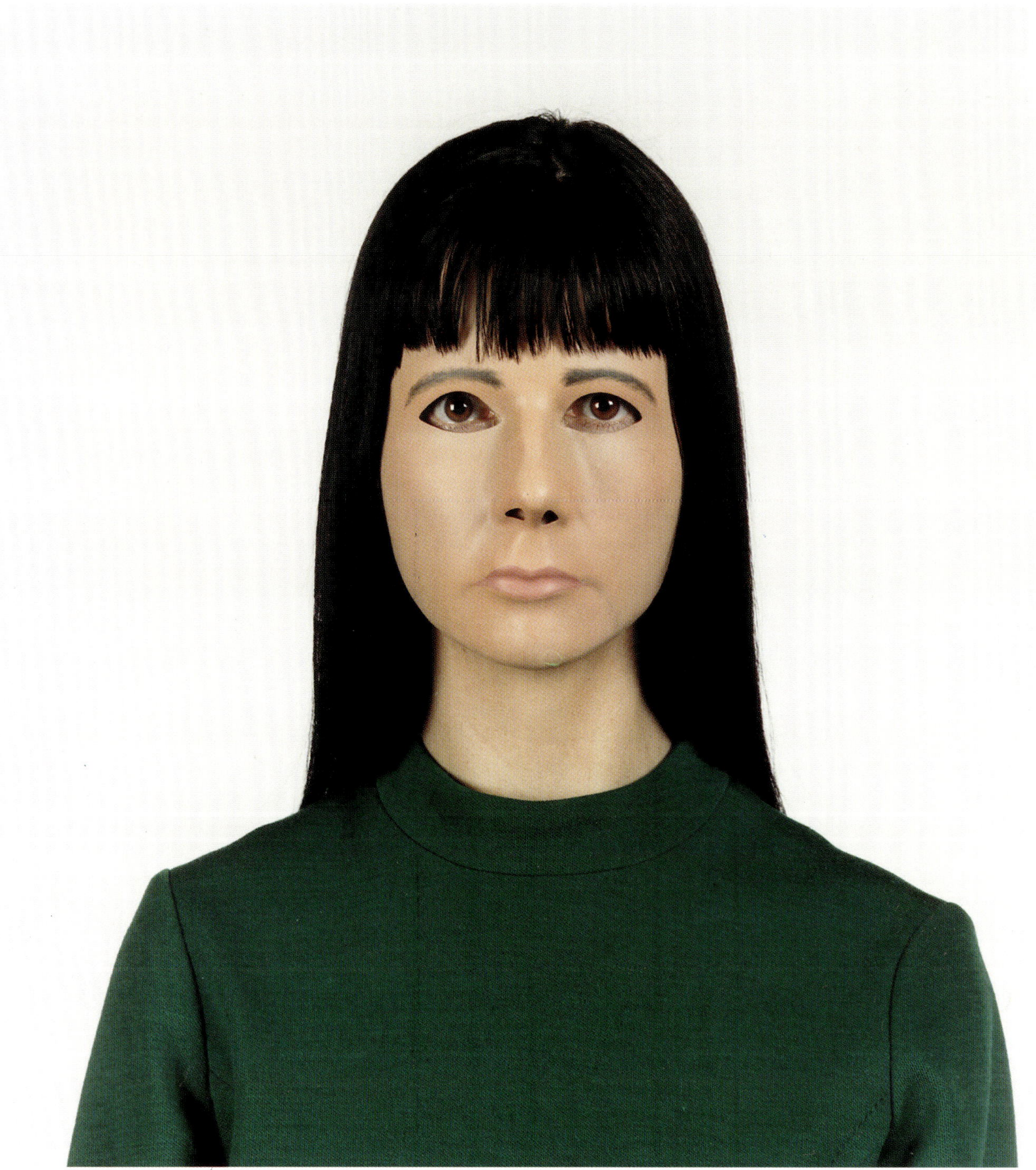

GILLIAN WEARING, SELF PORTRAIT, 2000, c-type print, 67 $^{11}/_{16}$ x 67 $^{11}/_{16}$"/ SELBSTPORTRÄT, C-Print, 172 x 172 cm.

THE ENCOUNTER WITH REALITY

GORDON BURN

If, as with Emerson, Williams seems to "ask the fact for the form," the form, once it comes, is free of the fact, is a d a n c e a b o v e the fact.
– Charles Tomlinson[1]

For some reason every time I applied myself to thinking about Gillian Wearing and her work, I found myself thinking about William Carlos Williams— Williams, the poet of inarticulate America; a poet who d i s t r u s t e d articulacy—and his elusive, famous little poem—only 16 words—"The Red Wheelbarrow":

so much depends
upon

a red wheel
barrow

glazed with rain
water

beside the white
chickens[2]

Like Wearing, Williams, a family doctor for most of his life in small-town New Jersey, believed in embrac-

ing the immediate and the local, the what-is-to-hand in the where-we-are. The great attraction of Williams' poetry was its insistence that intelligence is inseparable from the whole range of immediate, physical, bodily perception. He set out to develop a language that was "an action upon the real" rather than a discourse of abstractions about it.

The blocked verbal facility of the people he encountered daily on his rounds was for Williams a constant rush and excitement ("It's the anarchy of poverty / delights me..."),[3] and the artlessness of ordinary speech came to replace "high-end" aestheticized language and the conventional poetic formulas in his work. "Colleges and books only copy the language which the field and work-yard made," Emerson had said (in "The American Scholar," 1837). And "'the speech of Polish mothers' was where Williams insisted he got his English from"[4]: "Anything is good material for poetry. Anything. I've said it time and time again."[5]

"That words set in Jersey speech rhythms mean less but mean it with more finality," critic Hugh Kenner once observed was Williams' great technical perception.[6] Which reminded me of something Gillian Wearing has said about her own work's investment

---

GORDON BURN is a writer living in London. His most recent books are *On the Way to Work* (with Damien Hirst), and *The North of England Home Service*, a novel.

in the completely defenseless simplicity of personal speech, and its implicit belief in a kind of heroism among damaged people and diminished things: "I'm more interested in how other people can put things together, how people can say something far more interesting than I can."[7]

Starting out, I had an idea that the matter for this essay on the awkward and, in important ways, unknowable work of Gillian Wearing was going to consist of "found" material like the sometimes funny, sometimes vulgar, often banal and uncomfortable thoughts and words of strangers that she incorporates into her gnarly photographic and video art. And one day when I should have been at home working on what you have in front of you now, I stepped out of a London restaurant into driving rain. Diagonally opposite the restaurant was a second-hand bookshop, and I ducked in there for shelter. It was musty-smelling, with a dinging door-bell and flattened cardboard boxes on the floor to take up the wet. The owner was sitting in a low, busted chair in his topcoat with the collar pulled all the way up, playing bridge or patience or another card-game on a grey box computer.

My eye was almost immediately drawn to some white writing on a red spine: "I Wanted to Write a Poem by William Carlos Williams."[8] It was the first edition of a "talked" book, published in 1958. Set on their own in the middle of the first page were five lines of the poem from which the book got its title:

I wanted to write a poem
that you would understand.
For what good is it to me
if you can't understand it?
But you got to try hard—

This book stood next to a long-forgotten novel by Djuna Barnes. And, slipped between them, a skinny filling in this melancholy modernist sandwich, an issue of the University of Minnesota Pamphlets on American Writers, number 24, dated 1963, subject William Carlos Williams. The pamphlet fell open to page 24, where "The Red Wheelbarrow" was reproduced. Page 25 carried a poem I hadn't come across before but which, for reasons that to even

casual Wearing-watchers will seem obvious, wrote itself straight into this space:

Danse Russe

If when my wife is sleeping
and the baby and Kathleen
are sleeping
and the sun is a flame-white disc
in silken mists
above shining trees, –
if I in my north room
dance naked, grotesquely
before my mirror
waving my shirt round my head
and singing softly to myself:
"I am lonely, lonely.
I was born to be lonely,
I am best so!"
If I admire my arms, my face,
my shoulders, flanks, buttocks
against the yellow drawn shades, –

Who shall say I am not
the happy genius of my household?[2]

"In the *Video Diary* and *Video Nation* TV spots," Wearing has said, "you see people acting silly in their own homes—and that's since camcorders have come out. People have wanted to record themselves being wacky; this is the 'true' them. But they're doing it in private. I'm sure that many people have done a lot of dancing in their bedrooms, but taking that fantasy and putting it somewhere it's alien—that's where you can start questioning."[9]

The 25-minute video DANCING IN PECKHAM (1994) shows Wearing herself dancing to a soundtrack (Nirvana's "Smells Like Teen Spirit," Gloria Gaynor's "I Will Survive") that she is unspooling silently in her head. The "alien" environment the spectacle unfolds in is the placelessness of a small shopping mall arcade—a locus of the new form of solitude endemic in what Marc Augé has defined as "the space of non-place."

"A person entering the space of non-place [motorways, airport lounges, cineplexes, destination

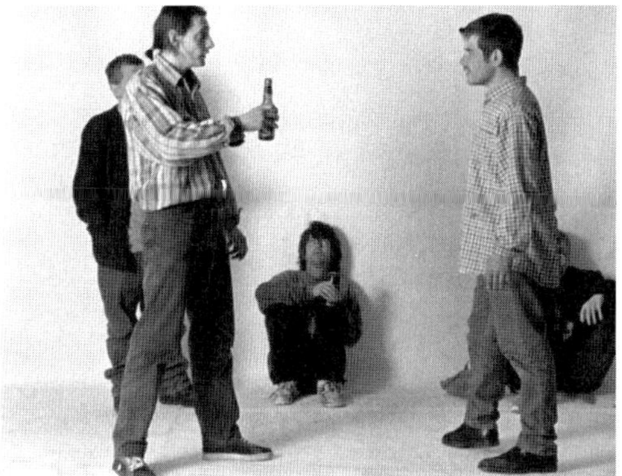
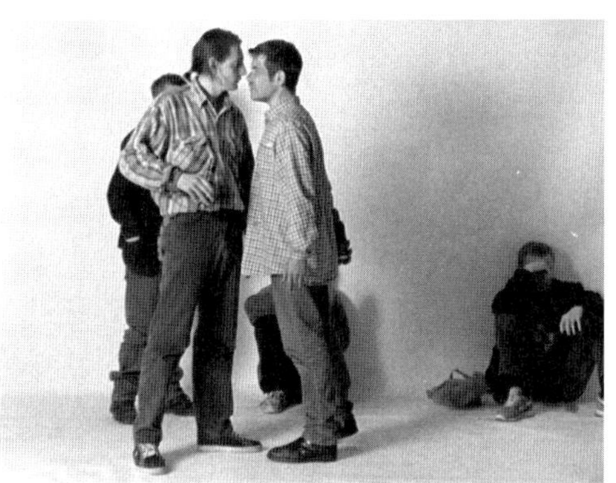
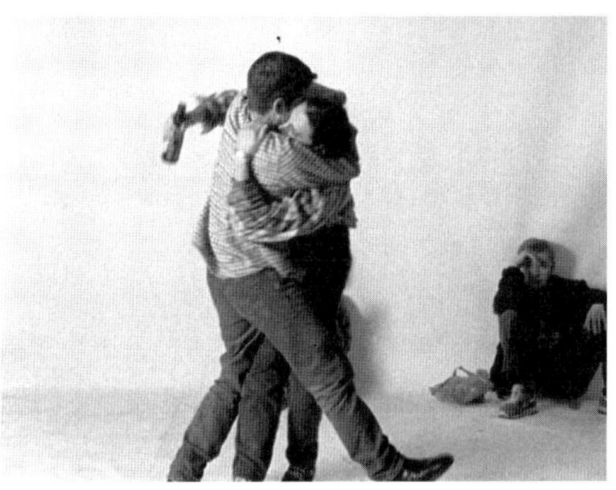
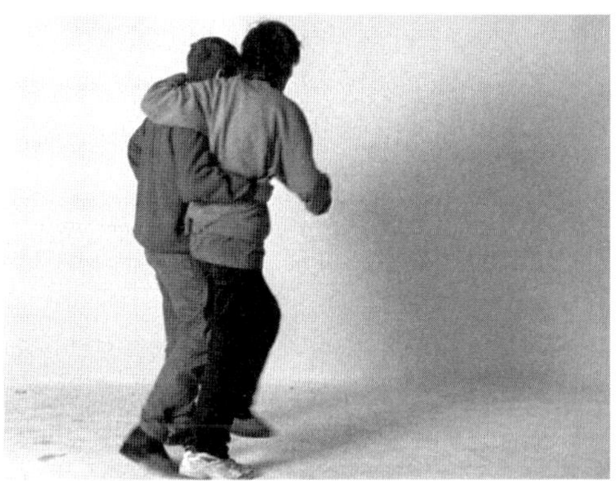

GILLIAN WEARING, DRUNK, 1999, stills from the 23-min. DVD 3-screen projection / BESOFFEN, Szenen aus der 23-minütigen DVD-Dreifachprojektion.

retail 'experiences'] is relieved of his usual determinants," Augé writes. "He obeys the same code as others, receives the same messages, responds to the same entreaties. The space of non-place creates neither singular identity nor relations; only solitude, and similitude."[10) To give vent to unembarrassed self-expression and self-display in such a non-place then becomes an act of willful and (this is the implication) punishable transgression.

It has become a commonplace in the environment of the image that images accumulate sensation around themselves the more they are reproduced and repeated; they grow an aura. And, thanks to a number of high-profile murder cases in Britain in recent years, a suggestion of the uncanny—the specter of death stalking through the center of life; the notion of demonistic or magic forces—has attached itself to suburban malls like the one where Wearing filmed herself disco-dancing in south London. (She had previously used the down-at-heel, no-longer-modern Peckham mall as a background in SIGNS THAT SAY WHAT YOU WANT THEM TO SAY AND NOT SIGNS THAT SAY WHAT SOMEONE ELSE WANTS YOU TO SAY, 1992–93).

In what was to be the last hour of her life, the popular television presenter Jill Dando was caught by CCTV cameras shopping for an ink cartridge for her printer in King's Mall, close to the BBC. The grainy stutter-frames of the three-year-old James Bulger walking through the central precinct of the Strand shopping center on Merseyside hand-in-hand with his two schoolboy killers became some of the most deeply ingrained images of recent times.

There is an aggression involved in every use of the camera. And inevitably there is an evidentiary quality—a stary cold stoniness—to the Dando and Bulger pictures. Although mechanically captured, they imply the slyness and patience of the snooper, the stalker, the lurking feral paparazzo photographer. They suggest the privileged view vouchsafed the killer, crouching, unseen, in the bushes in the front garden of Jill Dando's house at Gowan Avenue in Fulham.

Perhaps it was these conventions that Gillian Wearing was testing when she put on a bandage mask and had herself spy-cammed as she walked to the local shops for HOMAGE TO THE WOMAN WITH THE

GILLIAN WEARING, WESTERN SECURITY, 1995, stills from 30-min. DVD for 10 security monitors /
WESTLICHE SICHERHEITSMASSNAHMEN, Szenen aus der 30-minütigen DVD für 10 Überwachungsmonitoren.

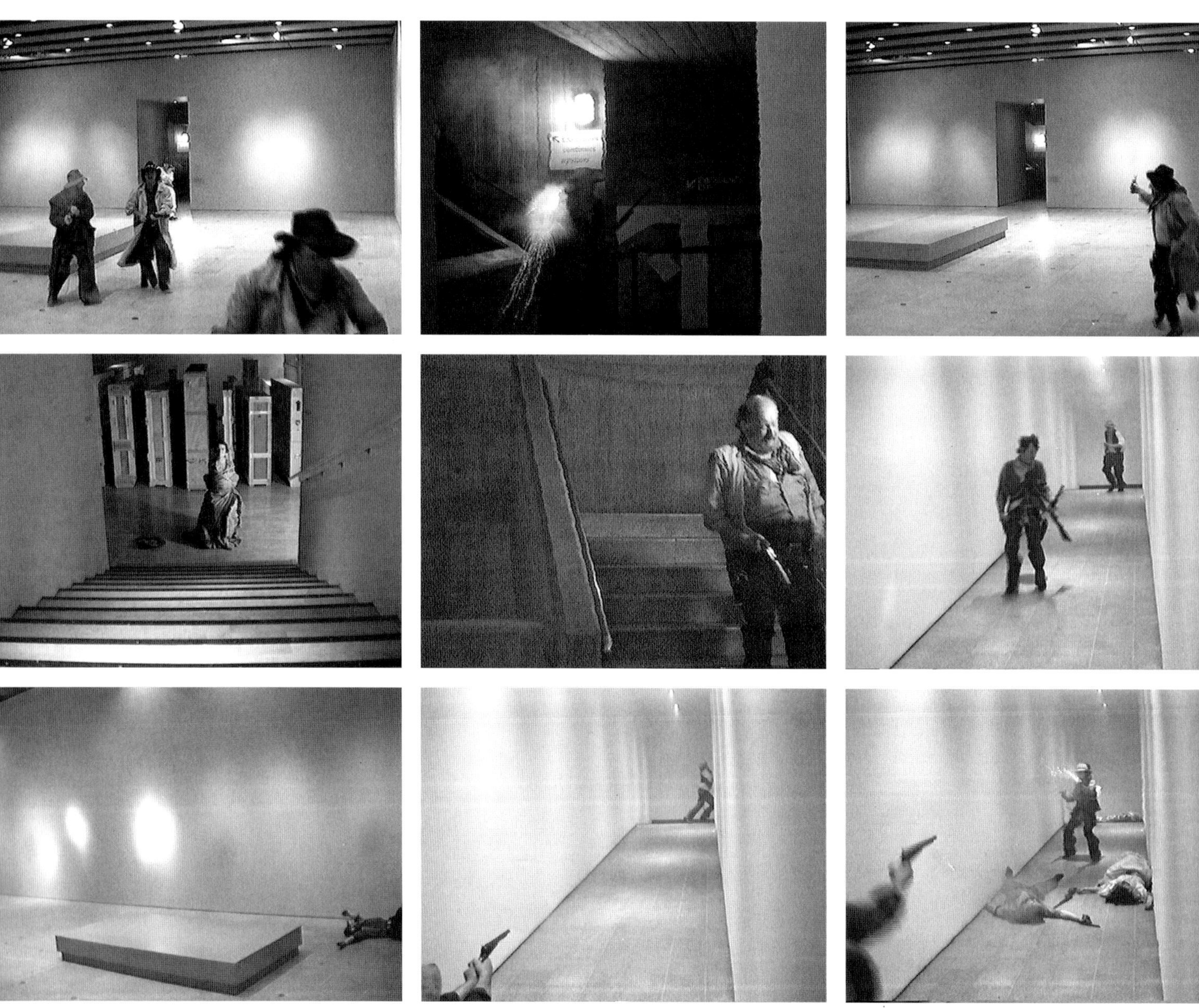

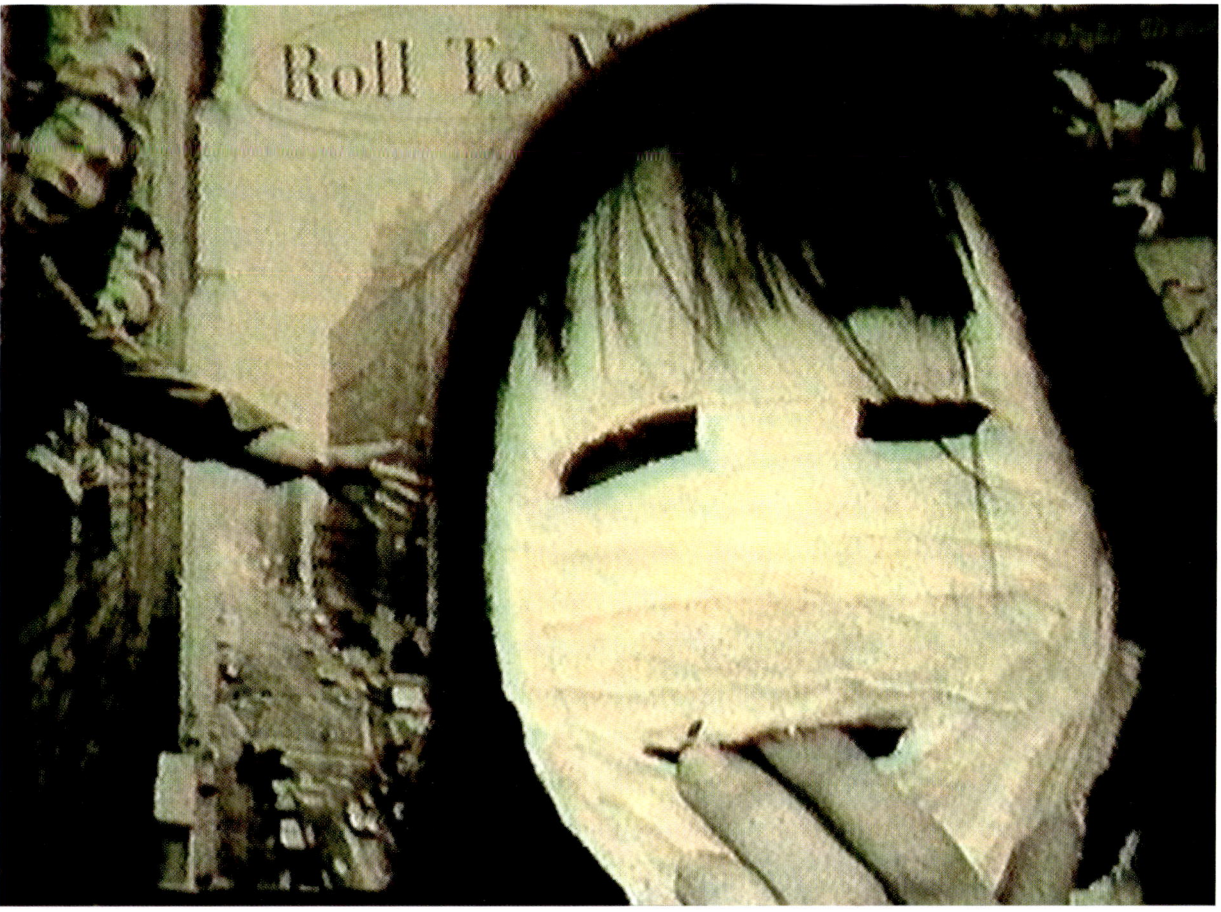

GILLIAN WEARING, HOMAGE TO THE WOMAN WITH THE BANDAGED FACE WHO I SAW YESTERDAY DOWN WALWORTH ROAD,
1995, still from 7-min. DVD for back projection / HOMMAGE AN DIE FRAU MIT DEM VERBUNDENEN GESICHT, DIE ICH GESTERN
AUF DER WALWORTH ROAD SAH, Szene aus der 7-minütigen DVD für Rückprojektion.

BANDAGED FACE WHO I SAW YESTERDAY DOWN WAL-
WORTH ROAD (1995). The visual vocabulary that, as
regular television grazers, we have all internalized—
the extreme graininess, the ethereal streaks and
smudges—is in evidence. The snatched quality of
such footage has come to be seen as a guarantee of
its authenticity. The rawness of the pictures (often
combined with ticking digits at the top of the frame
or the bottom) has become code for the real world
happening in real time—for reality caught off-guard,
in what we might think of as the in-between moments, when crimes and catastrophes happen. Much
of their power derives from the fact that they were
never meant to be seen. Only the calamitous events

to which they have become connected have led to
them being retrieved.

The difference in this instance is that Wearing
herself is the embodiment of the uncanny, if you accept the psychoanalytical interpretation of the uncanny as being "something that ought to have remained secret and hidden but which has come to
light"[11]—"a sense of something new, foreign and hos-
tile invading an old, familiar, customary world."[12]
And another difference: the woman in the bandage
mask returns the gaze; stares down the starers; she
looks back.

What is it with Wearing and masks? "Celebrity,"
John Updike has written, "is a mask that eats into the

face." Unlike a number of her friends and contemporaries among the Young British Artists pack, Gillian Wearing hasn't become a promiscuously photographed party presence, an instantly recognizable household face. In SELF PORTRAIT (2000), though, she wears a mask that reads as a photofake, digitally doctored version of her own features (it is in fact an actual mask made of her face). It has no physical texture; none of the complicated tonality of a living face; none of the greasy luster of living skin. The hard-shadowed eye sockets and deep caves of the nostrils are unnerving. The face appears virtual; incorporeal. Less Lara Croft than Larkin's stone effigy on an Arundel tomb.

In these ways SELF PORTRAIT, and the more recent self portraits as various members of her immediate family (SELF PORTRAIT AS MY MOTHER JEAN GREGORY, 2003, and so on) are reminiscent of the computer composites that Nancy Burson has made, using "wrinkle masks" taken from the family members of long-missing children to digitally "age" the children's faces in order to give an approximation of how they might look in the unlikely event of them still being alive.

In the work of an earlier generation of English artists—the portrait paintings of Francis Bacon and Lucien Freud, most notably—the body-shape is clearly modeled by the life inside it; there is a sense of internal pressure pushing the skin into its uniquely complex shape. But with Wearing, as with a number of other notable artists of her generation, you never know whether there is a (real) face or only a ghastly void behind the crude disguises and prosthetic masks.

In his 1991 novel, *Mao II,* Don DeLillo has the following passage: "He knew the boy was standing by the door and he tried to see his face in words, imagine what he looked like, skin and eyes and features, every aspect of that surface called a face, if we can say he has a face, if we believe there is actually something under the hood."[13]

"There are signs everywhere [in US fiction] of the end of what I would call the physiognomy tradition," the novelist Charles Baxter recently wrote. "In writers like Don DeLillo, there is the... suggestion that the individual face simply has no importance any more... In DeLillo we enter a world where we cannot really know much of anything, particularly about other people. Other people may have some sort of individual reality, but it is not very likely to appear on their faces or to be visible anywhere else... If there are no real individuals left, why bother describing their faces. You will have to find something else to describe."[14]

We have come to a point where more and more of us, not only the famous, benefit from packaging ourselves in congenial forms. The packaging, like the masking that is such a feature of Wearing's work, is a form of self-protection. Because it can be perilous to go out there as yourself in a time when personality has replaced output as the measure of fame.

Confess all on video. Don't worry, you will be in disguise. Intrigued? Call Oprah, Jerry, Kilroy, Trisha. Come on. You can be real or fake-real so people think they're seeing reality when they're seeing something they invent. We are all creatures of the electronic limbo. Call Gillian.

1) Charles Tomlinson, in his introduction to William Carlos Williams: *Selected Poems* (London: Penguin, 1976), p. 16.
2) From William Carlos Williams, *Collected Poems: 1909–1939*, vol. I, copyright 1938 by New Directions Publishing Corp. Reprinted by permission.
3) Opening lines of Williams' poem "The Poor."
4) Tomlinson, op. cit., p. 16.
5) "Mike Wallace asks William Carlos Williams Is Poetry a Dead Duck?," an interview published in *The New York Post*, 18 October 1957, also included by Williams in his long poem "Paterson," (Book V, 1958).
6) Hugh Kenner, cited by Tomlinson, op. cit., p. 16.
7) Interview with Donna De Salvo, in *Gillian Wearing* (London: Phaidon, 1999), p. 11.
8) William Carlos Williams, *I wanted to write a poem: the autobiography of the works of a poet,* reported and ed. by Edith Heal (Boston: Beacon Press, 1958).
9) Interview with Ben Judd in 1995, reproduced in *Gillian Wearing* (London: Phaidon, 1999), p. 119.
10) Marc Augé, *Non-Places: Introduction to an Anthropology of Supermodernity* (London: Verso, 1995), p. 94.
11) Friedrich Schelling, quoted in Anthony Vidler, *Rachel Whiteread's House,* ed. James Lingwood (London: Phaidon, 1995), p. 71.
12) Anthony Vidler, *The Architectural Uncanny: Essays in the Modern Unhomely* (Cambridge, MA: MIT Press, 1992), p. 7.
13) Don DeLillo, *Mao II* (London: Jonathan Cape, 1991), p. 203.
14) Charles Baxter, "Loss of Face," *The Believer*, issue 8, November 2003, p. 17.

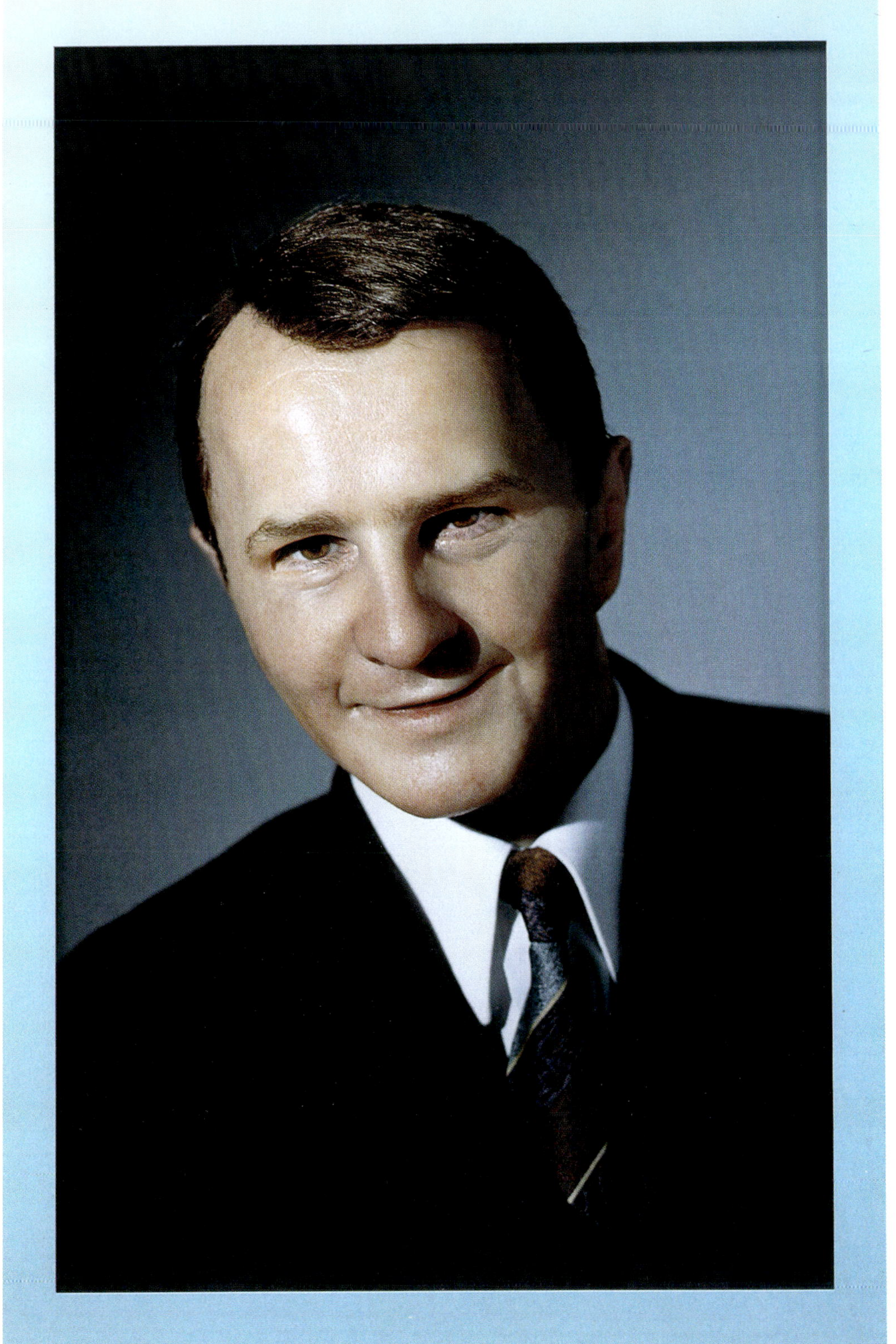

GILLIAN WEARING, SELF PORTRAIT AS MY UNCLE BRYAN GREGORY (ALBUM), 2003, digital c-type print, framed, 48 $^{13}/_{16}$ x 32 $^{1}/_{2}$" / SELBSTPORTRÄT ALS MEIN ONKEL BRYAN GREGORY, digitaler C-Print, gerahmt, 124 x 82,5 cm.

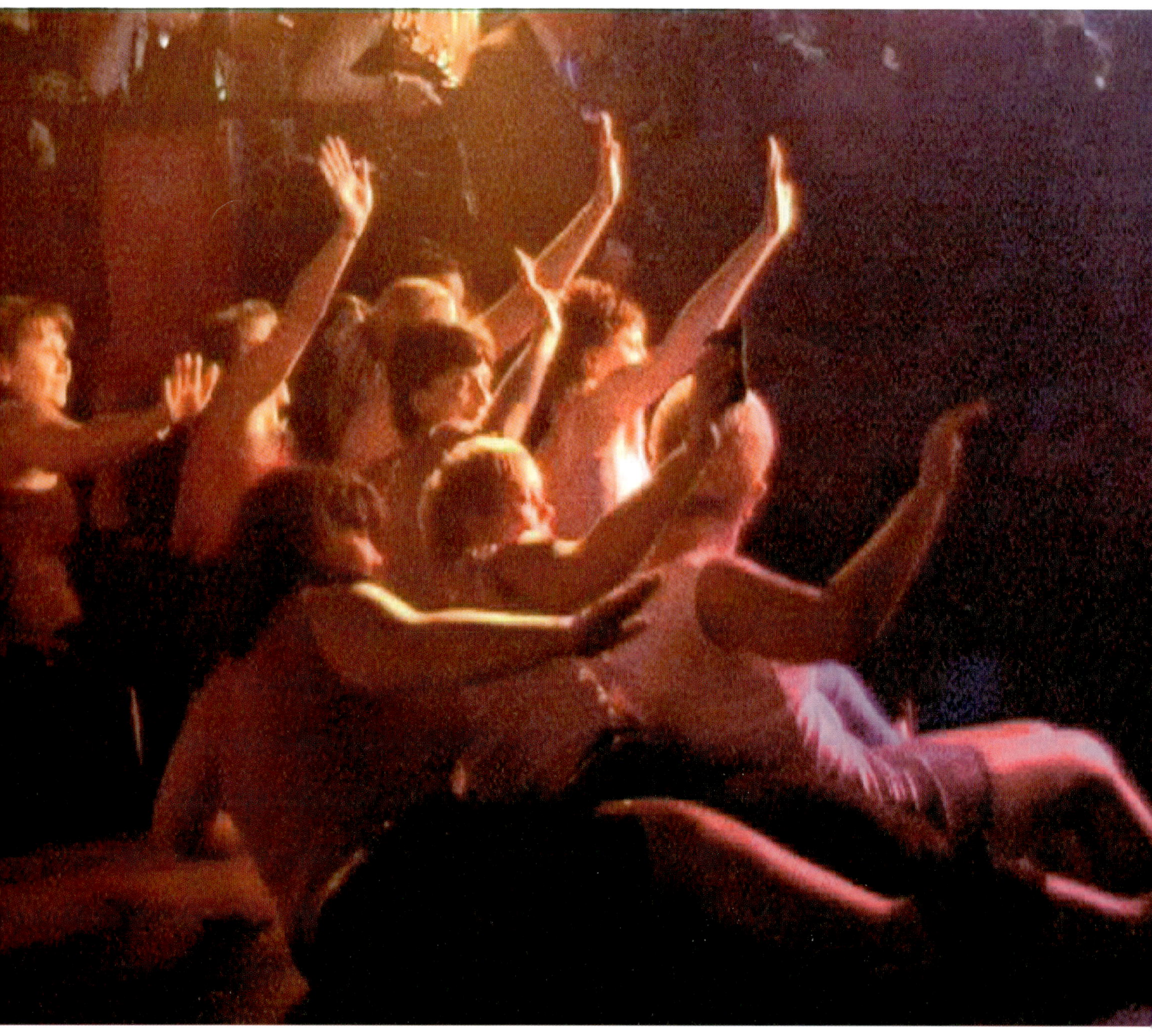

GILLIAN WEARING, BROAD STREET, 2001, still from multiple DVD projection of ca. 24 min. /
Szene aus der DVD-Mehrfachprojektion von ca. 24 Min.

*Wenn Williams wie Emerson «die Wirklichkeit
nach der Form zu fragen» scheint,
so ist die Form, kaum ist sie da, der Wirklichkeit enthoben,
ein Tanz über der Wirklichkeit.*
– Charles Tomlinson[1]

DIE BEGEGNUNG MIT DER WIRKLICHKEIT

GORDON BURN

Aus irgendeinem Grund begannen meine Gedanken jedesmal, wenn ich über Gillian Wearing und ihre Arbeit nachzudenken begann, um William Carlos Williams zu kreisen – um Williams, den Dichter des sprachlosen Amerika, ein Dichter, der der Sprachgewalt misstraute – sowie um Williams' flüchtiges, berühmtes, gerade mal sechzehn Worte umfassendes, kleines Gedicht «The Red Wheelbarrow» (Die rote Schubkarre):

so much depends	*so viel hängt ab*
upon	*von*
a red wheel	*einer roten Schub-*
barrow	*karre*

glazed with rain	*glänzend von Regen-*
water	*wasser*
beside the white	*bei den weissen*
chickens	*Hühnern*[2]

Wie Wearing bekannte sich auch Williams, der die meiste Zeit seines Lebens als Hausarzt in der Provinz von New Jersey praktizierte, zum Unmittelbaren und Lokalen, zum hier und jetzt greifbar Vorhandenen. Der besondere Reiz von Williams' Dichtung liegt in ihrem Beharren darauf, dass der Intellekt untrennbar mit der gesamten unmittelbaren, physischen, körperlichen Wahrnehmung verbunden ist. Er machte sich daran, eine Sprache zu entwickeln, die der Wirklichkeit entsprechen sollte, statt sich lediglich in Abstraktionen über sie zu ergehen.

Das gehemmte Sprachvermögen der Menschen, denen er tagtäglich bei seinen Hausbesuchen begeg-

---

GORDON BURN ist Schriftsteller und lebt in London. Seine zuletzt erschienenen Bücher sind *On the Way to Work* (mit Damien Hirst) und der Roman *The North of England Home Service*.

nete, ergriff und bewegte Williams immer wieder (*It's the anarchy of poverty / delights me...*[3]), und in seinem Werk sollte das Schlichte der Alltagssprache jede elitäre, kunstbewusste Ausdrucksweise und konventionelle poetische Formeln ersetzen: Wie schon Emerson meinte, kopieren Universitäten und Bücher ja lediglich die Sprache, die auf dem Feld und in der Werkstatt entsteht.[4] Und Williams selbst behauptete, sein Englisch von polnischen Müttern gelernt zu haben[5]: «Alles bietet gutes Material für Dichtung. Alles. Ich habe es immer wieder gesagt.»[6]

Dass Worte im typischen Sprechrhythmus New Jerseys zwar weniger aussagen, dies aber mit umso grösserer Bestimmtheit, war, wie der Literaturkritiker Hugh Kenner bemerkte, Williams' bahnbrechende technische Erkenntnis.[7] Was mich wiederum an etwas erinnerte, was Gillian Wearing über ihre Arbeit sagte, nämlich, dass sie der absolut wehrlosen Schlichtheit der individuellen Rede verpflichtet sei und ihr implizit ein Glaube an eine Art Heldentum der beeinträchtigten Menschen und Dinge innewohne: «Mich interessiert es mehr, wie andere Leute Dinge auf die Reihe bringen, wie sie etwas viel Interessanteres sagen können als ich.»[8]

Als ich anfing, dachte ich mir schon, dass das Material für diesen Beitrag über das seltsam sperrige und in wesentlichen Punkten schwer erkennbare Werk von Gillian Wearing aus «Vorgefundenem» be-

stehen würde, wie den mal komischen, mal vulgären, oft trivialen oder peinlich berührenden Gedanken und Worten von Fremden, die sie in ihre irritierende Photo- und Videokunst einbaut. Und eines Tages, als ich eigentlich zu Hause an diesem Text hätte arbeiten sollen, trat ich aus einem Londoner Restaurant in den peitschenden Regen hinaus. Schräg gegenüber befand sich ein Buchantiquariat, in dem ich Schutz suchte. Es roch muffig, die Türglocke klingelte, und auf dem Fussboden waren platt gedrückte Kartons ausgebreitet um das Wasser aufzusaugen. Der Antiquar sass im Überzieher mit hochgestelltem Kragen in einem kaputten niedrigen Sessel und spielte Bridge, Patience oder irgendein anderes Kartenspiel auf seiner grauen Computerkiste.

Fast sofort fiel mein Blick auf einen roten Buchrücken mit der weissen Aufschrift: «I Wanted to Write a Poem by William Carlos Williams». Es war die Erstausgabe eines Buches mit Gesprächen, das 1958 erschienen war. Auf der ersten Seite waren in der Mitte fünf Zeilen aus dem Gedicht abgedruckt, das dem Band den Titel gegeben hatte:

> *I wanted to write a poem*
> *that you would understand.*
> *For what good is it to me*
> *if you can't understand it?*
> *But you got to try hard—* [9]

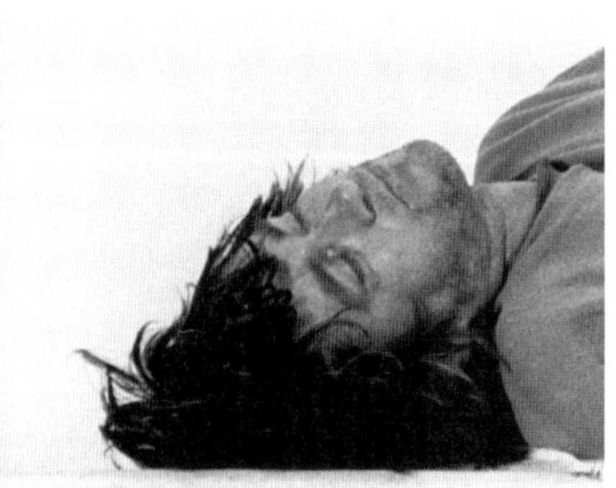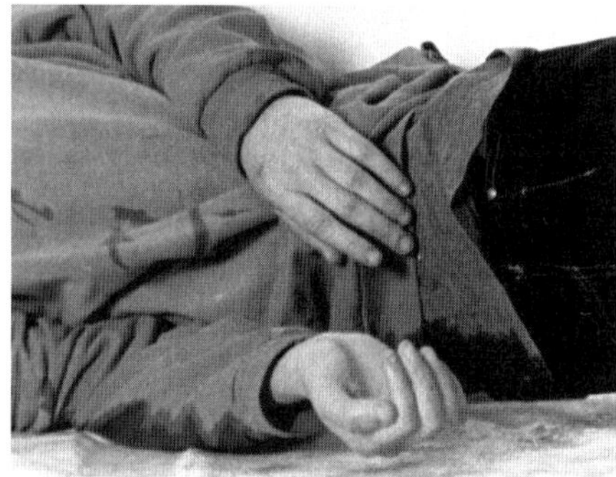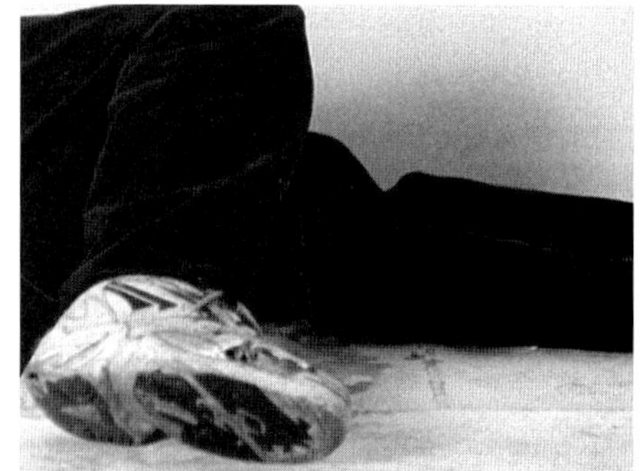

Der Band stand neben einem längst vergessenen Roman von Djuna Barnes. Und zwischen beiden eingeklemmt war, wie der magere Belag eines melancholisch modernistischen Sandwichs, ein Bändchen der *University of Minnesota* Reihe über amerikanische Schriftsteller: Band 24 aus dem Jahr 1963 über William Carlos Williams. Es öffnete sich gleich auf Seite 24, wo «The Red Wheelbarrow» abgedruckt war. Auf Seite 25 stand ein Gedicht, dem ich nie zuvor begegnet war, das sich aber – was jedem und jeder auch nur flüchtig mit Wearings Arbeit Vertrauten sofort einleuchten wird – wie von selbst hier einschob:

Danse Russe

If when my wife is sleeping
and the baby and Kathleen
are sleeping
and the sun is a flame-white disc
in silken mists
above shining trees, –
if I in my north room
dance naked, grotesquely
before my mirror
waving my shirt round my head
and singing softly to myself:
"I am lonely, lonely.
I was born to be lonely,
I am best so!"
If I admire my arms, my face,
my shoulders, flanks, buttocks
against the yellow drawn shades, –

Who shall say I am not
the happy genius of my household? [10]

«In den *Video Diary* - und *Video Nation* -TV-Spots», so Wearing, «sieht man, wie albern sich Leute in den eigenen vier Wänden aufführen – das ist so, seit die Camcorder auf dem Markt sind. Die Leute wollten schon immer sich selbst als Ausgeflippte dokumentieren; das ist ihr 'wahres' Gesicht. Sie tun das jedoch privat. Zweifellos gibt es unzählige Leute, die wie wild im eigenen Schlafzimmer herumgetanzt sind, aber erst wenn einer diese Phantasie irgendwohin verlegt, wo sie nicht hingehört, kann man beginnen, Fragen zu stellen.» [11]

In der 25-minütigen Videoarbeit DANCING IN PECKHAM (Tanzen in Peckham, 1994) tanzt Wearing selbst zu einem Soundtrack (Nirvanas «Smells Like Teen Spirit» und Gloria Gaynors «I Will Survive»), der sich lautlos in ihrem eigenen Kopf abspielt. Die «fremde» Umgebung, in der sich das Spektakel entfaltet, ist eine gesichtslose kleine Einkaufspassage – Schauplatz einer neuen Form von Einsamkeit, die im «Raum des Nicht-Ortes» (Marc Augé) um sich greift.

Eine Person, die den Raum des Nicht-Ortes [Autobahnen, Flughafenwartehallen, Multiplex-Kinos, «Erlebnis-Shopping»-Adressen] betrete, sei ihrer gewohnten Determinanten enthoben, schreibt Augé. Sie unterliege demselben Code wie andere, empfange dieselben Botschaften, leiste denselben Bitten Folge. Der Raum des Nicht-Ortes erzeuge weder eine einzelne Identität noch Beziehungen; nur Einsamkeit und Ähnlichkeit. [12] Sich an einem solchen Nicht-Ort ganz ungeniert dem persönlichen Ausdruck und der Selbstdarstellung hinzugeben gerät somit zu einer mutwilligen und (so wird nahe gelegt) strafbaren Übertretung.

In der heutigen Bilderwelt ist es zum Gemeinplatz geworden, dass Bilder immer mehr «Gefühlsinhalt» ansetzen, je häufiger sie reproduziert und wiederholt werden: Sie entwickeln eine Aura. Und dank einer Reihe Aufsehen erregender Mordfälle in Grossbritannien in den letzten Jahren verbindet sich mit dem typischen Vorstadt-Einkaufszentrum, das auch die Kulisse für Wearings Discotanz in Südlondon abgibt, mittlerweile ein Hauch des Unheimlichen – das Gespenst des Todes, das mitten durchs Leben geistert; Vorstellungen von dämonischen oder magischen Kräften. (Das heruntergekommene, veraltete Einkaufszentrum in Peckham hatte Wearing schon einmal als Kulisse gedient für SIGNS THAT SAY WHAT YOU WANT THEM TO SAY AND NOT SIGNS THAT SAY WHAT SOMEONE ELSE WANTS YOU TO SAY / Schilder, die das sagen, was man sagen will, und nicht Schilder, die sagen, was jemand anderer will, dass man sagt, 1992–93.)

In der, wie sich herausstellen sollte, letzten Stunde ihres Lebens wurde die populäre Fernsehmoderatorin Jill Dando von Überwachungskameras beim

Kauf einer Druckerpatrone in der King's Mall unweit des BBC-Studios aufgenommen. Und die grobkörnigen Aufnahmen des dreijährigen James Bulger, der Hand in Hand mit den beiden Schuljungen, die ihn später ermorden sollten, mitten durch das *Strand*-Shoppingcenter in Merseyside spaziert, haben sich im öffentlichen Bewusstsein Grossbritanniens so tief wie kaum ein anderes Bild der jüngeren Vergangenheit eingeprägt.

Mit jedem Einsatz der Kamera ist eine gewisse Aggression verbunden. Und zwangsläufig haben die Dando- und Bulger-Bilder die Qualität polizeilicher Ermittlungsphotos: Sie sind emotionslos und starr. Obwohl sie automatisch aufgenommen wurden, suggerieren sie die Gerissenheit und Geduld des Schnüfflers, des Voyeurs, des lauernden, raubtierhaften Paparazzos. Sie erinnern an die vorteilhafte Aussicht, die der Mörder genoss, als er unsichtbar im Gebüsch vor Jill Dandos Haus an der Gowan Avenue in Fulham lauerte.

Vielleicht waren es diese Konventionen, die Gillian Wearing auf die Probe stellte, als sie sich im Rahmen der Arbeit HOMAGE TO THE WOMAN WITH THE BANDAGED FACE WHO I SAW YESTERDAY DOWN WALWORTH ROAD (Hommage an die Frau mit dem verbundenen Gesicht, die ich gestern auf der Walworth Road sah, 1995) eine Verbandsmaske anlegte und sich auf dem Weg zu den örtlichen Geschäften von Überwachungskameras filmen liess. Die Bildsprache, die wir als regelmässige Fernsehkonsumenten alle verinnerlicht haben, ist unübersehbar: extreme Grobkörnigkeit, ätherische Streifen und Flecken. Der heimliche Charakter solcher Aufnahmen gilt inzwischen als Garant ihrer Authentizität. Das Unausgegorene solcher Bilder (oft verbunden mit tickenden digitalen Ziffern oben oder unten im Bild) ist inzwischen zur Chiffre einer Wirklichkeit geworden, die sich in Echtzeit abspielt – einer heimlich beobachteten Wirklichkeit der Augenblicke zwischendurch, in denen sich Verbrechen und Katastrophen ereignen. Ihre besondere Wirkung beruht zum grossen Teil darauf, dass sie nie dazu bestimmt waren, gesehen zu werden. Nur die verhängnisvollen Ereignisse, mit denen sie nachträglich in Zusammenhang gebracht wurden, haben dazu geführt, dass man sie ausgrub.

In diesem Fall besteht der Unterschied darin, dass Wearing selbst das Unheimliche verkörpert, wenn man die psychoanalytische Deutung des Begriffs akzeptiert, wonach das Unheimliche etwas ist, «was im Verborgenen hätte bleiben sollen und hervorgetreten ist»[13] oder ein «Gefühl, dass etwas Neues, Fremdes und Feindliches in die alte, vertraute, gewohnte Welt einbricht».[14] Aber da ist noch ein weiterer Unterschied: Die Frau mit der Verbandsmaske erwidert den Blick, zwingt den Blick derer, die sie anstarren, nieder, sie blickt zurück.

Was hat es mit Wearing und den Masken auf sich? Laut John Updike ist Berühmtheit eine Maske, die sich ins Gesicht frisst. Anders als manche ihrer Freunde und Zeitgenossen aus den Reihen der Young British Artists hat sich Gillian Wearing nicht bei jeder Gelegenheit und Party photographieren lassen und ist nicht zu einem sofort erkennbaren, allgegenwärtigen Gesicht geworden. In der Arbeit SELF PORTRAIT (Selbstporträt, 2000) trägt sie jedoch eine Maske, die wie eine photographische Fälschung, eine digital manipulierte Version ihrer Gesichtszüge wirkt. (Tatsächlich ist es eine exakte Maske ihres eigenen Gesichts.) Es fehlt die Struktur der Oberfläche, die komplexe Farbwirkung eines lebendigen Gesichts, der Fettschimmer lebender Haut. Die von dunklen Schatten umrandeten Augenhöhlen und die tiefen Nasenlöcher irritieren. Das Gesicht wirkt virtuell, unkörperlich, erinnert jedoch weniger an Lara Croft als an die steinernen Grabskulpturen in Philip Larkins Gedicht «An Arundel Tomb» (1956).

In dieser Hinsicht erinnert SELF PORTRAIT wie die neueren Selbstbildnisse, in denen Wearing in die Masken ihrer engeren Familienangehörigen schlüpft (ALBUM, 2003), an jene Computermontagen, die Nancy Burson mit Hilfe von «Faltenmasken» der Angehörigen von Kindern erstellte, die seit langem vermisst werden, um die Gesichter dieser Kinder digital «altern» zu lassen und so eine ungefähre Vorstellung davon zu erhalten, wie sie aussehen könnten, falls sie wider Erwarten noch am Leben wären.

In Arbeiten einer älteren Generation englischer Künstler – insbesondere in den gemalten Porträts von Francis Bacon und Lucien Freud – ist die körperliche Gestalt eindeutig durch das Leben in ihrem

GILLIAN WEARING, BROAD STREET, 2001, stills from multiple DVD projection of ca. 24 min. / Szenen aus der DVD-Mehrfach-Projektion von ca. 24 Min.

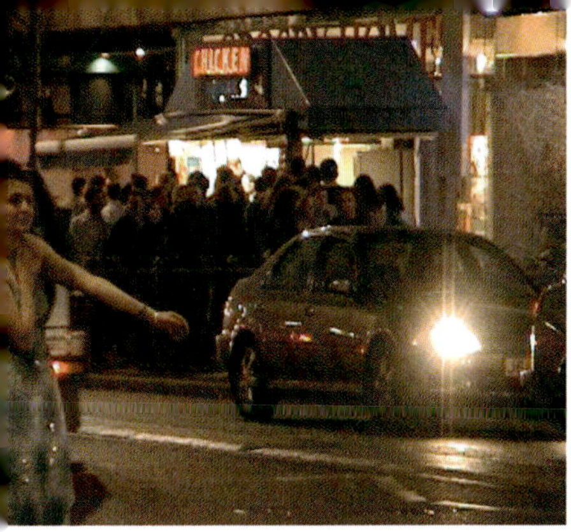

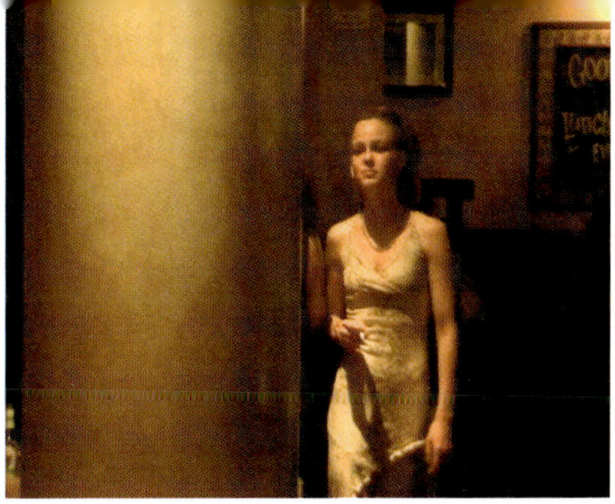

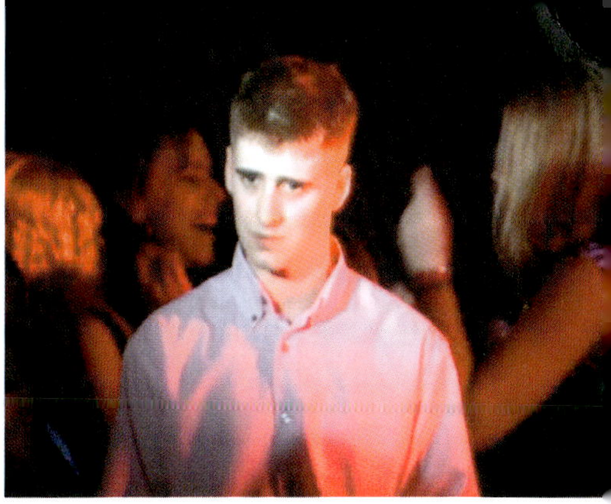

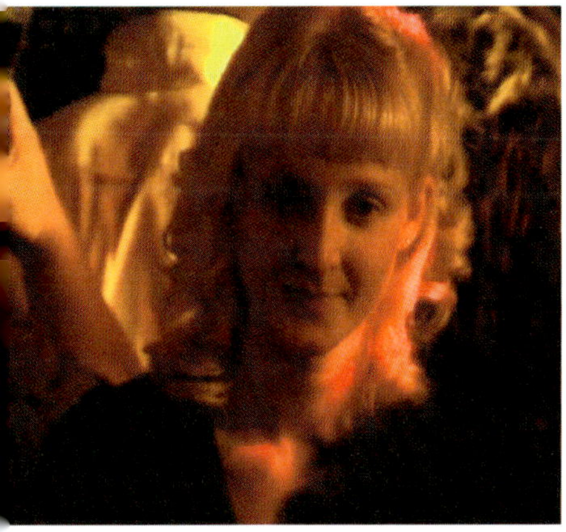

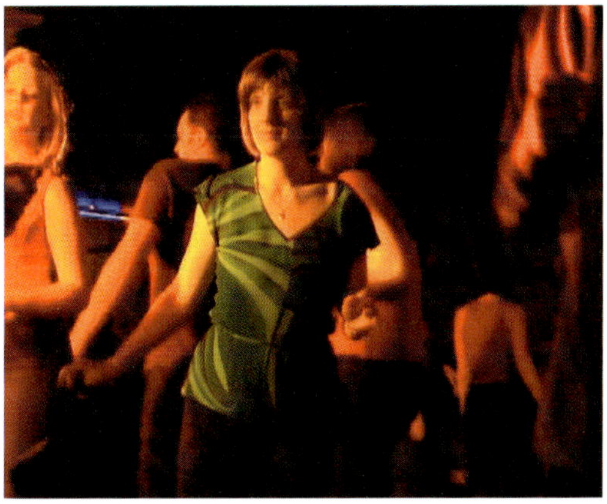

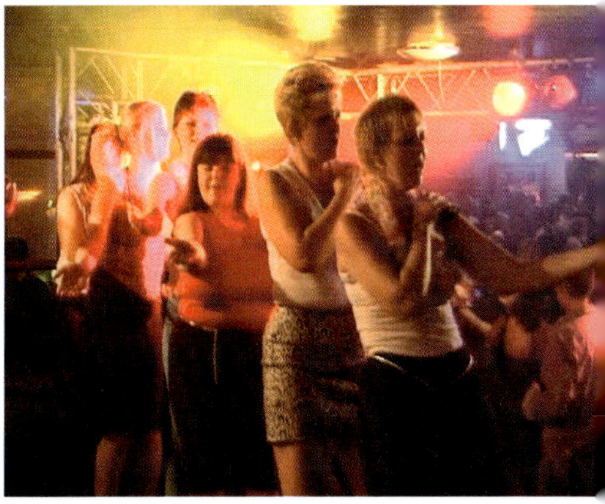

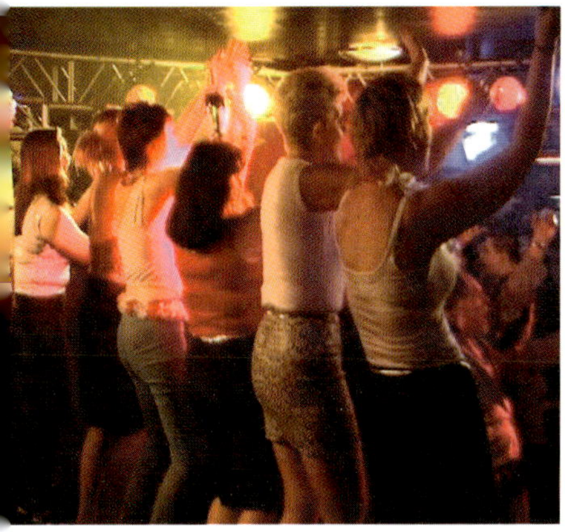

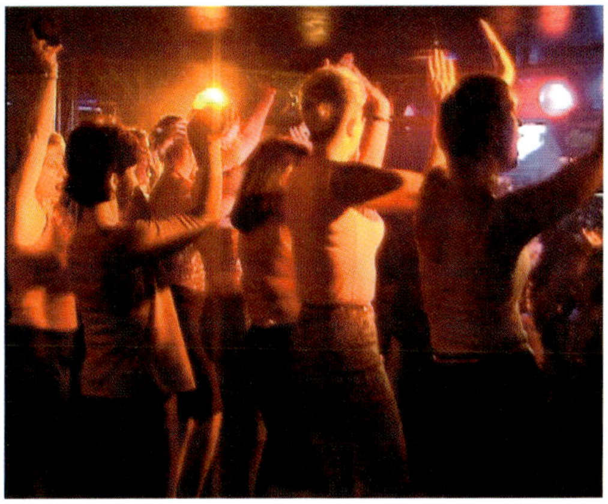

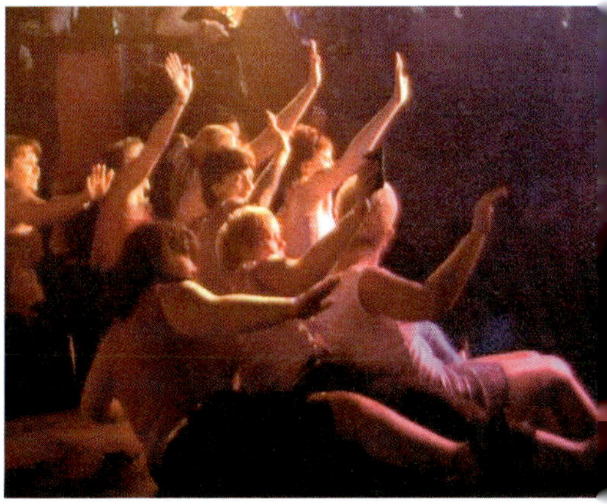

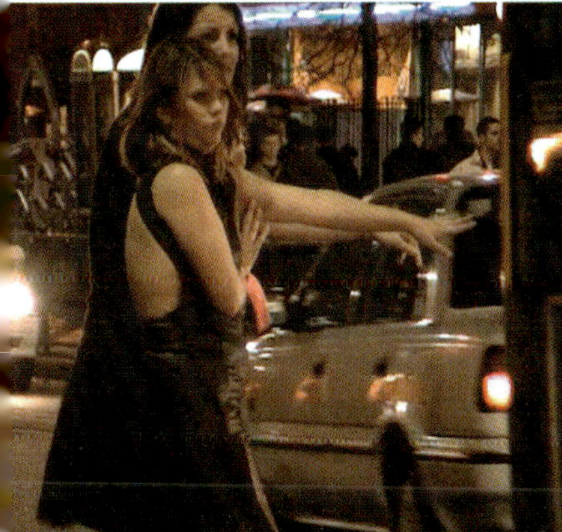 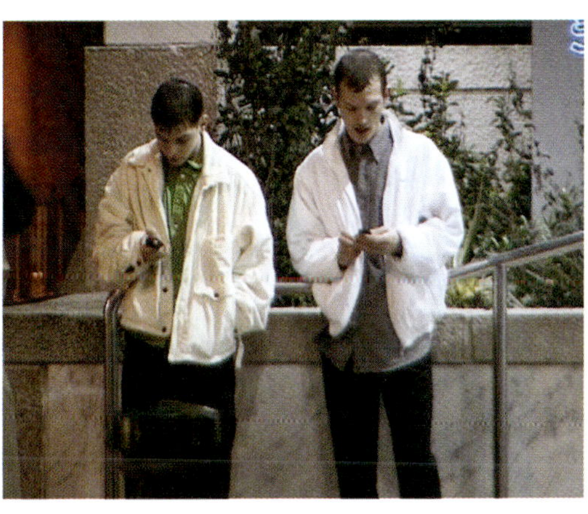 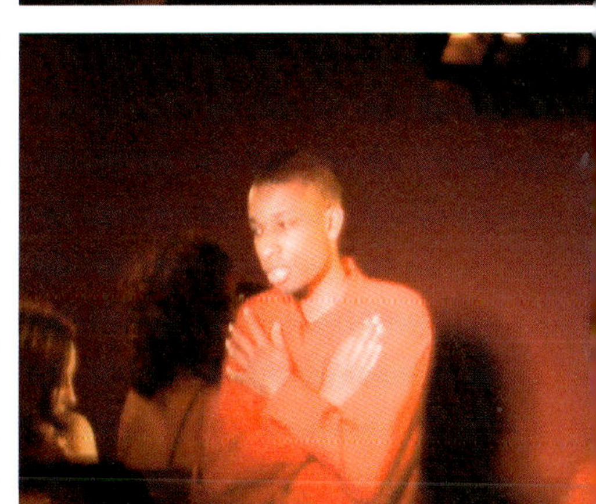

Innern bestimmt; man hat das Gefühl, dass ein innerer Druck die Haut in ihre einzigartig komplexe Form presst. Bei Wearing dagegen weiss man, wie bei einer Reihe anderer bekannter Künstlerinnen und Künstler ihrer Generation, nie, ob hinter den kruden Verkleidungen und prothetischen Masken ein (wirkliches) Gesicht steckt oder nur gespenstische Leere gähnt.

Im Don DeLillos Roman *Mao II* (1991) findet sich folgende Stelle: «Er wusste, dass der Junge an der Tür stand, und er versuchte, sein Gesicht in Worten zu sehen, sich vorzustellen, wie er aussah, Haut und Augen und Miene, jedes Detail dieser Fläche, die man Gesicht nennt, falls wir sagen können, dass er ein Gesicht hat, falls wir glauben, dass unter der Kapuze tatsächlich etwas ist.»[15]

Es gebe in der US-amerikanischen Literatur allenthalben Anzeichen für ein Ende dessen, was er die physiognomische Tradition nennen würde, meinte jüngst der Schriftsteller Charles Baxter. Bei Autoren wie Don DeLillo gewinne man den Eindruck, dass dem individuellen Gesicht schlicht keine Bedeutung mehr zukomme... Bei DeLillo würden wir eine Welt betreten, in der es nur noch wenige Gewissheiten gebe, insbesondere, was andere Menschen betreffe. Andere Menschen könnten durchaus eine eigene Wirklichkeit haben, diese würde sich aber kaum auf ihrem Gesicht abzeichnen oder sonstwie sichtbar sein... Wenn es aber gar keine echten Individuen mehr gebe, weshalb sollte man sich damit aufhalten, ihre Gesichter zu beschreiben? Man werde etwas anderes finden müssen, was zu beschreiben sich lohne.[16]

Wir sind an einem Punkt angelangt, wo immer mehr Leute, nicht nur die Berühmten, davon profitieren, in eine passende äussere Form schlüpfen zu können. Die Verpackung ist, wie die für Wearings Arbeiten so charakteristische Maskierung, eine Form des Selbstschutzes. Denn in Zeiten, da die Persönlichkeit das Werk als Massstab der Berühmtheit abgelöst hat, kann es gefährlich werden, sich als man selbst da draussen zu bewegen.

Beichte alles auf Video. Mach dir keine Sorgen, du wirst maskiert sein. Interessiert? Melde dich bei Oprah, Jerry, Kilroy, Trisha. Komm schon. Du kannst echt sein oder nur zum Schein echt, so dass die

Leute denken, sie sähen die Wirklichkeit, wo sie nur selbst Erfundenes sehen. Wir alle sind Geschöpfe der elektronischen Vorhölle. Melde dich bei Gillian.

(Übersetzung: Bram Opstelten)

1) Charles Tomlinson in seiner Einführung zu William Carlos Williams, *Selected Poems,* Penguin Books, London 1976, S. 16.
2) Zitiert nach der zweisprachigen Ausgabe, W. C. Williams, *Ausgewählte Gedichte,* hrsg. v. Joachim Sartorius, Rowohlt Taschenbuch, Reinbek bei Hamburg 2001 (ursprünglich bei Carl Hanser Verlag, München 1991).
3) Etwa «Die Anarchie der Armut ists, was mir gefällt...», Anfang des Gedichts «The Poor». (Übers.: Red.)
4) Ralph Waldo Emerson, in seiner Ansprache «The American Scholar» (Harvard 1837).
5) Tomlinson, op. cit., S. 16.
6) Aus «Mike Wallace asks William Carlos Williams Is Poetry a Dead Duck?», Interview in *The New York Post,* 18. Oktober 1957; von Williams 1958 ins 5. Buch des Gedichtes «Paterson» aufgenommen. Vgl. *Ausgewählte Gedichte,* op. cit., S. 622.
7) Hugh Kenner, zitiert in Tomlinson, op. cit., p. 16.
8) Interview mit Donna De Salvo in *Gillian Wearing,* Phaidon Press, London 1999, S. 11.
9) W. C. Williams, *I wanted to write a poem: the autobiography of the works of a poet,* aufgeschrieben und herausgegeben von Edith Heal, Beacon Press, Boston 1958. Etwa: *Ich wollte ein Gedicht schreiben / das du verstehen würdest. / Denn was nützt es mir / wenn du es nicht verstehst / Aber du musst es ernsthaft versuchen* – (Red.)
10) Copyright by New Directions Publishing Corp., Abdruck mit freundlicher Genehmigung.
Wenn, während meine Frau schläft / und das Baby und Kathleen / schlafen / und die Sonne als flammendweisse Scheibe / in seidigen Nebeln / über glänzenden Bäumen steht, – / wenn ich in meinem Nordzimmer / nackt tanze, grotesk / vor meinem Spiegel / mit dem Hemd um den Kopf wedle / und leise vor mich hin singe: / «Ich bin allein, allein, / ich bin zum Alleinsein geboren, / so ist mir am wohlsten!» / Wenn ich meine Arme, mein Gesicht bestaune, / meine Schultern, Flanken, Hinterbacken / vor den geschlossenen, gelben Jalousien, – // Wer wollte da sagen, ich sei nicht / der glückliche Schutzgeist meines Haushalts? (Red.)
11) Interview mit Ben Judd, 1995, in *Gillian Wearing,* Phaidon Press, London 1999, S. 119.
12) Marc Augé, *Non-Places: Introduction to an Anthropology of Supermodernity,* Verso, London 1995, S. 94. (Deutsche Ausgabe: *Orte und Nicht-Orte: Vorüberlegungen zu einer Ethnologie der Einsamkeit,* S. Fischer, Frankfurt am Main 1994. Das Zitat wurde aus dem Engl. übersetzt.)
13) Sigmund Freud, «Das Unheimliche», zitiert in Anthony Vidler, *unHEIMlich; Über das Unbehagen in der modernen Architektur,* Edition Nautilus, Hamburg 2002, S. 34.
14) Anthony Vidler, ebenda, S. 44.
15) Don DeLillo, *Mao II,* Kiepenheuer & Witsch, Köln 1992, S. 261.
16) Charles Baxter, «Loss of Face», *The Believer,* Nr. 8, November 2003, S. 17.

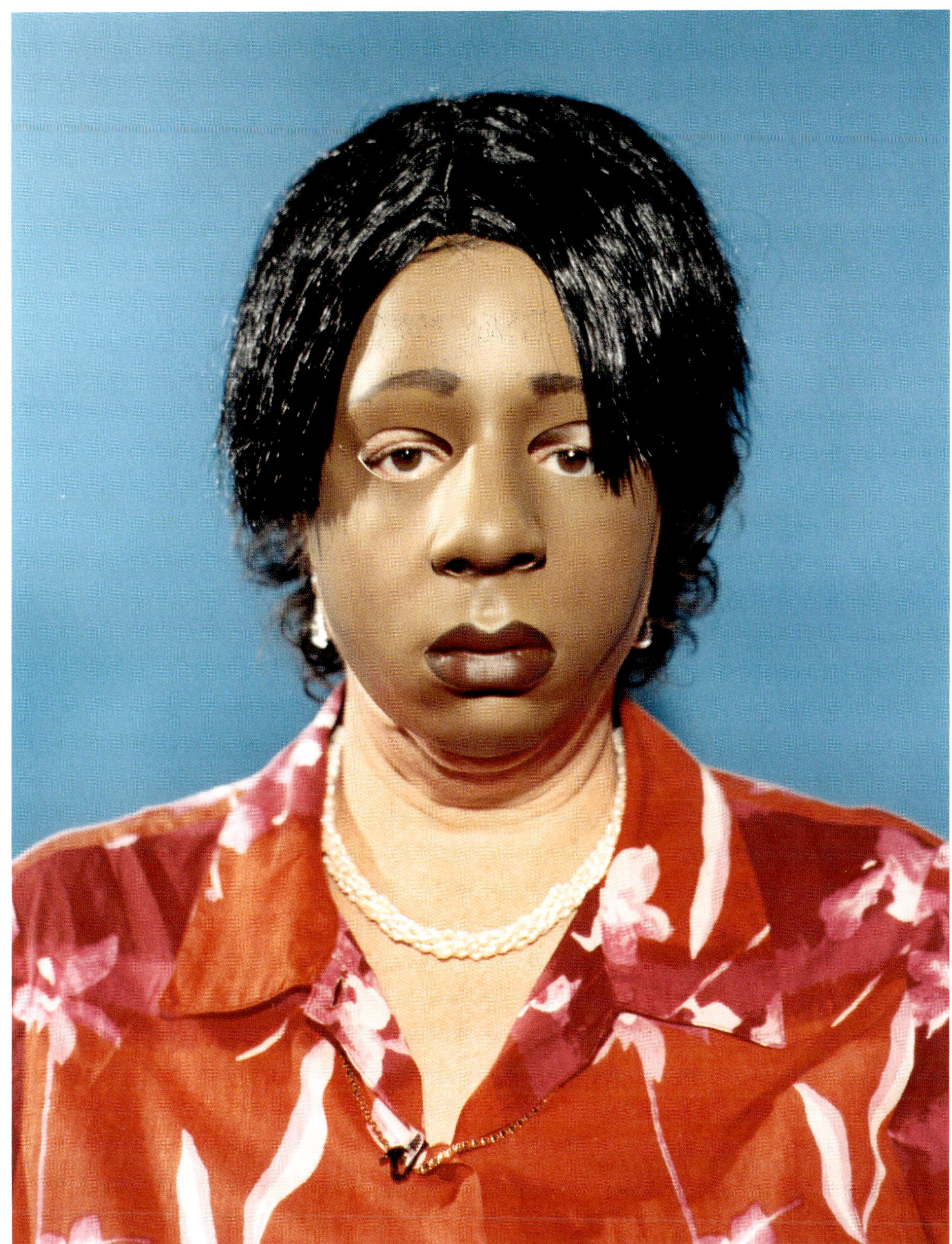

GILLIAN WEARING, *TRAUMA*, 2000, production still from 30-min. video with sound / *Aufnahme während der Produktion des 30-minütigen Videos mit Ton.*

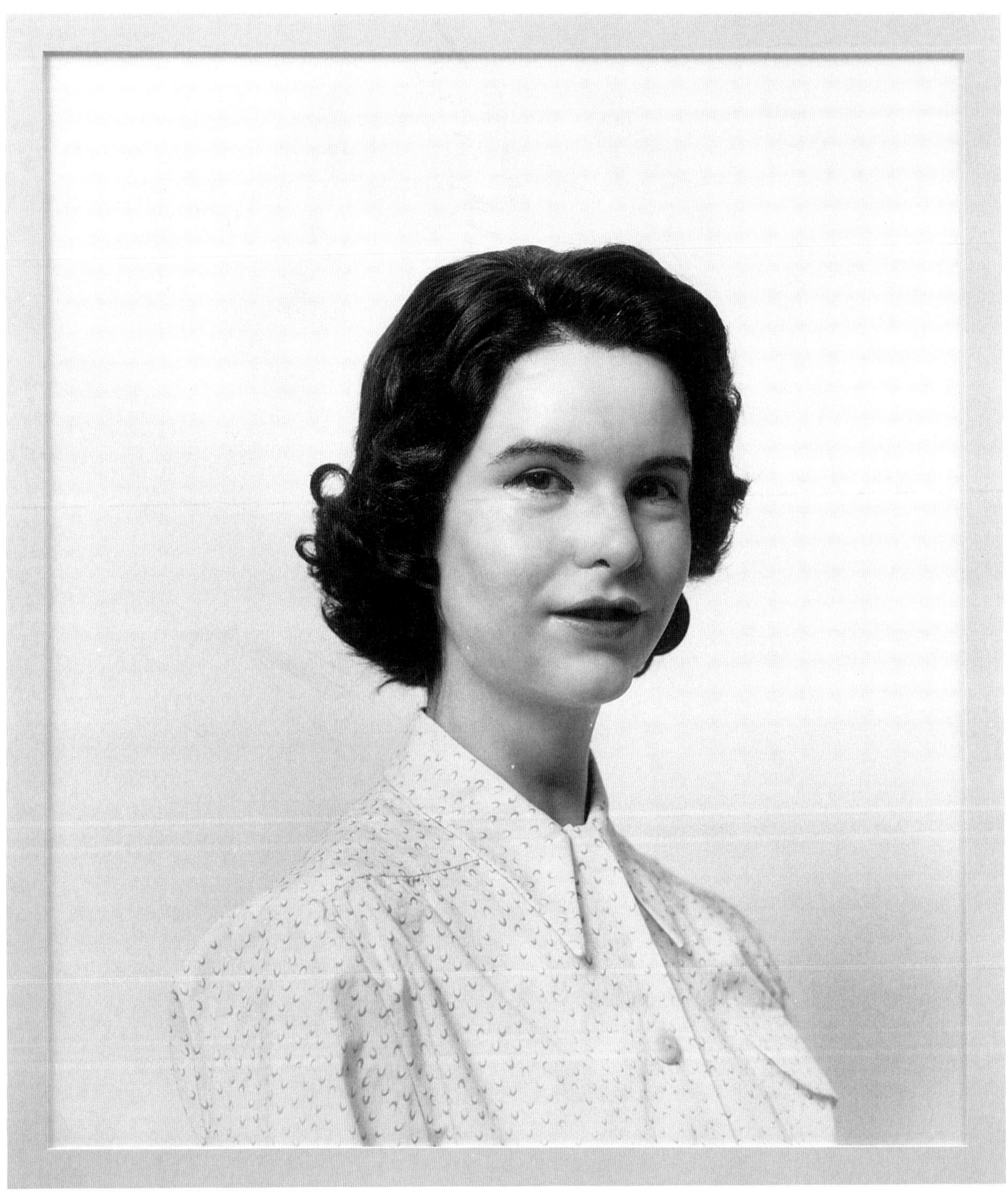

GILLIAN WEARING, SELF PORTRAIT AS MY MOTHER JEAN GREGORY (ALBUM), 2003, black-and-white print, framed, 58 ⅝ x 51 ³⁄₁₆" /
SELBSTPORTRÄT ALS MEINE MUTTER JEAN GREGORY, Schwarzweissabzug, gerahmt, 149 x 130 cm.

ALBUM SERIES (2003)

GILLIAN WEARING ON HER

GILLIAN WEARING & CAY SOPHIE RABINOWITZ

CAY SOPHIE RABINOWITZ: Tell me about ALBUM.

GILLIAN WEARING: When I was sorting through some old photographs I came across an image of my mother as a twenty-three-year-old. I've had the image for about twenty years. I noticed that my memory of the photo was very different from what I was looking at when I rediscovered the photograph in 2001. It was through this re-evaluation that I began to think about what I had projected onto the image of her and my consciousness of her age. It was strange that when I was younger I thought of her as older in the picture and when I returned to it, I realized that hers was the face of a young woman that I didn't recognize and hadn't seen before! It took my own aging to make me really appreciate and understand my mother as her younger self. I could see in the photograph my mother, myself, and someone I could never have known at that age.

It was a puzzle that motivated me to want to "be her" at that age and investigate the missing link concerning me, her, and that picture.

CSR: So you thought to construct a mask of her younger face and be her for your portrait of her?

GW: There was something she possessed in the picture that had to do with innocence. I guess it was this quality that I hoped to capture. It was a delicate procedure to try and convey the fragile, hopeful sense of innocence as well as the optimism of her life stretching before her. The mask that I had made of her face was in many ways the opposite of innocent, but my hope was that I could internalize her state of being at that age and, mainly with my eyes, posture and bearing, convince the viewer that I was her.

CSR: So you weren't only concerned with the photo as such, you were more concerned with the state of being?

GW: Definitely both. I needed the photo as an anchor or talisman, but I also wanted to explore something extra, something more than the photo. There was a level of empathy that I wanted to feel.

CAY SOPHIE RABINOWITZ is the Senior Editor of *Parkett* in New York.

C S R : Did that extend to some of the other images?

G W : My first concern was to work closely with the picture of my mum and it was truly the starting point that I felt the most connection to, having spent so much time thinking of this image. However, once I had begun working on it, and after two years of research as well as the extended production, I realized that I wanted to take the whole thing further and widen it to include the closest members of my family. The cohesion that held the work together for me was the age that everyone, including myself, was in the photographs I had selected.

C S R : So everyone was younger in the pictures you chose?

G W : Yeah, especially my mum, dad, and uncle. They were all at an age where they seemed hopeful and in some ways undefined by life's pressures. I mean with fewer responsibilities, a little more self-centered. They projected a more optimistic or idealized face to the world. At that time, particularly in studio portraits, this was expected and was more what would be conventionally portrayed. And having portraits of everyone at around the same age helped to equalize the relationship between all the family members and destroy the hierarchy.

C S R : So what about your brother and sister?

G W : My brother was taken from a snapshot that had been taken by my mother in 1991. I was fascinated by this picture and managed to keep hold of it for years, always wanting to make a work about it. It fulfils something I always wanted to investigate. This to me is a *vanitas* image.

It has something very classical as well as contemporary about it. It has all these incidental props which help create the narrative and portrait of the subject, in this case my brother. I worked with an excellent technical crew to construct a body suit of my brother and have a mask and wig made to enact this. It was the most physically demanding photo I created, as I had to wear the very heavy body suit for hours as well as adopt a very particular posture and gesture. All this, including the tattoo being painted on the arm of the body cast, was undertaken just to remake what was in effect a casual snapshot! Nothing could have been further from the truth—I was hot, in pain, and contorted for hours, as well as having to direct the whole shoot.

The picture of my sister was based on an amateur photographer's sitting. All through my teens I wanted to be my sister. So here was the opportunity to be her as I had idealized her, and the photographer had.

C S R : You are not only looking at your family; you're also looking at the nature of photography and its genres?

G W : Yes, that had always been a parallel interest for me whilst working on this. You can see how much photography has changed both technically and in relation to the form that had become acceptable as a mode of practice when each of the original pictures was taken.

C S R : Can you say more about that?

G W : In my parents' lifetime fewer cameras were available. In order to document oneself it was necessary to employ a studio photographer, and an air of formality as well as a standard convention of posing and presentation was expected. By the seventies the whole photographic process had become more accessible, making a snapshot aesthetic more accepted. So by the time my mother took the picture of my brother she could do so without censoring, or judging it too casual or familiar. Yet at his age she would have only considered being photographed within the conventions of the photograph in which I present her.

C S R : So the series of works assesses the state of photography as well as the emotional state of your family?

GW: Diane Arbus was taught by Lizette Model that the more specific you could be about yourself and the subjects you choose to photograph, the more universal you are. So for me this is an album of my family, but I think it also represents a family album that can be recognized by everyone. It's this aspect that also interests me. It's all the archetypes coming together, and in this case it's the element of each image being a "self-portrait" that gives it deeper meaning.

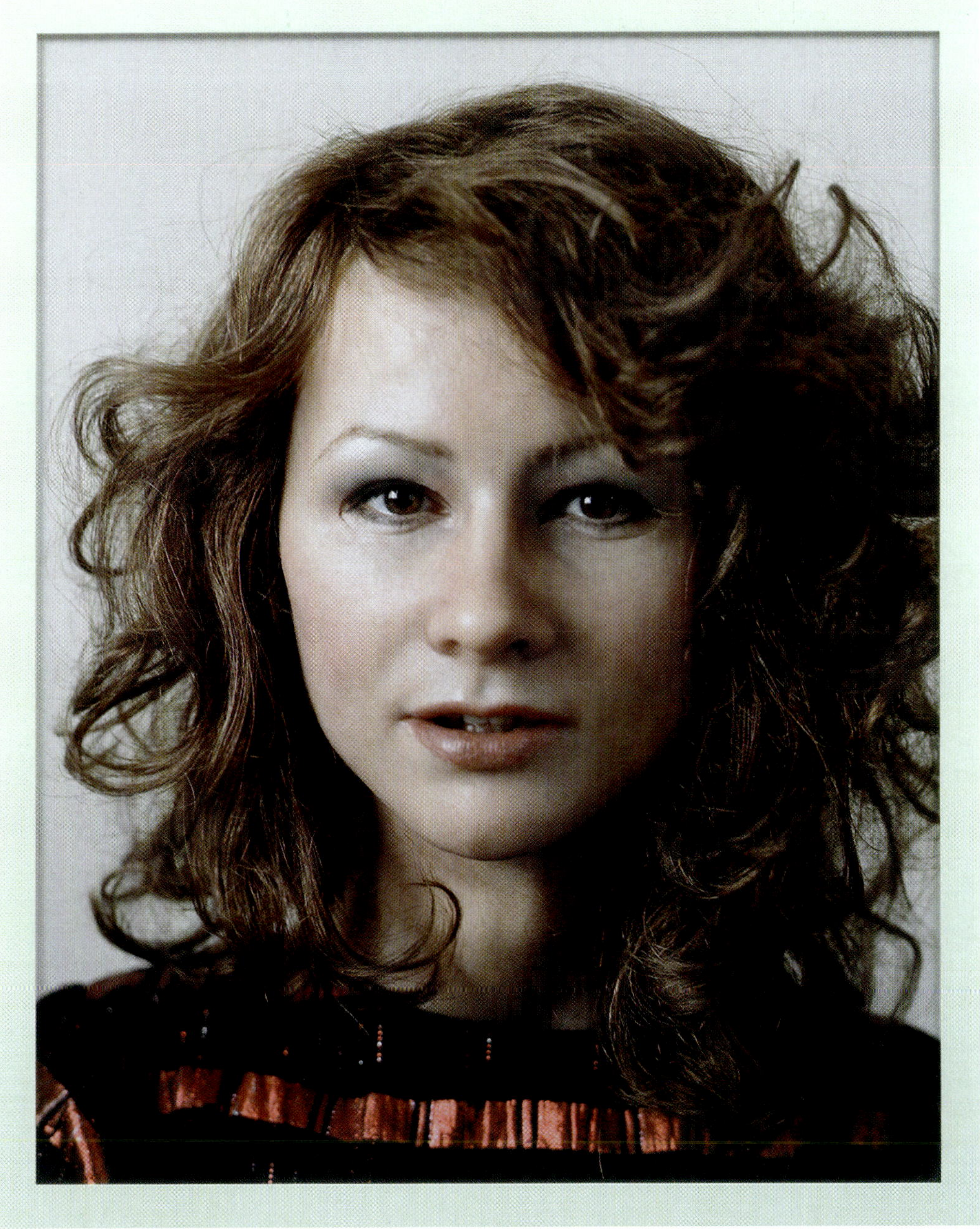

GILLIAN WEARING, SELF PORTRAIT AS MY SISTER JANE WEARING (ALBUM), 2003, digital c-type print, framed, 55 ½ x 45 ⅝" / SELBSTPORTRÄT ALS MEINE SCHWESTER JANE WEARING, digitaler C-Print, gerahmt, 141 x 116 cm.

ALBUM SERIE (2003)

GILLIAN WEARING & CAY SOPHIE RABINOWITZ

GILLIAN WEARING ÜBER DIE

CAY SOPHIE RABINOWITZ: Erzähl mir etwas über ALBUM.

GILLIAN WEARING: Beim Durchsehen alter Photographien stiess ich auf ein Bild meiner Mutter als Dreiundzwanzigjährige. Ich besass das Bild schon seit rund zwanzig Jahren. Mir fiel auf, dass meine Erinnerung an dieses Photo sich stark von dem unterschied, was ich vor mir sah, als ich es 2001 wieder fand. Dank diesem neuen Blick auf das Bild begann ich darüber nachzudenken, was ich darauf projiziert hatte und wie ich ihr Alter wahrnahm. Es war merkwürdig, dass ich sie, als ich selbst jünger gewesen war, auf diesem Bild für älter gehalten hatte. Als ich es jetzt wiedersah, wurde mir bewusst, dass ihr Gesicht das einer jungen Frau war, die ich nicht kannte und nie zuvor gesehen hatte! Ich musste selbst erst älter werden, um das jüngere Ich meiner Mutter wirklich wahrzunehmen. Ich konnte auf dem Photo meine Mutter sehen, aber auch mich selbst und jemanden, den ich in diesem Alter gar nicht hätte kennen können.

Es war ein Rätsel, das mich dazu brachte, «sie sein» zu wollen, in eben diesem Alter, um der fehlenden Verbindung zwischen mir, ihr und diesem Bild nachzuspüren.

CSR: So bist du darauf gekommen, eine Maske ihres jungen Gesichts herzustellen, um für dein Porträt von ihr in ihre Haut schlüpfen zu können?

GW: Sie hat etwas auf diesem Bild, das mit Unschuld zu tun hat. Ich denke, es war diese Qualität, die ich einzufangen hoffte. Es war eine heikle Aufgabe, diesen fragilen, hoffnungsvoll unschuldigen Eindruck wiederzugeben, aber gleichzeitig auch den Optimismus im Hinblick auf das noch vor ihr liegende Leben. Die Maske, die ich von ihrem Gesicht angefertigt hatte, war in vielerlei Hinsicht alles andere als unschuldig, aber ich hoffte, dass ich ihren Seinszustand in jenem Alter verinnerlichen könnte und den Betrachter – hauptsächlich mit den Augen, der Haltung und meinem Verhalten – davon würde überzeugen können, dass ich tatsächlich sie war.

CSR: Also ging es dir nicht nur um das Photo als solches, sondern mehr um den damit verbundenen Seelenzustand.

GW: Es ging ganz klar um beides. Ich war auf das Photo angewiesen wie auf einen Anker oder Talisman, aber ich wollte auch noch etwas anderes untersuchen, etwas über das Photo Hinausgehendes. Da war eine gewisse Empathie, die ich spüren wollte.

CAY SOPHIE RABINOWITZ ist *Parkett*-Redaktorin in New York.

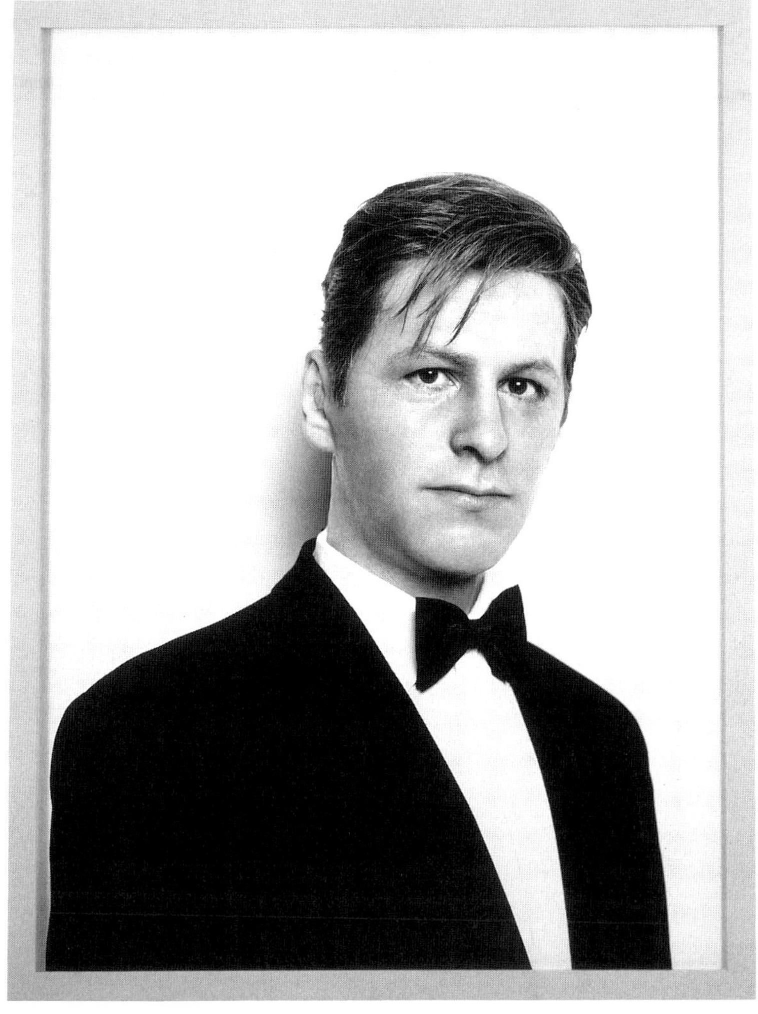

CSR: Gilt das auch für einige der anderen Bilder?

GW: Es ging mir in erster Linie darum, intensiv mit dem Bild meiner Mutter zu arbeiten, und es war tatsächlich der Ausgangspunkt, mit dem ich mich am engsten verbunden fühlte, nachdem ich so lange über dieses Bild nachgedacht hatte. Als ich jedoch mit der Arbeit daran begonnen hatte und zwei Jahre lang recherchiert sowie die langwierige Produktion in Angriff genommen hatte, wurde mir klar, dass ich die ganze Sache weiterziehen und auf die nächsten Familienmitglieder ausdehnen wollte. Der Kitt, der die Arbeit zusammenhielt, war für mich das Alter jedes Einzelnen auf den gewählten Photos, das gilt auch für mich selbst.

CSR: Dann waren also alle jünger auf den Bildern, die du wähltest?

GW: Ja, besonders meine Mama, mein Papa und mein Onkel. Sie alle waren in einem Alter, in dem sie voller Hoffnung schienen und irgendwie noch nicht von den Zwängen des Lebens bestimmt wurden. Ich meine, sie hatten weniger Verantwortung zu tragen und waren ein bisschen egozentrischer. Sie sahen optimistischer oder idealistischer in die Welt. Damals wur-

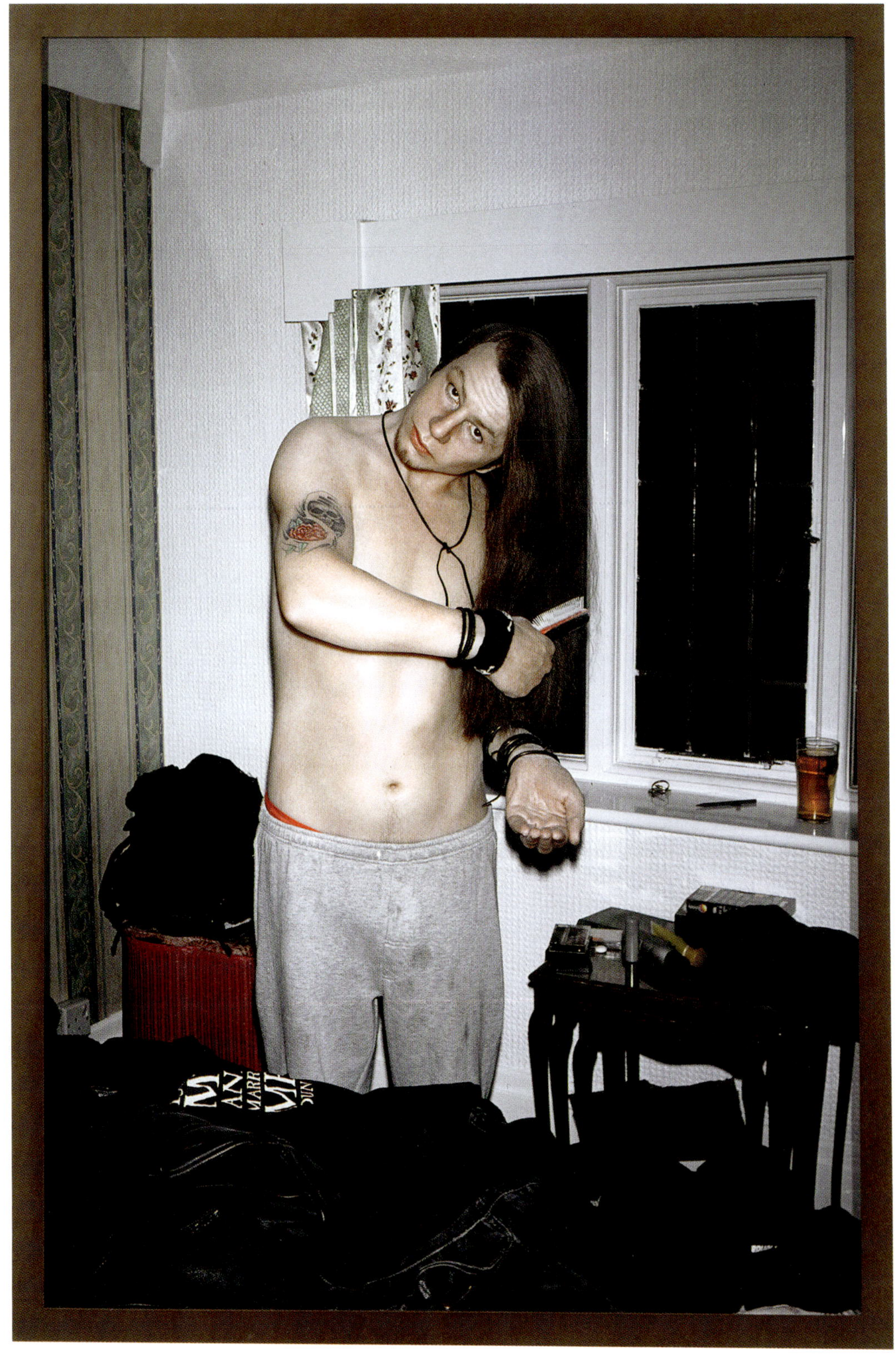

GILLIAN WEARING, SELF PORTRAIT AS MY BROTHER RICHARD WEARING (ALBUM), 2003, digital c-type print, framed, 75 ³/₁₆ x 51 ³/₈ " /
SELBSTPORTRÄT ALS MEIN BRUDER RICHARD WEARING, digitaler C-Print, gerahmt, 191 x 130,5 cm. (PHOTOS: MAUREEN PALEY INTERIM ART, LONDON)

de dies – besonders in professionellen Porträtaufnahmen – auch erwartet und gehörte zum konventionellen Porträt. Die Tatsache, dass alle auf ihrem Porträt ungefähr gleich alt waren, erleichterte es, die Beziehungen zwischen den Familienmitgliedern auszugleichen und die Hierarchie zu verwischen.

C S R : Wie war das mit deinem Bruder und deiner Schwester?

G W : Bei meinem Bruder nahm ich einen Schnappschuss, den meine Mutter 1991 gemacht hatte. Das Bild faszinierte mich und ich bewahrte es Jahre lang auf; ich wollte schon immer eine Arbeit über dieses Bild machen. Es löst etwas ein, was ich schon lange untersuchen wollte. Für mich ist es ein *Vanitas*-Bild. Es hat zugleich etwas zutiefst Klassisches und Zeitgenössisches. Da sind all diese zufälligen Requisiten, die dazu dienen, den narrativen Kontext und das Porträt, in diesem Fall meines Bruders, zu erzeugen. Ich arbeitete mit einem ausgezeichneten technischen Team zusammen, um die Körpermaske meines Bruders sowie die Gesichtsmaske samt Perücke herzustellen. Es war das körperlich anstrengendste Photo, das ich je gemacht habe. Und all das, einschliesslich der Tätowierung, die auf den Arm des Körperabgusses gemalt werden musste, um einen letztlich beiläufigen Schnappschuss zu rekonstruieren! Nichts hätte weiter von der Wahrheit entfernt sein können – ich schwitzte, hatte Schmerzen, musste Stunden lang in einer verrenkten Stellung aushalten und überdies noch die Aufnahme überwachen.

Was meine Schwester betrifft, stützte ich mich auf das Porträt eines Amateurphotographen. Als Teenager wäre ich immer gern meine Schwester gewesen. Hier kam also endlich die Gelegenheit in ihre Haut zu schlüpfen, so wie ich sie idealisiert hatte und wie der Photograph es getan hatte.

C S R : Du hast also nicht nur deine Familie im Blick, sondern auch die Photographie als solche und ihre Genres?

G W : Ja, das Interesse daran verlief immer parallel zu meiner Arbeit an dieser Serie. In der Zeitspanne, die vergangen ist und die punktuell in diesen Bildern sichtbar wird, erkennt man sowohl die Veränderung der Phototechnik wie jene der jeweils akzeptierten Form und Praxis zum Zeitpunkt jeder einzelnen Aufnahme.

C S R : Kannst du das näher erläutern?

G W : Zu Lebzeiten meiner Eltern gab es weniger Photoapparate. Wenn man sein Bild dokumentarisch festhalten wollte, musste man einen Berufsphotographen beauftragen; das war mit einer gewissen Formalität und einer konventionellen Pose und Präsentation verbunden. In den 70er Jahren wurde die Photographie leichter zugänglich und damit wurde auch die Ästhetik des Schnappschusses akzeptabel. Als meine Mutter also dieses Bild meines Bruders machte, konnte sie dies tun, ohne es zu zensurieren oder es für zu unbedeutend oder zu intim zu halten. Aber für sie selbst wäre in seinem Alter keine andere Form von Photographie denkbar gewesen als die konventionelle, in der ich sie darstelle.

C S R : Also ist in diesen Werken nicht nur die emotionale Befindlichkeit deiner nächsten Verwandten registriert, sondern auch der jeweilige Stand der Photographie?

G W : Diane Arbus hat von Lizette Model gelernt, dass man umso universaler ist, je spezifischer man auf sich selbst und seine eigenen Sujets eingeht. Deshalb ist dies für mich ein Familienalbum meiner eigenen Familie, aber ich glaube, dass jede und jeder darin sein Familienalbum wiedererkennen kann. Diesen Aspekt finde ich auch interessant. In einem solchen Album kommen alle Archetypen zusammen, und in diesem speziellen Fall ist es die Tatsache, dass jedes Bild ein «Selbstporträt» ist, die dem Ganzen tiefere Bedeutung verleiht.

(Übersetzung: Wilma Parker)

Edition for Parkett   GILLIAN WEARING

Sleeping Mask, 2004

Wax (reinforced by polymer resin), paint,

8 1/4 x 5 5/16".

Produced by Making Objects Ltd., London.

Edition of 60, signed and numbered.

Schlafende Maske, 2004

Wachs (verstärkt mit Polymerharz), Farbe,

21 x 13,5 cm.

Produktion: Making Objects Ltd., London.

Auflage: 60, signiert und nummeriert.

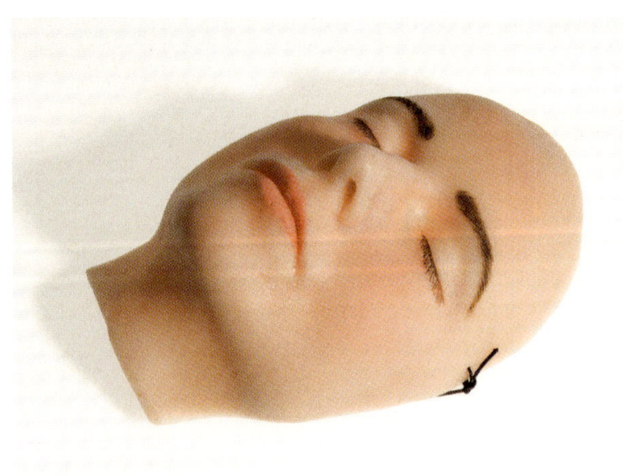

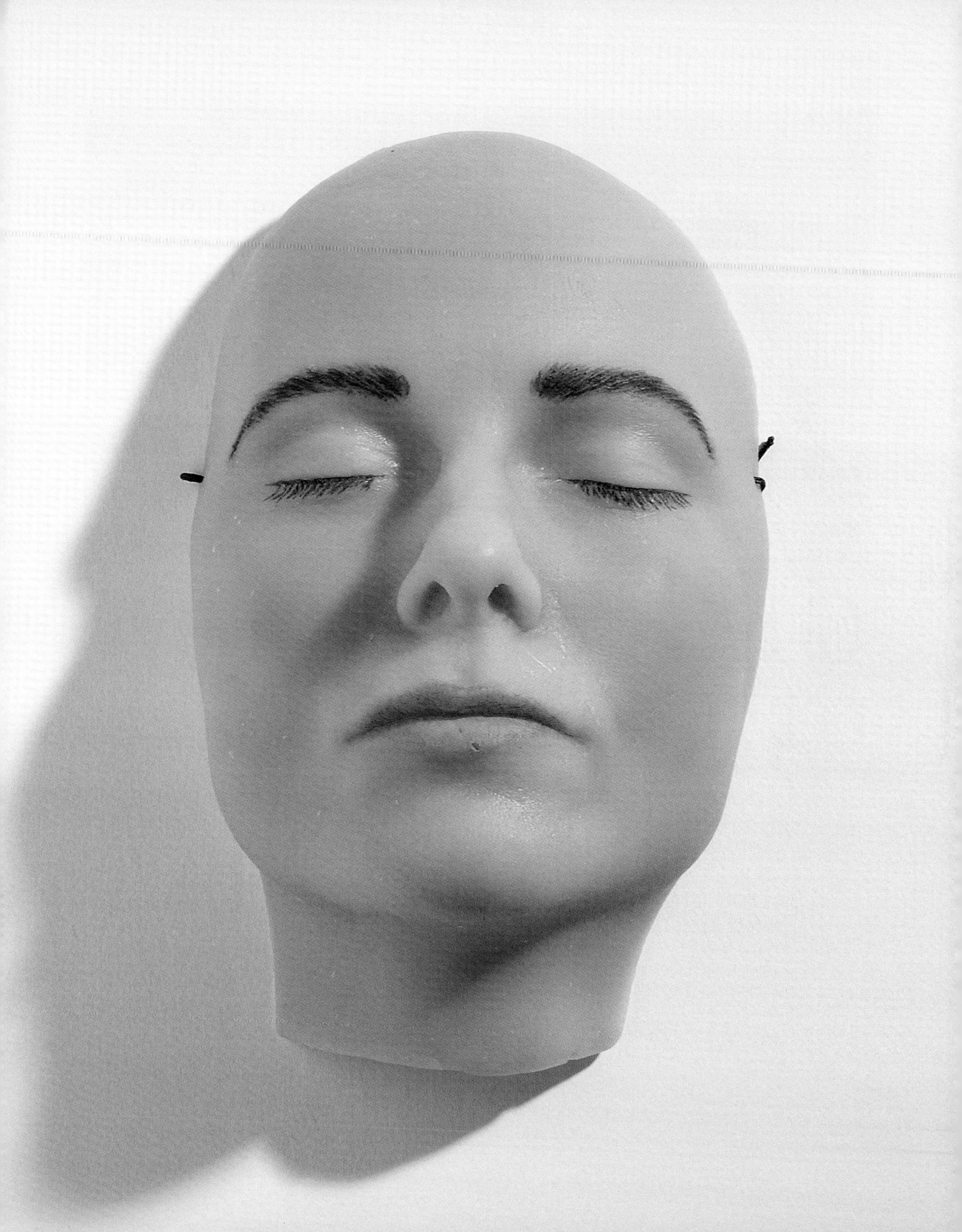

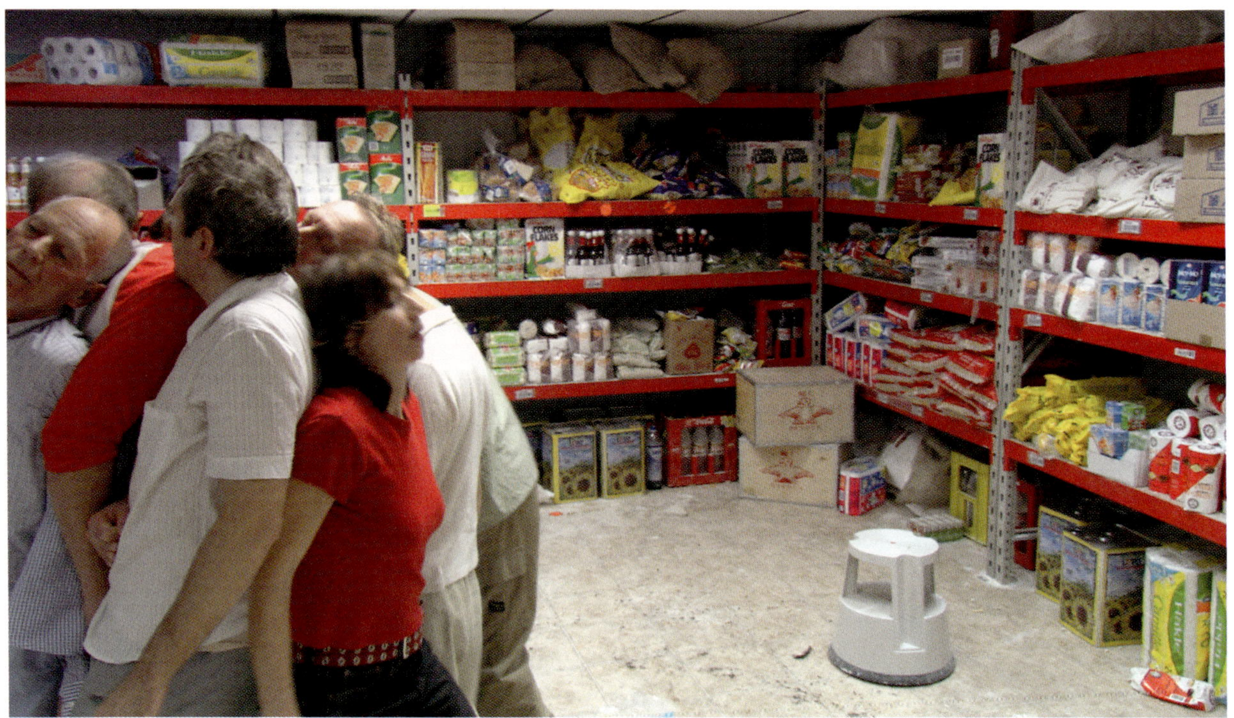

Choreography of Chaos

DOMINIC VAN DEN BOOGERD

In 2003 the Dutch artist Aernout Mik produced IN TWO MINDS at the Stedelijk Museum, together with theater company Toneelgroep Amsterdam. The work is a cross between theater, video, and installation—what the artist calls "a fifty-five-minute live exhibition."[1] Mik has become known for his video installations in which projection screens are incorporated into an architectonic mise en scène. Along with Doug

Aitken, Eija-Liisa Ahtila, and Douglas Gordon, he belongs to a generation of artists who explore the possibilities of split-screen cinema in a spatial setting. With IN TWO MINDS Mik returns to some of his earlier works, such as BLUE SINKHOLE (1995), which also involve live performances.[2]

IN TWO MINDS bears no resemblance to conventional theater. On entering we see no stage, no seats, but a real-life supermarket, complete with refrigerated compartments, shopping carts, and a rather grimy-looking prefab ceiling with built-in fluorescent

DOMINIC VAN DEN BOOGERD is an art critic and director of De Ateliers, Amsterdam.

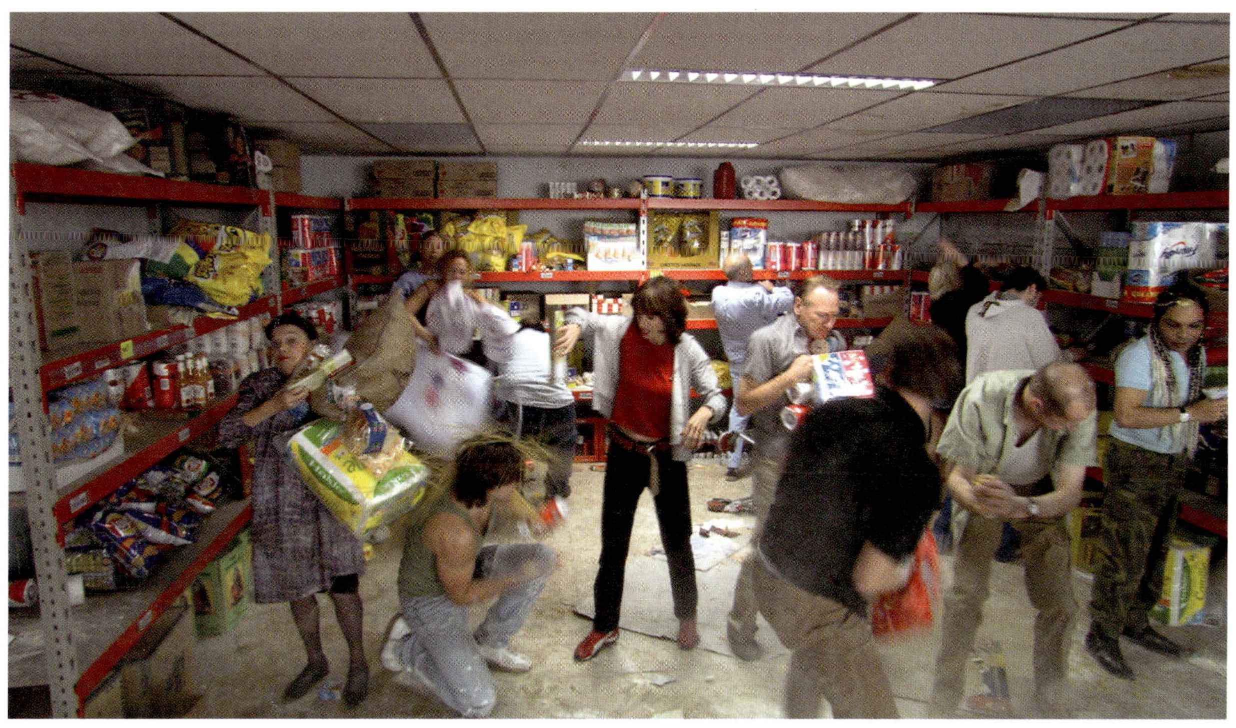

AERNOUT MIK, IN TWO MINDS, 2003, video stills from 55-minute live installation, coproduction with Toneelgroep and Stedelijk Museum, Amsterdam / VERUNSICHERT, Videostills aus der 55-minütigen Live-Installation.

Aernout Mik's
IN TWO MINDS

lights. All around us are shelves crammed with cans of olive oil, bottles of soda, packages of toilet paper. The merchandise is arranged without much logic. The stale interior surrounds us entirely; an exterior seems not to exist. A glass wall divides the space into two halves. Visitors find seats on boxes and crates and then peer through the glass.

The performance begins with the dull rumble of a current surge. All at once the glass wall turns into a projection screen. There appear video images that have been shot in the same supermarket. When the projection stops, the glass wall becomes transparent again and we are looking at events that take place behind it. The switch will occur countless times, always at unexpected moments—too fast, too late. We look at filmed scenes and live action alternately—both involving the same actors in the same surroundings. The video images show the environment as being slightly larger than it actually is. And so with each shift from projection surface to transparent wall, there is a shift in scale, as though the space is contracting and expanding. We get to see much more video than theater, but that is hardly noticeable. The two realities merge imperceptibly. In retrospect it is impossible to reconstruct what has happened live and what has been shown on the screen. Reflected in this is the way in which the mind works. In many of our recollections, after all, it is not clear what is based on our own experience and what is taken from secondhand information.

The supermarket is difficult to place. It could be a grocery store with marked-down lots of goods, perhaps in some "low-wage country," as they are called in the language of global capitalism. The airy clothing of those present suggests, in any case, a warm climate. Though supermarkets may be geared to local needs, they respond worldwide to a single order. Au-

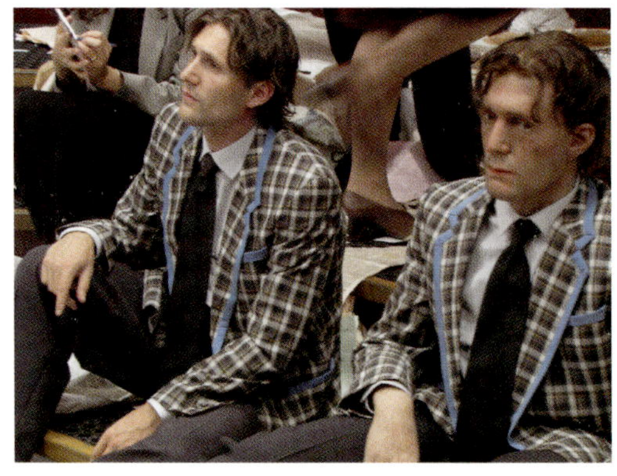

AERNOUT MIK, MIDDLEMEN, 2001, stills from video installation, Galerie Gebauer, Berlin / MITTELSMÄNNER, Videostills.

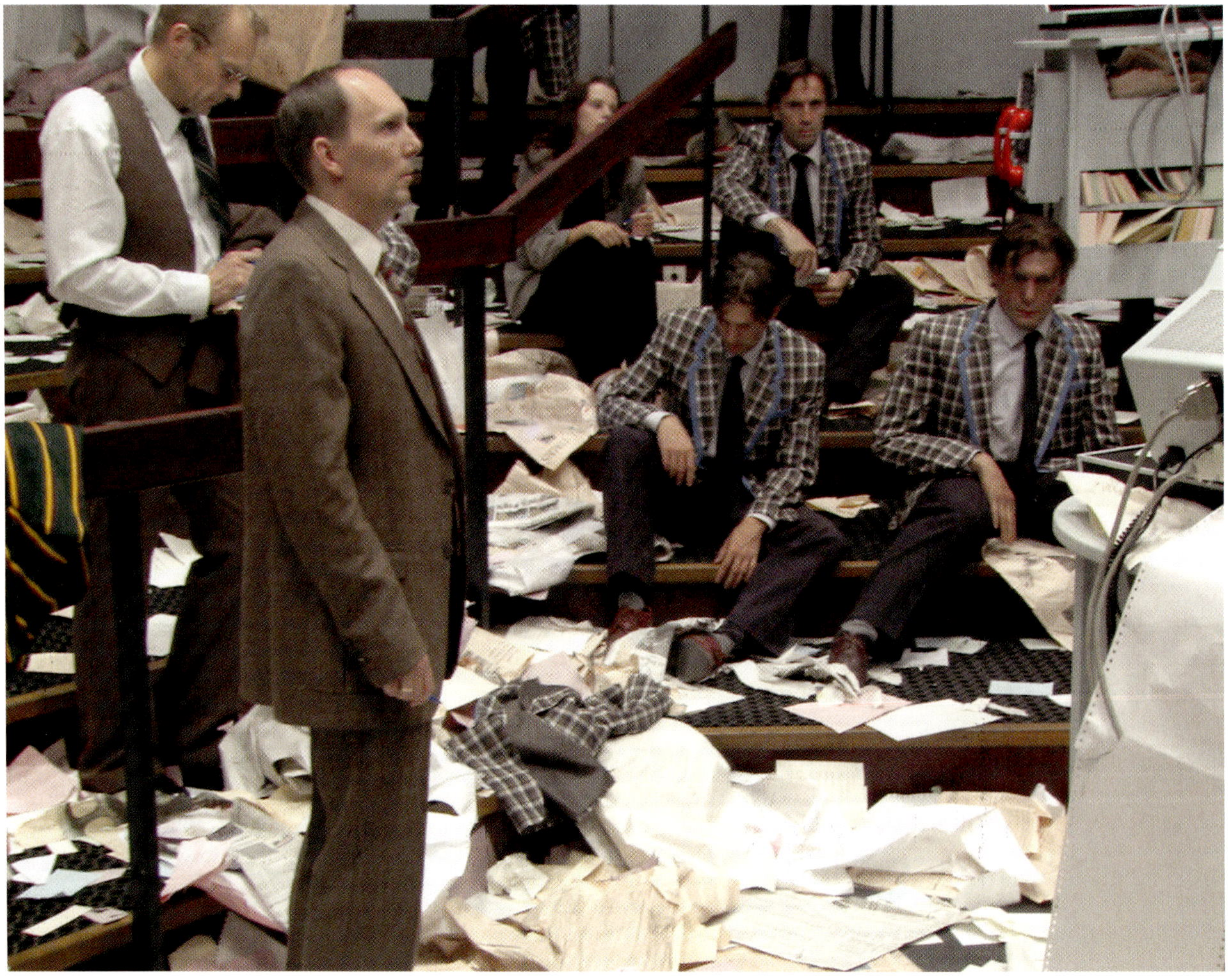

tomatically, the visitor inspects the products on the shelves. Everything is within reach. Do I want this? Consumerism never sleeps.

IN TWO MINDS unfolds before us like a mesmerizing theater of movement. A narrative line is absent or is at most suggested by a succession of schematic situations, as is often the case in Mik's work. It begins quietly. We see some employees kneeling on the floor, their heads hidden between the shelves, nearly swallowed up by the setting, and some clad in khaki, crawling around on their hands and knees. Others seem not to belong there: the half-naked youths, surrounded by empty bottles, bits of clothing, and cigarette butts, who are huddled together on mattresses and in sleeping bags. They look like squatters who have just found a new place to stay. Their pseudo-erotic cavorting is languid, blasé, halfhearted—if any people were ever in doubt about whether to do it or not, they certainly are. A hint of the illegal is distinctly evident. Repeatedly walking through the picture is a boy who has pulled his shirt over his head, as if he wanted to remain unrecognizable.

After these relatively calm scenes, the tempo suddenly accelerates. We see video images of a restless crowd busy removing items or tearing them out of their packaging. Also behind the glass wall there is some sense of feverish activity. Men and women are stuffing all kinds of things under their shirts, taking as much as they can. At the premiere, in early 2003, these scenes were particularly reminiscent of television images of social upheaval in Buenos Aires during the currency crisis. Such registrations of society's derailment, broadcast on television every night of the week, have become so familiar that they fail to stand out any longer. Aernout Mik discovers their unwritten choreography. People run back and forth, storage racks are knocked down. In the writhing mass, everyone seems overwhelmed and totally absorbed by the circumstances. The rapidly spreading decline makes the order among bodies, furniture, products less and less relevant.

There seems to be no end to the riot. In the work of Aernout Mik, disintegration is permanent. As we look at the images of people sitting on the floor, dazed in the midst of an unimaginable mess, the loud thumping of the plunderers can still be heard.

In his novel *In the Country of Last Things,* Paul Auster writes, "What strikes me as odd is not that everything is falling apart, but that so much continues to be there. It takes a long time for a world to vanish, much longer than you would think."[3] With Mik the derailment is irreparable, the decline interminable. We are faced with a continual loss of coherence and energy.

Two moments stand out. First, the moment at which the hectic film images suddenly stop and we stand eye to eye with several actors who stare at us motionlessly. Here the work of Dan Graham comes to mind, in particular his installations in which the roles of spectator and performer are reversed. The moment confronts us with the inactivity and the silence of the audience, with our "frozen vision" as Serge Daney called it. And second, a striking scene toward the end, when the bodies of the performers coagulate, as it were, into a compact group. This shuffling mass of sleepwalkers forms an "internally divided, heterogeneous organ" (Mik), comparable to the *Lebende-Leute-Skulptur* of ManfreDu Schu. Here we can discern Mik's preoccupation with the spatial, almost sculptural presence of the human body. Automatically our thoughts go back to Gilbert & George's THE SINGING SCULPTURE (1969), a five-hour performance held on the very museum stairway that led to IN TWO MINDS.

The behavior that is being displayed here is more predetermined than intentional. The movements seem slightly neurotic, compulsive. They escalate and de-escalate, as though driven by the remote control of some unknown force—inexplicably in our view, but evidently as a matter of course to those carrying out the movements. Actually, it shouldn't surprise us. The conduct of a specific group of people simply complies with a logic that is not always discernible to outsiders. Mik has tested the elasticity of social cohesion time and again in his works, with stockbrokers (MIDDLEMEN, 2001) and demonstrators (GLUTINOSITY, 2001). In all of his works, motives and aims are less important than body language. The motoric movements are somewhat mechanical. Professional acting, as found in the video installations of Catherine Sullivan or Stan Douglas, is hardly evident here. It could be considered ironic that several of the country's best actors, including Joop Admiraal and

Lineke Rijxman, participated without playing roles of significance: they have no lines, don't act, and don't portray anything. They operate merely within set conditions—as people do all their lives.

Here man is a "walk-on" rather than a personality, a nameless part of the crowd. In the writings of Samuel Beckett, man lives in a world which he has not created and which resists his efforts to make sense of it. Under the direction of Aernout Mik, it has become a fluid world, one of resilience, contracting and expanding but never changing fundamentally.

In the final scene of IN TWO MINDS, the video image switches unexpectedly from the cramped supermarket to a wave pool. The rhythm slows down. The heaving water is covered with dozens of mats, sloshed together like driftwood. Through the noise of the water, we hear the murmuring of actors stationed against the back wall. The incoherent sounds come closer, then become faint, rising and fading away. At the end of the performance, the group is suddenly standing in open space. Like the movable room in ORGANIC ESCALATOR (2000) this supermarket is a space that undergoes a metamorphosis: unnoticeably, the back wall has receded.

With IN TWO MINDS Aernout Mik creates a delicate balance between projected video images and live events, between recorded time and real time. Sometimes reality and the registration run parallel; sometimes one runs ahead of the other. As soon as we are on the verge of becoming engrossed in the film, we are confronted with the living reality of theater, and vice versa. We live in two worlds, the real and the unreal, the then and the now, that of facts and that of imagination—never knowing precisely which of the two we inhabit.

As in many of Mik's video installations, the relationship between cause and effect is gone. This is a world in full operation, yet without consequences. After every important movement, each decisive act, the course of events immediately backtracks or the focus shifts to minor considerations, to what Mik calls "occurrences that arise unintentionally in the body." This incessant delay of crucial developments produces an awareness that what is really going on here, what really matters, will remain elusive and unknowable. The great drama is taking placc elsewhere, off screen as it were. Actions, movements are drawn out endlessly until they finally congeal and come to a halt.

Though it may sound a bit desperate, the regime of minor considerations has a more or less tranquilizing effect in the work of Aernout Mik. In Mik's

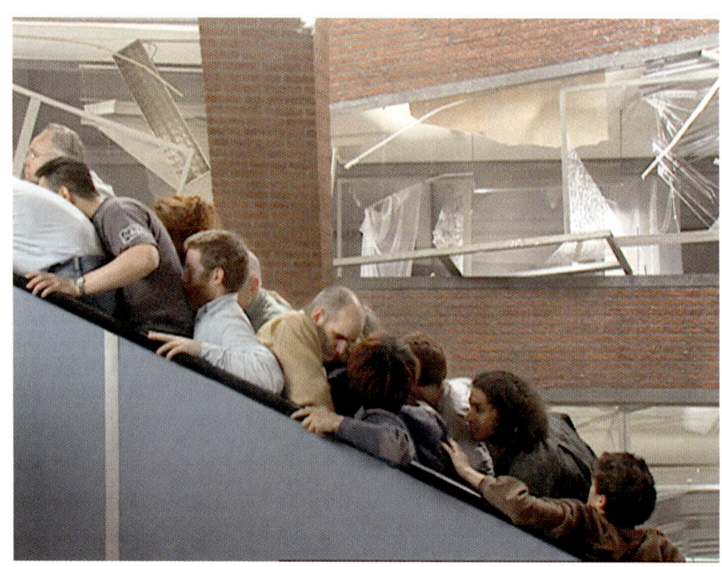

AERNOUT MIK, ORGANIC ESCALATOR, 2000,
still from video installation, Galerie Gebauer, Berlin /
ORGANISCHE ROLLTREPPE, Videostill.

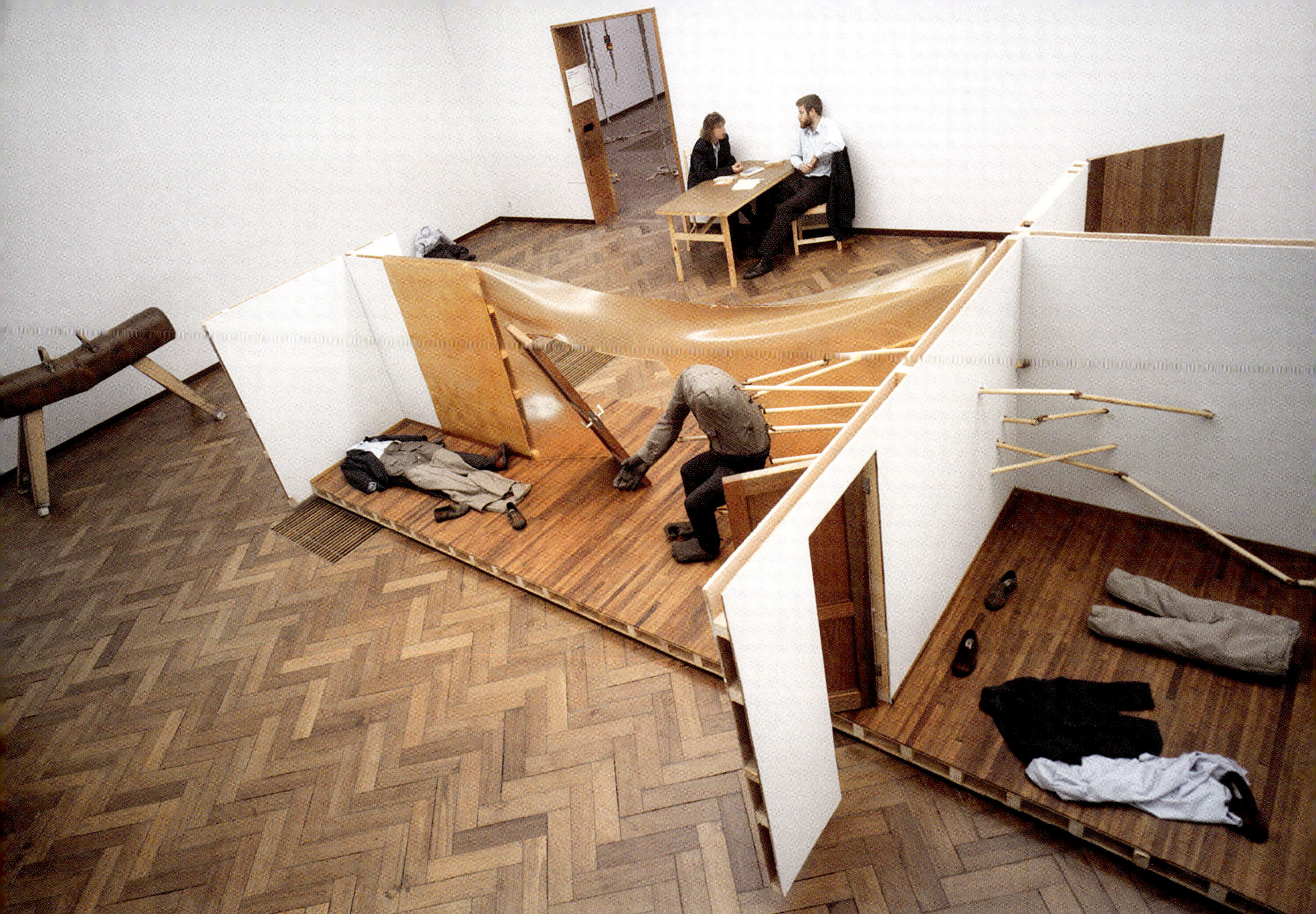

branch of global commerce, man survives on reflexes and automatisms, responding to some persistent, ruthless system. The derailments that we know from television images are stripped of their topical, social meaning. They have transformed into a ritual dance, a softly rocking *tableau vivant* that sharply conflicts with our notion of what is reasonable and sensible. Not only does the familiar supermarket resemble a wilderness; the subversive undermining of the consumer paradise—the stealing, plundering, squatting, destruction—has the effect of an anesthetic, as though no difference exists between the sight of an aquarium and television images of rebellion. It just keeps going on and on and on. "Droll thing life is," wrote Joseph Conrad, "that mysterious arrangement of merciless logic for a futile purpose."[4]

(Translation from the Dutch: Beth O'Brien)

1) This and all further quotes by the artist come from a conversation with the author in November 2002.
2) The live performance was carried out under the co-direction of Marjoleine Boonstra.
3) Paul Auster, *In the Country of Last Things* (London: Faber & Faber, 1987), pp. 28–29.
4) Joseph Conrad, *Heart of Darkness* (1902) (London: Penguin Classics, 1985), p. 112.

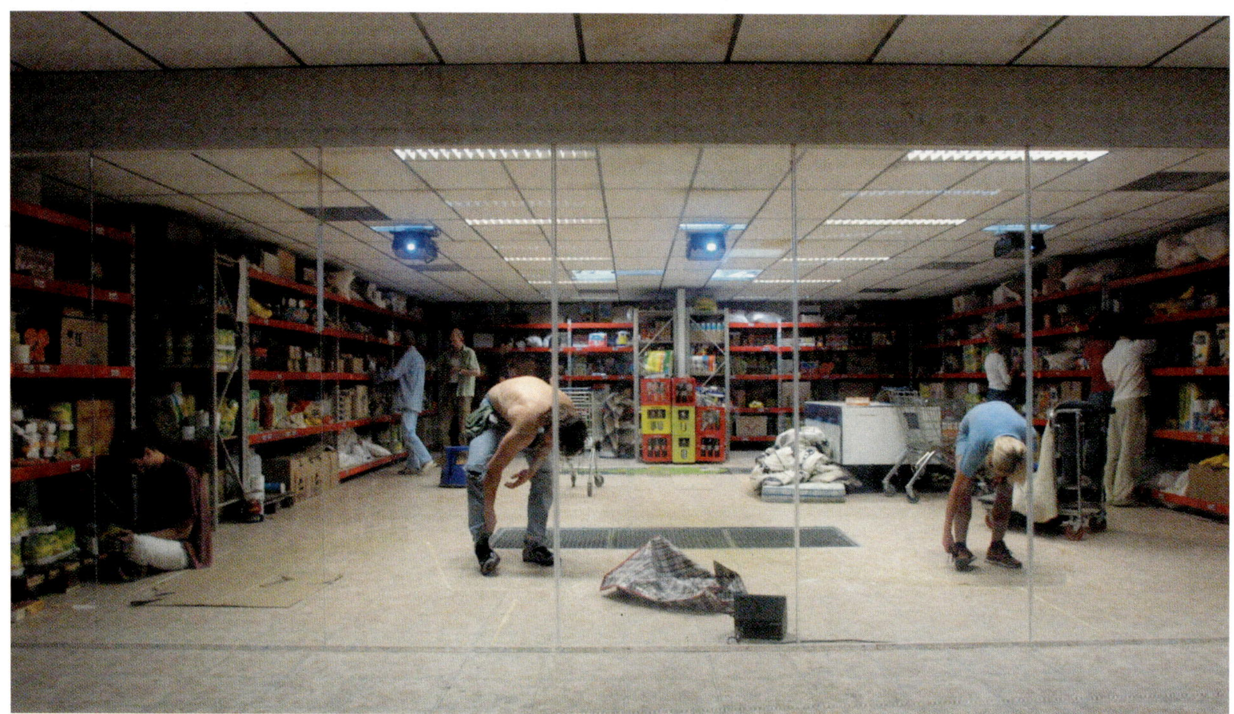

Choreographie des Chaos

DOMINIC VAN DEN BOOGERD

Im Jahr 2003 erarbeitete der niederländische Künstler Aernout Mik zusammen mit der Theatergruppe Toneelgroep Amsterdam im Stedelijk Museum IN TWO MINDS (Verunsichert). Es handelt sich um eine Mischung aus Theater, Video und Installation – der Künstler bezeichnet das Werk als «55-minütige Live-Schau.»[1] Mik hat sich mit Videoinstallationen

einen Namen gemacht, in denen Projektionsflächen zu integralen Bestandteilen einer architektonischen Inszenierung werden. Wie Doug Aitken, Eija-Liisa Ahtila und Douglas Gordon gehört er einer Generation von Künstlern an, welche die Möglichkeiten der auf mehrere Leinwände verteilten Projektion im Rahmen der Rauminstallation erkundet. Mit IN TWO MINDS nimmt Mik Bezug auf frühere Werke wie BLUE SINKHOLE (Blaues Senkloch, 1995), die ebenfalls mit Live-Performances einhergingen.[2]

DOMINIC VAN DEN BOOGERD ist Kunstkritiker und Direktor von De Ateliers, Amsterdam.

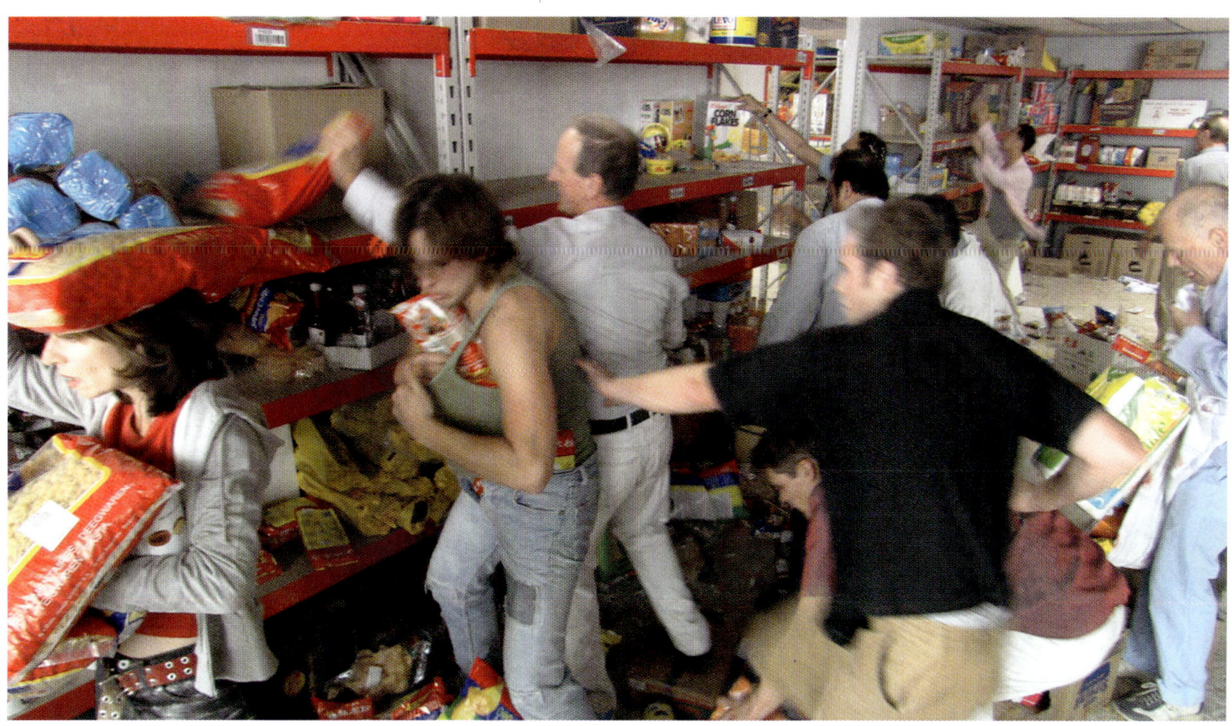

Aernout Miks
IN TWO MINDS

IN TWO MINDS hat keinerlei Ähnlichkeit mit konventionellem Theater. Wenn man den Raum betritt, sieht man weder eine Bühne noch Zuschauerränge, sondern einen echten Supermarkt samt Tiefkühlbereich, Einkaufswagen und einer schmutzig wirkenden, vorgefertigten Decke mit eingelassenen Neonröhren. Man ist von Regalen umzingelt, die voll gepackt sind mit Olivenölkanistern, Mineralwasserflaschen und Toilettenpapier. Die Anordnung der Waren ist nicht besonders logisch. Der muffige Innenraum umschliesst uns vollkommen, als gäbe es überhaupt keine Aussenwelt. Der Raum wird in der Mitte durch eine Glaswand unterteilt. Die Besucher nehmen auf Kisten und Kartons Platz und spähen durch das Glas auf die andere Seite.

Die Performance beginnt mit dem dumpfen Grollen brandender Wellen. Unvermittelt wird die Glaswand zur Projektionsfläche. Es erscheinen Videobilder, die im selben Supermarkt aufgenommen wurden. Sobald die Projektion aufhört, wird die

Glaswand wieder durchsichtig und man sieht, was dahinter vorgeht. Dieser Wechsel findet unzählige Male statt, immer unerwartet – zu früh oder zu spät. Wir schauen uns abwechselnd die gefilmten Szenen und das Live-Geschehen an – es handelt sich jedoch immer um dieselben Darsteller in derselben Umgebung. Auf den Videobildern ist der Raum etwas grösser dargestellt als in Wirklichkeit. Daher findet bei jedem Wechsel von der Projektionsfläche zur transparenten Wand eine Massstabsveränderung statt, als würde sich der Raum abwechselnd ausdehnen und wieder schrumpfen. Wir bekommen weitaus mehr Videobilder als Theaterszenen zu sehen, aber das ist kaum wahrnehmbar. Die beiden Realitäten vermischen sich und im Rückblick ist es unmöglich zu sagen, was live geschah und was auf der Projektionswand gezeigt wurde. Darin widerspiegelt sich die Art, wie unser Gehirn funktioniert: Bei vielen Erinnerungen lässt sich nämlich nachträglich nicht mehr klar ausmachen, was wir selbst erfahren haben und was aus zweiter Hand stammt.

Der Supermarkt lässt sich nur schwer lokalisieren. Es könnte ein Lebensmittelgeschäft mit herabgesetzter Ware sein, vielleicht in einem «Billiglohnland», wie das in der Sprache des globalen Kapitalismus heisst. Die leichte Kleidung der Anwesenden lässt jedenfalls auf ein warmes Klima schliessen. Auch wenn Supermärkte auf lokale Bedürfnisse ausgerichtet sind, folgen sie doch weltweit denselben Regeln. Der Besucher begutachtet automatisch die Waren in den Regalen. Alles ist in Reichweite. Möchte ich das kaufen? Das Konsumbedürfnis kommt nie zur Ruhe. IN TWO MINDS entfaltet sich vor unseren Augen

wie ein faszinierendes Bewegungstheater. Eine Handlung fehlt oder wird, wie oft in Miks Arbeiten, allenfalls durch eine Abfolge schematischer Situationen angedeutet. Das Werk beginnt ruhig. Wir sehen am Boden kniende Angestellte, deren Köpfe hinter den Regalen verschwinden, so dass sie fast ganz von der Umgebung verschluckt werden. Einige sind khakifarben gekleidet und kriechen auf allen Vieren herum. Andere scheinen nicht hierher zu gehören: halbnackte Jugendliche, die, umgeben von leeren Flaschen, Kleidungsstücken und Zigarettenkippen, dicht aneinander gedrängt auf Matratzen und in Schlafsäcken herumsitzen. Sie sehen aus wie Hausbesetzer, die soeben eine neue Bleibe gefunden haben. Ihre pseudoerotischen Spielereien sind träge, gelangweilt, halbherzig – wenn jemals jemand unschlüssig war, ob er es tun sollte oder nicht, dann sie. Ein Hauch von Illegalität hängt in der Luft. Immer wieder läuft ein Junge durchs Bild, der sein Hemd über den Kopf gezogen hat, als wolle er unerkannt bleiben.

Nach diesen relativ ruhigen Szenen beschleunigt sich das Ganze plötzlich. Wir sehen Videobilder einer hektischen Menschenmenge, die damit beschäftigt ist, Waren aus Regalen und Verpackungen zu reissen. Auch hinter der Glaswand herrscht fieberhafte Aktivität. Männer und Frauen stopfen alle möglichen Dinge unter ihre Hemden und raffen zusammen, was sie kriegen können. Bei der Premiere Anfang 2003 fühlte man sich unweigerlich an Fernsehbilder von Plündereien in Buenos Aires während der Währungskrise erinnert. An diese allabendlich im Fernsehen ausgestrahlten Bilder einer aus den

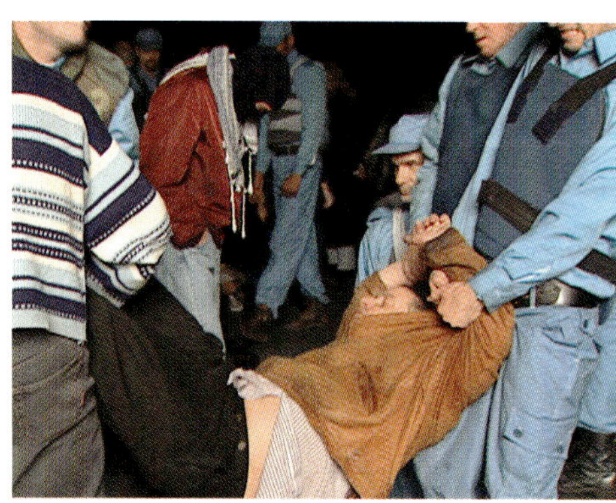
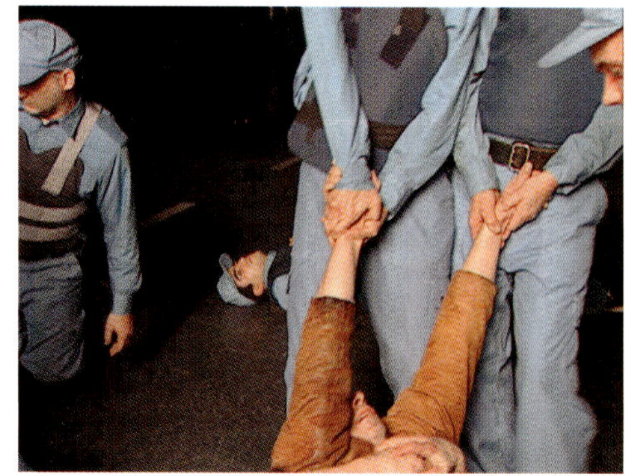

Fugen geratenen Gesellschaft haben wir uns so sehr gewöhnt, dass sie uns gar nicht mehr besonders aufrütteln. Aernout Mik macht ihre ungeschriebene Choreographie sichtbar. Die Leute rennen hin und her, Regale werden umgestossen. In der wogenden Masse scheinen alle vom Geschehen überwältigt und total absorbiert zu sein. Durch die rapide fortschreitende Zerstörung wird jede bestehende Ordnung von Körpern, Einrichtungsgegenständen und Waren zunehmend bedeutungslos.

Der Tumult scheint kein Ende zu nehmen. In Aernout Miks Arbeiten ist der Zerfall ein Dauerzustand. Während wir Bilder von Leuten sehen, die wie betäubt inmitten eines unvorstellbaren Chaos auf dem Boden sitzen, ist immer noch der Lärm zu hören, den die Plünderer veranstalten. In seinem Roman *Im Land der letzten Dinge* schreibt Paul Auster: «Was mir merkwürdig vorkommt, ist nicht, dass alles in die Brüche geht, sondern dass so vieles sich erhält. Es dauert lange, bis eine Welt verschwindet, viel länger, als man meinen sollte.»[3] Bei Mik ist die Entgleisung irreparabel, der Niedergang unaufhaltsam. Wir haben es mit einem fortlaufenden Verlust an Kohärenz und Energie zu tun.

Zwei Momente stechen heraus. Erstens, der Augenblick, als die hektischen Filmbilder plötzlich zum Stillstand kommen und wir Aug in Auge mehreren Schauspielern gegenüberstehen, die uns regungslos anstarren. Man fühlt sich dabei an Dan Grahams Arbeiten erinnert, vor allem an jene Installationen, bei denen die Rollen von Zuschauer und Darsteller vertauscht werden. Wir sind in diesem Moment mit der stummen Untätigkeit des Publikums konfrontiert, mit unserem «starren Blick», wie Serge Daney es nannte. Zweitens, die beeindruckende Szene gegen Ende der Performance, als die Körper der Darsteller gleichsam zu einer kompakten Masse verschmelzen. Diese träge Masse von Schlafwandlern bildet ein «innerlich gespaltenes, heterogenes Organ» (Mik), vergleichbar mit der *Lebende-Leute-Skulptur* von ManfreDu Schu. Hier zeigt sich Miks Faszination für die räumliche, beinahe skulpturale Präsenz des menschlichen Körpers. Automatisch erinnern wir uns an THE SINGING SCULPTURE (Die singende Skulptur, 1969) von Gilbert & George, eine fünfstündige Performance, die auf derselben Museumstreppe stattfand, über die man zu IN TWO MINDS gelangte.

Das hier gezeigte Verhalten ist mehr vorgegeben als intentional. Die Bewegungen wirken etwas neurotisch, zwanghaft. Sie werden heftiger und wieder schwächer, wie von einer unbekannten Macht gesteuert – für uns unerklärlich, aber für jene, die sie ausführen, ganz selbstverständlich. Das sollte uns eigentlich nicht überraschen. Das Verhalten einer bestimmten Gruppe von Menschen folgt oft einer Logik, die sich Aussenstehenden nicht erschliesst. Mik hat in seinen Arbeiten wiederholt die Elastizität des sozialen Zusammenhalts erkundet: in MIDDLEMEN (Mittelsmänner, 2001) mit Börsenmaklern und in GLUTINOSITY (Klebrigkeit, 2001) mit Demonstranten. In seinem ganzen Werk sind Motive und Ziele immer weniger wichtig als die Körpersprache. Die motorischen Bewegungen sind dabei eher mechanisch. Professionelle Schauspielerei wie in den Videoinstallationen von Catherine Sullivan oder Stan Douglas ist hier kaum erkennbar. Man könnte

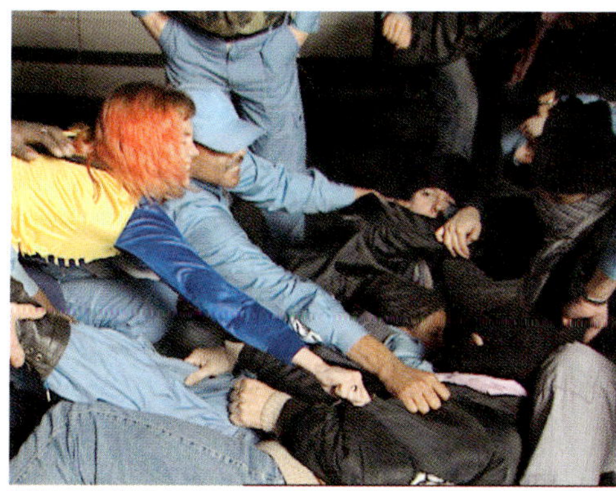
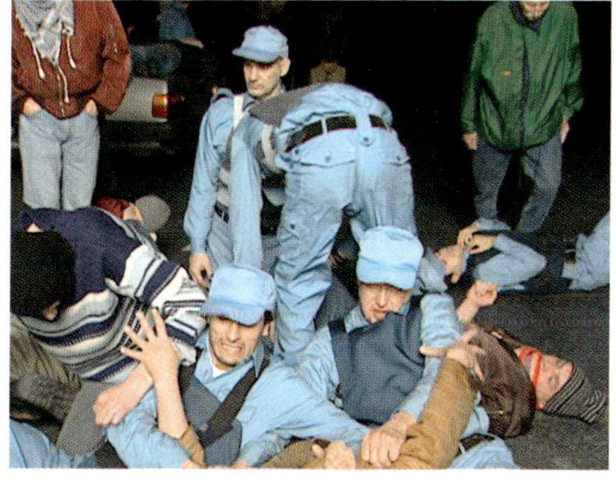

es als Ironie auffassen, dass einige der besten Schauspieler des Landes, etwa Joop Admiraal und Lineke Rijxman, mitwirkten ohne bedeutende Rollen zu spielen: Sie haben keinen Text, spielen nicht und stellen nichts dar. Sie bewegen sich bloss innerhalb vorgegebener Bedingungen – wie Menschen es oft ihr ganzes Leben lang tun.

Hier ist der Mensch mehr Statist als Persönlichkeit, ein namenloses Gesicht in der Masse. In Samuel Becketts Stücken lebt der Mensch in einer Welt, die er nicht geschaffen hat und die sich seinen Bemühungen, ihr einen Sinn abzugewinnen, widersetzt. Unter der Regie von Aernout Mik wird die Welt fliessend und elastisch; sie schrumpft und wächst, ändert sich aber niemals grundlegend.

In der Schlussszene von IN TWO MINDS wechselt das Videobild überraschend vom überfüllten Supermarkt zu einem Wellenschwimmbecken. Der Rhythmus verlangsamt sich. Auf der wogenden Wasserfläche schwimmen Dutzende von Matten, die wie Treibholz gegeneinander schwappen. Durch das Wassergeräusch hindurch ist das Gemurmel von Schauspielern zu hören, die der Rückwand entlang Aufstellung genommen haben. Die unzusammenhängenden Geräusche kommen näher, werden schwächer, schwellen an und verklingen wieder. Am Ende der Performance stehen die Darsteller plötzlich im offenen Raum. Wie der bewegliche Raum in ORGANIC ESCALATOR (Organische Rolltreppe, 2000) macht auch der Supermarkt eine Verwandlung durch: Die Rückwand ist unbemerkt zurückgewichen.

Aernout Mik erzeugt mit IN TWO MINDS ein fragiles Gleichgewicht zwischen Videobildern und Live-Geschehen, zwischen aufgezeichneter Zeit und Echtzeit. Manchmal laufen Wirklichkeit und Film parallel, dann wieder eilt das eine dem anderen voraus. Kaum beginnt uns der Film zu fesseln, werden wir wieder in die Live-Realität des Theaters gestossen – und umgekehrt. Wir leben in zwei Welten, der realen und der irrealen, der einstigen und der jetzigen, der Welt der Tatsachen und jener der Phantasie, und wir wissen dabei nie genau, in welche der beiden wir gehören.

Wie in so vielen von Miks Videoinstallationen ist die Verknüpfung von Ursache und Wirkung verschwunden. Es ist eine voll funktionierende Welt, die

aber jeglicher Konsequenz entbehrt. Nach jedem wichtigen Vorgang, jeder entscheidenden Handlung, nehmen die Ereignisse eine Kehrtwendung oder die Aufmerksamkeit verschiebt sich auf nebensächliche Faktoren, auf Dinge, die, so Mik, «unwillkürlich im Körper ablaufen». Dieses unaufhörliche Hinauszögern jeder entscheidenden Entwicklung erweckt den Eindruck, dass das, was hier wirklich vorgeht und zählt, sich uns immer entziehen und rätselhaft bleiben wird. Das grosse Drama spielt sich anderswo ab, sozusagen im Off. Alle Handlungen und Bewegungen werden endlos in die Länge gezogen, bis sie schliesslich erstarren und zum Stillstand kommen.

Es mag etwas verzweifelt klingen, aber die Dominanz der nebensächlichen Faktoren hat in Aernout Miks Arbeiten eine mehr oder weniger beruhigende Wirkung. In Miks Filiale der globalen Handelswelt überlebt der Mensch, indem er mit Reflexen und Automatismen auf ein gleichbleibend unbarmherziges System reagiert. Die chaotischen Szenen, die wir aus dem Fernsehen kennen, haben hier ihre aktuelle, gesellschaftliche Bedeutung eingebüsst und sind zu einem rituellen Tanz geworden, einem sanft wogenden *Tableau vivant*, das unserer Vorstellung davon, was vernünftig und sinnvoll ist, aufs Heftigste widerspricht. Nicht nur gleicht der vertraute Supermarkt einer Wildnis; das subversive Unterlaufen des Konsumparadieses – das Stehlen, Plündern, Besetzen, Verwüsten – hat auch eine narkotisierende Wirkung, als gäbe es keinen Unterschied zwischen dem Anblick eines Aquariums und Fernsehbildern von sozialen Unruhen. Es geht einfach immer weiter und weiter und weiter. «Eine seltsame Sache, das Leben», schrieb Joseph Conrad, «diese geheimnisvolle Anordnung gnadenloser Logik für ein nichtiges Ziel.»[4]

(Übersetzung aus dem Englischen: Irene Aeberli)

1) Dieses und alle weiteren Zitate des Künstlers stammen aus einem Gespräch mit dem Autor vom November 2002.
2) Bei der Live-Performance führte Marjoleine Boonstra gemeinsam mit dem Künstler Regie.
3) Paul Auster, *Im Land der letzten Dinge*, Rowohlt Taschenbuch Verlag, Reinbek bei Hamburg 1992, S. 37.
4) Joseph Conrad, *Herz der Finsternis*, Haffmans Verlag, Zürich 1992, S. 135.

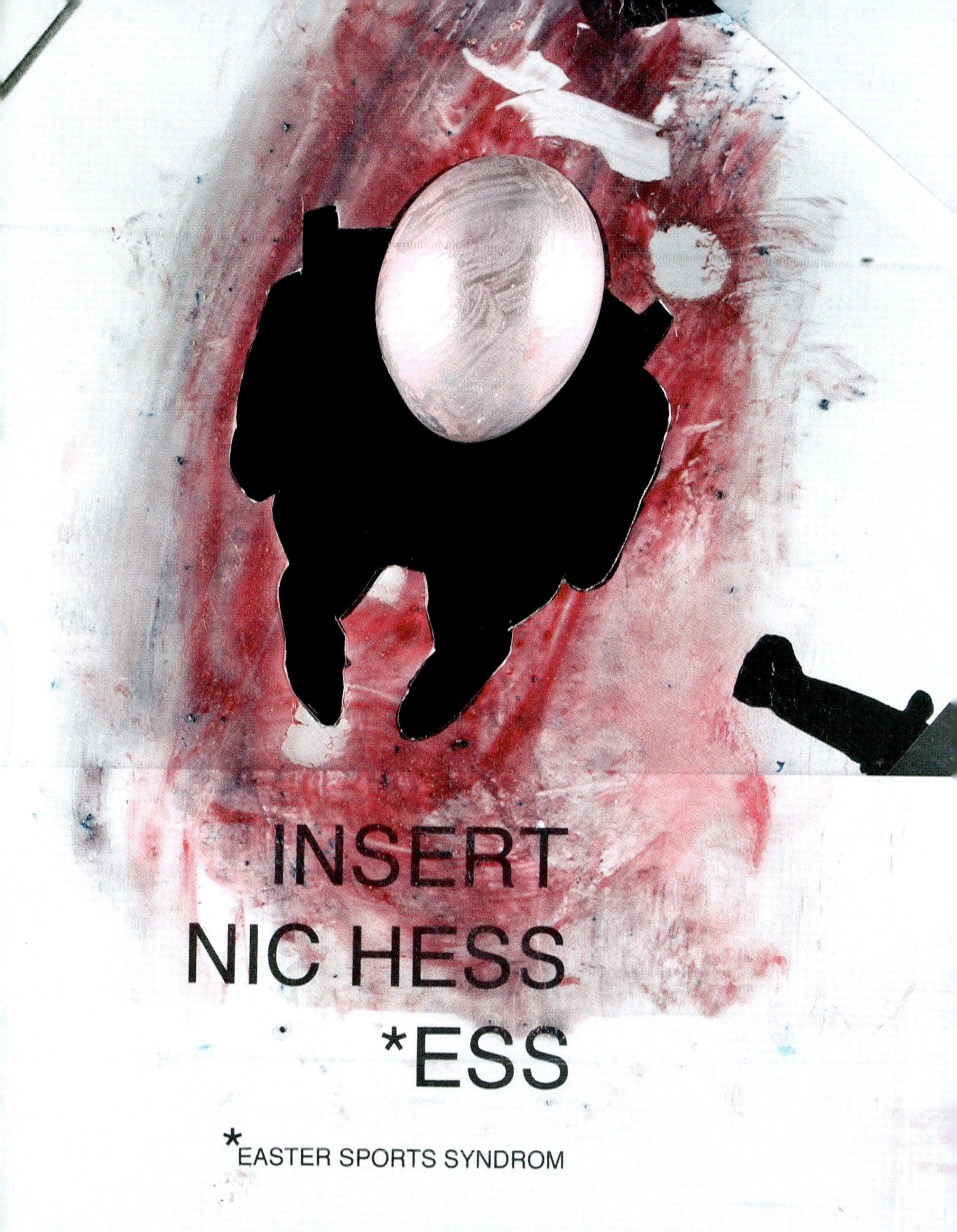
INSERT
NIC HESS
*ESS
*EASTER SPORTS SYNDROM

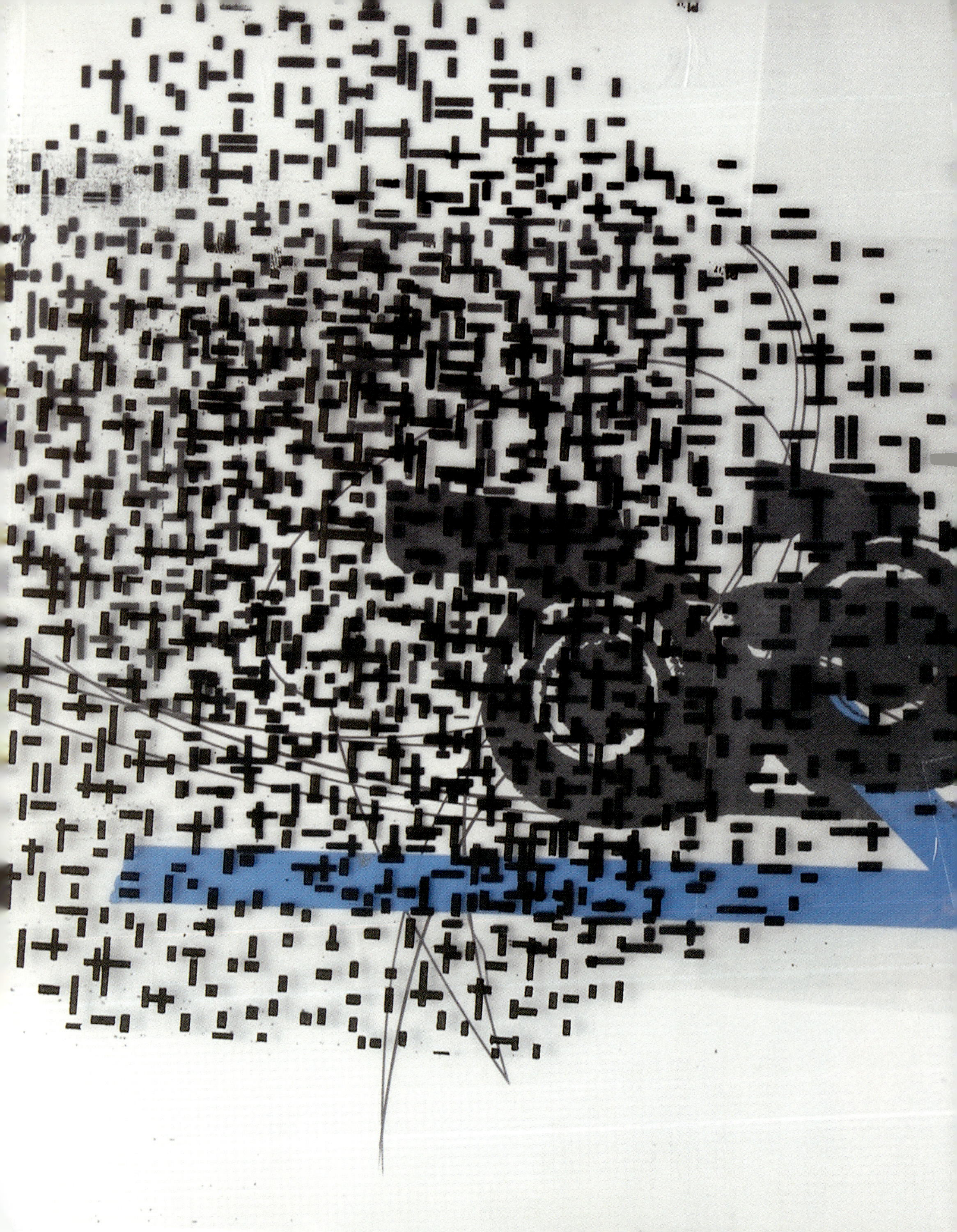

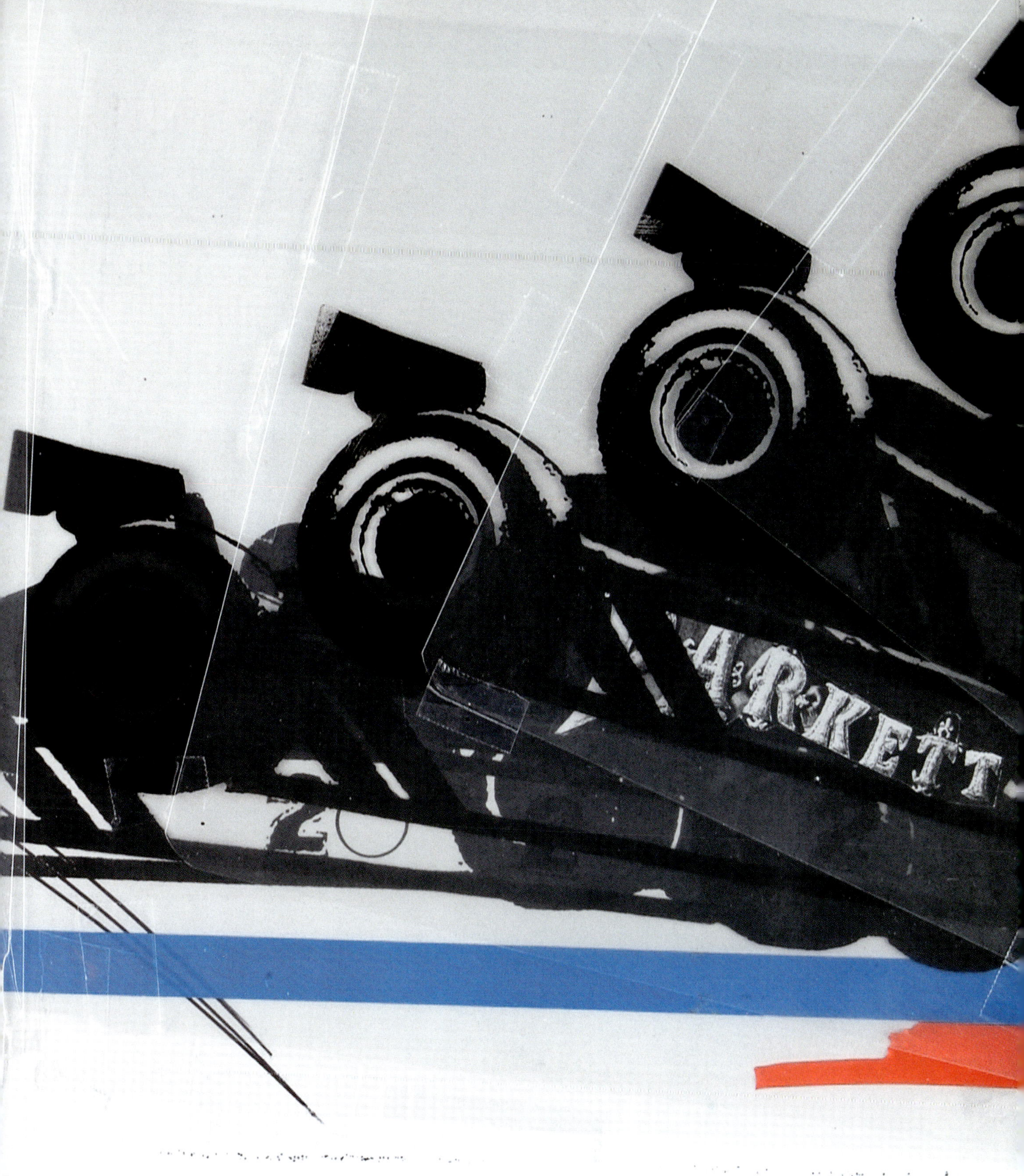
ARKETT

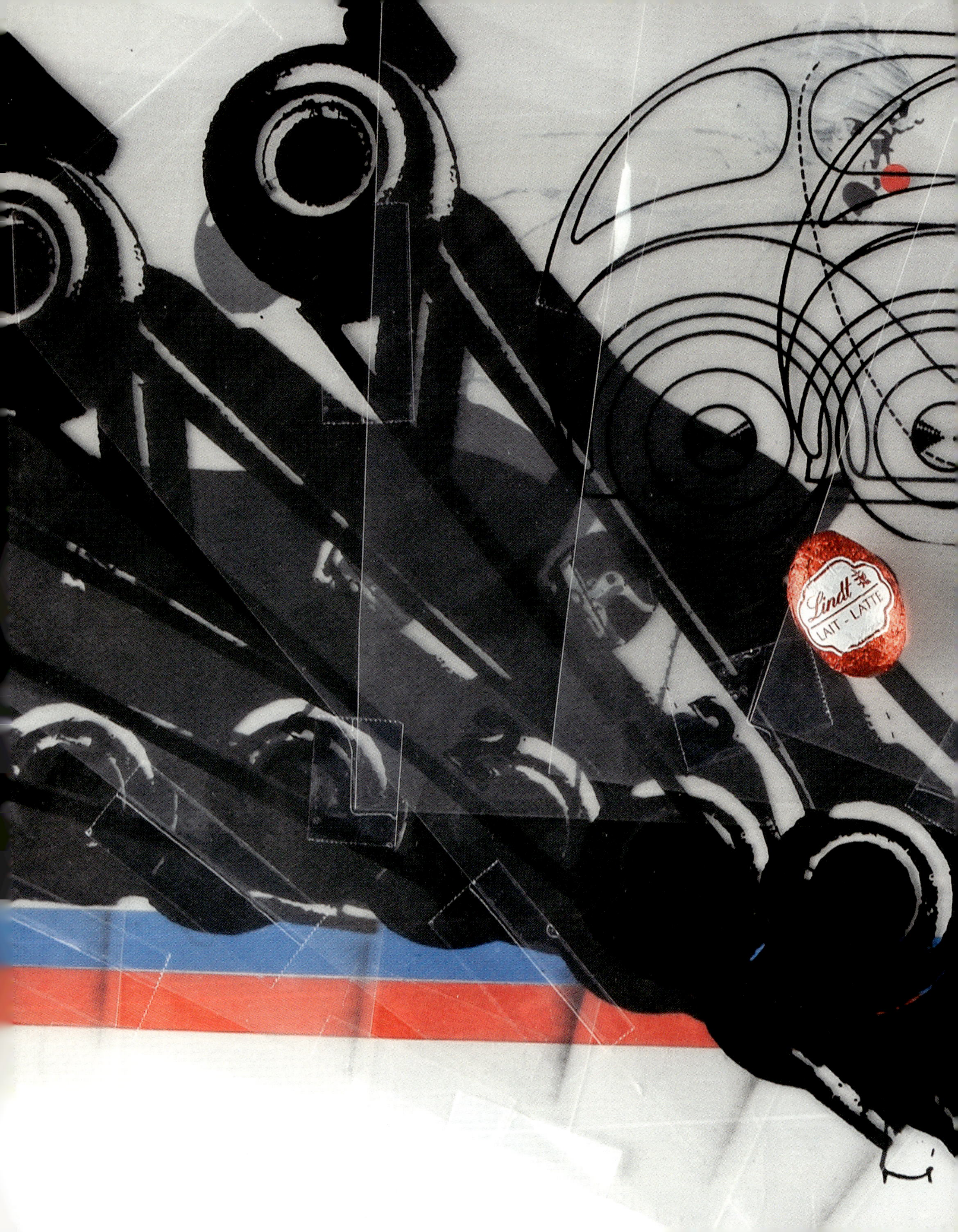

Lindt
LAIT - LATTE

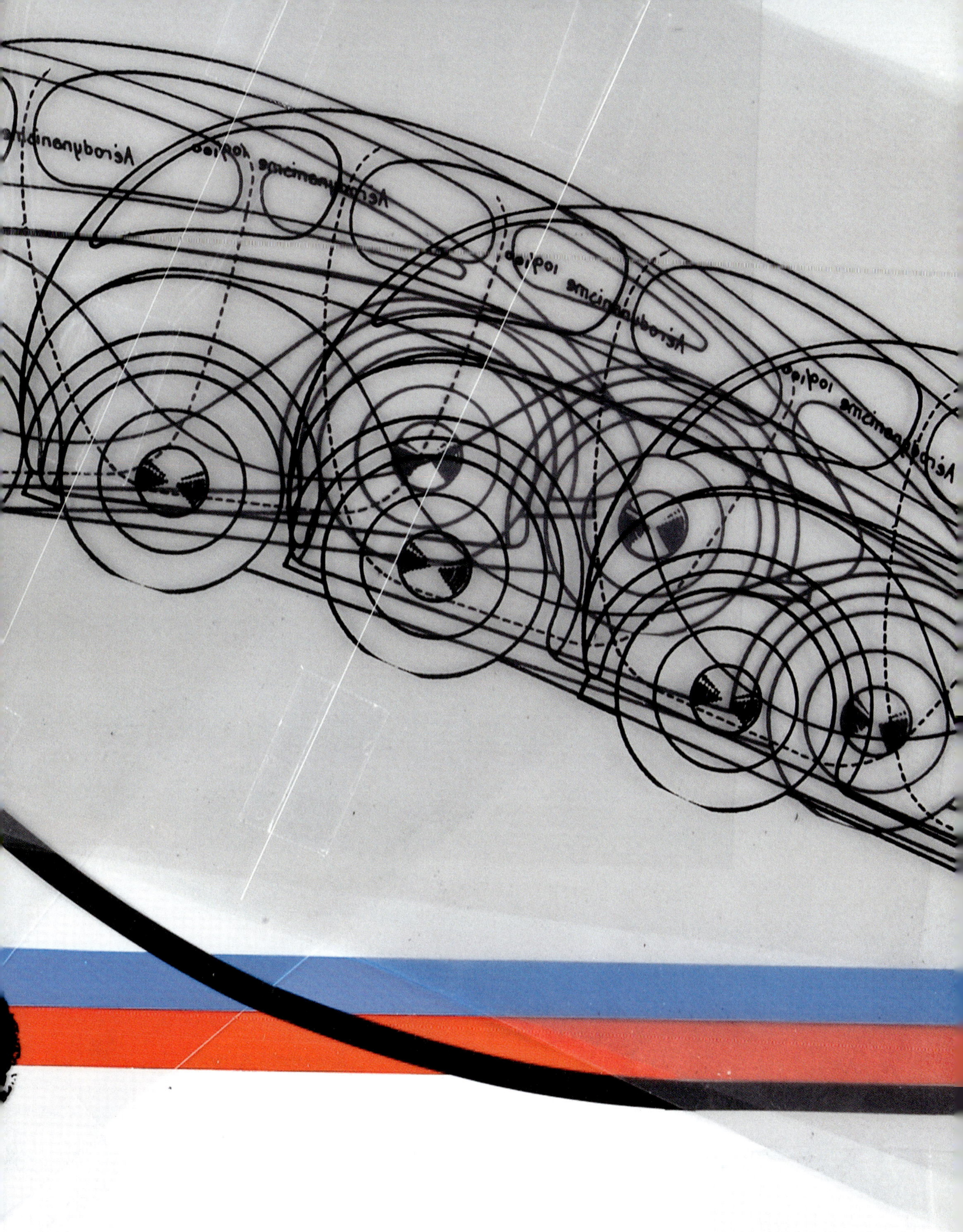

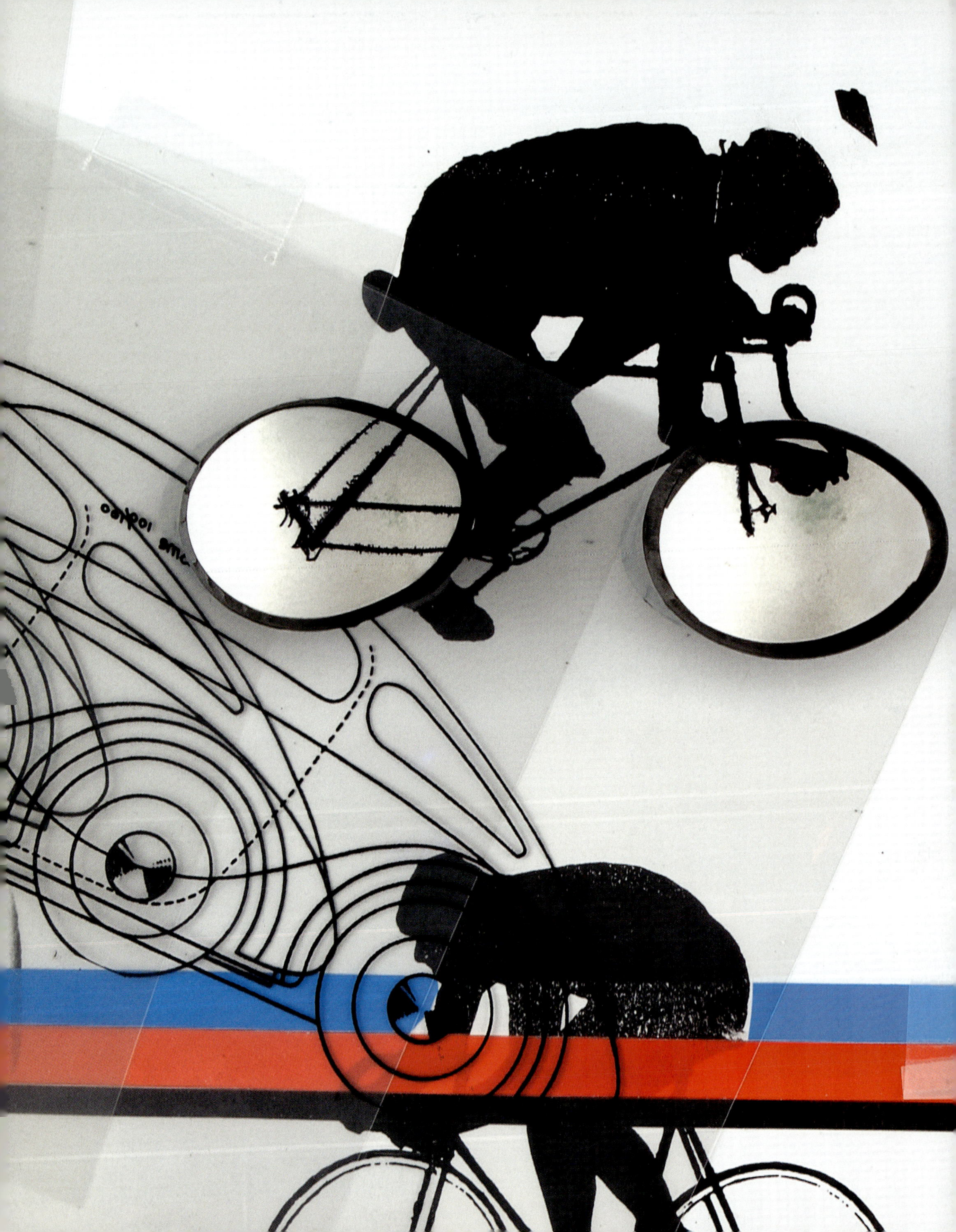

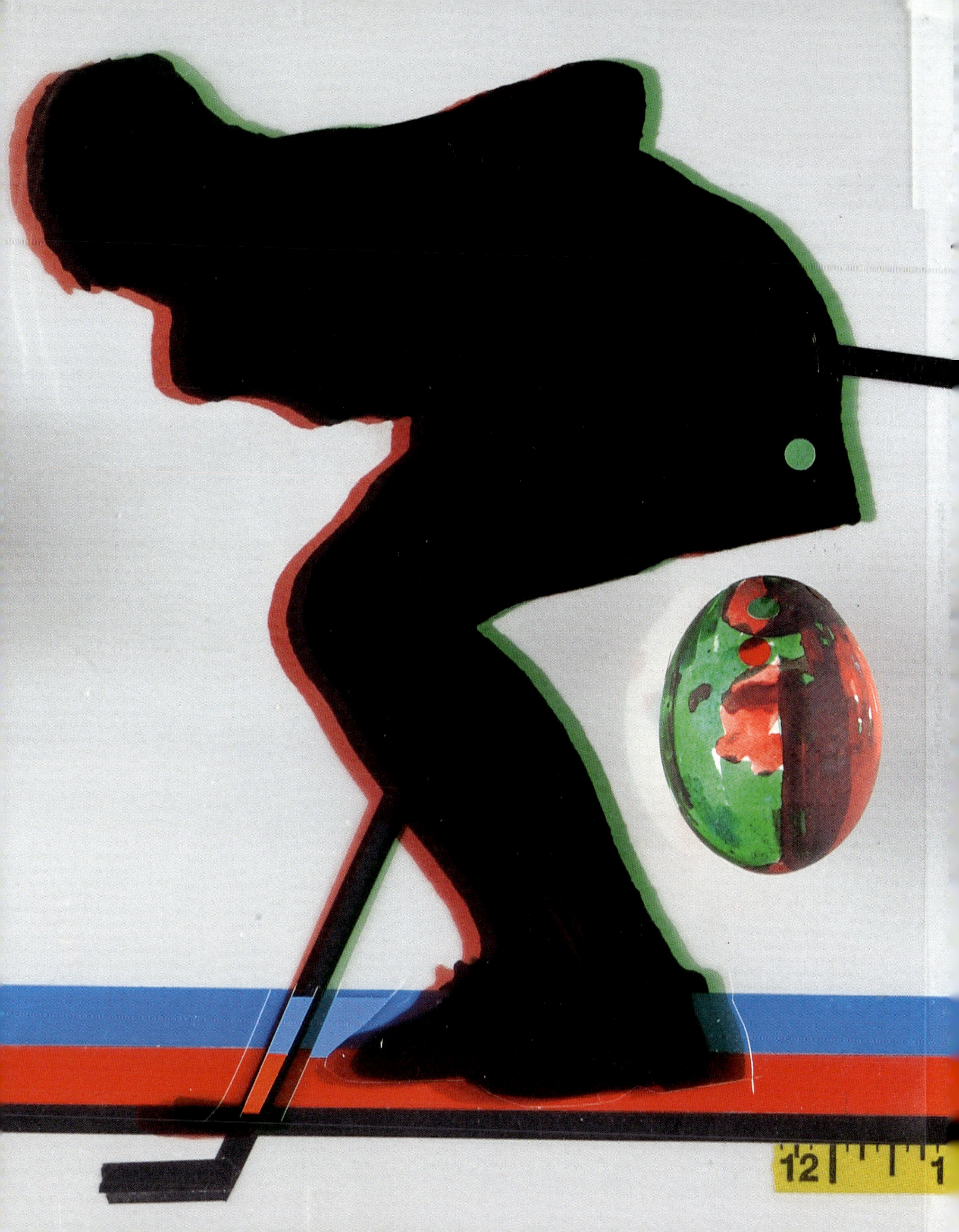

12

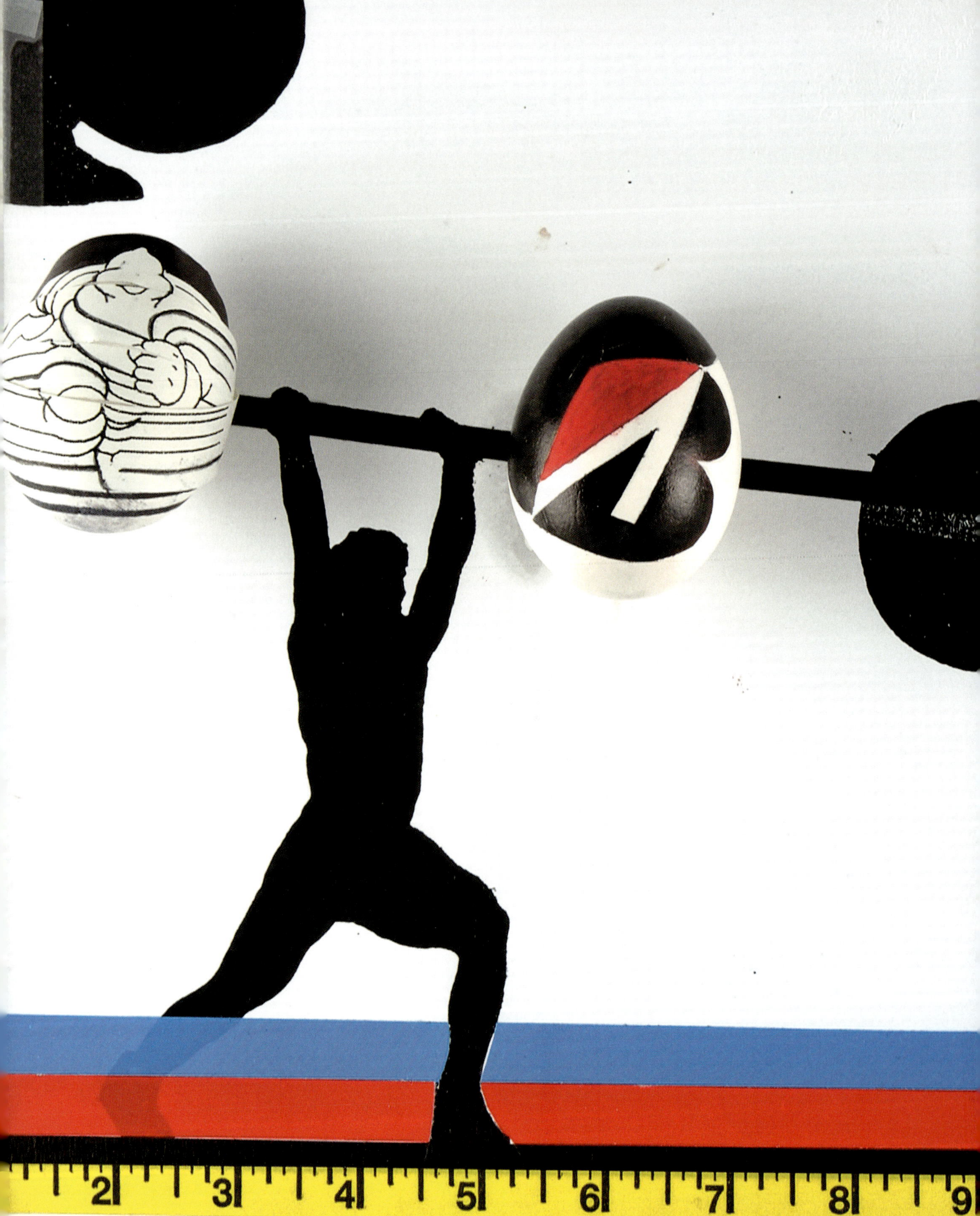

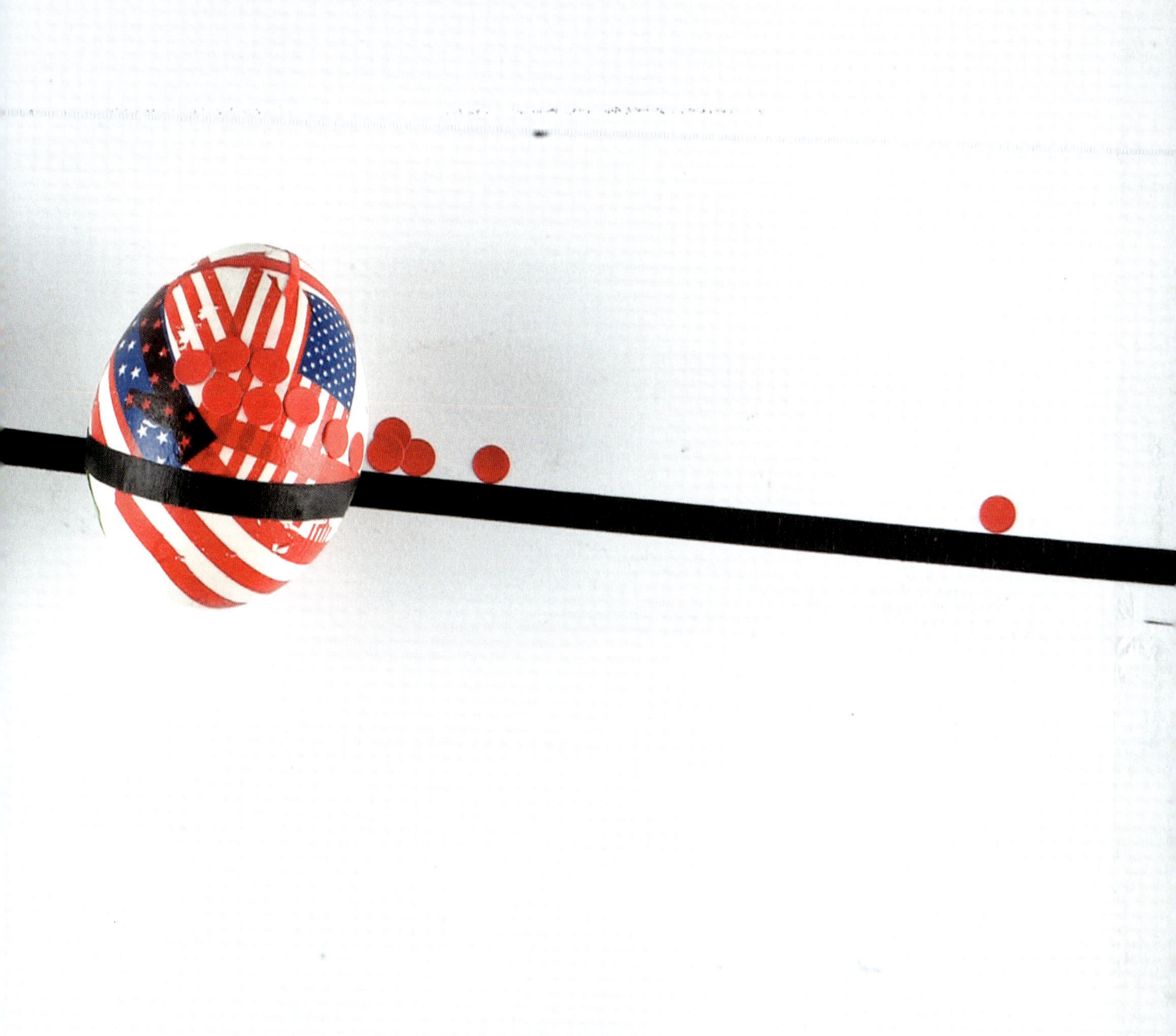

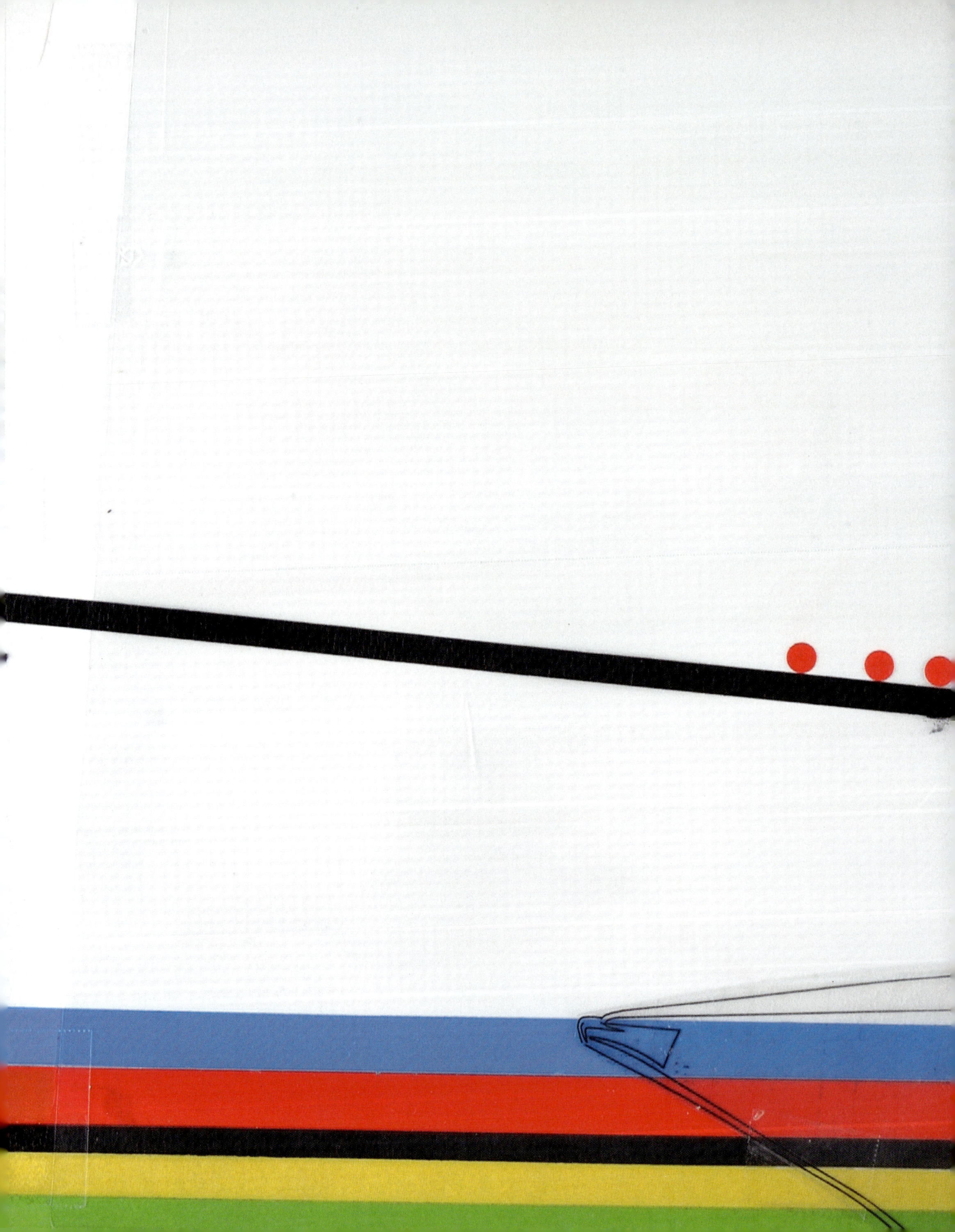

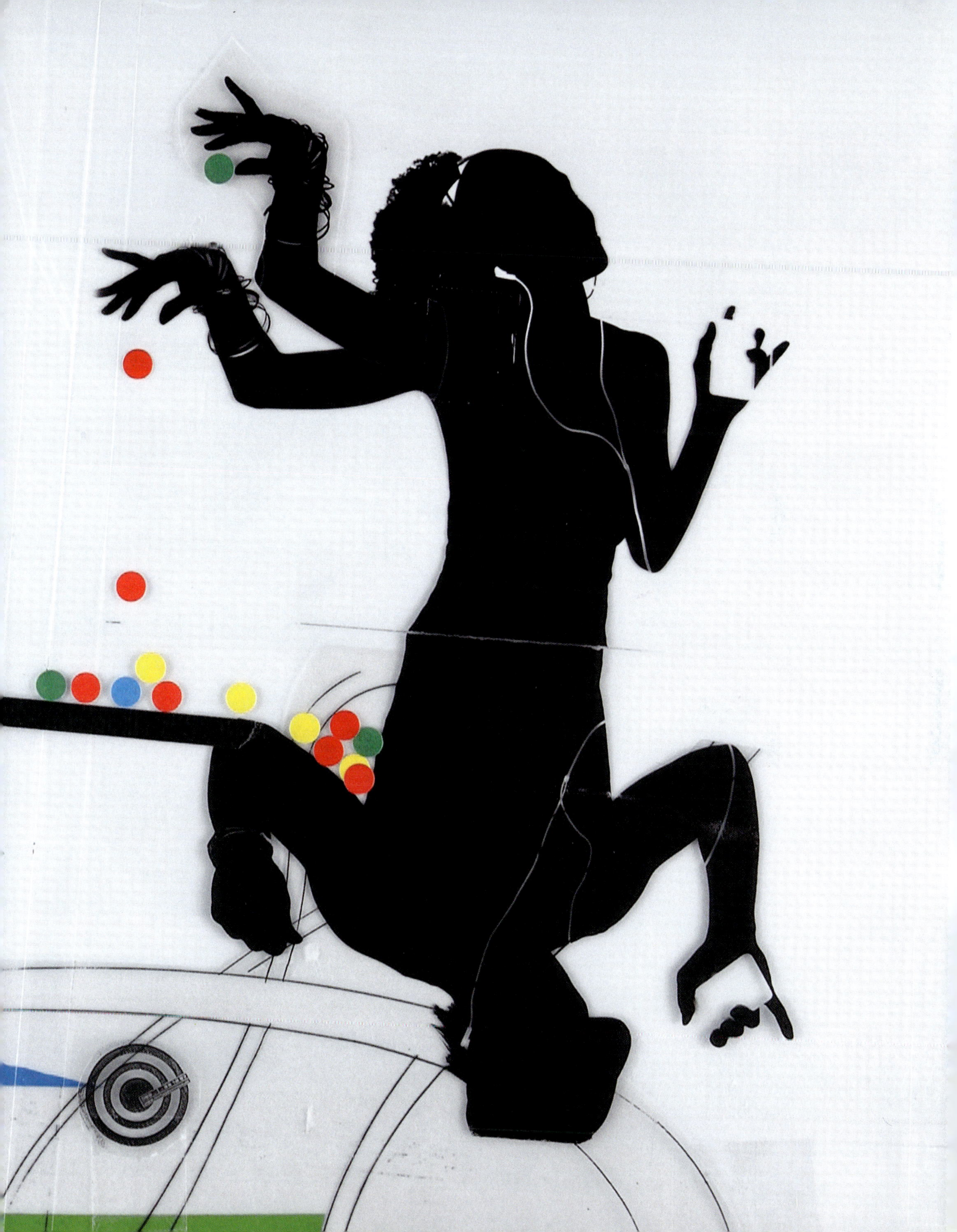

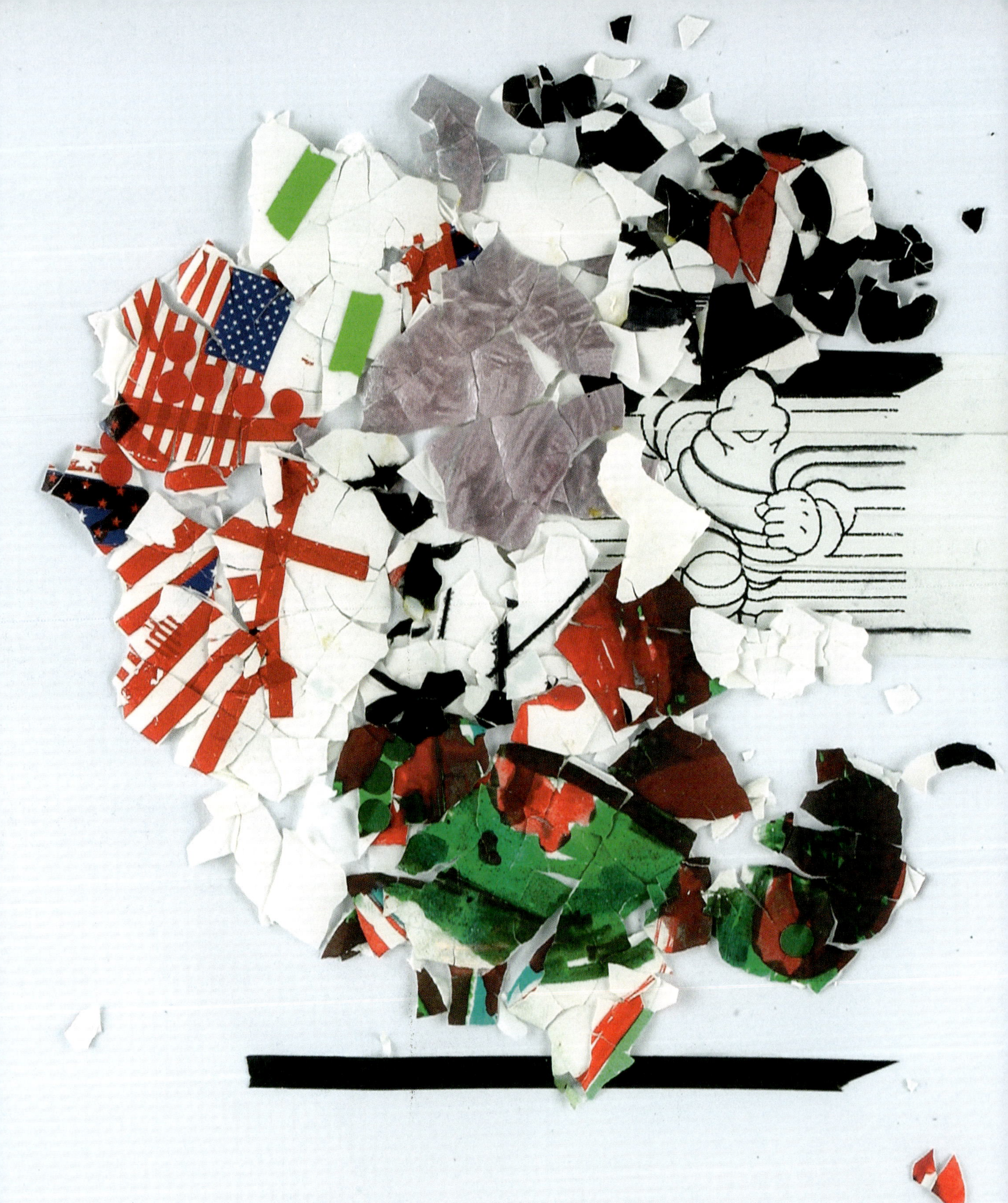

Horror Vacui*

THE SUBJECT AS IMAGE IN MARK LECKEY'S "PARADE"

CATHERINE WOOD

John Currin once described Picasso's invention of Cubism as a manifestation of his voracious drive to see, spread out on one plane of vision, the "ass, breasts, and vulva" of the female nude. Alongside his prolific output of paintings, Picasso designed sets and costumes for a number of theater productions, notably for Diaghilev's street ballet, *Parade* (1917). Constructed from flat canvases, these costumes flaunted their image quality at the expense of the performer's ability to move, tilting the image surface fully towards the viewer's eye. The artist's conception was literally, in this case, of a mobilized "parade" for the eye; an awkward striv-

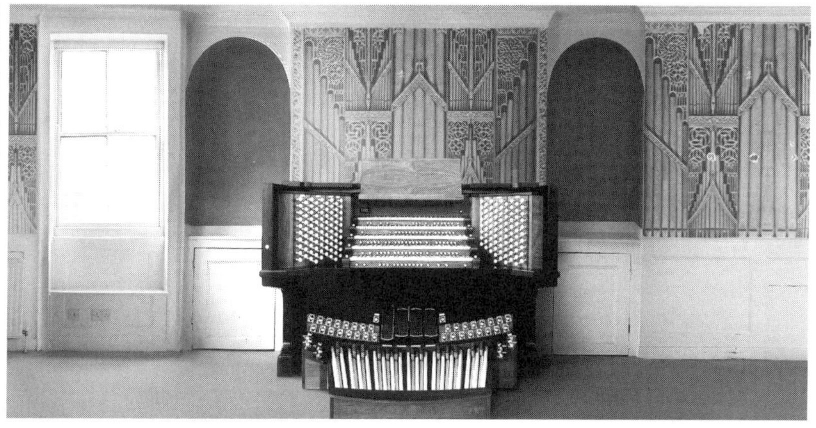

MARK LECKEY, PARADE, 2003, *video projection still.*
("PARADE" WAS COMMISSIONED BY FILM AND VIDEO UMBRELLA IN ASSOCIATION WITH THE
BRIGHTON PHOTO BIENNIAL)

ing offering maximum visual apprehension. The figures were presented to be watched, the sense in which "parade" is a noun, at the same time that they were actively showing themselves or "parading," a verb. It is with the same reflexive self-awareness of the solicitous and passive act of being seen that Mark Leckey spreads out the image for the viewer's eye in his film,

PARADE (2003), the title of which was suggested to him by the name of a pornographic magazine.

Leckey's video works to date— FIORUCCI MADE ME HARDCORE (1999), WE ARE UNTITLED (2001), and PARADE—represent the human subject striving to spread itself out into a reduced dimensionality. His subjects dance, take drugs, and dress up in

* The phrase *horror vacui* is defined in the *Oxford English Dictionary* as "the dislike of leaving empty spaces, e.g. in an artistic composition," and is used by Siegfried Kracauer in his essay "Those Who Wait" (1922) to describe a "fear of emptiness" at the core of urban existence. See *The Mass Ornament* (Cambridge, MA: Harvard University Press, 1995), p. 132.

CATHERINE WOOD is Curator of Performance at Tate Modern and Tate Britain, London.

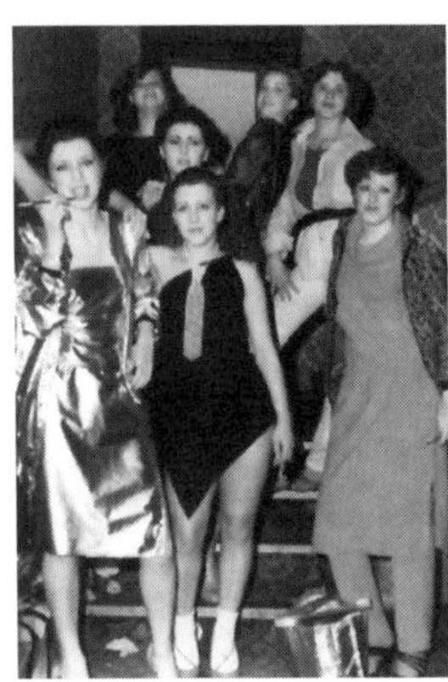

their attempts to transcend the obstinate physicality of the body and disappear in abstract identification with the ecstasy of music, or the seamlessness of the image.

Leckey's treatment of his medium is identical with what he represents. His subject is embedded in the moving image surface to such an extent that it is impossible to unpick observed truth from manipulated fiction. The artist intervenes in the frenetic, angular movement of a dancing boy in FIORUCCI..., speeding up the loop to push his subject to maniacal possession by the music; in PARADE, he double-layers the cosmetic treatment of his own face using make-up and Photoshop techniques, and cuts and pastes the four walls of his room in order to flatten architectural space onto a single visual plane. The empirical facility of the video medium is deliberately undone as Leckey mines its fantastical potential instead: obfuscating documentation with cheap disco and horror effects— dry ice or strobe lighting—and dragging time against the momentum of the medium by directing participants to strike still poses as though they are standing for a long-exposure photograph.

In these ways, Leckey pulls apart what Deleuze has described as the homogenizing effect of the movement-image which connects "any-instant-whatevers" into a coherent sequence simply by feeding them through evenly paced moments of time, and undoes Walter Benjamin's conception of the democratic capture of the photograph which involuntarily reveals an "optical unconscious." In form and content, PARADE favors an old fashioned idea of unconsciousness to do with dreams and visions. As in FIORUCCI..., Leckey's complex weaving of material disrupts any sense of an external, rational, or abstract progression of time, infusing the narrative progression with subjective qualities so that it unfolds to resemble different moments played out, at times hazily and at other times with piercing clarity, in someone's head.

Where artists such as Paul Pfeiffer or Douglas Gordon use loops and freeze-frame to point to the formal properties of the medium, Leckey's use of video revokes the logic of modernism. He works in film as William Blake, in his time, worked with the illustrated book: both artists are fascinated by their medium's potential to thread movement through images, to find an art form that approximates to the capacity of the imagination.

PARADE is staged entirely inside an artificial studio space. Built from layer upon layer of film, photographic or performed image surface against a black backdrop, each element is placed with symbolic weight and intention. The film's mutating looped structure, combined with its more or less continuous impression of panning around inside an enclosed space, gives it a claustrophobic quality. There is a passing glimpse of yellow-white daylight which might appear as a kind of "daybreak" from the film's darkness, but this circular structure does not connote "cyclical" naturalness. Rather, PARADE deals with delusional vision. Its subject's cycle is a fruitless one which describes the continuous transition from the consumption of images to internal subjective vision to external presentation of image and back again.

It is an unnatural mechanism that propels this hallucinatory cycle. Midway through the loop, the camera eye rests on a gleaming shop window. Passing through the hieroglyph of the black and gold shop sign (reading "Elle: Exclusive Design for Men"), Leckey presents himself holding a shoe from the display, fetishistically rubbing its lustrous surface. Earlier in the piece a close-up of the matted texture of Leckey's gelled hair is contrasted sharply with the smooth faces of model girls' billboard perfection. Similarly, in this passage, the artist's own flesh appears vulnerable and real next to the deep gloss of treated animal skin. It is as though rubbing the shoe— the palpable frisson of the two surfaces—conjures a genie in the lamp which transmutes Leckey's physical self into seamless, fantasy image. Like Baudelaire's women who in their rice powder and kohl resemble "marble statuary," he now resembles a mannequin with perfect tawny skin, pale pink lips, and whitened, eyeliner-rimmed eyes.

It is astonishing that the result is not camp. The fusion of the artist's image with the flat visual plane is so complete that there is no protrusion of conflicting truths, no comedy. In this final image, physicality and gender are ironed out as every detail is pushed to the surface. At the end of the sequence, Leckey remains still, holding the left hand side of his jacket open to show its beautifully tailored red lining. The flagrant ostentation of this pose is analogous to pornographic display and there are obvious connotations of feminine sexuality with the showing of internal redness. But with every surface turned towards the frontal plane the feminized subject's self-image has an allover charged quality which drains it of sexuality altogether. As though a record player suddenly slows and grinds to a halt, the soundtrack also drains out, dragging down its high notes away from transcendence. Leckey buttons up his jacket and dissolves into the red background before the loop begins again.

* * *

Leckey has often appeared in his own work, but PARADE is most akin to a self-portrait. Rather than presenting a coherent identity, though, the film proposes its subject to be lost in a struggle to distinguish between interiority and surface. In PARADE, the artist-subject's transformation of self-image goes way beyond the appropriation of weekend wear by football hooligans, as Leckey has described in his text-based project "The Casuals," or the striving to "pass" for affluent or feminine normalcy in Jennie Livingston's documentary about Harlem drag-queen balls, *Paris Is Burning* (1991). Here, the artist transcends economics and gender as he stands stock still within a group of ghostly cardboard cutout figures, attempting to camouflage himself as one among many pictures.

The artist's desire to both create and inhabit the image points to the difficulty of separating the traditional domain of art from the vehicle of dominant ideology. According to Guy Debord, the image is inextricably bound up with the defining characteristic of the capitalist "spectacle" and its perpetual, mirage-like unobtainability. In the mysterious and brooding atmosphere of this piece, Leckey rewrites the narrative of capitalist logic, replacing it with the enabling fantasy of magic. PARADE both fantasizes and manifests the artist's ability to possess the interiorlessness of the image.

But in the heart of the piece, Leckey inserts a shot of himself walking around what appears to be a cavernous church space. An artificially matched soundtrack of footsteps echoing on a stone floor adds an impression of spatial depth to the scene. The empty space and the sound delay force awareness of an alternative dimension, prompting consideration of what it means if, in order to be recognized, the individual must aspire to the condition of the inanimate image. In merging with the spectacle and becoming image, the artist-subject achieves the fantasy of transcendent abstraction, whilst inevitably becoming unobtainable to himself. This scenario makes the artist-subject ultra-visible, but leaves internal subjectivity to lurk in an imperceptible dimension. PARADE shows itself as a succession of seductive and beautiful images, but at its core, it is a lament.

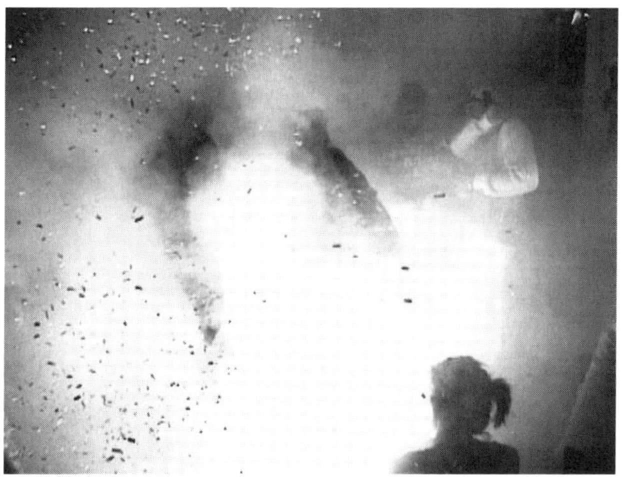

MARK LECKEY, WE ARE UNTITLED, 2001, still from 8-min. DVD /
Szene aus der 8-minütigen DVD.

*Horror Vacui**

DAS SUBJEKT ALS BILD IN MARK LECKEYS «PARADE»

CATHERINE WOOD

John Currin hat einmal gesagt, Picasso habe den Kubismus deshalb erfunden, weil er von der unersättlichen Lust besessen gewesen sei, «den Arsch, die Titten und die Vagina» des weiblichen Aktes in einer einzigen Bildebene vor sich ausgebreitet zu sehen. Neben seiner ungeheuren Bilderproduktion entwarf Picasso auch Bühnenbilder und Kostüme für eine Reihe von Theaterproduktionen, insbesondere für Diaghilews Strassenballett *Parade* (1917). Die Kostüme bestanden aus Leinwandflächen, die immer dem Betrachter zugewandt sein sollten; sie trugen also ihren Bildcharakter gewissermassen auf Kosten der Beweglichkeit der Darsteller vor sich her. Dem Künstler ging es in diesem Fall buchstäblich um eine bewegliche «Parade» für das Auge: ein etwas unbeholfenes Bemühen um ein Höchstmass an optischer Erfassbarkeit. Die Figuren wurden als Anschauungsobjekte vorgeführt, waren also Elemente

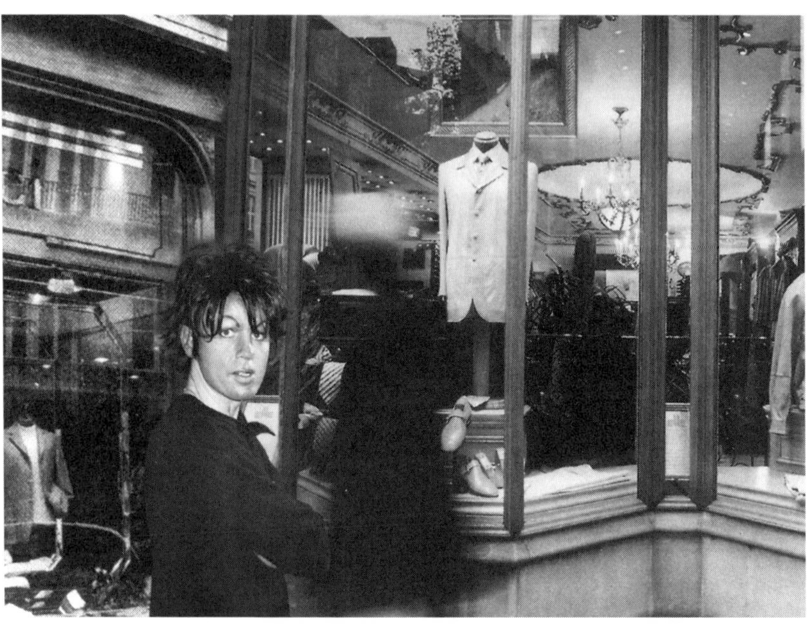

MARK LECKEY, PARADE, 2003, video still.
(«PARADE» ENTSTAND IM AUFTRAG VON FILM AND VIDEO UMBRELLA UND
DER PHOTOGRAPHIE-BIENNALE BRIGHTON)

* Siegfried Kracauer verwendete den Begriff des *Horror Vacui* in seinem Essay «Die Wartenden» (1922), um damit die für das Grossstadtleben wesenhafte «Angst vor dem Schrecken der Leere» zu beschreiben. (Kracauer, *Das Ornament der Masse: Essays,* Suhrkamp, Frankfurt am Main 1963.)

CATHERINE WOOD ist Kuratorin für Performancekunst der Tate Modern und Tate Britain Gallery, London.

einer «Parade», führten sich aber gleichzeitig selbst aktiv vor und «paradierten». Dasselbe reflexive Selbstbewusstsein eines aktiv inszenierten und gleichzeitig passiven Gesehenwerdens entfaltet Mark Leckey in seinem Film PARADE (2003) vor dem Auge des Betrachters – die Anregung zum Filmtitel lieferte der Name eines Pornoheftes.

Leckeys bisherige Videoarbeiten – FIORUCCI MADE ME HARDCORE (1999), WE ARE (2000) und PARADE – zeigen, wie das menschliche Individuum nach Ausbreitung in beschränkten Dimensionen strebt. Die gezeigten Personen tanzen, nehmen Drogen und machen sich fein im Bemühen darum, die hartnäckige Materialität des Körper-

lichen hinter sich zu lassen und sich in
einer abstrakten Identifikation mit der
Ekstase der Musik oder der Grenzen-
losigkeit des Bildes zu verlieren.

Leckey setzt das Medium Video in
einer Art und Weise ein, die sich mit
dem Dargestellten deckt. Das Subjekt
ist bei ihm so sehr Teil der lebendigen
Bildfläche, dass sich unmöglich unterscheiden lässt, was beobachtete Tatsache ist und was manipulierte Fiktion.
In FIORUCCI... nimmt der Künstler auf
die ausgelassene Kreisbewegung eines
tanzenden Jungen Einfluss, indem er
die Videoschleife beschleunigt und das
dargestellte Subjekt zu einem manisch
Musikbesessenen macht. In PARADE
erweitert er die kosmetische Veränderung des eigenen Gesichts mit Schmin-
ke durch digitale Photoshop-Bearbei-
tung um eine zusätzliche Ebene und
ordnet die vier Wände seines Zimmers
mittels «Ausschneiden» und «Einfü-
gen» neu, bis der architektonische
Raum schliesslich zur zweidimensio-
nalen Bildfläche wird. Das empirisch
Simple des Mediums Video unterläuft
Leckey ganz gezielt, indem er das
phantastische Potenzial des Mediums
nützt, wenn er etwa Dokumentarisches
mit billigen Disko- und Horroreffekten
– Trockeneis oder Stroboskoplicht –
vernebelt oder, ganz gegen den Strich
des Mediums, die Zeit dehnt, indem er
Mitwirkende anweist, eine starre Haltung einzunehmen, als würden sie für
ein Photo mit langer Belichtungszeit
posieren.

Auf diese Weise reisst Leckey auseinander, was Deleuze als die vereinheit-
lichende Wirkung des «Bewegungs-Bil-
des» beschrieben hat, das «beliebige
Momente» zu einer Sequenz ver-
knüpfe, indem es sie einfach in gleich-
mässigen Zeitabständen aufeinander
folgen lasse, und er demontiert Walter

Benjamins Auffassung, dass die Photographie demokratisch sei, da sie unwillkürlich ein «Optisch-Unbewusstes»
offenbare. Formal wie inhaltlich be-
vorzugt PARADE einen altmodischen
Begriff des Unbewussten, der mit Träumen und Visionen einhergeht. Wie
schon in FIORUCCI... unterbindet
Leckey durch sein vielschichtiges Ver-
weben des Materials jedes Erleben
eines äusseren, rationalen oder abstrakten Zeitverlaufs und spickt den
Handlungsablauf mit subjektiven Merk-
malen, so dass es den Anschein hat, als
spielten sich die verschiedenen Momente mal verschwommen, mal gesto-
chen scharf im Kopf einer Person ab.

Während Künstler wie Paul Pfeiffer
und Douglas Gordon mit Videoschlei-
fen und eingefrorenen Bildern arbeiten, um die formalen Eigenschaften
des Mediums zu unterstreichen, erteilt
Leckey der Logik der Moderne in seinen Videoarbeiten eine Absage. Er
arbeitet mit dem Film wie William
Blake seinerzeit mit dem illustrierten
Buch: Beide sind fasziniert von der
Möglichkeit, die Bewegung im Bild zu
integrieren und eine Kunstform zu
finden, die unserer Vorstellungskraft
ähnelt. PARADE spielt ausschliesslich
im künstlichen Studioraum. In der
mehrschichtigen Überlagerung photo-
graphischer, filmischer oder szenisch
dargestellter Bilder vor schwarzem Hintergrund hat jedes Element seinen
gezielten symbolträchtigen Platz. Die
ständigen Wechsel und Wiederholun-
gen des Films und der Eindruck eines
unablässigen Hin- und Herschwenkens
der Kamera im geschlossenen Raum
haben eine klaustrophobische Wirkung.
Einmal ist kurz etwas gelbweisses
Tageslicht zu erblicken, was wie ein
Hereinbrechen des Tages ins Dunkel
des Films anmuten mag, doch diese

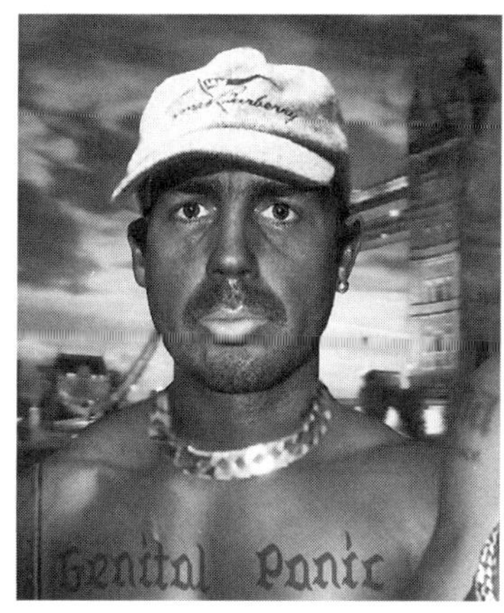

MARK LECKEY, WE ARE UNTITLED,
2001, photograph of the artist-actor /
Photo des Künstlers als Schauspieler.
(PHOTO: BEN BRETT)

zirkuläre Struktur hat absolut nichts
mit einem natürlichen Zyklus zu tun.
Thema von PARADE ist vielmehr das
Trügerische der visuellen Wahrnehmung. Das Zyklische dieses Themas ist
ein ergebnisloses Kreisen, das den
ständigen Wechsel vom Bildkonsum
über die innere subjektive Sicht zur
äusseren Bildpräsentation und wieder
zurück nachzeichnet.

Der halluzinatorische Zyklus wird
von einem unnatürlichen Mechanis-
mus angetrieben. Auf halbem Weg
durch die Filmschleife heftet sich das
Kameraauge auf ein leuchtendes Schau-
fenster. Durch die Hieroglyphe des
schwarzgoldenen Ladenschildes hindurch (die Aufschrift lautet *Elle: Exclusive Design for Men*) präsentiert sich

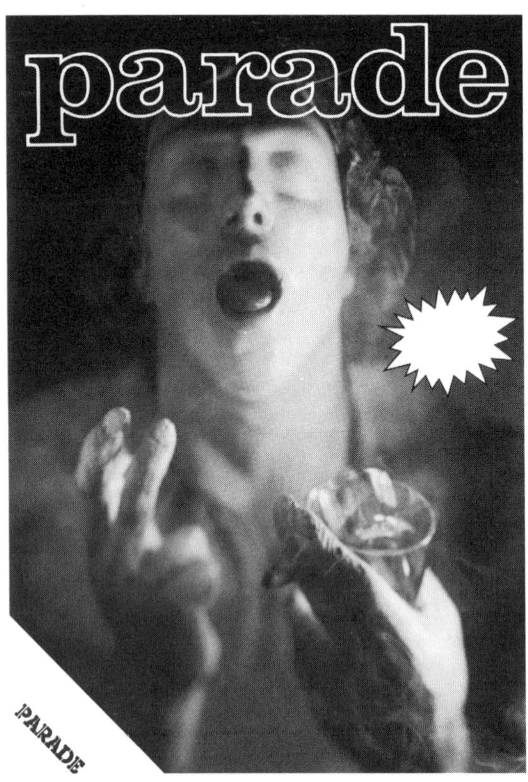

Cover of "Parade" Magazine /
Titelblatt der Zeitschrift «Parade».

Leckey selbst: Er hält einen Schuh der Auslage in der Hand und streicht wie ein Fetischist über die glänzende Oberfläche. An früherer Stelle im Video steht eine Nahaufnahme von Leckeys matt wirkendem, mit Gel behandeltem Haar in scharfem Kontrast zur glatten Gesichtshaut makelloser Werbemodels. In der Einstellung mit dem Schuh wirkt die Haut des Künstlers selbst ähnlich verwundbar und real neben dem tiefen Glanz der verarbeiteten Tierhaut. Es ist, als würde durch das Reiben des Schuhs – das förmlich spürbare Knistern der beiden Oberflächen – ein Geist in der Lampe (beziehungsweise im Schuh) beschworen, was Leckeys äussere Gestalt übergangslos in eine Phantasiefigur verwandelt. Wie die Frauen bei Baudelaire, die dank Reispuder und schwarzen Augenkonturen «Marmorstatuen» gleichen, ähnelt er nun einer Schaufensterpuppe mit perfekt gebräuntem Teint, blassrosa Lippen und weisslich geschminkten, lidstrichumrandeten Augen.

Es ist erstaunlich, dass das Ganze nicht *camp* wirkt. Das Bild des Künstlers verschmilzt so total mit der flachen Bildebene, dass keinerlei Widerspruch oder Komik entsteht. Dadurch dass sich jedes Detail auf die Fläche drängt, wird im definitiven Bild alles Körperliche und Geschlechtliche ausgelöscht. Am Ende der Einstellung steht Leckey unbeweglich und hält die linke Seite seines Jacketts auf und gibt den Blick auf das wunderbar geschneiderte rote Futter frei. Das schamlos Prahlerische dieser Pose würde auch zu einer pornographischen Darbietung passen und das Vorzeigen innerer Röte erinnert offenkundig an weibliche Sexualität. Doch da alle möglichen Ansichten zu einer einzigen frontalen Ansicht vereint sind, wird das Persönlichkeitsbild des feminisierten Subjekts derart allumfassend aufgeladen, dass es jedweden sexuellen Charakter verliert. Wie bei einem Plattenspieler, der plötzlich langsamer wird und zum Stillstand kommt, wobei die Melodie abstirbt, die hohen Töne tiefer werden und ihre Transzendenz verlieren. Leckey knüpft sein Jackett zu und löst sich im roten Hintergrund auf, ehe die Schleife wieder von vorne beginnt.

* * *

Mike Leckey tritt oft selbst in seinen Werken auf, aber von all seinen Arbeiten kommt PARADE einem Selbstporträt am nächsten. Statt einer in sich geschlossenen Identität präsentiert der Film jedoch ein Subjekt, das sich im verzweifelten Bemühen aufreibt, zwischen Innerlichkeit und Oberfläche zu unterscheiden. In PARADE geht die Verwandlung des Persönlichkeitsbildes des Künstler-Subjekts weit über das hinaus, was Leckey in seinem Text über *The Casuals* (1999) beschreibt – Hooligans, die in exklusiv stilvoller Freizeitkleidung auftraten –, aber auch über das in Jennie Livingstons Dokumentarfilm *Paris is Burning* (1991) geschilderte Bestreben von Transvestiten in Harlem, als gut betucht und weiblich durchzugehen. Hier lässt der Künstler alles Ökonomische und Geschlechtliche hinter sich, wenn er regungslos

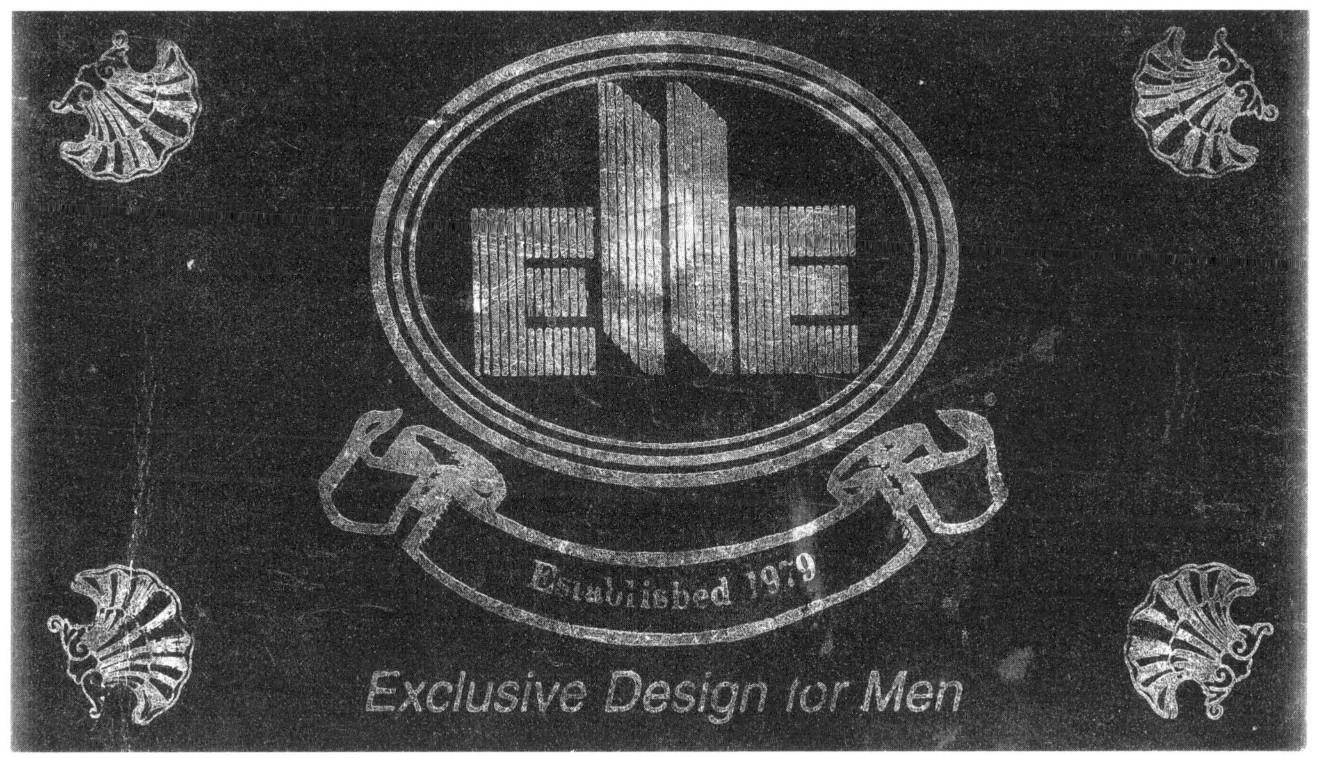

MARK LECKEY, PARADE, 2003, video still.

inmitten einer Gruppe geisterhafter Pappkameraden steht und sich selbst als eines unter vielen Bildern auszugeben versucht.

Das Bedürfnis des Künstlers, Bilder zu schaffen und gleichzeitig in ihnen zu «leben», deutet auf die Schwierigkeit hin, den traditionellen Bereich der Kunst vom Medium der herrschenden Ideologie abzugrenzen. Nach Guy Debord ist das Bild untrennbar mit dem für den Kapitalismus charakteristischen «Spektakel» und dessen ewiger, trugbildartiger Unerreichbarkeit verbunden. In der geheimnisvoll brütenden Atmosphäre dieser Arbeit schreibt Leckey die Geschichte der kapitalistischen Logik um und ersetzt sie durch die beflügelnde Phantasie des Magischen. PARADE phantasiert und bezeugt zugleich die Fähigkeit des Künstlers, den fehlenden Innenraum des Bildes zu besetzen.

Als Herzstück der Arbeit fügt Leckey jedoch eine Szene ein, in der die Figur des Künstlers selbst einen, so scheint es, höhlenartigen Kirchenraum durchschreitet. Ein künstlich abgestimmter Soundtrack mit dem Geräusch von Schritten auf Steinplatten vermittelt den Eindruck raumlicher Tiefe. Der leere Raum und das nachhallende Geräusch zwingen uns eine weitere Dimension wahrzunehmen und lassen uns darüber nachdenken, was es heisst, wenn das Individuum den Zustand eines unbeseelten Bildes anstreben muss, um Anerkennung zu finden. Indem es mit dem Spektakel verschmilzt und Bild wird, realisiert das Künstler-Subjekt eine Vorstellung transzendenter Abstraktion, wird dabei jedoch für sich selbst unerreichbar. Dieses Szenario macht das Künstler-Subjekt zwar extrem sichtbar, verbannt seine innere Subjektivität jedoch in eine unsichtbare Dimension. PARADE tritt als eine Folge verführerischer und wunderschöner Bilder auf, im Kern aber ist es ein Klagelied.

(Übersetzung: B. Opstelten / W. Parker)

IN EVERY EDITION OF PARKETT, TWO CUMULUS CLOUDS, ONE FROM AMERICA, THE OTHER FROM EUROPE, FLOAT OUT TO AN INTERESTED PUBLIC. THEY CONVEY INDIVIDUAL OPINIONS, ASSESSMENTS, AND MEMORABLE ENCOUNTERS—AS ENTIRELY PERSONAL PRESENTATIONS OF PROFESSIONAL ISSUES.

OUR CONTRIBUTORS TO THIS ISSUE ARE NEW YORK WRITER *CAROLEE THEA* AND *GABRIELE SCHOR*, AN ART CRITIC FOR THE "NEUE ZÜRCHER ZEITUNG," WHO TEACHES MODERN AND CONTEMPORARY ART AT THE UNIVERSITIES OF VIENNA AND SALZBURG.

Joan Jonas

CAROLEE THEA

While new strategies and languages for negotiating artistic expression, critique, and concern continue to evolve, some older models are holding their ground. Performance art, for example, has been a volatile art form in which artists have responded to current concerns. It is a strategy that generates ideas and re-examines the contemporary from new viewpoints. In the sixties, performance was considered a permissive activity for formal and intellectual excursions to reveal new layers of meaning. In the words of RoseLee Goldberg, the curator and historian of performance, "performance art ... retains a tentativeness that allows the obsessions of our cultural moment to seep from its edges."[1] Considered transgressive, performative works counter the familiar, formal, and social goals with their assumption of a non-material primacy over the aesthetic. In many cases, the work explored various realities across the divide of high and popular culture while, through enigma and ephemerality, it aimed to upset routine bourgeois thinking.

For several decades, in inquiries using the body, gender, sexuality, and material from other cultures, the pioneering artist Joan Jonas has continued her work, often out of view. At present she teaches media and performance at MIT and is frequently invited to do exhibitions, mostly in Europe. Recently, however, she was invited to compose a new work for The Moore Space in Miami, Florida and to participate in her retro-

---

CAROLEE THEA is the author of *Foci: Interviews with 10 International Curators* (New York: Apexart, 2001).

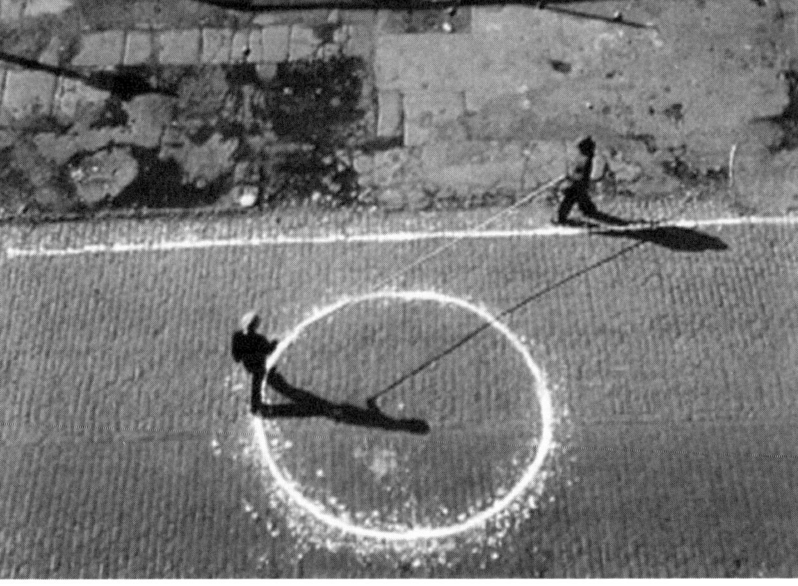

*JOAN JONAS, SONGDELAY, 1973,
still from 16-mm film on DVD / Szene aus dem
auf DVD übertragenen
16-mm-Film.
(VIDEO STILLS: COURTESY ELECTRONIC
ARTS INTERMIX, NEW YORK)*

words, "I didn't see a major difference between a poem, a sculpture, a film, or a dance. A gesture has for me the same weight as a drawing: draw, erase, draw, erase—memory erased."[2] A storyteller, or rather a picture-builder, she imbricates cultural and mythological epics with personal narrative, video, and other media. In most of her work, as early as in MIRROR PIECE (1967), Jonas examines space and perceptual phenomena while merging elements of

moving through a stark, windswept landscape. Her performers struggle over and over with their fluttering coats, battling the gusts. The 16-mm film—silent, black-and-white, jerky, and sped-up—evokes early cinema, while its content locates it in spare late-sixties Minimalism. (The camera work and editing was done in collaboration with Peter Campus.) In SONGDELAY (1973), another early performance film, Jonas is concerned with stripping down the medium and foregrounding the figure and its ritualistic movements in space.

VOLCANO SAGA (1987) begins with rituals of the everyday that the artist links to myths, sagas, and fairy tales. Based on the thirteenth-century Icelandic Laxdeala saga, the work is a narrative reverie, a televisual retelling of a

*JOAN JONAS, WIND, 1968,
stills from 16-mm film on DVD.
Camera: Peter Campus;
edited by Peter Campus and Joan Jonas.*

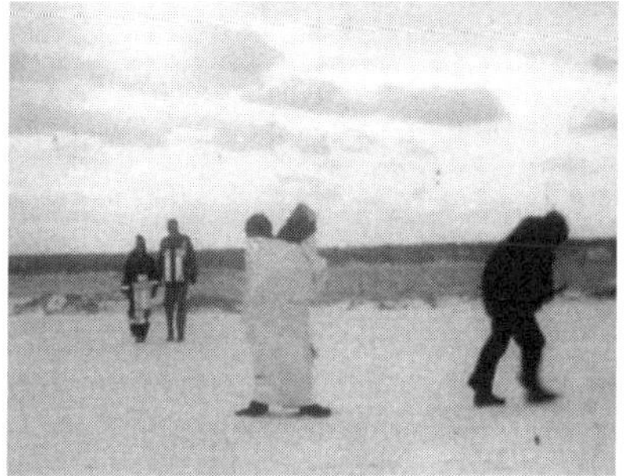

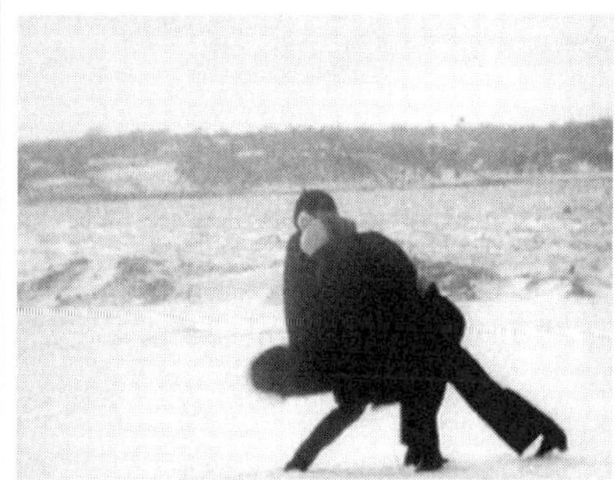

spective at the Queens Museum in New York City. As well, Jonas' first New York performance in over a decade revisits the myth of Helen of Troy at The Kitchen, a space that since the seventies has been a leader in presenting performance, dance, and multimedia visual culture.

In her complex installations that include drawing, poetry, sculpture, film, video, performance, and dance, Jonas analyzes and re-synthesizes the action and interaction of the performing body and its transformations. In her own

dance, Japanese Noh and Kabuki, drawing, and sculpture.

By employing live projections, single-channel video, and asynchronous picture and/or sound sequences, Jonas reveals the manipulative potential of film and video techniques. In her groundbreaking video VERTICAL ROLL (1972) an interrupted electronic signal causing a vertical roll on the monitor was transformed into a formal device to dislocate space and fracture the recorded image. For WIND, a 1968 work, Jonas focuses on a group of performers

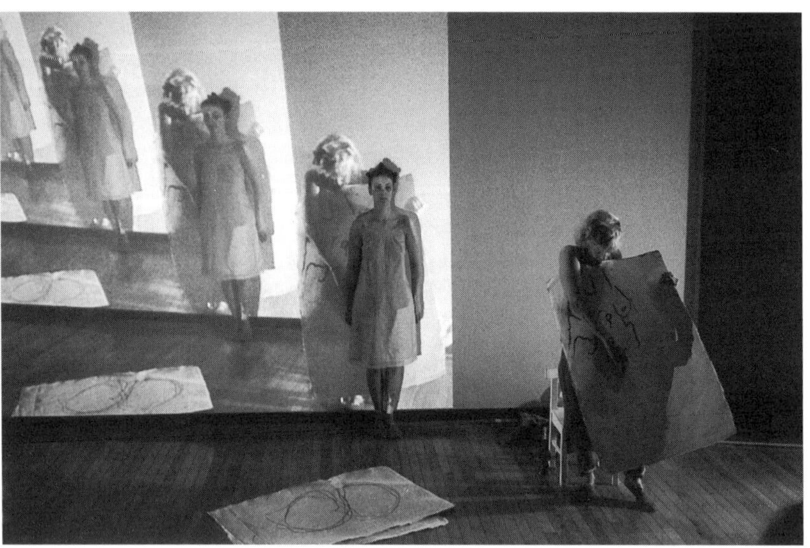

medieval myth about a young woman (played by Tilda Swinton) whose dreams foretell the future. Shot in the dramatic natural landscapes of Iceland and in New York, the performance-based work uses ancient dream analysis as a starting point for a densely textured tale in which the young woman's interpreter (played by Ron Vawter) hears her dreams and sees their meaning. Jonas employs multilayered digital effects to create a ritualistic dreamscape of the young woman's imagination and desires. The ghostly overlays of other-worldly images and mythical text imbue this work with a haunting beauty.

The principal structuring element of Jonas' work has been the simultaneity of live performance and video imagery; by switching back and forth and shifting the gaze, one mode or object supplements the other. Borrowing narratives or poems, objects, cameras, bodies, and movement, the artist cre-ates a patchwork of the esoteric and mundane to reveal symptoms of the present.

Continuing to accommodate a widening inquiry into familiar patterns of narration, in 2002 Jonas created a work for "Documenta 11" based on an epic poem in confrontation with the disjunctive tensions of our postcolonial world. While much of the artwork in Kassel was concentrated in a documentary mode, a significant number of artists sought ways of translating the moment into the kinds of languages necessary for shaping the production of new and different forms of knowledge to complement the contemporary upheaval of received realities and ideas.

In that work, LINES IN THE SAND, the artist took as her starting point "Helen in Egypt," an epic poem by H.D., the Imagist poet Hilda Doolittle. The canonical Helen myth, based on the tale of a war fought at Troy for a woman stolen from the Greeks, has for centuries been preferred over a lesser-known version in which Helen remained in Egypt the whole time and never set foot in Troy. The true cause of the war was thus disguised by a more romantic, appealing, and palatable idea that dissimulated the actual reality of a brutal war. In H.D.'s poem, Helen continually questions the reality of her own myth, and Jonas questions the cause of wars in general. In the case of Troy, Jonas surmises that the likely reason for the war could be found in the more mundane ongoing tensions between Greece and Troy over access to trade routes in the Black Sea.

More material for the weaving of LINES IN THE SAND was found by Jonas in H.D.'s writing sessions during her analysis with Freud (as recorded in her book *Tribute to Freud*), in which the poet examined, with Freud, aspects of her "peculiar" experience of writing on the wall while recuperating in Corfu from her divorce from the poet Richard Aldington. In her performance, Jonas entwines the performative act of wall-writing with the Helen myth, while also incorporating a text from yet another culture. Within this text, as a play within a play, the artist inserts the ancient Irish epic, the *Tain*, a tale embedded in the larger herocycle of Cuchullain. Building her own narrative, she incorporates a multilayered reality alongside the Helen myths—a shadow of a shadow. For example, in the segment titled *Pillow Talk*, a newly wed Irish king and queen are in bed discussing which of them has the most possessions. Their often humorous dialogue echoes the trade war between Greece and Troy while demonstrating how personal arguments over possessions begin at home. In drawing these two myths together, Jonas enacts the political and the personal while intimating the contemporary.

The performance aspect of Jonas' work embroils us in the mirror world of vertiginous realities. Jonas develops her own emblematic and striking visual and theatrical vocabulary by synthesizing ritualized gestures and objects like masks, costumes, and mirrors. The back-and-forth of the artist drawing on the ground or walls with chalk attached to a branch, and performers in masks and costumes enacting stylized dance-like repetitive moves, contrast with the monitors projecting a glut of oversized imagery which includes digital patterns, shadows, sarcophagi being pulled by trucks (in a reference to Egypt as a postmodern Las Vegas), and audio

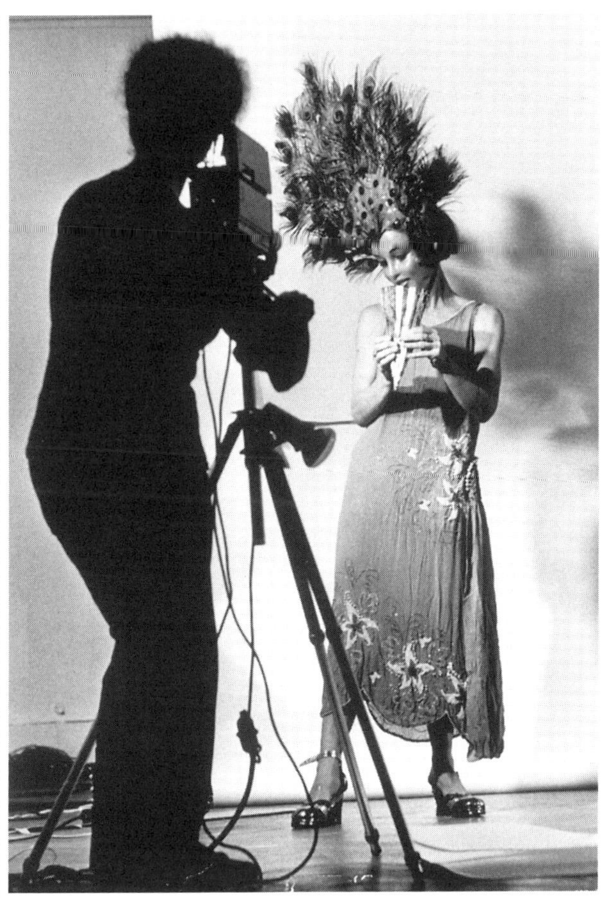
JOAN JONAS, ORGANIC HONEY'S VERTICAL ROLL, 1972/1973, production still, Musée Galliera, Paris. (PHOTO: BEATRICE HEILIGERS)

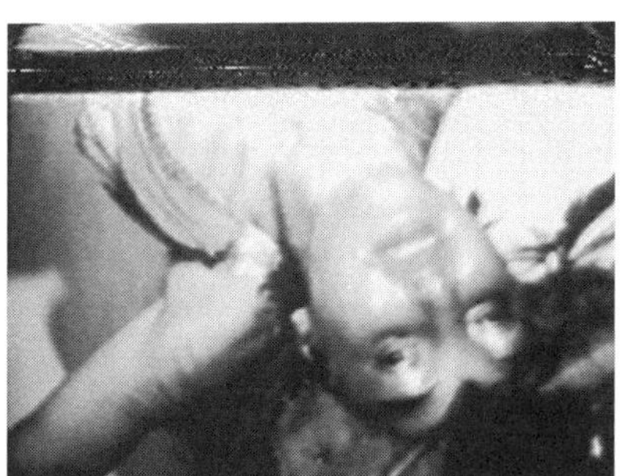
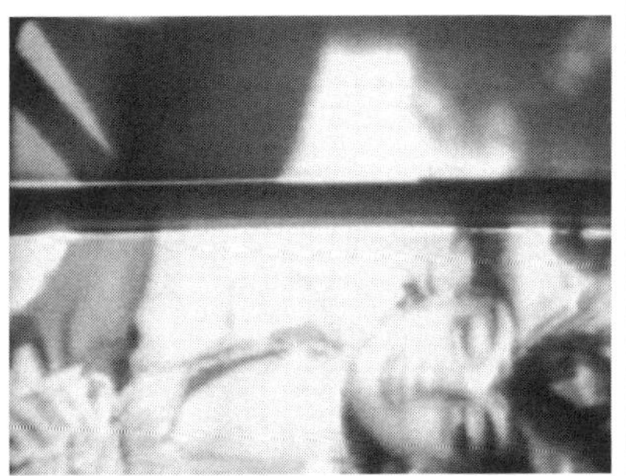
JOAN JONAS, VERTICAL ROLL, 1972, video stills.
(COURTESY ELECTRONIC ARTS INTERMIX, NEW YORK)

contrasts between Erik Satie and rock music. Combining past myths with the present, Jonas juxtaposes time and idea to create more tensions for the viewer, who, meandering through a set comprising monitors, drawings, and objects, gradually untangles the web.

Paralleling the interactivity of modern life, as in the play of virtual reality or cyberspace, Jonas' work offers the illusion of constant movement and refocus, as an implied action between gazer and other, to create restless motion in a fragmentary dream. As a participatory game, the artist's work involves us in ways that are subliminal, challenging, and assaulting. Yet, within her systematically constructed grounding, the multilayerings gain directness, as their intensity and uniqueness transport us through time and place.

Finally, LINES IN THE SAND plays out a kind of scenario in an intelligible formal and political language that attempts to highlight the political upheavals in contemporary society. While Jonas' signature contribution is ephemeral, it enhances re-cognition of ideas that intellectuals and artists, both inside and outside the "advanced" economies, continue to grapple with.

1) RoseLee Goldberg, *Performance: Live Art Since 1960* (New York: Harry N. Abrams, 1998), p. 11.
2) *Joan Jonas, Scripts and Descriptions 1968–1982,* ed. Douglas Crimp (Berkeley: University Art Museum/Eindhoven: Stedelijk Van Abbemuseum, 1983), p. 137.

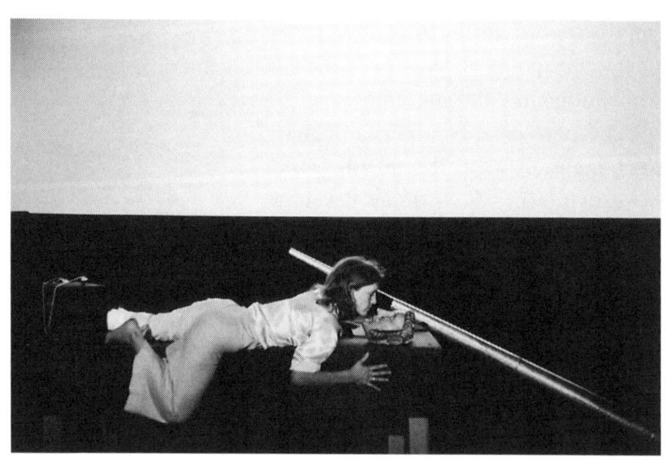

Joan Jonas

CAROLEE THEA

Trotz des Aufkommens neuer Strategien und Sprachen im Zusammenhang mit künstlerischen Ausdrucksformen, Kunstkritik und Kunstfragen behaupten manche älteren Modelle ihre Stellung. Die Performance beispielsweise ist eine flüchtige Kunstform, mit der Künstler jeweils auf aktuelle Themen reagieren. Sie ist eine produktive, ideenreiche Strategie, die das Zeitgenössische einer Prüfung unter neuen Gesichtspunkten unterzieht. Die aus der Fluxus-Bewegung der 60er Jahre hervorgegangene Performancekunst galt ursprünglich als freizügige Methode, um auf formalen und intellektuellen Umwegen neue Bedeutungs-

CAROLEE THEA schreibt für verschiedene Kunstpublikationen und ist Autorin von *Foci: Interviews with 10 International Curators,* Apex Art, New York 2001.

schichten aufzudecken. Laut RoseLee Goldberg, der auf Performance spezialisierten Kuratorin und Kunsthistorikerin, «hat die Performancekunst noch immer etwas Tentatives, das den Obsessionen unserer kulturellen Gegenwart erlaubt, an den Rändern einzusickern».[1] Die als grenzüberschreitend geltenden, performativen Arbeiten widersetzen sich den vertrauten formalen und gesellschaftlichen Zielen durch die Annahme, dass das Nicht-Materielle Vorrang habe vor dem Ästhetischen. Oft erkundete die Performance verschiedene Realitäten beidseits der Kluft zwischen Hoch- und Populärkultur, wobei sie mit ihrem rätselhaften und flüchtigen Charakter bürgerliche Denkgewohnheiten vor den Kopf stossen wollte.

Joan Jonas, eine Pionierin der Performancekunst, untersuchte jahr-

zehntelang – oft völlig unbeachtet – Körper, Geschlecht, Sexualität und Material aus anderen Kulturen. Sie unterrichtet zurzeit Multimedia- und Performancekunst am MIT und wird oft eingeladen Ausstellungen zu gestalten, vor allem in Europa. Erst kürzlich bat man sie, ein neues Werk für *The Moore Space* in Miami zu realisieren und an einer Retrospektive im Queens-Museum in New York mitzuwirken. Ausserdem greift Jonas mit ihrer seit über zehn Jahren ersten Performance in New York einmal mehr auf die Sage der Schönen Helena zurück – und zwar in *The Kitchen,* einem seit den 70er Jahren führenden Ort in Sachen Performance-, Tanz- und Multimediakunst.

In ihren komplexen Installationen, welche Zeichnungen, Lyrik, Skulptur, Film, Video, Performance und Tanz umfassen, analysiert Jonas die Aktion und Interaktion des an der Performance beteiligten Körpers und seiner Verwandlungsformen und führt sie zu neuen Synthesen. Wie sie selbst sagt: «Ich konnte keinen wesentlichen Unterschied sehen zwischen einem Gedicht, einer Skulptur, einem Film oder dem Tanz. Eine Gebärde hat für mich ebenso viel Gewicht wie eine Zeichnung: zeichnen, auslöschen, zeichnen, auslöschen – gelöschte Erinnerung.»[2] Als Erzählerin von Geschichten oder besser noch: Erbauerin von Bildern

Durch den Einsatz von Live-Projektionen, Einkanalvideos und asynchronen Bild- und/oder Tonsequenzen lässt Jonas das manipulative Potenzial der Film- und Videotechnik sichtbar werden. Ihr bahnbrechendes Video VERTICAL ROLL (1972), in welchem ein gestörter elektronischer Impuls ein vertikales Rollen des Bilds auf dem Monitor auslöste, wurde zum formalen Instrument, das den Raum aus den Fugen hob und das aufgezeichnete Bild zerhackte. WIND (1968) zeigt eine

Schnitt erfolgten in Zusammenarbeit mit Peter Campus.) In SONGDELAY (Songverzögerung, 1973), einem weiteren frühen Performancefilm, geht es Jonas darum, das Medium von jedem Ballast zu befreien und die Gestalt und deren rituelle Bewegungen im Raum in den Vordergrund zu stellen.

VOLCANO SAGA (Vulkan-Sage, 1987) beginnt mit Alltagsritualen, welche die Künstlerin mit Mythen, Sagen und Märchen in Verbindung bringt. Die von der isländischen Laxdal-Sage aus

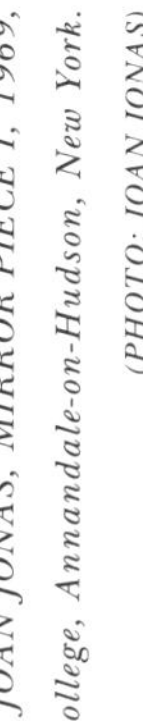

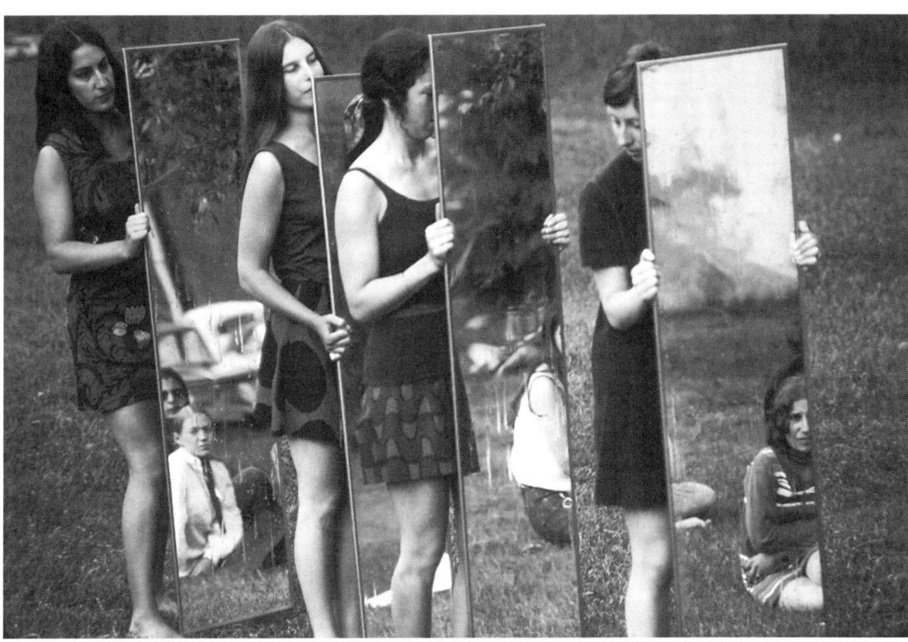

verzahnt sie kulturelle und mythologische Epen mit privaten Begebenheiten, Videobildern und anderen Medien. Fast immer geht Jonas räumlichen und wahrnehmungsbedingten Phänomenen nach und lässt dabei Elemente aus Tanz, Zeichnung, Skulptur oder dem japanischen No- und Kabuki-Theater einfliessen. Das war schon bei MIRROR PIECE (Spiegelstück, 1967) der Fall.

Gruppe von Darstellern, die sich durch eine kahle, windgepeitschte Landschaft bewegen. Sie kämpfen gegen die Böen an und mühen sich dabei unablässig mit ihren flatternden Mänteln ab. Der 16-mm-Film – ohne Ton, schwarzweiss, holprig und im Zeitraffer ablaufend – erinnert an die Frühzeit des Kinos, obwohl sein Inhalt auf den kargen Minimalismus der späten 60er Jahre verweist. (Kameraführung und

dem dreizehnten Jahrhundert ausgehende Arbeit ist eine erzählerische Träumerei, eine televisionäre Nacherzählung der mittelalterlichen Legende von einer jungen Frau (gespielt von Tilda Swinton), die in ihren Träumen die Zukunft sieht. Der auf der Form der Performance aufgebaute Film wurde in den dramatischen Naturlandschaften Islands sowie in New York gedreht. Er macht alte Traumdeutungen zum Ausgangspunkt einer dicht gewobenen Geschichte, in welcher der Traumdeuter (gespielt von Ron Vawter) die Träume der jungen Frau anhört und deren Bedeutung erkennt. Mit Hilfe von vielschichtigen digitalen Effekten lässt Jonas eine rituelle Traumlandschaft der Phantasien und Sehnsüchte der jungen Frau entstehen. Die geisterhaften Überblendungen überirdischer Bilder und mythischer Worte verleihen dem Werk eine geheimnisvolle Schönheit.

Das wichtigste Strukturelement in Jonas' Arbeiten ist der simultane und komplementäre Einsatz von Live-Performance und Videobildern, der den Blick rasch hin und her wechseln lässt. Durch das Beiziehen von Geschichten oder Gedichten, Objekten, Kameras, Körpern und Bewegung erzeugt die Künstlerin ein Patchwork aus esoterischen und alltäglichen Elementen, das Symptome unserer Zeit sichtbar macht.

Im Bestreben, immer weiter gefasste Untersuchungen in vertraute Erzählmuster einzupassen, schuf Jonas 2002 für die «Documenta 11» ein Werk, in welchem sie ein episches Gedicht den ungeheuren Spannungen unserer postkolonialen Welt gegenüberstellte. Zwar waren viele Arbeiten in Kassel dem Dokumentarischen verpflichtet, doch eine beträchtliche Zahl von Kunstschaffenden suchte doch nach Möglichkeiten, den Moment in einer Sprache zu erfassen, die neue und andere Formen des Wissens möglich machen und den aktuellen Umsturz überlieferter Realitäten und Ideen ergänzen sollten.

In jener Arbeit – LINES IN THE SAND (Spuren im Sand, 2002) – nahm die Künstlerin das Epos «Helen in Egypt» zum Ausgangspunkt, ein Werk der Dichterin H.D. (Hilda Doolittle), die zum Kreis der Imagisten zählt. Die

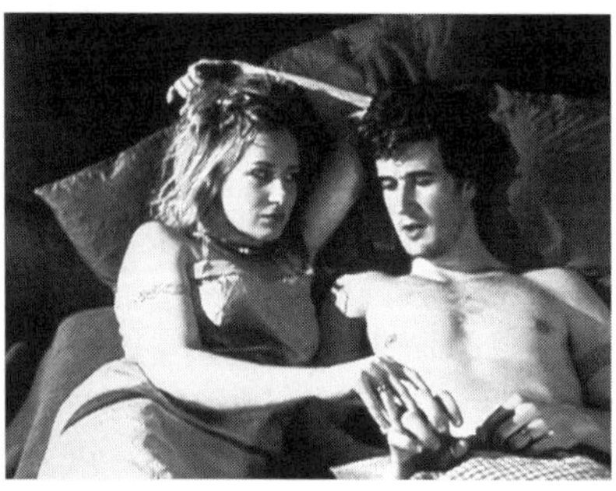

bekannte Version der Sage, derzufolge der Raub der Griechin Helena durch die Troer zur Belagerung Trojas führte, hatte jahrhundertelang Vorrang vor der weniger bekannten Version, laut der Helena die ganze Zeit über in Ägypten blieb und nie einen Fuss auf trojanischen Boden setzte. Der wahre Kriegsgrund wurde also durch ein romantisches, attraktives und appetitlicheres Argument verschleiert, das die harte Realität des brutalen Krieges kaschierte. In Doolittles Gedicht zweifelt Helena ständig an der Realität ihres eigenen Mythos. Jonas zieht die Ursachen von Kriegen ganz allgemein in Zweifel. Im Fall von Griechenland und Troja vermutet sie, dass der wahre Kriegsgrund wohl eher im profaneren Konflikt um den Zugang zu den Handelswegen im Schwarzen Meer zu suchen sei.

Weiteres Material für LINES IN THE SAND fand Jonas in Doolittles Sitzungsaufzeichnungen ihrer Analyse bei Freud (im Buch *Tribute to Freud*), in denen die Dichterin mit Freud verschiedene Aspekte des «seltsamen» Erlebnisses erörtert, dass ihr eine Schrift

an der Wand erschienen war, als sie sich in Korfu von ihrer Scheidung von Richard Aldington erholte. In ihrer Performance verknüpft Jonas den performativen Akt des «Schreibens auf der Wand» mit der Sage von Helena und zieht zusätzlich noch einen Text aus einer anderen Kultur bei. Gleichsam als Schauspiel im Schauspiel integriert die Künstlerin das altirische Epos *Tain* in die Performance (eine Geschichte, die Teil der Heldensage von Cuchullain ist). Sie webt ihre eigene Geschichte und lässt um die Helena-Mythen herum eine vielschichtige Realität entstehen – den Schatten eines Schattens. So unterhält sich in einem Abschnitt mit dem Titel *Pillow Talk* (Kissengeflüster) ein jung vermähltes irisches Königspaar im Bett darüber, wer von beiden mehr Besitztümer habe. Dieser oft witzige Dialog erinnert an den Handelskrieg zwischen Griechenland und Troja und zeigt zugleich, dass Besitzstreitigkeiten im eigenen Haus anfangen. Indem sie die beiden Sagen miteinander verknüpft, zeigt Jonas politische und persönliche Aspekte auf und spielt dabei auf die Gegenwart an.

Die Performance-Elemente von Jonas' Arbeit verstricken uns in eine Spiegelwelt Schwindel erregender Wirklichkeiten. Durch die Kombination von ritualisierten Gesten und Objekten wie Masken, Kostüme und Spiegel entwickelt Jonas ihr eigenes typisches visuelles und schauspielerisches Vokabular. Die Künstlerin, die mit einer an einem Ast befestigten Kreide hin und her geht und auf den Boden oder die Wände zeichnet, und die Darsteller, die in Masken und Kostümen stilisierte, tanzähnliche, repetitive Bewegungen vollführen, stehen im Kontrast zu den Monitoren, die eine Flut übergrosser

Bilder an uns vorbeiziehen lassen. Dazu gehören auch digitale Muster, Schatten oder von Lastwagen gezogene Sarkophage – eine Anspielung auf Ägypten als eine Art postmodernes Las Vegas – sowie ein Soundtrack, der von Erik Satie bis zu Rockmusik reicht. Indem sie alte Sagen mit der Gegenwart verbindet, stellt Jonas Zeiten und Ideen nebeneinander um die Spannung für den Betrachter zu erhöhen, der, während er zwischen den Monitoren, Zeichnungen und Objekten herumwandert, das Geflecht allmählich entwirrt.

Vergleichbar mit der Interaktivität des modernen Lebens, wie sie in der virtuellen Realität oder im Cyberspace zum Ausdruck kommt, vermittelt Jonas' Werk die Illusion der ständigen Bewegung und Neuausrichtung als implizite Interaktion zwischen Betrachter und Betrachtetem und erzeugt damit den ruhelosen Eindruck eines Traumfragments. Das Werk lädt zum Mitspielen ein und bezieht uns auf unterschwellige, provozierende und stürmische Art mit ein. Doch innerhalb der systematisch konstruierten Grundstruktur werden die Vielschichtigkeiten zunehmend direkter, während uns ihre Intensität und Einzigartigkeit durch Zeit und Raum tragen.

Schliesslich spielt LINES IN THE SAND eine Art Szenario durch, und zwar in einer verständlichen formalen und politischen Sprache, die versucht, die politischen Umwälzungen in der heutigen Gesellschaft deutlich aufzuzeigen. Jonas' sehr persönlicher Beitrag bleibt zwar ephemer, doch er erleichtert das Verständnis von Ideen, mit denen sich Intellektuelle und Künstler in Industrie- und anderen Ländern nach wie vor herumschlagen.

(Übersetzung: Irene Aeberli)

1) RoseLee Goldberg, *Performance: Live Art Since 1960* (New York: Harry N. Abrams, 1998), S. 11.
2) *Joan Jonas, Scripts and Descriptions 1968–1982*, Hrsg. Douglas Crimp (Berkeley: University Art Museum / Eindhoven: Stedelijk Van Abbemuseum, 1983), S. 137.

JOAN JONAS, LINES IN THE SAND, 2002, performance, Documenta 11, Kassel.
(PHOTO: WERNER MASCHMANN)

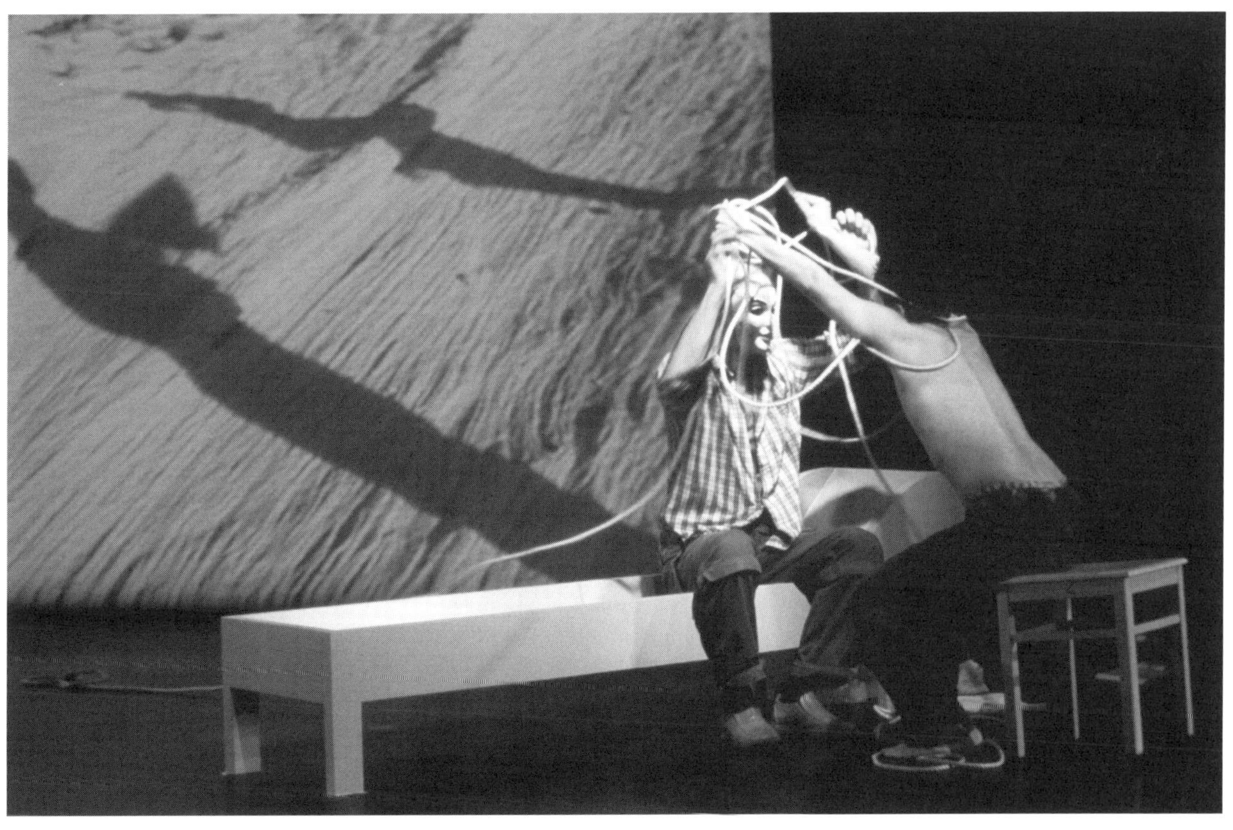

IN JEDER AUSGABE VON PARKETT PEILT EINE CUMULUS-WOLKE AUS AMERIKA UND EINE AUS EUROPA DIE INTERESSIERTEN KUNSTFREUNDE AN. SIE TRÄGT PERSÖNLICHE RÜCKBLICKE, BEURTEILUNGEN UND DENKWÜRDIGE BEGEGNUNGEN MIT SICH – ALS JEWEILS GANZ EIGENE DARSTELLUNG EINER BERUFLICHEN AUSEINANDERSETZUNG.

IN DIESEM BAND ÄUSSERN SICH *GABRIELE SCHOR*, KUNSTKRITIKERIN DER «NEUEN ZÜRCHER ZEITUNG» UND DOZENTIN FÜR MODERNE UND ZEITGENÖSSISCHE KUNST AN DEN UNIVERSITÄTEN WIEN UND SALZBURG, SOWIE DIE PUBLIZISTIN *CAROLEE THEA* AUS NEW YORK.

HYBRIDITÄT, EROS UND TOD

GABRIELE SCHOR

Synthetische Stoffe sind für zeitgenössische Kunstwerke oft die Bedingung ihrer Entstehung. Mehr noch: Es ist gerade ihre spezifische Materialität, die Künstler zu aussergewöhnlichen Formen und Dimensionen inspiriert. Welches Material sonst hätte Anish Kapoor ermöglicht seine gigantische Installation MARSYAS (2002) in der Tate Modern über den Köpfen der Besucher schweben zu lassen, wenn nicht das elastische, aber extrem feste Material einer Kunstfaser?[1]

Heute durchdringen Kunststoffe wie eine *force majeure* all unsere Lebensbereiche. Für Roland Barthes ist «Plastik» jedoch «weniger eine Substanz als vielmehr die Idee ihrer endlosen Umwandlung, es ist, wie sein gewöhnlicher Name anzeigt, die sichtbar gemachte Allgegenwart. Und gerade darin ein wunderbarer Stoff: Das Wunder ist allemal die plötzliche Konvertierung der Natur. Das Plastik bleibt ganz von diesem Erstaunen durchdrungen: Es ist weniger Gegenstand als Spur einer Bewegung.»[2]

In den 90er Jahren liess diese Spur der Bewegung ein signifikantes Erscheinungsbild der zeitgenössischen Plastik aus diversen Kunststoffen erkennen, das Dirk Luckow in einer sensibel kuratierten Schau präsentierte. Es waren ausschliesslich abstrakte Formen amorpher, biomorpher und monolithischer Ausprägung zu sehen. Ihre synthetisch gelackten Oberflächen strahlten glänzende Sinnlichkeit aus. Vertreten waren unter anderen Thomas Rentmeister, Elke Baulig, Thomas Grünfeld und Asta Gröting. Ihre Formen wirkten zuweilen wie glitschige Amöben. Gemeinsam war diesen Arbeiten das Zurücktreten des erzählerischen Inhalts hinter die

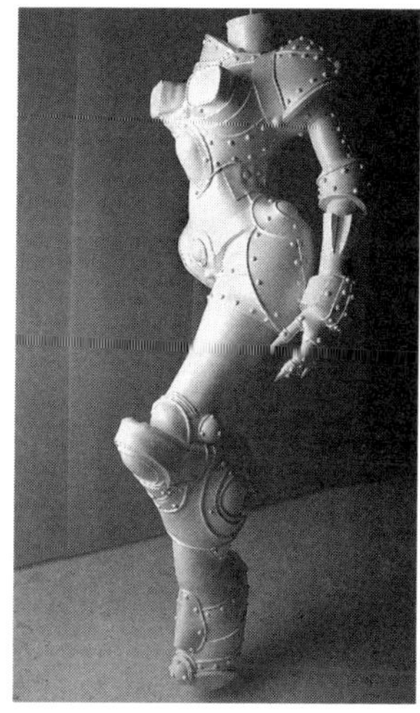

blanken Oberflächen und reduzierten Formen.[3)]

Anhand der Werke von fünf Künstlern, deren Arbeiten mir in Wien aufgefallen sind, möchte ich zeigen, dass sich einige Jahre später auch noch eine andere – narrative – Richtung herausgebildet hat. An der Schwelle zum einundzwanzigsten Jahrhundert offenbaren sich die vielfältigen Anwendungsgebiete des Kunststoffs. Mit den Themen Hybridität, Eros und Tod wird eine Art Gegenpol zu den gegenstandslosen, morphologisch inspirierten Formen der 90er Jahre umrissen.

Die 1964 in Südkorea geborene Künstlerin Lee Bul setzt sich mit der Hybridität des Cyberspace auseinander, in der das Virtuelle real und die Realität virtuell ist. Sie entwirft Fabelwesen, zum Beispiel riesige weisse Monster, deren überdimensionale Flügel, lange Fangarme und spitze Klauen sie aus Polyurethanplatten schneidet und in Anspielung auf die antike Mythologie «Sirenen» nennt. Was in der Antike ein Monster war, wird in der Zeit der Raumfahrt zum Cyborg, jener berüchtigten Kreuzung zwischen Mensch und Maschine. Bul modelliert ihre CYBORGS als Kriegerinnen im Rüstungskorsett mit spitzen Brüsten und engen Taillen. Sie wirken sexy, kampfbereit und unerbittlich. Die Maschinenwesen oder kybernetischen Organismen entstammen dem Repertoire der massenmedialen Unterhaltungsindustrie Seouls, der Welt der Sciencefiction, der japanischen *Manga*-Comics und der koreanischen *Anime*-Figuren. In ihnen manifestieren sich Mythen, Ideologien und Phantasien, etwa der Wahn technologischer Perfektion und Allmacht. Meistens werden die Fabelwesen von jungen – männlichen – Programmierern entwickelt. Die arche-

typischen Bilder des Weiblichen erscheinen voll Ambiguität: Die Frau ist verführerisch und bedrohlich, kontrollierbar und monströs, schwach und allmächtig. Bul greift diese Phantasien auf und unterläuft sie. Ihre Cyborgs aus weissem Silikonguss sind Torsi ohne Kopf, mit nur einem Arm oder einem Bein. So, wie sie – etwa in der Ausstellung «The Divine Shell» – von der Decke der Ausstellungsräume hängen, scheinen sich Buls Silikon-Figuren im Cyberspace zu bewegen.[4)] Schon deshalb ist Bul auf leichtes Material angewiesen, das ihr diese künstlerische Freiheit gewährt.

Während Lee Bul die Verquickung des Realen und des Virtuellen im Cyberspace aufspürt, kreuzt Brian Jungen zwei verschiedene kulturelle Sphären miteinander, nämlich die Kultur der amerikanischen Massenproduktion mit jener der kanadischen *Dâne-Zaa-(First Nations-)*Indianer, welchen der 1970 geborene Künstler selbst angehört. Seine hybriden Skulpturen nennt er PROTOTYPES FOR NEW UNDERSTANDING (1998–2003). Jungen zerlegt die besonders unter Jugendlichen populären Nike-Air-Jordan-Basketballschuhe und näht deren Bestandteile aus Gummi, Kunststoff und Leder zu neuen Formen zusammen. Die zwischen der ethnologischen Aura zeremonieller Masken von Nordwestküstenindianern und dem Déjà-vu ihrer vertrauten Materialität oszillierenden Objekte wirken irritierend. Die Farben Schwarz, Rot und Weiss der Nike-Schuhe entsprechen zugleich den beliebten Farben der traditionellen Kunst der *First Nations*-Indianer, die in den letzten fünfzehn Jahren ein vielfältiges Revival erfahren hat. Jungens Rekodifizierung eines Massenproduktes mit dem *native style* der Nordwest-

küsten-Indianer verweist kritisch darauf, dass die regional und kulturell spezifische Bedeutung von Objekten durch die Massenvermarktung völlig verwässert und aufgelöst wird.[5)]

Zwei andere Künstlerinnen widmen sich dem Eros. Während Barbara Kuntz auf der Suche nach der latenten Erotik in der Natur ist, befasst sich Deborah Sengl mit der manifesten Ekstase in der Pornographie. Kuntz erforscht die Welt der Früchte, Schoten, Samenkapseln und Blüten von meist exotischen Pflanzen und zeichnet deren Öffnungen, Rundungen und Wölbungen. Vom Zeichnen einer kleinen getrockneten Fruchtkapsel der afrikanischen Wassernuss nähert sie sich über Transformation und Vergrösserung der Skulptur. Früher haftete den Objekten die materialbedingte Schwere der Majolika an. Seit der Hinwendung zum Kunststoff 1997, erfährt Kuntz eine weitaus grössere künstlerische Entfaltungsmöglichkeit. Ein komplexes Produktionsverfahren mit Styropor, Metallstäben sowie einem Gemisch aus Glasfaser und Kunstharz erlaubt der Künstlerin das natürlich vorhandene statische Gleichgewicht der Pflanzen auch skulptural herzustellen.

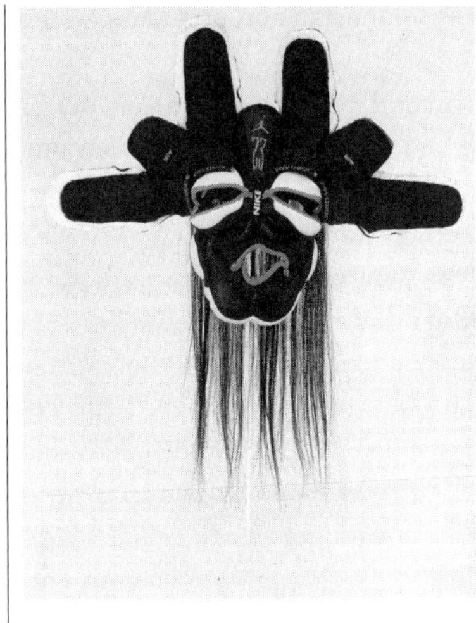

Die perfekt lackierte Oberfläche, oft in der Signalfarbe eines flammenden Rot, betont die erotische Ausstrahlungskraft der vegetabilen Formen. Wir sehen uns konfrontiert mit reiner botanischer Formenlust. [6]

Im Atelier der 1974 in Wien geborenen Künstlerin Deborah Sengl stapeln sich Pornohefte und Männermagazine. Sie dienen ihr seit einigen Jahren als Inspirationsquelle für ihren pornographischen Zyklus ORIONTARNUNGEN (seit 1999). Begonnen hat es mit der Entdeckung des Spielzeugs Pyssla, das Kindern ermöglicht mit bunten Plastiksteckperlen beliebige Bilder zusammenzusetzen. Sengl faszinierte es, diese beiden Bildebenen zu kreuzen, einerseits das unschuldige, naive Material der bunten Steckperlen und andrerseits das von Männerphantasien strotzende, obszöne Repertoire der Hochglanzmagazine. Fellationierende rote Lippen, volle rosige Brüste, gespreizte fleischfarbene Beine, schwarze Strapse und Strümpfe, aufgerissene blaue Augen und schneeweiss spritzendes Sperma erfahren durch die kindlich anmutenden Plastikperlen eine Dekontextualisierung. Die von der Pornoindustrie instrumentalisierten Posen und Stellungen verlieren so an Präzision und Schärfe und damit auch ihren rein funktionellen Charakter. Sengl sagt dazu: «Man könnte meinen, dass genau dieses Phänomen von ‹Sehen- und Nichtsehenwollen› die Grundzüge unseres zwiespältigen Umgangs mit Erotik und Sexualität charakterisiert.» [7]

Im Oktober 2000 zeigte das Wiener Museum für Angewandte Kunst (MAK) in nur einem Raum eine beeindruckende Installation aus Säcken. Sechzig Stück, körpergross, aus knallorangem, PVC-beschichtetem Stoff – nicht sofort als Leichensäcke zu erkennen, da die schrill leuchtende Farbe in Europa nicht mit dem Tod assoziiert wird. In Südafrika werden in diesen *bodybags* Leichen transportiert. Das kalte Neonlicht liess den gesamten Keller wie eine Leichenhalle erscheinen. Die gezeigten Säcke waren klinisch rein, ihre schwarzen Reissverschlüsse noch nicht zugezogen. Doch die vorläufige Abwesenheit jeglicher Spur menschlichen Leids liess dieses nur umso schriller anwesend sein. Der 1968 in Südafrika geborene Künstler Kendell Geers nennt seine Installation SONG OF THE PIG (Schweinegesang, 2000). Wobei «pig / Schwein» als pejoratives Synonym für diktatorische oder autoritäre Instanzen bis hin zu den die Befehle konkret ausführenden Personen steht. Geers begann 1985 zu studieren und in Bezug auf die Apartheid meint er: «Jeder von uns in Johannesburg konnte von ihnen [den Organen der Obrigkeit] gerufen werden. Und jeder von uns kann auch heute an anderen Orten ihre Rufe hören.» [8] Insofern allegorisiert SONG OF THE PIG nicht nur die früheren Verhältnisse in Johannesburg, sondern auch aktuelle Situationen in Israel, im Irak und überall, wo Menschen aus sozialen oder politischen Gründen sterben müssen.

Eine der wohl prägnantesten Arbeiten aus Kunststoff, die ich gesehen habe, ist Brian Jungens riesiges, an die zehn Meter langes Walskelett, das unlängst in der Wiener Secession gezeigt wurde. Es ist aus unzähligen weissen Plastikstühlen, die in Kanada *monoblock chairs* genannt werden, zusammengebaut. Aus jenen weissen Plastikstühlen also, deren stereotype Ästhetik uns an jedem noch so weit entfernten und idyllischen Urlaubsort aufgedrängt wird. Wie schon bei den erwähnten PROTOTYPES FOR NEW UNDERSTANDING nützt Jungen auch hier ein gewöhnliches, überall erhältliches industrielles Produkt als Ausgangsmaterial für seine Kunst. Jungen wollte mit einem besonders künstlichen Material etwas deutlich Organisch-Morphologisches darstellen. Mit dem Walskelett ist ihm das gelungen: Es hat die verblüffend naturalistische Aura eines Präparats in einem Naturhistorischen Museum.

Die von Roland Barthes erkannte «Spur der Bewegung» wird uns wohl weiterhin mit überraschenden Ideen und Formen erstaunen.

1) vgl. *Parkett* Nr. 69, 2003.
2) Roland Barthes, «Plastik», in: *Mythen des Alltags*, Suhrkamp, Frankfurt am Main 1964, S. 79.
3) Dirk Luckow, *Plastik,* Ausstellungskatalog, Württembergischer Kunstverein, Stuttgart 1997.
4) Lee Bul, «The Divine Shell», Ausstellung in der BAWAG Foundation, Wien 2001.
5) Brian Jungen in einem E-Mail an die Autorin, 6. Februar 2004.
6) Agness, «Tutto è scherzo d'amore», Ausstellung in der Pfalzgalerie Kaiserslautern, 2004.
7) Deborah Sengl im Gespräch mit der Autorin, 8. Februar 2004.
8) Kendell Geers im Gespräch mit der Autorin, 5. Oktober 2000.

HYBRIDITY, EROS, AND DEATH

GABRIELE SCHOR

Synthetic materials often determine the making of contemporary works of art. In fact, it is the specific nature of these materials that inspires artists to venture into exceptional shapes and dimensions. What else but the extreme elasticity and sturdiness of polyester fibers could have permitted Anish Kapoor to suspend his gargantuan MARSYAS sculpture (2002) above visitors' heads at Tate Modern?[1]

Synthetics have infiltrated virtually all aspects of our lives. To Roland Barthes, however, plastic is "more than a substance, [it] is the very idea of its infinite transformation; as its everyday name indicates, it is ubiquity made visible. And it is this, in fact, which makes it a miraculous substance: a miracle is always a sudden transformation of nature. Plastic remains impregnated throughout with this wonder: it is less a thing than the trace of a movement."[2]

In the nineties, such traces of movement significantly influenced the appearance of contemporary sculpture made of plastic materials, as demonstrated in Dirk Luckow's sensitively curated show of abstract amorphous, biomorphic, and monolithic forms.[3] A radiant sensuality emanated from the synthetic high-gloss surfaces of works by such artists as Thomas Rentmeister, Elke Baulig, Thomas Grünfeld, and Asta Gröting. Some of the shapes had

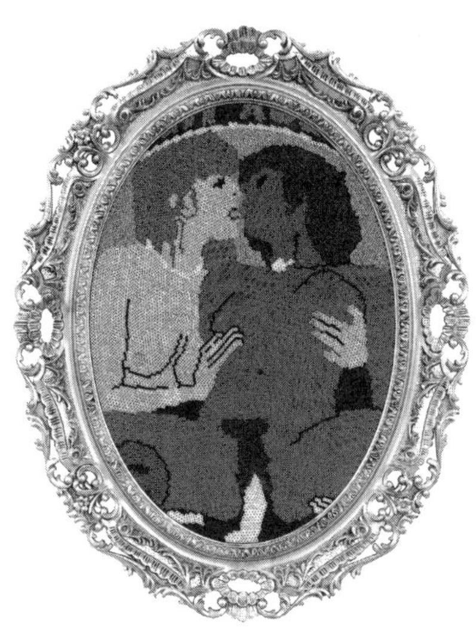

DEBORAH SENGL, ORIONTARNUNG, 2001, Plastikperlen in Rahmen, 91 x 71 cm / plastic beads in frame, 35 $^{13}/_{16}$ x 28".
(PHOTO: WERNER SCHRÖDL)

the look of slithery amoebas. Common to all of them was the constraint of narrative content in favor of shiny surfaces and reduced shapes.

Five artists, whose work attracted my notice at exhibitions in Vienna, can serve to illustrate the thesis that a different—narrative—approach has acquired currency at the threshold of the twenty-first century, their work revealing the diversity of uses to which plastic lends itself as a material. Applied to the study of hybridity, eros, and death, their oeuvre represents a kind of antipode to the nonobjective, morphologically inspired forms of the nineties.

South Korean artist Lee Bul, born in 1964, investigates the hybridity of cyberspace, where the virtual is real and reality virtual. She invents mythical creatures, such as gigantic white monsters, whose outsized wings, tentacle-like arms, and sharp claws she cuts out of synthetic resin, and which she calls "sirens" in allusion to ancient mythology. The cyborgs of space travel, those notorious hybrids between man and machine, have superseded the monsters of antiquity. Bul models her "cyborgs" as women warriors in armored corsets with pointed breasts and cinched waists. They are sexy, bellicose, and merciless. These cybernetic organisms stem from the repertoire of Seoul's mass-media entertainment in-

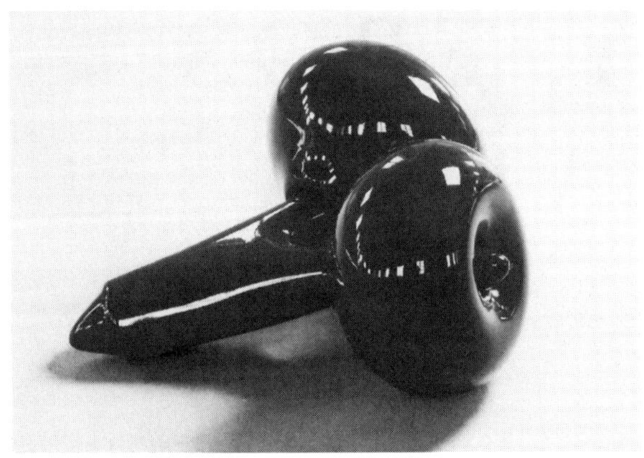

dustry, the world of science fiction, Japanese manga comics, and Korean anime. They embody myths, ideologies, and fantasies, including the mania of technological perfection and omnipotence. As a rule, it is young male programmers who develop such mythical beings. Ambivalence characterizes their archetypal image of the feminine: woman is seductive and menacing, controllable and monstrous, weak and omnipotent. Bul exploits these fantasies and undermines them. Take for example her 2001 Vienna exhibition "The Divine Shell"[4]: Her cyborgs, cast in white silicone, are headless torsos, with only one arm or one leg. Suspended from the ceiling of an exhibition venue, they seem to be moving in cyberspace. That alone is reason enough for Bul to rely on a lightweight material in order to ensure the artistic freedom of her work.

While Lee Bul explores the fusion of real and virtual phenomena, Brian Jungen, born in 1970, crossbreeds two cultural spheres: the phenomenon of American mass production and the art of the Canadian *Dàne-Zaa* (First Nations) Indians, the tribe to which his mother belonged. He calls his hybrid sculptures PROTOTYPES FOR NEW UNDERSTANDING (1998–2003). Jungen has dismembered Nike Air Jordans, so popular among young people, and restitched the components of rubber, plastic, and leather into new shapes. These objects make a disturbing impression that oscillates between the ethnological aura of the Northwest Coast Indians and the déjà vu of their familiar materials. The black, red, and white of the classic Nike shoes also correspond to the colors favored in the traditional art of the First Nations, which has enjoyed a wide-ranging comeback over the past fifteen years. Jungen's re-codification of a mass product with the "native style" of the Northwest Coast Indians draws critical attention to the fact that the regional

and culturally specific meaning of objects is utterly diluted, adulterated, and undermined by mass marketing.[5]

Two other artists devote themselves to eros: Barbara Kuntz tracks down the latent eroticism of nature, while Deborah Sengl addresses manifest ecstasy in pornography. Kuntz studies the fruit, pods, seed capsules, and blossoms of mostly exotic plants and renders their openings, curves, and bulges in her drawings. Her picture of a small, dried capsule of the African waternut almost becomes sculpture through transformation and enlargement. Initially her objects had the weightiness of majolica, due to their materials, but in 1997, when Kuntz began working with plastics, she substantially extended the range of her artistic freedom. A complex process of production with Styrofoam, metal rods, and a blend of glass fibers and synthetic resin has enabled the artist to capture the natural static balance of plants in sculptural form. The perfectly enameled surfaces, often in an emblematic flaming red, underscore the erotic expressiveness of vegetable shapes. We are confronted with a pure delight in botanical forms.[6]

Porn and men's magazines are piled up in the studio of the artist Deborah Sengl, born in Vienna in 1974. For a

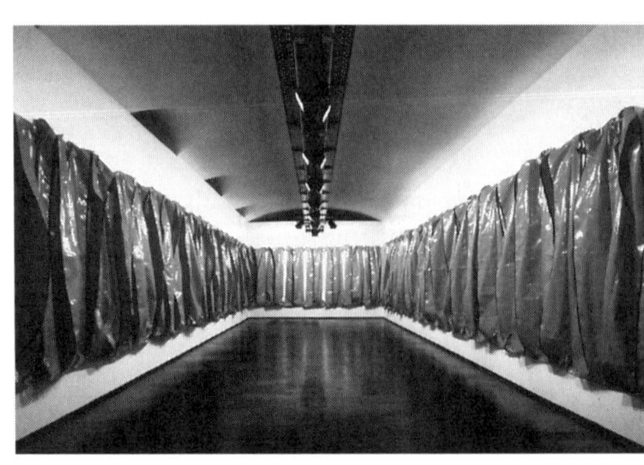

number of years they have been the source of inspiration for her pornographic cycle ORIONTARNUNGEN (since 1999, ongoing). The work began with her discovery of Pyssla, colorful plastic beads with which children can invent and make their own pictures. Sengl was fascinated with the idea of mixing two visual levels: the innocent, naive material of colorful beads on one hand, and on the other, the obscene repertory of high-gloss mags steeped in male fantasies. Ruby lips performing fellatio, voluptuous pink breasts, flesh-colored legs spread apart, black straps and stockings, wide-open blue eyes, and squirting snow-white semen are all decontextualized by the childlike character of the plastic beads. Poses and positions instrumentalized by the porn industry lose their precision and sharpness—and therefore their purely functional character as well. As Sengl notes, "it actually seems as if this phenomenon of 'seeing and not wanting to see' defines the fundamental traits of our ambivalence toward eroticism and sexuality."[6]

In October 2000, the Viennese Museum of Applied Arts (MAK) showed a striking installation of bags in one single room. The sixty bags, each the size of a body and made of orange-colored, PVC-coated fabric, were not immediately identifiable as body bags because Europeans do not associate the garish, luminous orange with death. But in South Africa, they transport corpses. The cold neon light in the cellar installation made the room feel like a morgue. The bags on display were clinically sanitary, their black zippers not yet closed. The pro tempore absence of all traces of human suffering, however, served only to reinforce their impact. Born in South Africa in 1968,

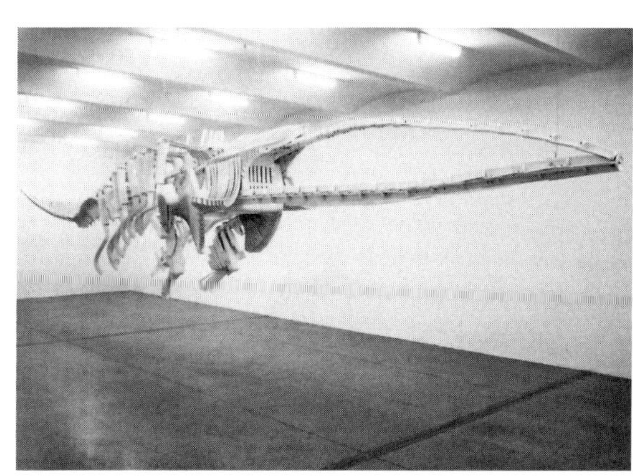

the artist Kendell Geers calls his installation SONG OF THE PIG (2000), the word "pig" functioning as a pejorative synonym covering the entire range of dictatorial or authoritarian institutions, including the functionaries who actually execute the orders. Geers started university in 1985. In reference to apartheid, he remarks, "Any one of us in Johannesburg might be summoned by them. And today we can all also hear their summons elsewhere."[7] In this respect, SONG OF THE PIG is not only an allegory of former conditions in Johannesburg, but also of current conditions in Israel or Iraq or any other place where people are dying because of social and political abuse.

One of the most striking works made of plastic that I have seen is Brian Jungen's colossal, almost-30-foot skeleton of a whale, recently on view at the Vienna Secession. It is pieced together out of innumerable white plastic chairs, known in Canada as "monoblock chairs": in other words, those white plastic chairs whose stereotypical aesthetic is inescapable even in the most remote and idyllic vacation paradise. As in the above-mentioned PROTOTYPES FOR NEW UNDERSTANDING, Jungen again exploits an ordinary, easily accessible industrial product as the point of departure for his art. Jungen wanted to create something obviously organic and morphological out of a conspicuously artificial material. He has succeeded in doing just that, for the skeleton radiates a startlingly naturalistic aura, as if it were a specimen in a museum of natural history.

The "traces of movement" that Barthes describes will undoubtedly long continue to astonish us with remarkable ideas and shapes.

(Translation: Catherine Schelbert)

1) See *Parkett*, no. 69, 2003.
2) Roland Barthes, "Plastic," in *Mythologies,* trans. Annette Lavers (New York: Hill and Wang, 1981), p. 97.
3) Dirk Luckow, *Plastik*, Württembergischer Kunstverein, Stuttgart, 1997.
4) Lee Bul, "The Divine Shell," BAWAG Foundation, Vienna, 2001.
5) Brian Jungen, email to the writer, 6 February 2004.
6) Agness, "Tutto è scherzo d'amore," exhibition, Pfalzgalerie Kaiserslautern, Kaiserslautern, 2004.
7) Deborah Sengl in conversation with the writer, 8 February 2004.
8) Kendell Geers in conversation with the writer, 5 October 2000.

BALKON

A Whole Life in One Minute

TINEKE REIJNDERS

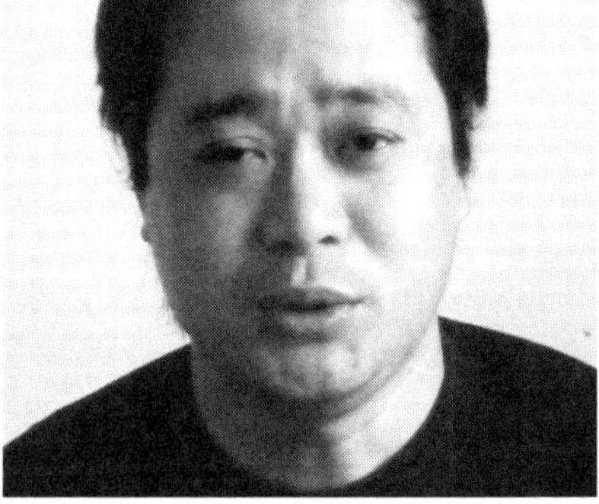

"What's your name?" The guy is trying to say his name but he stutters, stutters. The monitor shows his talking head, the soundbox is full of his repeated attempts, and both create an increasingly uncomfortable feeling. His features are Chinese, so the pronunciation strikes higher and lower tones; the chafing tension turns to an impression of experimental vocal music. The concert goes on for fifty-nine seconds—to be concluded gloriously in the sixtieth second with his impeccably spoken name. Gu Yue, a young artist from Xia-

TINEKE REIJNDERS is an Amsterdam-based art historian and critic.

men, provides with CAN NOT SPEAK (2002) a witty counterpart to Gary Hill's PRIMARILY SPEAKING (1981–1983), while demonstrating that one minute can be painfully long.

Video pieces of one minute are no recent invention, but since the one-minute rule was set for a competition in Amsterdam some five years ago, it has become a cherished format for a young generation of artists all over the world. Sixty seconds help to make video the truly democratic tool it claimed to be from the beginning.

When Jos Houweling, director of the Sandberg Institute in Amsterdam, organized the first One Minutes Awards

in 1999, the competing artists were mainly students and former students from his post-graduate institute. But word of the contest quickly spread, partly thanks to the various nationalities of the students. The following year, artists from around the world sent their One Minutes to Amsterdam hoping for a nomination. The participation of the Western world may not be surprising, but the enrollment of Chinese artists is remarkable. It is likely that soon a One Minutes Awards event

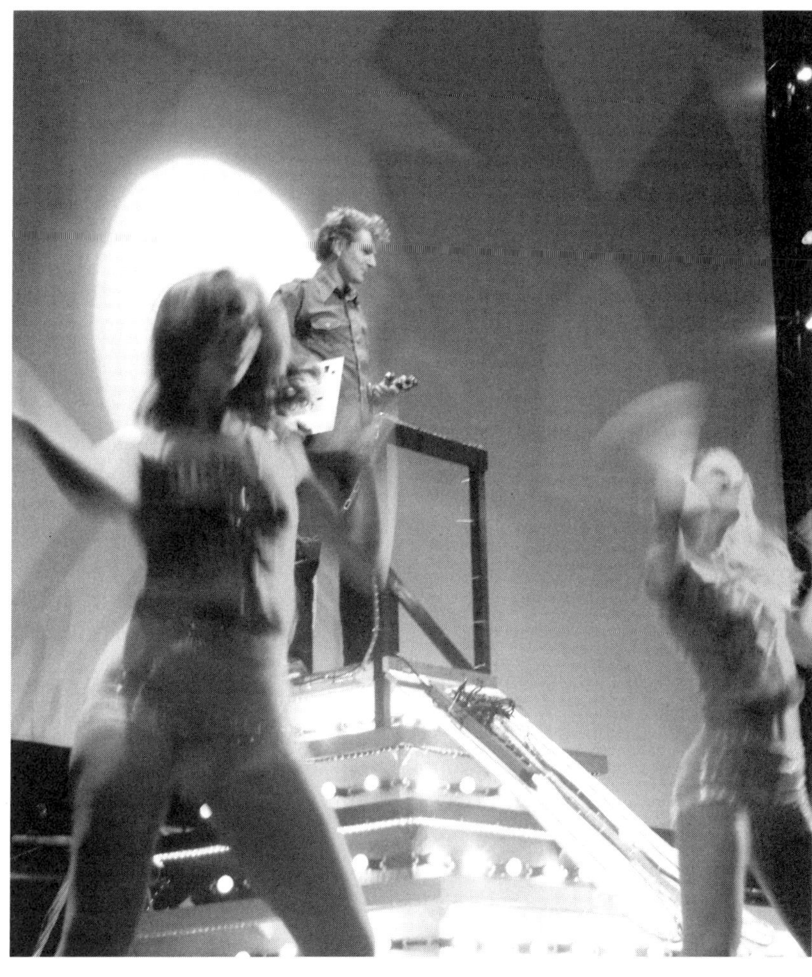

will take place in China. Better proof of the accessible, low-key, and communicative format of these short video works can hardly be found. For China has become a full-fledged partner in this domain, while in general the country stands apart, like many other non-Western countries, from the regular global art network, despite some powerful exceptions. "Use video as a pencil," was the visionary slogan long ago. It has become that simple indeed.

The chance to shine on an international platform brings thousands of tapes and DVDs every year. You will find videographics, social drama, funny stories, filmic or sound comments, narratives, soap appropriations, suspense, loops, calm observations, reflections on life, all condensed into a time span that is shorter than the visual arts average and longer than TV shorts. Of course not every One Minute is a masterpiece. Often the most denuded and simple scripts are remembered best. The wide diversity of genres is divided into a number of categories. The artists designate the category in which they wish to submit their work, and with the help of jury members, a selection of nominees is made.

The fun of the creation is reflected in the show ballet and make-believe Hollywood style of the Awards evening at the Paradiso club in Amsterdam. Last time even Tommies (The One Minutes Sculptures) accompanied the prize money. But most impressive was the fraternal, humanitarian atmosphere. This was partly due to the participation of the juniors. Since 2002 the European Cultural Foundation and UNICEF have participated in the activities of the One Minutes Foundation. These organizations enable teams of young artists to set up workshops for schoolchildren (aged twelve to eighteen) in cities that could use an impulse in the peaceful domain of art. Junior films have been made in Casablanca, Londonderry, Berlin, and Tbilisi,

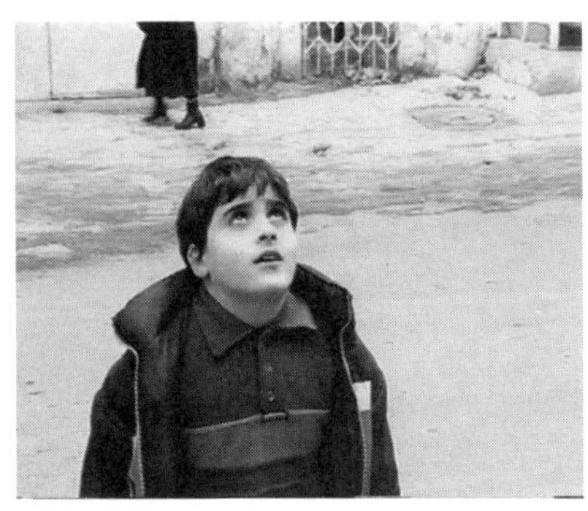

and more cities will follow. In each local workshop pupils from different regions cooperate. In Casablanca, for instance, children were gathered from Morocco, Algeria, and Tunis.

While the two official foundations were smart enough to seek participation, the network underlying the One Minutes is mainly rooted in personal contacts. Professor Qin Jian, jury member and responsible for the One Minutes Awards in China, teaches at Xiamen University. In 1999 the Chinese European Art Center (CEAC) was established in this city of Southeastern China. Under the wing of the University of Xiamen, with Qin Jian as a driving force, the CEAC is directed by its founder, Dutch-Icelandic Ineke Gudmundsson who curates exhibitions of Western and Chinese artists alike. Since teachers and students from the Sandberg Institute were invited to lecture and to give video workshops, the video camera was introduced as a tool for art—albeit semi-legally, because until recently art education in China still advocated traditional media. (This year a new media department was launched in Xiamen.) An overwhelming enthusiasm for the One Minutes

emerged. Eager to know what is going on abroad, Chinese students and artists were delighted to learn that their small art pieces function on an international platform. Video proves to be a smart key. Who would have been aware of the talent of Gu Yue or of Meiya Lin, were it not for the One Minutes Competition, and the fact that compilations of selected works are sent to new-media institutes and are broadcast by TV stations? Meiya Lin contributed BREATHER (2003), a piece of uncanny poetry. Accompanied by lighthearted music, fatty grey-green planes of concrete pass by, now and then interrupted by beamlike elevations. On the distant horizon a strip of light promises the escape the viewer longs for so fiercely. By pointing the camera into the air, this student managed to transform the gloomy neighborhood she walked through each morning on her way to art school, into a metaphoric obstacle race with a wider perspective.

Remarkably it was television that spread the idea of the One Minutes in China. CCTV regularly gave coverage to the non-profit CEAC and showed interest in video art. A team came over to Amsterdam for the Awards of 2001. Westerners could easily overlook the importance of CCTV, whose two channels serve more than a billion viewers. After the emission in China, the One Minutes attracted considerable publicity, and at least one city received nationwide attention for its invitation to compete for the municipal awards. One of the winners of a digital camera was an eighty-year-old woman who managed to tell the story of her entire life in one minute.

While TV is now hailed as a sworn friend of video art, another jury member, Emir Kusturica, warned the audience against the hegemony of this

medium's standards. For those who enjoyed his unforgettable film *Underground* (1995) on TV, where the film enjoyed wide acclaim, his remark was a bit confusing.

This skepticism reminds us of the old days of video art. As soon as video became portable in the mid-sixties, it was considered an appropriate weapon against authority, in different forms. First it questioned the hegemony of TV and advertising, then the dominance of white male artists. On a formal level probably the most conspicuous characteristic of early video art has been the analytical approach of the time factor. Combining real time and recorded time, disconnecting the monitor image from the real time experience, using slow motion, departing from synchronism, and introducing imperceptible time delays are some of the strategies for sensorial and psychological experiences. Often single-channel videotapes did not suffice. Artists began building installations to enhance the physical and mental effects. These spatial extensions established video art definitively in the institutional context and thwarted the expectation that artists could send their tapes to the exhibi-

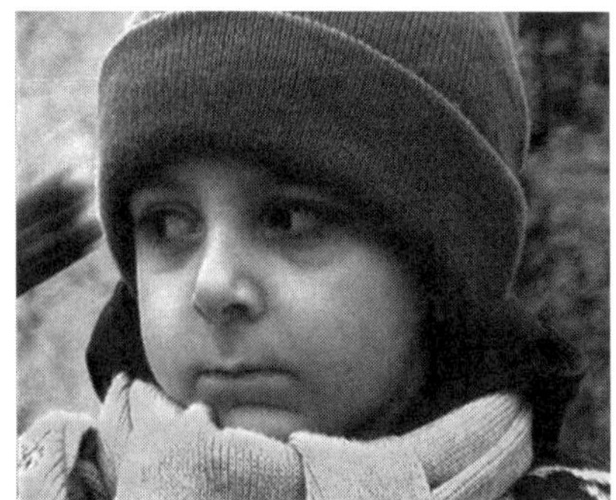

tion venue or festival, without the necessity of attendance. This informal distribution, which had become obsolete in the eighties, is now the basis of the One Minutes' success.

The playful use of the one-minute model appeals to a generation that may have lost interest in the time regime of concept-oriented video art. Often complaints resound about the supposed heavy load of time-consuming video art classics. Experimental is not a fashionable epithet anymore if it goes against the taste of the public. Video art should please and captivate. In younger eyes television bears the same emotional value as the playthings from their childhood. Western youth grew up with music videoclips; advertising by now has, albeit with irony, heroic connotations and the gender question is warmly ignored.

Therefore most of the nominated One Minutes have a funny, lighthearted plot and sometimes a serious twist in the end. KOFFIEZETAPPARAAT (1999), by German/Dutch Helmut Dick, shows the artist urinating into the reservoir of an operating coffee maker; the boiling drops fall on a hairy cactus which gradually shrinks. Few videos create such a strong sense of smell. Besides showing interest in human behavior or in cultural phenomena, One Minutes often comment on the phenomenon of movement. In GINZA (2002) neat-looking pedestrians on a crossing in Tokyo all of a sudden start to run, sometimes alone, sometimes in small groups. The observation is absurd from the beginning to the end, even if you know that Michal Butink wiped the traffic lights out. Allard Zoetman captured a wonderful event on a public playground. Little children group a bunch of shopping trolleys into a turning carousel that

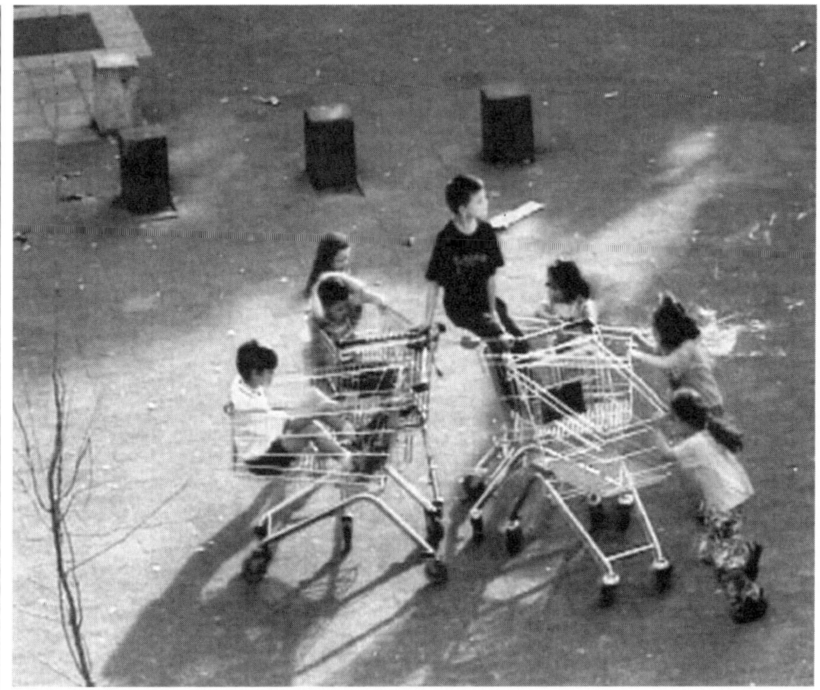

ALLARD ZOETMAN, HOMO ECCO PART II, 2002, video still.

turns faster and faster (HOMO ECCO PART II, 2002). With a different mood altogether, Yael Bartana filmed the gradual and mysterious stopping of all the cars in a tunnel on a highway—a modest hint to a memorial day in Israel.

What distinguishes the junior videos from those of the adults is their unhampered, un-ironical cry for a better world. In 2002 the fourteen-year-old Armenian Gor Baghdasaryan won a prize with his plea for a weapon-free society. In his video children proudly brandish their wooden Kalashnikovs and revolvers. First reluctantly, then gradually persuaded, they throw the toy guns in a heap and set it on fire. The workshops also stimulate theatrical ingenuity. David Djindjikhachvili, a graduate of the Sandberg Institute, conducted the workshop in Tbilisi, the town from which his family had to emigrate. The teenager George Baramidze offered eloquent proof of the Georgian capital's reputation as a habitat of theater. His winning One Minute portrays the lighthearted drama of a kid who comes home from school to find the front door locked. His mother answers neither the doorbell nor the telephone. In the next shot we see her in the kitchen, intensely rehearsing the gestures of the Ketchup song. The music prevents her from hearing anything else. In the final shot the boy speaks to the camera in confidence, stating that you should never leave a child outside (DON'T LEAVE CHILD OUT, 2003).

Sixty-second videos may mean little for a sophisticated art discourse, but as casual carriers of freedom and democracy, they have at least begun to break down political and cultural barriers.

(Translation from the Dutch: Beth O'Brien)

TINEKE REIJNDERS

Das ganze Leben in einer Minute

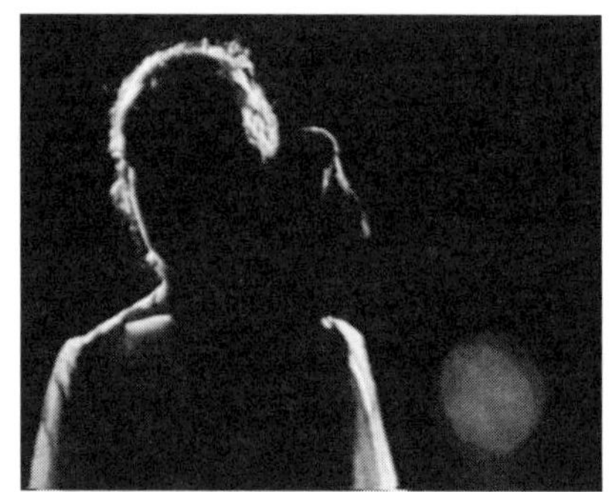

«Wie heisst du?» Der Bursche will seinen Namen sagen, bringt jedoch nur ein wiederholtes Stottern hervor. Auf dem Monitor ist dabei sein Kopf zu sehen, aus dem Lautsprecher hört man die wiederholten Artikulationsversuche, und beides zusammen lässt ein zunehmend unbehagliches Gefühl aufkommen. Das Gesicht ist das eines Chinesen, und sein Tonfall schwankt zwischen ziemlich hohen und tieferen Tönen; schliesslich kippt die aufreibende Spannung und man meint ex-

---

TINEKE REIJNDERS ist Kunsthistorikerin und Kritikerin und lebt in Amsterdam.

perimenteller Vokalmusik zu lauschen. Das Konzert dauert 59 Sekunden und endet in der sechzigsten glanzvoll mit dem perfekt ausgesprochenen Namen. Gu Yue, ein junger Künstler aus Xiamen, präsentiert mit CAN NOT SPEAK (Kann nicht sprechen, 2002) ein witziges Gegenstück zu Gary Hills PRIMARILY SPEAKING (Erstes Sprechen, 1981–1983) und zeigt, wie quälend lang eine Minute sein kann.

Einminütige Videoarbeiten sind keine neue Erfindung, aber seit vor etwa fünf Jahren in Amsterdam ein entsprechender Wettbewerb stattfand, erfreut sich dieses Format bei jungen Kunstschaffenden auf der ganzen Welt grosser Beliebtheit. Die Beschränkung auf 60 Sekunden trägt dazu bei, Video zu dem wahrhaft demokratischen Medium zu machen, welches es seit jeher zu sein behauptet.

1999 veranstaltete Jos Houweling, Leiter des Sandberg-Instituts in Amsterdam, die ersten «One Minutes Awards». Teilgenommen haben damals hauptsächlich Studierende und Absolventen seines Instituts für postgraduelle Studien. Doch die Nachricht verbreitete sich wie ein Lauffeuer, zum Teil auch, weil seine Studenten den verschiedensten Nationalitäten ange-

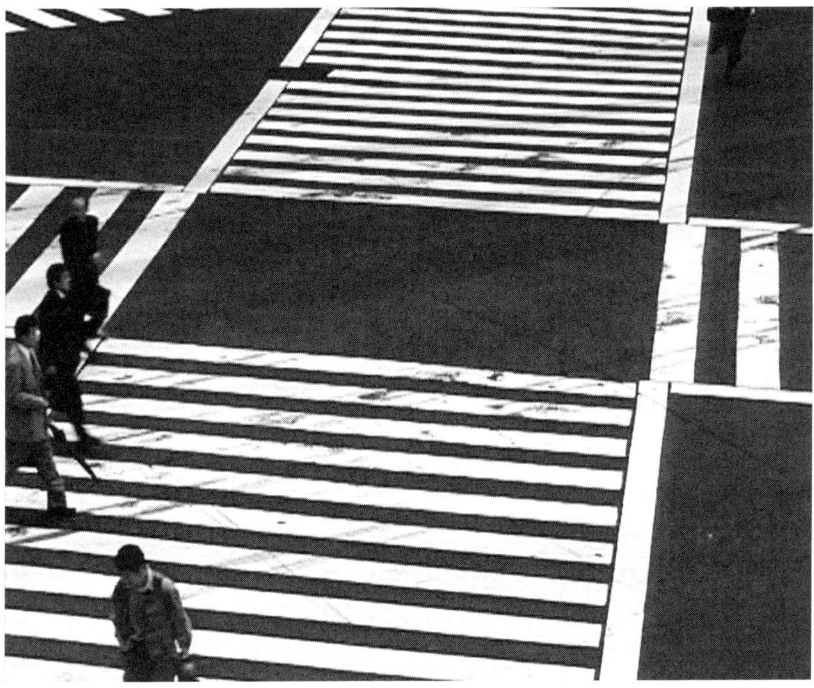

hörten. Im Jahr darauf trafen Minutenvideos von Künstlern aus aller Welt in Amsterdam ein. Das rege Interesse im Westen überrascht wohl kaum, aber die zahlreichen Anmeldungen chinesischer Künstler waren doch bemerkenswert. Wahrscheinlich wird bald ein *One Minutes*-Wettbewerb in China ausgeschrieben. Einen besseren Beweis für das leicht zugängliche, unkomplizierte und kommunikative Format dieser Kurzvideos könnte es jedenfalls nicht geben. Denn China ist in diesem Bereich zum vollwertigen Partnerland geworden, obschon es wie viele andere nichtwestliche Staaten sonst abseits des globalen Kunstbetriebs steht – mit wenigen gewichtigen Ausnahmen. Vor langer Zeit verkündete ein visionärer Slogan, Video sei wie ein Bleistift zu benützen. Nun ist es tatsächlich so einfach geworden.

Die Aussicht, sich auf einer internationalen Plattform hervorzutun, führt jedes Jahr zur Produktion Tausender von Videobändern und DVDs. Da gibt es Videografik, Sozialdramen, lustige Geschichten, filmische oder akustische Kommentare, Erzählungen, Soap-Parodien, Suspense, Loops, ruhige, nachdenkliche Beiträge und Betrachtungen über das Leben: alles in eine Zeitspanne gepresst, die kürzer ist als das durchschnittliche Videokunstwerk und länger als ein TV-Kurzbeitrag. Natürlich ist nicht jedes Minutenvideo ein Meisterwerk. Oft bleiben die schnörkellosesten und einfachsten Arbeiten am besten in Erinnerung. Die grosse Vielfalt der Genres ist in eine Anzahl Kategorien unterteilt, in welche die Künstler ihre Arbeit selbst einreihen. Durch eine Jury wird dann eine Auswahl preiswürdiger Werke getroffen. Der Spass am Kreativen spiegelt sich auch in der Preisverleihung im Pseudo-Hollywood-Stil samt Showballett im Club Paradiso in Amsterdam. Das letzte Mal wurden neben dem Preisgeld sogar Tommies (The One Minutes-Sculptures) vergeben. Am eindrücklichsten war jedoch die ungezwungene freundschaftliche Atmosphäre. Dies war unter anderem der Teilnahme der Nachwuchstalente zu verdanken. Seit 2002 unterstützen die Europäische Kulturstiftung und UNICEF die Tätigkeit der *One Minutes Foundation*. Die drei Organisationen ermöglichen es Teams von jungen Künstlern, in Städten, die Impulse aus dem friedlichen Gebiet der Kunst gebrauchen können, Workshops für Schülerinnen und Schüler im Alter von zwölf bis achtzehn Jahren durchzuführen. So entstanden bereits Schülervideos in Casablanca, Londonderry, Berlin und Tiflis. Workshops in weiteren Städten werden folgen. In jedem Workshop arbeiten Schüler aus verschiedenen

Regionen zusammen – in Casablanca beispielsweise Kinder aus Marokko, Algerien und Tunesien.

Obwohl die beiden offiziellen Stiftungen so klug waren, ihre Mitwirkung anzubieten, basiert das Netzwerk der *One Minutes Foundation* vorwiegend auf persönlichen Kontakten. Professor Qin Jian, Jurymitglied und Verantwortlicher für den *One Minutes*-Wettbewerb in China, unterrichtet an der Universität Xiamen. 1999 wurde in dieser südostchinesischen Stadt das Chinese European Art Center (CEAC) gegründet. Qin Jian war dabei eine treibende Kraft. Das unter der Aufsicht der Universität Xiamen stehende CEAC wird von dessen niederländisch-isländischer Gründerin Ineke Gudmundsson geleitet, die Ausstellungen westlicher und chinesischer Künstler organisiert. Da Lehrer und Studierende des Sandberg-Instituts eingeladen wurden Vorlesungen zu halten und Videoworkshops zu leiten, wurde die Videokamera als künstlerisches Ausdrucksmittel eingeführt – wenn auch nur inoffiziell, denn im Kunstunterricht in China werden nach wie vor die traditionellen Medien propagiert. (Das Institut für neue Medien an der Universität Xiamen besteht erst seit diesem Jahr.) Die Idee der Minutenvideos stiess auf grosse Begeisterung. Die chinesischen Studenten und Kunstschaffenden, die sehr offen sind für alles, was im Ausland läuft, waren hoch erfreut, dass ihre kleinen Kunstwerke in einem internationalen Umfeld Anklang fanden. Video öffnet also auch Türen. Wer hätte ohne den *One Minutes*-Wettbewerb je vom Talent eines Gu Yue oder einer Meiya Lin erfahren? Kompilationen ausgewählter Werke zirkulieren nämlich an Instituten für neue Medien und werden von Fernsehstationen ausgestrahlt. Mit BREATHER (Atempause, 2003) gelang Meiya Lin ein Werk, das unheimlich poetisch wirkt. Von heiterer Musik untermalt, ziehen speckige graugrüne Betonflächen vorüber, die dann und wann von balkenartigen Erhebungen unterbrochen werden. Ein Lichtstreifen am Horizont verheisst einen Ausweg, den der Zuschauer verzweifelt herbeisehnt. Indem sie die Kamera nach oben richtete und einen weiten Blickwinkel wählte, gelang es der Studentin, das trostlose Quartier, das sie jeden Morgen auf dem Weg zur Kunsthochschule durchqueren musste, in ein metaphorisches Hindernisrennen zu verwandeln.

Erstaunlicherweise wurde der *One Minutes*-Wettbewerb in China durch das Fernsehen bekannt. Der Staatssender CCTV berichtete regelmässig über das nicht kommerzielle Chinese European Art Center und bekundete

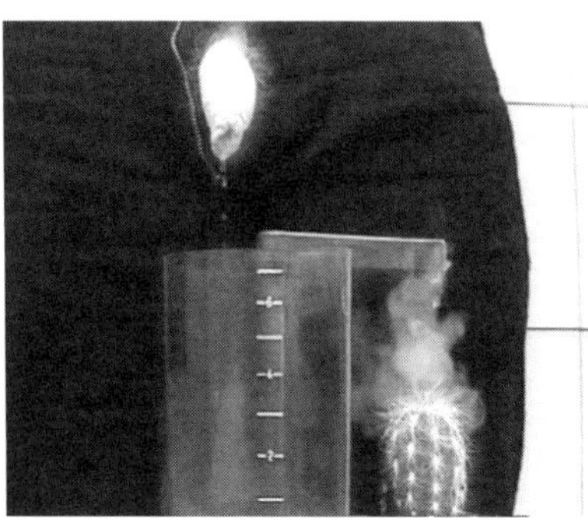

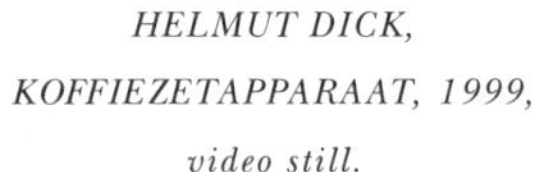
HELMUT DICK,
KOFFIEZETAPPARAAT, 1999,
video still.

Interesse an der Videokunst. Zur Preisverleihung 2001 schickte er sogar ein Team nach Amsterdam. Im Westen ist man sich der Bedeutung von CCTV, dessen zwei Kanäle mehr als eine Milliarde Zuschauer erreichen, kaum bewusst. Nach dem Fernsehbericht waren die Minutenvideos gross im Gespräch und zumindest eine chinesische Stadt fand landesweit Beachtung, weil sie einen kommunalen Wettbewerb für ihre Einwohner veranstaltete. Zu den Gewinnern einer Digitalkamera gehörte eine Achtzigjährige, die Aufsehen erregte, da sie die Gelegenheit nutzte um in einer Minute ihr ganzes Leben zu erzählen.

Obschon das Fernsehen heute als grosser Freund der Videokunst gepriesen wird, warnte das Jurymitglied Emir Kusturica die Zuschauer vor den dominanten Standards dieses Mediums. Wer seinen unvergesslichen Film *Underground* (1995) im Fernsehen gesehen hat, wo er äusserst erfolgreich war, mag diese Äusserung wohl eher als verwirrend empfunden haben.

Diese Skepsis erinnert an die Frühzeit der Videokunst. Als Mitte der 60er Jahre die tragbare Videokamera aufkam, galt das neue Medium zunächst als geeignete Waffe im Kampf gegen Autoritäten. Zuerst stellte es die Dominanz von Fernsehen und Werbung in Frage, dann jene der weissen, männlichen Künstler. Das Auffälligste an der frühen Videokunst war auf formaler Ebene wohl der analytische Umgang mit dem Faktor Zeit. Die Kombination von Echtzeit und aufgezeichneter Zeit, die Trennung von Monitorbild und Echtzeiterfahrung, der Einsatz von Zeitlupe, die Abwendung von der Synchronizität und das Einbauen unmerklicher Verzögerungen sind solche Strategien, die besondere sensorische und

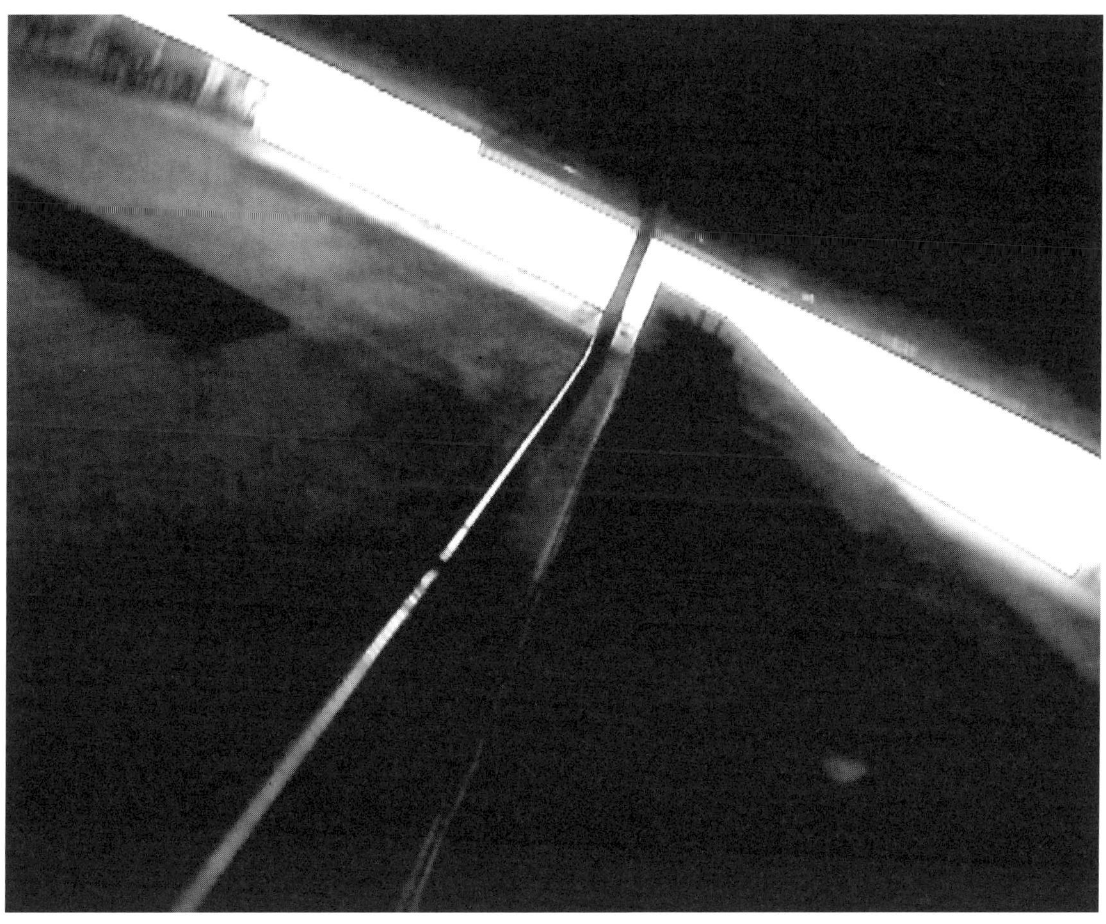

psychische Erfahrungen ermöglichen. Oft genügten Einkanalvideos jedoch nicht und bald schon bauten die Künstler Installationen, um die physische und geistige Wirkung ihrer Werke zu erhöhen. Dank dieser räumlichen Erweiterungen etablierte sich die Videokunst endgültig im institutionellen Kontext und durchkreuzte die Erwartung, dass Künstler ihre Videofilme an Ausstellungsorte oder Festivals senden könnten, ohne dort persönlich zu erscheinen. Diese informelle Art der Verbreitung, die seit den 80er Jahren zunehmend an Bedeutung verlor, ist heute die Grundlage für den Erfolg der Minutenvideos.

Der spielerische Umgang mit dem Ein-Minuten-Modell spricht eine Generation an, die sich vermutlich nicht mehr dafür interessiert, wie die konzeptorientierte Videokunst mit dem Zeitfaktor umging. Oft hört man Klagen über die angeblich schwerfälligen, zeitraubenden Klassiker der Videokunst. «Experimentell» ist kein taugliches modisches Etikett mehr, wenn dabei der Publikumsgeschmack verfehlt wird. Videokunst soll gefallen und faszinieren. Für junge Leute hat das Fernsehen denselben emotionalen Wert wie die Spielsachen aus der Kindheit. Die Jugend im Westen ist mit Musikvideos aufgewachsen; der Werbung haftet mittlerweile etwas Hehres an, auch wenn dabei ein Schuss Ironie im Spiel ist, und die Geschlechterfrage wird freundlich ignoriert.

Daher haben die meisten nominierten Minutenvideos einen witzigen, unbeschwerten Plot, der mitunter am Ende eine ernste Wendung nimmt. KOFFIEZETAPPARAAT (Kaffeemaschine, 2000), ein Evergreen des Deutsch-Niederländers Helmut Dick, zeigt, wie der Künstler in den Wassertank einer laufenden Kaffeemaschine uriniert; die kochenden Tropfen fallen auf einen haarigen Kaktus, der allmählich einschrumpft. Wenige Videos vermitteln einem derart stark den Eindruck eines Geruchs. Neben menschlichem Verhalten oder kulturellen Phänomenen thematisieren Minutenvideos häufig die Bewegung. In Michal Butinks GINZA (2002) beginnen adrett gekleidete Fussgänger auf einer Kreuzung in Tokio ganz plötzlich zu rennen, teils einzeln, teils in kleinen Gruppen. Die Situation ist von Anfang bis Ende absurd, selbst wenn man weiss, dass Butink sämtliche Verkehrsampeln aus dem Video getilgt hat. Allard Zoetman hat eine wunderbare Begebenheit auf einem öffentlichen Spielplatz festgehalten: Kinder schieben ein paar Einkaufswagen zu einem Karussell zusammen, das sich immer schneller dreht (HOMO ECCO TEIL II, 2002).

Yael Bartana dagegen filmte, wie in einem Autobahntunnel alle Autos auf geheimnisvolle Weise allmählich zum Stillstand kommen – eine leise Anspielung auf einen Gedenktag in Israel.

Was die Nachwuchsvideos von jenen der Erwachsenen unterscheidet, ist ihr vorbehaltloses, nicht ironisches Verlangen nach einer besseren Welt. 2002 erhielt der vierzehnjährige Armenier Gor Baghdasaryan einen Preis für seinen Appell für eine waffenlose Gesellschaft. In seinem Film präsentiercn Kinder stolz ihre Kalaschnikows und Revolver aus Holz. Dann werfen sie die Spielzeugwaffen crst nur widerstrebend, dann ziemlich entschlossen auf einen Haufen und stecken diesen in Brand. In den Workshops wird auch schauspielerischer Ideenreichtum entwickelt. David Djindjikhachvili, ein Absolvent des Sandberg-Instituts, leitete den Workshop in Tiflis, jener Stadt also, aus der seine Familie einst emigrierte. Der Teenager George Baramidze machte dabei dem Ruf der georgischen Hauptstadt als Theaterstadt alle Ehre. Sein siegreiches Video skizziert das kleine Drama eines Kindes, das nach der Schule nach Hause kommt und die Haustür verschlossen findet. Seine Mutter reagiert weder auf das Läuten der Türglocke noch auf das Klingeln des Telefons. In der nächsten Einstellung sehen wir sie in der Küche, wo sie intensiv die Gebärden zum Ketchup-Song übt. Dabei hört sie nichts ausser ihrem Lieblingslied. In der Schlusseinstellung zieht der Junge die Kamera ins Vertrauen und sagt, man sollte nie ein Kind vor der Tür stehen lassen (DON'T LEAVE CHILD OUT, 2003).

Die 60-Sekunden-Videos mögen für den akademischen Diskurs keine grosse Bedeutung haben, doch als informelle Boten von Freiheit und Demokratie sorgen sie immerhin dafür, dass politische und kulturelle Mauern langsam zu bröckeln beginnen.

(Übersetzung: Irene Aeberli)

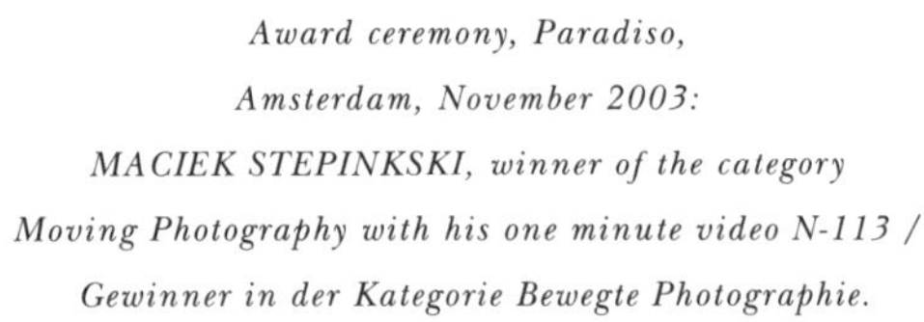

Award ceremony, Paradiso,
Amsterdam, November 2003:
MACIEK STEPINKSKI, winner of the category
Moving Photography with his one minute video N-113 /
Gewinner in der Kategorie Bewegte Photographie.

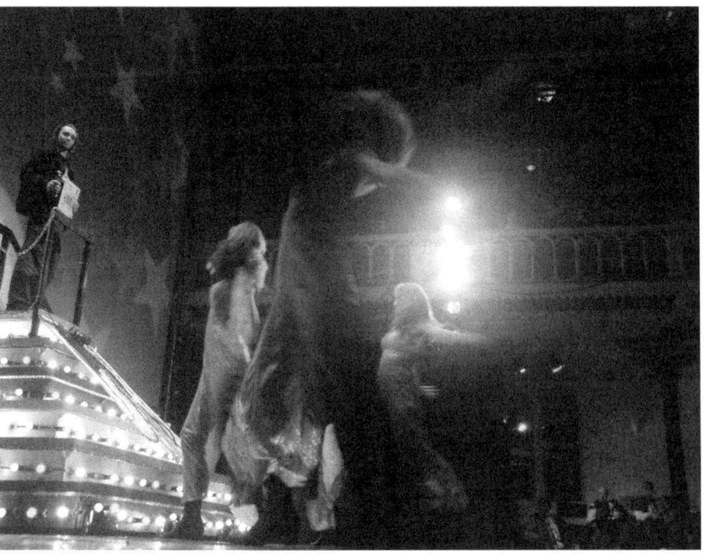

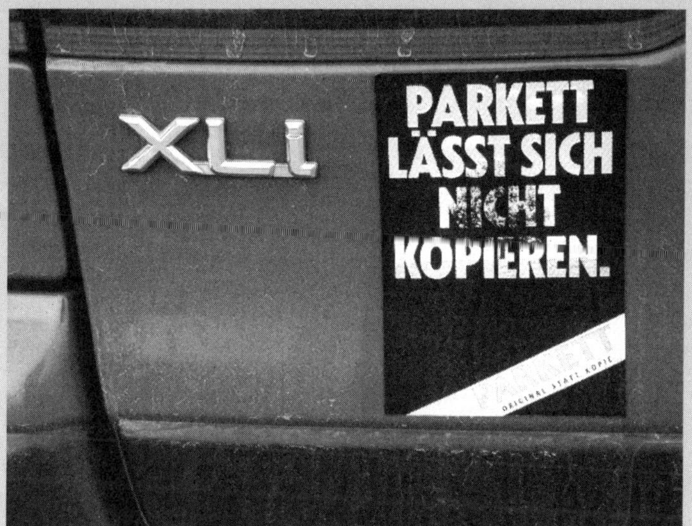

Garderobe

'gär-₁drōb

Parkett lässt sich nicht kopieren! –
Vom Plakat (Parkett 49) zum handlichen Aufkleber! /
Parkett is inimitable! –
from poster (Parkett 49) to handy little sticker.

Competition in Parkett 69 – Solution and Winners

The mystery passage is found in the novel *Middlesex* by Jeffrey Eugenides. It is on p. 262 in the paperback edition (Picador, 2003) and on page 325 in the German translation (Rowohlt, 2003).

And the lucky winners are:
• The first prize, a one-year subscription to Parkett, goes to *Amanda Douberley from Austin, Texas,* the only reader to send in the right answer.
• Our freshly launched, one-off plausibility prize (one updated Postcardbox with 146 postcards of Parkett Editions) goes to *Vanessa Muth from Berlin,* for the most imaginative wrong answer. Brett Easton Ellis's *Glamourama* is indeed a highly plausible answer with its nonstop, fast-paced parade of brand names.

Congratulations!

Wettbewerbsfrage aus Heft 69 – Auflösung und Gewinner

Die gesuchte Passage stammt aus dem Roman *Middlesex* von Jeffrey Eugenides. Sie findet sich auf S. 325 der gebundenen deutschen Ausgabe (Rowohlt, 2003) und S. 262 der englischen Taschenbuchausgabe (Picador, 2003).

Die glücklichen Gewinnerinnen sind:
• Gewinnerin eines Parkett-Jahresabos, mit der einzigen richtigen Einsendung, ist *Amanda Douberley aus Austin, Texas.*
• Gewinnerin unserer aktualisierten Postcardbox (146 Postkarten der Parkett-Editionen) ist *Vanessa Muth aus Berlin,* und zwar mit der plausibelsten falschen Antwort: Sie tippte auf Brett Easton Ellis' *Glamourama*, was uns aufgrund von Ellis' geradezu manischer Auflistung bekannter Markennamen plausibel und preiswürdig erschien.

Herzliche Gratulation und vielen Dank fürs Mitmachen!

20 YEARS OF PARKETT
ESSAY BY BORIS GROYS
ARTISTS' PAGES
SPECIAL COLLABORATION:
ALEX KATZ

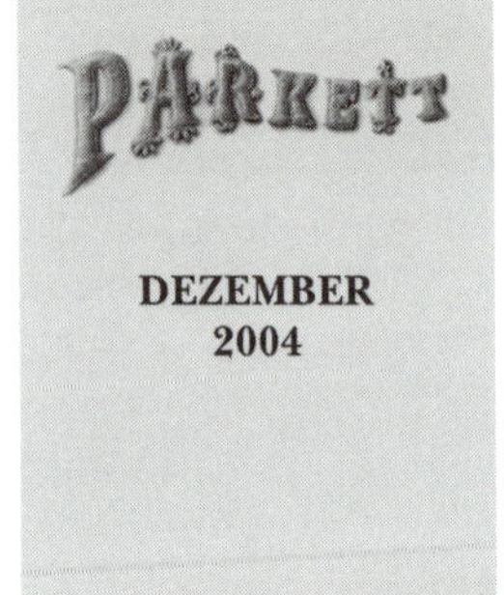

No. 72 - ISBN 3-907582-32-2

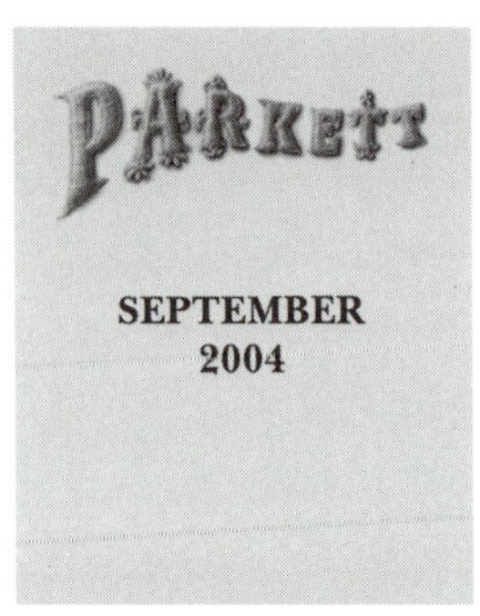

No. 71 - ISBN 3-907582-31-4

OLAF BREUNING
RICHARD PHILLIPS
KEITH TYSON

20 YEARS OF PARKETT
ESSAY BY NICOLAS BOURRIAUD
ARTISTS' PAGES
SPECIAL COLLABORATION:
PIPILOTTI RIST

CHRISTIAN MARCLAY
WILHELM SASNAL
GILLIAN WEARING
SHERBURNE, SCHAFFNER, VERGNE
DAILEY, SZYMCZYK, JANSEN; CAMERON
BURN, WEARING/RABINOWITZ
INSERT: **NIC HESS**
GREG HILTY: **REBECCA WARREN**
D. VAN DEN BOOGERD: **AERNAUT MIK**
LES INFOS: C. WOOD ON **MARK LECKEY**
CUMULUS: C. THEA, G. SCHOR
BALKON: TINEKE REIJNDERS
20 YEARS OF PARKETT: ESSAY BY
JOHANNA BURTON, ARTISTS' PAGES
SPECIAL COLLABORATION: **FRANZ WEST**

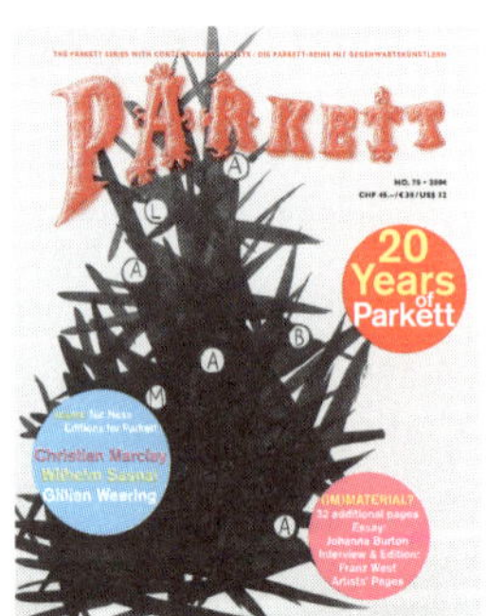

No. 70 - ISBN 3-907582-20-9

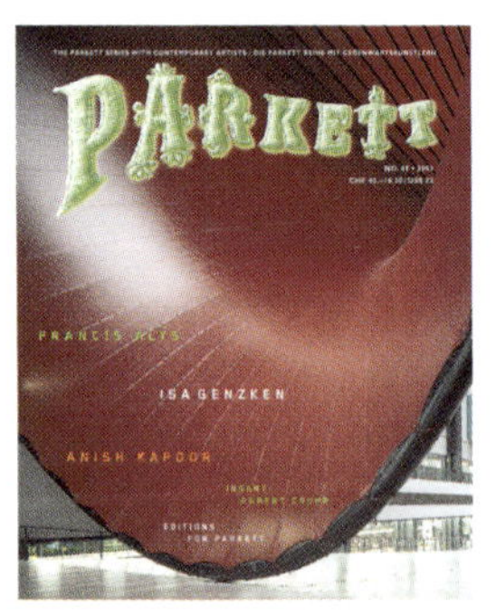

No. 69 - ISBN 3-907582-19-5

FRANCIS ALŸS
ISA GENZKEN
ANISH KAPOOR
SCOTT, ANTON, STORR, HEISER
LEE, KRAJEWSKI, BRYSON
FORSTER, WARNER
INSERT: **ROBERT CRUMB**
KAISER: **AMELIE VON WULFFEN**
COMER: **SWETLANA HEGER**
INQUIRY: CONSENSUS/KONSENS
CUMULUS AMERICA: J. PEARSON
CUMULUS EUROPE: E. TRONCY
BALKON: SERGIO RISALITI

FRANZ ACKERMANN
EIJA-LIISA AHTILA
DAN GRAHAM
FOGLE, DECTER, STANGE, ILES, ELFVING
KOCH, GUAGNINI/SCHNEIDER, MACDONALD
DI BARTOLOMEO, ROSENBERG MILLER
INSERT: **JONATHAN MONK**
D. KURJAKOVIC: **BOJAN SARCEVIC**
H. U. OBRIST: **BERNARD FRIZE**
G. JANSEN: **DIRK SKREBER**
LES INFOS: J. MURPHY
CUMULUS: C. RABINOWITZ, J. HOFFMANN
BALKON: HANS RUDOLF REUST

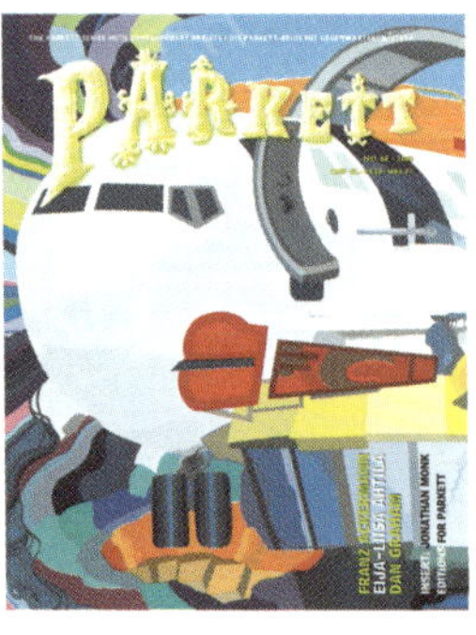

No. 68 - ISBN 3-907582-18-7

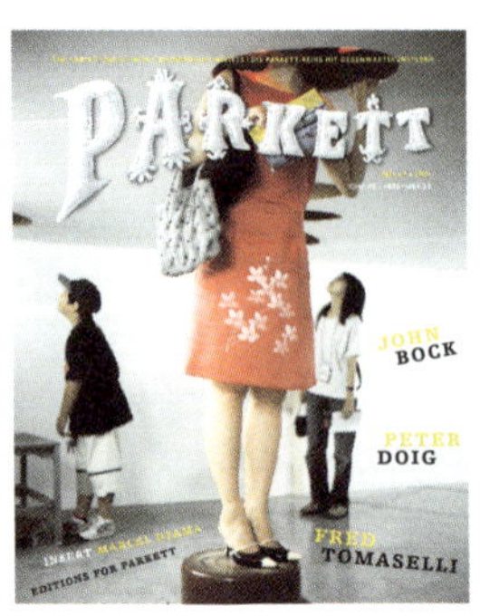

No. 67 - ISBN 3-907582-17-9

JOHN BOCK
PETER DOIG
FRED TOMASELLI
HOFFMANN, BIRNBAUM, AVGIKOS
BONAVENTURA, FUCHS, RUF
CAMERON, RONDEAU, PINCHBECK
INSERT: **MARCEL DZAMA**
T. SELVARATNAM: **SIMON STARLING**
S. OMLIN: **HANNE DARBOVEN**
VISCHER/HERZOG: SCHAULAGER BASEL
LES INFOS: H. BÖHME ON **WANG FU**
CUMULUS: FIRSTENBERG, KERSTING
BALKON: DANIELE MUSCIONICO

ARTISTS' EDITIONS FOR PARKETT SUBSCRIBERS
WWW.PARKETTART.COM

The PARKETT Series is created in collaboration with artists, who contribute an original work available exclusively to the subscribers in the form of a signed limited SPECIAL EDITION. The available works are also reproduced in each PARKETT issue.

Each SPECIAL EDITION is available by order from any one of our offices in New York or Zurich. Just fill in the details below and send this card to the office nearest you. Once your order has been processed, you will be issued with an invoice and your personal edition number. Upon receipt of payment, you will receive the SPECIAL EDITION. (Please note that supply is subject to availability. PARKETT does not assume responsibility for any delays in production of SPECIAL EDITIONS. Postage is not included.)

☐ As a subscriber to PARKETT, I would like to order the following Special Edition(s), signed and numbered by the artist.

PARKETT No.	ARTIST	NAME:
PARKETT No.	ARTIST	ADDRESS:
PARKETT No.	ARTIST	CITY:
PARKETT No.	ARTIST	STATE/ZIP:
PARKETT No.	ARTIST	COUNTRY:
PARKETT No.	ARTIST	PHONE:

☐ I have indicated my way of payment on the reverse side of this form.

Send this form to the PARKETT office nearest you:

PARKETT PUBLISHERS 155 AV. OF THE AMERICAS NEW YORK, NY 10013 PHONE (212) 673-2660 FAX (212) 271-0704

PARKETT VERLAG QUELLENSTRASSE 27 CH-8031 ZÜRICH TELEFON +41-1-271 81 40 FAX +41-1-272 43 01

Visit our website: www.parkettart.com

 70

KÜNSTLEREDITIONEN FÜR PARKETT-ABONNENTEN
WWW.PARKETTART.COM

Die PARKETT-Buchreihe entsteht in Zusammenarbeit mit Künstlern, die eigens für die Abonnenten einen Originalbeitrag in Form einer limitierten und signierten EDITION gestalten. Diese Editionen sind auch in der Zeitschrift abgebildet und können mit dieser Bestellkarte in jedem unserer Büros in Zürich, Frankfurt oder New York bestellt werden. Sie erhalten dann Ihre persönliche Editionsnummer und eine Rechnung. Sobald wir Ihre Zahlung erhalten haben, schicken wir Ihnen Ihre Edition(en). Lieferung solange Vorrat. PARKETT übernimmt keine Verantwortung für allfällige Verzögerungen bei der Herstellung der Vorzugsausgaben. Versandkosten und MwSt (Schweiz) nicht inbegriffen.

☐ Ich bin PARKETT-Abonnent(in) und bestelle folgende EDITION(EN), nummeriert und vom Künstler signiert:

PARKETT Nr.	KÜNSTLER/IN	NAME:
PARKETT Nr.	KÜNSTLER/IN	STRASSE:
PARKETT Nr.	KÜNSTLER/IN	PLZ/STADT:
PARKETT Nr.	KÜNSTLER/IN	LAND:
PARKETT Nr.	KÜNSTLER/IN	TEL.:

☐ Meine Zahlungsweise habe ich auf der Rückseite angegeben.

Senden Sie die Bestellkarte an das PARKETT-Büro in Ihrer Nähe:

PARKETT VERLAG QUELLENSTRASSE 27 CH-8031 ZÜRICH TELEFON +41-1-271 81 40 FAX +41-1-272 43 01

PARKETT PUBLISHERS 155 AV. OF THE AMERICAS NEW YORK, NY 10013 PHONE (212) 673-2660 FAX (212) 271-0704

Besuchen Sie unsere Website: www.parkettart.com

☐ I wish to subscribe to the PARKETT Series, starting with issue no. ______

☐ I wish to send a gift subscription, starting with issue no. ______ (a gift card in my name will be sent to the recipient):

  ☐ for 1 year (3 issues) at US $ 80 (USA/Canada), € 82 (Europe), € 98 (Rest of the World)

  ☐ for 2 years (6 issues) at US $ 145 (USA/Canada), € 150 (Europe), € 188 (Rest of the World)

  ☐ for 3 years (9 issues) at US $ 205 (USA/Canada), € 212 (Europe), € 278 (Rest of the World)

  ☐ for 1 year (3 issues) at the special student discount (US $ 65 for USA/Canada, € 67 for Europe). A copy of my student ID is enclosed.
  Postage included. All prices subject to change.

☐ I wish to complete my PARKETT library and order the following issue(s):

  No. ____
  at € 30 each (up to no. 43: € 20; no. 44–48: € 28), postage not included. Within the USA & Canada $ 32 (up to no. 43: $ 22.50; no. 44–48: $ 29), add postage: $ 5 (USA), $ 10 (Canada). (Sold out: No. 1–10, 12, 13, 16, 17, 19, 22, 25, 26, 27, 29–31, 35, 36, 38, 45).

☐ I wish to order ______ copies of the newly updated PARKETT Postcard Set with Text Booklet on MoMA Show. Featuring all artists' editions made for PARKETT since 1984 and a booklet with essays by Deborah Wye (Chief Curator Illustrated Books and Prints at MoMA) and Susan Tallman. 146 color postcards, booklet with 2 texts, color reproductions of 64 PARKETT covers. 64 p., packed in a box, 6¼ x 4¾ x 2⅜", € 30 (USA $ 30) per set, plus postage.

NAME: _______________________________________

ADDRESS: ____________________________________

CITY: ____

STATE/ZIP/COUNTRY: __________________________

TEL.: _______________ FAX: _________________

E-MAIL: ______________________________________

GIFT RECIPIENT: ______________________________

ADDRESS: ____________________________________

CITY: ____

STATE/ZIP: ___________________________________

COUNTRY: ____________________________________

☐ Charge my Visa Card   ☐ Mastercard   ☐ AMEX

Card No. ⎢⎢⎢⎢⎢⎢⎢⎢⎢⎢⎢⎢⎢⎢⎢⎢ Expiration date ______

☐ Payment enclosed (US check or money order)   ☐ Bill me

DATE _______________________________________

SIGNATURE __________________________________

Send this form to the PARKETT office nearest you:

PARKETT PUBLISHERS   155 AV. OF THE AMERICAS   NEW YORK, NY 10013   PHONE (212) 673-2660   FAX (212) 271-0704

PARKETT VERLAG   QUELLENSTRASSE 27   CH-8031 ZÜRICH   TELEFON +41-1-271 81 40   FAX +41-1-272 43 01

Visit our website: www.parkettart.com

PARKETT

ABONNIEREN, VERVOLLSTÄNDIGEN ODER VERSCHENKEN SIE DIE UMFASSENDSTE BUCHREIHE ÜBER GEGENWARTSKÜNSTLER – WWW.PARKETTART.COM

70

☐ Ich abonniere die PARKETT-Reihe ab Nr. ______

☐ Ich verschenke ein PARKETT-Abonnement ab Nr. ______ (Der/die Beschenkte erhält eine Geschenkkarte in meinem Namen)

  ☐ für 1 Jahr (3 Bände) zu: € 78 (Deutschland), CHF 116.– (Schweiz), € 82 (übriges Europa)

  ☐ für 2 Jahre (6 Bände) zu: € 140 (Deutschland), CHF 216.– (Schweiz), € 150 (übriges Europa)

  ☐ für 3 Jahre (9 Bände) zu: € 200 (Deutschland), CHF 312.– (Schweiz), € 212 (übriges Europa)

  ☐ für 1 Jahr (3 Bände) zum Studenten-Sonderpreis (Deutschland: € 65 /Schweiz: CHF 96.– / übriges Europa: € 67). Eine Kopie meines gültigen Studentenausweises lege ich bei.
  Preise einschliesslich Versandkosten. Preisänderungen vorbehalten.

☐ Ich möchte meine PARKETT-Bibliothek vervollständigen und bestelle die folgenden noch erhältliche(n) Ausgabe(n):

  Nr. ____
  zu je € 30 / CHF 45.– (bis Nr. 43: € 20 / CHF 30.–; Nr. 44–48: € 28 / CHF 39.–), zzgl. Versandkosten (vergriffen: Nr. 1–10, 12, 13, 16, 17, 19, 22, 25, 26, 27, 29–31, 35, 36, 38, 45).

☐ Ich bestelle ______ Ex. des aktualisierten PARKETT-Postkarten-Sets mit Textbüchlein zur MoMA-Ausstellung. Mit Postkarten der seit 1984 von Künstlern für PARKETT geschaffenen Editionen. Das Textbüchlein enthält 2 Essays zur Ausstellung im MoMA, New York, von Deborah Wye (Chefkuratorin für illustrierte Bücher und Grafik am MoMA) und Susan Tallman. 146 Farbpostkarten, Büchlein mit zwei Texten, Farbabb. von 64 PARKETT-Titelblättern u.a.m. 64 S., in bunter Schachtel, 16 x 12 x 6 cm. € 30 / CHF 45.– pro Set, zzgl. Versandkosten.

NAME: _______________________________________

STRASSE: ____________________________________

PLZ/STADT: __________________________________

LAND: _______________________________________

TEL.: _______________ FAX: _________________

E-MAIL: ______________________________________

BESCHENKTE(R): ______________________________

STRASSE: ____________________________________

PLZ/STADT: __________________________________

LAND: _______________________________________

☐ Ich zahle mit Visa   ☐ Eurocard/Mastercard   ☐ AMEX

Karten Nr. ⎢⎢⎢⎢⎢⎢⎢⎢⎢⎢⎢⎢⎢⎢⎢⎢ Gültig bis ____________

☐ Mein Scheck über CHF/€ ________________________ liegt bei.

☐ Bitte senden Sie mir eine Rechnung.

DATUM ______________________________________

UNTERSCHRIFT _______________________________

Senden Sie die Bestellkarte an das PARKETT-Büro in Ihrer Nähe:

PARKETT VERLAG   QUELLENSTRASSE 27   CH-8031 ZÜRICH   TELEFON +41-1-271 81 40   FAX +41-1-272 43 01

PARKETT PUBLISHERS   155 AV. OF THE AMERICAS   NEW YORK, NY 10013   PHONE (212) 673-2660   FAX (212) 271-0704

Besuchen Sie unsere Website: www.parkettart.com

ANGELA BULLOCH
DANIEL BUREN
PIERRE HUYGHE
REBENTISCH, WILSON, PRINZHORN
RORIMER, GINGERAS, BUREN/HUYGHE
MILLAR, OBRIST, HOBBS
T. NICHOLS GOODEVE/G. BRUNO
E. DIMENDBERG: **ALLAN SEKULA**
LES INFOS: ROBERTO OHRT ON
MONICA BONVICINI
CUMULUS AMERICA: NATO THOMPSON
CUMULUS EUROPA: GREG HILTY

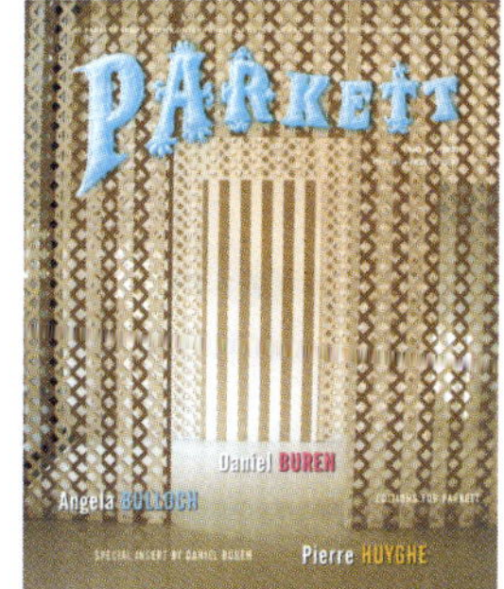

No. 66 - ISBN 3-907582-16-0

JOHN CURRIN
LAURA OWENS
MICHAEL RAEDECKER
SEWARD, VAN DE WALLE, BERG
FERGUSON, THOMSON, WEISSMAN
VERSCHAFFEL, MYERS, EGGERS
INSERT: **LOU REED**
KURT W. FORSTER: **JEFF WALL**
STORR: **DIETER ROTH & D. IANNONE**
K. BITTERLI: **HUBBARD/BIRCHLER**
LES INFOS: CHRISTINA VÉGH
CUMULUS: O. WESTPHALEN, T. HAHN
BALKON: SHEENA WAGSTAFF

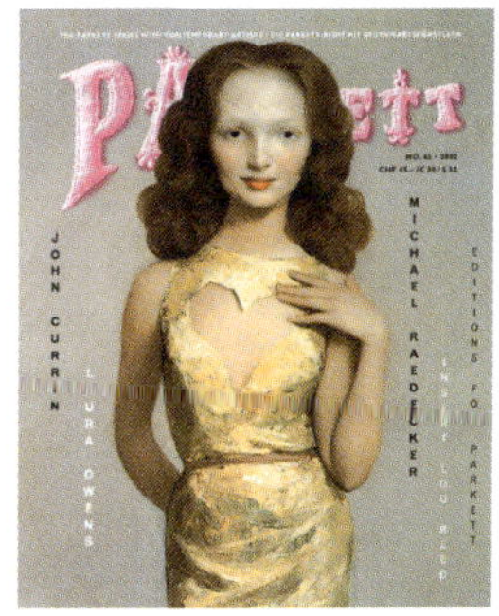

No. 65 - ISBN 3-907582-15-2

OLAFUR ELIASSON
TOM FRIEDMAN
RODNEY GRAHAM
BLOM, MORGAN, CAMERON, MATSUI
WATERS/FRIEDMAN, COOKE, HALE
INSERT: **AMY SILLMAN**
VÉRONIQUE D'AUZAC:
XAVIER VEILHAN
INTERVIEW:
A.M. HOMES: **CHRIS VERENE**
HAKAN NILSSON: **ANNIKA LARSSON**
INQUIRY/UMFRAGE:
LEARNING FROM "DOCUMENTA"

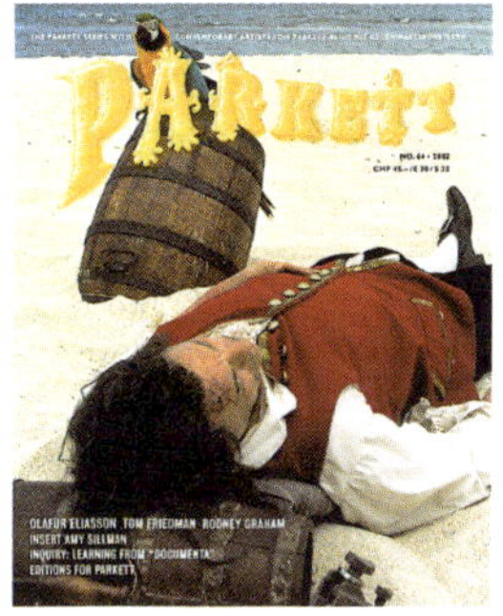

No. 64 - ISBN 3-907582-14-4

TRACEY EMIN
WILLIAM KENTRIDGE
GREGOR SCHNEIDER
BARBER, MUIR, PREECE
GUNNING, STEWART, GOLDBERG
PUVOGEL, LOOCK
INSERT: **JEREMY BLAKE**
CLAUDIA SPINELLI: **FABRICE GYGI**
RAINER FUCHS: **KATHARINA GROSSE**
ADRIAN DANNATT: **THE THREE**
CUMULUS: CHRISTIAN RATTEMEYER
DANIEL BIRNBAUM
BALKON: MICHAEL OPPITZ

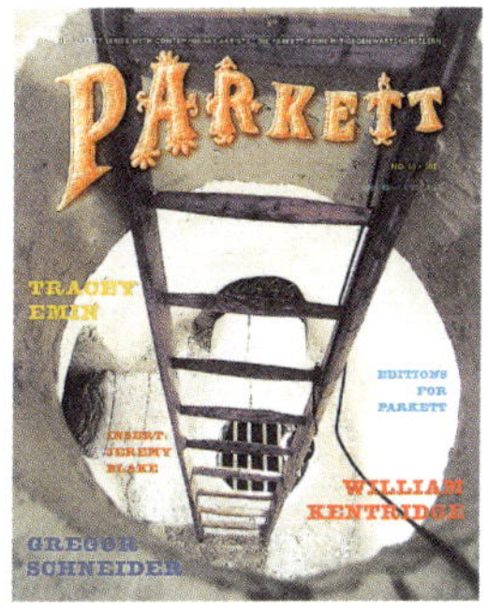

No. 63 - ISBN 3-907582-13-6

JOHN WESLEY
TACITA DEAN
THOMAS DEMAND
MILLAR, CARABELL, SCHWARZ
NORDEN, KÖNIG/STOCKEBRAND
HAINLEY, SEARLE, RUBY, HEISER
INSERT: **G. STEINER & J. LENZLINGER**
PHILIP URSPRUNG: **ALLAN KAPROW**
RUSSELL FERGUSON: **GLEN WILSON**
EDWARD A. SCHEER: **MIKE PARR**
LES INFOS: DAVID GREENBERG
CUMULUS: G. CARMINE, S. DIETZ

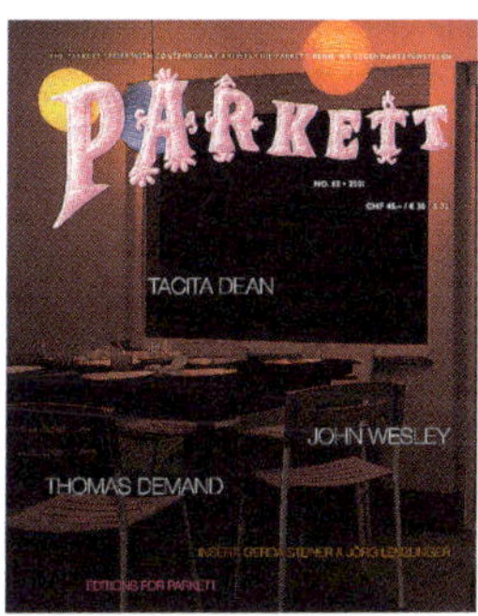

No. 62 - ISBN 3-907582-12-8

BRIDGET RILEY
LIAM GILLICK
SARAH MORRIS
MATTHEW RITCHIE
KUDIELKA, HICKEY
GILLICK, STEMMRICH, WOLLEN
NICHOLS GOODEVE, KLEIN
PRINZHORN, RABINOWITZ
GALISON/JONES, MARCUS
ELISABETH KLEY: **PAUL LINCOLN**
CUMULUS: O. ENWEZOR, M. WARNER
BALKON: STELLA ROLLIG

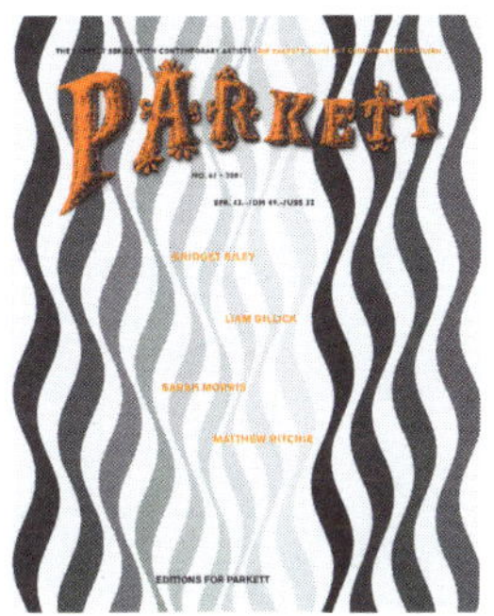

No. 61 - ISBN 3-907582-11-X

CHUCK CLOSE
DIANA THATER
LUC TUYMANS
PROSE, CLOSE/PEYTON, SHIFF
CLOSE/CURIGER, ARRHENIUS
HASLINGER, GILBERT-ROLFE
HOPTMAN, MOSQUERA, REUST
INSERT: **SHIRANA SHAHBAZI**
GREG HILTY: **JEREMY DELLER**
HOWARD SINGERMAN: **DAVID BUNN**
LES INFOS: T. DE DUVE—INTERVIEW
CUMULUS: F. WARD, H. U. RECK

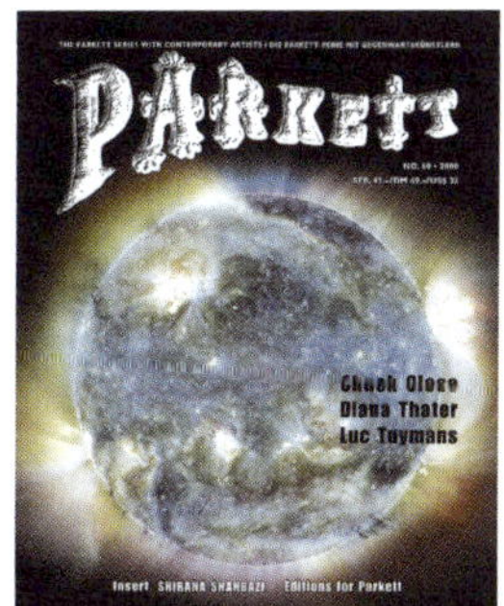

No. 60 - ISBN 3-907582-10-1

MAURIZIO CATTELAN
YAYOI KUSAMA
KARA WALKER
BOURRIAUD, GINGERAS, BONAMI
PANHANS-BÜHLER, MATSUI, POLLOCK
DUBOIS SHAW, JANUS, WALKER
INSERT: **ANDREAS ZÜST**
VINCENT KATZ
F. BRONFEN: **ANNETTE MESSAGER**
JAN AVGIKOS: **ANNA GASKELL**
LES INFOS: ALI SUBOTNICK
CUMULUS: M. ROWELL, L. FÖLDENYI
BALKON: MICHELLE NICOL

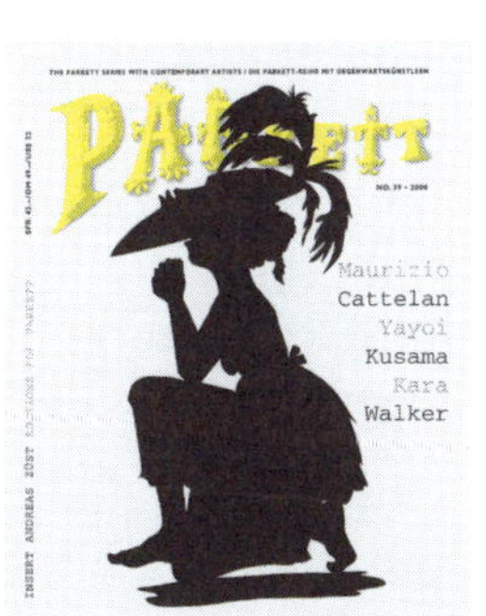

No. 59 - ISBN 3-907582-09-8

JAMES ROSENQUIST
SYLVIE FLEURY
JASON RHOADES
RUSSELL, KOONS/ROSENQUIST
HULTEN, FELIX, GLENN, LOBEL
DANNATT, RUF, KOETHER, FERGUSON
ORTH, SCHEIDEMANN/HERMANN
INSERT: **HENRY BOND**
G. WILLIAMS: **JANE & LOUISE WILSON**
S. ZIZEK, PAUL D. MILLER & CHRIS OFILI
LES INFOS: ANNA HELWING
CUMULUS: D. ROBBINS, H. TEERLINCK
BALKON: KNUT EBELING

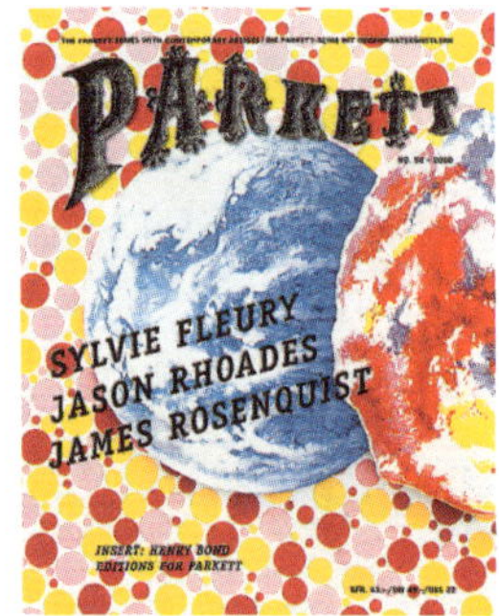

No. 58 - ISBN 3-907582-08-X

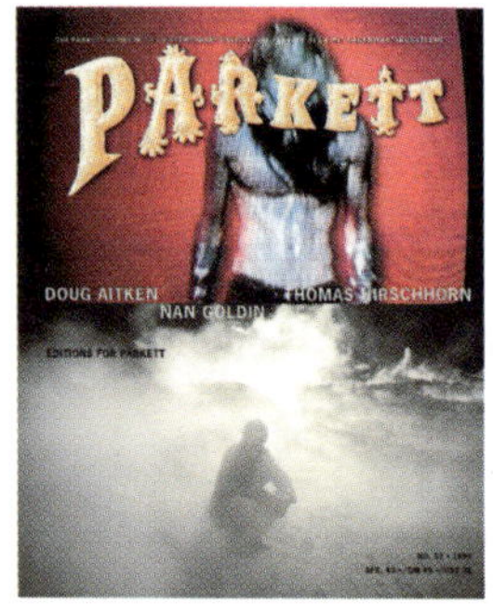

No. 57 - ISBN 3-907582-07-1

DOUG AITKEN
NAN GOLDIN
THOMAS HIRSCHHORN
ROBERTS, BONAMI, VAN ASSCHE
LEBOVICI, DANTO, LIEBMANN
FRIIS-HANSEN, HAKERT, EISENBERG
FLECK, GINGERAS, VERGNE, STEINWEG
D. GREENBERG: **DONALD BAECHLER**
ANDREA KROKSNES: **LOUISE LAWLER**
LIONEL BOVIER: **JOHN MILLER**
LES INFOS: RUDOLF SCHMITZ
CUMULUS: H.U. OBRIST, C. BUTLER
BALKON: J. STEINER/ANNELISE COSTE

ELLSWORTH KELLY
VANESSA BEECROFT
JORGE PARDO
KELLEIN, FER, MAURER, RIMANELLI
BRYSON, TAZZI, SEWARD, AVGIKOS
FERGUSON, VÉGH, VAN WINKEL
FRANGENBERG, BUSH
GREG HILTY: **CERITH WYN EVANS**
THOMAS Y. LEVIN: **CHRISTIAN MARCLAY**
LYNNE COOKE: **DIANA THATER**
LES INFOS: DIANE LEWIS
CUMULUS: A. DANNATT, P. NEDOMA

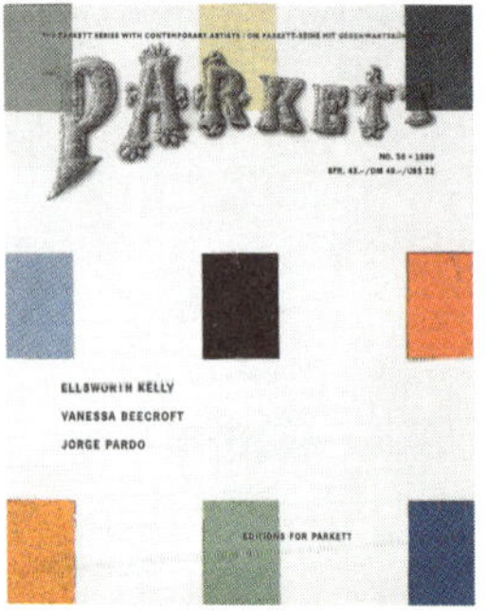

No. 56 - ISBN 3-907582-06-3

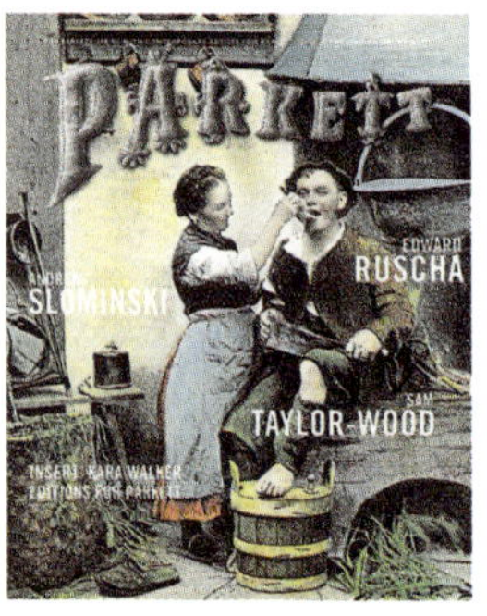

No. 55 - ISBN 3-907582-05-5

EDWARD RUSCHA
ANDREAS SLOMINSKI
SAM TAYLOR-WOOD
PERRONE, HIGGIE, SINGERMAN
SCHENKER, SCANLAN, SPECTOR, FREY
HEYNEN, GROYS/FUNCKE/HOFFMANN
BRONFEN, BONAMI, LAJER-BURCHARTH
INSERT: **KARA WALKER**
BORIS GROYS: **PAVEL PEPPERSTEIN**
RUDOLF SCHMITZ: **ALEXANDER KLUGE**
BEATRIX RUF: **EIJA-LIISA AHTILA**
CUMULUS: M. NICOL, S. ROLNIK

RONI HORN
MARIKO MORI
BEAT STREULI
SCHORR, GUNNARSSON, GOROVOY, LEWIS
SPECTOR, BRYSON, NAKAZAWA, NICHOLS
GOODEVE, STALS, DANTO, AMANO, SMITH
INSERT: **MATTHEW RITCHIE**
VINCENT KATZ: **ALEX KATZ**
H. BREDEKAMP: **STEPHAN VON HUENE**
PAUL D. MILLER: **SHIRIN NESHAT**
LES INFOS:
OKWUI ENWEZOR & WILLIAM KENTRIDGE
CUMULUS: VALÉRIA PICCOLI, MARIA LIND

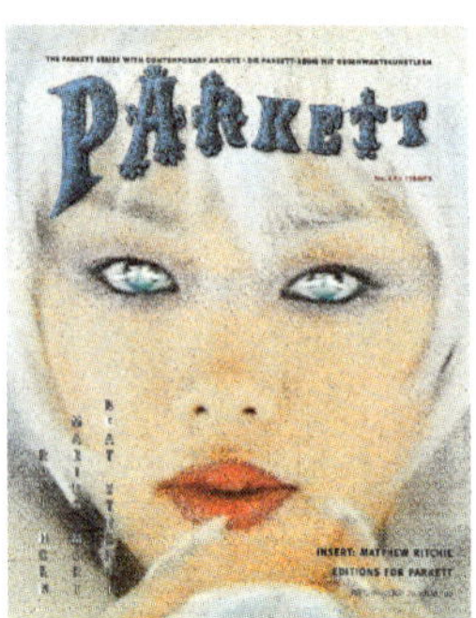

No. 54 - ISBN 3-907582-04-7

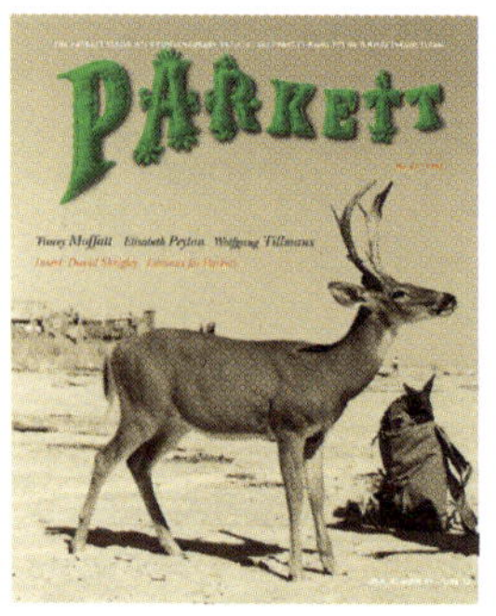

No. 53 - ISBN 3-907582-03-9

TRACEY MOFFATT
ELIZABETH PEYTON
WOLFGANG TILLMANS
MARTIN, LAJER-BURCHARTH, RIMANELLI
PILGRIM, URSPRUNG, LIEBMANN, MATSUI
WAKEFIELD, BUDNEY, NESBITT, ZIEGLER
INSERT: **DAVID SHRIGLEY**
C. BERNARD: **JOHAN GRIMONPREZ**
BERNARD MARCADÉ: **ROBERT GOBER**
LES INFOS DE L'ENFER: V. LIEBERMANN
CUMULUS: BLESSING, AUPETITALLOT
BALKON: STEINER/MAGNAGUAGNO

KAREN KILIMNIK
MALCOLM MORLEY
UGO RONDINONE
SCHORR, BÜRGI, JUNCOSA
MORLEY, LEBENSZTEJN, BONAMI
VERWOERT, HOPTMAN
INSERT: **THOMAS BAYRLE**
ED WHITE: **JEAN MICHEL OTHONIEL**
NEVILLE WAKEFIELD: **RICHARD SERRA**
GILDA WILLIAMS: **GILLIAN WEARING**
R. GRESKOVIC: **MERCE CUNNINGHAM**
CUMULUS: WALKER, KURZMEYER
BALKON: CECILIA VICUÑA

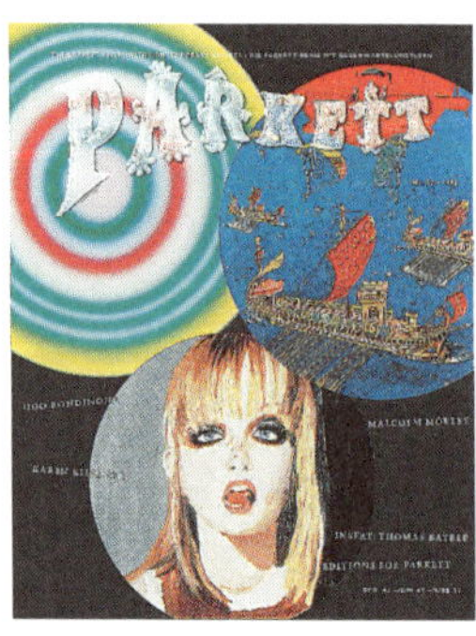

No. 52 - ISBN 3-907582-02-0

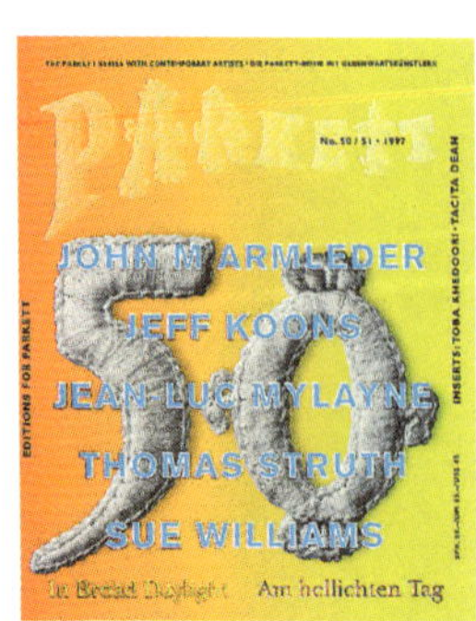

50/51 - ISBN 3-907582-00-4

JOHN M ARMLEDER, JEFF KOONS
JEAN-LUC MYLAYNE
THOMAS STRUTH, SUE WILLIAMS
DI PIETRANTONIO, BOVIER, MUNIZ
SEWARD, LOERS, NICHOLS GOODEVE
COOKE, DION, ARNAUDET, MYLAYNE
CURIGER, LINGWOOD, OKUTSU, BRYSON
SCHJELDAHL, NESBIT, DANNATT, CAMHI
INSERTS: **TOBA KHEDOORI, TACITA DEAN**
ONFRAY: **H. RIGAUD**, NICOL: **SAM SAMORE**
MURPHY, VAN DER WALLE, STEINER
KURT W. FORSTER: **FRANK GEHRY**
CUMULUS: COLEMAN, BIRNBAUM

LAURIE ANDERSON
DOUGLAS GORDON
JEFF WALL
FLOOD, BEZZOLA, FERGUSON
GILLICK/GORDON, BRYSON
PONTBRIAND, SCHORR, ANDERSON
BURCKHARDT, BUDNEY
INSERT: **SILVIA BÄCHLI**
COLIN DE LAND: **JOHN WATERS**
ROBERT STORR: **SEYDOU KEITA**
D. SALVIONI: **CLEGG & GUTTMANN**
CUMULUS: KITTELMANN, MEYER

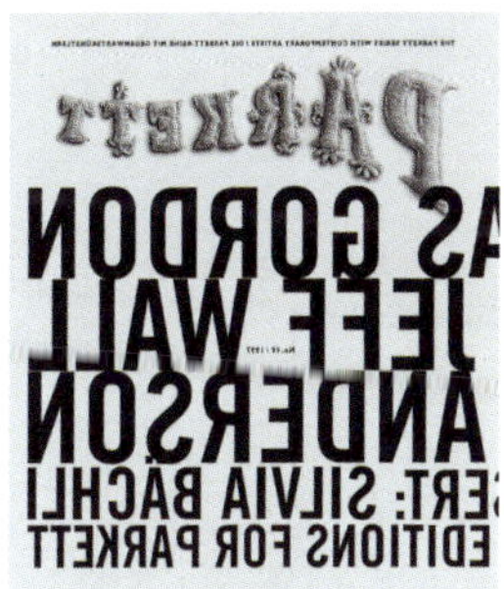

No. 49 - ISBN 3-907509-99-4

GARY HUME
GABRIEL OROZCO
PIPILOTTI RIST
BOVIER, MUIR, FOGLE, BONAMI
DE ZEGHER, SPECTOR, URSPRUNG
BABIAS, COLOMBO, ANDERSON
INSERT: **RUDY BURCKHARDT**
V. KATZ: **RUDY BURCKHARDT**
MARK VAN DER WALLE:
CHARLES LONG & STEREOLAB
FAYE HIRSCH: **BRUCE CONNER**
CH. DOSWALD: **IAN ANÜLL**
CUMULUS: LEGGAT, SCHNEIDER

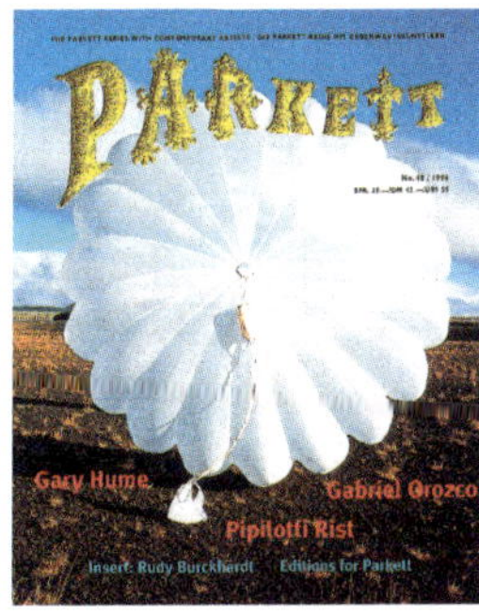

No. 48 - ISBN 3-907509-98-6

TONY OURSLER
RAYMOND PETTIBON
THOMAS SCHÜTTE
COOKE, RICHARD, NERI
LEWIS, GROYS, ALS, RUGOFF
GOODEVE, SEARLE, MARI, REUST
WAKEFIELD, LOOCK, JANUS
INSERT: **ZOE LEONARD & CHERYL DUNYE**
JURI STEINER: **EMMA KUNZ**
M. WECHSLER: **CHRISTOPH RÜTIMANN**
SUSAN MORGAN: **DIANE ARBUS**
CUMULUS: PRINCENTHAL, BOVIER/CHERIX

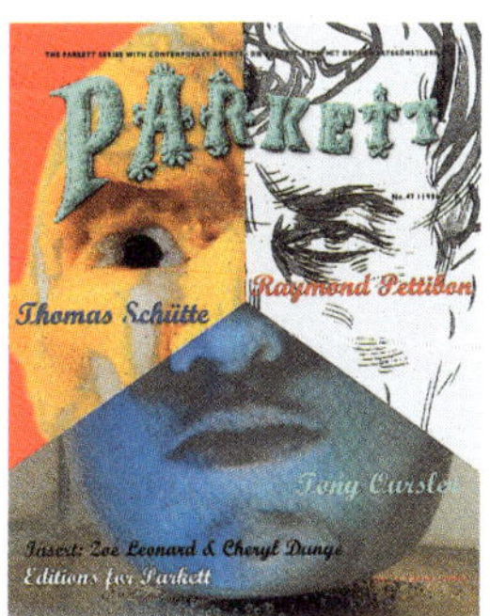

No. 47 - ISBN 3-907509-97-8

RICHARD ARTSCHWAGER
CADY NOLAND
HIROSHI SUGIMOTO
DEITCHER, SCHAFFNER, FORSTER
MUNIZ, ARMSTRONG, RELYEA
BOGDAN, GOODEVE, NICKAS
BRYSON, RUGOFF, DENSON
INSERT: **JOHN M ARMLEDER**
ROLAND WÄSPE: **ERWIN WURM**
D. BIRNBAUM: **ÖYVIND FAHLSTRÖM**
LES INFOS DU PARADIS: ROBERT FLECK
CUMULUS: MILLER, VETTESE
BALKON: MARTIN HELLER

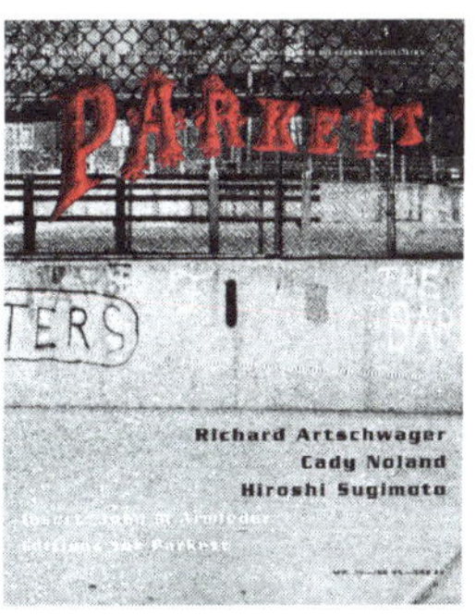

No. 46 - ISBN 3-907509-96-X

VIJA CELMINS
ANDREAS GURSKY
RIRKRIT TIRAVANIJA
PRINCENTHAL, LEWIS, SILVERTHORNE
SHIFF, CRIQUI, BURCKHARDT, WAKEFIELD
SCHORR, MELO, GILLICK, FLOOD, STEINER
INSERT: **HANS DANUSER**
LES INFOS: LIAM GILLICK /DOUGLAS GORDON
LYNNE COOKE, DAVID DEITCHER
DANIEL KURJAKOVIC: **MARIE JOSÉ BURKI**
NAN GOLDIN: **PETER HUJAR**
NOEMI SMOLIK: **ANDREAS SLOMINSKI**
JASON SIMON: **MARK DION**
LUK LAMBRECHT: **MARK LUYTEN**

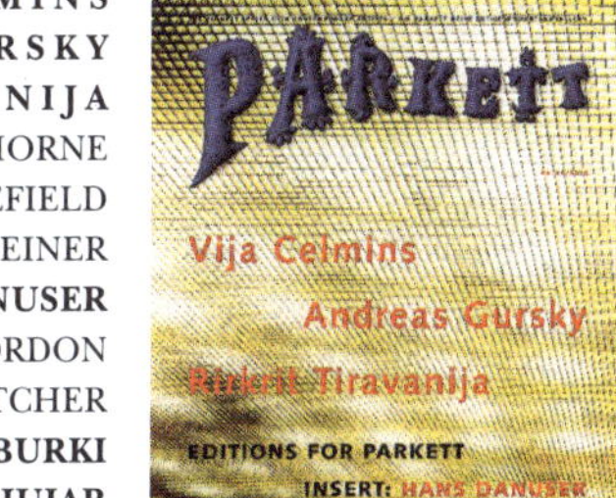

No. 44 - ISBN 3-907509-94-3

JUAN MUÑOZ
SUSAN ROTHENBERG
LYNNE COOKE, ALEXANDRE MELO
JAMES LINGWOOD, GAVIN BRYARS
ROBERT CREELEY, INGRID SCHAFFNER
JEAN-CHRISTOPHE AMMANN
MARK STEVENS, JOAN SIMON
INSERT: **ROBERT SMITHSON**
NEVILLE WAKEFIELD
MICHELLE NICOL: **CARSTEN HÖLLER**
H.U. OBRIST: **FABRICE HYBERT**

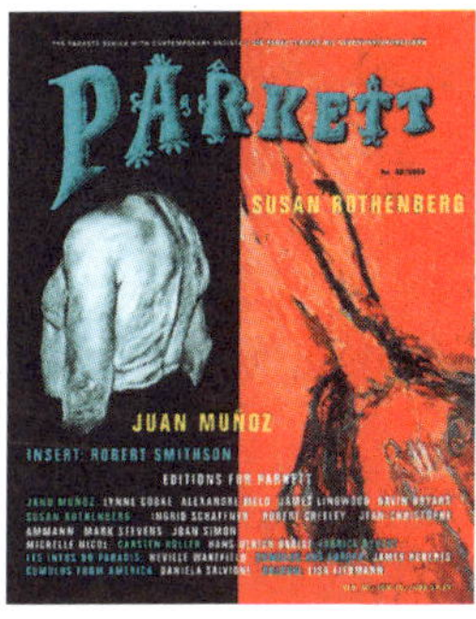

No. 43 - ISBN 3-907509-93-5

LAWRENCE WEINER
RACHEL WHITEREAD
B. ADAMS, F. RICHARD
D. SCHWARZ, D. SALVIONI
E. LEFFINGWELL, L. RELYEA
N. WAKEFIELD, R. SCHMITZ
T. FAIRBROTHER, S. WATNEY
INSERT: **NAN GOLDIN**
VINCE LEO: **ROBERT FRANK**
C. RITSCHARD: **MARKUS RAETZ**

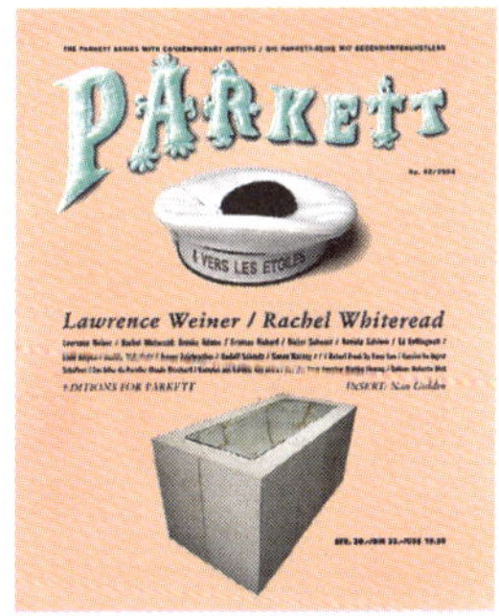

No. 42 - ISBN 3-907509-92-7

FRANCESCO CLEMENTE
GÜNTHER FÖRG
PETER FISCHLI/DAVID WEISS
DAMIEN HIRST
JENNY HOLZER
REBECCA HORN
SIGMAR POLKE
HOLLAND COTTER, BORIS GROYS
MAX WECHSLER, DAVID RIMANELLI
JOAN SIMON, GORDON BURN
GILBERT LASCAULT, WERNER SPIES
BICE CURIGER, JEFF PERRONE
G. ROGER DENSON, VIK MUNIZ
DAVE HICKEY

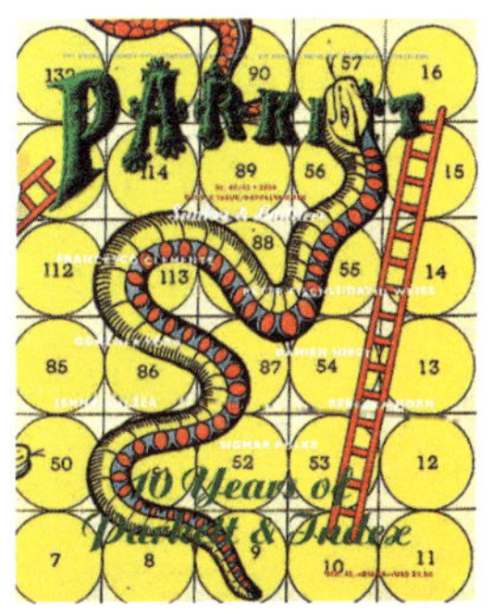

40/41 - ISBN 3-907509-90-0

CHARLES RAY
FRANZ WEST
K. KERTESS, CH. KNIGHT
P. SCHJELDAHL, R. STORR
J. AVGIKOS, A. HUBER
M. PRINZHORN, E. SCHLEBRÜGGE
HARALD SZEEMANN
D. ZACHAROPOULOS
INSERT: **PIPILOTTI RIST**
JEAN BAUDRILLARD
HANS RUDOLF REUST: **LUC TUYMANS**
PARKETT INQUIRY:
CHERCHEZ LA FEMME PEINTRE

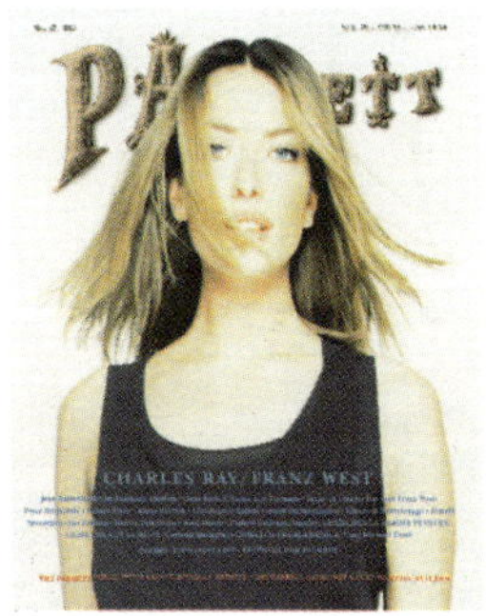

No. 37 - ISBN 3-907509-87-0

ILYA KABAKOV
RICHARD PRINCE
BORIS GROYS, ROBERT STORR
JAN THORN-PRIKKER
CLAUDIA JOLLES, EDMUND WHITE
SUSAN TALLMAN, DANIELA
SALVIONI, KATHY ACKER
INSERT: **TATSUO MIYAJIMA**
GUDRUN INBODEN: **ASTA GRÖTING**
LYNNE COOKE: **GARY HILL**
PATRICK McGRATH: **STEPHEN ELLIS**

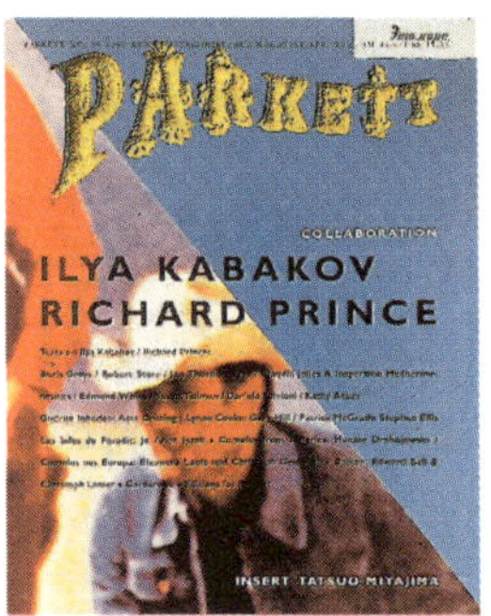

No. 34 - ISBN 3-907509-84-6

IMI KNOEBEL
SHERRIE LEVINE
RUDOLF BUMILLER
RAINER CRONE/DAVID MOOS
LISA LIEBMANN, DANIELA SALVIONI
ERICH FRANZ, HOWARD SINGERMANN
INSERT: **DAMIEN HIRST**
SHEENA WAGSTAFF: **VIJA CELMINS**
JIM LEWIS: **LARRY CLARK**
LIAM GILLICK: **BETHAN HUWS**
THOMAS KELLEIN: **WALTER DE MARIA**

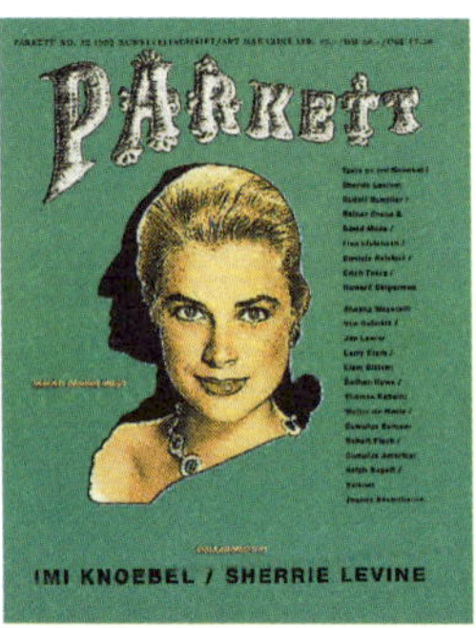

No. 32 - ISBN 3-907509-82-X

FRANZ GERTSCH
THOMAS RUFF
H. FRIEDEL, U. LOOCK
I. MICHAEL DANOFF
A. WALLACH. R. M. MASON
M. FREIDUS, J. JOHNEN
T. FAIRBROTHER/N. BRYSON
INSERT: **LIZ LARNER**
JAMES LEWIS: **RICHARD PRINCE**
DAVID HICKEY: **THE INVISIBLE**
DRAGON/DER UNSICHTBARE
DRACHEN
P. TAYLOR: **JAMES ROSENQUIST**

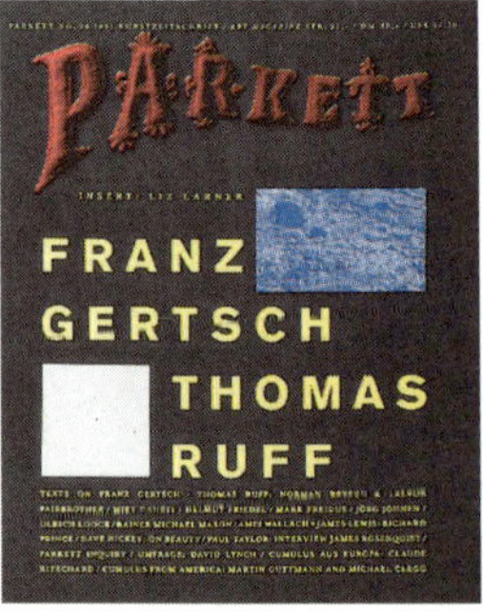

No. 28 - ISBN 3-907509-78-1

ALEX KATZ
JOHN RUSSELL, BROOKS ADAMS
DAVID RIMANELLI, FRANCESCO
CLEMENTE, MICHAEL KRÜGER
RICHARD FLOOD, PATRICK FREY
CARL STIGLIANO, BICE CURIGER
GLENN O'BRIEN
INSERT: **WILLIAM WEGMAN**
LISA LIEBMAN: **ROBERT GOBER**
JACQUELINE BURCKHARDT:
GIULIO ROMANO

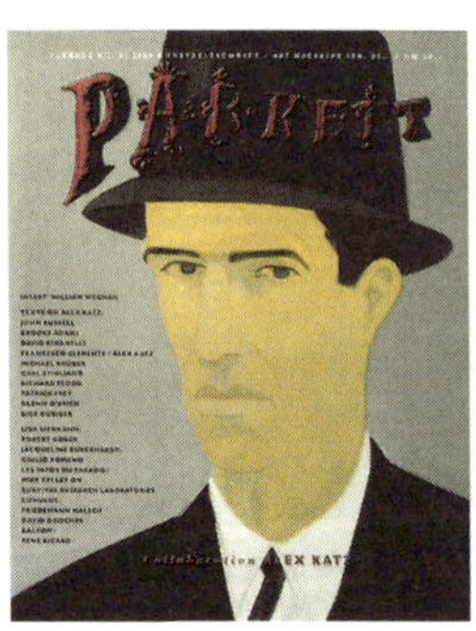

No. 21 - ISBN 3-907509-71-4

MARIO MERZ
MARLIS GRÜTERICH, JEANNE
SILVERTHORNE, DEMOSTHENES
DAVVETAS, HARALD SZEEMANN
DENYS ZACHAROPOULOS
INSERT: **GENERAL IDEA**
MAX KOZLOFF: **GILLES PERESS**
FRIEDEMANN MALSCH:
GEORG HEROLD
BRUNELLA ANTOMARINI:
FRANCESCA WOODMAN

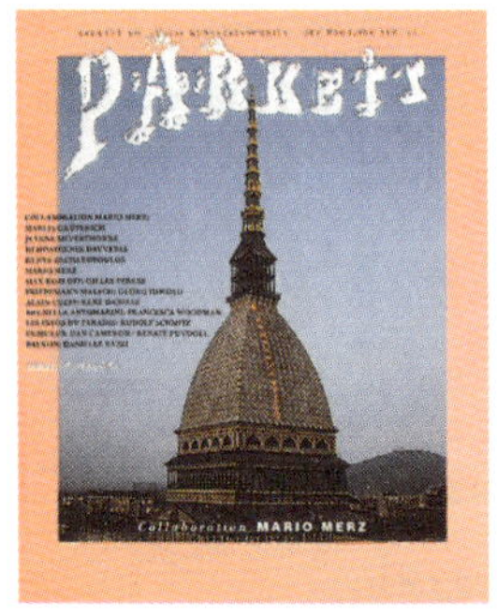

No. 15 - ISBN 3-907509-65-X

GILBERT & GEORGE
DUNCAN FALLOWELL
MARIO CODOGNATO
JEREMY COOPER
DEMOSTHENES DAVVETAS
WOLF JAHN
INSERT: **ROSEMARIE TROCKEL**
ROBERT STORR: **NANCY SPERO**
HAIM STEINBACH: **MANIFESTO**
JÖRG ZUTTER: **THOMAS HUBER**

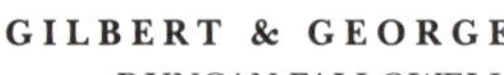

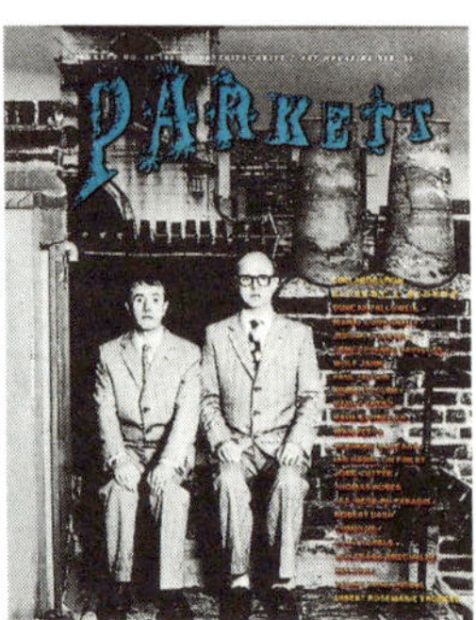

No. 14 - ISBN 3-907509-64-1

GEORG BASELITZ
REMO GUIDIERI
DIETER KOEPPLIN
ERIC DARRAGON
RAINER MICHAEL MASON
FRANZ MEYER, JOHN CALDWELL
INSERT: **BARBARA KRUGER**
GRAY WATSON: **DEREK JARMAN**
CAROL SQUIERS:
PHOTO OPPORTUNITY
ROSETTA BROOKS:
TROY BRAUNTUCH

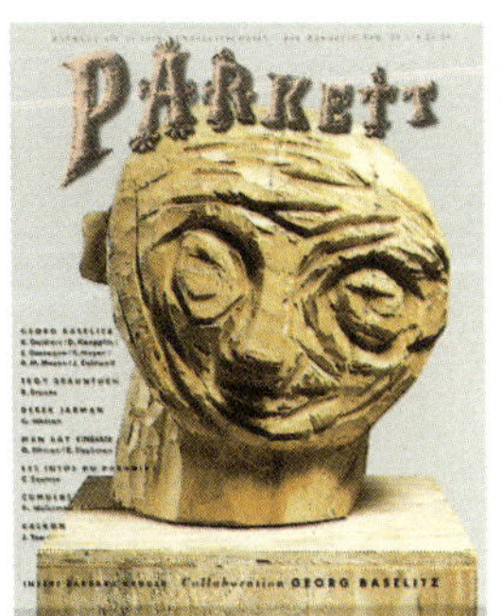

No. 11 - ISBN 3-907509-61-7

Each volume of PARKETT is created in collaboration with artists, who contribute an original work specially made for the readers of PARKETT. The works are available in a signed and numbered Special Edition. Prices are subject to change. Postage is not Included.

EDITIONS FOR PARKETT

Jeder PARKETT-Band entsteht in Collaboration mit Künstlern, die eigens für die Leser von PARKETT Originalbeiträge gestalten. Diese Vorzugsausgaben sind als nummerierte und signierte Editionen erhältlich. Preisänderungen vorbehalten. Versandkosten und MwSt. (Schweiz) nicht inbegriffen.

Büchergestell. Armierungsstahl, Plexiglas, vier Räder,
120 x 60 x 30 cm.
Auflage: 99, signiertes und nummeriertes Zertifikat.
CHF 4400 / € 2900

2 X 20 YEARS OF PARKETT, 2004
Bookshelf. Reinforcing steel, Plexiglas, four wheels,
47 ¼ x 23 ⅝ x 11 ¹³/₁₆".
Edition of 99, signed and numbered certificate.
$ 3500 / € 2900

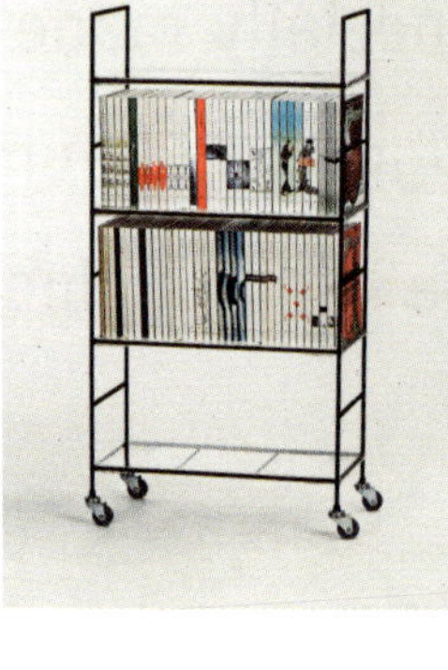

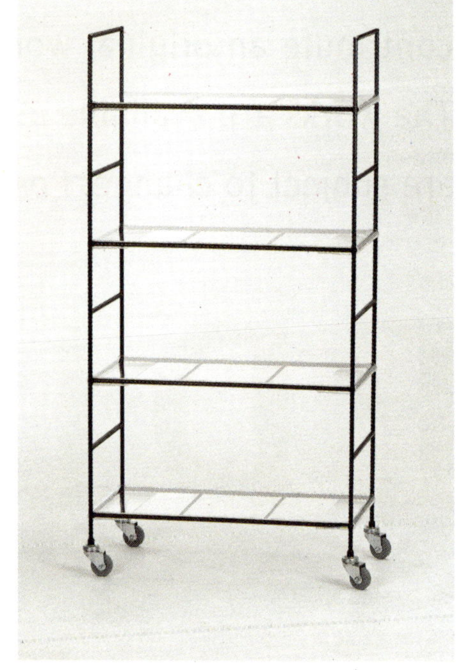

THIS WHEELED COMPANION TO THE GLOBETROTTER'S
"POUCH FOR PARKETT" (1993) WILL HOUSE ALL THE
VOLUMES OF PARKETT THROUGH 2024.

NACH DEM SACKERL FÜR UNTERWEGS FOLGT DIE
BEWEGLICHE «LIBRAIRIE EN APPARTEMENT» MIT
PLATZ FÜR ALLE PARKETTBÄNDE BIS 2024.

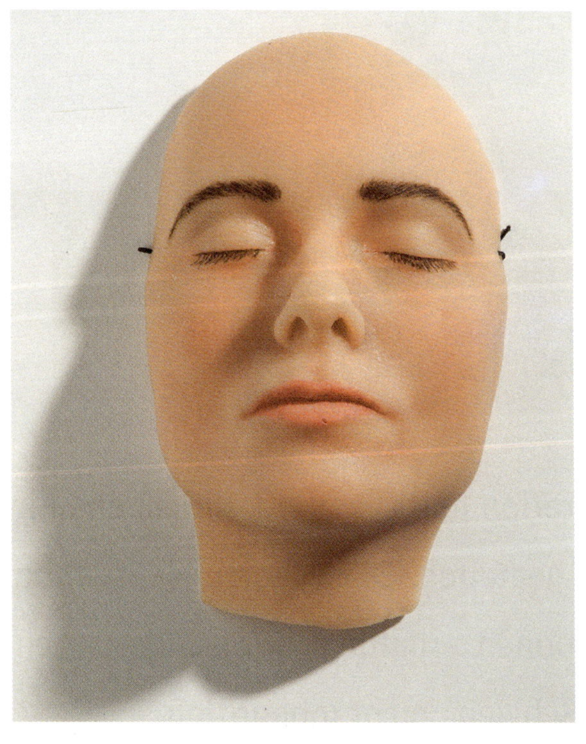

PARKETT 70
GILLIAN WEARING
SLEEPING MASK, 2004
Wax (reinforced by polymer resin), paint, 8 ¼ x 5 ⁵/₁₆".
Produced by Making Objects Ltd., London.
Edition of 60, signed and numbered.
$ 1600 / € 1350

SCHLAFENDE MASKE, 2004
Wachs (verstärkt mit Polymerharz), Farbe, 21 x 13,5 cm.
Produktion: Making Objects Ltd., London.
Auflage: 60, signiert und nummeriert.
CHF 2100 / € 1350

INVERTING THE COTHURNUS, FROM FOOT TO FACE, FROM
SOUND TO SILENCE, FROM THE SWAGGER OF CONCEIT TO
THE TRUTHFULNESS OF DISGUISE.

UNDURCHDRINGLICHE OFFENBARUNG: DIE MASKE VERWEI-
GERT DEN BLICK UND VERWEIST IN DIE TRANSZENDENZ.

PARKETT 70
CHRISTIAN MARCLAY
MY BAD EAR, 2004

Life-size bronze cast
by Modern Art Foundry, Astoria, NY.
Edition of 60, signed and numbered.
$ 1100 / € 900

MEIN SCHLECHTES OHR, 2004

Bronze, Abguss im Massstab 1:1.
Guss: Modern Art Foundry, Astoria, NY.
Auflage: 60, signiert und nummeriert.
CHF 1400 / € 900

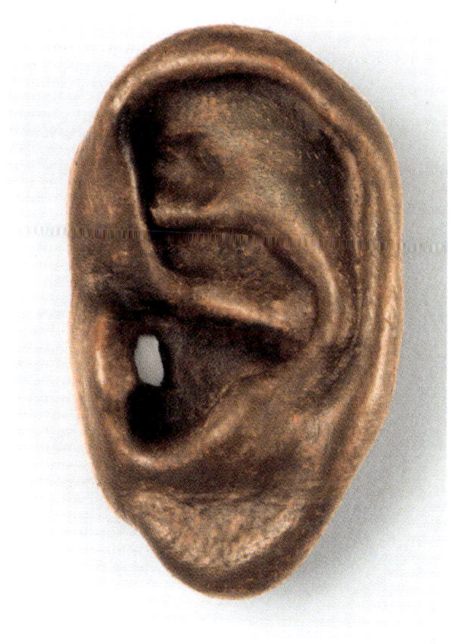

PARKETT 70
WILHELM SASNAL
CONCORDE IS DEAD, 2004

Color contact print from engraved negative
on Kodak paper, 12 5/8 x 18 7/8".
Edition of 60, signed and numbered.
$ 950 / € 800

Farbphotographie mit (auf dem Negativ)
eingravierter Schrift,
Kontaktabzug auf Kodakpapier, 32 x 48 cm.
Auflage: 60, signiert und nummeriert.
CHF 1200 / € 800

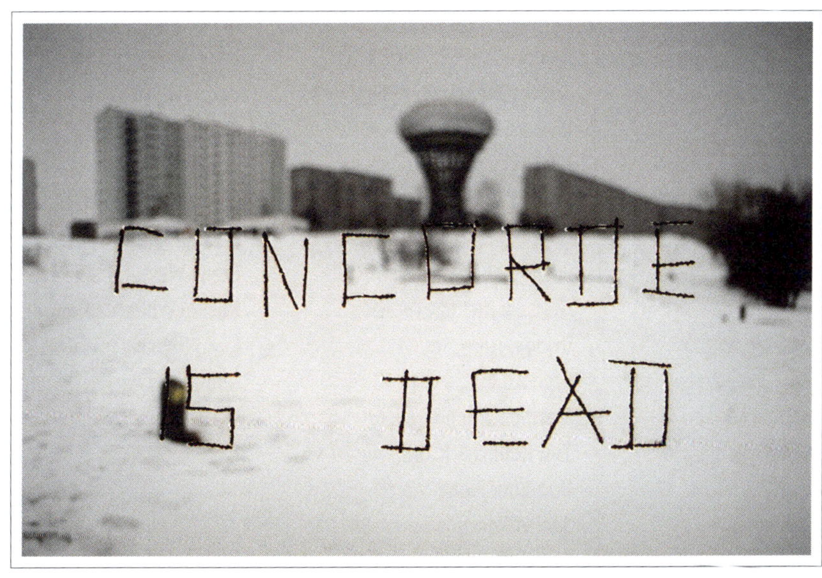

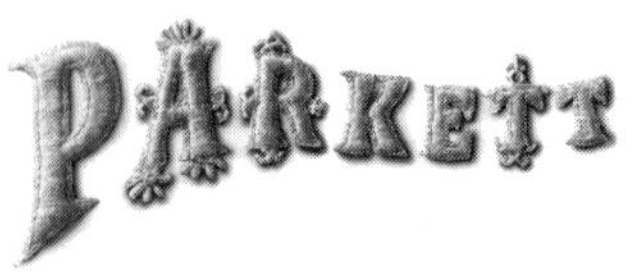

ARTISTS' MONOGRAPHS & EDITIONS / KÜNSTLERMONOGRAPHIEN & EDITIONEN

FOR AVAILABILITY SEE NEXT PAGE / LIEFERBARKEIT SIEHE FOLGENDE SEITE

Franz Ackermann, vol. 68
Eija-Liisa Ahtila, vol. 68
Doug Aitken, vol. 57
Francis Alÿs, vol. 69
Laurie Anderson, vol. 49
John Armleder, vol. 50/51
Richard Artschwager, vol. 23, vol. 46
John Baldessari, vol. 29
Stephan Balkenhol, vol. 36
Matthew Barney, vol. 45
Georg Baselitz, vol. 11
Vanessa Beecroft, vol. 56
Ross Bleckner, vol. 38
John Bock, vol. 67
Alighiero e Boetti, vol. 24
Christian Boltanski, vol. 22
Louise Bourgeois, vol. 27
Olaf Breuning, vol. 71
Angela Bulloch, vol. 66
Daniel Buren, vol. 66
Sophie Calle, vol. 36
Maurizio Cattelan, vol. 59
Vija Celmins, vol. 44
Francesco Clemente, vol. 9 & 40/41
Chuck Close, vol. 60
Enzo Cucchi, vol. 1
John Currin, vol. 65
Tacita Dean, vol. 62
Thomas Demand, vol. 62
Martin Disler, vol. 3
Peter Doig, vol. 67
Marlene Dumas, vol. 38
Olafur Eliasson, vol. 64
Tracey Emin, vol. 63
Eric Fischl, vol. 5
Peter Fischli /

David Weiss, vol. 17, 40/41
Sylvie Fleury, vol. 58
Günther Förg, vol. 26 & 40/41
Tom Friedman, vol. 64
Katharina Fritsch, vol. 25
Liam Gillick, vol. 61
Isa Genzken, vol. 69
Franz Gertsch, vol. 28
Gilbert & George, vol. 14
Robert Gober, vol. 27
Nan Goldin, vol. 57
Felix Gonzalez-Torres, vol. 39
Douglas Gordon, vol. 49
Dan Graham, vol. 68
Rodney Graham, vol. 64
Andreas Gursky, vol. 44
David Hammons, vol. 31
Thomas Hirschhorn, vol. 57
Damien Hirst, vol. 40/41
Jenny Holzer, vol. 40/41
Rebecca Horn, vol. 13 & 40/41
Roni Horn, vol. 54
Pierre Huyghe, vol. 66
Gary Hume, vol. 48
Ilya Kabakov, vol. 34
Anish Kapoor, vol. 69
Alex Katz, vol. 21, 72
Mike Kelley, vol. 31
Ellsworth Kelly, vol. 56
William Kentridge, vol. 63
Karen Kilimnik, vol. 52
Martin Kippenberger, vol. 19
Imi Knoebel, vol. 32
Jeff Koons, vol. 19, 50/51
Jannis Kounellis, vol. 6
Yayoi Kusama, vol. 59

Wolfgang Laib, vol. 39
Sherrie Levine, vol. 32
Sarah Lucas, vol. 45
Christian Marclay, vol. 70
Brice Marden, vol. 7
Mario Merz, vol. 15
Tracey Moffatt, vol. 53
Mariko Mori, vol. 54
Malcolm Morley, vol. 52
Sarah Morris, vol. 61
Juan Muñoz, vol. 43
Jean-Luc Mylayne, vol. 50/51
Bruce Nauman, vol. 10
Cady Noland, vol. 46
Meret Oppenheim, vol. 4
Gabriel Orozco, vol. 48
Tony Oursler, vol. 47
Laura Owens, vol. 65
Jorge Pardo, vol. 56
Raymond Pettibon, vol. 47
Elizabeth Peyton, vol. 53
Richard Phillips, vol. 71
Sigmar Polke, vol. 2, 30 & 40/41
Richard Prince, vol. 34
Michael Raedecker, vol. 65
Markus Raetz, vol. 8
Charles Ray, vol. 37
Jason Rhoades, vol. 58
Gerhard Richter, vol. 35
Bridget Riley, vol. 61
Pipilotti Rist, vol. 48, 71
Matthew Ritchie, vol. 61
Tim Rollins & K.O.S., vol. 20
Ugo Rondinone, vol. 52
James Rosenquist, vol. 58
Susan Rothenberg, vol. 43

Thomas Ruff, vol. 28
Edward Ruscha, vol. 18 & 55
Gregor Schneider, vol. 63
Wilhelm Sasnal, vol. 70
Thomas Schütte, vol. 47
Cindy Sherman, vol. 29
Roman Signer, vol. 45
Andreas Slominski, vol. 55
Beat Streuli, vol. 54
Thomas Struth, vol. 50/51
Hiroshi Sugimoto, vol. 46
Philip Taaffe, vol. 26
Sam Taylor-Wood, vol. 55
Diana Thater, vol. 60
Wolfgang Tillmans, vol. 53
Rirkrit Tiravanija, vol. 44
Fred Tomaselli, vol. 67
Rosemarie Trockel, vol. 33
James Turrell, vol. 25
Luc Tuymans, vol. 60
Keith Tyson, vol. 71
Kara Walker, vol. 59
Jeff Wall, vol. 22 & 49
Andy Warhol, vol. 12
Gillian Wearing, vol. 70
Lawrence Weiner, vol. 42
John Wesley, vol. 62
Franz West, vol. 37, 70
Rachel Whiteread, vol. 42
Sue Williams, vol 50/51
Robert Wilson, vol. 16
Christopher Wool, vol. 33

vol.	Collaboration			vol.	Collaboration			vol.	Collaboration		
71	Olaf Breuning	m	e	55	Andreas Slominski	m		37	Franz West	m	e
	Richard Phillips	m	e		Sam Taylor-Wood	m		36	Stephan Balkenhol		
	Keith Tyson	m	e	54	Roni Horn	m	e		Sophie Calle		
70	Christian Marclay	m	e		Mariko Mori	m		35	Gerhard Richter		
	Wilhelm Sasnal	m	e		Beat Streuli	m		34	Ilya Kabakov	m	
	Gillian Wearing	m	e	53	Tracey Moffatt	m			Richard Prince	m	
69	Francis Alÿs	m			Elizabeth Peyton	m		33	Rosemarie Trockel	m	
	Isa Gentzken	m	e		Wolfgang Tillmans	m			Christopher Wool	m	
	Anish Kapoor	m		52	Karen Kilimnik	m	e	32	Imi Knoebel	m	
68	Franz Ackermann	m	e		Malcolm Morley	m	e		Sherrie Levine	m	
	Eija-Liisa Ahtila	m	e		Ugo Rondinone	m	e	31	David Hammons		
	Dan Graham	m	e	50/51	John Armleder	m		31	Mike Kelley		
67	John Bock	m	e		Jeff Koons	m	e	30	Sigmar Polke		
	Peter Doig	m	e		Jean-Luc Mylayne	m		29	John Baldessari		
	Fred Tomaselli	m	e		Thomas Struth	m		29	Cindy Sherman		
66	Angela Bulloch	m	e		Sue Williams	m		28	Franz Gertsch	m	
	Daniel Buren	m	e	49	Laurie Anderson	m	e		Thomas Ruff	m	
	Pierre Huyghe	m	e		Douglas Gordon	m		27	Louise Bourgeois		
65	John Currin	m			Jeff Wall	m			Robert Gober		
	Laura Owens	m	e	48	Gary Hume	m		26	Günther Förg		
	Michael Raedecker	m	e		Gabriel Orozco	m			Philip Taaffe		
64	Olafur Eliasson	m			Pipilotti Rist	m		25	Katharina Fritsch		e
	Tom Friedman	m		47	Tony Oursler	m			James Turrell		e
	Rodney Graham	m			Raymond Pettibon	m		24	Alighiero e Boetti	m	
63	Tracey Emin	m	e		Thomas Schütte	m	e	23	Richard Artschwager	m	
	William Kentridge	m		46	Richard Artschwager	m		22	Christian Boltanski		
	Gregor Schneider	m			Cady Noland	m			Jeff Wall		
62	Tacita Dean	m	e		Hiroshi Sugimoto	m		21	Alex Katz	m	
	Thomas Demand	m		45	Matthew Barney	m		20	Tim Rollins + K.O.S.	m	
	John Wesley	m	e		Sarah Lucas	m		19	Martin Kippenberger		
61	Liam Gillick	m			Roman Signer		e		Jeff Koons		
	Sarah Morris	m	e	44	Vija Celmins	m		18	Ed Ruscha	m	
	Bridget Riley	m			Andreas Gursky	m		17	Fischli/Weiss		
	Matthew Ritchie	m	e		Rirkrit Tiravanija	m	e	16	Robert Wilson		
60	Chuck Close	m		43	Juan Muñoz	m		15	Mario Merz	m	
	Diana Thater	m	e		Susan Rothenberg	m		14	Gilbert & George	m	
	Luc Tuymans	m	e	42	Lawrence Weiner	m	e	13	Rebecca Horn		
59	Maurizio Cattelan	m			Rachel Whiteread	m		12	Andy Warhol		
	Yayoi Kusama	m	e	40/41	Francesco Clemente	m		11	Georg Baselitz	m	
	Kara Walker	m			Fischli/Weiss	m		10	Bruce Nauman		
58	Sylvie Fleury	m			Günther Förg	m		9	Francesco Clemente		
	Jason Rhoades	m			Damien Hirst	m		8	Markus Raetz		
	James Rosenquist	m			Jenny Holzer	m		7	Brice Marden		
57	Doug Aitken	m	e		Rebecca Horn	m		6	Jannis Kounellis		
	Nan Goldin	m			Sigmar Polke	m		5	Eric Fischl		
	Thomas Hirschhorn	m		39	Felix Gonzalez-Torres	m		4	Meret Oppenheim		
56	Vanessa Beecroft	m			Wolfgang Laib	m		3	Martin Disler		
	Ellsworth Kelly	m		38	Ross Bleckner			2	Sigmar Polke		
	Jorge Pardo	m	e		Marlene Dumas			1	Enzo Cucchi		
55	Edward Ruscha	m		37	Charles Ray	m					

m = available monograph / erhältliche Monographie, e = available edition / erhältliche Edition
Delivery subject to availability at time of order / Lieferung solange Vorrat

PARKETT IN BOOKSHOPS (Selection)

PARKETT IS AVAILABLE IN 500 LEADING ART BOOKSHOPS AROUND THE WORLD. FOR FURTHER INFORMATION CONTACT:
PARKETT GIBT ES IN 500 FÜHRENDEN KUNSTBUCHHANDLUNGEN AUF DER GANZEN WELT. FÜR WEITERE INFORMATIONEN WENDEN SIE SICH BITTE AN:
PARKETT VERLAG, QUELLENSTRASSE 27, CH-8031 ZÜRICH, TEL. +41-1 271 81 40, FAX 272 43 01, WWW.PARKETTART.COM;
PARKETT, 155, AVENUE OF THE AMERICAS, 2ND FLOOR, NEW YORK, N.Y. 10013, PHONE +1 (212) 673-2660, FAX 271-0704, WWW.PARKETTART.COM

NORTH & SOUTH AMERICA, ASIA, AUSTRALIA

DISTRIBUTOR / VERTRIEB
D.A.P. (DISTRIBUTED ART PUBLISHERS)
155 AVENUE OF THE AMERICAS, 2ND FLOOR,
NEW YORK, NY 10013

USA

AUSTIN, TX
BOOK PEOPLE
603 N. LAMAR

BERKELEY, CA
BERKELEY ART MUSEUM
2625 DURANT AVENUE
CODY'S BOOKS
2454 TELEGRAPHE AVENUE

BEVERLY HILLS, CA
RIZZOLI
9501 WILSHIRE BOULEVARD

BOSTON, MA
INSTITUTE OF CONTEMPORARY ART
955 BOYLSTON STREET
TRIDENT BOOKSELLERS
338 NEWBURY STREET

BUFFALO, NY
TALKING LEAVES
3158 MAIN STREET

CAMBRIDGE, MA
MIT PRESS BOOKSTORE
292 MAIN STREET

CHICAGO, IL
ART INSTITUTE OF CHICAGO
104 S. MICHIGAN
MUSEUM OF CONTEMPORARY ART
220 EAST CHICAGO AVENUE
QUIMBY'S
1854 W. NORTH AVENUE
SMART MUSEUM OF ART
5550 S. GREENWOOD AVENUE

CINCINNATI, OH
CONTEMPORARY ARTS CENTER
115 E. 5TH STREET

COLUMBUS, OH
COLUMBUS MUSEUM OF ART
372 COMMONS MALL
WEXNER CENTER BOOKSTORE
30 W. 15TH STREET

CORAL GABLES, FL
BOOKS & BOOKS
296 ARAGON ROAD

HOUSTON, TX
BRAZOS BOOKSTORE
2421 BISSONNET
CONTEMPORARY ARTS MUSEUM
5216 MONTROSE BOULEVARD
MENIL COLLECTION
1520 SUL ROSS

HUNTINGTON, WV
HUNTINGTON MUSEUM OF ART
2033 MCCOY ROAD

LOS ANGELES, CA
BOOKSOUP
8818 SUNSET BOULEVARD
MUSEUM OF CONTEMPORARY ART
250, S. GRAND
UCLA / ARMAND HAMMER MUSEUM OF ART
10899 WILSHIRE BOULEVARD

MIAMI, FL
BOOKS & BOOKS
296 ARAGON AVENUE, CORAL GABLES
MUSEUM OF CONTEMPORARY ART
770 N.E. 125TH STREET NORTH MIAMI

MINNEAPOLIS, MN
THE WALKER ART CENTER BOOKSTORE
VINELAND PLACE

NEW YORK, NY
GUGGENHEIM DOWNTOWN MUSEUM
575 BROADWAY
MUSEUM OF MODERN ART
11 W. 53RD STREET
NEW MUSEUM OF CONTEMPORARY ART
583 BROADWAY
RIZZOLI
454 WEST BROADWAY
SAINT MARK'S BOOKSTORE
31 3RD AVENUE

OAKLAND, CA
DIESEL, A BOOKSTORE
5433 COLLEGE AVENUE

OAK PARK, MI
BOOK BEAT LTD.
26010 GREENFIELD

OMAHA, NE
JOSLYN ART MUSEUM
2200 DODGE STREET

PHILADELPHIA, PA
AVRIL 50
3406 SANSOM STREET
WATERSTONE BOOKSELLERS
2191 HORNIG ROAD

PITTSBURGH, PA
CARNEGIE INSTITUTE
4400 FORBES AVENUE

PORTLAND, OR
POWELL'S BOOKS
7 NW 9TH STREET

PROVIDENCE, NY
ACCIDENT OR DESIGN
128 N. MAIN STREET
RHODE ISLAND SCHOOL OF DESIGN
2 COLLEGE STREET, 1765

SAN ANTONIO, TX
SLOAN / HALL SAN ANTONIO
5930 BROADWAY

SAN FRANCISCO, CA
A CLEAN WELL LIGHTED PLACE
601 VAN NESS AVENUE
CITY LIGHTS BOOKSHOP
261 COLUMBUS AVENUE
SAN FRANCISCO MUSEUM OF MODERN ART,
MUSEUMBOOKS
151 3RD STREET, 1ST FLOOR

ST. LOUIS, MO
LEFT BANK BOOKS
399 NORTH EUCLID

SANTA MONICA, CA
ARCANA
1229 3RD STREET PROMENADE
HENNESSEY & INGALLS BOOKS
1254 3RD STREET PROMENADE

ST. PAUL, MN
HUNGRY MIND BOOKSTORE
1648 GRAND AVENUE

SEATTLE, WA
UNIVERSITY BOOKSTORE
4326 UNIVERSITY WAY

WASHINGTON D.C.
NATIONAL GALLERY OF ART
6TH STREET & CONSTITUTION AVENUE, NW

CANADA / KANADA

CALGARY
TREPANIER BAER GALLERY
105 999 8TH STREET SW

MONTREAL
ARTEXTE
3575 STREET LAURENT
OLIVIERI LIBRAIRIE BOOKSTORE
185 STREET CATHERINE WEST

TORONTO
ART GALLERY OF ONTARIO
317 DUNDAS STREET WEST
ART METROPOLE
788 KING STREET WEST
DAVID MIRVISH BOOKS ON ART
596 MARKHAM STREET

VANCOUVER
VANCOUVER ART GALLERY
750 HORNBY STREET

AUSTRALIA / AUSTRALIEN

DARLINGHURST
EAST SYDNEY BOOKSTORE
THE DOME, THE ELAN BUILDING
1 KINGS CROSS ROAD

SYDNEY
MUSEUM OF CONTEMPORARY ART
140 GEORGE STREET, CIRCULAR QUAY NORTH
GLEE BOOKS
191 GLEBE POINT ROAD, GLEBE

NEW ZEALAND / NEUSEELAND

AUCKLAND
PROPAGANDA
2 CARR ROAD, MT ROSKILL

ASIA / ASIEN

JAPAN

TOKYO
AOYAMA BOOK CENTRE, SHIBUYA-KU
COSMOS AOYAMA GARDEN FLOOR B2F
5-53-97, JINGUMAE
ART & BOOKS
2-1-13-307
TAKANAWA, MINATO-KU
WATARI MUSEUM OF CONTEMPORARY ART,
ON SUNDAYS BOOKSHOP
376 JINGUMAE SHIBUYA-KU

SINGAPORE / SINGAPUR
PAGE ONE BOOKSTORE
20 KAKI BUKIT VIEW TECHPARK

GREAT BRITAIN / GROSSBRITANNIEN

DISTRIBUTOR / VERTRIEB
CENTRAL BOOKS
99, WALLIS ROAD
LONDON E9 5LN

BRISTOL
ARNOLFINI BOOKSHOP
16 NARROW QUAY

LONDON
BORDERS BOOKSHOP
120 CHARING CROSS ROAD

BORDERS BOOKSHOP
203–207 OXFORD STREET
CAMDEN ARTS CENTRE
ARKWRIGHT ROAD
HAYWARD GALLERY
SOUTH BANK
IAN SHIPLEY BOOKSHOP
70 CHARING CROSS ROAD
INSTITUTE OF CONTEMPORARY ARTS
12 CARLTON HOUSE TERRACE
THE MALL
SERPENTINE GALLERY
KENSINGTON GARDENS
TATE MODERN
BANKSIDE
ZWEMMER LTD. ART BOOKS
24 LITCHFIELD STREET

IRELAND / IRLAND
DUBLIN
DOUGLAS HYDE GALLERY
TRINITY COLLEGE

GERMANY / DEUTSCHLAND
DISTRIBUTOR / VERTRIEB
GVA VERLAGSSERVICE GÖTTINGEN
PF 2021
D-37010 GÖTTINGEN
BERLIN
BÜCHERBOGEN AM SAVIGNYPLATZ
STADTBAHNBOGEN 593
GALERIE 2000 KUNSTBUCHHANDLUNG
KNESEBECKSTRASSE 56/58
WALTHER KÖNIG BUCHHANDLUNG, MUSEUM FÜR
GEGENWARTSKUNST
IM HAMBURGER BAHNHOF INVALIDENSTRASSE 50–51
WIENS LADEN & VERLAG
LINIENSTRASSE 158 (HOF)
WASMUTH GMBH & CO.
PFALZBURGERSTRASSE 43–44
BREMEN
BEIM STEINERNEN KREUZ GMBH
BEIM STEINERNEN KREUZ 1
DÜSSELDORF
LITERATUR BEI RUDOLF MÜLLER
NEUSTRASSE 38
WALTHER KÖNIG BUCHHANDLUNG
HEINRICH-HEINE-ALLEE 15
FRANKFURT
KUNST-BUCH, KUNSTHALLE SCHIRN
RÖMERBERG 7
WALTHER KÖNIG BUCHHANDLUNG
DOMSTRASSE 6
HAMBURG
HELMUT VON DER HÖH BUCHHANDLUNG
GROSSE BLEICHEN 21
SAUTTER + LACKMANN BUCHHANDLUNG
ADMIRALITÄTSTRASSE 71/72
HANNOVER
MERZ KUNSTBUCHHANDLUNG
KURT-SCHWITTERS-PLATZ
KARLSRUHE
HANS MENDE BUCHHANDLUNG
KARLSTRASSE 76
KÖLN
SCHADEN.COM BUCHHANDEL
BURGMAUER 10
WALTHER KÖNIG BUCHHANDLUNG
EHRENSTRASSE 4
KIOSK-BUCH-EVENT GMBH
IM MEDIAPARK 7
MÜNCHEN
HANS GOLTZ BUCHHANDLUNG
FÜR BILDENDE KUNST
TÜRKENSTRASSE 54
ILKA KÖNIG BUCHHANDLUNG
MAXIMILIANSTRASSE 35

L. WERNER BUCHHANDLUNG
RESIDENZSTRASSE 18
NÜRNBERG
WALTHER KÖNIG BUCHHANDLUNG
LUITPOLDSTRASSE 5
STUTTGART
LIMACHER BUCHHANDLUNG
KÖNIGSTRASSE 28 / KÖNIGSBAU

SPAIN / SPANIEN
BARCELONA
LAIE – CAIXAFÒRUM
MARQUES DE COMILLAS 6–8
LAIE – CCCB (CENTRE DE CULTURA
CONTEMPORÀNIA DE BARCELONA)
MONTALEGRE 5
MADRID
MUSEO NACIONAL REINA SOFIA
C/ SANTA ISABEL, 52

FRANCE / FRANKREICH
PARIS
CENTRE POMPIDOU, FLAMMARION 4
26, RUE JACOB
GALERIE NATIONALE DU JEU DE PAUME
1, PLACE DE LA CONCORDE
LIBRAIRIE DU MUSÉE D'ART MODERNE
9, RUE GASTON DE SAINT-PAUL
CHRISTOPH DAVIET-THERY,
LIVRES & ÉDITIONS D'ARTISTES
10, RUE DUCHEFDELAVILLE
COLETTE
213, RUE SAINT-HONORÉ

ITALY / ITALIEN
MILANO
A&M BOOKSTORE
30, VIA TADINO
ROMA
GALLERIA NAZIONALE D'ARTE MODERNA
131, VIA DELLE BELLE ARTI
GALLERIA PRIMO PIANO
203, VIA PANISPERNA

NORWAY / NORWEGEN
OSLO
THE NATIONAL MUSEUM OF CONTEMPORARY ART
BANKPLASSEN 4 / SKATTEFOG

PORTUGAL
LISBOA
MODULO CENTRO DIFUSOR DE ARTE
CALÇADA DOS MESTRES 34 A–B
PORTO
MODULO CENTRO DIFUSOR DE ARTE
AV. BOAVISTA 854

SWEDEN / SCHWEDEN
STOCKHOLM
KULTURHUSET KONSTIG
MEDIA & KONSTBOKHANDEL
SERGELS TORG 3
MODERNA MUSEET
SKEPPSHOLMEN
GÖTEBORG
GÖTEBORGS KONSTMUSEUM
GÖTAPLATSEN / AVENYN

TURKEY / TÜRKEI
ISTANBUL
ROBINSON CRUSOE BOOKS PUSULA PRODUCTIONS
389 ISTIKAL CADDESI BEYOGLU

**NETHERLANDS, BELGIUM
AND LUXEMBURG**
DISTRIBUTOR / VERTRIEB
IDEA BOOKS
NIEUWE HERENGRACHT 11
NL-1011 RK AMSTERDAM

NETHERLANDS / NIEDERLANDE
AMSTERDAM
ART BOOK
VAN BAERLESTRAAT 126
ATHENAEUM NIEUWSCENTRUM
SPUI 14–16
ROBERT PREMSELA BOOKSHOP
VAN BAERLESTRAAT 78
GRONINGEN
SCHOLTENS / WRISTERS BOOKSHOP
FULDENSTRAAT 20
ROTTERDAM
DONNER BOOKSHOP
LIJNBAAN 150

BELGIUM / BELGIEN
ANTWERPEN
F.N.A.C.
GROENPLAATS
BRUXELLES
TROPISMES LIBRAIRIES
GALERIE DES PRINCES 11
GENT
COPYRIGHT BOOKSHOP
JACOBIJNENSTRAAT 8

LUXEMBOURG / LUXEMBURG
LUXEMBOURG
CASINO LUXEMBOURG
41, RUE NOTRE-DAME

SWITZERLAND / SCHWEIZ
DISTRIBUTOR / VERTRIEB
SCHEIDEGGER & CO. C/O AVA
CENTRALWEG 16
CH-8910 AFFOLTERN A. A.
BASEL
FONDATION BEYELER
BASELSTRASSE 77, RIEHEN
GALERIE STAMPA
SPALENBERG 2
JÄGGI BUCHHANDLUNG
FREIE STRASSE 32
KUNSTHALLE BASEL
KLOSTERGASSE 5
BERN
STAUFFACHER BUCHHANDLUNG
IM KUNSTMUSEUM
HODLERSTR. 12
LUZERN
RÄBER BÜCHER AG
FRANKENSTRASSE 7-9
GENÈVE
LIBRAIRIE PAYOT
5, RUE DE CHANTEPOULET
MENDRISIO
GABRIELE CAPELLI LIBRERIA ARCHITETTURA
4, VIA NOBILI BOSIA
ST. GALLEN
RÖSSLITOR BÜCHER
WEBERGASSE 5
ZÜRICH
CALLIGRAMME BUCHHANDLUNG
HÄRINGSTRASSE 4
HOWEG BUCHHANDLUNG
WAFFENPLATZ 1
KUNSTGRIFF BUCHHANDLUNG
LIMMATSTRASSE 270
KUNSTHAUS ZÜRICH
HEIMPLATZ 1
KUNSTKIOSK
LIMMATQUAI 31
ORELL FÜSSLI KRAUTHAMMER
MARKTGASSE 12
ORELL FÜSSLI BUCHHANDLUNG
FÜSSLISTRASSE 4
SCALO BOOKS & LOOKS
WEINBERGSTRASSE 22 A
SEC 52 BUCHHANDLUNG
JOSEFSTRASSE 52

E X H I B I T I O N S

ZÜRICH

ARS FUTURA	Bleicherweg 45	DANIELE BUETTI	18.5.–17.7.2004
GALERIE AG	8002 Zürich	ART 35 BASEL	16.6.–21.6.2004
	Tel. 01 201 88 10	ALEXANDRA VOGT	26.8.–16.10.2004
	www.arsfutura.com	CHIARA DYNYS	28.10.–23.12.2004
	info@arsfutura.com	OLAF BREUNING	6.1.–5.3.2005
ELISABETH	Müllerstrasse 57	Italian Studies / The Quest for Excitement	
KAUFMANN	8004 Zürich	SHAHRYAR NASHAT	8.5.–4.7.2004
	Tel./Fax 043 322 01 15	SEASON OPENING:	
	elkauf@yahoo.com	MARTIN DISLER	ab 25.8.2004
GALERIE LELONG	Predigerplatz 10–12	EDUARDO CHILLIDA	**Juni–Juli 2004**
	8001 Zürich	ART 35 BASEL, Hall 2.0 Stand S 3	**16.6.–21.6.2004**
	Tel. 01 251 11 20	URSULA VON RYDINGSVARD	**September–Oktober 2004**
	www.galerie-lelong.com		
	galerie.lelong@dplanet.ch		
MAI 36 GALERIE	Rämistrasse 37	RITA MC BRIDE	30.4.–5.6.2004
	8001 Zürich	FILIPA CÉSAR. CRISTINA IGLESIAS.	
	Tel. 01 261 68 80	ON KAWARA. MATT MULLICAN.	
	www.artgalleries.ch/mai36	PEDRO CABRITA REIS. THOMAS RUFF.	
	mai36@artgalleries.ch	HIROSHI SUGIMOTO.	11.6.–24.7.2004
		ART 35 BASEL	16.6.–21.6.2004
MARK MÜLLER	Gessnerallee 36	ReConstructing Painting	
	8001 Zürich	(Gruppenausstellung)	12.6.–24.7.2004
	Tel. 01 211 81 55	ART 35 BASEL – KünstlerInnen der Galerie	
	www.markmueller.ch	ART Unlimited – FRANCIS BAUDEVIN	16.6.–21.6.2004
	mark.mueller@dplanet.ch		
SEMINA RERUM	Cäcilienstrasse 3	DAGMAR VARADY / RENÉE CHABOT	27.5.–9.7.2004
IRÈNE PREISWERK	8032 Zürich	MICHEL GRILLET	26.8.–16.10.2004
	Tel. 01 251 26 39	ERIK STEFFENSEN /	
	www.seminarerum.ch	DAVID SCHLATTER	22.10.–4.12.2004
	ipreiswerk@bluewin.ch		
GALERIE PROARTA	Bleicherweg 20	SAM FRANCIS (1923–1994)	
	8002 Zürich	Paintings from 50's and 60's	18.5.–10.7.2004
	Tel. 01 202 02 02	SUSI KRAMER	26.8.–25.9.2004
	www.proarta.ch		
	proarta@proarta.ch		

E X H I B I T I O N S

BOB VAN ORSOUW	Limmatstrasse 270 Tel. 01 273 11 00 www.bobvanorsouw.ch mail@bobvanorsouw.ch	ANTON HENNING eleven almost impeccable paintings ART 35 BASEL OLAV CHRISTOPHER JENSSEN New Paintings	 22.5.–24.7.2004 16.6.–21.6.2004 28.8.–2.10.2004
ANNEMARIE VERNA	Neptunstrasse 45 8032 Zürich Tel. 01 262 38 20 www.annemarie-verna.ch office@annemarie-verna.ch	JERRY ZENIUK Recent Paintings DONALD JUDD	 25.5.–10.7.2004 21.9.–6.11.2004
JAMILEH WEBER	Waldmannstrasse 6 8001 Zürich Tel. 01 252 10 66 www.jamilehweber.com info@jamilehweber.com	FRANK STELLA Moby Dick – Waves – Imaginary Places ART 35 BASEL, Halle 2.0 Stand F2 MICHAEL BIBERSTEIN, Paintings	 7.5.–3.7.2004 16.6.–21.6.2004 26.8.–9.10.2004
BRIGITTE WEISS	Müllerstrasse 67 8004 Zürich Tel. 01 241 83 35 www.likeyou.com/brigitteweiss brigitteweiss@bluewin.ch	CHRISTIAN VETTER SHAAN SYED	7.5.–10.7.2004 25.8.–9.10.2004

BASEL

NICOLAS KRUPP	Erlenstrasse 15 4058 Basel Tel. 061 683 32 65 www.nicolaskrupp.com nic@nicolaskrupp.com	ANGELA DE LA CRUZ Liste 04 Summer Group Show DANIEL HUNZIKER	29.4.–26.6.2004 15.6.–20.6.2004 1.7.–21.8.2004 27.8.–16.10.2004

ST. GALLEN

WILMA LOCK	Schmiedgasse 15 9000 St. Gallen Tel. 071 222 62 52 wilmalock@freesurf.ch	BERNARD FRIZE Nouvelles Peintures Sommerpause nach Vereinbarung geöffnet	 19.5.–17.7.2004 bis 7.9.2004

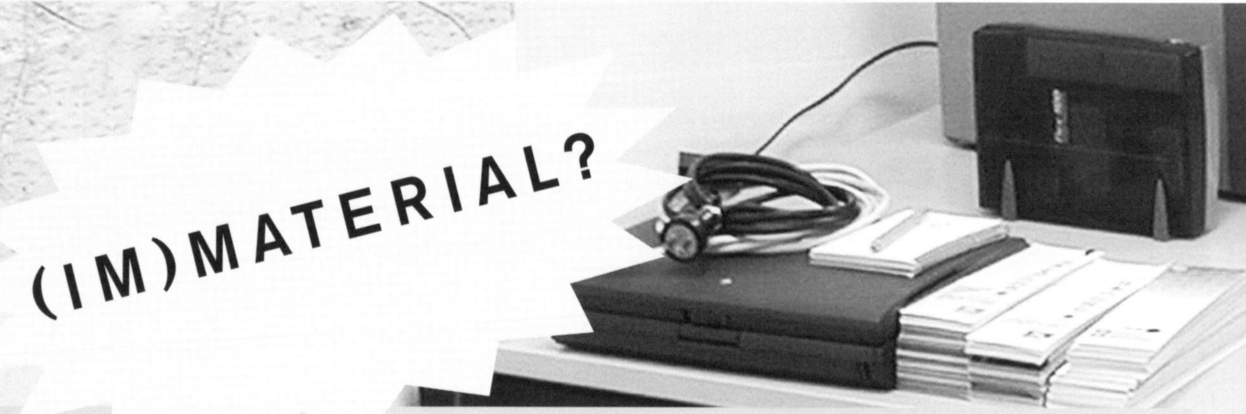

A SERIES OF THREE ESSAYS ON THE WHYS AND WHEREFORES OF MATERIALS IN CONTEMPORARY ART

BY

JOHANNA BURTON	NO. 70
NICOLAS BOURRIAUD	NO. 71
BORIS GROYS	NO. 72

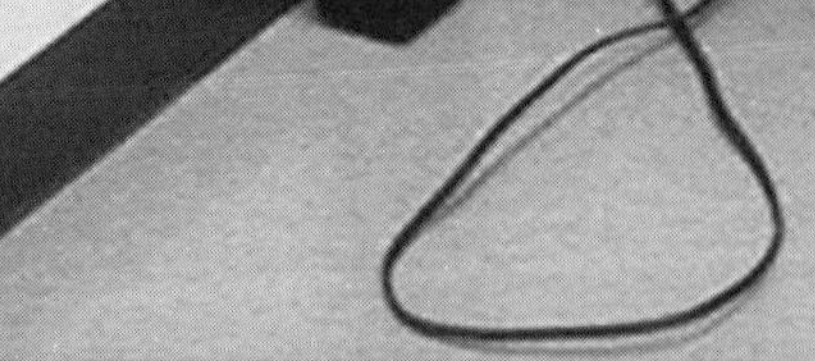

You are welcome to join us at the following events and exhibitions: >>>>>>>>>>>>

ART BASEL, JUNE 15 – 21, 2004 >>>>>>>>>>>>>>>>>

>>>>>>>>>>>>>>>> **LONDON, FRIEZE ART FAIR, October 14 – 18, 2004** >>>>>

ART BASEL MIAMI BEACH, December 2 – 5, 2004 >>>>>>>>>>>>>>>>>

FOR DETAILS AND UPDATES, SEE >>>>>>>>>>

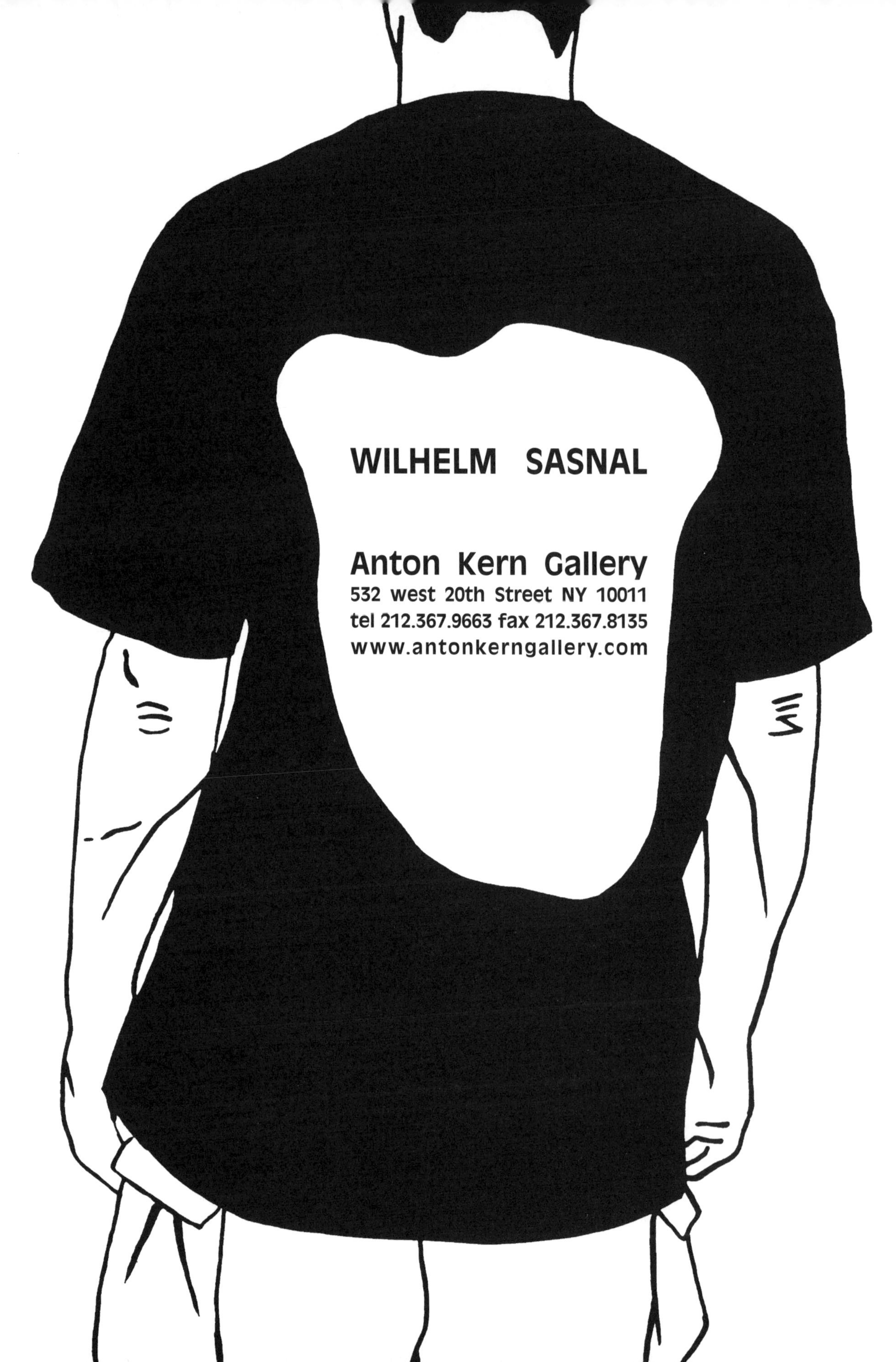

WILHELM   SASNAL

Anton Kern Gallery
532 west 20th Street NY 10011
tel 212.367.9663 fax 212.367.8135
www.antonkerngallery.com

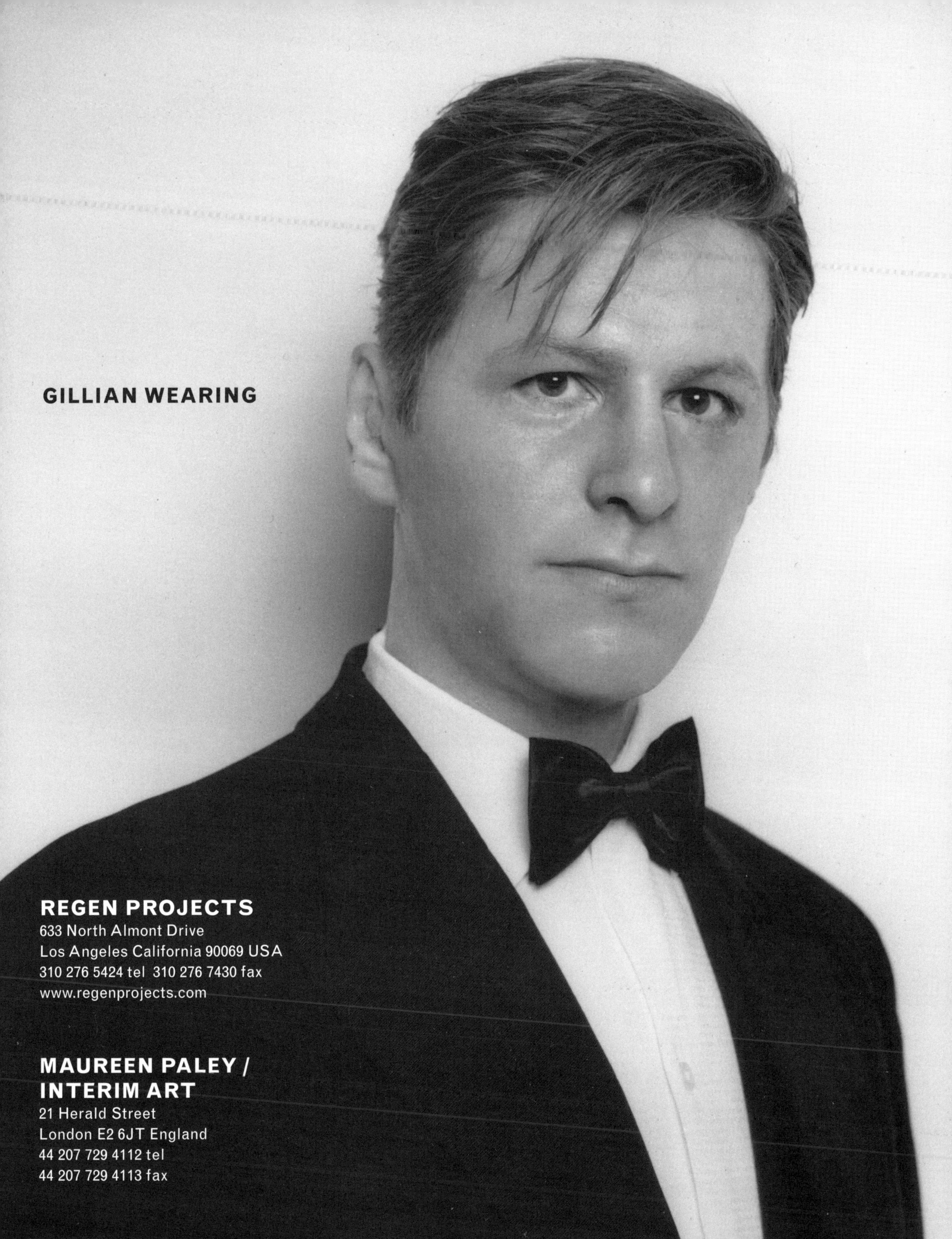

GILLIAN WEARING

REGEN PROJECTS
633 North Almont Drive
Los Angeles California 90069 USA
310 276 5424 tel 310 276 7430 fax
www.regenprojects.com

MAUREEN PALEY /
INTERIM ART
21 Herald Street
London E2 6JT England
44 207 729 4112 tel
44 207 729 4113 fax

REBECCA WARREN

Maureen Paley Interim Art, London. + 44 20 7729 4112
Donald Young Gallery, Chicago. + 1 312 455 0100
Matthew Marks Gallery, New York. + 1 212 243 0200
Galerie Daniel Buchholz, Köln. + 49 221 257 4946

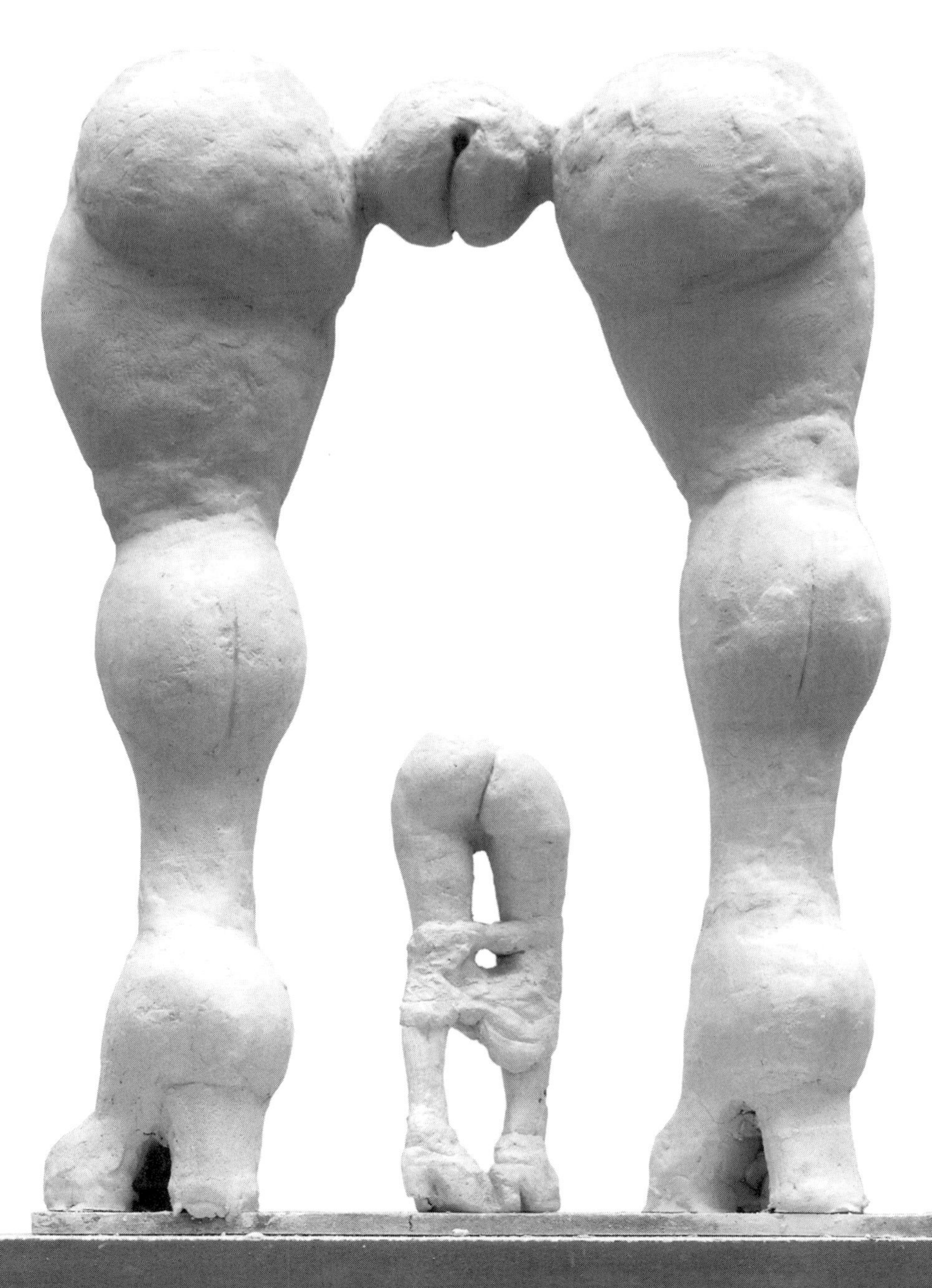

CHRISTIAN MARCLAY

13.6.–5.9.2004

KUNSTMUSEUM THUN

Kunstmuseum Thun, Thunerhof, Hofstettenstrasse 14, CH-3602 Thun
Öffnungszeiten: Di–So 10–17 Uhr, Mi 10–21 Uhr, Mo geschlossen
www.kunstmuseumthun.ch, kunstmuseum@thun.ch

THE PROJECT

JOSÉ DAMASCENO

MARIA ELENA GONZÁLEZ

NIC HESS

GLENN KAINO

KIM SOOJA

DANIEL JOSEPH MARTINEZ

JULIE MEHRETU

AERNOUT MIK

KORI NEWKIRK

YOSHUA OKON

PAUL PFEIFFER

WILLIAM POPE.L

JESSICA RANKIN

PETER ROSTOVSKY

TRACEY ROSE

JASON SALAVON

CRISTIÁN SILVA

STEPHEN VITIELLO

MARTÍN WEBER

New York
37 West 57th Street, 3rd Floor
New York, NY 10019
T: 212-688-4673
F: 212-688-1589

Los Angeles
6086 Comey Street
Los Angeles, CA 90034
T: 323-939-3777
F: 323-939-3553

www.elproyecto.com
mail@elproyecto.com

Nic Hess
Guten Morgen Deutschland!
Haus der Kunst München
26/03/2004 – 06/06/2004

GALERIE GRIEDERVONPUTTKAMER Sophienstr. 25 10178 Berlin
Tel +49 (30) 28 87 93 80   Fax +49 (30) 28 87 93 81   jvonputtkamer@gmx.net

SERGE ZIEGLER GALERIE Tel +41 (79) 409 49 36 Fax +41 (1) 251 25 46
info@zieglergalerie.com www.zieglergalerie.com

EIJA-LIISA AHTILA
CHANTAL AKERMAN
GIOVANNI ANSELMO
JOHN BALDESSARI
LOTHAR BAUMGARTEN
DARA BIRNBAUM
CHRISTIAN BOLTANSKI
MARCEL BROODTHAERS
DANIEL BUREN
MAURIZIO CATTELAN
JAMES COLEMAN
TONY CRAGG
RICHARD DEACON
TACITA DEAN
THIERRY DE CORDIER
RINEKE DIJKSTRA
DAVID GOLDBLATT
DAN GRAHAM
PIERRE HUYGHE
CRISTINA IGLESIAS
WILLIAM KENTRIDGE
STEVE MCQUEEN
MARISA MERZ
ANNETTE MESSAGER
JUAN MUÑOZ
MARIA NORDMAN
GABRIEL OROZCO
GIULIO PAOLINI
GIUSEPPE PENONE
GERHARD RICHTER
ANRI SALA
THOMAS SCHÜTTE
THOMAS STRUTH
NIELE TORONI
JEFF WALL
LAWRENCE WEINER
FRANCESCA WOODMAN

MARIAN GOODMAN GALLERY

24 WEST 57TH STREET NEW YORK, NY 10019
TEL: 212-977-7160 FAX: 212-581-5187

GALERIE MARIAN GOODMAN

79, RUE DU TEMPLE PARIS, FRANCE 75003
TEL: 33-1-4804-7052 FAX: 33-1-4027-8137

WWW.MARIANGOODMAN.COM

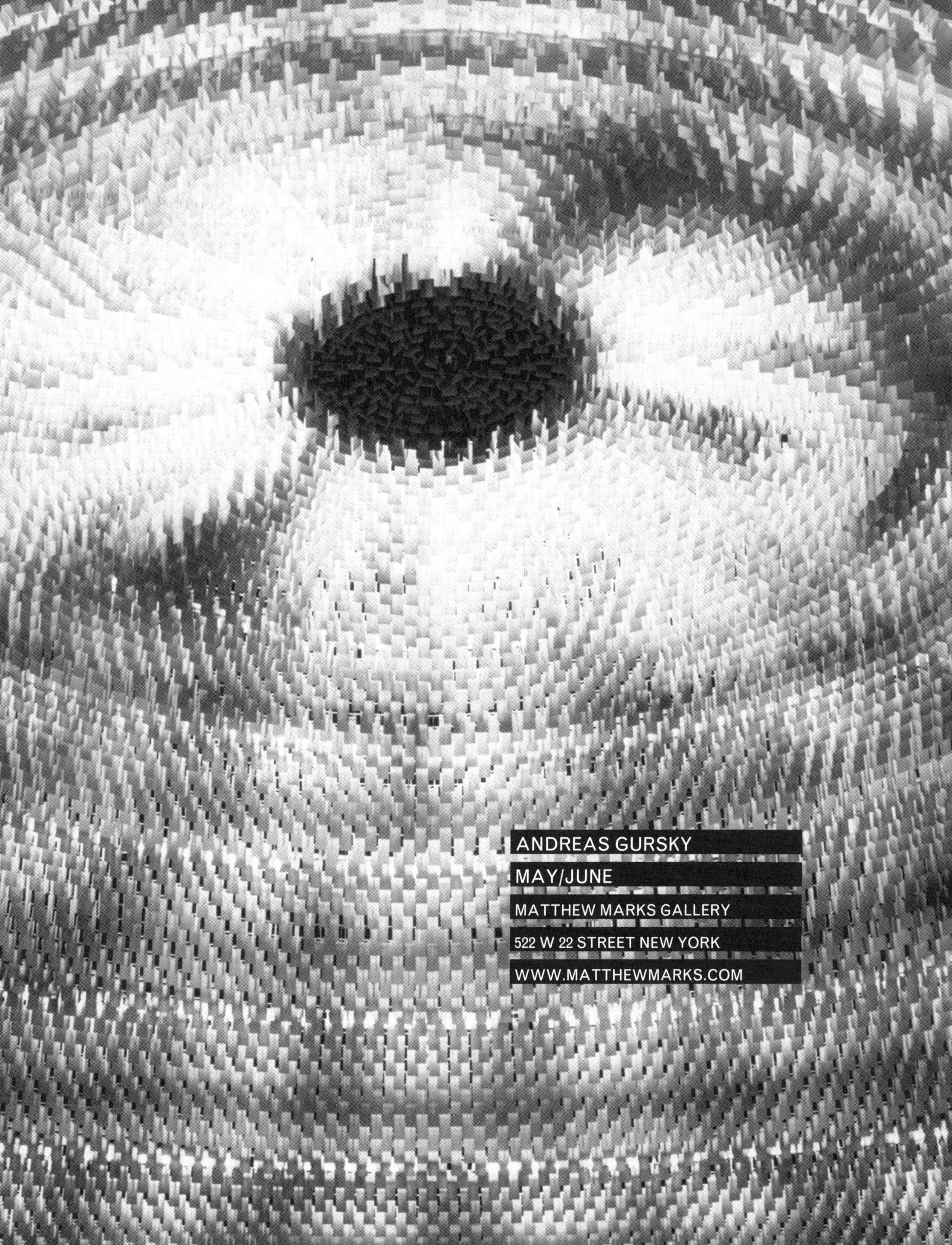
ANDREAS GURSKY
MAY/JUNE
MATTHEW MARKS GALLERY
522 W 22 STREET NEW YORK
WWW.MATTHEWMARKS.COM

GILBERT & GEORGE
LONDON E1 PICTURES
JUNE - JULY 2004
GALERIE THADDAEUS ROPAC
BEAUBOURG, 75003 PARIS TEL: 331 4272 9900 FAX: 331 4272 6166 www.ropac.net

ANRI SALA FOR
HAUSER & WIRTH ZÜRICH LONDON

May 13 - June 30

ISAAC JULIEN

June 16 - 21

Art | 35 | Basel

Hall 2.1 Stand R3 (New Location)

ART UNLIMITED

PEP AGUT

Bertozzi & Casoni
Donald Baechler
Alighiero Boetti
Greg Bogin
Francesco Clemente
Greg Colson
Nicola De Maria
Wim Delvoye
Graham Gillmore
Toland Grinnell
Peter Halley
Guillermo Kuitca
Wolfgang Laib
Jonathan Lasker
Richard Long
Malcolm Morley
Vik Muniz
Tom Sachs
David Salle
Julian Schnabel
Philip Taaffe
Not Vital
Andy Warhol
William Wegman

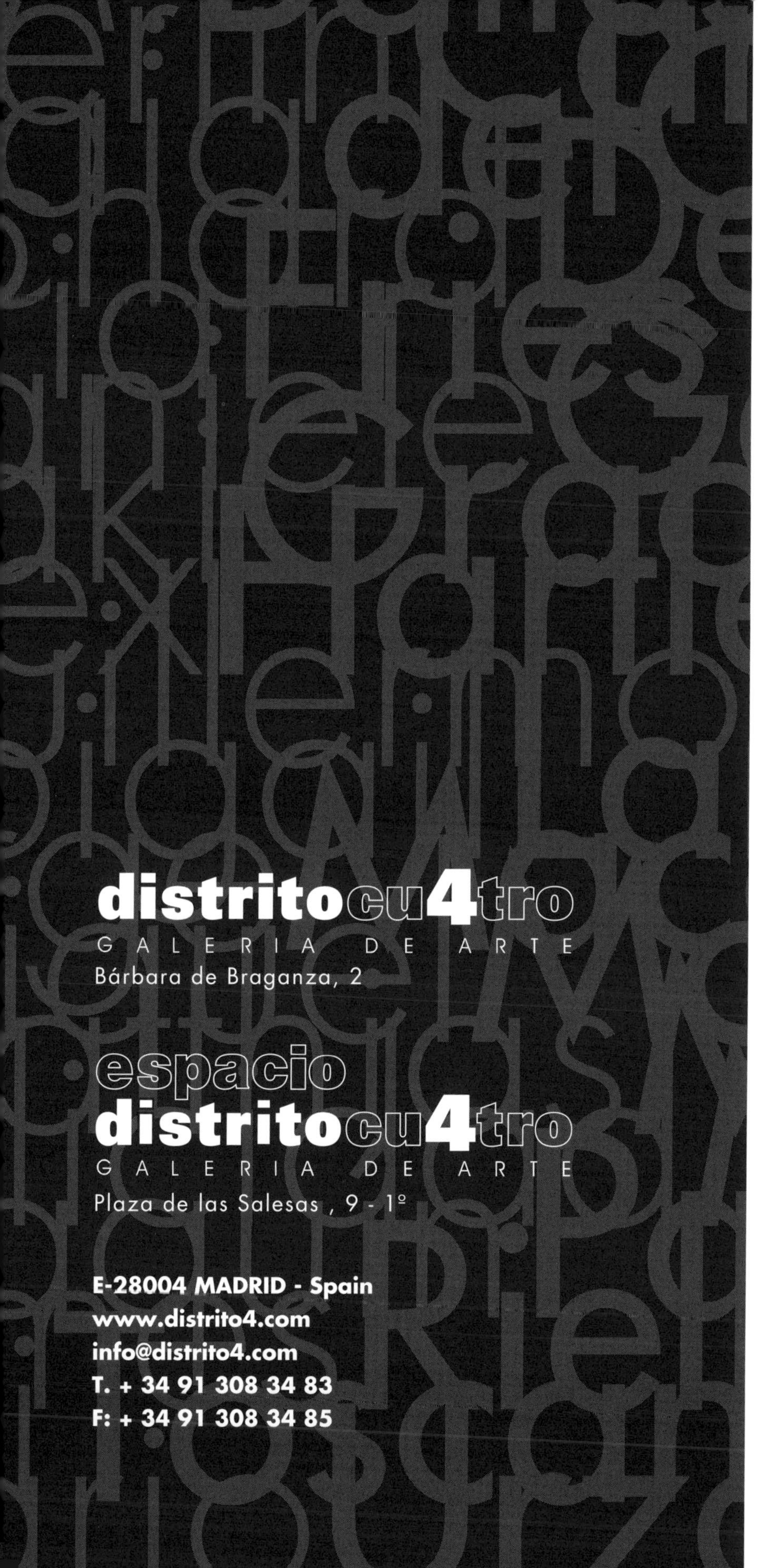

J.M.**Ballester**

Merlin**Carpenter**

Maia**delCastillo**

Richard**Deacon**

Pia**Fries**

Daniele**Galliano**

Iñaki**Gracenea**

Alex**Hartley**

Guillermo**Kuitca**

Abigail**Lane**

Jorge**Macchi**

Miquel**Mont**

Matthias**Müller**

Felicidad**Moreno**

Joaquín**Pacheco**

James**Rielly**

Rui**Toscano**

Dario**Urzay**

Abramovic Accardi Acconci Ackermann Rita Adler Albers Alys Amer Andre Anselmo Appel Araki Arman Armleder Arp Artigas Artschwager Astore Bach Baj Baldessari Balka Balla Barceló Barclay Barry Becher Beecroft Berkhemer Bertrand Beuys Bissier Bochner Boetti Boltanski Bonvicini Borghi Brauner Breitz Breuning Buetti Buren Burri Calder Calle Calzolari Capogrossi Cardiff&Bures Miller Caro Cascella Pietro Casorati Castellani Castro Cattelan Cesar Charlton Christo Clegg&Guttmann Colla Coplans Corbijn Cornell Costa Pietro Costa Vece Cragg Crewdson Davey De Bruyckere De Dominicis De Luca Degas Demand Depero DiCorcia Dijkstra Dine Dion Doig Dorazio Du Dumas Durant Dynys Eliasson Elmgreen&Dragset Emin Fabro Fautrier Favelli Festa Fischli&Weiss Flavin Fontana Forg Francis Franco Fritsch Fulton Gabellone Gallizio Gastini Geers Gentilini Ghibaudo Giacometti Giardini Gilardi Giletta Goldin Gonzalez-Foerster Gordon Gormley Graham Dan Graham Rodney Granular Synthesis Grosz Guaita Gursky Hains Hakansoon Hartung Hatoum Hernandez Hill Hirschhorn Hirst Hofer Honert Horn Horowitz Huan Huebler Hugonnier Indiana Joffe Jorn Judd Kapoor Kcho Kelley Kentridge Kersels Kiefer Kienholz Klein Micha Klein Yves Kline Franz Kneffel Koivisto Kosuth Kounellis Kulik Kuri Kusama Lago Laib Lambie Laplante Lawler Leger Leoncillo Linke Lipchitz Lo Savio

Locher Long Longo Lucas Lutz Luy Magnelli Mainolfi

Man Ray Mannikko Manzoni Manzù Marden Margolles

Marini Marisaldi Martinez Martini Marzouk Masbedo

Masson Mastroianni Mathieu Matta Mattiacci Mazzucconi

McCarthy McCaslin Melotti Meredith-Vula Merz Gerhard

Merz Mario Messina Michaux Migliora Mirò Mocellin

Mochetti Modica Modigliani

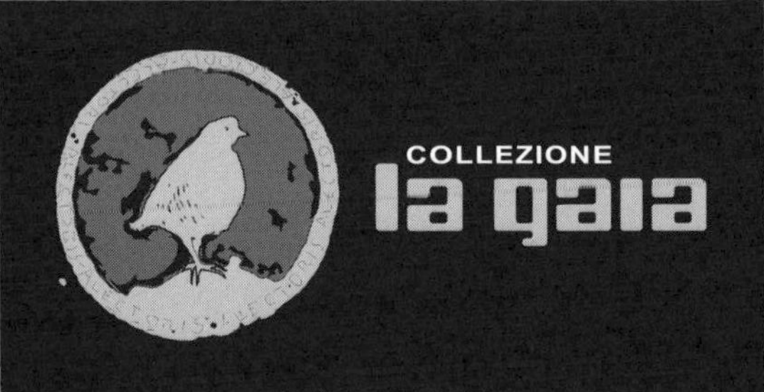

Moffatt Moholy-Nagy Mondino Morandi Mori Morimura Moro Morris Mthethwa Mucha Muehl Nahmad Nam June Paik Nannucci Nauman Neshat Nicholson Niedermair Nitsch Noble&Webster Noland Novelli Oehlen Olaf Oldenburg Opie Catherine Opie Julian Oppenheim Ortega Oursler Paci Paladino Palermo Pane Paolini Pascali Patella Paulucci Penone Perino&Vele Piacentino Pierson Pistoletto Pitz Pivi Poliakoff Polke Pomodoro Arnaldo Pomodoro Giò Ponzio Prince Prinz Ragalzi Rama Rauschenberg Reinhardt Rielly Riopelle Rossi Rosso Rotella Ruckriem Ruscha Ryman Sachs Salvo Samore Sander Scarpitta Schifano Schlegel Schneider Schutte Schwitters Scognamiglio Segal Semper Serrano Severini Sierra Signorini Skoglund Skreber Slominski Smith Kiki Smith Melanie Smith Paul Solano Sorin Soulages Spagnulo Spoerri Stadtbaumer Starling Steinbach Struth Stuart Sugimoto Takis Ter Heijne Tesi Thek Thomas Tillmans Tiravanija Tobey Torelli Toscani Trockel Tunick Tuttle Tuttofuoco Twombly Uecker Uklanski Uncini United Aliens Van Dongen Van Lamsweerde Van Lieshout Van Oost Varga Weisz Varotsos Vedova Velickovic Venet Viola Vostell Wall Wallace Warhol Wegman Wesselmann West White Zandomeneghi Zhen Zorio

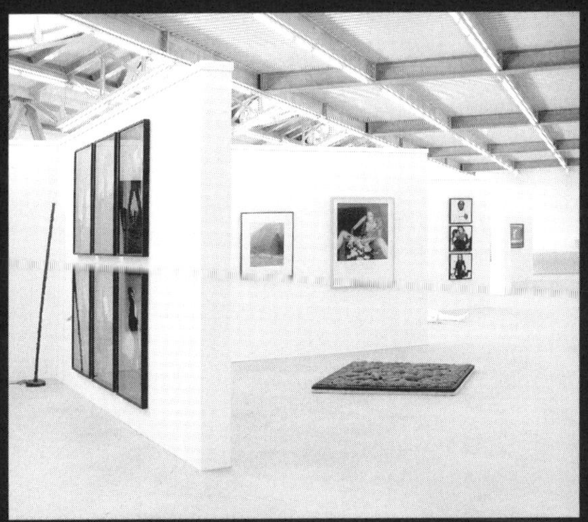

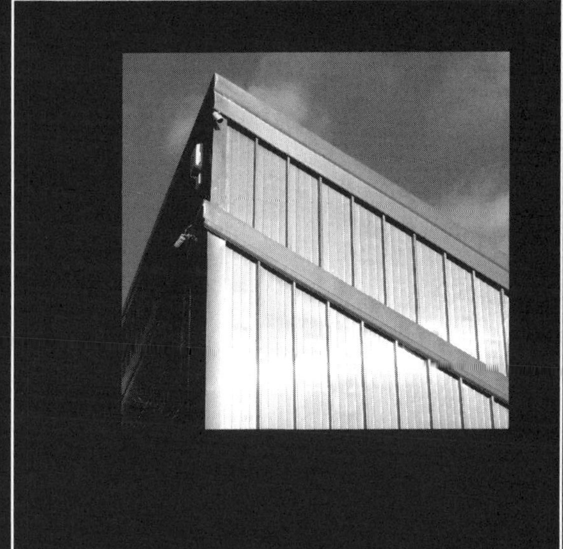

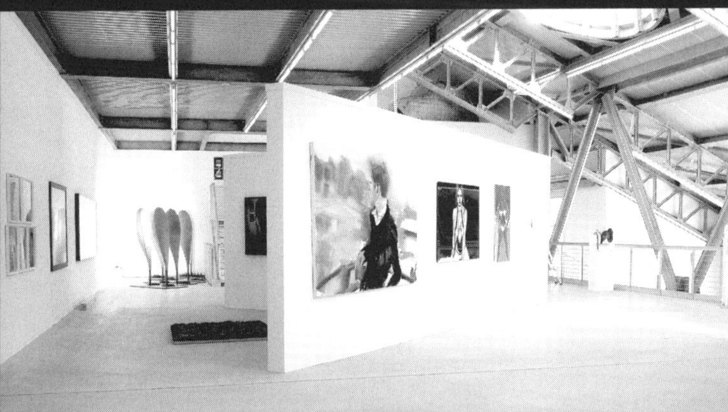

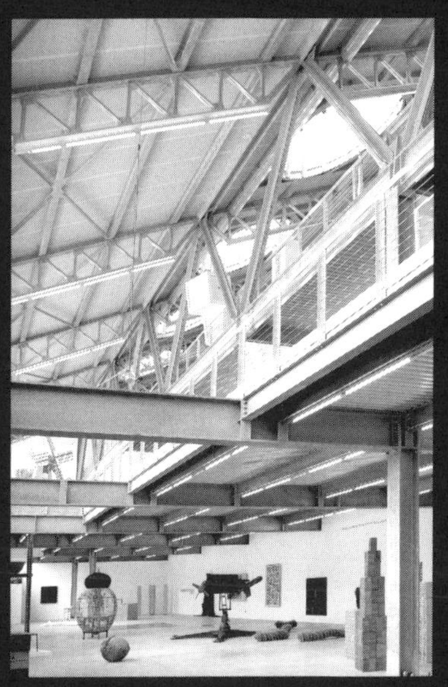

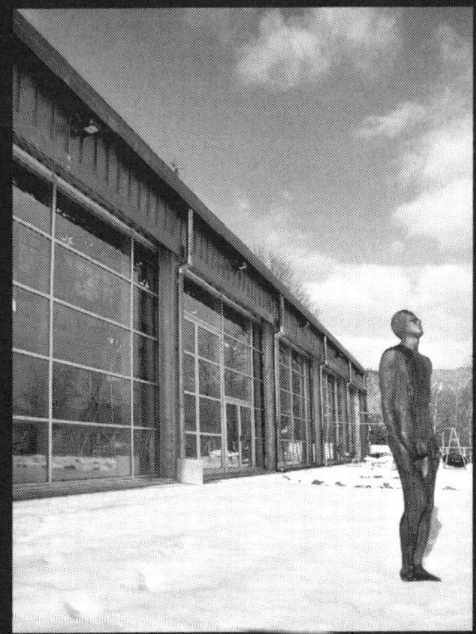

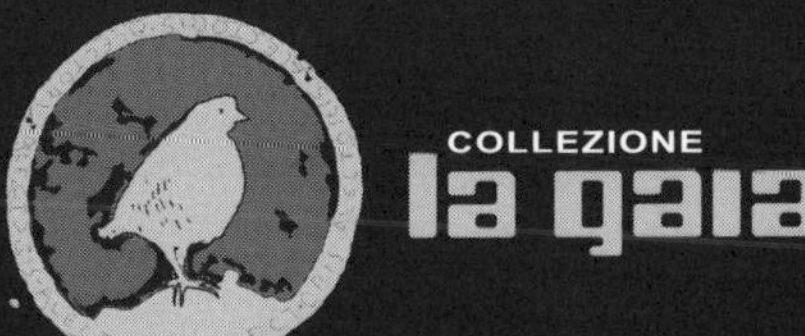

COLLEZIONE
la gaia

20,21

Galerie Edition Kunsthandel GmbH
Meisenburgstraße 169–173
45133 Essen
Tel. **+49 2 01 871 00-0**
Fax **+49 2 01 871 00-10**
info@2021art.com
www.2021art.com

Di–Fr 10–18 · Sa 11–16
und nach Vereinbarung

29|5 – 24|7|04

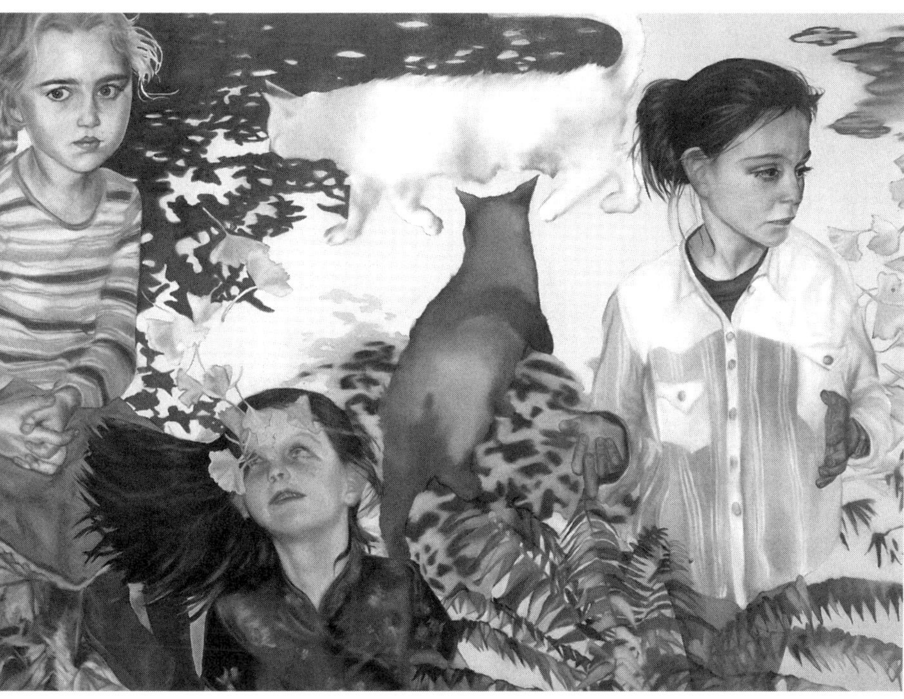

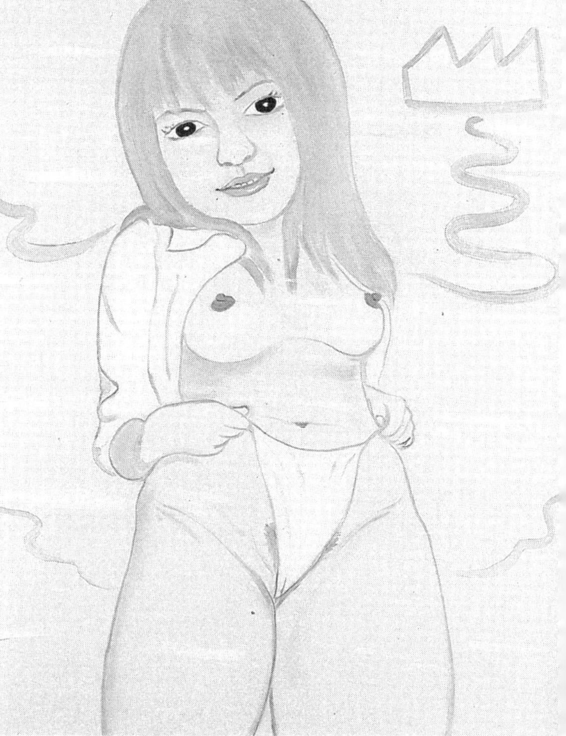

Nicky Hoberman
Playtime

Masahiko Kuwahara
Paintings

Nicky Hoberman: *Atomic Kittens*, 2003
oil on canvas, 183 x 275 cm

Masahiko Kuwahara: *Land Development*, 2002
oil on canvas, 100 x 80,3 cm

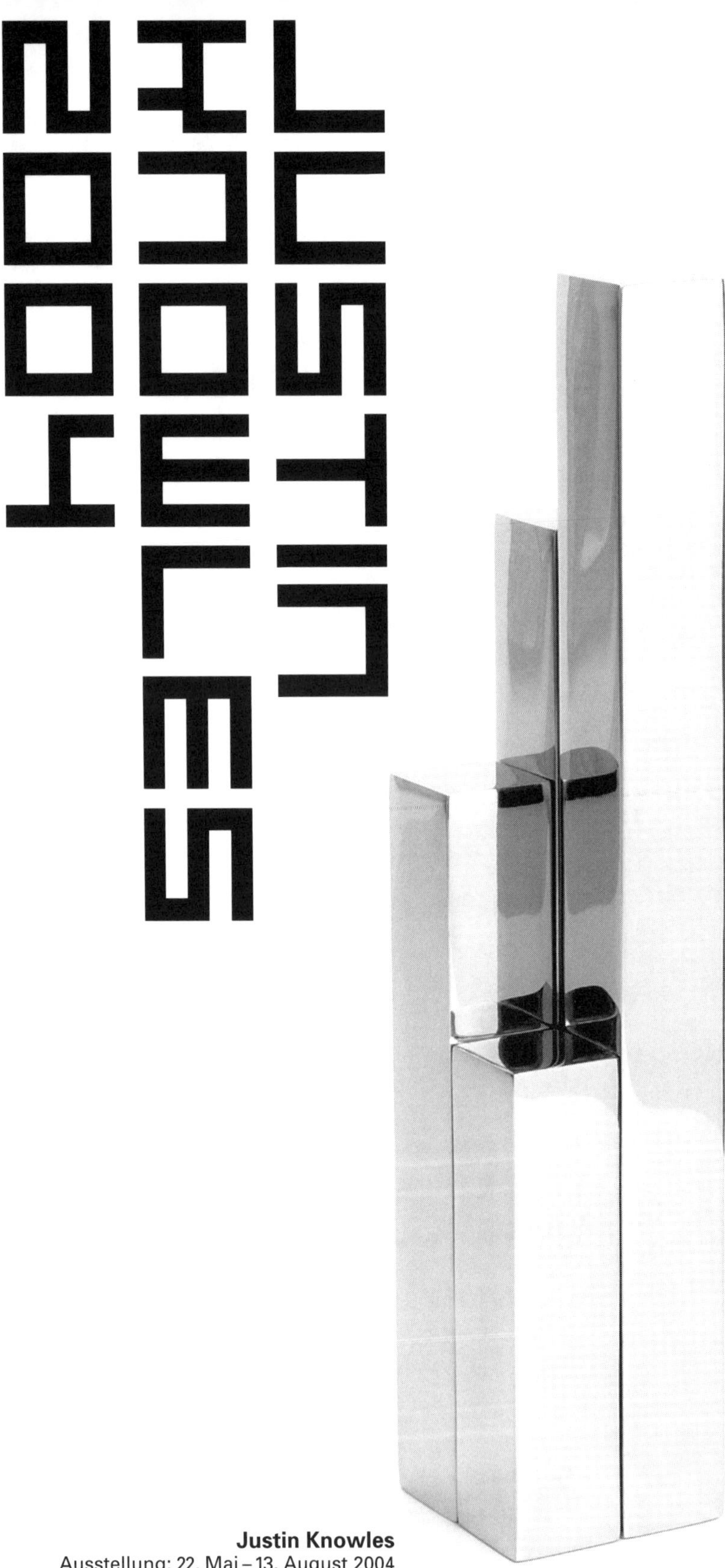

Justin Knowles
Ausstellung: 22. Mai – 13. August 2004
(außer 26. Juli – 7. August 2004)

Exhibition: 22 May – 13 August 2004
(closed: 26 July – 7 August 2004)

Graf & Schelble Galerie
Spalenvorstadt 14, CH-4003 Basel
www.grafschelble.ch
www.justinknowles.co.uk

James Cohan Gallery

INGRID CALAME
IAN DAWSON
TRENTON DOYLE HANCOCK
YUN-FEI JI
RICHARD LONG
BEATRIZ MILHAZES
RON MUECK
ROXY PAINE
RICHARD PATTERSON
HIRAKI SAWA
YINKA SHONIBARE
ROBERT SMITHSON
ERICK SWENSON
FRED TOMASELLI
BILL VIOLA
WIM WENDERS

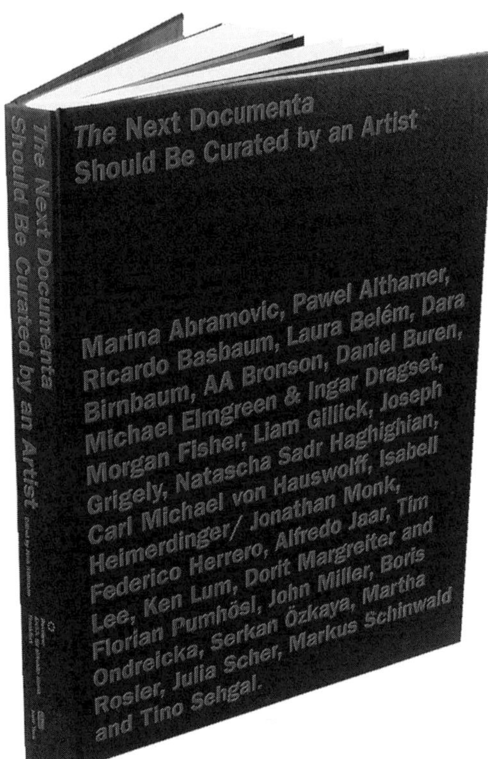

NEW BOOK!

THE NEXT DOCUMENTA SHOULD BE CURATED BY AN ARTIST

AN E-FLUX PROJECT CO-PUBLISHED WITH REVOLVER (ARCHIV FÜR AKTUELLE KUNST)

Curated by Jens Hoffmann

Designed by Christoph Steinegger / INTERKOOL

Hardcover, 88 pages, 8 x 9.75 inches

$24.95   ISBN 3-936919-05-4

With essays by Marina Abramovic, Pawel Althamer, John Baldessari, Ricardo Basbaum, Laura Belém, Dara Birnbaum, Daniel Buren, AA Bronson, Michael Elmgreen & Ingar Dragset, Morgan Fisher, Liam Gillick, Joseph Grigely, Natascha Sadr Haghighian, Carl Michael von Hauswolff, Federico Herrero, Isabel Heimerdinger, Alfredo Jaar, Tim Lee, Ken Lum, Dorit Margreiter, John Miller, Jonathan Monk, Florian Pumhösl, Martha Rosler, Julia Scher, Markus Schinwald, Tino Sehgal, Lawrence Weiner, and selections from an open forum.

© e-flux, Revolver and Jens Hoffmann, 2004

 e·flux

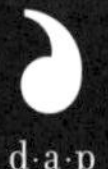

HELMUT LANG

metallic skirts
photographed by Juergen Teller
Paris ★ New York, N.Y. - S/S 04
WWW.HELMUTLANG.COM

MAI 36 GALERIE

RITA MCBRIDE
30 April – 5 June 2004

**Filipa César · Cristina Iglesias · On Kawara
Matt Mullican · Pedro Cabrita Reis
Thomas Ruff · Hiroshi Sugimoto**

11 June – 24 July 2004

Art | 35 | Basel 16 – 21 June 2004

Rämistrasse 37, CH-8001 Zürich, www.mai36.artgalleries.ch
Tel. +41 1 261 68 80, Fax +41 1 261 68 81, mai36@artgalleries.ch

---

SYLVIE FLEURY

12. JUNI – 31. JULI 2004

RICHARD PRINCE

28. AUGUST – 9. OKTOBER 2004

MARTIN BOYCE

GALERIE EVA PRESENHUBER

WWW.PRESENHUBER.COM
TEL: +41 (43) 444 70 50 / FAX: +41 (0) 43 444 70 60
LIMMATSTRASSE 270, POSTFACH 1517, CH–8031 ZURICH
Öffnungszeiten: Di-Mi, Fr 12-18, Do 12-20, Sa 11-16 Uhr

DOUG AITKEN, EMMANUELLE ANTILLE, MARTIN BOYCE, ANGELA BULLOCH, VERNE DAWSON, MARIA EICHHORN, URS FISCHER, PETER FISCHLI/DAVID WEISS, SYLVIE FLEURY, LIAM GILLICK, CANDIDA HÖFER, KAREN KILIMNIK, RICHARD PRINCE, GERWALD ROCKENSCHAUB, UGO RONDINONE, DIETER ROTH, JEAN-FRÉDÉRIC SCHNYDER, BEAT STREULI, FRANZ WEST, SUE WILLIAMS

BERNIER / ELIADES

11, EPTACHALKOU, GR–11851 ATHENS • TEL: + 30 210 341 39 35–7, FAX: + 30 210 341 39 38
E-mail: bernier@bernier-eliades.gr • www.bernier-eliades.gr

JUNE– SEPTEMBER 2004

GILBERT & GEORGE

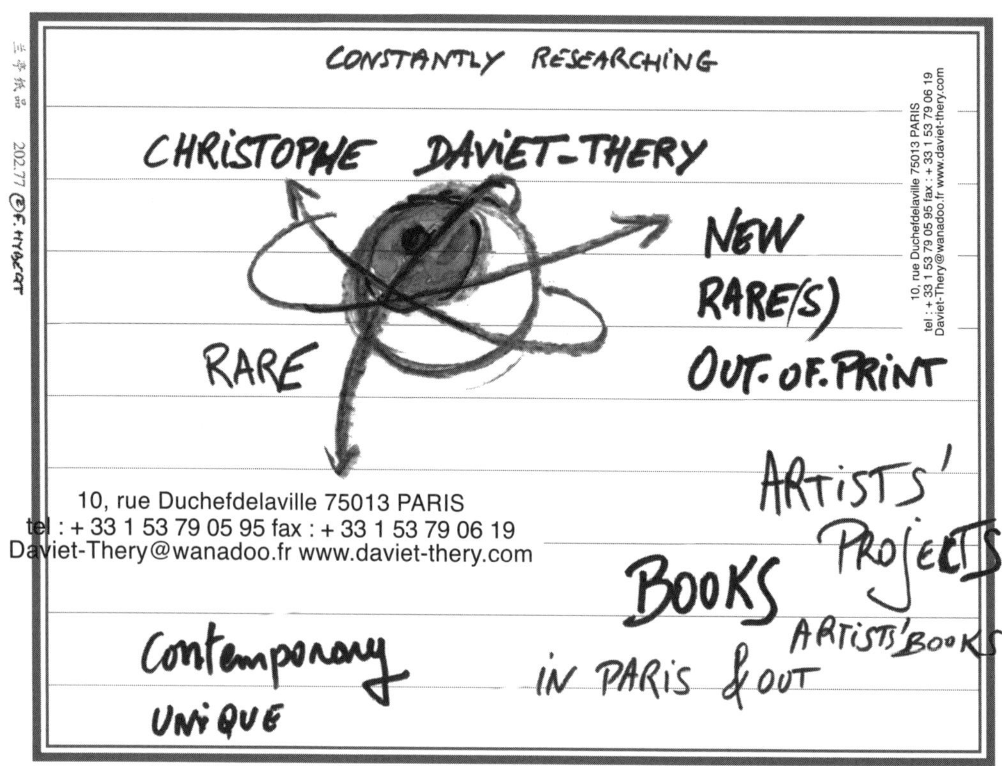

GALERIE   BOB   GYSIN

www.bg-galerie.ch

AUSSTELLUNGSSTRASSE 24, 8005 ZÜRICH
T +41-1-278 40 60—F +41-1-278 40 50—INFO@BG-GALERIE.CH

Bob Gramsma - Neue Installationen
11. Juni - 31. Juli 2004

Teresa Chen - GORGEOUS!
26. August - 23. Oktober 2004

DI–FR 13–18—SA 11–16

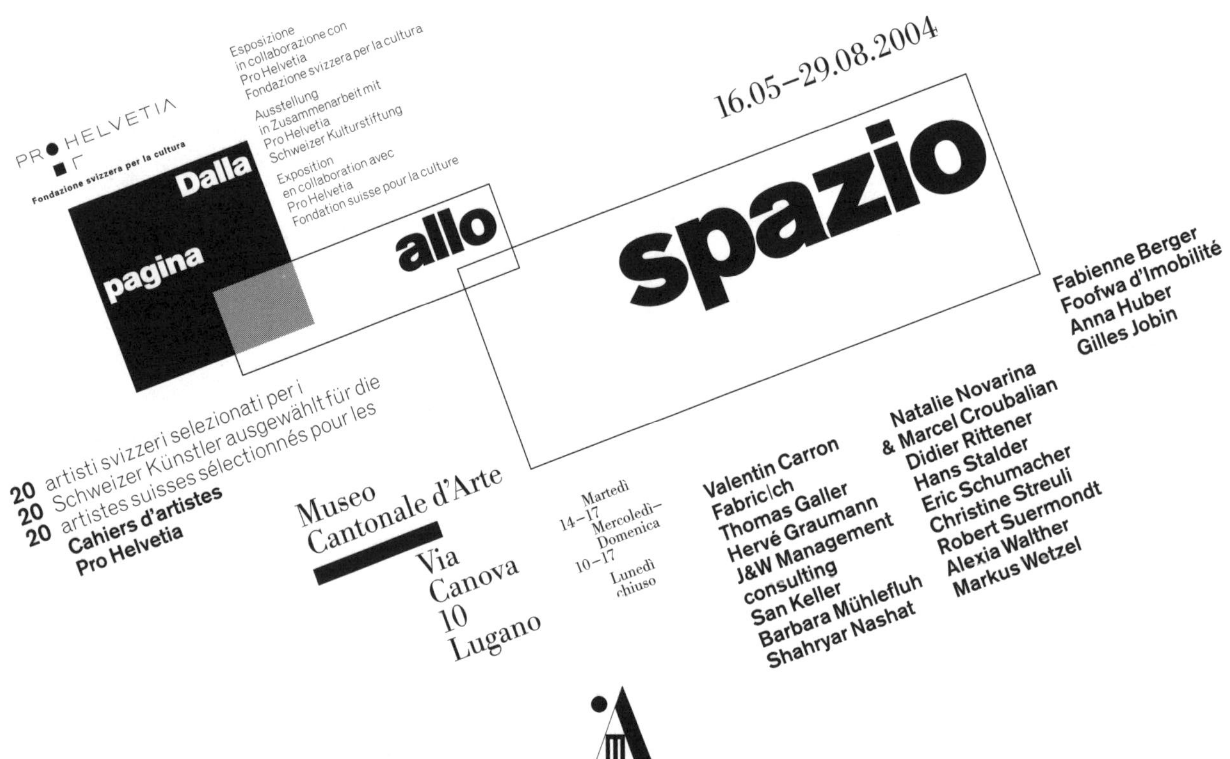

PRO HELVETIA
Fondazione svizzera per la cultura
Esposizione in collaborazione con Pro Helvetia Fondazione svizzera per la cultura
Ausstellung in Zusammenarbeit mit Pro Helvetia Schweizer Kulturstiftung
Exposition en collaboration avec Pro Helvetia Fondation suisse pour la culture
16.05–29.08.2004
Dalla pagina allo spazio
Fabienne Berger
Foofwa d'Imobilité
Anna Huber
Gilles Jobin
20 artisti svizzeri selezionati per i
20 Schweizer Künstler ausgewählt für die
20 artistes suisses sélectionnés pour les
Cahiers d'artistes
Pro Helvetia
Museo Cantonale d'Arte
Via Canova 10 Lugano
Martedì 14–17 Mercoledì–Domenica 10–17 Lunedì chiuso
Valentin Carron
Fabric|ch
Thomas Galler
Hervé Graumann
J&W Management consulting
San Keller
Barbara Mühlefluh
Shahryar Nashat
Natalie Novarina & Marcel Croubalian
Didier Rittener
Hans Stalder
Eric Schumacher
Christine Streuli
Robert Suermondt
Alexia Walther
Markus Wetzel

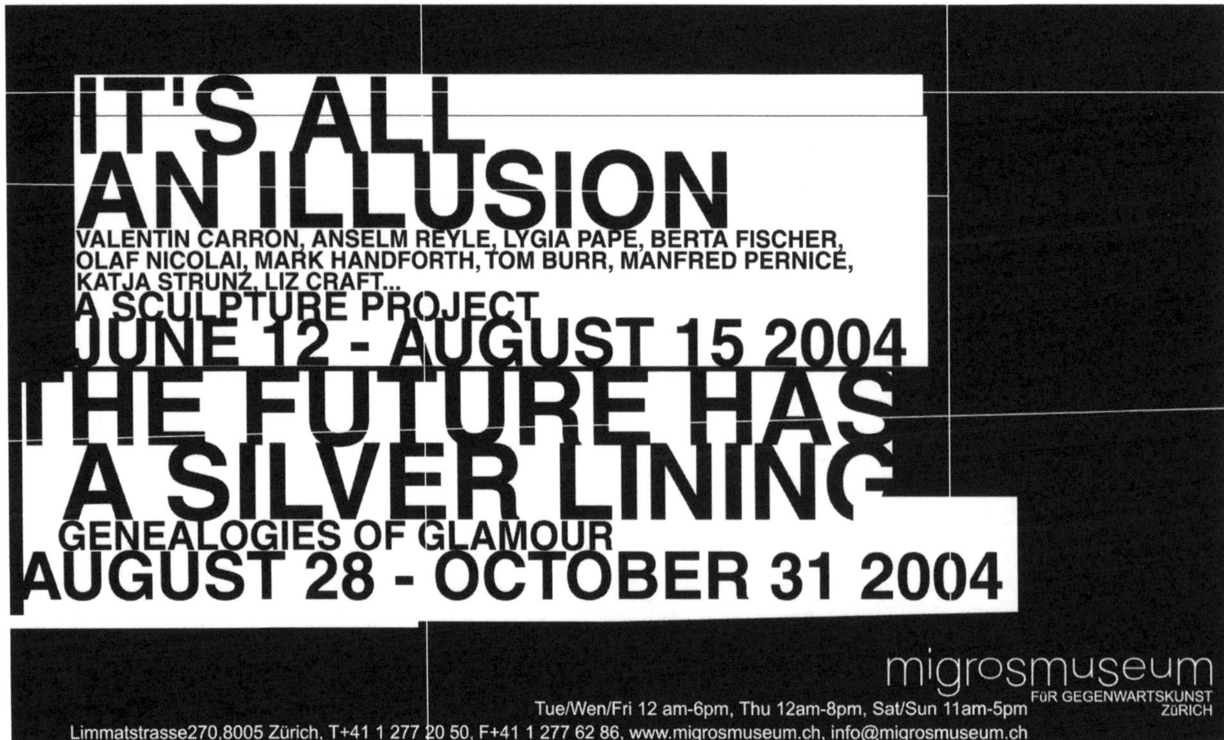

IT'S ALL AN ILLUSION
VALENTIN CARRON, ANSELM REYLE, LYGIA PAPE, BERTA FISCHER, OLAF NICOLAI, MARK HANDFORTH, TOM BURR, MANFRED PERNICE, KATJA STRUNZ, LIZ CRAFT...
A SCULPTURE PROJECT
JUNE 12 - AUGUST 15 2004
THE FUTURE HAS A SILVER LINING
GENEALOGIES OF GLAMOUR
AUGUST 28 - OCTOBER 31 2004
migrosmuseum
FüR GEGENWARTSKUNST ZüRICH
Tue/Wen/Fri 12 am-6pm, Thu 12am-8pm, Sat/Sun 11am-5pm
Limmatstrasse270, 8005 Zürich, T+41 1 277 20 50, F+41 1 277 62 86, www.migrosmuseum.ch, info@migrosmuseum.ch

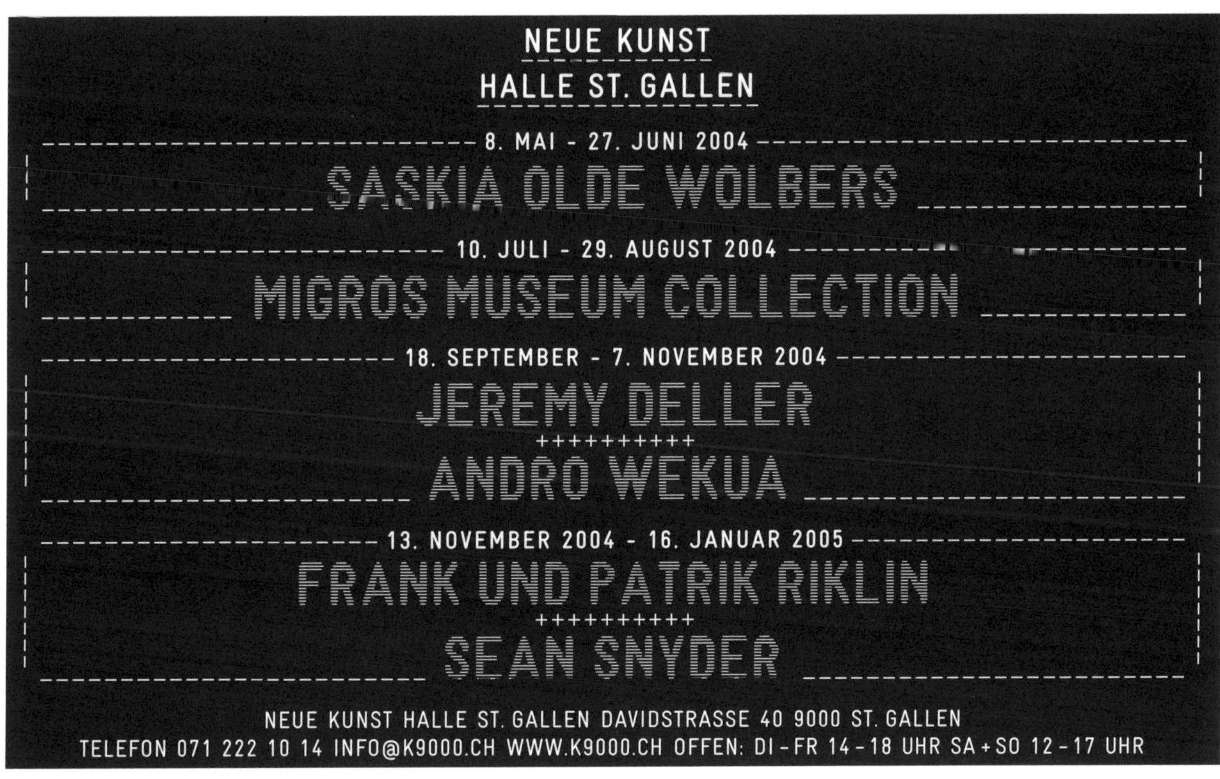

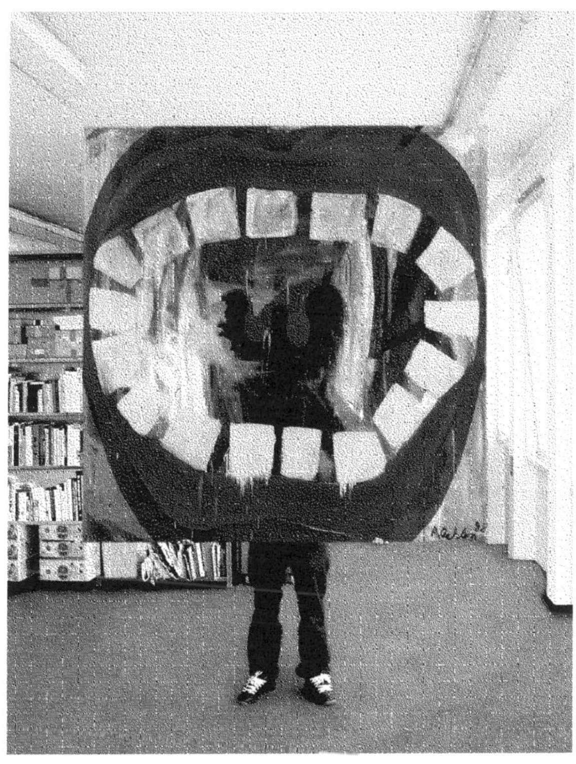

Albert Oehlen

Peintures / Malerei

1980 – 2004

Musée cantonal des Beaux-Arts Lausanne
18.6. – 5.9.2004

Palais de Rumine Place de la Riponne 6 CH-1014 Lausanne
T +41(0)21 316 3445 F +41(0)21 316 3446 musee.beaux-arts@serac.vd.ch

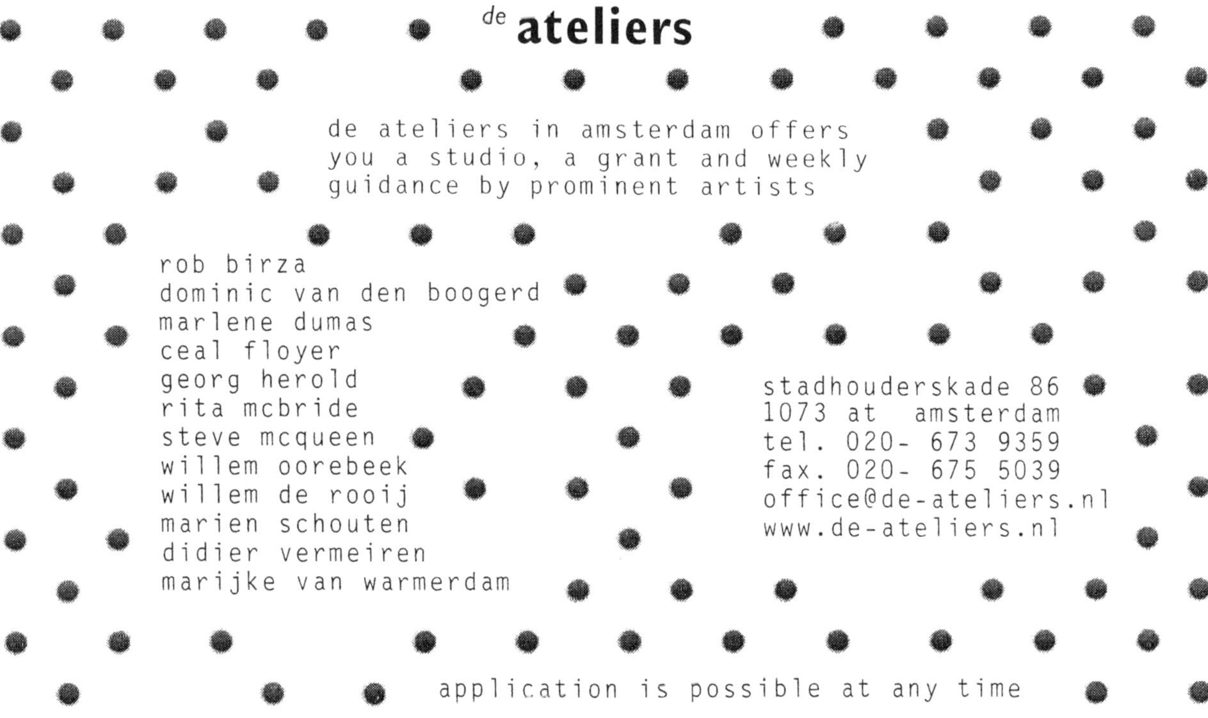

de ateliers

de ateliers in amsterdam offers
you a studio, a grant and weekly
guidance by prominent artists

rob birza
dominic van den boogerd
marlene dumas
ceal floyer
georg herold
rita mcbride
steve mcqueen
willem oorebeek
willem de rooij
marien schouten
didier vermeiren
marijke van warmerdam

stadhouderskade 86
1073 at amsterdam
tel. 020- 673 9359
fax. 020- 675 5039
office@de-ateliers.nl
www.de-ateliers.nl

application is possible at any time

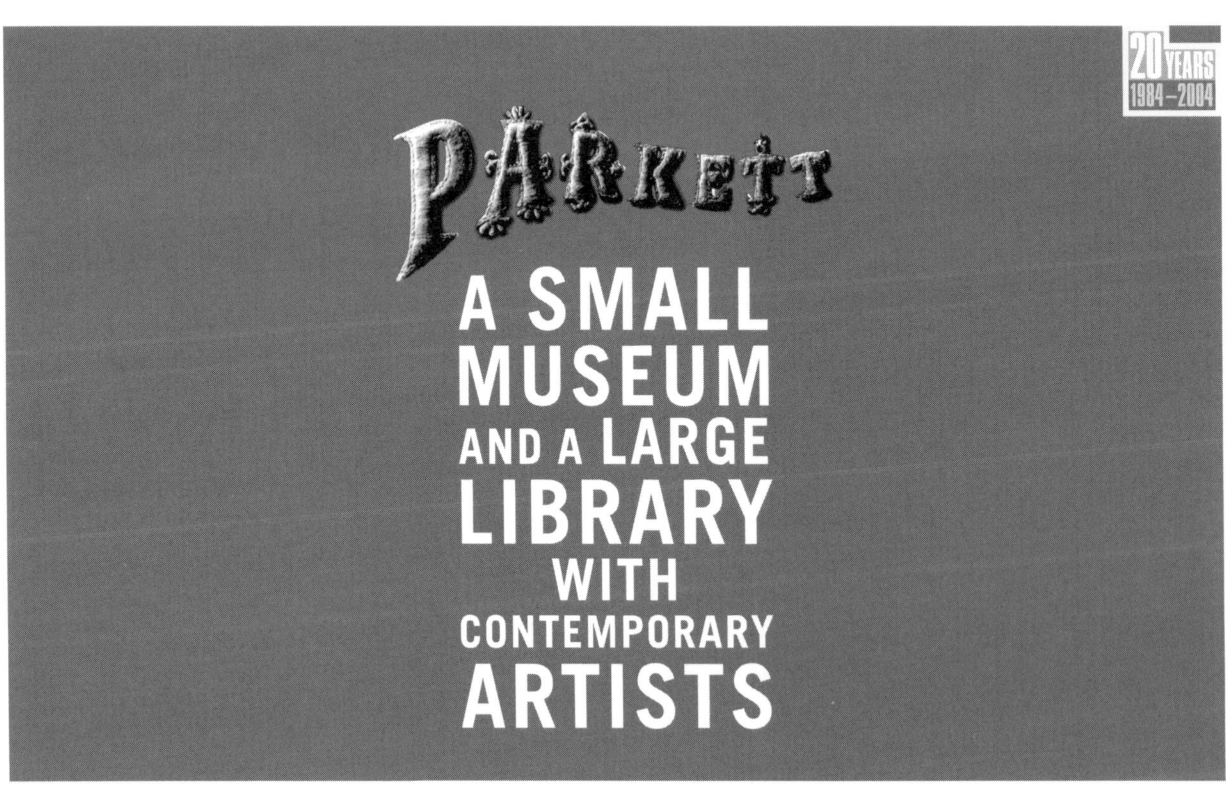

20 YEARS
1984–2004

PARKETT

A SMALL
MUSEUM
AND A LARGE
LIBRARY
WITH
CONTEMPORARY
ARTISTS

Louise
Bourgeois

March 13 – September 12, 2004

DAROS EXHIBITIONS

Löwenbräu-Areal	Thursday and Friday	June 14, 16, 17, 18 *(Art Basel)*
Limmatstrasse 268	3 p.m. to 7 p.m.	12 noon to 7 p.m.
CH-8005 Zürich	Saturday and Sunday	August 1, closed
T: +41 1 447 70 00	1 p.m. to 5 p.m.	September 4 *(Lange Nacht der Museen)*
F: +41 1 447 70 10		7 p.m. to 2 a.m.
www.daros.ch		

DAROS

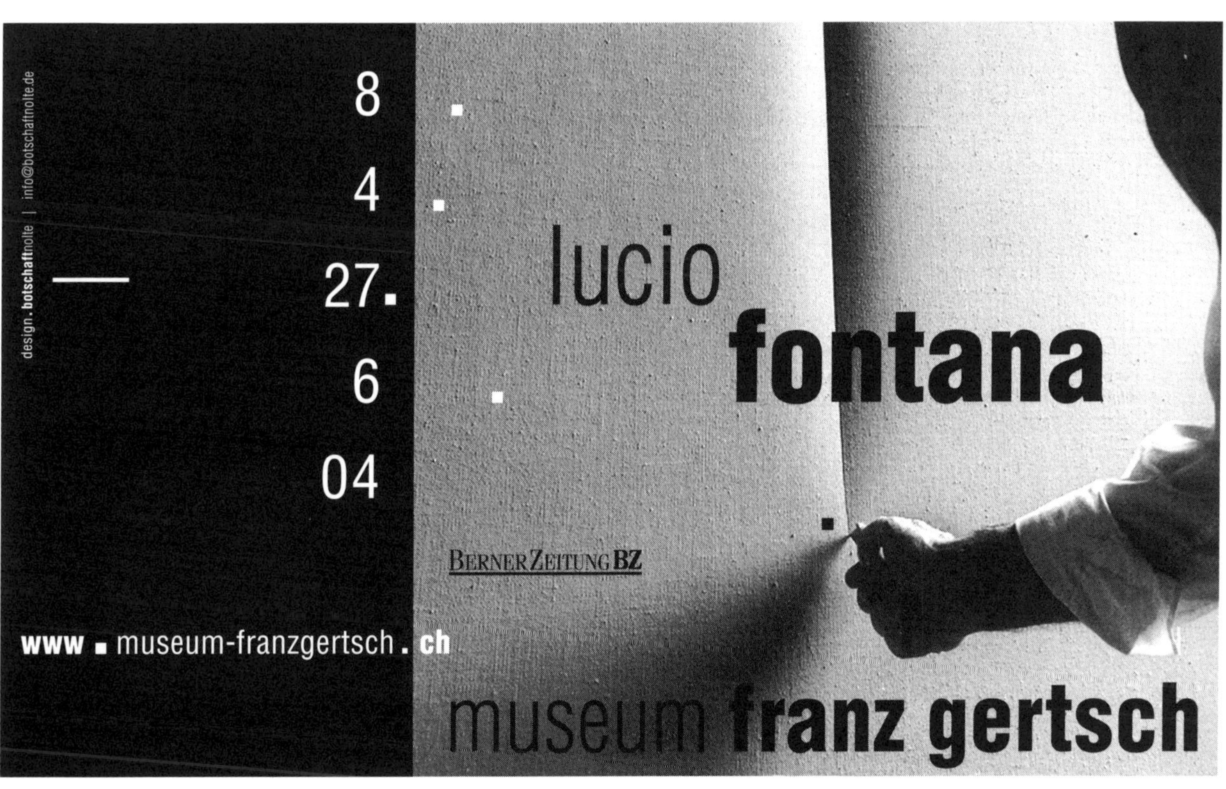

Art | 35 | Basel | 16–21 | 6 | 04

Art Galleries at Art 35 Basel | **A** | **303 Gallery** New York | **Acquavella** New York | **Air de Paris** Paris | **Aizpuru** Madrid, Sevilla | **Alexander and Bonin** New York | **de Alvear** Madrid | **Ammann** Zürich | **Andréhn-Schiptjenko** Stockholm | **Andriesse** Amsterdam | **Arndt & Partner** Berlin | **Ars Futura** Zürich | **Art & Public** Genève | **Artiaco** Napoli | **B** | **von Bartha** Basel | **Berggruen** San Francisco | **Bernier / Eliades** Athens | **Beyeler** Basel | **Bischofberger** Zürich | **Blau** München | **Blum** New York, Zürich | **Blum & Poe** Los Angeles | **Bonakdar** New York | **Brito Cimino** São Paulo | **Brown** New York | **Brusberg** Berlin | **Buchholz** Köln | **Buchmann** Lugano, Köln | **C** | **C & M** New York | **c/o-Gerhardsen** Berlin | **CAAW** Beijing | **Campaña** Köln | **Capitain** Köln | **carlier gebauer** Berlin | **Carzaniga + Ueker** Basel | **Cheim & Read** New York | **Cobo** Sevilla | **Cohan** New York | **Coles** London | **Contemporary Fine Arts** Berlin | **Continua** San Gimignano | **Cooper** New York | **Corkin / Shopland** Toronto | **Crousel** Paris | **D** | **Dabbeni** Lugano | **De Cardenas** Milano | **De Carlo** Milano | **Denise René** Paris | **Di Meo** Paris | **Ditesheim** Neuchâtel, Genève | **E** | **Ecart** Genève | **Eigen + Art** Berlin, Leipzig | **F** | **Fischer** Düsseldorf | **Foksal** Warsaw | **Fontana** Milano | **Fortes Vilaça** São Paulo | **Fraenkel** San Francisco | **Friedman** London | **Friedrich** Basel | **Frith Street** London | **G** | **Gagosian** New York | **Galerie 1900-2000** Paris | **Galerie de France** Paris | **Galerie St. Etienne** New York | **Galleria dello Scudo** Verona | **Gasser & Grunert** New York | **Gelink** Amsterdam | **Gladstone** New York | **Gmurzynska** Köln, Zug | **González** Madrid | **Goodman Gallery** Johannesburg | **Goodman Marian** New York, Paris | **Grässlin** Frankfurt | **Gray** Chicago, New York | **Greve** Köln, Milano, Paris, St. Moritz | **Guerra** Lisboa | **H** | **Haas & Fuchs** Berlin | **Hauser & Wirth** Zürich | **Hécey** Luxembourg | **Hengesbach** Köln, Wuppertal | **Hetzler** Berlin | **Hilger** Wien, Paris | **Hoppen** London | **Hoss** Paris, Bruxelles | **Houk** New York | **Hufkens** Bruxelles | **Hutton** New York | **Hyundai** Seoul | **I** | **Interim Art** London | **Invernizzi** Milano | **J** | **Jablonka** Köln | **Jacobson** London, San Francisco | **Janda** Wien | **Janssen Michael** Köln | **Janssen Rodolphe** Bruxelles | **Johnen / Schöttle** Köln, München | **Juda** London | **K** | **Kaplan** New York | **Kargl** Wien | **Kelly** New York | **Kerlin** Dublin | **Kern** New York | **Kewenig** Köln | **Kicken** Berlin | **Kilchmann** Zürich | **Klosterfelde** Berlin | **Klüser** München | **König** Wien | **Koyama** Tokyo | **Koyanagi** Tokyo | **Kraus** New York | **Krinzinger** Wien | **Krugier** Genève, New York | **Kukje** Seoul | **Kulli** Zürich | **L** | **L.A. Louver** Venice | **La Città** Verona | **Lahumière** Paris | **Lambert** Paris, New York | **Landau** Montreal | **Leavin** Los Angeles | **Lehmann** Dresden | **Lelong** Zürich, New York | **Linder** Basel | **Lisson** London | **Löhrl** Mönchengladbach | **Lorenzo** Madrid | **Luhring Augustine** New York | **M** | **m Bochum** Bochum | **Mai 36** Zürich | **Mann** New York | **March** Valencia | **Marconi** Milano | **Marks** New York | **Marlborough** Zürich, London | **Mathes** New York | **Maubrie** Paris | **Mayer** Düsseldorf, Berlin | **Mayor** London | **McKee** New York | **Meert Rihoux** Bruxelles | **Meier** San Francisco | **Metro Pictures** New York | **Meyer Riegger** Karlsruhe | **Meyer-Ellinger** Frankfurt | **Millan** São Paulo | **Miller** New York | **Minini** Brescia | **Miro** London | **Mitchell-Innes & Nash** New York | **Modern Institute** Glasgow | **Moeller** New York | **Müller** Zürich | **Munro** Hamburg | **N** | **nächst St. Stephan** Wien | **Nagel** Köln, Berlin | **Nahmad Helly** London | **Nelson** Paris | **Neu** Berlin | **neugerriemschneider** Berlin | **New Art Center** Salisbury | **Nolan / Eckman** New York | **Nordenhake** Berlin, Stockholm | **Nothelfer** Berlin | **O** | **OMR** Mexico D.F. | **Orangerie-Reinz** Köln | **Oxley9** Sydney | **P** | **PaceWildenstein** New York | **Painter** Santa Monica | **Pauli** Lausanne | **Paviot** Paris | **Perrotin** Paris | **Persano** Torino | **Petzel** New York | **Piccadilly** London | **Prats** Barcelona | **Presenhuber** Zürich | **Produzentengalerie** Hamburg | **R** | **Rech** Paris | **Reckermann** Köln | **Regen Projects** Los Angeles | **Reynolds** London | **Ricke** Köln | **Riis** Oslo | **Ropac** Paris, Salzburg | **Rosen** New York | **S** | **S65** Aalst | **SCAI** Tokyo | **Scalo** Zürich, New York | **Scheibler** Köln | **Schipper & Krome** Berlin | **Schlégl** Zürich | **Schulte** Berlin | **ShanghART** Shanghai | **Shugoarts** Tokyo | **Sikkema** New York | **Skarstedt** New York | **Skopia** Genève | **Sonnabend** New York | **Sperone Westwater** New York | **Sprüth / Magers** Köln, München | **Stähli** Zürich | **Stampa** Basel | **Starmach** Cracow | **Stein** Milano | **Stolz** Berlin | **Strina** São Paulo | **Szwajcer** Antwerpen | **T** | **Taka Ishii** Tokyo | **Tanit** München | **Tega** Milano | **Templon** Paris | **The Project** New York | **Thomas** München | **Tolksdorf** Frankfurt | **Trisorio** Napoli | **Tschudi** Glarus | **U** | **Ubu** New York | **Utermann** Dortmund | **V** | **van Orsouw** Zürich | **Verna** Zürich | **Villepoix** Paris | **W** | **Waddington** London | **Wallner** Copenhagen | **Walter** Basel, Zürich | **Washburn** New York | **Weber Jamileh** Zürich | **Weiss** Berlin | **Welters** Amsterdam | **Werner** New York, Köln | **White Cube** London | **Wuethrich** Basel | **Y** | **Young** Chicago | **Z** | **Zeno X** Antwerpen | **Ziegler** Zürich | **Zwirner** New York | **Zwirner & Wirth** New York |

Art Edition, Galleries | **Alexander** New York | **Art of this Century** New York | **Artelier** Graz | **Borch Jensen** Copenhagen | **Cristea** London | **Crown Point** San Francisco | **Fanal** Basel | **Gemini** Los Angeles, New York | **Item** Paris | **Knust** München | **Lelong Editions** Paris, Zürich, New York | **Nitsch** New York | **Noire** San Sebastiano Po | **Pace Prints** New York | **Paragon** London | **Polígrafa** Barcelona | **Putman** Paris |

Art Statements, Artists, Galleries | **Dirk Bell** BQ, Köln | **Pierpaolo Campanini** Kaufmann Francesca, Milano | **Valentin Carron** Praz-Delavallade, Paris | **Sunah Choi** Neff, Frankfurt | **Roe Ethridge** Kreps, New York | **Juan Pedro Fabra** Brändström & Stene, Stockholm | **The Icelandic Love Corporation** i8, Reykjavik | **Dr. Lakra** kurimanzutto, Mexico D.F. | **Mai-Thu Perret** Pia, Bern | **Alex Pollard** Mummery, London | **Marcin Maciejowski** Meyer Kainer, Wien | **Aleksandra Mir** Jousse, Paris | **Anselm Reyle** Nourbakhsch, Berlin | **Matthew Ronay** Staerk, Copenhagen | **Steven Shearer** Noero, Torino | **Tino Sehgal** Mot, Bruxelles | **Torbjörn Vejvi** Raucci / Santamaria, Napoli | List in formation | Index April 2004

Art Unlimited | Art Film |

Tuesday, June 15, 2004 | **Vernissage** | by invitation only
Monday, June 21, 2004 | **Professional Day** | by invitation only

The Art Show – Die Kunstmesse
Art 35 Basel, MCH Messe Basel AG, CH-4005 Basel
Fax +41/58-206 26 86, info@ArtBasel.com, www.ArtBasel.com

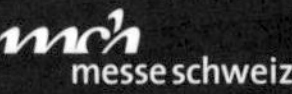

ART FORUM
BERLIN

18-22 September 2004
The International Fair
for Contemporary Art

Berlin Exhibition Grounds, Halls 18-20
daily 12-8 p.m.
Opening 17 September 2004, 4-9 p.m.

www.art-forum-berlin.com

Messe Berlin

Kunst

2004

Zürich

12–15 November 2004

10th International Contemporary Art Fair

ABB Hall 550

Zürich-Oerlikon

Phone +41 1 381 00 52

mail@kunstzuerich.ch

www.kunstzuerich.ch

LISTE 04
THE YOUNG ART FAIR IN BASEL

June 15–20, 2004
Open hours: 1 p.m. to 9 p.m.

Opening reception: Monday, June 14, 6 p.m. to 10 p.m.
Burgweg 15, CH-4058 Basel
T/F: ++41/61/692 20 21, info@liste.ch, www.liste.ch
A project in the workshop community Warteck pp

49 GALLERIES FROM 19 COUNTRIES: new at LISTE*

AUSTRIA: Michael Hall, Vienna. **BELGIUM:** Drantmann, Brussels. **CANADA:** Tracey Lawrence*, Vancouver. **DENMARK:** Christina Wilson, Copenhagen. **FRANCE:** &:gb agency, Paris. Corentin Hamel*, Paris. Loevenbruck, Paris. Maisonneuve, Paris. **GERMANY:** Frehrking Wiesehöfer, Cologne. Vera Gliem, Cologne. Karin Guenther, Hamburg. Iris Kadel*, Karlsruhe. Johann König, Berlin. Sies + Höke, Dusseldorf. Jan Winkelmann*, Berlin. **GREAT BRITAIN:** aspreyjacques, London. doggerfisher, Edinburgh. Kate MacGarry*, London. Mobile Home, London. Vilma Gold, London. VTO, London. **GREECE:** Unlimited Contemporary Art, Athens. **HOLLAND:** Ellen de Bruijne Projects, Amsterdam. Diana Stigter, Amsterdam. Upstream*, Amsterdam. **ITALY:** 404 Arte Contemporanea, Naples. Maze, Torino. T293*, Naples. Zero, Milano. **JAPAN:** Kodama, Osaka. **LITHUANIA:** IBID Projects, Vilnius/London. **LUXEMBOURG:** Alimentation Générale/Art Contemporain, Luxembourg. **NORWAY:** Fotogalleriet*, Oslo. **POLAND:** Raster*, Warsaw. **SLOVENIA:** Gregor Podnar, Ljubljana. **SWEDEN:** ALP/Peter Bergman, Stockholm. **SWITZERLAND:** ausstellungsraum25, Zurich. Evergreene*, Geneva. Judin Belot*, Zurich. Nicolas Krupp, Basel. **TURKEY:** Galerist*, Istanbul. **USA:** Cohan and Leslie, New York. John Connelly Presents*, New York. Daniel Hug*, Los Angeles. maccarone inc., New York. moniquemeloche, Chicago. peres projects*, Los Angeles. Daniel Reich*, New York. Team, New York.

Main sponsor: **E. GUTZWILLER & CIE, BANQUIERS, Basel**

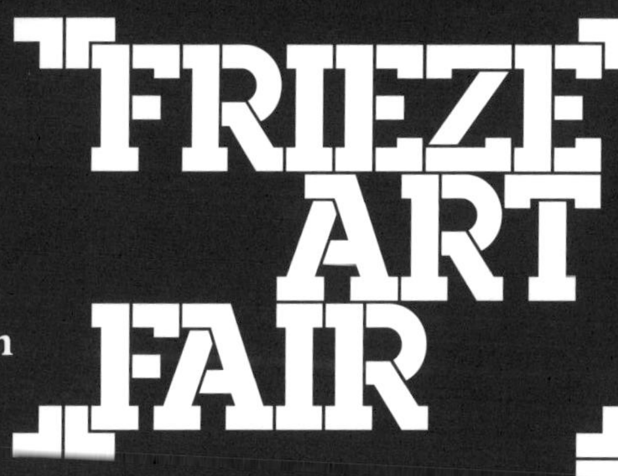
FRIEZE
ART
FAIR

art ɟɹnʞuɐɹɟ 2005

Young Arts Fair
Avantgarde, Modern, Edition

April 29 - May 2

11 a.m. to 8 p.m., last day to 6 p.m.
Messe Frankfurt, Hall 1, City Entrance
www.artfrankfurt.de
Phone + 49 69 75 75 - 66 64

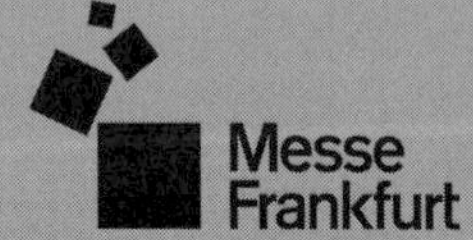

Art | Basel | Miami Beach
2–5 | 12 | 04

✳ UBS

The International Art Show – La Exposición Internacional de Arte
Art Basel Miami Beach, CH-4005 Basel
Fax +41/58-206 31 32, MiamiBeach@ArtBasel.com, www.ArtBasel.com

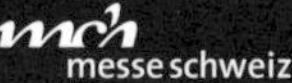

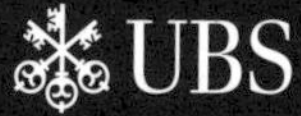

DIE ZÜRCHER GALERIEN – THE ZURICH GALLERIES

Season Opening August 25 / 26 / 27, 2004

www.dzg.ch Current Exhibitions – Represented Artists – City Map

KUNST ZÜRICH AUSSERSIHL

Previews: August 25, 2004

Art-Magazin, Rolf Müller
Militärstrasse 42, 8004 Zürich

Havana, B. Liaskowski
Dienerstrasse 30, 8004 Zürich

Mark Müller
Gessnerallee 36, 8001 Zürich

Hubert Bächler
Müllerstrasse 47, 8004 Zürich

Esther Hufschmid
Rotwandstrasse 52, 8004 Zürich

Römerapotheke, Philippe Rey
Langstr. 136, 8004 Zürich

Marlene Frei Galerie & Edition
Zwinglistrasse 36 (Hof), 8004 Zürich

Elisabeth Kaufmann
Müllerstrasse 57, 8004 Zürich

Staub (g*fzk!)
Rotwandstr. 39 (Hof), 8004 Zürich

Bob Gysin
Ausstellungsstrasse 24, 8005 Zürich

Susanna Kulli
Dienerstrasse 21, 8004 Zürich

Brigitte Weiss
Müllerstrasse 67, 8004 Zürich

ZÜRICH INNENSTADT

Previews: August 26, 2004

Annamarie M. Andersen
Bodmerstrasse 8, 8002 Zürich

gz8, Irène Ringier
Ob. Zäune 8, 8001 Zürich

Scalo
Schifflände 32, 8001 Zürich

ars Futura
Bleicherweg 45, 8002 Zürich

Lazertis
Universitätstrasse 9, 8006 Zürich

Schlégl - Nicole Schlégl
Minervastrasse 119, 8032 Zürich

Arteba Fine Art
Forchstrasse 127, 8032 Zürich

Lelong Zürich
Predigerplatz 10 - 12, 8001 Zürich

semina rerum - Irène Preiswerk
Cäcilienstrasse 3, 8032 Zürich

Art Forum Ute Barth
Kartausstrasse 8, 8008 Zürich

Lutz & Thalmann
Wettingerwies 2 B, 8001 Zürich

Stähli. Zürich. Galerie & Edition
Stampfenbachstrasse 59, 8006 Zürich

Werner Bommer
Kirchgasse 25, 8001 Zürich

Mai 36
Rämistrasse 37, 8001 Zürich

Jörg Stummer
Kapfsteig 31, 8032 Zürich

Commercio
Mühlebachstrasse 2, 8008 Zürich

Maurer
Münstergasse 14 + 18, 8001 Zürich

Jamileh Weber
Waldmannstrasse 6, 8001 Zürich

Elten & Elten - Am Hottingerplatz
Wilfriedstr.19 + Gemeindestr. 51, 8032 Zürich

Proarta AG
Bleicherweg 20, 8002 Zürich

Kunstsalon Wolfsberg
Bederstrasse 109, 8002 Zürich

Patrik Fröhlich
Kirchgasse 33, 8001 Zürich

Susanna Rüegg, galerie & poesie
Schipfe 39, 8001 Zürich

Renée Ziegler
Rämistrasse 34, 8001 Zürich

LÖWENBRÄUAREAL UND UMGEBUNG

Previews: August 27, 2004

Hauser & Wirth Zürich
Limmatstrasse 270, 8005 Zürich

Bob van Orsouw
Limmatstrasse 270, 8005 Zürich

Caratsch de Pury & Luxembourg
Limmatstrasse 264, 8005 Zürich

Peter Kilchmann
Limmatstrasse 270, 8005 Zürich

Eva Presenhuber
Limmatstrasse 270, 8005 Zürich

Fabian & Claude Walter
Limmatstrasse 270, 8005 Zürich

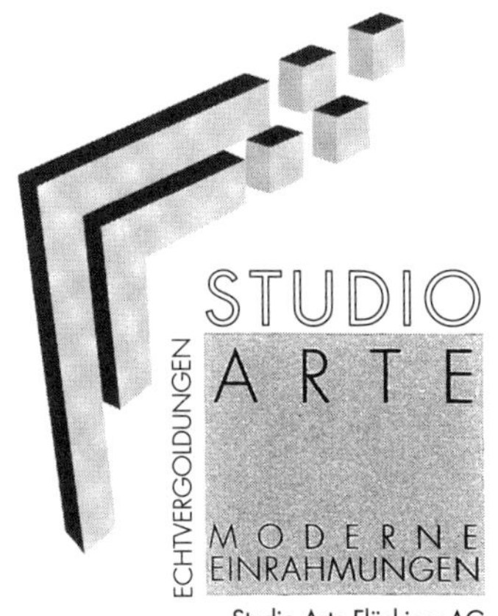

MODERNE EINRAHMUNGEN

Studio Arte Flückiger AG
Stauffacherquai 46, 8004 Zürich
Telefon 01-245 86 00
Telefax 01-241 35 85
E-Mail: studio.arte.ag@bluewin.ch

WIR HABEN ALLE RAHMEN FÜR DIE AUSSTELLUNGEN DER

PARKETT - EDITIONEN IM MUSEUM LUDWIG, KÖLN,

IM LOUISIANA MUSEUM, DÄNEMARK, IM HILL SIDE FORUM,

TOKIO, UND IM MUSEUM OF MODERN ART, NEW YORK,

HERGESTELLT.

ZU UNSEREN KUNDEN ZÄHLEN:

KUNSTSAMMLER, MUSEEN, GALERIEN, INDUSTRIE UND PRIVATE.

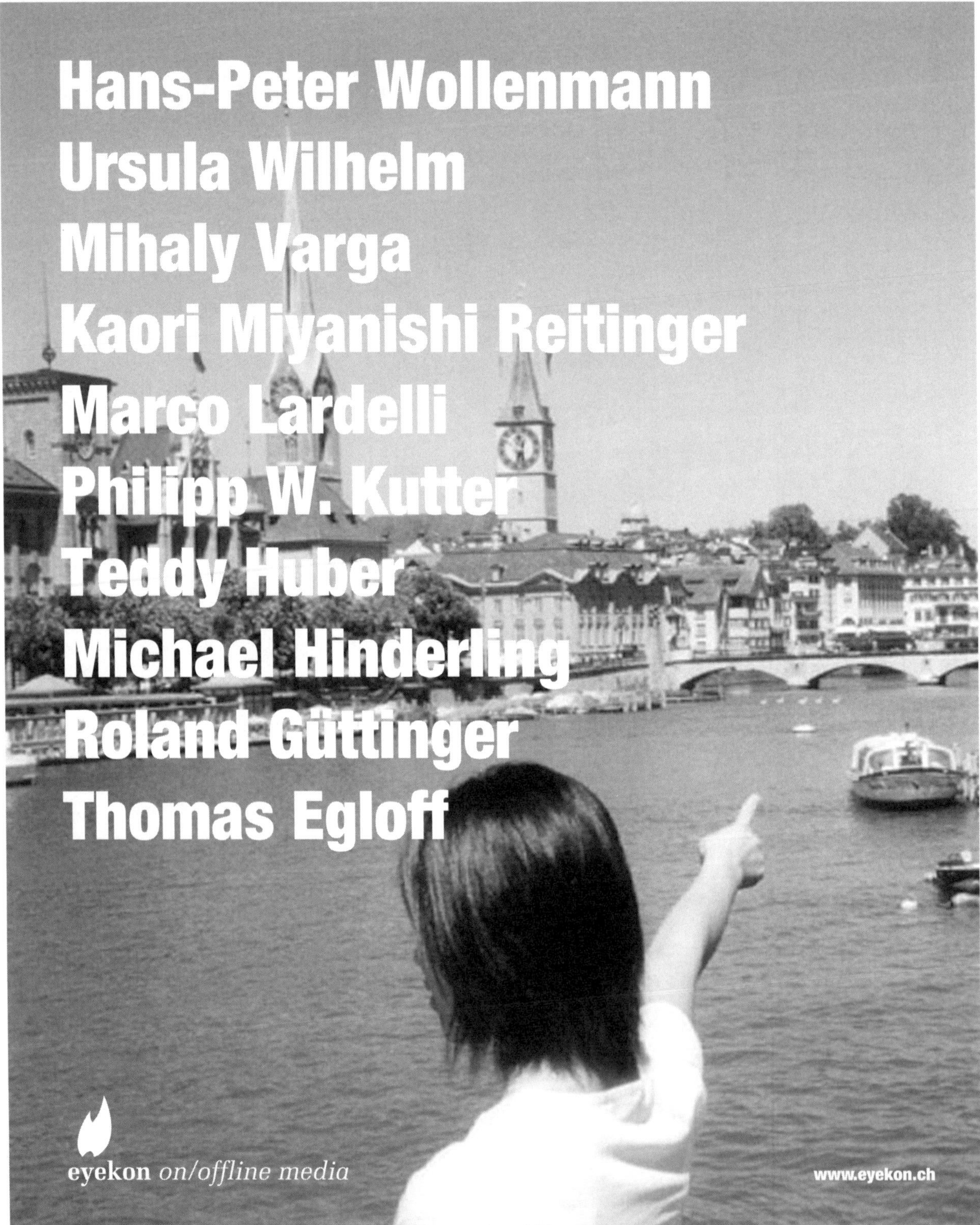

Hans-Peter Wollenmann
Ursula Wilhelm
Mihaly Varga
Kaori Miyanishi Reitinger
Marco Lardelli
Philipp W. Kutter
Teddy Huber
Michael Hinderling
Roland Güttinger
Thomas Egloff
eyekon on/offline media
www.eyekon.ch

«Je mehr Sie den ganzen Druck uns überlassen, desto weniger spüren Sie ihn.»

Um den Druck von unseren Kunden zu nehmen, haben wir unser *Projektmanagement* massiv ausgebaut. Damit evaluieren wir bereits in der Planungsphase alle nötigen und geeigneten Produktionspartner. Und führen perfekt Regie während des ganzen Projektes: von der umfassenden *Druckvorstufe* über den intern oder extern ausgeführten Druck bis hin zur Datenverwaltung. Während des ganzen Prozesses minimieren wir mögliche Informationsverluste und Kosten und optimieren die Druckpräzision und das Zeitmanagement. So können unsere Kunden aufwändige und unproduktive Koordinations- und Kontrollaufgaben sparen und uns ganz vertrauen. Damit ist die Zürichsee Druckereien AG für jeden Auftraggeber und für jedes Druckprojekt immer der richtige Partner.

Das freut unsere Kunden, unsere ehemaligen Konkurrenten und uns natürlich auch.

Mit freundlichen Grüssen
Zürichsee Druckereien AG

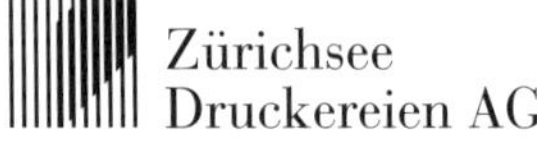

Heini Strehler, Geschäftsführer

Zürichsee
Druckereien AG

Seestrasse 86
CH-8712 Stäfa
www.zsd.ch

Telefon 01 928 53 03
Telefax 01 928 52 00
E-Mail: info@zsd.ch

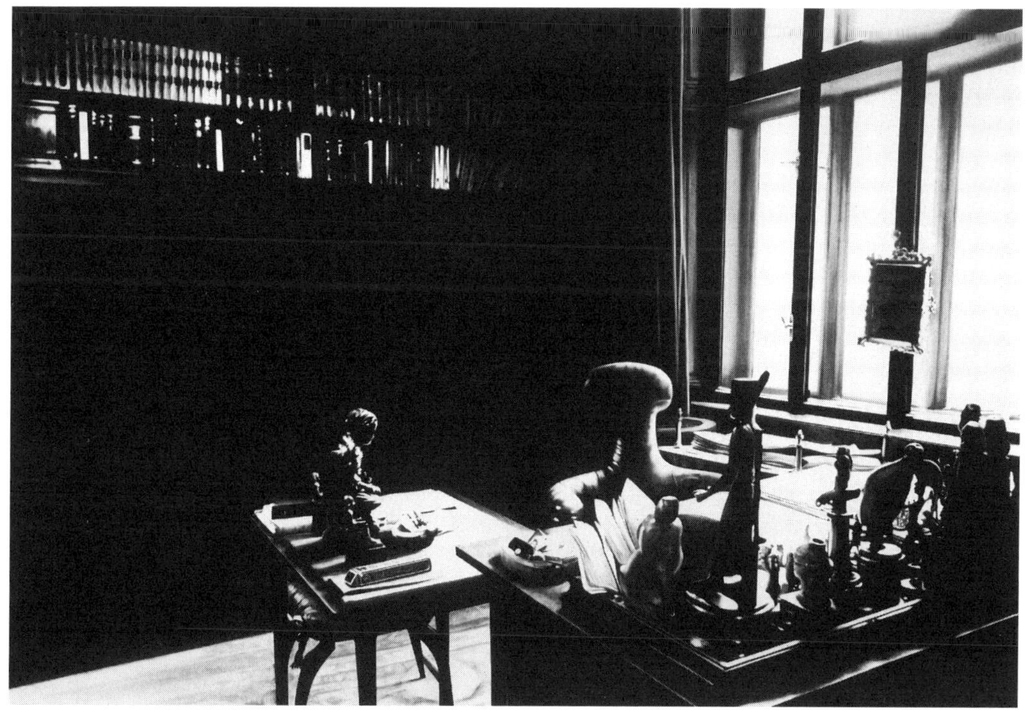

The Freud Cycle
Robert Longo

A Series of 13 digital pigment
prints on rag paper, sizes
from 81 x 60 to 113 x 177 cm
Published 2004 by
Edition Schellmann,
München-New York and
Harry Jancovici Editions, Paris

Catalog available

Edition Schellmann
New York: 210 11th Avenue
Tel 212-219 1821
Fax 212-941 9206
München: Römerstrasse 14
Tel 089-33 1717
Fax 089-33 2800

www.editionschellmann.com

S I

SPRING, SUMMER + FALL 2004

FIVE BILLION YEARS
WITH FRANÇOIS CURLET, PHILIPPE DECRAUZAT,
CEAL FLOYER, TONY MATELLI, JONATHAN MONK AND
HIROSHI SUGIMOTO
MARCH 10 – APRIL 30 2004

CHRISTOPH BÜCHEL
JUNE 1 – AUGUST 7 2004

THE LAST PAINTING SHOW CURATED BY OLIVIER MOSSET
SEP – OCT 2004

+ NEW SI EDITIONS BY
SHIRANA SHABAZI, OLAF BREUNING, NIC HESS AND OTHERS

+ OTHER EXHIBITIONS AND EVENTS (SEE WEBSITE)

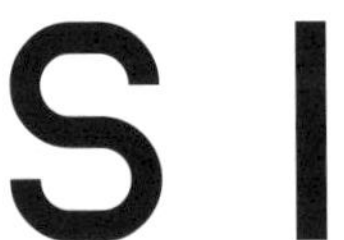

SWISS INSTITUTE - CONTEMPORARY ART
495 BROADWAY 3RD FLOOR / NEW YORK NY 10012
TUESDAY – SATURDAY 11 A.M. – 6 P.M. / p 212 925 2035 / f 212 925 2040
www.swissinstitute.net / info@swissinstitute.net

SHAKE Zurich/Belgrade/Lüneburg
ID TROUBLES · Halle für Kunst Lüneburg 15/05/04-11/07/04
Halil Altindere, Fernando Alvim, Art & Language, Annelise Coste, Minerva Cuevas, Harun Farocki, Ghazel, Helbling & Marušić, Miodrag Krkobabić, Andreja Kulunčić, Oliver Musovik, Tanja Ostojić, Anny & Sibel Öztürk, Erzen Shkololli, Milica Tomić, Andro Wekua, Stephen Willats, Jun Yang

SHAKE Linz & Nice
STAATSAFFÄRE · O.K Centrum für Gegenwartskunst 28/05/04-25/07/04
SHAKE · Villa Arson - Centre National d'Art Contemporain 03/07/04-10/10/04
Adel Abdessemed, Dennis Adams, Saâdane Afif, Kader Attia, Stéphane Bérard, Candice Breitz, Jota Castro, Wong Hoy Cheong, Antonio Gallego, Jens Haaning, Robert Jelinek-State of Sabotage, Sandra Kogut, Dorit Margreiter, Lisl Ponger, Julian Rosefeldt, Juan Esteban Sandoval,Tim Sharp, Ross Sinclair, Social Impact, Stalker, Niek van de Steeg, Ben Vautier, Luca Vitone, Jun Yang

RE:LOCATION
SHAKE

SHAKE Bucharest
SHAKE THE LIMITS · CIAC & Muzeul Naţional de Artă Contemporană 05/06/04-25/07/04
Daniel Blaufuks, Pavel Brăila, João Paulo Feliciano, Ângela Ferreira, Veli Grano, Teodor Graur, Tellervo Kalleinen, Mihaela Kavdanska, Dominik Lejman, Ciprian Mureşan, Cristian Pogăcean, Rassim, Miguel Soares, Time'sUp, Roi Vaara

SHAKE Trnava
RE:LOCATION SHAKE · Galéria Jána Koniarka 05/06/04-31/08/04
Azorro, Christoph Büchel, Simone Decker, EVA & ADELE, Volker Eichelmann & Jonathan Faiers & Roland Rust, Oliver Sadovský & Matúš Vallo, Milan Tittel; project 'PuBLIC CoMMISSION'

SHAKE Luxembourg
RE:LOCATION ACADEMY / SHAKE SOCIETY · Casino Luxembourg 19/06/04-26/09/04
Irina Botea, Hsia-Fei Chang, Jon Mikel Euba, Esra Ersen, Iratxe Jaio, Charlotte Karlsson, Aurelio Kopainig, Vlad Nanca, Isa Riedl, Mia Rosasco, Janek Simon, Veronika Šramatyová

SHAKE Gdańsk
HAMLET OR (RATHER) MUCH ADO ABOUT NOTHING? · Centrum Sztuki Współczesnej Łaźnia 26/06/04-15/08/04
Azorro, Oskar Dawicki, Roman Dziatkiewicz, Grzegorz Klaman, Felix Kubin, Marysia Lewandowska & Neil Cummings, Robert Rumas, Grzegorz Sztwiertnia, Julita Wójcik, Piotr Wyrzykowski

SHAKE NIGHT 09/07/04
Television programme 10 p.m. – midnight CEST / 11 p.m. – 1 a.m. EEST

www.re-location.org

Curators: Adam Budak, Zoran Erić, Laurence Gateau, Viera Jančeková, Enrico Lunghi, Heike Munder, Genoveva Rückert, Maria Rus Bojan, Bettina Steinbrügge

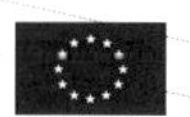
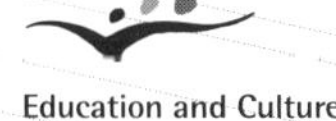
Education and Culture

Culture 2000

Casino Luxembourg - Forum d'art contemporain, Luxembourg (L) · Centrul Internaţional pentru Artă Contemporană & Muzeul Naţional de Artă Contemporană, Bucharest & Fundaţia ArtStudio, Cluj (RO) · Centrum Sztuki Współczesnej Łaźnia, Gdańsk (PL) · Galéria Jána Koniarka, Trnava (SK) · migros museum für gegenwartskunst, Zurich (CH) & Halle für Kunst, Lüneburg (D) · O.K Centrum für Gegenwartskunst, Linz (A) · Villa Arson - Centre National d'Art Contemporain, Nice (F)

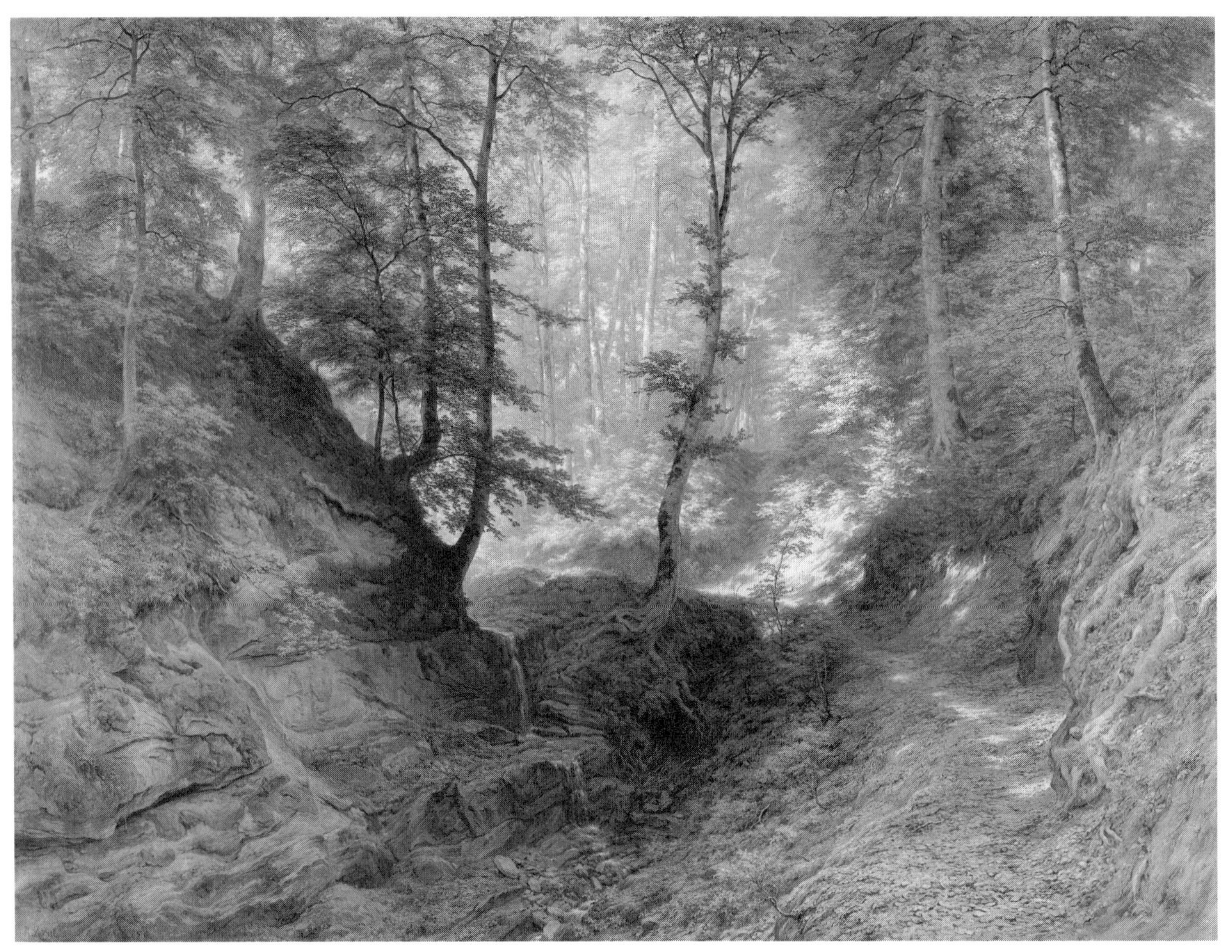

Robert Zünd (1828–1909)
June 12 – September 26, 2004

Rudolf Blättler "Schwarzes Haus II"
May 25 – November 14, 2004

Dominique Goblet, Lorenzo Mattotti,
Stefano Ricci, Caroline Sury
exhibition in collaboration with
Comix Festival Fumetto
May 1 – Juli 18, 2004

Andreas Glauser "Random Room"
June 12 – August 8, 2004

Kunstmuseum Luzern Museum of Art Lucerne
Europaplatz 1 (KKL Level K) CH–6002 Luzern Tel. +41 (0)41 226 78 00
Infotel. +41 (0)41 226 78 78 www. kunstmuseumluzern.ch

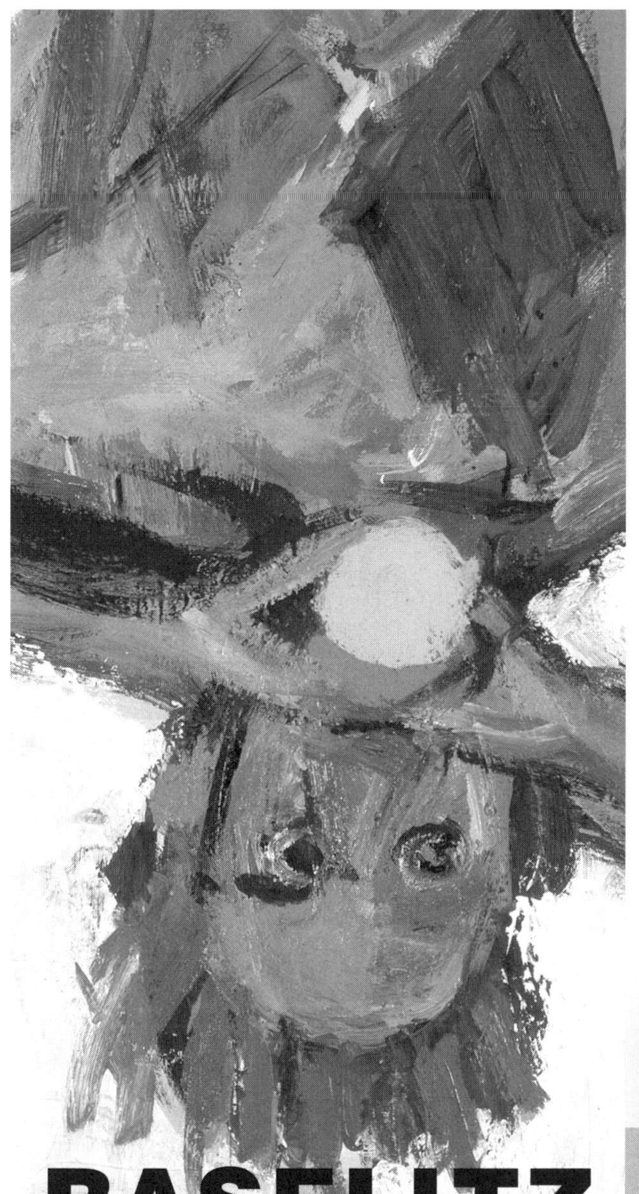

BASELITZ
BILDER, DIE DEN KOPF VERDREHEN
EINE RETROSPEKTIVE · BILDER UND SKULPTUREN VON 1959 BIS 2004
2. APRIL BIS 8. AUGUST 2004
KUNST- UND AUSSTELLUNGSHALLE
DER BUNDESREPUBLIK DEUTSCHLAND
MUSEUMSMEILE · 53113 BONN · FRIEDRICH-EBERT-ALLEE 4 · U-BAHN-STATION HEUSSALLEE
TEL 0228/9171-200 · WWW.BUNDESKUNSTHALLE.DE · INFO@KAH-BONN.DE
ÖFFNUNGSZEITEN: DI + MI 10 – 21 UHR · DO – SO 10 – 19 UHR
MO GESCHLOSSEN · FREITAGS KOSTENLOSER EINTRITT FÜR SCHULKLASSEN
PHOTOKONTAKT
BENJAMIN KATZ : GEORG BASELITZ

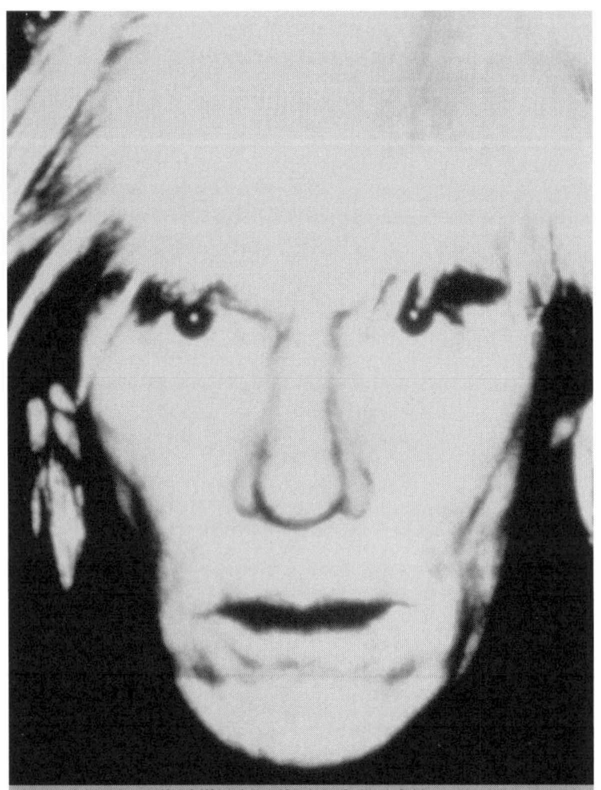
Andy Warhol, Self-Portrait, 1986. © 2004, Andy Warhol Foundation/Pro Litteris, Zürich

Andy Warhol
Self-Portraits

Kunstverein St. Gallen
Kunstmuseum
13. Juni – 12. September 04

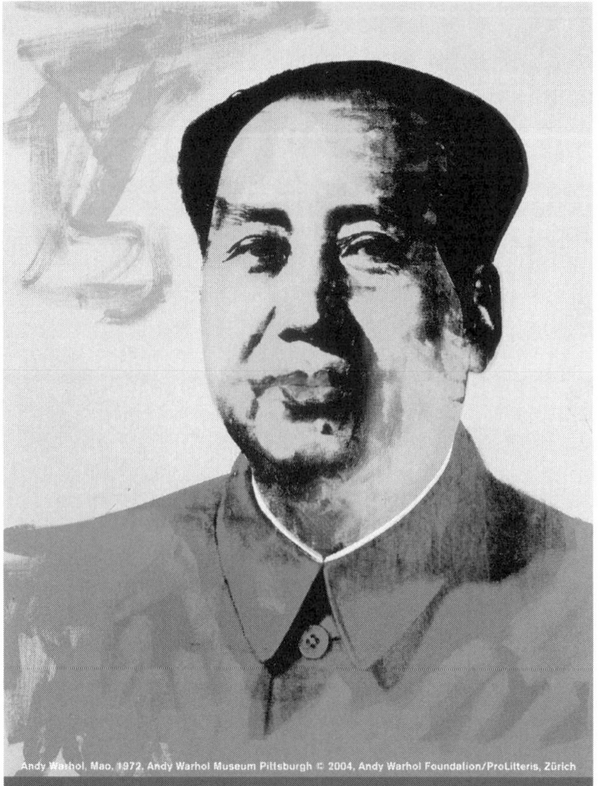
Andy Warhol, Mao, 1972, Andy Warhol Museum Pittsburgh © 2004, Andy Warhol Foundation/ProLitteris, Zürich

Andy Warhol
The Late Work

13. Juni – 12. September 04

KUNSTMUSEUM
LIECHTENSTEIN

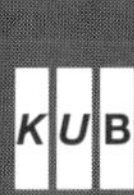

12. Juni bis 5. September 2004

JENNY HOLZER

Kunsthaus Bregenz
Karl Tizian Platz
A-6900 Bregenz
Telefon +43-(0)55 74-485 94-0
www.kunsthaus-bregenz.at

Dienstag – Sonntag 10 – 18 Uhr
Donnerstag 10 – 21 Uhr

**Während der Bregenzer Festspiele
(21. Juli – 22. August 04),
täglich** 10 – 21 Uhr

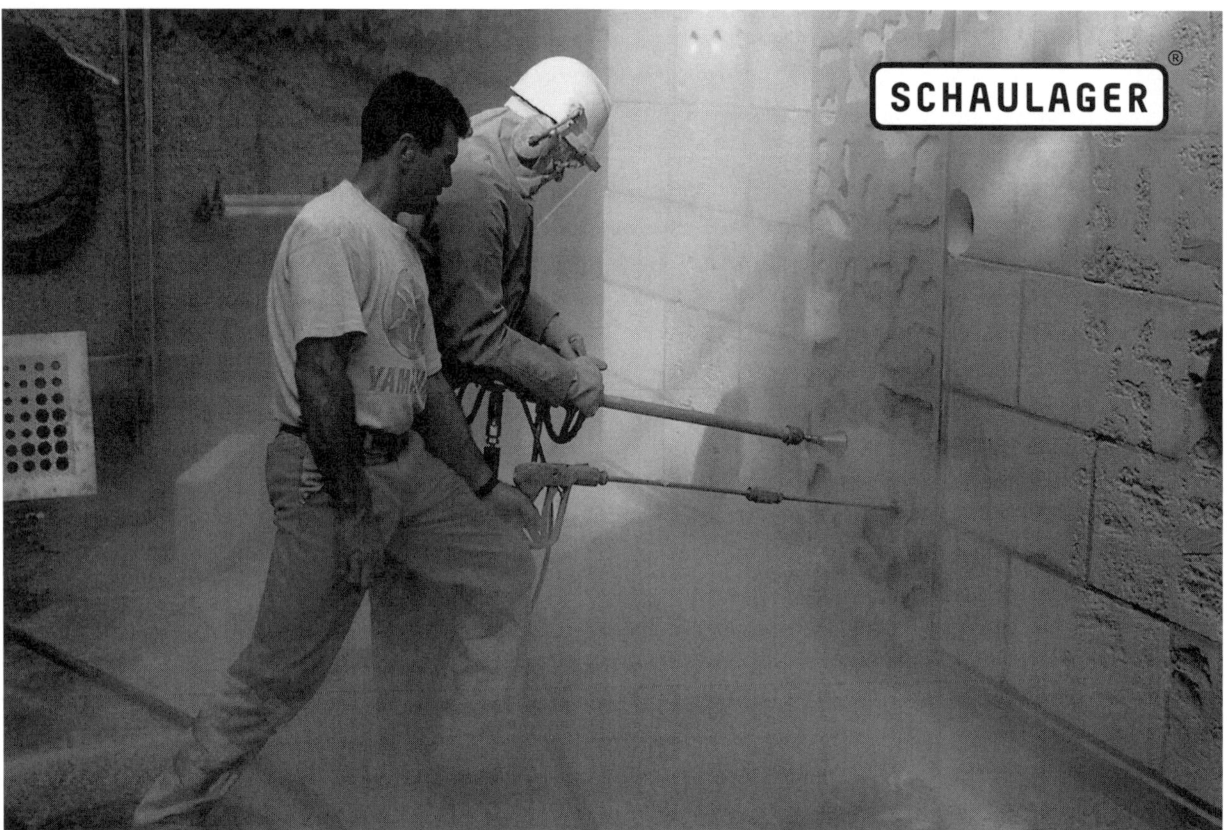

HERZOG & DE MEURON

NO. 250

EINE AUSSTELLUNG
8. MAI BIS 12. SEPTEMBER 2004

Schaulager Ruchfeldstrasse 19 CH-4142 Münchenstein/Basel
T +41 61 335 32 32   F +41 61 335 32 30   www.schaulager.org

LAURENZ-STIFTUNG

Bregenz Kunsthaus

Jenny Holzer | Secret

12.6. – 5.9.04

Di–So 10–18, Do 10–21; 21.7.–22.8. 10–21 Uhr | T (+43-5574) 485 94-0
www.kunsthaus-bregenz.at

40 km ↓

St.Gallen Kunstmuseum

Andy Warhol | Self-Portraits

13.6. – 12.9.04

Di–Fr 10–12, 14–17 Uhr; Mi bis 20 Uhr; Sa/So 10–17 Uhr | T (+41-71) 242 06 71
www.kunstmuseumsg.ch

70 km ↓

Vaduz Kunstmuseum Liechtenstein

Andy Warhol | The Late Work

13.6. – 12.9.04

Di–So 10–17 Uhr, Do 10–20 Uhr | T (+423) 235 03 00
www.kunstmuseum.li

40 km ↓

Chur Bündner Kunstmuseum

Giovanni Segantini | Zeichnungen

5.6. – 5.9.04

Di–So 10–17 Uhr, Do 10–20 Uhr | T (+41-81) 257 28 68
www.buendner-kunstmuseum.ch

40 km ↑

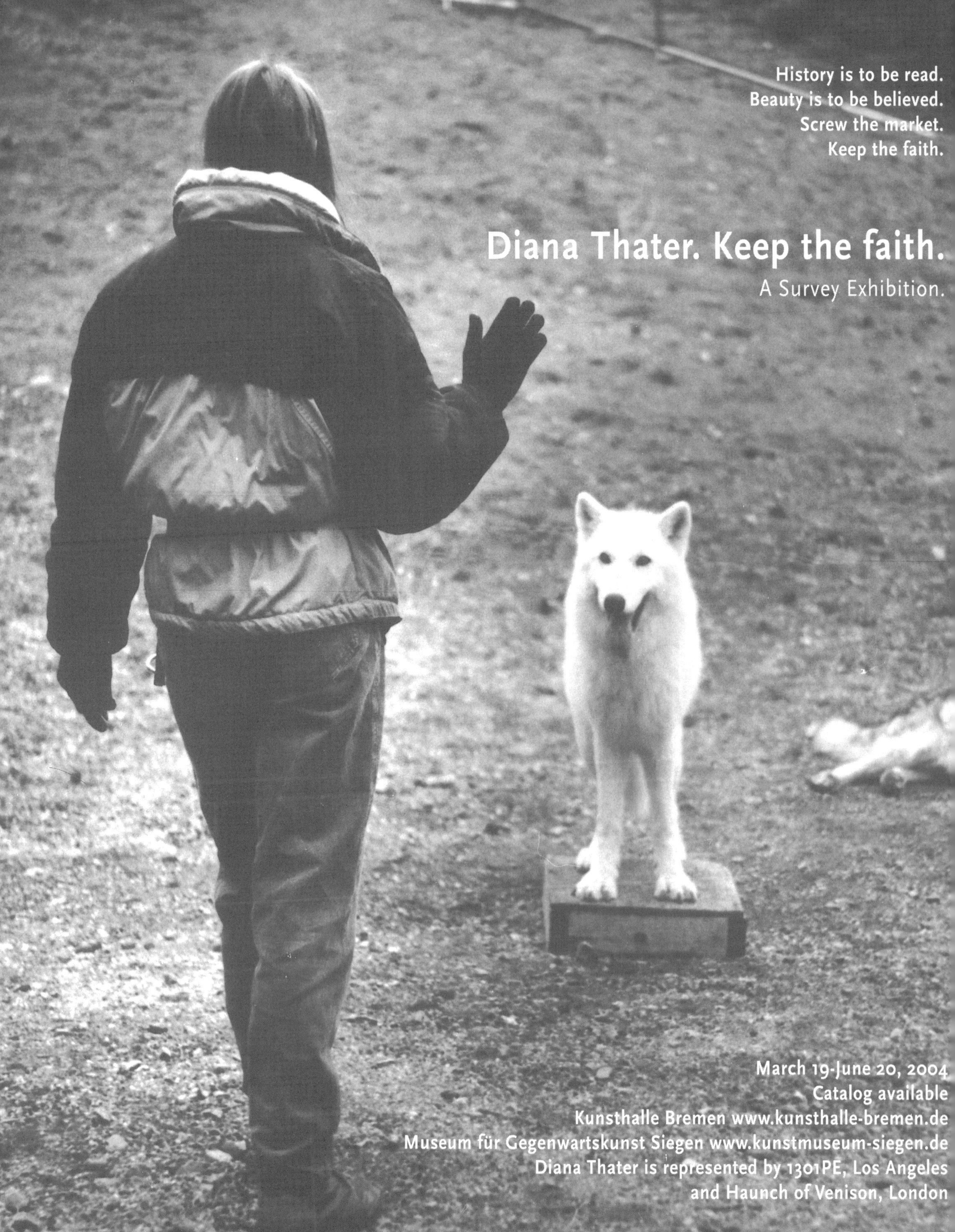

History is to be read.
Beauty is to be believed.
Screw the market.
Keep the faith.

Diana Thater. Keep the faith.
A Survey Exhibition.

March 19-June 20, 2004
Catalog available
Kunsthalle Bremen www.kunsthalle-bremen.de
Museum für Gegenwartskunst Siegen www.kunstmuseum-siegen.de
Diana Thater is represented by 1301PE, Los Angeles
and Haunch of Venison, London

MAX BECKMANN

APRIL – MAY 2004

ALIGHIERO E BOETTI

JUNE – AUGUST 2004

CARATSCH de PURY & LUXEMBOURG

LIMMATSTRASSE 264 CH - 8005 ZÜRICH
TEL 41-1-276 80 20   FAX 41-1-276 80 21
MONTAG - FREITAG 10 - 6   SAMSTAG 11 - 5

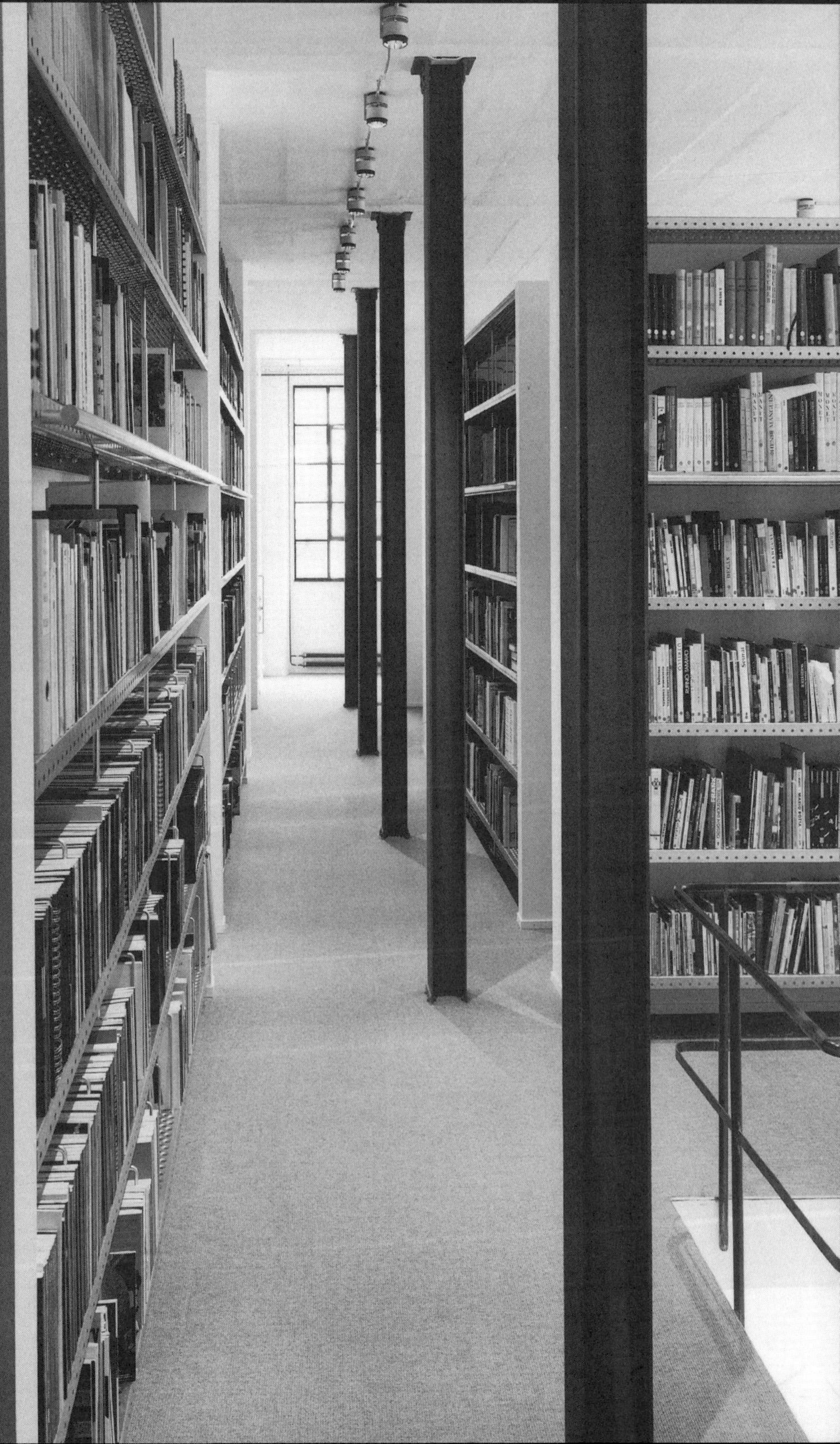

jean-luc
verna

'Vous n'êtes pas un peu beaucoup maquillé ? – non'
Works on paper from 1994 to 2003 _ In collaboration with Air de Paris, Paris

18_03_04-01_05_04

raymond
pettibon

Selected works from 1982 to 2003 & Speaks Volumes, 1995

BFAS
Blondeau Fine Art Services

5 rue de la Muse
1205 Geneva _ Switzerland
T +41 (0)22 544 95 95
F +41 (0)22 544 95 99
■ contact _ Philippe Davet
philippe@bfasblondeau.com

■ exhibition
THU-FRI 14h-18h30
SAT   11h-17h
■ offices
MON-FRI 9h-12h30 / 14h-18h30

Claes Oldenburg
Coosje van Bruggen

Images à la Carte

April 24 – July 2   534 West 21st Street
A full-color book by the artists has been published in connection with the exhibition.

Paul D. Miller a.k.a.
DJ Spooky that Subliminal Kid

Path is Prologue

May 26 – June 18   521 West 21st Street

Art Basel 2004

June 16 – June 21   Hall 2, Stand R4

Paula Cooper Gallery

534 West 21st Street New York NY 10011   T 212 255 1105   F 212 255 5156

info@paulacoopergallery.com

THOMAS AMMANN FINE ART AG ZURICH

CY TWOMBLY

JUNE 14 – SEPTEMBER 30, 2004

RESTELBERGSTRASSE 97 · CH-8044 ZÜRICH · TEL +41 1 360 51 60 · FAX +41 1 360 51 61
WWW.AMMANNFINEART.COM · DA@AMMANNFINEART.COM

frank stella

moby dick – waves – imaginary places

may 7 – july 3, 2004

art 35'04 *booth 2.0 f2*
june 16 – 21, 2004

michael biberstein

paintings

august 26 – october 9, 2004

galerie jamileh weber

waldmannstrasse 6 · ch–8001 zürich
tel +41 1 252 10 66 · fax +41 1 252 11 32
www.jamilehweber.com · info@jamilehweber.com

FRANZ WEST
2 X 20 JAHRE PARKETT, 2004

Büchergestell. Armierungsstahl, Plexiglas, vier Räder,
120 x 60 x 30 cm.

Auflage: 99, signiertes und nummeriertes Zertifikat.

CHF 4400 / € 2900

2 X 20 YEARS OF PARKETT, 2004

Bookshelf. Reinforcing steel, Plexiglas, four wheels,
47 1/4 x 23 5/8 x 11 13/16".

Edition of 99, signed and numbered certificate.

$ 3500 / € 2900

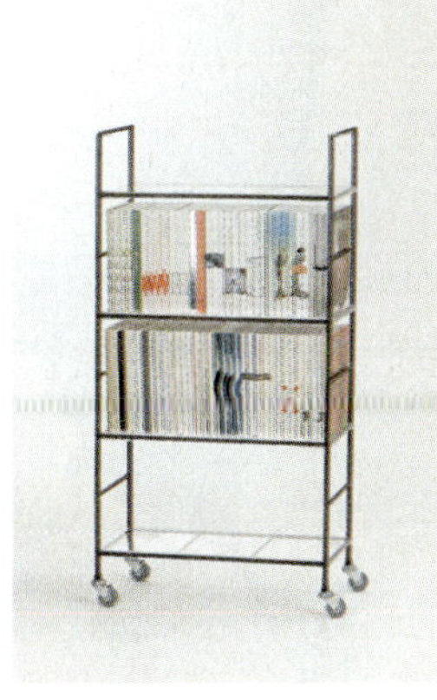

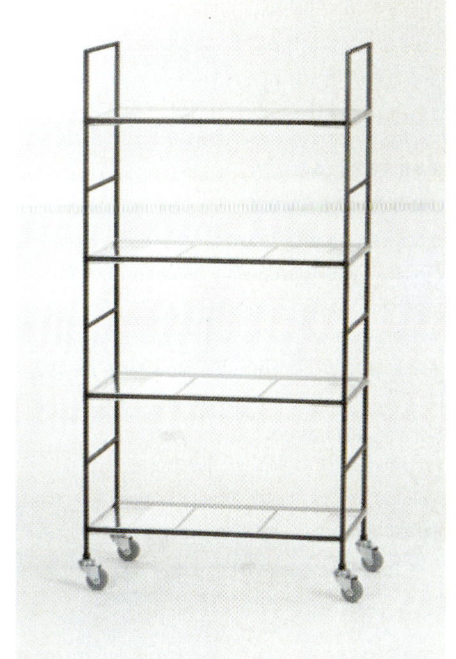

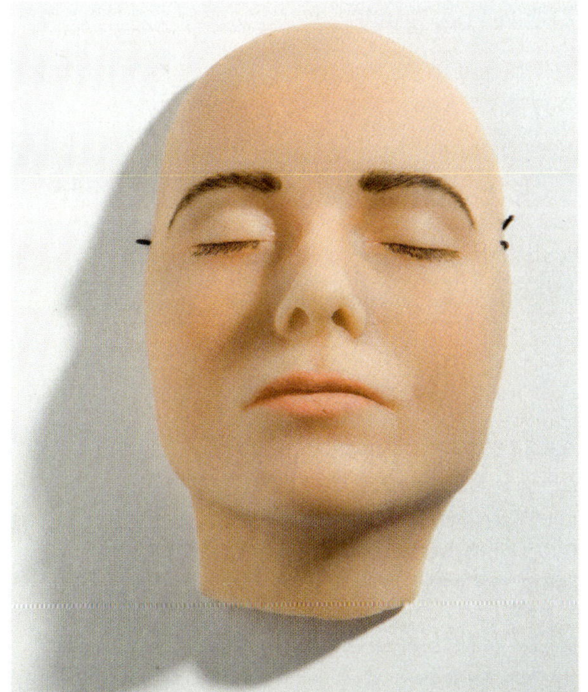

GILLIAN WEARING
SLEEPING MASK, 2004

Wax (reinforced by polymer resin), paint, 8 1/4 x 5 5/16".
Produced by Making Objects Ltd., London.
Edition of 60, signed and numbered.

$ 1600 / € 1350

SCHLAFENDE MASKE, 2004

Wachs (verstärkt mit Polymerharz), Farbe, 21 x 13,5 cm
Produktion: Making Objects Ltd., London.
Auflage: 60, signiert und nummeriert.

CHF 2100 / € 1350

PARKETT 62
JOHN WESLEY
BOYFRIENDS, 2001
6-color silkscreen on Coventry 290 gm²;
paper size 31 x 38", image size 28 x 35".
Printed by Bob Blanton, Brand X Editions, New York
Edition of 70, signed and numbered, **$ 1050 / € 980**

Siebdruck (6 Farben) auf Coventry 290 gm²;
Papierformat 87,7 x 96,5 cm; Bild 71 x 89 cm.
Gedruckt von Bob Blanton, Brand X Editions, New York
Auflage: 70, signiert und nummeriert, **CHF 1500.– / € 980**

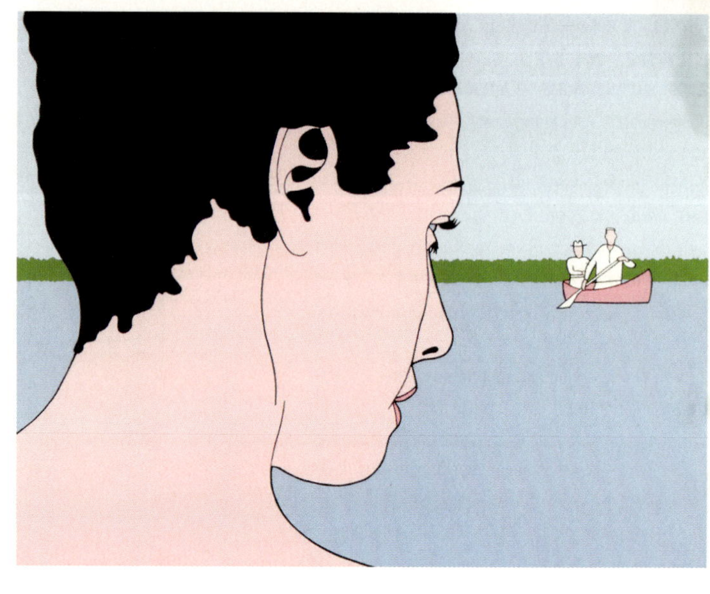

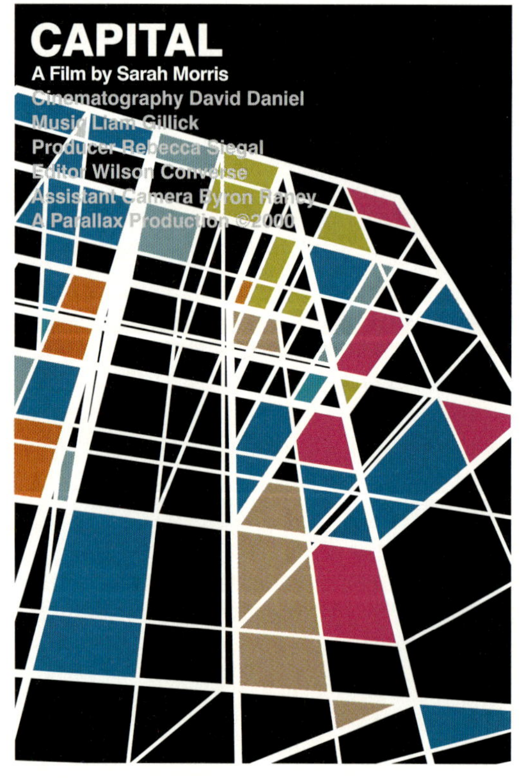

PARKETT 61
SARAH MORRIS
CAPITAL (A FILM BY SARAH MORRIS), 2001
8-color silkscreen on 300 gm² Somerset satin, 60 x 40".
Designed by Sarah Morris/Peter Saville, printed by Coriander Studio Ltd., London.
Edition of 70, signed and numbered, **$ 1380 / € 1270**

Siebdruck (8 Farben) auf 300 gm² Somerset-Satin, 150 x 100 cm.
Design Sarah Morris/Peter Saville, gedruckt bei Coriander Studio Ltd., London.
Auflage: 70, signiert und nummeriert, **CHF 1950.– / € 1270**

PARKETT 63
TRACEY EMIN
SELF-PORTRAIT, 12.11.01
Unique color print from original Polaroid;
all images taken on the same day.
Image size 7 $^7/_8$ x 7 $^7/_8$", paper size 15 $^3/_4$ x 15 $^3/_4$".
Edition of 80, signed and numbered, **$ 990 / € 910**

SELBSTPORTRÄT, 12.11.01
Abzug einer Polaroidaufnahme, Unikat;
alle Aufnahmen entstanden am gleichen Tag.
Bildgrösse 20 x 20 cm, Papierformat 40 x 40 cm.
Auflage: 80, signiert und nummeriert, **CHF 1400.– / € 910**

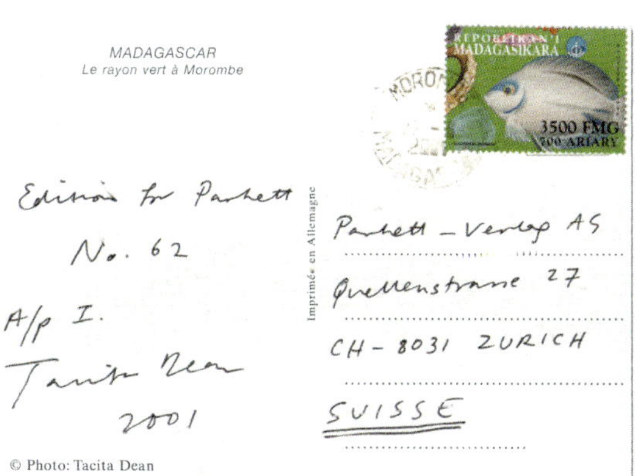

PARKETT 62
TACITA DEAN
THE GREEN RAY, 2001
Color postcard, 105 x 148,5 mm.
Printed by Steidl Verlag, Göttingen, Germany.
Edition of 100, signed, numbered, stamped, and posted in Morombe,
Western Madagascar **$ 410 / € 380**

Farbpostkarte, 105 x 148,5 mm
Gedruckt bei Steidl Verlag, Göttingen.
Auflage: 100, signiert, nummeriert, mit Poststempel aufgegeben in
Morombe, West-Madagaskar, **CHF 580.– / € 380**

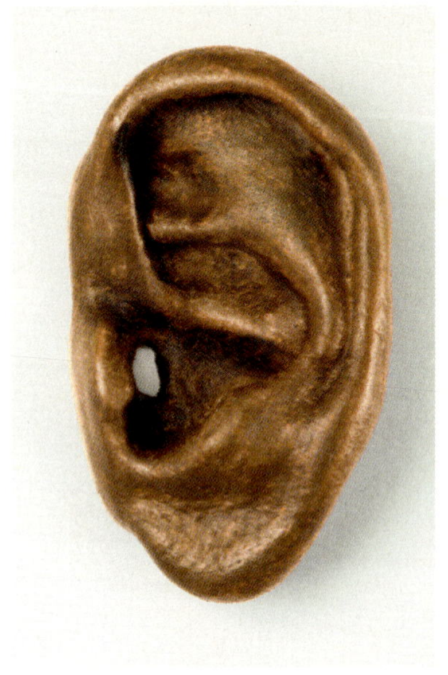

PARKETT 70
CHRISTIAN MARCLAY
MY BAD EAR, 2004

Life-size bronze cast
by Modern Art Foundry, Astoria, NY.
Edition of 60, signed and numbered.
$ 1100 / € 900

MEIN SCHLECHTES OHR, 2004

Bronze, Abguss im Massstab 1:1.
Guss: Modern Art Foundry, Astoria, NY.
Auflage: 60, signiert und nummeriert
CHF 1400 / € 900

PARKETT 70
WILHELM SASNAL
CONCORDE IS DEAD, 2004

Color contact print from engraved negative
on Kodak paper, 12 5/8 x 18 7/8".
Edition of 60, signed and numbered.
$ 950 / € 800

Farbphotographie mit (auf dem Negativ)
eingravierter Schrift,
Kontaktabzug auf Kodakpapier, 32 x 48 cm.
Auflage: 60, signiert und nummeriert.
CHF 1200 / € 800

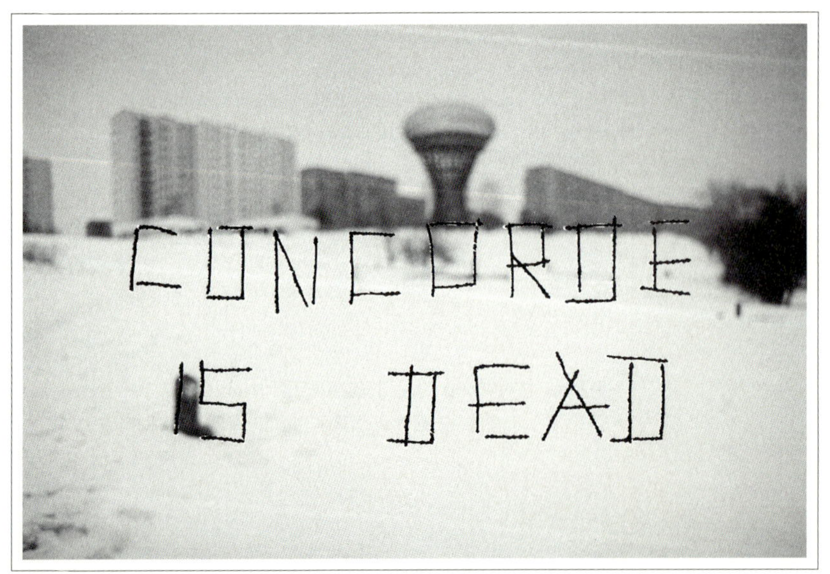

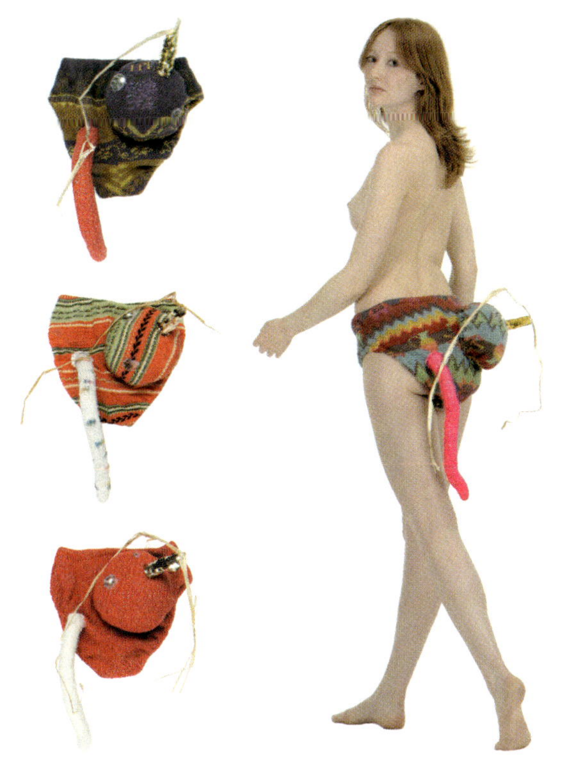

PARKETT 67

JOHN BOCK

**GEOMETRISCHER ORT DER 2 MIO. $ KNÖDELKNIK-
KERBOCKERMIGRÄNEHITSHITBITSSOUFFLÉVISAGE,
DRIN STROHMULMIGE ISOQUANTE TOUCHIERT
GOLDENE BILANZREGEL + INSOLVENZSNOB, 2003**

Unikat-Unterhose, Strickmaterial, Goldpailletten, Strohhalm, Silikon,
Hasenkötel, Migränetablette.
Auflage: 60, signiertes und nummeriertes Zertifikat.
CHF 1400.– / € 920

Unique underpants, knitted fabric, gold sequins, straw, silicone, bunny
droppings, migraine pill.
Edition of 60, signed and numbered certificate.
$ 1000 / € 920

PARKETT 67

PETER DOIG

GASTHOF, 2003

7-color etching with aquatint, 26 x 22'',
on Hahnemühle 300 gm², natural white, 31 x 26''.
Printed by Hope Sufferance Press, London.
Edition of 70, signed and numbered.
$ 1300 / € 1200

Radierung und Aquatinta (7 Farben), 66 x 55,5 cm,
auf Hahnemühle 300 gm², naturweiss, 73 x 63 cm.
Gedruckt bei Hope Sufferance Press, London.
Auflage: 70, signiert und nummeriert.
CHF 1800.–/ € 1200

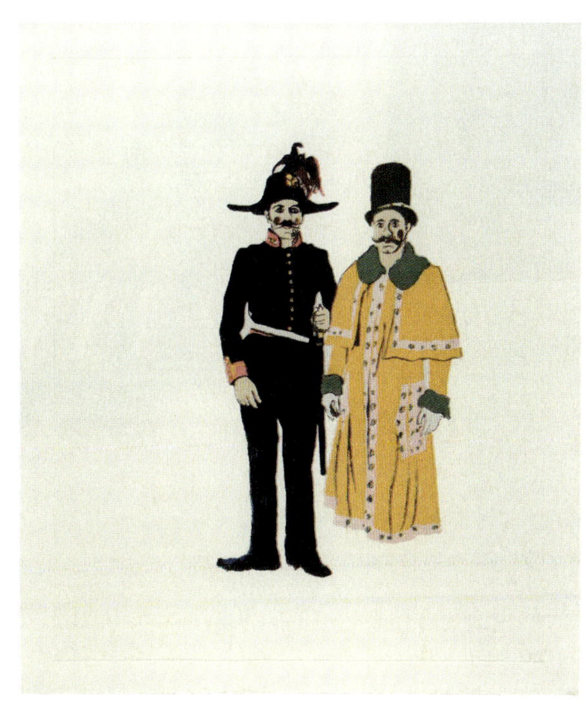

PARKETT 49
LAURIE ANDERSON
HEARRING, 1997
Earring with playable sound message
(approx. 20 sec.), brass, copper, circuit board,
loudspeaker, lithium battery,
plexiglas, wires, approx. size: 3 ³/₈ x 1 ³/₄ x 1''.
Jewelry by Josiah Dearborn; engineering design Bob Bielecki.
Ed. 150, with monogram and numbered, **$ 430 / € 390**

HEARRING, 1997
Ohrring mit abspielbarem Tonstück (ca. 20 Sek.),
Messing, Kupfer, Chip, Lautsprecher, Lithiumbatterie, Plexiglas, Elektrodraht,
Grösse ca. 8,5 x 4,5 x 2,5 cm.
Juwelierarbeit: Josiah Dearborn. Technikdesign: Bob Bielecki.
Ed. 150, mit Monogramm und nummeriert, **CHF 600.– / € 390**

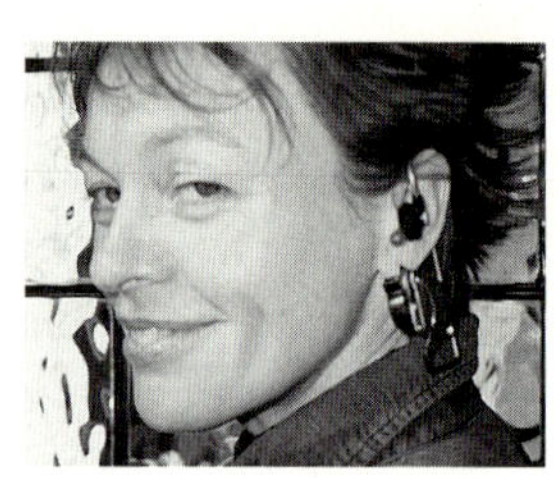

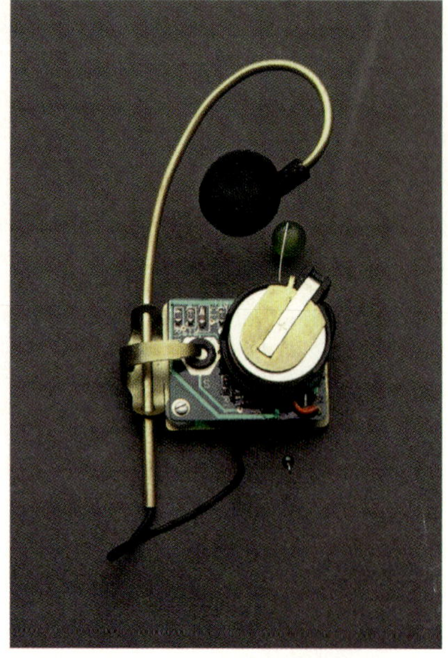

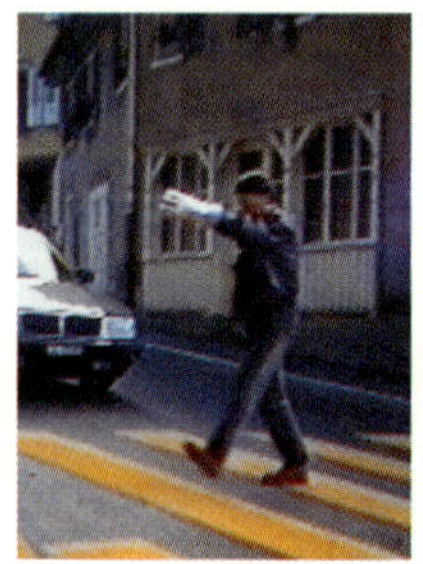

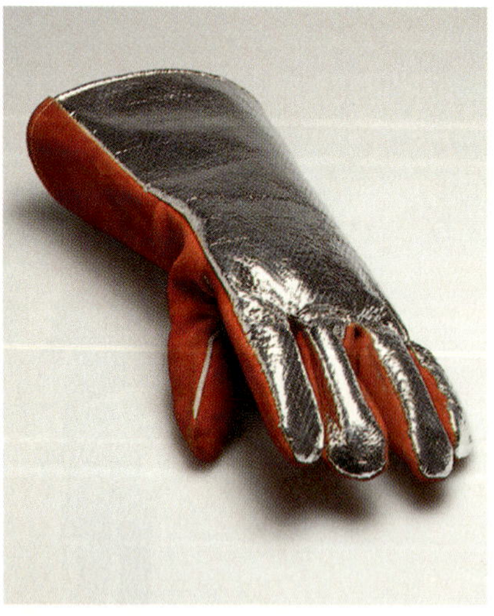

PARKETT 45
ROMAN SIGNER
FEUERWEHRHANDSCHUH MIT PHOTO, 1995
Handfläche aus hitzebeständigem Spezialspaltleder, Handrücken
aus hitzereflektierendem, aluminisiertem KEVLAR-Gewebe 550 g/m2,
isolierendes Wollfutter, Länge 35 cm,
Photographie aus einem Video von Aleksandra Signer, ca. 13 x 18 cm
Ed. 80, signiert und nummeriert, **CHF 750.– / € 490**

FIREMAN'S GLOVE WITH PHOTOGRAPH, 1995
Standard fireman's glove with heat-resistant red suede palm, heat-reflecting,
aluminized KEVLAR back, 550 g/m2, insulating woolen lining,
length 13 ³/₄'', still from a video by Aleksandra Signer, approx. 5 ¹/₈ x 7 ¹/₈''.
Ed. 80, signed and numbered, **$ 530 / € 490**

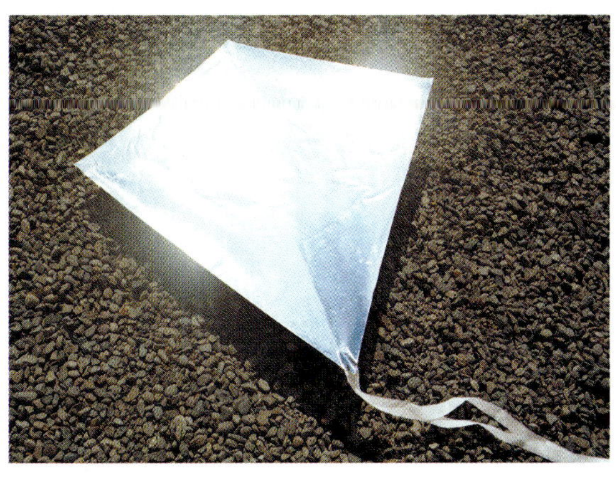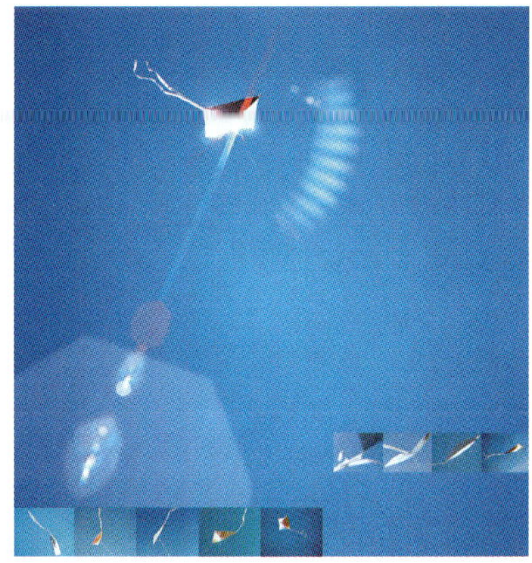

PARKETT 57

DOUG AITKEN

DECREASE THE MASS AND RUN LIKE HELL, 1999

Mirror kite, ca. 34 x 33 $^1/_2$", tail 37 $^3/_8$",

with poster of flying kite, ca. 20 x 15 $^5/_8$".

Edition of 60, stamped and numbered, **$ 700 / € 650**

DIE MASSE VERKLEINERN UND RENNEN WIE DER TEUFEL, 1999

Spiegeldrachen, ca. 86,5 x 85 cm, Schwanz 95 cm,

und Plakat mit fliegendem Drachen, 51 x 39,6 cm.

Auflage 60, mit Prägestempel und nummeriert, **CHF 990.– / € 650**

FEATHER THE LIGHT AND CAST A SPELL: THIS
KITE PREYS ON REFLECTION.

LICHTHUNGRIGER LUFTFLITZER HÄNGT SEINEN
REFLEXIONEN NACH.

MIRACULUM HELVUM MAGNUM.

PARKETT 50/51

JEFF KOONS

**INFLATABLE BALLOON FLOWER
(YELLOW), 1997**

PVC, approx. 51 x 59 x 70".

Manufactured by Schultes, Vienna.

Edition of 100, signed and numbered,

$ 3900 / € 3600

**AUFBLASBARE BALLONBLUME
(GELB), 1997**

PVC, ca. 128 x 148 x 180 cm.

Hergestellt bei Schultes, Wien.

Auflage: 100, signiert und nummeriert,

CHF 5500.– / € 3600

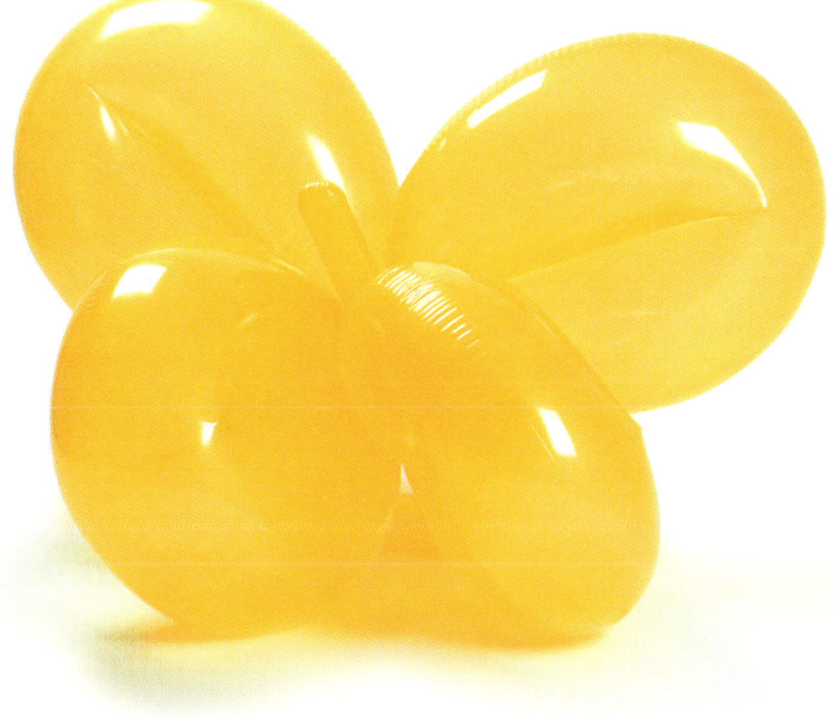

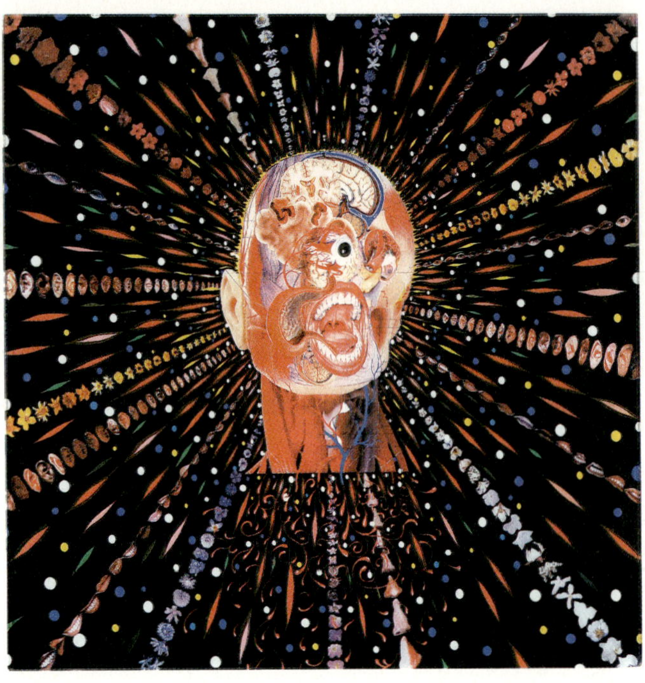

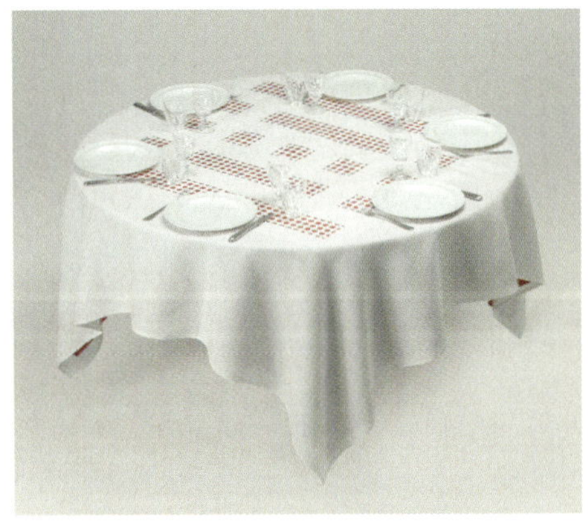

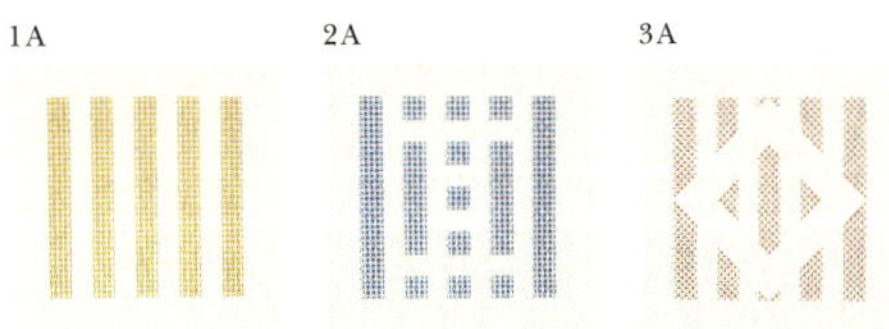

1A   2A   3A

PARKETT 68

DAN GRAHAM

**FUN FOR KIDS AT MY WORK IN
A PARK IN MANHATTAN, 2003**

Piezo Ultrachrome Pigment on Hahnemühle paper, 13 x 16 ½''.

Printed by Laumont Editions, New York.

Photograph by Rosalind Cutforth.

Edition of 60, signed and numbered on the reverse.

$ 1400 / € 1200

Piezo-Ultrachrome-Pigmentdruck auf Hahnemühle, 33 x 42 cm.

Gedruckt bei Laumont Editions, New York.

Photographie von Rosalind Cutforth.

Auflage: 60, auf der Rückseite signiert und nummeriert.

CHF 1800 / € 1200

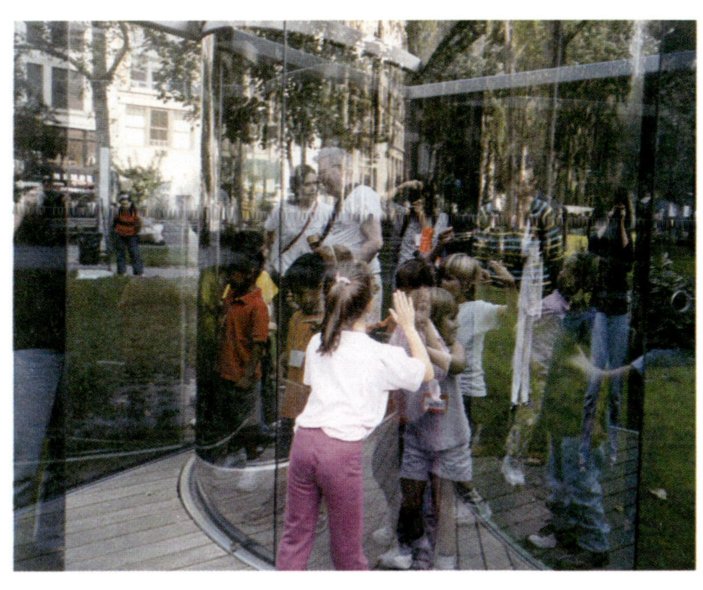

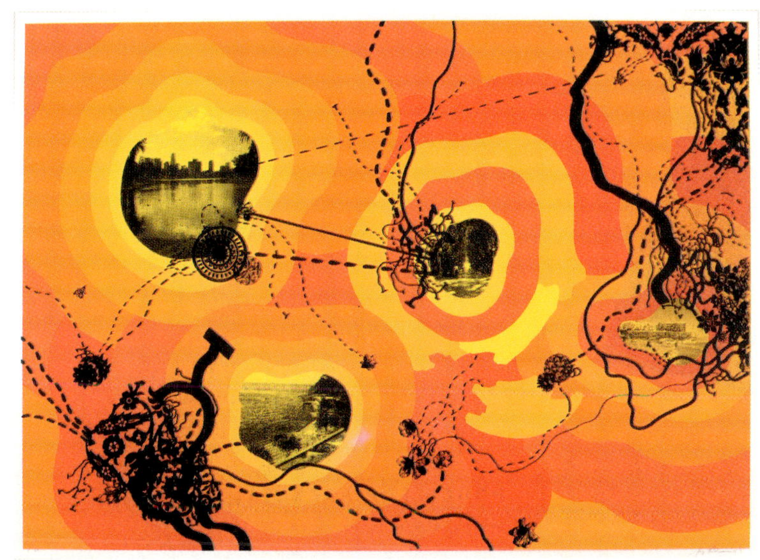

PARKETT 68

FRANZ ACKERMANN

PEAK SEASON, 2003

Siebdruck (10 Farben) auf Somerset 300 gm²;
Blattformat 50 x 70 cm, Bildformat 48 x 68 cm.

Druck: Werkstatt für Kunstsiebdruck München.

Auflage: 70, signiert und nummeriert.

CHF 1700.– / € 1100

10-color silkscreen print on Somerset 300 gm²;
paper size 19 ¹¹⁄₁₆ x 27 ⁹⁄₁₆'', image size 18 ⁷⁄₈ x 26 ³⁄₄''.

Printed by Werkstatt für Kunstsiebdruck Munich.

Edition of 70, signed and numbered.

$ 1400 / € 1100

PARKETT 44
RIRKRIT TIRAVANIJA
UNTITLED, 1995 (450/375)
Gold-rimmed Ray Ban glasses with engraving on the lenses:
LONG RIVER   A SINGLE LINE
ORANGE SAFFRON   AT TWILIGHT
Ed. 80, numbered, with signed certificate, **$ 530 / € 490**

OHNE TITEL, 1995 (450/375)
Metallbrille Ray Ban mit Gravur auf den Gläsern:
LONG RIVER   A SINGLE LINE
ORANGE SAFFRON   AT TWILIGHT
Ed. 80, nummeriert, mit signiertem Zertifikat, **CHF 750.– / € 490**

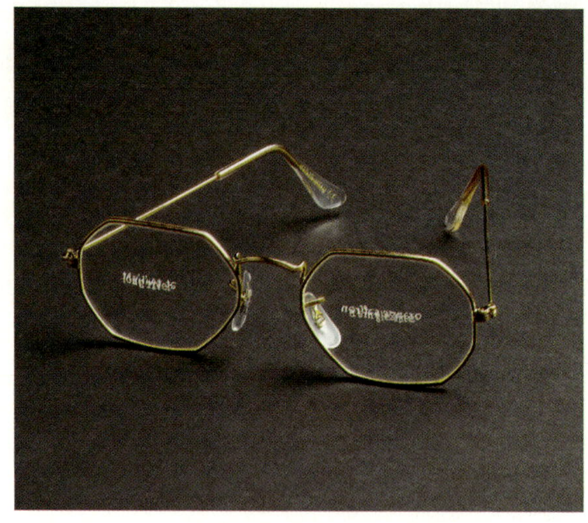

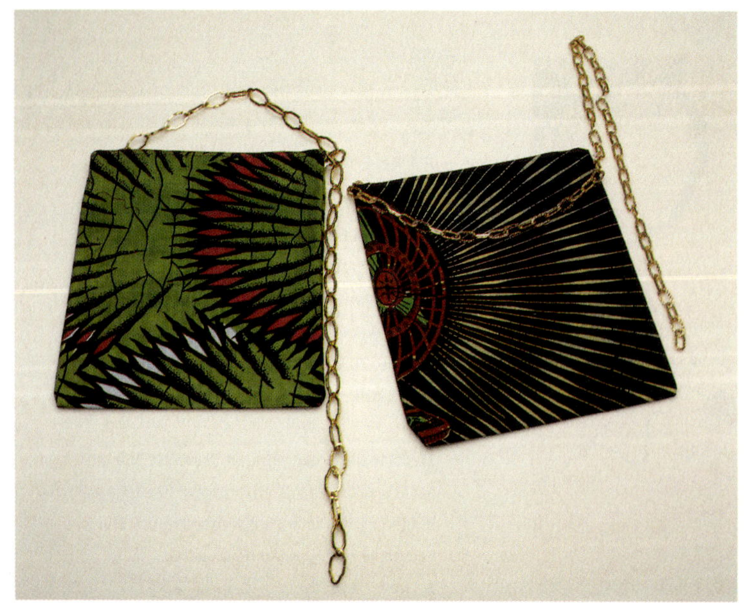

PARKETT 37
FRANZ WEST
ETUI FÜR PARKETT, 1993
Bedruckte afrikanische Baumwollstoffe, Kette,
Ed. 180, signiert und nummeriert, **CHF 250.– / € 160**

POUCH FOR PARKETT, 1993
Printed African fabric, chain, Ed. 180,
signed and numbered, **$ 180 / € 160**

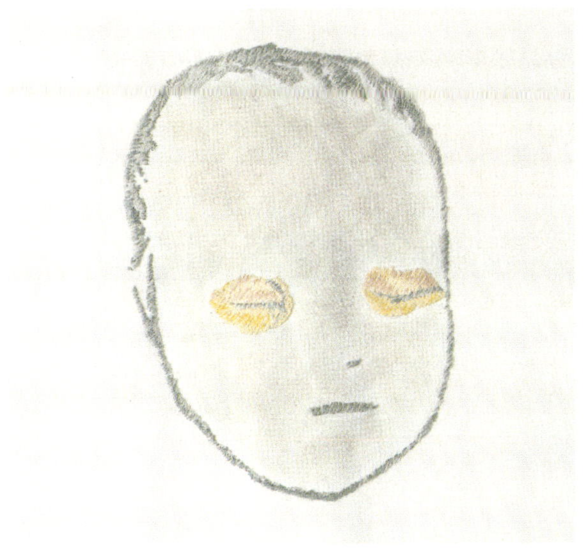

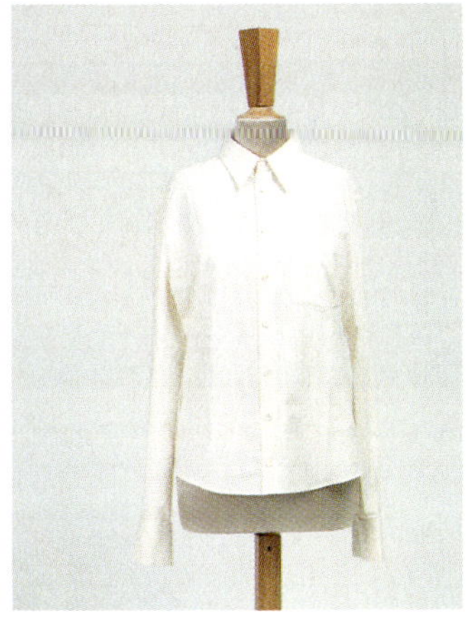

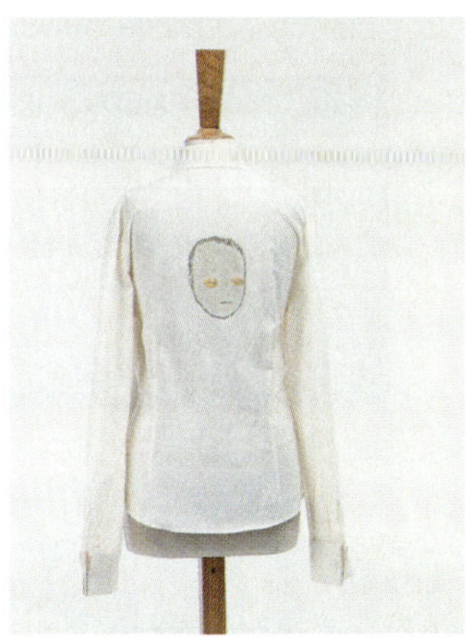

PARKETT 60
LUC TUYMANS
SILENCE, 1990–2000
Men's cotton shirt with reproduction of the artist's
painting SILENCE, 1991.
Shirt design by Walter van Beirendonck, 3 sizes (S, M, L).
Silkscreen version printed by Lorenz Boegli, Zurich.
Edition of 99, signed and numbered, **$ 570 / € 520**

STILLE, 1990–2000
Baumwoll-Herrenhemd mit Reproduktion
des Bildes SILENCE, 1991.
Hemddesign Walter van Beirendonck,
3 Grössen (S, M, L).
Siebdruck-Version gedruckt bei Lorenz Boegli, Zürich.
Auflage: 99, signiert und nummeriert, **CHF 800.– / € 520**

PARKETT 59
YAYOI KUSAMA
INFINITY NETS, 2000
Silkscreen print on mirror, 10 x 8 $^1/_4$".
Edition of 70, signed and numbered on the back,
$ 950 / € 920

UNENDLICHKEITSNETZE, 2000
Siebdruck auf Spiegel, 25,5 x 21 cm.
Auflage: 70, auf der Rückseite signiert und nummeriert,
CHF 1400.– / € 920

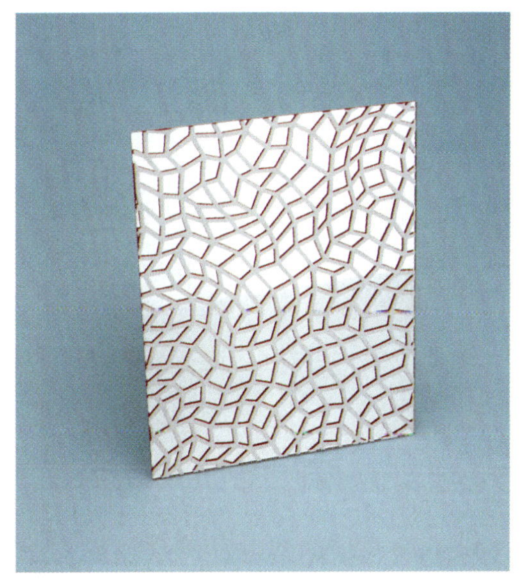

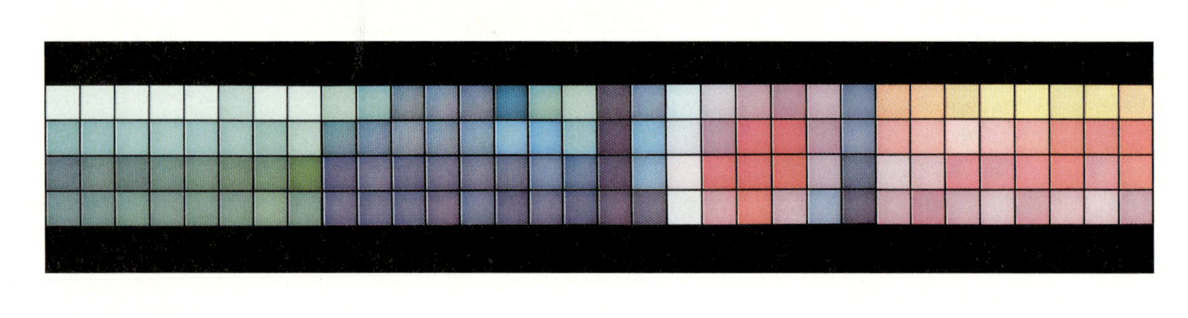

PARKETT 66
ANGELA BULLOCH
HORIZONTAL TECHNICOLOUR:
STILLS WITH NEGATIVE SPACE, 2002
C-print, 12 $^3/_{16}$ x 46" (image 8 $^7/_{16}$ x 42 $^7/_{16}$")
Printed by Philippe Laumont, Laumont Editions, New York
Edition of 80, signed and numbered, **$ 990 / € 920**

C-Print, 31 x 116, 8 cm (Bild 21,5 x 107,8 cm)
Produziert bei Philippe Laumont, Laumont Editions, New York
Auflage: 80, signiert und nummeriert, **CHF 1400 / € 920**

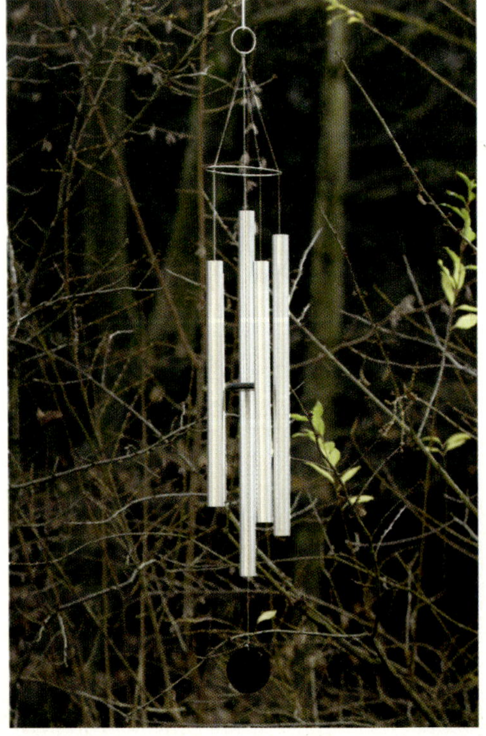

PARKETT 66
PIERRE HUYGHE
ALL BUT ONE, 2002
Windchime for outdoor use, 5 hand-tuned aluminum tubes, 1 $^3/_8$" diameter each;
top hanging ring 2"; black cord, black wood striker, engraved aluminum wind
plate, 4" diameter, overall length 55 $^1/_8$"; overall diameter 8"
Manufactured by Jeff Kile, Grace Note Windchimes, Mariposa, California
Edition of 70, signed and numbered certificate, **$ 1280 / € 1180**

ALLE AUSSER EINEM, 2002
Freiluft-Windglockenspiel , 5 handgestimmte Aluminiumrohre von je 3,5 cm
Durchmesser; Aufhängering 5 cm Durchmesser, schwarze Kordelschnur, schwarze
Holzscheibe als Klangklöppel, gravierte Windscheibe aus Aluminium, 10 cm Durch-
messer, Gesamthöhe 140 cm; Gesamtdurchmesser 20,5 cm
Hergestellt von Jeff Kile, Grace Note Windchimes, Mariposa, California
Auflage: 70, signiertes und nummeriertes Zertifikat, **CHF 1800 / € 1180**

PARKETT 69
ISA GENZKEN
AL DENTE, 2003

Italienische Keramik, Lack, Kunststoff.
Je individuell von Hand gestalteter Teller
mit zwei Spielzeugfiguren (Kuh und Dinosaurier),
ca. 30 x 20 x 26 cm.
Auflage: 74, signiertes und nummeriertes Zertifikat.
$ 1200 / € 1000

Italian ceramic, lacquer, plastic.
Plate with two toy figures (cow and dinosaur),
each unique and handmade by the artist,
ca. 11 $^{13}/_{16}$ x 7 $^{7}/_{8}$ x 10 $^{1}/_{4}$".
Edition of 74, signed and numbered certificate.
CHF 1500 / € 1000

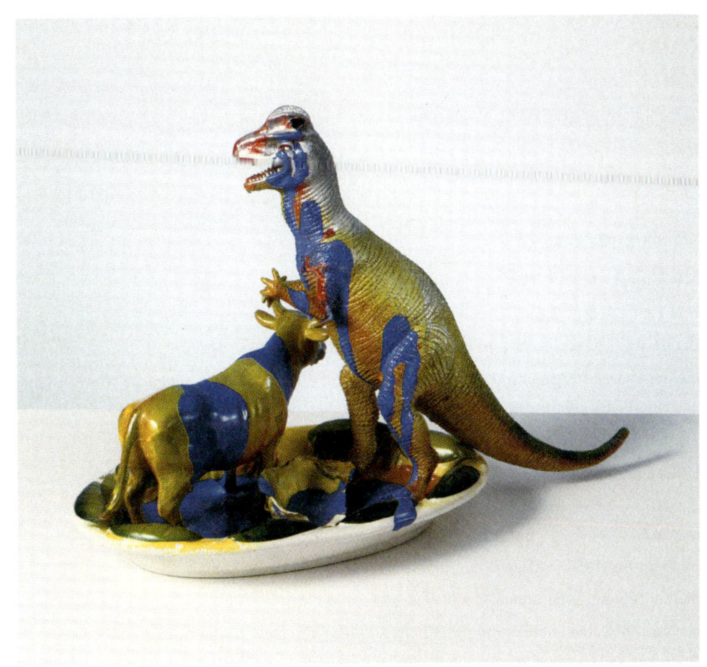

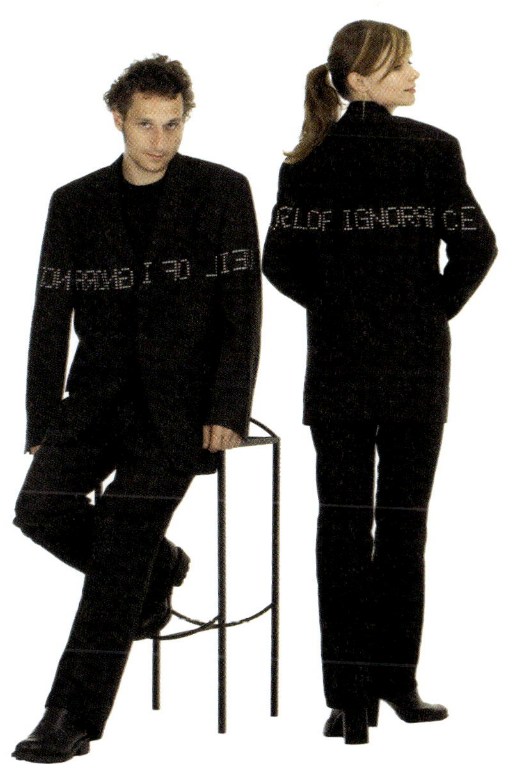

PARKETT 68
EIJA-LIISA AHTILA,
VEIL OF IGNORANCE, 2003

Pure wool jacket with text printed on front (mirror-inverted) and back.
Handprinted silkscreen lettering by Atelier für Siebdruck Lorenz Boegli, Zurich.
Available in 5 sizes (see size table below). Edition of 70, signed certificate.
$ 1400 / € 1200

Reines Wolljackett mit aufgedrucktem Text vorn und hinten (vorne spiegelverkehrt).
Handbedruckt bei Atelier für Siebdruck Lorenz Boegli, Zürich.
Erhältlich in 5 Grössen (siehe untenstehende Tabelle).
Auflage: 70, signiertes Zertifikat. **CHF 1800 / € 1200**

Measurements in cm / Masse in cm:

Men's Sizes / Herrengrössen: Continental European	US/UK	shoulder width / Schulterbreite	back width/ Rückenbreite	back length Rückenlänge	sleeve length / Ärmellänge	chest measurement Brustumfang /
48	38	62	48	77	65	110
C 96	38 short	62	48	75	63	114
50	40	64	49	79	66	114.5
C 100	40 short	64	49	76	64	116.5
52	42	66	51	81	67	117

PARKETT 65
LAURA OWENS
UNTITLED, 2002
Handprinted 10-color lithograph on tan BFK Rives with three collage
elements: one handpainted with watercolor on blue Magnani Pescia, two on white
BFK Rives, the color of the moon will vary with each print, 18 x 12"
Printed by Ed Hamilton, Hamilton Press, Venice, California
Edition of 70, signed and numbered on the back, **$ 1350 / € 1250**

OHNE TITEL, 2002
Handgedruckte 10-Farben-Lithographie auf getöntem BFK Rives mit drei Collage-
Elementen: eines handbemalt mit Wasserfarbe auf Magnani Pescia (Blau), zwei auf
weissem BFK Rives, die Farbe des Mondes variiert von Blatt zu Blatt, 45,8 x 30,6 cm
Gedruckt bei Ed Hamilton, Hamilton Press, Venice, Kalifornien
Auflage: 70, rückseitig signiert und nummeriert, **CHF 1900.– / € 1250**

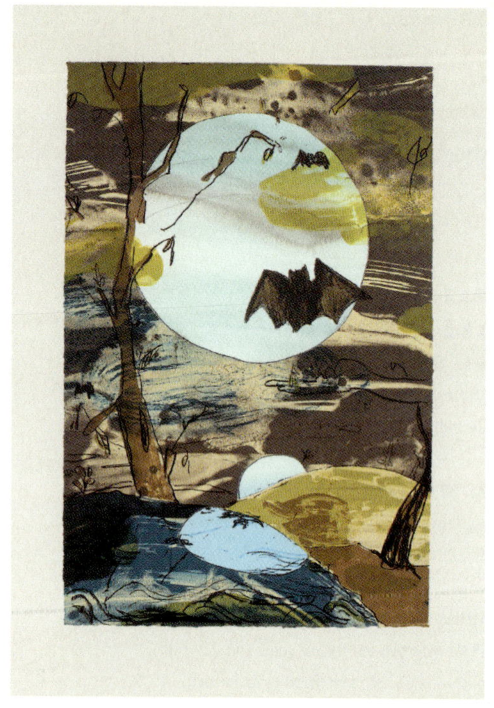

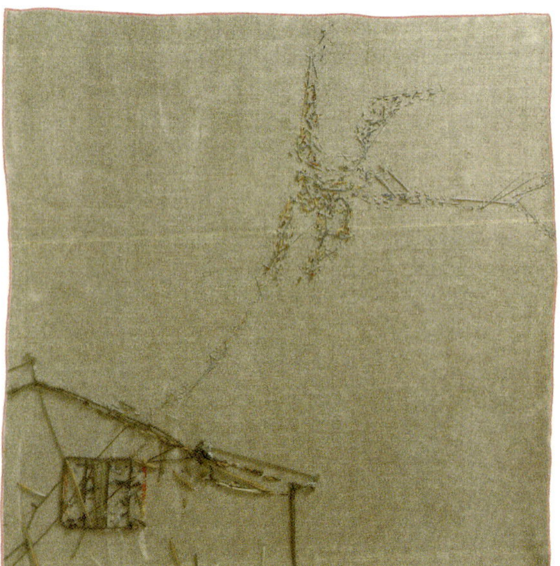

PARKETT 65
MICHAEL RAEDECKER
THE OTHER SIDE, 2002
13-color silkscreen print on pure silk satin scarf
with handrolled border, 33 $^1/_2$ x 33 $^1/_2$"
Detail from the back of the painting INCOMPLETE (2002)
Produced by Fabric Frontline, Zurich
Edition of 99, signed and numbered certificate,
$ 550 / € 500

13-Farben-Siebdruck auf Seidensatinfoulard,
handrouliert, 85 x 85 cm
Produktion: Fabric Frontline, Zürich
Ausschnitt der Rückansicht des Bildes INCOMPLETE (2002)
Auflage: 99, signiertes und nummeriertes Zertifikat,
CHF 770.– / € 500

PARKETT 61
MATTHEW RITCHIE
THE BAD NEED, 2001
Adhesive-backed vinyl, ca. 36^1/$_4$ x 40^1/$_4$'',
to be installed at a height of 41^1/$_2$'' o.c. on a wall surface
(with a minimum size of 96 x 72'') painted with the
eggshell acrylic paint supplied as part of the edition.
Accompanied by an annotated artist's book.
Edition of 70, signed and numbered, **$ 1380 / € 1270**

Vinylfolie mit Haftbeschichtung, ca. 91 x 101 cm, zur
festen Installation auf einer Höhe von 105 cm (Bildmit-
te) auf einer (mindestens 244 cm hohen und 183 cm breiten)
eierschalenfarben gestrichenen Wand. Die Acrylfarbe ist
Bestandteil der Edition.
Begleitbuch mit Anmerkungen des Künstlers.
Auflage: 70, signiert und nummeriert, **CHF 1950.– / € 1270**

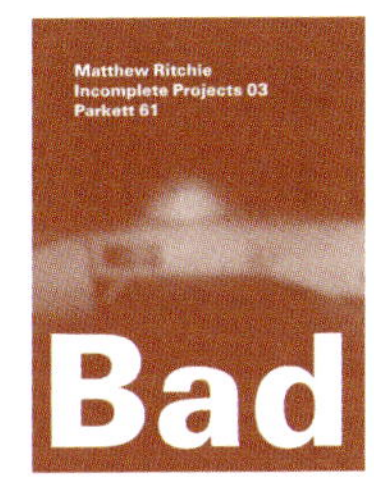

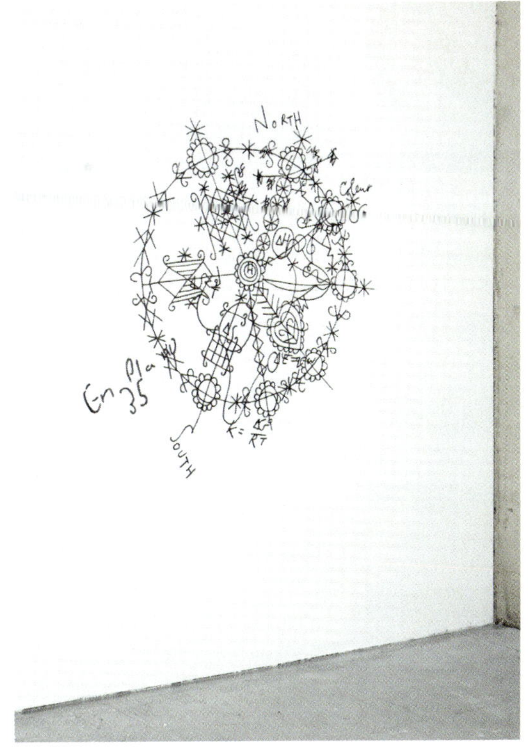

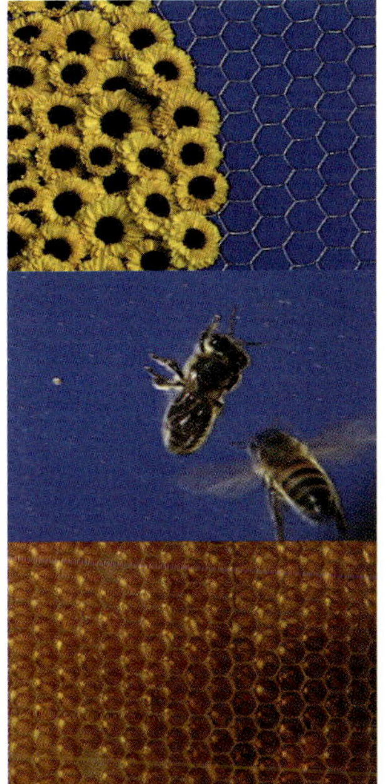

PARKETT 60
DIANA THATER
UNTITLED, 2000
DVD (Digital Video Disc)
with endless loop.
Edition of 150,
signed and numbered, **$ 430 / € 390**

OHNE TITEL, 2000
DVD (Digital Video Disc),
Endlos-Schlaufe.
Auflage: 150,
signiert und nummeriert, **CHF 600.– / € 390**

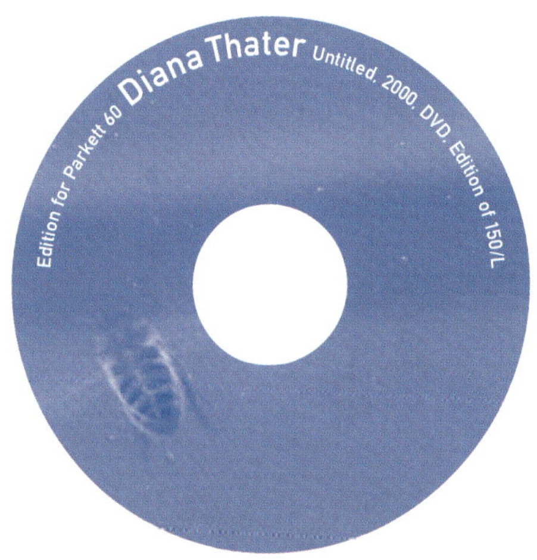

DEAR PARKETT SUBSCRIBER, DEAR READER,

On the occasion of Parkett's 20-year anniversary, it gives us great pleasure to present this latest survey of currently available artists' editions. The Parkett exhibition at the Museum of Modern Art in New York (2001) was the most complete presentation of all the editions that artists had so far made especially for Parkett. The exhibition has since traveled to the Whitechapel Art Gallery, London, and other places.

The Kunsthaus Zurich will feature all Parkett editions in a special exhibition from October 8, 2004 to January 2005. Full documentation is available in the newly updated box containing color postcards of all 146 editions and a booklet with two essays on the MoMA show. Visit our website at www.parkettart.com, which includes among other features an extensive search engine on all artists and the 1000 Parkett texts published up to now.

Beatrice Fässler in Zurich or Monika Condrea in New York will be happy to answer any questions you may have regarding Parkett's Musée en Appartement. Orders may be placed online (SSL secured) as well as by phone, fax or mail (see yellow order form in each issue). Prices are subject to change, postage and packaging are not included; orders will be filled on a first-come first-serve basis.

Yours sincerely,

SEHR GEEHRTE ABONNENTIN, SEHR GEEHRTER ABONNENT,
LIEBE PARKETT-LESER,

Anlässlich des 20-jährigen Parkett-Jubiläums freuen wir uns sehr, Ihnen diesen neuesten Überblick über die zurzeit erhältlichen Künstlereditionen zu geben. Die Parkett-Ausstellung im Museum of Modern Art in New York (2001) war die bisher vollständigste Präsentation aller bis dahin von Künstlerinnen und Künstlern eigens für Parkett geschaffenen Editionen. Inzwischen wurde die Ausstellung auch in der Whitechapel Art Gallery, London, und an anderen Orten gezeigt.

Das Kunsthaus Zürich wird vom 8.Oktober 2004 bis Januar 2005 alle Parkett-Editionen in einer Sonderschau präsentieren. Die Künstlereditionen sind umfassend in der mit 146 Farbpostkarten soeben neu komplettierten Postkartenbox dokumentiert, welche nach wie vor das Textbüchlein mit zwei Essays zur MoMA-Ausstellung enthält. Besuchen Sie auch unsere Website, www.parkettart.com, wo u.a. eine Suchmaschine zu allen Künstlern und den über 1000 bis heute veröffentlichten Texten zur Verfügung steht.

Für alle Fragen zu Parketts Musée en Appartement steht Ihnen Beatrice Fässler in Zürich jederzeit gerne zur Verfügung. Ihre Bestellung können Sie uns online (Site ist SSL-zertifiziert), per Telefon, Fax oder Post (siehe gelben Antwortschein in jeder Ausgabe) zukommen lassen. Preisänderungen bleiben vorbehalten. Versand, Verpackungskosten und MWSt. (Schweiz) sind nicht inbegriffen. Die Lieferung erfolgt in der Reihenfolge des Bestelleingangs solange Vorrat.

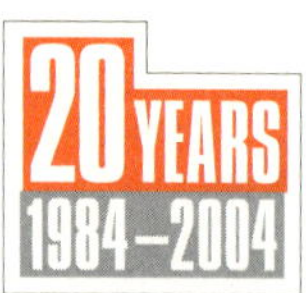

Mit freundlichen Grüssen
Dieter von Graffenried
Publisher/Verleger

Bice Curiger
Editor-in-Chief/Chefredaktorin

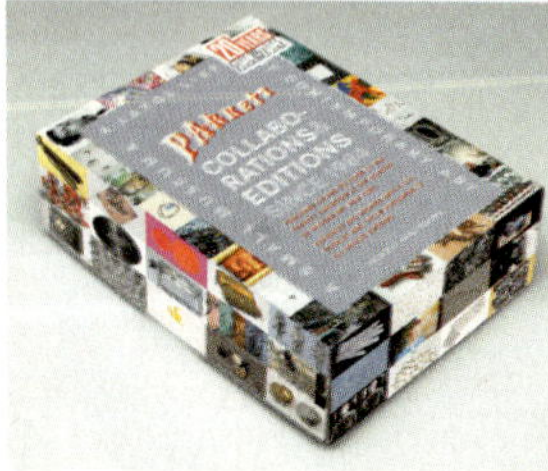

NEWLY UPDATED
POSTCARD SET
WITH TEXT BOOKLET
ON MOMA SHOW
146 color postcards,
booklet of 64 pages.
CHF 45.– / $ 30 / € 30
ISBN 3-907582-23-3

Parkett Verlag AG
Quellenstr. 27
8031 Zürich
Tel. +41-1-271 81 40
FAX +41-1-272 43 01

Parkett PUBLISHERS
155 AV. of the Americas
New York, NY 10013
phone (212)673-2660
FAX (212)271-0704
www.parkettart.com